D0392125

KNIGHT'S ILLUSTRATIONS FOR TODAY

Walter B. Knight

MOODY PRESS
CHICAGO

DEDICATION

To my wife, Alice Marie Knight, who collaborated with me in writing this book and also contributed illustrations of special interest to children and children's workers, I affectionately dedicate this book.

FOREWORD

In writing *Knight's Illustrations for Today*, it has been my undeviating aim to make it a crowning work of my life—the most helpful book of its kind yet to appear. I believe that its up-to-dateness, its freedom from archaisms and circumlocutions, and its inclusion of sections which are seldom if ever found in similar books will be readily seen by those who read it. Its relevance to our contemporary world should greatly enhance its value and usefulness to pastors, teachers, speakers and writers. Many of the illustrations conclude with a Bible verse which scripturally clinches the illustration.

May the use of this book bring illumination and inspiration to many and cause unsaved ones to turn to the Saviour for His mercy and forgiveness.

To God be the glory,
Great things He hath done!

WALTER B. KNIGHT

PREFACE

Our Lord Jesus demonstrated the value of illustrations. His messages were based on illustrations, or parables, which made the truth He taught crystal clear. Profound truths concerning His kingdom were revealed in the parables which He gave by the seaside. He was a Master in the use of illustrations.

People who have no knowledge of spiritual things lack spiritual understanding. Their souls are darkened and they need illustrations as windows to allow the light to shine into their mind and heart. The wise sower of the Word will spice his messages with illustrations if he would win souls to Christ.

Often listeners will remember an illustration even though they may forget the message. Thus the truth is fastened in the mind and not lost. Illustrations make profound truth easy to understand so even the simple ones may comprehend. And deep thinkers find truth more palatable when it is served on the golden platter of a story.

God endows certain men with special gifts for the edification of the entire church. Such a man is Walter B. Knight, the author of *Knight's Illustrations for Today*. When a young man in Orlando, Florida, he began writing as a news correspondent. He received his training for the gospel ministry at Mercer University, Macon, Georgia, and has been exceedingly successful as a pastor, both in the North and South. In selecting his illustrations for this new book, he has dipped into his deep well of experience as a pastor, public speaker and writer. His three previous books of illustrations have become a household staple of ministers of all churches and denominations, who have used them to enhance their messages and to make them more effective. Certainly many thousands of pastors and public speakers will welcome this new and fresh book of illustrations.

These illustrations are treasures which will prove most helpful to all public speakers, pastors and writers who use them. They are gleaned from fresh, up-to-date, everyday, common-life experiences which are exciting enough to make them newsworthy.

RALPH W. NEIGHBOUR

CONTENTS

ACCOUNTABILITY

"Did I Reach the Last One?"

Years ago James Blackman went as a missionary to India. He gave himself in utter abandonment to Christian service. During an epidemic of cholera, hundreds of the nationals were stricken with the dreadful disease. With no thought of his safety, Blackman went into the isolation wards of the hospitals, ministered to the sick and the dying, and told them of the Saviour's love and sacrifice for the sin of the world.

In time he succumbed to cholera. As his life ebbed away, he asked deliriously, "Did I reach the last one? Did I reach the last one?"

Our acccountability to God will be great if we fail to do our best to reach the unsaved myriads at home and in the regions beyond.

* * *

"Give an Account of Your Stewardship"

Fritz Kreisler stated, "I was born with music in my system and knew musical scores instinctively before I knew my ABC's. It was a gift from God. Music is too sacred to be sold, so I have never looked upon the money I earn as my own. It is public money, entrusted to my care for proper disbursement. I never spend it in high living or for selfish pleasure. How can I squander money on myself while there is so much misery, so much hunger in the world?"

Let us hold our dollars in trust for God, knowing that we must give an account to Him for how we use or misuse them.

* * *

Businessmen Awaking

R. G. LeTourneau said, "The most encouraging sign on the horizon today is the fact that businessmen are waking up to their responsibility to God and are beginning to prove that Christianity is practical."

Used or Misused Talents

In an effort to cause his son to desist from versifying, the father of Isaac Watts threatened him with physical punishment. Poetry, however, was in the soul of the boy, and he could no more repress the God-given talent than he could refrain from breathing.

After the reading of the Scripture one morning, the Watts family knelt for prayer. Just then Isaac pointed to a mouse running up the bell rope and exclaimed:

"There was a mouse for want of stairs,
Ran up a rope to say his prayers!"

The children began to snicker. Observing the grieved expression on his father's face, and anticipating the threatened punishment, Isaac ran to him and pleaded:

"O Father, Father, pity take!
And I will no more verses make!"

While still a boy, Isaac Watts became a Christian. Using his divinely given talent, he gave to the church some of its most soulful hymns—hymns which will bless and challenge God's children as long as time lasts. Among them are: "Alas! and Did My Saviour Bleed?" "Joy to the World!" "Am I a Soldier of the Cross?" and "Jesus Shall Reign."

To each one of His children God has given some *special* talent. Each one will give account to God for how he uses or misuses his talent: "So then every one of us shall give account of himself to God" (Rom. 14:12).

* * *

Why Not?

Some parents say, "We will not influence our children in making choices and decisions in the matter of religion." Why not? TV and radio will. The press will. The movies will. Their neighbors will. We use our influence over flowers, vegetables and cattle. Shall we ignore our God-given responsibilities to our children?

J. Edgar Hoover

ALCOHOLISM

Spurns a Million Dollars

Asked by a news correspondent why he didn't have beer in Disneyland, Walt Disney replied, "It just doesn't seem appropriate for Disneyland."

An associate of Disney said, "A brewery offered a million dollars to get in, but Walt turned them down."

* * *

"It Is a Mistake"

Said Dr. Donald R. Young, staff member of the Menninger Foundation, "It is a mistake to describe alcoholism as a disease, because it makes the alcoholic feel he is not morally responsible for his behavior. It is important, some assume, to remove some of the social stigma from alcoholism by calling it a disease."

If alcoholism is a disease, why are millions of dollars spent annually to persuade people to run the risk of contracting such a devastating malady?

Our nation's yearly expenditure of $13.5 billion for intoxicating liquors far exceeds what is given for the churches of the nation.

* * *

Children or Booze, Which?

Recently, the tragic, heartrending end of a broken home was written in juvenile court, Cleveland, Ohio. A thirty-two-year-old alcoholic father gave up his children for adoption. His wife, who suffered periods of depression, was often abused by her drinking husband. She took her life just before she was to be hospitalized for the fourth time.

Judge Gagliardo asked the father, "Does alcohol mean more to you than your children? You are still a young man. Your life isn't over yet. You have two beautiful children. You do not need any more reason to live. Do you realize that when I sign this order, you will never again be able to see your children, touch them, kiss them, hold them close to you, or know where they are and what they are doing?"

Tears ran down the alcoholic's cheeks. He nodded and mumbled that he understood.

Then the judge said, "It is the order of this court that your children are now placed in the permanent care and custody of the division of child welfare."

Childhood has no deadlier enemy than alcohol. Though popularized and protected, it is a merciless destroyer. Saddest of all, it is a heaven-blocking sin: "Know ye not that the unrighteous shall not inherit the kingdom of God? . . . nor thieves, nor covetous, nor drunkards" (I Cor. 6:9-10).

* * *

The Liquor Industry's Best Boost

A report entitled "Alcohol Problems: A Report to the Nation," prepared by the Cooperative Commission on the Study of Alcoholism, states, "If America adopts a national policy permitting youths easy access to alcohol in carefully controlled settings, it is likely there will be fewer alcoholics."

The report's most astounding recommendations call for prompt lowering of the legal drinking age to eighteen, and the encouragement of teenage drinking at social and church gatherings.

Dr. Samuel A. Jeanes, legislative chairman of the New Jersey Council of Churches, has urged U.S. senators from his state to investigate the report, adding, "The liquor business has never had a better boost for its business than has come through this report paid for by the taxpayers of America."

The cost of the federally financed six-year study by the commission was one million dollars. This nonsensical report revealed tragic waste of money and deplorable failure to deal with an evil which is increasingly enmeshing youth in crime, undermining their health and destroying their character.

* * *

Impairment of Judgment

A brochure of the Metropolitan Life Insurance Company stated, "Two alcoholic drinks are enough to cause a definite impairment of the judgment and reactions of many people. Alcohol and gasoline are a dangerous combination. In fact, this combination accounts for about 50 percent of all fatal traffic accidents today."

Cause of One-Half of Fatal Crashes

A symposium of the National Academy of Engineering Traffic Safety reported: "Alcoholism is a critical cause of automobile deaths and injuries in the United States."

Dr. William Haddon, Jr., the associate director of the Chronic Disease Services of the New York Department of Health, affirmed, "There is overwhelming evidence that about one-half of our fatal crashes are initiated at least in part by the prior use of alcohol."

* * *

A Chief Cause of Unhappiness

J. C. Penney said, "I have a sincere conviction that liquor is one of the chief causes of unhappiness, both to the people who drink and to those who are near and dear to them. Early in my life I decided not to touch liquor even in moderation, and I have adhered to this resolution. I am grateful for God's help during periods of stress when I might have been tempted to drink had I relied on human strength alone."

* * *

I Cast My Vote

Upton Sinclair declared, "I cast my vote against social drinking. I will not keep a dog in my house that bites one out of every five or nine people who stop to pet it. Nor will I sanction alcohol, because it dooms or harms one out of every five or nine who drink."

* * *

Depth of Despair

Can we fathom the depth of despair and remorse felt by those who, in fits of anger, commit horrible crimes including murder? Take the case of Joseph ———, a father who took the life of his drunken son who staggered into the house and became abusive and threatening. Something seemed to snap in the father's mind. His son's worthlessness, brought on by drink, drove him to commit that tragic deed. In prison the father collapsed from remorse and sorrow.

"Dad, We Took Your Liquor"

"Who hath woe? . . . wounds without cause?" Youths, fathers, mothers, wives, husbands. None escape the consequences of the deadly, heaven-obstructing evil—alcohol!

Four young people were recently killed in a traffic accident. They had been drinking, and a father vowed, "I'll kill the bartender who sold them liquor!"

Going to his cupboard for a drink, he found a note which had been written by his dead daughter: "Dad, we took some of your liquor. We knew you wouldn't care."

* * *

Any Is Too Much

Recently James M. Forester, a nineteen-year-old prelaw student, hanged himself in an abandoned barn. The sad deed followed a misunderstanding with a girl friend who had criticized him for drinking *too much*.

Alcoholism begins with the first drink. The imbibing of any amount of alcohol is *too much*, and could be hazardous. Play safe! Abstain totally!

* * *

America's No. 1 Thug Running Amuck

Dr. Horace E. Chandler, in *Christianity Today*, declared, "For each dollar of liquor revenue collected, taxpayers are paying more than eleven dollars to offset the baneful results of the alcoholic beverage traffic.

"Americans squander $13.5 billion a year on the liquor itself. Absenteeism and various other industrial losses devour another billion. The states, in taking care of alcoholics in hospitals, asylums, jails and welfare grants, drain the public purse unmercifully. Clearly America's No. 1 thug is running amuck, and every citizen, abstainer or drinker, is suffering from his attacks. Contrary to popular belief, even a small amount of alcohol can be dangerous."

* * *

On the Losing Side

In his book *Twenty-six Years on the Losing Side*, Conrad S. Jensen, a former New York City police inspector, says,

"Our jails, at tremendous expense to the taxpayers, are filled with people who are there because of booze. Alcoholics may eventually comprise half of the jail population because of offenses committed in connection with drinking."

* * *

Liquor Outlets Versus Churches

Dr. J. Allen Blair wrote in *The Perils of Alcohol*, "America spends annually some thirteen and one-half billion dollars for alcoholic beverages. There are about 300,000 churches in the United States, but 441,800 liquor establishments. Every true American and every child of God ought to hate alcohol and stand against it."

* * *

Why He Abstained

Dr. Andrew Ivy said, "For others, I abstain from alcohol. I desire to avoid completely any responsibility for causing my own children or the sons and daughters of other parents to become victims of alcoholism and all the other tragedies that result from the use of alcoholic beverages."

* * *

The Children's Enemy

Some years ago a man under the influence of liquor entered his home. He tried to remove the wedding ring from his wife's finger so he could sell it for more liquor. The wife resisted him, and he stabbed her to death. He was tried and condemned to hang.

The man had three children—aged twelve, nine and five. Before his execution, the children visited him. "Good-bye, Papa," they said as they wept. The oldest child said, "You were a good papa before you began drinking. You loved us and you loved Mamma. You didn't mean to kill Mamma, did you, Papa?"

Have little children a deadlier and more merciless enemy than strong drink?

* * *

Singers Must Be Fit

Said Lily Pons, Metropolitan Opera star, "Singers are like athletes. If singers are not fit physically, they cannot sing well. We must be an example. Drinking does not give anything to people. It is destructive. Why do so many people feel that they must drink as others do? 'Just to be sociable,' they say. When I am served a cocktail, I refuse it."

* * *

Drink and Lincoln's Death

On the last day of his life, Lincoln said, "We have abolished slavery. Our next great task will be the overthrow and suppression of the legalized liquor traffic. It is morally, socially, and politically wrong. This demon—alcohol—has gone forth, like the Egyptian angel of death, to slay, if not the firstborn, the fairest born in every family."

That night Lincoln went to Ford's Theatre. John Wilkes Booth, an actor, stopped by Peter Taltavul's saloon to fortify himself with liquor to nerve him to carry out the dark deed—the assassination of the President! When Booth entered Ford's Theatre, he found the way clear to where the president sat. Lincoln's bodyguard, John F. Parker, had slipped away to have a drink at the same saloon.

* * *

It Could Be You

Donald Hewitt, M.D., said, "No scientist or doctor can tell any person whether or not he will become an alcoholic addict after he has taken the first drink. Everyone who takes even one drink of any alcoholic beverage thereby becomes a potential alcoholic addict. There is absolutely no guarantee that, once he has taken the first drink, he will be able to call a halt."

* * *

A Psychiatrist in Need of a Psychiatrist

Dr. Morris Chafetz, a Harvard University psychiatrist, advocates the teaching of the techniques of social drinking in public schools. Speaking in a New York conference on "Alcohol and Food in Health and Disease," he said, "It would be a good idea for students to practice drinking in elementary schools and continue through college."

12

Gov. Harold E. Hughes of Iowa, a former alcoholic, said, "This psychiatrist ought to consult a psychiatrist. I disagree with him a *thousand* percent. Children ought to be taught the great danger involved in the use of alcohol, not how to drink it."

Said Mrs. Fred J. Tooze, president of the Women's Christian Temperance Union, "The Chafetz plan would turn public schools into schools for alcoholism and double this country's ten million alcoholics and problem drinkers."

* * *

Men of Extinction

An unhappy woman wrote a letter to a columnist complaining that her husband thought it funny to make her pet cat drunk by pouring liquor in its milk. "The poor creature staggers in circles and falls in a heap, and is rapidly losing its hair on the liquor diet," she lamented. Letters denouncing the husband for cruelty to animals began to pour into the newspaper office.

A man who imbibes liquor is not considered hurt, but sophisticated. How quickly do men of *distinction* who are enslaved to alcohol become men of *extinction!*

* * *

Teenage Drinking

Said Richard E. Hunton, M.D., in *Upward*, "I have become greatly alarmed and distressed by the recent reports of teenage drinking. I am alarmed because many of these young people will become the future leaders, and they are subjecting their minds and bodies to a poisonous influence from which most of them will never completely recover.

"I am alarmed because many of them will bring death on the highway to some of our dearest friends and relatives; because one out of every ten of our teenagers will eventually become an alcoholic; because these teenagers have chosen to bring sorrow to their families and friends; because teenagers from many of our finest families have chosen to celebrate the birth of Christ with drinking parties which are often terminated by the police.

"We in medicine have the distasteful opportunity to see 'men and women of distinction' become bums, prostitutes, wreck victims, shooting and stabbing victims, and succumb to delirium tremens.

"When we see the broken homes, the orphans, the diseased minds and bodies, the poverty, the rapes, the pregnant high school girls, the ruined lives, and the blasted ambitions—all because of drinking—we label as the ultimate in deception and malicious lying the totally false claim that 'it's smart to drink!' It's about as smart as taking rat poison or playing Russian roulette!"

* * *

Free Built-in Commercials

Someone asked Terrence O'Flaherty, columnist, "What do you mean when you state that there are no hard liquor commercials on television?

"Almost every movie I have seen for the past twenty-five years has had built-in commercials for drinking. No brand names, of course, but it doesn't matter what you drink as long as you drink. At first it was scotch or champagne. Now it's everything.

"For the past five or six years, television has followed suit. Why should the liquor industry pay for commercials when they are getting this much free advertising in a more effective part of the program? And why is it that only the hero and the good guys drink—men of distinction? The villians never seem to drink on TV.

"I object to the over-glorification of liquor and the disparagement of those who don't drink. I object to the implication that drinking is an important part of the 'good life.' "

Adapted from *San Francisco Chronicle*

* * *

They Had Both Been Drinking

"They had both been drinking." Thus began the tragic story of a medical doctor who had murdered his wife.

The doctor had a fine practice and a splendid army record. When the officers entered his $50,000 suburban home, they found him intoxicated and incoherent. Then he lapsed into a coma.

13

When he was questioned later, the doctor said, "We were both drinking. We quarreled over money. Then a free-for-all fight ensued. I whacked her in the face, and she fell over dead!"

* * *

Supervised Teenage Cocktail Parties

Thomas F. A. Plaut, a researcher in Stanford University's cooperative commission, has recently completed a five-year, $1,100,000 federally financed study of alcoholism.

Millions throughout the land disagree with what Plaut recommended—supervised teenage cocktail parties to prevent alcoholism among them.

* * *

Seeing Themselves as They Are

A police magistrate in Philadelphia has a novel way of sobering some of the alcoholics who are daily brought into the station. He lines them up before a large mirror so they can see themselves as they are—bleary-eyed, filthy and ragged. Some of them are humiliated. Some are amused. A few realize that they need God's help.

* * *

It's All Fuzzy

"I've been drinking since I was sixteen years old and all the trouble I have ever been in happened when I was drunk," said jailed Martin U. Still, Jr., an ex-convict, who recently killed a woman. Later, when he learned what he had done, he said, "I was shocked when the officers told me I had murdered someone. It's all fuzzy in my mind."

* * *

"When Can I Start to Drink, Dad?"

Editorialized the *Moody Monthly* magazine: "The alcoholic beverage industry is never more convincing—or dangerous—than when it puts on its good citizen costume and talks about respectable use of liquor. In this role its script generally calls for judicious reference to mature drinking, good judgment, and enjoyment of the finer things of life. It is a smooth and plausible approach and often gets by unchallenged.

"In Portland, Oregon, there recently appeared a particularly obnoxious Father's Day ad by a nationally known distiller which aroused several members of the Hinson Memorial Baptist Church. Headed 'When Can I Start to Drink, Dad?' the distiller's message implied that boys become mature enough to drink as soon as they learn to drink sensibly and moderately.

"The pastor, Dr. Herbert E. Anderson, ran a rebuttal advertisement in the *Portland Oregonian* and the *Portland Journal*. In answering the question 'When can I start to drink, Dad?' with '*Never!*' reminding that use of intoxicants produces moral ruin and misery, and that taking up social drinking is like playing Russian roulette with a revolver that has five of its six chambers empty, it quoted the historian Toynbee: 'Out of twenty-one civilizations preceding this one, nineteen have been destroyed by a mixture of atheism, socialism, materialism and alcoholism.' "

* * *

"I Like It!"

Said General Robert E. Lee, "Whiskey? I like it! I always did, and that is the reason I never use it."

* * *

The Main Cause

J. Elmer Morgan said, "Drinking in moderation is not the solution to the liquor problem. It is the main cause of it."

* * *

Desist

Alcoholism begins with the first drink! Desist! Play safe!

* * *

The Greatest Criminal

Dr. Albert Schweitzer stated, "Drink is commercially our greatest wastrel; socially it is our greatest criminal; morally and religiously it is our greatest enemy."

14

The Most Degrading

William McKinley declared, "The liquor business is the most degrading and ruinous of all human pursuits."

* * *

Later Than We Think

Jasper A. Huffman stated in *Christianity Today*, "It is much later than we think in regard to combating an enemy that is within our own nation. Alcoholism is more dangerous and deadly than any danger from outside."

* * *

Industrial Loss

Thomas P. Vassaux, nationally known counselor on industrial alcoholism, stated, "Business and industry lose $2 billion a year because of problem drinkers."

* * *

A National Emergency

Said Dr. William C. Menninger, Menninger Clinic, Topeka, Kansas, "If any other disease [other than alcoholism] affected our citizens so much, a national emergency would be declared."

Who They Are

The Center of Alcohol Studies, Rutgers University, established the following: "Eighty million adult Americans—71 percent of the population over twenty-one— drink intoxicating beverages."

* * *

A Great Discovery

Testified Jerry G. Dunn, executive director of the People's City Mission, Lincoln, Nebraska, "I discovered that God is for the alcoholic at the conclusion of a two-year drunk when I picked up a Bible in my cell in a Texas prison more than sixteen years ago."

* * *

A Cause of Family Trouble

According to a Gallup Poll on Alcoholism and its related problems, 12 persons out of every 100 say alcohol has been a cause of trouble in their families. Twenty-two percent favor prohibiting the sale of all beer, wine and liquor throughout the United States.

ASSURANCE

All Christians Are Saints

A *Moody Monthly* editorial stated: "Essentially this is the simple teaching of the Word of God—that God's children are ... saints here and now; that sainthood for believers in Christ is not a far-off gleam of hope for the few but a reality for every Christian, and that God is working day by day to make us saints with saintly lives.

"Interestingly, the Catholic Confraternity edition of the New Testament contains a glossary which states that the term 'saint' in Bible times was applied to all believers.

"Saints are not those who achieve salvation but those who receive the salvation of God through faith in Christ. Though pinpointing grievous spiritual and moral shortcomings among the Corinthian Christians, Paul began his letter by reminding them that they were 'saints' (I Cor. 1:2)."

How unsaintly and unchristlike are many of God's children at times!

* * *

God Is a Reality

A socially prominent woman asked Dr. William Evans, "What shall I do? Everything concerning God is as dark to me as a starless night."

Dr. Evans replied, "Act as if God is a reality, and you will come to know that He is."

Later she said to Dr. Evans, "I followed your instruction. It works! Now God is to me a bright and living reality!"

Although we cannot explain God, we can experience Him: "O taste and see that the LORD is good" (Ps. 34:8).

15

The Everlasting Arms

Have you ever tried to visualize what occurs in a plane when a crash seems inevitable? Here's a firsthand answer:

After my wife and I boarded the plane in Guatemala City for Miami, we streaked northward. As we neared the Florida coast, which sometimes is stormy, our jet suddenly began to wobble crazily! Light objects in the overhead racks began to fly about in all directions. The scene was one of pandemonium.

Some called audibly on God for help. Some prayed silently. Many screamed when the plane suddenly lunged downward!

Though the earthward plunge lasted only a few seconds, it seemed like a lifetime. Then, as if upheld by some buoyant power, the plane leveled off and shot forward. We made a safe landing.

How precious and assuring to God's children in times of peril is the sure promise: "The eternal God is thy refuge, and underneath are the everlasting arms" (Deut. 33:27).

W. B. K.

* * *

No Hell Where Jesus Is

A bright African boy heard the story of Jesus and trusted Him as His Saviour. How happy he was!

Later the boy became ill and called for the missionary. He said, "I am very happy! I hope I will not get well again."

"Why?" asked the missionary in astonishment.

The boy replied, "Because I would like to go soon to heaven where I shall see Jesus and be with Him always."

To test the reality of the boy's faith, the missionary asked, "What would you do if Jesus were not in heaven?"

"I would follow Him," said the boy.

"What if Jesus went to hell? What would you do then?"

The boy replied, "Ah, missionary, there is no hell where Jesus is!"

Told by ALICE MARIE KNIGHT

"The People That Do Know"

One day Miss Irene Webster-Smith, whose challenging life story is told by Russell T. Hitt in *Sensei*, was asked, "Do you know the Lord Jesus Christ as your personal Saviour and Friend?"

Momentarily Miss Webster-Smith was nonplussed. If she had been asked, "Are you a Christian?" she would have given a confident affirmative answer. Being honest, she replied, "I don't think I know Him like that."

We all need an experimental knowledge of Christ to outride the storms of our turbulent times: "The people that do know their God shall be strong, and do exploits" (Dan. 11:32).

* * *

A General's Request

"What do you want us to give you that we may be protected from Russian aggression?" asked the Secret Defense Committee of General Lemay.

Without hesitancy, the general replied, "Men who know God! Men who know how to pray!"

* * *

When Stars Have Passed Away

The stars shine over the mountains,
The stars shine over the sea;
The stars look up to the mighty God,
The stars look down on me.

The stars shall last for a million years,
A million years and a day;
But God and I will live and love,
When the stars have passed away.

ROBERT LOUIS STEVENSON

* * *

"My Lord and My God"

I once attended a magnificent rendering of Handel's *Messiah* by a choir of several hundred voices in the Royal Albert Hall, London. The friend who accompanied me was a dear saint of God, then in his seventies.

When the "Hallelujah Chorus" reached its climax, "King of kings, and Lord of lords," my friend could hardly contain himself. Tears streamed from his eyes

16

and he whispered to me, "That is my Saviour they are singing about!" I shall never forget the meaning he put into that word *my*.

What joy will be in our hearts if we, like Thomas, can say, "My Lord and my God!"

LESLIE D. WEATHERHEAD

* * *

Whom

Through the years a faithful minister had memorized much of God's Word. In old age much of it slipped from his mind. Some days before his homegoing, he could recall only a portion of one verse: "I know whom I have believed." On the day he passed confidently and radiantly into the presence of his Lord, his last word was *whom*. This was enough! *Whom* was death's Conqueror—Jesus. His promise is sure: "Because I live, ye shall live also" (John 14:19).

Told by R. E. NEIGHBOUR

* * *

Experimental Knowledge

A Christian served on a parliamentary commission with Prof. Thomas H. Huxley. One Sunday they stayed together in a little country inn.

"I suppose you are going to church this morning," said Huxley.

"I am. I always go to church on the Lord's Day," replied the Christian.

Huxley said, "Suppose you sit down and talk with me about religion—simple, experimental religion."

Sensing something of heart hunger in the great scientist, the associate replied, "If you mean it, I will." Then he spoke out of a rich, experimental knowledge of the saving and satisfying power of Christ.

Huxley listened intently. Grasping the hand of the Christian, he said with deep feeling, "If I could believe what you have said about the cross of Christ and His pardoning love, I would be willing to give my right hand."

This is *certain*: "And ye shall seek me, and find me, when ye shall search for me with all your heart" (Jer. 29:13).

* * *

The Unknown Future

We do not know what the future holds: "Thou knowest not what a day may bring forth" (Prov. 27:1). We do know, however, the One who holds the future, and in His hand reposes all power in heaven and in earth.

ATHEISM

It Just Happened

A Sunday school teacher said to her class of juniors, "Some say that the moon, the stars, the sun and the planet on which we live—the earth—just happened, and that there was no all-wise and all-powerful Creator who made them. I hold in my hand a small wristwatch. Suppose I would say, 'This wristwatch just happened. Its screws, its springs, its wheels, its case, its hands, its face and its crystal began to twirl and twist and finally came together just as you see it in my hand.' Why, you would say, 'Poor teacher! A cog has slipped in her mind.' You would be right if I should make such a claim for my watch. Yet people who are otherwise sensible and intelligent say

the universe just happened. They deny that a great and mighty God created all things and established order throughout the universe."

Told by ALICE MARIE KNIGHT

* * *

A Minister Who Believes

Robert Ingersoll, the self-acclaimed agnostic, at intervals attended the preaching services of a minister who believed the Bible and faithfully preached it. A friend asked him, "What does this mean, Bob? You are an avowed agnostic, and you go to hear a minister who believes in God and the Bible."

Ingersoll replied, "It is true that I am an agnostic, but once in a while I like to listen to a man who actually believes what he preaches and practices what he preaches."

* * *

Blinded Minds

Dr. Alfred E. Emerson, professor at the University of Chicago, averred, "We have to give up our belief in anthropomorphic spirits and in gods with evil or beneficent attitudes toward individuals, together with the necessity of special rituals for their propitiation."

Said Dr. Hudson Hoagland, professor of physiology at Boston University, "To accept a faith in a personal deity, who has specific concern for personal problems of good and evil, is simply not possible for many persons. Mystification both humbles and challenges, but for many of us it cannot . . . yield a basis for positive faith."

To myriads, however, God is experimentally precious. They know that He is "merciful and gracious." He is a kind, loving heavenly Father.

Christ also is precious to those who make room in their hearts for Him: "Unto you . . . which believe he is precious" (I Peter 2:7). To them He is an ever present, never failing Friend who enters feelingly into their sorrows and trials.

"O taste and see that the Lord is good: blessed is the man that trusteth in him" (Ps. 34:8).

* * *

Theological Windbags

Dr. Carl F. H. Henry declared, "The Christian world today confronts theology without Christ as its climax; theology without the theos [God]; theology without logos [reason]. Ours is, in very fact, a time of antitheological theology, where modernism is politically a volcano and theologically a windbag."

* * *

"In the Beginning God"

Newspapers over the nation gave wide publicity to the Egyptian find of Prof. Elwyn L. Simons, a professor of geology at Yale University—an incomplete skull alleged to be from eight to ten million years older than any previously uncovered and said to be a major connecting link in the evolution of primates. Researchers who studied the fragmented skull estimated its age to be twenty-eight million years. Such conjectural claims tax the faith of the layman.

Said *Time* magazine (Nov. 24, 1967) in an imaginative report of the find, "Swinging down from a tree in the lush forest that stood in what is now the Fayum desert region in Egypt, the little creature reached the riverside and began to drink. Suddenly it was attacked and eaten by a crocodile-like reptile that rose without warning from the water. All that the predator left behind was the victim's head, which sank to the bottom and became embedded in the sand." Amusing indeed is this hypothetical drama!

We do not speak disparagingly of men of science. We are amazed, however, by fantastic surmises and guesses about what occurred millions of years ago. In contrast, how profound and satisfying is the factual statement of the Bible: "In the beginning God created the heaven and the earth. God created man in his own image, in the image of God created he him" (Gen. 1:1, 27).

Dr. Henry M. Morris, head of the department of engineering at Virginia Polytechnic Institute, insisted, "There is not one shred of genuine evidence in science or Scripture for the validity of evolution."

* * *

A National Disaster

A news correspondent asked J. Edgar Hoover, "What would you consider a national disaster?"

Hoover replied, "For a nation conceived under God, it would be a great disaster to deny in any respect the presence, power, guidance and protection of God."

A living faith in the living God keeps people on an even keel—mentally, morally and emotionally. The French philosopher Rousseau stated, "If there wasn't a God, we would have to invent one to keep people sane."

18

Fighting a Nonentity

Mahatma Gandhi was importuned to organize and promote an anti-God cult. Gandhi replied, "It amazes me to find an intelligent person who fights against something in which he does not at all believe."

* * *

"Which Way Shall I Take?"

The daughter of an arrogant and defiant unbeliever was critically ill. The girl's mother was a devout Christian. Often she had prayed for the daughter's conversion. The daughter weakened progressively. As she neared death, she said to her father, "Daddy, Mother has often tried to get me to become a Christian, but your influence has kept me from trusting Christ to save me from sin. I know I am going to die, and I am not ready to die. Am I to follow your infidelity, or am I to take my mother's God, and trust her Saviour to save me?"

The father was deeply moved. He greatly loved his daughter. Weeping, he said, "Daughter, my infidelity holds out no hope for you in this dark hour. In God's name, turn from it. Take your mother's God and your mother's Christ and your mother's Bible."

* * *

Man Is Incurably Religious

In her book *Twenty Letters to a Friend*, Svetlana Alliluyeva, the daughter of Joseph Stalin, repeatedly expresses her faith in God. The *New York Times Service*, in commenting upon her upbringing in an atheistic society and the futile effort of the Soviets to extirpate faith in God, said, "It is the doctrine of atheism, not faith in God, that is dying in the Soviet Union. The human spirit instinctively reaches out for the support and reassurance of the Supreme Being, and nothing that any man-made apparatus can do will destroy faith. Churches can be burned and pulpits silenced, but above the ashes and beyond the silence the believer presses on."

Fools

A Christian mother lay on her deathbed. Her husband had predeceased her. The mother said to her little girl, "Mother won't be with you much longer. Promise me that you will love and serve Jesus and read your Bible every day."

After her mother's death, the little girl was taken to the home of her grandfather who was not a Christian. One day he saw his little granddaughter reading her Bible. He began to ridicule it, asking, "Why do you read the Bible?"

"Why, Grandpa, to learn about God," she replied.

"There is no God," he said.

The little girl was deeply hurt. She said, "Grandpa, you're a fool!"

Her grandfather became very angry.

She explained, "Grandpa, I didn't call you a fool, but the Bible does. It says, 'The fool hath said in his heart, There is no God.'"

Told by ALICE MARIE KNIGHT

* * *

The Unknown One

One day Mark Twain took his little daughter on his knee and told her about all the rulers and prominent men he had met in his travels. She listened attentively. When he had finished, she said, "Daddy, you know everybody but God, don't you?"

* * *

Life Dead on Our Hands

Dr. Carl Jung, renowned psychiatrist, commented on the neurosis of emptiness, "Men cut themselves off from the root of their being, from God, and then life turns empty, inane, meaningless, without purpose. When meaning goes, value goes and life turns dead on our hands."

* * *

Satanic Sweetness

"And no marvel; for Satan himself is transformed into an angel of light" (II Cor. 11:14).

One day I entered into conversation with a preacher who belonged to a strange and dangerous cult. At first he displayed

19

much satanic sweetness. Then I insisted on an answer to the question "Have you at any time seen yourself as a lost sinner in need of the Saviour and God's forgiveness?"

Tearing off, as it were, his mask, he disclosed his unbelief in hell and the new birth through faith in Christ. He became very angry and spoke abusively of me and of all ministers and churches in general. He seemed to be utterly destitute of love and compassion.

The Bible says, "To the law and to the testimony: if they speak not according to this word, it is because there is no light in them" (Isa. 8:20).

W. B. K.

* * *

"I Have Changed"

Nehru, late prime minister of India, who was perhaps the most articulate agnostic of this century, said, "I have changed. I now believe that the human mind is hungry for something deeper, in terms of moral and spiritual development, without which all the material advance may not be worthwhile."

Jesus said, "Man shall not live by bread alone, but by every word of God" (Luke 4:4).

* * *

On Way to Becoming Fertilizer

Said Huxley, "Man is nothing but a protoplasmic agglomeration on the way to becoming fertilizer."

How different is God's appraisal of man. As a spiritual being crowned with glory and honor, endowed by God with an intellect and a "living soul," man is of incalculable worth and precious to God: "For what is a man profited, if he shall gain the whole world, and lose his own soul?" (Matt. 16:26).

* * *

Pressed with Evangelistic Fervor

Stated Dr. Elton Trueblood, professor of philosophy at Earlham College, England, "Never in my life have I known a time when the attacks on the gospel were as vicious as they are now. I see about me a far more militant atheism than I have ever known, and I see it pressed with evangelistic fervor. Some of the most damaging attacks on the validity of the gospel are coming from those who claim some kind of marginal connection with Christianity."

* * *

Bravo!

The Council of Bishops of the Methodist Church has joined battle with the God-is-dead theologians.

Reaffirming belief "in the living God," the council issued the following statement: "In a day of confused religious philosophies, some of them purporting to be Christian, it seems urgent to reaffirm our abiding faith in the living God who is the Father of our Lord Jesus Christ, who moves purposefully in human history, and before whom each of His children has inescapable moral and spiritual responsibility."

Sunday School Times

* * *

Where Christian Doctrines Are Massacred

In editorializing on the fact that so-called Christian institutions of learning often make the most vicious attacks upon the Bible, the *Chicago Daily News* said, "We are struck by the hypocrisy and treachery of these attacks on Christianity. Men may say what they please about religion, but is there no place in which to assail Christianity but a divinity school? Is there no one to write infidel books except the professors of Christian theology? Is a theological seminary an appropriate place for a general massacre of Christian doctrines?"

* * *

"It's Hard to Be an Agnostic"

When his trusted plane, *Spirit of St. Louis,* was midway on its transatlantic flight between New York and Paris, Col. Charles A. Lindberg began to think of the smallness of man and the deficiency of his devices, and the greatness and marvels of God's universe. He mused, "It's hard to be an agnostic here in the *Spirit of St. Louis* when so aware of the frailty of man's devices. If one dies, all God's creation goes on existing in a plan so

20

perfectly balanced, so wondrously simple, and yet so incredibly complex, that it is beyond our comprehension. There's the infinite magnitude of the universe, the infinite detail, and man's consciousness of it all—a world audience to what, if not to God?"

The psalmist said, "When I consider thy heavens, the work of thy fingers, the moon and the stars, which thou hast ordained; what is man, that thou art mindful of him?" (Ps. 8:3-4).

* * *

An Insistent Question

Prof. Hannes Alfven, astrophysicist at the Swedish Institute of Technology, Stockholm, stated, "In the beginning there was an original cloud, magnetized and perhaps a light year, six trillion miles in diameter."

The professor must answer an insistent, paramount question: Where did the original cloud come from, and who put it there?

How spiritually and intellectually satisfying is the profound factual statement of the Bible: "In the beginning God created the heaven and the earth" (Gen. 1:1).

The *Pilgrim*

* * *

OK for Calm Waters

Some years ago two fishermen were fishing from an anchored rowboat on the Niagara River. One was an avowed atheist. The other was a devout Christian.

The anchor slipped and the boat began to move in the swift current toward the falls. The atheist, realizing their danger, yelled to his companion, "God, help us! Man, bend to the oars, or we'll surely go over the falls!"

They began to row desperately and finally turned the boat to the shore.

With a puzzled look on his face, the Christian said, "I thought you were an atheist. Why did you call on God?"

"Well," the other replied, "atheism is OK for calm waters, but not when you're drifting toward Niagara Falls!"

Told by RALPH W. NEIGHBOUR

* * *

Definite Plan

Astronaut John Glenn said, "Could the universe have just happened? I can't believe that. The universe was a definite plan. This is one big thing in space that shows me there is a God."

* * *

Then the Universe Would Be God

Said Dr. George David, physicist, "If the universe could create itself, it would embody the power of a Creator, and we should be forced to conclude that the universe itself is God."

* * *

An Explosion in Printing Shop

Biologist Edwin Conklin averred, "The probability of life originating from accident is comparable to the probability of an unabridged dictionary resulting from an explosion in a printing shop."

* * *

Convinced

Dr. Paul Amos Moody, professor of zoology, University of Vermont, stated, "The more I study science the more I am convinced that this world and the universe have a definite design, and design suggests a Designer."

* * *

Only Fair

Paul Harvey, journalist, declared, "If it is our intention to keep God out of the schools, then let us keep atheistic professors from promoting their godless religion, too."

21

BIBLE

Joshua's Long Day

The Bible tells us there was once a long day almost double in length: "And the sun stood still, and the moon stayed, until the people had avenged themselves on their enemies. . . . So the sun stood still in the midst of heaven, and hasted not to go down about a whole day" (Joshua 10:13).

Professors Pickering of Harvard University and Saunders of Greenwich, England, the site of an astronomical observatory, have demonstrated the veracity of the Bible by careful astronomical computation. They discovered that a day of twenty-four hours is missing.

The "Joshua day" plus the lacking forty minutes recorded in Isaiah—"I will bring again the shadow of the degrees . . . ten degrees backward" (38:8)—account for the missing twenty-four-hour day.

Greece, Egypt, China and Mexico all have records of this long day in the past. For a long time this long day had been denied. Now it has been proven.

Adapted from *News*

* * *

Keen Edge Blunted

A teenager complained, "Year in and year out in religious classes we have talked about God and Jesus and the apostles and all the same old stories. Now we should switch from what happened long ago and think about the problems in the world today."

Unless our study of God's Word and the heroes of the "faith which was once delivered unto the saints" ultimates in our practicing and applying the truths of God's Word to human needs, the truths will lose their keen cutting edge and challenge.

We are to be "doers of the word, and not hearers only" (James 1:22).

* * *

A Flickering Taper

A conceited young fellow said to an aged minister, "You believe in the inspiration of the whole Bible, don't you?

He replied, "I surely do."

The youth said, "The Bible is hardly a flickering taper."

The minister said, "Do you mean to say that groping mankind would see any better if the taper were put out?"

The psalmist said, "Thy word is a lamp unto my feet, and a light unto my path" (Ps. 119:105).

* * *

"The Paths of the Sea"

Some years ago, *Reader's Digest* had a most interesting article about the discovery of an oceanographer. Before his disclosure, westward and eastward ocean traffic often collided, with resultant loss of life and cargo.

One day the oceanographer read in the Bible: "The fowl of the air, and the fish of the sea, and whatsoever passeth through the paths of the seas" (Ps. 8:8). He resolved, "If the seas have paths, I am going to discover them."

The oceanographer pursued his self-appointed task and discovered the ocean's paths. He charted them and gave directions for oceangoing traffic to move in specified paths, with resultant diminishing of collisions.

* * *

God's Word Has Stood the Test

"After forty-five years of scholarly research in biblical textual studies and language study," said the late Robert Dick Wilson, Ph.D., professor of Semitic Philology at Princeton Theological Seminary, "I have come now to the conviction that no man knows enough to assail the truthfulness of the Old Testament. Wherever there is sufficient documentary evidence to make an investigation, the statements of the Bible, in the original text, have stood the test."

* * *

All I Need to Know

Martin Luther declared, "I have made a covenant with my God that He send me neither visions, dreams, nor even angels. I am well satisfied with the gift of Holy Scriptures which gives me abundant instruction and all that I need to know

22

both for this life and for that which is to come."

God has spoken His ultimate word "by [in] his Son" (Heb. 1:2). He tells us to "hear him" (Luke 9:35). That Word is changeless and true: "For ever, O LORD, thy word is settled in heaven" (Ps. 119:89).

* * *

When the Scholars Differ

Dr. R. A. Torrey, biblical scholar and Hebraist, said, "The truly wise man is he who always believes the Bible against the opinions of any man, whether scientist, philosopher or theologian. If the Bible says one thing and any man or body of men say another thing, the truly wise man will say, 'The Bible is the Word of Him who cannot lie.' "

* * *

Why the Bible Is Rejected

A missionary in India put a drop of water from the allegedly sacred Ganges River beneath a microscope and said to a Hindu, "Take a look."

The Hindu was horrified when he saw tiny wriggling, creeping things in the water.

"In seeking spiritual rest and forgiveness of sin, you and myriads of people in India bathe in water like this," said the missionary.

Later the Hindu came and bought the microscope from the missionary. He threw it violently on the pavement and broke it. Then he walked silently away. Many people reject God's Word because it reveals hidden sins and the vileness of the unchanged heart of man—"deceitful . . . and desperately wicked" (Jer. 17:9).

* * *

The Bible Breeds Unrest

When Martin Luther was still in a monastery, struggling with his doubts and dissatisfactions, one of his teachers said, "Do not read the Bible. Study the writings of the church fathers. They will give you the whole marrow of the Bible. Reading the Bible breeds unrest."

The preceptor unintentionally conveyed certain truths about the Bible. It does breed unrest in those who are under the rule and dominance of sin: "The wicked are like the troubled sea, when it cannot rest" (Isa. 57:20).

* * *

Born Again by the Word

Richard Blackaby, a Canadian soldier who was critically wounded in World War II, gave this testimony: "I lay in a shell hole for fifteen hours, unable to get up. I felt in my pocket for a cigarette. All that I could find was a little New Testament which someone had given me, and I had never read. I began to read the book of Matthew. Later I continued to read it while convalescing in the hospital. The little Book changed my life! Shortly I will return to the front, but I will not return alone. Christ will be with me!"

"Being born again . . . by the word of God, which liveth and abideth for ever" (I Peter 1:23).

Told by an army chaplain

* * *

Triumphant in Crises

Capt. Eddie Rickenbacker testified, "I probably would not be here today if it had not been for the spiritual light and the moral power derived from the Bible. It has carried me through many crises of life."

* * *

Its Tranquilizing Power

Dr. Klaus Thomas said, "After twenty-five years of pastoral and psychiatric practice, I cannot have any doubt about the overwhelming harmonizing, health-restoring, and transforming power of the Bible's message and of a geniune Christian faith."

* * *

Clean Christians and Dirty Bibles

In Latin America, evangelical churches are known as "the churches of the dirty Bibles." How complimentary! Usually members of evangelical churches in Latin America are poverty-stricken, hard-working manual laborers. With dirty fingers they leave smudges on the pages of their Bibles.

23

Oh, for more churches where the poor read Bibles!

"I have esteemed the words of his mouth more than my necessary food" (Job 23:12).

Told by JOHN W. BRAWAND,
Wycliffe Bible Translators

* * *

The Indestructible Word

God's Word has been published, in whole and in part, in 1,216 languages and dialects. More than 3,000 translators are currently working in 130 countries. William Tyndale was among the pioneer translators of God's Word into the language of the people. He was banished from England as a heretic. He fled to Wittenberg, Germany. There he translated the New Testament from the Greek into English. His New Testament was printed in the city of Worms. When the New Testaments were smuggled into England, Henry VIII decreed that all of them be confiscated and burned. The tyrannical king had Tyndale arrested in Antwerp, Belgium. After sixteen months' imprisonment, Tyndale was tried for heresy and judged guilty. He was burned at the stake on August 6, 1536.

The burning of God's Word kindled a glowing love for it in the hearts of His children. And so "the word of God grew and multiplied" (Acts 12:24). Thank God! "The word of God is not bound" (II Tim. 2:9). We are to *proclaim* it: "Preach the word" (II Tim. 4:2); *practice* it: "Be ye doers of the word" (James 1:22); and *promulgate* it: "This gospel shall be preached throughout the whole world" (Mark 14:9).

* * *

Corrupting God's Word

How interesting and rewarding is the study of words—their etymology and their use.

The word *corrupt* described what the street peddlers of ancient Greece, who sold wine and other things, used to do. These hucksters were notorious for adulterating their wine and thus shortchanging their customers.

Paul had in mind the unscrupulous practice of those peddlers when he wrote, "We are not as many, which corrupt the word of God" (II Cor. 2:17).

Great havoc is done by those who compromise, or adulterate, God's eternal Word. The inspired writers of God's Word spoke most severely of them: "For there are . . . crept in unawares . . . ungodly men, turning the grace of our God into lasciviousness, and denying the only Lord God, and our Lord Jesus Christ" (Jude 4).

* * *

Moving World Toward God

The novelist Joseph Conrad said, "With the right word and the right accent; with a lever long enough, and with a fulcrum strong enough, and a place to stand, I can move the world."

God's children can say, "With the Word of God as our lever, the church as our fulcrum, and Jesus Christ as our place to stand, we can move the world toward God."

* * *

How It Is Translated

It is interesting to know how the Wycliffe Bible Translators translate the Bible into the language of Indian tribes in Central and South America.

"God loves" is translated "God hurts in His heart for us." "Doubt" becomes "thinking two things." "Our hope is in God" is translated "We hang on God." "Heap coals of fire on his head" is translated "Make him ashamed by your kindness."

Extreme caution must be exercised in translating the Bible into multitonal words, because often only the inflection of the voice indicates which word is meant. For instance, "sinner" is almost synonymous with "a fat person." One day a teacher said, "God loves the sinner." A look of bewilderment clouded the Indians' faces. They thought the missionary said, "God loves a fat person." None of them were fat, so they concluded that they were not the objects of God's love.

Told by JOHN W. BRAWAND,
Wycliffe Bible Translators

A Source of Strength

In his inaugural address, John F. Kennedy quoted the following verse which he said had been a source of strength to him through the years: "They that wait upon the LORD shall renew their strength; they shall mount up with wings as eagles; they shall run, and not be weary; and they shall walk, and not faint" (Isa. 40:31).

* * *

The Revealing Spade

Italian archaeologists working with the Israeli Department of Antiquities recently discovered in the ancient theater at Caesarea a tablet bearing the names of Pontius Pilate and Tiberius. This is the first archaeological find to mention the Roman governor. Until this discovery our knowledge of Pontius Pilate was limited to the gospel narratives and the writings of the Jewish historian Josephus.

Dr. Abraham Biran, Director of Antiquities, stated, "Once again the veracity of the Old and New Testaments has been established."

* * *

The Reverse Is True

Solomon Richter said, "The Bible is a set of scruples, imposed on the framework of humanity, to keep it from functioning normally."

The reverse is true. Every "thou shalt" or "thou shalt not" of the Bible is designed for the highest spiritual and physical welfare of man. When the Bible says, "Thou shalt not . . . ," it is saying, "Do thyself no harm."

* * *

Teaching from Early Childhood

Emperor Haile Selassie declared, "From early childhood I was taught to appreciate the Bible, and my love for it increases with the passing of time. All through my troubles I have found it a source of infinite comfort. Today man sees all his hopes and aspirations crumbling before him. He is perplexed and knows not whither he is drifting. But he must realize that the Bible is his refuge and the rallying point of humanity. In it

man will find the solution of his present problems and guidance for his future action. Unless he accepts the Bible and its great message, he cannot hope for salvation. I glory in the Bible."

Baptist Standard

* * *

Archaeology Has Convinced Many

Dr. R. V. D. Magoffin, a past president of the Archaeological Institute of America, said, "Archaeology has converted both laity and clergy. No longer do they fear that archaeological investigation will overturn the Bible statements. Thus far the finds have confirmed them, or have opened confirmatory possibilities."

* * *

Religious Quackery

Dr. A. W. Tozer stated, "Beware of the widely prevalent, man-devised 'do-it-yourself religions,' which are basically a hash of religious quackery."

Isaiah said, "To the law and to the testimony: if they speak not according to this word, it is because there is no light in them" (8:20).

* * *

The Indestructible Word

Centuries ago a council of bishops decreed, "We forbid the common people to possess any of the Books of the Old or New Testament."

Little did they think that the time would come when the common people in many lands would possess and be able to read God's Word in their own language.

John Wycliffe was the first translator of the Bible into English. He has been called "the morning star of the Reformation."

Many of Wycliffe's followers were burned at the stake because they possessed and read the English Bible. Fifty years after Wycliffe's death, his grave was torn open, his body was burned, and his ashes were thrown into a brook near his old church.

Tides of bitterness and intolerance have ebbed and flowed around God's imperishable Word through the centuries. But the rage and cruelties of its enemies could not stop the spread of the Bible, nor prevent the masses from obtaining and reading it.

"But the word of the Lord endureth for ever" (I Peter 1:25).

* * *

Convinced

When William Gladstone was prime minister of Britain, he refused to appoint Dr. A. H. Sayce, a noted expert on Assyriology, as professor of history at Oxford University because he held some critical views about the Bible, doubting the historical accuracy of some Old Testament stories.

When the great scholar went to the Near East to take part in archaeological research, his views changed. As he excavated the ruins of Bible lands and discovered ancient records paralleling biblical stories and incidents, he became convinced that the Bible is historically right. He openly acknowledged his firm belief in the accuracy and integrity of the Scriptures.

MARIANO DI GANGI,
in *Sunday School Times*

* * *

Koran Memorized

"What are you taught in your school?" a visiting missionary asked a small Muslim boy in a village school in Turkey.

"The Koran, sir. We memorize the Koran in Arabic," said the boy.

"Only the Koran? Do you not also study history, literature and philosophy?" asked the missionary.

"Only the Koran," he replied. "When we finish elementary school, we come here and begin to memorize the Koran in Arabic. It takes years, but when we have finished the task, we are Islamic priests."

"And do you understand it?"

"It is not necessary to understand it. The Koran has the sacred writings of Muhammad the prophet, and when we recite them from memory, we are qualified to be priests."

A Mutilated Bible

A modernistic minister became pastor of a church in Ireland. He began to speak disparagingly of portions of the Bible. As time passed, faith in some of the eternal verities of God's Word was undermined.

One day a prominent member of his church, who was critically ill, sent for the minister.

"Shall I read some from the Bible to you and pray with you?" he asked.

"Yes," said the dying man.

The wife brought the minister a Bible. As he opened it, he discovered that some entire books were missing, some chapters were gone from other books, and some of the verses were cut out. It was a shamefully mangled Bible.

The startled clergyman exclaimed, "Have you not a better Bible than this one?"

Accusingly the dying man said, "When you came to this parish, I had a *whole* Bible. But when you told us that a certain book was fictional, I cut it out of my Bible. When you told us that a chapter was not true, I removed it. When you told us that some of the stories were fables, I cut them out too. There is little of my Bible left except the two covers."

Told by WILLIAM McCARRELL

* * *

Contemporary and Timely

A religious colporteur in the Middle East was arrested, brought into a local police court and charged with selling what appeared to be highly inflammatory political propaganda. After examining the strange book carefully, the judge demanded, "Where is that man Paul who wrote this book of Romans? Bring him into this court!"

The colporteur explained to the judge that the apostle Paul died almost two thousand years ago. The judge was difficult to convince. Finally he said, "Here, you sign a statement declaring you will be personally responsible for everything written in this book of Romans. This document is too contemporary and its significance too timely not to have some-

26

one personally responsible for its contents."

Many people do not have the insight of that Muslin judge. They look upon the Bible as an ancient book, more or less unrelated and irrelevant to our time. They honor it with high-sounding praise, but do not believe it with their hearts. They quote it, but they do not live it.

Told by EUGENE A. NIDA

* * *

Settled on the Book

I entered the world's great library doors,
I crossed their acres of polished floors,
I searched and searched their stacks and nooks,
But I settled at last on the Book of books: The Bible.

* * *

A Two-Way Conversation

A missionary observed an African Christian sitting beneath a tree and reading his Bible. He always read a verse and then looked up. The missionary asked, "Why do you keep looking up when you read your Bible?"

"I look at God's Book and let God talk to me," said the native, "and then I look up and talk to Him."

* * *

Spiritually Starved

Following an autopsy on a six-month-old boy, Dr. Luther Adelson, chief Cuyahoga County (Ohio) pathologist, and Coroner Samuel Gerber ruled that the death of the baby was homicide by starvation.

The coroner said, "While battered babies are a seemingly more common occurrence, this is not so. It is only that battered babies are more easily detected. Infant starvation is rarely seen while it is in progress. Acts of omission whereby the child is deprived of adequate nutrition are equally or more dangerous to the child's welfare and equally culpable under the law."

Many newborn babes in Christ are spiritually starved through failure to obey the command "As newborn babes, desire the sincere milk of the word, that ye may grow thereby" (I Peter 2:2).

* * *

Increasingly Precious

Fanny Crosby said, "My love for the Holy Bible and its sacred truth is stronger at ninety than it was at nineteen."

Said the psalmist, "O how love I thy law! It is my meditation all the day" (Ps. 119:97).

* * *

No Controversy

After many years of exploration and excavation in Palestine, Dr. Nelson Glueck, archaeologist, rabbi and president of the Hebrew Union College, said, "It may be stated categorically that no archaeological discovery has ever controverted a biblical reference. Scores of archaeological findings have been made which confirm in clear outline or in exact detail historical statements in the Bible. And, by the same token, proper evaluation of biblical descriptions has often led to amazing discoveries. They form tesserae in the vast mosaic of the Bible's almost incredibly correct historical memory."

* * *

The Greatest Hope for Survival

At his eightieth birthday party at Miami Beach, David Ben-Gurion, the first prime minister of Israel, called for an international study of the Bible by Jewish children. "It is the Bible that has kept us alive all these centuries, and it is the Bible that holds the greatest hope for our survival in the future," he said.

* * *

It Works

An astronomer called a skilled mechanic to repair the giant telescope in his observatory. During the lunch hour, the astronomer saw the mechanic reading his Bible. "Why do you read that?" he asked. "You don't even know who wrote some of it."

The mechanic replied, "You use multiplication tables and logarithm charts, don't you?"

27

"Of course I do," the astronomer replied.

"Do you know who wrote them?" he asked.

"No," the astronomer replied. "I don't need to know who wrote them. I trust them because they work."

"Well," the mechanic declared, "I trust the Bible for the same reason. It works!"

Told by WILLIAM MCCARRELL

* * *

"And the Word of God Increased"

Dr. Eugene A. Nida, the translation secretary of the American Bible Society, said, "We have reached a new epoch in Bible translation. Instead of translations being made by missionaries who are not always familiar with colloquialisms and shades of meaning in exotic languages, translations are being done increasingly by trained indigenous Christians. At present, some three thousand worldwide translators are at work."

* * *

Archaeology Confirms Bible

Many years ago Robert Ingersoll, the self-acclaimed atheist, rejected the Bible because there was no corroborative evidence outside the Bible to prove the historic genuineness of some of its records. If Ingersoll lived today, he would have to conjure up other excuses for rejecting God's inspired Word.

In recent years, archaeologists have unearthed records of ancient peoples and civilizations which parallel and substantiate the historicity of the biblical record of ancient people and events.

In excavating at the site of ancient Ur, in 1929, archaeologists sank a deep shaft down through various strata of ancient civilizations. In coming to a stratum of alluvial clay, which was eight feet thick, they discovered that it was entirely free from fragments of any kind. Below it were discovered pottery of an ancient type and neolithic flint instruments.

The alluvial stratum was so corroborative of the biblical story of the flood that archaeologist Sir Charles Leonard Woolley said, "The deposit could be due only to a flood of such exceptional dimensions that it completely wiped out an earlier race and culture and was, indeed, the flood of the Bible story. Whether the flood covered the inhabited world as known to Noah, or had a much wider range may, in the present state of our knowledge, be left an open question."

Dr. Harold J. Ockenga has stated, "Wherever the spade has dug; wherever it has turned over an ancient civilization; wherever it has brought to light some ancient monument; wherever it has unearthed anything that has to do with a name, an event, or a place of the Bible, it has vindicated the Bible."

* * *

The Wrong Weapons

Clarence Hall, a World War II correspondent, testified, "I can never think of the boons and benefits that the Bible invariably brings without thinking of Shimmabuke, a tiny village I came upon as a war correspondent in Okinawa.

"Thirty-five years before, an American missionary en route to Japan had stopped there, just long enough to make two converts—Shosei Kina and his brother Mojon. He left a Bible with them and passed on. For thirty years they had no contact with any other Christian missionary, but they made the Bible come alive. They taught the other villagers until every man, woman and child in Shimmabuke became Christians.

"Shosei Kina became the headman of the village, and Mojon the chief teacher. In his school the Bible was read daily. The precepts of the Bible were law in the village. In those thirty years there developed a Christian democracy in its purest form.

"When the American Army came across the island, an advance patrol came to the village compound with guns leveled. The two old men stepped forth, bowed low and began to speak. An interpreter explained that the old men were welcoming the Americans as fellow Christians. The GIs were flabbergasted. They sent for their chaplain. He came with officers of the Intelligence Service. They toured the village. They were astounded at the spotlessly clean homes and streets and the gentility of the inhabitants. The

28

other Okinawan villages they had seen were filthy, and the people were ignorant and poverty-stricken.

"Later I strolled through Shimmabuke with a tough army sergeant. He said, 'I can't figure it out—this kind of people coming from a Bible and a couple of old guys who wanted to live like Jesus Christ. *Maybe we have been using the wrong kind of weapons to make the world over!*'"

* * *

When the Pilgrim Comes to the Valley

Henry Van Dyke said of the Bible, "No man is poor or desolate who has this treasure for his own. When the landscape darkens and the trembling pilgrim comes to the valley of the shadow, he is not afraid to enter. He takes the rod and the staff of Scripture in his hand. He says to his friend and comrade, 'Good-bye. We shall meet again!' Comforted by that support, he goes toward the lonely pass as one who walks through darkness into light!"

* * *

No Binding Chains

The apostle Paul, bound with chains in Rome, wrote about the Word of God which cannot be bound. Wicked men have tried to bind it with the chains of indifference or to banish it with ridicule into permanent exile. The Bible is the Magna Charta of our liberties. All the hopes of mankind are in Christ who is presented to us in the priceless Word of God.

JOHN RUSKIN

The Living Word

A biology teacher held up a little seed and said to his class, "I know the proportionate chemical elements in this seed—its hydrogen, carbon, nitrogen and so forth. If I made a seed of identical chemical proportions and planted it, its elements would only be absorbed in the soil. But if I plant in good soil this seed that God has made—with its inherent life principle—it will become a plant."

The Bible looks like other books. It is different, however. It has a life-giving ingredient. It "liveth and abideth for ever" (I Peter 1:23). It imparts spiritual life to all who receive it in their hearts.

* * *

Window of Hope

Timothy Dwight said, "The Bible is the window of hope through which we look into eternity."

* * *

The Bible Reads Me

Johann Wolfgang von Goethe, the German poet and dramatist, testified, "I read all kinds of books, including sacred books, but the Bible stands alone because it reads me."

* * *

Above All

Martin Luther stated, "I put the Scriptures above all the sayings of the fathers, angels, men and devils. Here I take my stand."

CARE, GOD'S

A Measured Gift from God

We breathe eighteen times a minute, about 26,000 times a day. Each breath that we take is a measured gift of life from God.

Job said, "Who knoweth not in all these that the hand of the LORD hath wrought this? In whose hand is the soul of every living thing, and the breath of all mankind" (Job 12:9-10).

"Oh that men would praise the LORD for his goodness, and for his wonderful works to the children of men!" (Ps. 107:8).

Daniel brought this accusation against the pagan ruler Belshazzar: "The God in whose hand thy breath is, and whose are all thy ways, hast thou not glorified" (Dan. 5:23).

* * *

One of Nature's Smallest Creatures

General Motors, one of the world's largest corporations, came to the aid of one of nature's smallest creatures—a mother house wren.

Fifteen-year-old Susan Crawshaw of Waco, Texas, wrote General Motors a letter, saying, "My father owns a Chevrolet pickup. He likes it very much. A house wren has made a nest in the truck. She has already laid three eggs and there may be more any moment. Naturally my mother and I will not let my father drive the pickup, because he might break the eggs. So would you please send us another pickup to drive while the eggs are hatching? Any color will do."

General Motors responded instantly and delivered a new truck to Susan's home. In it there was a sign to be placed on the nesting pickup: Quiet! Birds hatching! Do not drive! The loaned truck remained with the Crawshaws until the baby wrens learned how to fly.

God quickly responds to the needs of His children. No need, however small, is overlooked by Him.

* * *

My Times

My times are in Thy hand:
Lord, I am glad;
No place more safe and sure
Was ever found;
No greater, wiser mind has ever planned
My times.

My happy times and harrowing times,
My times of darkness and despair,
And times when I am made to wait:
All these are in
Thy hand.

My times—Thy hand,
Twin thoughts of consolation these,
The secret of serenity
For all the passing days.

* * *

Sufficient for the Day

Oh, ask not thou, "How shall I bear
    The burden of tomorrow?"
Sufficient for the day its care,
    Its evil and its sorrow;
God imparteth by the way,
    Strength sufficient for the day.

Your Mother Was Right

A shivering, hungry little boy stood in front of a restaurant in Liverpool. A sea captain placed his hand on the boy's shoulder and asked, "What are you doing here, my boy?"

The boy replied, "I am hungry, sir."

The captain said, "Come with me, my boy, and be my guest."

As they were eating, the captain asked, "Where are your parents?"

The boy replied, "My mother died when I was four, and I haven't seen my father since."

"Who takes care of you?" asked the captain.

"Well, sir," replied the boy hesitantly, "just before my mother died she said, 'Jesus will take care of you.'"

The captain said, "Your mother was right. The good Lord provided for you tonight, didn't He?"

Told by ALICE M. KNIGHT

* * *

"Somebody Cares"

As Fannie Edna Stafford listened intently to her pastor's sermon, a sentence in his message went like an arrow to her heart: "The great need of this weary world is to know that somebody cares."

Late that Sunday night, the pastor's message lingered in her mind. She was so deeply impressed with the thought of God's love and concern for His children that she resolved to put the truth into a poem. She began to write "Somebody Cares," and finished it the next day. Homer Rodeheaver put it to music:

Somebody knows when your heart aches,
    And everything seems to go wrong;
Somebody knows when the shadows
    Need chasing away with a song.
Somebody knows when you're lonely,
    Tired, discouraged and blue;
Somebody wants you to know Him,
    And know that He dearly loves you.

30

No Need for Two to Stay Awake

During the aerial bombardment of London in World War II, an old lady refused one night to move from the top front room of a house where she had lived for twenty years. In explaining why she refused to seek seemingly safer quarters, she said, "I say my prayers to God every night. I know that He sees and hears me and will take care of me. Since God never sleeps or slumbers, I see no need for both of us to stay awake."

"I will both lay me down in peace, and sleep: for thou, LORD, only makest me dwell in safety" (Ps. 4:8).

RALPH W. NEIGHBOUR

* * *

Song of the Sparrow

I'm only a little sparrow,
 A bird of low degree,
My life is of little value,
 But the dear Lord cares for me.

He gives me a coat of feathers,
 It is very plain, I know,
Without a speck of crimson,
 For it was not made for show.

But it keeps me warm in winter,
 And it shelters me from the rain,
Were it bordered with gold and purple,
 Perhaps it would make me vain.

And now that the springtime cometh,
 I will build me a little nest,
With many a chirp of pleasure,
 In the spot I like the best.

I have no barn or storehouse,
 I neither sow nor reap,
God gives me a sparrow's portion,
 And never a seed to keep.

* * *

Tell God Only

Early in his career, God seemed to say to George Müller, "Tell no one about your needs. Only trust Me to supply them!" From that moment, Müller dedicated himself to the ministry of prayer.

When in his seventies, Müller testified, "God has answered thousands of specific prayers. Often He answered them immediately. At other times He delayed the answer. I knew that the answer would come in God's good time and manner."

Let us remember that delays are not denials to our prayers. Sometimes denials are answers to our prayers: "Ye know not what ye ask" (Matt. 20:22). "Likewise the Spirit also helpeth our infirmities: for we know not what we should pray for as we ought" (Rom. 8:26).

This is certain: "No good thing will he withhold from them that walk uprightly" (Ps. 84:11). God will give what is best for His children!

* * *

In His Hands

My times are in Thy gracious hand,
 I'm glad my times are there;
There's much I do not understand,
 Enough that Thou dost care.

My times are in Thy guiding hand,
 And this my peace would be;
For Thou wilt guide as Thou hast planned,
 And that will prosper me.

My times are in Thy giving hand,
 Thus till my race is run,
Till I reach the heavenly land,
 Of cares I need have none.

J. DANSON SMITH

* * *

I Only Know

I know not where His islands lift
 Their fronded palms in air,
I only know I cannot drift
 Beyond His love and care.

And so beside the silent sea,
 I wait the muffled oar.
No harm from Him can come to me
 On ocean or on shore.

JOHN GREENLEAF WHITTIER

31

CHILDREN

(See also Parental Responsibility)

Don't Grow Weeds

Luther Burbank, the horticulturist, once warned, "If we had paid no more attention to our plants than we have to our children, we would now be living in a jungle of weeds."

Phillips Brooks said, "He who helps a child helps humanity with an immediateness which no other help given to a human creature, in any other stage of human life, can possibly give again. We never stand so tall as when we stoop to help a little child."

Parents' Magazine reported, "Modern psychologists and psychiatrists are convinced that the chances for healthy mental development are largely determined during the first six years of a child's life."

Say commented, "It is a well-established fact that the seeds of insanity are sown from the ages of one to six."

We bring them, Lord, in thankful hands,
    And yield them up to Thee;
Joyful that we ourselves are Thine,
    Thine let our children be.

ALICE M. KNIGHT

* * *

"Mommy, Wrap Me up in You!"

Every child yearns for loving care and a feeling of security.

Little Gloria was out playing one day, when she suddenly stopped and ran into the kitchen. With outstretched arms, she said, "Mommy, wrap me up in you!"

Mother took Gloria in her arms and sat down in a rocking chair. Soon Gloria was asleep.

The mother said later, "As I rocked her, I felt a great need of assurance of God's tender care. With childlike simplicity I prayed, 'Dear Lord, wrap me up in You.' "

ALICE MARIE KNIGHT

* * *

Headlines

How suggestive are the captions of recent magazine articles on children written by leading educators, psychiatrists and psychologists: "The First Five Years Shape All of Life"; "Behavior Is Set by Five"; "Baby's First Year Is the Growingest"; "Train Citizens in the Cradle"; "Don't Wait for the School Bell"; "Age Five Is Old Psychologically"; "Combat Crime in Infancy."

* * *

Make Certain They Attend

J. Edgar Hoover advised, "If we are to make progress in the fight against crime, make certain that the children of the nation regularly attend Sunday school and church. Regardless of parents' religious convictions, they owe it to their children to give them the opportunity of regularly attending Sunday school and church. The hope of the nation lies in a return to the faith of our fathers."

* * *

Two and a Half Conversions

Moody once reported the results of one of his meetings thus: "Two and a half conversions."

A friend asked, "Two adults and a child, I suppose?"

"No," replied Moody, "two children and an adult. The children gave their whole lives. The adult had only half a life to give."

* * *

Bless Passersby

A minister was entertained in the home of a missionary in Mexico. One morning as he passed the bedroom of little three-year-old Margarite, he heard her pray for her loved ones by name and close her prayer thus: "Heavenly Father, please bless all the people who pass by my house."

The minister said later, "I had been observing the expressions of sorrow and helplessness of those passing Margarite's house. I had felt their great need, but I did not pray for them until led to do so by little Margarite."

Told by ALICE M. KNIGHT

"In Christ's Stead"

During the last twelve years of his pastorate, Dr. Albert William Beaven gave a five-minute sermon to the children before the morning worship service. As the children passed before him to go to a specially reserved place for them, each child looked at him and smiled. He always gave a smile in return.

One morning he failed to return the smile of a little, curly-headed, four-year-old girl. She left the procession and ran to her mother, sobbing. After quieting the little one, her mother asked why she had cried. She replied, "I smiled at God, and He didn't smile back at me!"

Later Dr. Beaven said, "Just think of it! For her I stood for God. I had failed with my smile and the world became dark for her!"

God's servants are His ambassadors. They stand before the people "in Christ's stead" (II Cor. 5:20). What a privilege! What a responsibility!

Long ago Jethro said to Moses, "Be thou for the people to God-ward" (Exodus 18:19).

Told by ALICE M. KNIGHT

* * *

The Lambs Too

An aged pastor in Scotland persistently refused to admit children into the membership of his church, even though they professed faith in Christ.

An elder, who was a sheepherder, invited the pastor to visit his ranch. When he came, the elder began to herd the sheep into the fold, but he allowed only the sheep to enter. Using a big stick, he roughly thrust back the lambs.

The pastor exclaimed, "How cruel! Why aren't you allowing the lambs to enter the protective sheepfold? They need the shelter far more than the older sheep."

"I'm doing just what you do at the church to the lambs—the children," said the elder.

18—Knights Illustrations

The pastor never again tried to shut out the little ones who trusted Jesus as their Saviour.

Told by ALICE MARIE KNIGHT

A Delinquent Society

Professor Walter A. Lunden of Iowa State University said, "In all probability the delinquent is a normal person living in a delinquent society. Few analyze the delinquency problem in terms of a state of society in which normative standards of conduct and belief have weakened or disappeared."

* * *

"Don't Send Your Child to Sunday School"

Many readers were startled when they read at the top of a page in a religious journal these words in large boldface letters, "Don't send your child to Sunday school. Anyone who does that does the child a great disservice."

Following the unusual statement, the meaning was cleared up by this statement in small print, "Don't *send* your child. *Take* him."

"I was glad when they said unto me, Let us go into the house of the LORD" (Ps. 122:1).

United Evangelical

* * *

Limitless Potentialities

Limitless potentialities for either good or evil are wrapped up in a baby.

On March 24, 1820, a baby girl was born in a village in New York State. When only a few weeks old, she became totally blind.

Her blindness was obviously a part of God's inscrutable plan for her life. Her physical blindness opened her spiritual eyes to the One whose presence and power rested mightily on her. The baby grew into womanhood and lived to be ninety-five years old. During the long span of years God used her to bring spiritual life and inspiration to countless millions by some six thousand hymns she wrote, hymns which will inspire and challenge many millions as long as time lasts. Her name, you ask? Fanny J. Crosby.

Adapted from *Canadian Baptist*

* * *

Pricelessly Precious Children

One day when Dr. J. Wilbur Chapman was in Tiffany's store in New York City, he heard a salesman say, "Madam, this pearl is worth seventeen thousand dollars."

Interested, Dr. Chapman said to the salesman, "Please let me see the pearl which is worth seventeen thousand dollars."

Dr. Chapman looked intently at the gem. As he left the store, he mused, *Suppose Tiffany would say to me, "Dr. Chapman, we are sending all the precious pearls and diamonds and rubies in our store to your home. We want you to take care of them tonight."* I would instantly get in touch with the police department and ask for the department's most trusted officers to guard my home during the night.

Then, as he walked along, Dr. Chapman thought, *But I have a nine-year-old boy in my home, and Jesus asked, "For what is a man profited, if he shall gain the whole world, and lose his own soul?"* [*Matt. 16:26*]. *If I had all the pearls, rubies and diamonds in the world, my little boy would be worth infinitely more than them.*

When he told about the incident later, Dr. Chapman said, "We all would tremble if we had millions of dollars' worth of jewels in our homes just for one night. How can we go up to our heavenly Father if the children are not with us?"

Told by ALICE M. KNIGHT

* * *

"From a Child Thou Hast Known the Scriptures"

Little Ruthie and Bruce, ages three and five, delighted to visit grandpa. Grandpa was happy to see them. He repeated nursery rhymes to them. The children couldn't readily identify the characters of whom the rhymes spoke. Grandpa said, "They don't know much."

Mother, who had sat silently, said, "They do know something." Then she said to Bruce, "Quote Romans 3:23." Having quoted it, Bruce asked, "Grandpa, shall I quote some other verses?" He quoted fifteen more verses, and Ruth quoted some in between.

Grandpa was thrilled! Later, he took them to nearby neighbors and relatives to show them how well the children knew the Scriptures. As the children quoted God's Word, it entered the heart of grandpa, blessing and enriching him as it had never done.

"Out of the mouth of babes . . . thou hast perfected praise" (Matt. 21:16).

Told by ALICE MARIE KNIGHT

* * *

The Dropouts

Solomon O. Lichter warned in his book *The Drop-Outs*, "Forty percent of American children discontinue school before high school graduation. At the current rate, seven and one-half million students will quit school during this decade. The dropouts represent a tragic waste of potential resources of our young people at a time when our country needs their fullest productivity."

* * *

God's Loveliest Things

When God makes a lovely thing,
The dearest and completest,
He makes it little, don't you see,
For little things are sweetest.

Little birds, little flowers,
Little diamonds, little pearls,
But the dearest things on earth
Are His little boys and girls.

* * *

"I Do Understand"

"Teacher, isn't it nice that God told us the ages of people who served Him in the Bible?" said Larry.

"Why do you think so, Larry?" asked the teacher.

"Here's why. I'm eight years old and I've accepted Jesus as my Saviour. When I told my mother about it, she said, 'Larry, you don't understand yet. You're too young.' I think grownups are wrong when they think eight-year-old boys and girls are too young to understand about being a Christian. When I grow up, I'm going to be a minister. The boys and girls in my church will sure feel good when I tell them I trusted Jesus as my Saviour when I was eight years old."

Told by ALICE M. KNIGHT

34

Learning Life's Lessons

There! little girl; don't cry.
  They have broken your doll, I know;
    And your teaset blue,
    And your playhouse, too,
  Are things of the long ago;
    But childish troubles will soon pass
      by,
      There! little girl; don't cry.

There! little girl; don't cry.
  They have broken your slate, I know;
    And the glad, wild ways
    Of your schoolgirl days
  Are things of the long ago;
    But life and love will soon come by,
      There! little girl; don't cry.

There! little girl; don't cry.
  They have broken your heart, I know;
    And the rainbow gleams
    Of your youthful dreams
  Are things of the long ago;
    But Heaven holds all for which you
      sigh,
      There! little girl; don't cry.

JAMES WHITCOMB RILEY

* * *

From Childhood

John Quincy Adams said, "The earlier my children begin to read the Bible, the more confident will be my hope that they will become useful citizens."

Paul said of Timothy, "From a child thou hast known the holy scriptures, which are able to make thee wise unto salvation through faith . . . in Christ Jesus" (II Tim. 3:15).

* * *

Prayer at the Birth of a Child

Lord, You know how earnestly I have asked for this child. Be present now and keep us in Your hand.

Let me never forget that You who have given this life have commanded us to bring up children to love and obey You. Grant me Your strength day by day and give me the assurance of Your presence.

Give me a glad, warm and understanding heart, a heart of love. Help me to be patient when things go wrong. . . . And if I should become too busy, remind me that there is more to being a mother than homely tasks. Help me to keep a loose hold on material things that I may cling to You.

Make me faithful in introducing Jesus Christ to my child. Of all the favors I would ask, the chief is that he will find Christ and find Him glorious.

Dear God, it is not easy to be a mother. Thank You for this child, for trusting me with this new life. Thank You for Your power. I put myself and this babe in Your hands. For Jesus' sake. Amen.

CATHARINE BRANDT, in *Moody Monthly*

* * *

"If It Weren't for You and Daddy"

Little Johnny said, as he rode in the family car, "Mommy, if it weren't for you and Daddy, I wouldn't know where we should turn."

Long ago the psalmist showed the same trust when he asked, "Whom have I in heaven but thee? And there is none upon earth that I desire beside thee" (Ps. 73:25).

* * *

The Baby

Where did you come from, baby dear?
Out of everywhere into the here.

Where did you get your eyes so blue?
Out of the sky as I came through.

What makes the light in them sparkle and
  spin?
Some of the starry spikes left in.

Where did you get that little tear?
I found it waiting when I got here.

What makes your forehead so smooth and
  high?
A soft hand stroked it as I went by.

What makes your cheek like a warm
  white rose?
Something better than anyone knows.

Whence that three-cornered smile of bliss?
Three angels gave me at once a kiss.

Where did you get that pearly ear?
God spoke, and it came out to hear.

Where did you get those arms and hands?
Love made itself into hooks and bands.

Feet, whence did you come, you darling
   things?
From the same box as the cherubs' wings.

How did they all just come to be you?
God thought about me, and so I grew.

But how did you come to us, you dear?
God thought of you, and so I am here.

GEORGE MACDONALD

*   *   *

"Mother, Who Made God?"

One day a six-year-old boy asked,
"Mother, who made God?"

Instantly his mother's face expressed
astonishment and chagrin. She said curt-
ly, "What an awful question to ask. You
had better run along and play."

In the same community another boy
asked his mother, "Did God make Himself?"

His mother prayed silently. Taking off
her wedding ring, she gave it to her son
and asked, "Where does this ring begin
and where does it end?"

The boy answered, "There is no starting place or stopping place to a ring."

The mother said, "Just so it is with
God. There is no beginning and no end
to God. He always has been and always
will be!"

The Bible says, "From everlasting to
everlasting, thou art God" (Ps. 90:2).

Told by ALICE M. KNIGHT

*   *   *

Tomorrow

I saw tomorrow marching by
  On little children's feet;
Within their forms and faces read
  Her prophecy complete.

I saw tomorrow look at me
  From little children's eyes;
And thought how carefully we'd teach
  If we were really wise.

MYRTLE G. BURGER

*   *   *

Blood Ankle-deep

Sing a song of TV
  For the little ones,
Four and twenty jailbirds
  Packing tommy guns!

When the scene is finished
  The blood is ankle-deep.
Wasn't that a pretty dish
  To send the kids to sleep?

Quoted by a federal
prison director before
the Senate subcommittee
on juvenile delinquency

*   *   *

That's a Junior!

Dr. Clate Risley stated, "A junior is
teachable, lovable, moldable and unpre-
dictable. That's a junior and more, but
not for long. There is no time to lose
from physical birth to win him to Christ,
and early turn his restless energies into
right channels."

Jesus said, "But whoso shall offend
[cause to stumble] one of these little ones
which believe in me, it were better for
him that a millstone were hanged about
his neck, and that he were drowned in
the depth of the sea" (Matt. 18:6).

*   *   *

"Now Call the Children"

Jesus sat by the roadside
Many years ago,
And said, "Now call the children
And let them come to Me."
The children all came running,
Their eyes with love aglow,
And sat down there beside Him
And clustered at His knee.

I wish that I had been there,
I wish I could have seen
The loving smile on Jesus' face
When all the children came.
I wish I could have heard Him,
As He lingered on the green,
And smiled upon the children,
And called them each by name.

ANNE CAMPBELL

*   *   *

Greatness Manifested

One Christmas Eve, as the world-famed
scientist Dr. Albert Einstein sat in his
home, some children sang carols outside.
When the caroling ceased, the children

36

knocked at his door. "We are collecting money to buy Christmas presents," they said.

Einstein replied, "Wait a moment."

Putting on his scarf and overcoat, he took his violin from its case and joined the children. He accompanied them on his violin as they sang "Silent Night."

Children need love and encouragement.

* * *

"Why, It's Mine!"

"This is a gift from my son to you," said Dr. A. B. Simpson as he handed an orange to a little girl who was ill. Gratefully she received it.

Dr. Simpson then asked, "Whose orange is that?"

The little girl said, "Why, it's mine. You just gave it to me and I said thank you."

"That's right," said Dr. Simpson. "When I offered you the orange, you reached forth your hand and took it. You didn't believe that I would snatch it back, did you?"

"No," said the little girl. "I knew that you would give it to me."

Then Dr. Simpson told her that God, in love and mercy, offers eternal life and a home in heaven to all who will receive them by faith. "As you received that orange, won't you now receive Jesus as your Saviour?"

A serious look came on the girl's face. Then, smiling broadly, she said, "I will."

As Dr. Simpson joyfully went his way, he knew that he had been the instrument used by God to bring salvation to that little girl.

Told by Alice M. Knight

* * *

Feed My Lambs

If among the older people
    You may not be apt to teach,
"Feed My lambs," said Christ, our Shepherd,
    "Place the food within their reach."
And it may be that the children
    You have fed with trembling hand
Will be found among your jewels
    When you reach Emanuel's land.

Why Little Peter Didn't Cry

When four-year-old Peter was hospitalized for the first time for an operation, he was put in a room all by himself. When Mom and Dad left him that night, they were worried, thinking that he would cry for them.

This didn't happen. When the nurse turned out the light in Peter's room and walked down the hallway, she heard a clear childish voice singing:

"Jesus loves me, this I know,
    For the Bible tells me so!"

The eyes of many patients became moist with tears. Peter's song of assurance brought God's presence comfortingly near to them, too.

Told by Alice M. Knight

* * *

Scarred

Dr. Alonzo Yerby, New York City's commissioner of hospitals, said recently, "More than 300 babies born in the city in 1965 suffered from narcotics addiction. They inherited the addiction through their mothers. The babies fought to kick the habit in the first days of life. Some of them died. Others survived. Doctors used drugs or synthetic opiates to bring them through. There is strong reason to believe that another 400 to 500 children were born to narcotics addicts in 1965 and the rate of neonatal narcotics addiction is rising."

Babies are gifts from God: "Lo, children are an heritage of the Lord: and the fruit of the womb is his reward" (Ps. 127:3). How essential it is to give them a good start. How reprehensible before God and man are parents who vitiate and enfeeble the babies by their sins.

* * *

Youth

Gay hope is theirs, by fancy fed,
    Less pleasing when possessed;
The tear forgot as soon as shed,
    The sunshine of the breast.
Theirs robust health as fresh as dew,
    Wild wit, invention ever new,

37

And lively thought of vigor born;
The carefree day, the easy night,
The spirits keen, the slumber light,
That flies with approach of morn.

T. GRAY

* * *

How the Child Is Lost

Many boys and girls are lost without being kidnapped, thus causing a nation-wide search for them. They are lost without any dramatic excitement. Still, they are lost.

Fathers lose their boys by being so pre-occupied with business and unimportant social engagements that there is no time left to be a confidant and a companion to the boys.

Mothers lose their daughters by being so engrossed with things of no lasting worthwhileness that no time is left to pray with them and play with them and enter understandingly into their problems.

The church, too, loses many of the boys and girls by neglecting to provide wholesome, character-building recreation and by failing to challenge them with places of responsibility and leadership in the church.

And so fathers, mothers, and the church are sadly looking for lost boys and girls whom they might have kept if they had invested some time and shown real concern for their spiritual welfare.

Adapted from *Child Welfare Magazine*

* * *

Accompanied—Unaccompanied

The *Lutheran Leader* commented, "If a child goes to church alone, there is about a 15 percent chance of doing something religiously for the child. If the father goes, too, there is an 85 percent chance the child will remain in the church."

How inspirational it is when parents attend church with their children and sit with them, all uniting their hearts and voices in the worship of God. The memory of it becomes permanently etched on the children's hearts and will help them to fight the battles of life courageously and victoriously.

Impressionable Years

Dr. C. W. Hall, Director and Professor of Bible and Religious Education, University of Texas, said, "A study of the home backgrounds of three hundred happily married individuals and of three hundred divorced individuals reveals the fact that often the atmosphere of the home during the early impressionable years of a child's life determines his later success or failure in marriage. In other words, a successful or unsuccessful marriage is usually forecast in childhood."

* * *

Emotional Pattern Fixed

The *International Journal of Religious Education* said, "By the time a child is five or six, his emotional pattern and habit structure are fixed. Of course, variations in development can be expected in one direction or the other, but in general the pattern has become permanently set. It is surprising that the Protestant church has not kept pace with what is known about the sensitivity and receptivity of these younger children. Preventive treatment is better than remedial medicine."

* * *

Concentrate upon Home Environment

Judge Joe Glasser stated, "It is important for parents to concentrate upon the family environment. This is especially true during the first six years of their children's lives, while basic behavior patterns are being established. . . . I am firmly convinced that almost 95 percent of the juvenile delinquents are such because of environmental factors and improper parental guidance during the critical age above set forth."

The Bible says, "Teach the young women . . . to love their children, to be discreet, . . . keepers at home" (Titus 2:4-5).

* * *

When God Made a Child

When God made the child He must have begun early in the morning. He watched the golden hues of the rising sun chase away the darkness. Then He chose the azure of the heavens for the color of

38

the child's eye, the crimson of the cloud to paint its cheeks, and the gold of the morning for its flowing tresses. He beheld the dewdrops on the flowers, and from the rose and lily and daffodil and daisy gathered nectar wherewith to put sparkle in the eyes and merry smiles upon the lips of the child. He listened to the songbirds as they sang and warbled and whispered, and strung the harp of childhood with notes now soft and low, now sweet and strong.

He saw the little lambs among the flocks romp and play and skip, and He put play into the child's heart. He saw the silvery brook and listened to its music and ripples as it coursed its way over sandy bed and mossy stone, and He made the laughter of the child like the ripple of the brook. He saw the angels of light as upon wings of love they hastened in holy duty, and He put innocence in the child-heart and formed its soul in purity and love.

And having made the child, He sent it out to bring joy in the home, laughter on the green, and gladness everywhere. He sent it to the home and said to the parents, "Nourish and bring up this child for Me." He sent it to the church and said, "Teach it My love and law." He sent it to the state, saying, "Deal tenderly with it, and it will bless and not curse thee." He sent it to the nation and said, "Be good to the child. It is thy greatest asset and thy hope."

GEORGE W. RIDEOUT

* * *

Ten Rules for Raising Delinquent Children

The police department of Houston, Texas, gave the following ten rules for producing delinquent children:

1. Begin with infancy to give the child everything he wants. In this way he will grow up to believe the world owes him a living.

2. When he picks up bad words, laugh at him. This will make him think he's cute. It will also encourage him to pick up "cuter" phrases that will blow the top off your head later.

3. Never give him any spiritual training. Wait until he is twenty-one and then let him "decide for himself."

4. Avoid use of the word *wrong*. It may develop a guilt complex. This will condition him to believe later, when he is arrested for stealing a car, that society is against him and he is being persecuted.

5. Pick up everything he leaves lying around—books, shoes and clothes. Do everything for him so that he will be experienced in throwing all responsibility on others.

6. Let him read any printed matter he can get his hands on. Be careful that the silverware and drinking glasses are sterilized, but let his mind feast on garbage.

7. Quarrel frequently in his presence. In this way he will not be shocked when the home is broken up later.

8. Give a child all the spending money he wants. Never let him earn his own. Why should he have things as tough as you had them?

9. Satisfy his every craving for food, drink and comfort. Denial may lead to harmful frustration.

10. Take his part against neighbors, teachers, policemen. They are all prejudiced against your child.

* * *

"How Can I Love Him?"

Little Cheryl asked, "Daddy, do you love Jesus?"

Daddy replied, "My dear little girl, Jesus is dead. He died long ago on a cross. How can I love Him? I have never seen Him."

Cheryl was nonplussed. She thought seriously. Then she asked, "Daddy, how old was I when mother died?"

"You were only six months old, Cheryl —a wee baby," he said.

"Daddy, I don't remember ever seeing my mother, but you have told me wonderful things about her and tried to get me to love her. So I love her, Daddy, even though I have never seen her that I can remember."

Tears began to trickle down Daddy's face. He put his arms around Cheryl and said, "God has spoken to me by you. Do ask Jesus to give me a new heart so I can love Him."

That prayer was soon answered.

Told by ALICE MARIE KNIGHT

Young and Old Heads

In the *Sunday School Times,* Joseph Edwin Harris said, "When a boy or girl truly accepts the Saviour, God does not change a young head or a young heart into an old one. A little child of six prayed, 'Dear Lord, please make me the kind of boy You were when You were six.' That was a wise prayer."

* * *

Educators Should Know Better

Edward T. Mattson, a state crime bureau officer in Minnesota, commented, "The alarming increase of crime stems from the social theories of educators who should know better. They have failed to instill fear of punishment in children and have argued that punishment would not deter crime. Punishment may not be the entire answer but it is a big portion of it.

We must change the thinking of juveniles so they will realize that they will get caught and face the penalty for their crimes."

The Bible says, "Foolishness is bound in the heart of a child; but the rod of correction shall drive it far from him" (Prov. 22:15).

* * *

Until They Are Seven

Francis Xavier, Spanish Jesuit missionary, said, "Give me the children until they are seven and anyone may have them afterward."

* * *

A Cancer

J. Edgar Hoover warned, "Juvenile delinquency is a cancer, eating away at the moral fiber of our entire nation."

CHOICE

Old Whiskers Spurns $20,000

If you were offered $19,219.68 or an existence as an almost penniless wino, which would you accept? Clint Westcott, age fifty-one, accepted the latter. His cronies called him Old Whiskers. How interesting is his story!

Clint was a bearded, flop-hatted bum, attired in rags. For ten years Old Whiskers had resided among the weeds on a slope at the base of a cliff in Los Angeles. His home had no walls, floors or ceiling—just a broken-down chair, an old mattress, a campfire, and several large rocks for his "guests" to sit on.

In his earlier years Clint was an industrious person. He ran a service station in Burnt Hills, New York, which he abandoned in 1953 when he headed west. The station was sold in 1961 for $15,124.38 and the money was banked to Westcott's credit by a New York court. Accumulated interest brought the deposit to nearly $20,000.

Attorney John P. Brown saw a story in the *Schenectady Gazette* about Old Whiskers and immediately contacted him. When told of his fortune, he turned his back on it. He said, "I'd rather stay at the bottom of the barrel. Give me a dollar. I'll take it, buy a little drink and a little smoke. But I don't want that money. Sure, I want to get out of the weeds. But I have no thought of moving out now."

Few people would reject earthly riches as did Old Whiskers, but multitudes spurn God's gift of eternal life "through Jesus Christ our Lord" (Rom. 6:23).

* * *

Trotsky's Choice

At the beginning of the century, two young Russian Jews were invited to a noonday service in a little Methodist church in New York City. One of them, Abraham Silberstein, accepted the invitation. He heard the gospel, received Christ as his Saviour and became a missionary to the Jews. The other young man, known later as Leon Trotsky, refused to enter the church. He returned to Russia and dedicated his life to atheistic communism. Ultimately he fell into disfavor with the party, fled from Russia to Mexico, and was murdered there in 1940.

"Choose you this day whom ye will serve" (Joshua 24:15).

Blue Jacket and Gray Trousers

A fable is told about a man who lived in a borderline state during the Civil War. He wanted to show that he was sympathetic toward both the North and the South, so he wore the blue jacket of a Union soldier and the gray trousers of a Confederate soldier.

All went well for a while. Then one day, when a fierce battle was raging, the Union soldiers shot him in the trousers, and the Confederate soldiers shot him in the coat.

The hapless man was a straddler, divided in his loyalty. He didn't take an all-out stand for either side, but swayed between two opinions.

Each one of us must make a decision either for Christ or against Him. Jesus said, "He that is not with me is against me" (Luke 11:23).

Told by WILLIAM McCARRELL

* * *

It Must Be Voluntary

After Japan's defeat in World War II, the emperor offered, among other things, to make Christianity the state religion. General MacArthur instantly rejected the offer, saying, "No individual or nation must be made to conform to any religion. It must be done voluntarily."

"Choose you this day whom ye will serve" (Joshua 24:15).

* * *

A Disastrous Choice

George Bernard Shaw, the Irish dramatist and critic, commented, "The trouble with Christianity is not that it has failed, but that it has never really been tried."

In speaking of the ills of the world, he said, "The trouble with the world is that when it had a choice, it chose Barabbas instead of Christ. Barabbas hasn't satisfied. It might be a good idea to try Christ."

Throughout the centuries, thank God, myriads of trustful ones have obeyed the command "O taste and see that the LORD is good" (Ps. 34:8). They have proven experimentally His saving, sanctifying and satisfying power!

"I'd Still Be Your Missionary"

James Chalmers, missionary to New Guinea, said, "Recall the twenty-one years; give me back all its experiences—the shipwrecks and the times when I stood in the face of death, surrounded by savages with their spears flying about me and clubs knocking me to the ground—give it all back to me and I'd still be your missionary."

* * *

Which Made the Wisest Choice?

Few of us have ever heard of John Livingstone. He was the brother of the famous missionary David Livingstone. When John Livingstone died, he was one of the wealthiest men in Ontario. The two boys grew up together in Scotland and received the same home instruction. In time each made a choice about his own life. John determined to acquire wealth, rather than follow Christ. David obeyed the command of Christ: "If any man will come after me, let him deny himself, and take up his cross, and follow me" (Matt. 16:24).

John lived in luxury and wealth. David died in a miserable hut in Africa. When John died, however, there was only a brief note in the obituary column, telling of his passing and of his being a brother of David Livingstone.

ALICE MARIE KNIGHT

* * *

A Harder Question

A man once asked Dr. Joseph Parker, "Why did Jesus choose Judas Iscariot to be His disciple?"

"I do not know," replied Dr. Parker, "but I have a harder question—why did Jesus choose me?"

* * *

Aaron Burr's Choice

Years ago an old man died on Staten Island, homeless and friendless. He had once been one of America's most brilliant lawyers and the vice-president of the United States. In his youthful years he decided against Christ, although he was convinced of sin and of his need of the Saviour.

In the wake of that tragic decision, there followed a life of crime and treasonable acts, culminating in the murder of Alexander Hamilton.

You ask for his name? It was Aaron Burr.

What decision have you made in reference to the destiny-determining question "What shall I do then with Jesus which is called Christ?" (Matt. 27:22)?

Told by RALPH W. NEIGHBOUR

CHRISTIAN EXAMPLE

(See also Influence)

His Example

David Livingstone said, "Religion is not a matter of fits, starts and stops, but an everyday affair."

Richard Cecil stated, "Example is more forceful than precept. People look at me six days a week to see what I mean on the seventh day."

In emphasizing the disparity between the preaching and the daily living of a popular pastor, Henry Ward Beecher said, "He preaches cream and lives only skim milk."

Lord Peterborough said concerning his contact with the French theologian Fénelon, "He is a magnetic creature. I was forced to get away from him as fast as I possibly could, or else he would have made me pious."

* * *

A Better Second Baseman

Bobby Richardson, star second baseman for the New York Yankees and an active Christian layman, was asked, "Does being a Christian make you a better second baseman?"

He replied, "Trying to be a good Christian has made me a better father, and my wife says it has made me a better husband. So, if being a Christian has made me a better man, I would say it has made me a better second baseman."

* * *

Testimony and Evidence

A Jewish lawyer attended a church service. He listened incredulously to the testimonies by some known to him for their shady deals and failure to meet their honest obligations.

"How did you like the testimonies?" a man asked him at the close of the service. He replied, "To a lawyer there is a vast difference between testimony and evidence."

What we are speaks louder than what we say.

* * *

Twenty-five Dollars and Board

A farmer advertised for a helper. A man answered the ad and asked, "How much do you pay?"

"Twenty-five dollars a week and board," replied the farmer.

"What kind of board?" asked the applicant.

"Well," said the good-natured farmer who was a picture of health, "I eat it."

"I'll take the job," said the applicant. The farmer was a good advertisement of the food he gave to his workmen.

Do others in observing your life hunger for Jesus, the bread of life?

Told by BRUCE SLACK

* * *

Practicing Christians

Some years ago I was asked to recommend to a rental agent the splendid Christian ladies who compose the Southside Witness to Israel in Chicago. I wrote, "These ladies are practicing Christians."

The agent inquired, "What's a practicing Christian?"

I replied, "A practicing Christian is a debt-paying, neighbor-loving, law-abiding, Christ-glorifying person—a person who practices what he preaches."

Are you a practicing Christian?

If We Lived The Christian Way

Dr. William Sadler, renowned specialist in nervous diseases, said, "If people lived in a truly Christian way, half the diseases would drop off tomorrow morning, and we would have a new superior race of human beings."

* * *

God's Exhibit

In courts of justice, lawyers present various items in evidence, such as guns, knives and clubs. They are labeled exhibits 1, 2, 3, and so on.

The healed and delivered maniac of Gadara was God's "exhibit," testifying to the saving and healing power of the Lord Jesus. Each one whom Christ saves is an exhibit attesting to His mightiness to break the shackles of sin.

Christ stoops to the "guttermost" to save men to the uttermost: "He is able . . . to save them to the uttermost that come unto God by him" (Heb. 7:25).

* * *

"Are You Jesus?"

One time Chaplain Raymond Lilly, the Black Samaritan, was visiting the children in a ward in the Cook County Hospital, Chicago. He spoke cheerfully to them, told them about Jesus and gave them little gifts.

One of the patients, a little boy who had been seriously injured in an automobile accident, was from a very poor home. Chaplain Lilly showed special kindness to the boy, and then he passed on to other children. He hadn't gone far when the little boy beckoned him to come back.

"What is it, my boy?" asked Lilly.

The boy said, "I just want to ask you if you are Jesus Christ."

* * *

Will She Hold Out?

There was a young woman who was only a nominal church member. She was disliked by the Christians with whom she worked, and hated by the non-Christians. She was mean, domineering and destructively critical.

One day the young woman was saved.

Then there was a marked change in her life. Some with whom she worked said, "Now that she's got religion, we'll see if it works and if she holds out."

Hearing what had been said, the new convert went to those whom she had treated so meanly and said, "I long with all my heart to show you my Saviour by my changed life and ways. I am sorry for all the mean things I have said and done." As time passed, all her fellow workers saw true Christlikeness in her words and deeds.

R. E. NEIGHBOUR

* * *

Showing What God Is Like

As Dr. Ida Scudder made her morning rounds in a hospital in Vellore, India, a Muslim woman asked her, "Tell me. I want to know. Why didn't you lose your temper with me the time I spoke so abusively of you?"

Before the doctor could reply, a Hindu woman in the next bed said, "Don't you know why? Her God is long-suffering and slow to anger, and she is like her God."

Baptist Standard

* * *

The Difference

There is a vast difference between a Christlike Christian and a so-so, or merely professing, Christian.

Dr. Courtland Myers was a Christlike Christian. One day he boarded a train to fill a preaching engagement in a distant city. After he took a seat, he began to read. Sitting behind him was an elderly lady with four poorly dressed children. One of them began to reach up and push the back of Dr. Myers' seat.

Dr. Myers' first impulse was to speak roughly to the boy and put him in his place. Instead, he spoke kindly to him and bought candy for him and the other children. Then he told them stories.

Several hours passed. As the train neared Dr. Myers' destination, a well-dressed gentleman approached him and said, "The other passengers and I have observed with admiration your kindness to these children. That's real Christianity!"

"I do not understand," said Dr. Myers.

The gentleman said, "You did not know it, but the elderly lady with these children is not their mother. Their mother is in the baggage car in her casket."

Let us never forget that others are watching us. They will turn from us with revulsion if we fail to practice what we profess.

Christlike Christians bring honor to Christ in all that they say and do.

* * *

Amazing Changes Occur

What amazing changes are worked in us when we penitently turn from sin to Christ.

A Hindu woman was converted by hearing the Word of God. She was terribly persecuted by her husband.

A missionary asked her, "How do you react to the cruel treatment of your husband?"

Smiling, she replied, "Sahib, I try to cook better food for him. When he speaks unkindly to me, I answer softly. I want to show him that when I became a Christian, I became a better wife and mother."

In time a change occurred in her husband. He had been able to withstand the preaching of the missionary. He could not withstand the *practicing* of his Christlike wife. She had the joy of winning him to Christ.

Told by CLAUDE A. RIES

Wanted: Christlike Christians

John R. Mott stated, "I find that the greatest hindrance of the gospel taking effect in the hearts and consciences of unbelievers is the un-Christlikeness of some who profess to know Christ. If a hundred people would make it their main business to be Christlike in love, sympathy and forgiveness, increasing numbers of the unsaved ones would come to Christ for His mercy and forgiveness."

* * *

Living Epistles

A bishop asked some village people in India, who were candidates for baptism, "What is it to be a Christian?"

To his surprise, the new converts said, "To live like Mr. Murray." Mr. Murray was the missionary who had shown them the way of life in Christ.

Paul said of some of God's children, "Ye are our epistles . . . known and read of all men" (II Cor. 3:2).

* * *

A Daily Matter

John H. Glenn testified, "I don't look upon religion as a fire escape—something to be used only in times of emergency. To me religion is a way of life, something to live by daily, on an even keel."

CHRISTMAS

A Grim, Defiant Wall

As the Yuletide dawns in Berlin, a grim, defiant wall of stone and barbed wire, erected by hatred and distrust, separates free West Berlin from enslaved East Berlin. On the west side of the wall, hundreds of Christmas trees, aglow with fifty thousand varicolored lights, silently proclaim the birth of the light of the world, Jesus. On the other side, no Christmas trees or Christmas lights are seen. Instead, the wall is illuminated by giant floodlights to spot any attempted escapes to the West. What an affront to freedom-loving people everywhere!

Atheistic Communists do not believe in the One whose coming into the world is commemorated at Christmastime. There are many, however, in the enslaved part of Berlin in whose hearts the spirit of Christmas reigns—the spirit of love, hope, cheer, kindness, forgiveness, brotherhood and goodwill toward all mankind.

* * *

Condescending Love

In his book *When Iron Gates Yield,* Geoffrey Bull tells of spending Christmas Eve in a Tibetan inn, en route to a Communist prison. He went into a stable to feed the horses and mules.

He says, "My boots squashed in the

manure and straw. The fetid smell of the animals was nauseating. I thought, *To think Christ came all the way from heaven to some wretched eastern stable, and what is more, to think He came for me! How* men beautify the cross and crib as if to hide the fact that at birth we resigned Him to the stench of beasts and at death exposed Him to the shame of rogues! God forgive us!"

* * *

The Christ Child

When the evils of the earth were greatest
  The Christ Child came from afar.
When the night of the world was darkest
  Shone forth the Bethlehem star:
Glory and peace was its message,
  Love and good will to men—
A peace beyond their making,
  And love beyond their ken.

ANNIE JOHNSON FLINT

* * *

The Untaken Gift

For some years the *Chicago Daily News* printed on its front page each Christmas Eve a cartoon by the Nobel prize winner Vaughan Shoemaker. It showed beneath a beautifully decorated Christmas tree an unopened package which was labeled "Eternal Life." The title of the cartoon was "The Untaken Gift." John 3:16 was quoted in the cartoon.

God in goodness gave Christ to the world. Now He offers eternal life to all who will receive it: "And whosoever will, let him take the water of life freely" (Rev. 22:17).

* * *

How God Did It

One day as a scientist watched some ants in his garden scurrying about, he thought, *Will time come when man can communicate his thoughts to an ant?*

As the scientist pondered the question, he related it to another question: How can the infinite God reveal Himself and convey His thoughts to finite man? Suddenly he exclaimed, "I see it! The God of the universe, infinitely high in His being and thoughts, had to become a man to teach men to know Him and His thoughts."

Jesus, the Son of God, "was made flesh, and dwelt among us" (John 1:14).

* * *

How God Revealed Himself

A missionary and a Buddhist priest were walking together in an Indian village, discussing their religions. The missionary accidentally stepped on an anthill. The Buddhist priest said sharply, "Be careful. You may have killed some of my ancestors."

The missionary replied apologetically, "I am very sorry. I didn't see the anthill. How can I tell the ants that I am sorry and ask their forgiveness?"

The priest thought awhile. Then he said, "There is only one way to do it. You would have to be born an ant and crawl around with them. Then you could tell them that you didn't mean to hurt them."

The missionary said, "That's why Jesus came to earth. He was born as a man and lived among us for thirty-three years so He could tell us that God loved us and sent Him to die for us. There was no other way for God to reveal Himself to us than to become one of us in the person of His Son Jesus."

Told by HERBERT MITCHELL

* * *

I Too Must Sing

Ah, dearest Jesus, holy Child,
Make Thee a bed, soft, undefiled
Within my heart that it may be
A quiet chamber kept for Thee.
My heart for very joy doth leap,
My lips no more can silence keep,
I, too, must sing with joyful tongue
That sweetest ancient cradle song:
"Glory to God in the highest heaven,
Who unto man His Son hath given,"
While angels sing with pious mirth
A glad new year to all the earth.

MARTIN LUTHER

* * *

What Christ Has Wrought

In extending Christmas greetings to the members of the American Legion and

45

their families, a Jewish department chaplain said, "These best wishes come from one who, though not of the Christian faith, shares in the hopes and the dreams of his fellow legionnaires that some day people will learn to live in peace and in goodwill toward one another.

"At this time of the year all people, regardless of race or creed, suddenly receive an impulse from God. Walls that divide people disappear. Everyone responds more favorably to visits of the angels of goodness, mercy, justice and kindness. It is the season when hatred goes down the drain. Charity, sympathy and kindness become the dominant attributes. God hovers over the family table, in the office, in the shop and in the marketplace. The baser impulses in us sink to a new low. There is peace instead of disquiet, love instead of hate. Violence and distrust of others are far removed from us amidst Christmas actions and attitudes. We resolve never to go back to hating and hurting, and live forever in love, goodwill and peace."

Christians are grateful that they can give credit to Jesus Christ whose coming effected these wonderful changes!

Told by an army chaplain

* * *

"Take It, John"

A sorrowful wife stood just outside a psychopathic ward in a great hospital. Her husband, a patient in the hospital, was with her. He looked vacantly into space as she pleaded, "John, here's a Christmas present for you. Take it, John, and look at it."

John made no move. Again the plea was made. "John, dear, all of us at home thought you would like your present so much. Look at it, John. Isn't it nice?"

The loving, urging voice failed to reach John's mind. He was powerless to grasp the meaning of a Christmas gift.

Millions in the world today are like John. They refuse God's great gift of love —the Saviour. There is this difference, however, between that mentally sick man and those who refuse God's gift: he didn't

knowingly refuse the gift offered to him, but many people deliberately and knowingly refuse the gift of God—the Saviour and eternal life.

Jesus said, "Ye will not come to me, that ye might have life" (John 5:40).

Told by a hospital chaplain

* * *

What Child Is This?

What Child is this who, laid to rest,
    On Mary's lap is sleeping?
Whom angels greet with anthems sweet,
    While shepherds watch are keeping?

This, this is Christ the King
    Whom shepherds guard and angels sing;
Haste, haste to bring Him laud,
    The Babe, the Son of Mary.

So bring Him incense, gold and myrrh.
    Come, peasant, king, to own Him.
The King of kings salvation brings;
    Let loving hearts enthrone Him.

Raise, raise your song on high;
    The virgin sings her lullaby.
Joy, joy, for Christ is born,
    The Babe, the Son of Mary.

* * *

The Afterglow

After the carols have ended
    And the gifts have been placed away,
The candles burned out their brightness
    And the snow has melted to gray;
After the holly has withered
    And the berries have all turned brown,
The carpets sparkled with tinsel
    When the needles came tumbling down,
With all the merriment ending
    And the embers are burning low,
May the Christ, the Heart of Christmas,
    Fill and brighten the afterglow.

* * *

Eternity's Intersection

Dr. Robert Lee said, "Christmas is the joyous celebration of eternity's intersection with time: 'When the fulness of the time was come, God sent forth his Son, made of a woman' (Gal. 4:4)."

CHURCH

(See also Worship)

Tarry Awhile

If after kirk ye bide a wee,
There's some wad like to speak to ye,
If after kirk ye rise and flee,
We'll all seem cold and stiff to ye.
The one that's in the seat with ye
Is stranger here than ye, may be;
All here hae got their fears and cares,
Add ye your soul unto their prayers,
    Be ye an angel unawares.

* * *

Animated Question Marks

David K. Wachtel stated, "Trier, the hometown of Karl Marx, boasted that it had more religious buildings than any other town of its size in Europe. In spite of all its religious activities, it was spiritually dead. The theologians of the era prided themselves in their critical study of the Scriptures—spending lifetimes chewing little morsels of doubt. They sought to glorify themselves, rather than Christ.

"The cross, the empty tomb, love divine and grace unlimited are lost without simple faith to appropriate them. Men who are filled with questions and doubts cannot crusade. Who would risk all or die for a question mark? The failure of the church helped to produce Karl Marx, Adolf Hitler and their successors."

* * *

Us Only

Dr. Harry A. Ironside chuckled as he spoke of a small church which was identified with an exclusive "splinter" denomination. The members cut out some gold letters and fastened them on the wall in the front of the church. The letters said JESUS ONLY.

One day a gust of wind blew away the letters *JES*. Then the sign read US ONLY.

The Sure Foundation

Mexico City has been called "The Artificial City." It is built, so to speak, in the bottom of a bowl, and is encircled by towering mountains. A certified Mexican guide told a group of sight-seers that mammoth pumps are in continuous operation, pumping water from beneath the city, out over the mountains.

Some structures in the city are gradually and perceptibly sinking. A few have sunk so low and become so crooked that they have long since been abandoned to their fate. They are grim reminders of the possible fate of other structures which may also be abandoned to a similar fate unless some way is devised to save them.

The large Catholic cathedral in the city is discernibly sinking in some sections.

The world-famed Iglesia de Guadalupe is sinking in some sections, too. How impressed I was as I observed the awesome sight! Concrete has been injected beneath subsiding foundations, but to no avail.

All stone-and-mortar churches are nonabiding. The living church, which Jesus Christ founded upon Himself, the sure foundation, is abiding: "For other foundation can no man lay than that is laid, which is Jesus Christ" (I Cor. 3:11).

The church which Christ founded is built, not with stone and mortar, but with living stones—born-again boys and girls, men and women. Peter attested to this wonderful truth: "Ye also, as lively [living] stones, are built up a spiritual house, an holy priesthood" (I Peter 2:5).

* * *

The Primary Objective

Robert L. Slater, president of John Hancock Mutual Life Insurance Company, said, "The church's primary objective should be the regeneration of the individual. Improvements in the environment should take a secondary position, because without regeneration all is ultimately lost."

You Ask Me Why?

You ask me why I go to church?
I gave my heart a careful search:
Because I need to breathe the air where
There's an atmosphere of prayer.
I need the hymns the churches sing;
They set my faith and hope awing;
They keep old truth in memory green,
Reveal the worth of things unseen.

* * *

Functioning as a Political Party

In *U.S. News,* Dr. Walter G. Couch, Jr., of Wichita, Kansas, said, "The truth is that the National Council of Churches has a long record of attempting to function as a political party instead of a religious fellowship, and it is doing so with money given by millions of Christians who heartily disagree with the pronouncements of its General Board and General Assembly."

* * *

The Only Remedy

A cartoon in a Canadian daily showed a hand holding a loaf of bread. On the hand were the words "the church." On the loaf was the word "Christ." Underneath the cartoon were these words: "The church has nothing else to offer." In offering Christ to the world, the church offers the only remedy for its spiritual ills.

Prairie Overcomer

* * *

Two Visions of the Church

In the book *The Shepherd of Hermas,* written early in the Christian era, the shepherd has two visions of the church: as a feeble old woman slumped in a chair and as a beautiful young woman seated on a throne.

The destructively critical enemies of the church see it decadent, weak and moribund. Those who love the church see it established and sustained by God, fulfilling, though imperfectly, His purposes and remaining precious to the head of the church, Christ.

Baptist Standard

Nonparticipating Spectators

A reporter asked Bud Wilkinson, former football coach at the University of Oklahoma and director of the President's Physical Fitness Program, "What would you say is the contribution of modern football to physical fitness?"

Wilkinson flashed, "Absolutely nothing!"

"Would you care to elaborate?" asked the nonplussed reporter.

"Certainly," replied Wilkinson. "I define football as twenty-two men on the field desperately needing rest and forty thousand people in the stands desperately needing exercise!"

How applicable to the average church is this appraisal of modern football. The overwhelming majority in the church are nonparticipating spectators, at ease in God's Zion. Too many Christians have the let-George-do-it attitude! God says, "Awake thou that sleepest" (Eph. 5:14).

Told by HOWARD G. HENDRICKS,
in *Moody Monthly*

* * *

Not on Sunday Night

O Lord, I thank Thee for the love
That makes my life so bright.
For this I praise Thee Sunday morn,
But not on Sunday night.

I'm glad to hear our choir chant
Thy praise, and know it's right.
On Sunday morn I hear them sing,
But not on Sunday night.

I like to hear our pastor speak,
His views are sound and right.
They feed my soul on Sunday morn,
But not on Sunday night.

At eleven A.M., I stroll to church,
In Sunday garb bedight,
But Lord, I crave my easy chair
And slippers Sunday night.

Lord, bless our church, and help to arm
Our preacher's soul with might,
To charge the sinful ramparts of
My empty pew on Sunday night.

48

"Thou Hast a Few Names"

A psychologist gave this general criticism of the church: "The church of today is like an autumn leaf, dry and dead, but retaining its form and structure."

His appraisal may be true of some churches, but, thank God, not all: "Thou hast a few names even in Sardis which have not defiled their garments" (Rev. 3:4).

There is bright hope for even a decadent church if its members will follow the directive of the head of the church, Christ: "Remember . . . from whence thou art fallen, and repent, and do the first works" (Rev. 2:5).

* * *

Busy Beavers

Dr. A. W. Tozer, in *Moody Monthly*, said, "Pastors boast that their church is a 'live' church, pointing to their church bulletin as proof—some activity scheduled for every night and several meetings during the day. A great many of these time-consuming activities are useless and others plain ridiculous. 'But,' say the busy beavers who run the religious squirrel cages, 'they provide fellowship and they hold our people together.' If this is the best thing churches can offer to hold the people together, they are not Christian churches in the New Testament meaning of the word.

"The center of attraction in the true church is Jesus Christ. If the many activities engaged in by the average church led to the salvation of sinners or the perfecting of believers they would justify themselves, but they do not. My observations have led me to the belief that many, perhaps most, of the activities engaged in by the average church contribute nothing to the true work of Christ on earth. I hope I am wrong, but I am afraid I am right."

* * *

Why She Was Unimpressed

An elderly lady was being conducted through a great cathedral in Europe. The guide spoke of its beauty of design, calling special attention to its statues and wonderful paintings.

The old lady was unimpressed. At the conclusion of the tour, she asked the guide, "How many souls have been saved here this year?"

"My dear lady," said the embarrassed guide, "this is a cathedral, not a chapel."

Churches have no reason for existence if they fail to bring souls to God and give the gospel of Christ to the ends of the earth.

Gospel Banner

* * *

Blest Be the Tie

Henry Ward Beecher said, "Climbers of the Alps fasten themselves together with a rope for safety. Our joining ourselves with someone else is conducive to our safety: 'Two are better than one; because they have a good reward for their labour. For if they fall, the one will lift up his fellow: but woe to him that is alone when he falleth; for he hath not another to help him up' [Eccles. 4:9-10].

"Christianity is a social thing. One reason why Christ instituted the church was that there might be a bond between all of His followers."

Blest be the tie that binds
Our hearts in Christian love.

* * *

How We Lost the Glow

A member of a Scottish congregation said to a visiting minister, "I can worship God and enter the holy of holies just as easily in my garden on the mountainside as I can in a church pew."

The two men were sitting before a fireplace in which the embers of coal glowed cheerily. Silently the minister went to the fireplace, took the tongs and lifted a single glowing coal from the fire and placed it alone on the hearth. Soon it turned to a black ash.

The church-neglecting Scot said, "Ah, ye need na say a word. I understand wha' ye mean. I canna worship alone any more than I can live alone. I'll be in me place at the kirk next Sunday."

God's children suffer irreparable loss when they habitually absent themselves from the fellowship of others of like precious faith, without cause. They easily become cold, critical and unbelieving when they disobey the command "Let us consider one another to provoke unto love . . . not forsaking the assembling of ourselves together, as the manner of some is; but exhorting one another" (Heb. 10:24-25).

Told by HADDON W. ROBINSON

* * *

Overorganized, Underagonized

The theology of the following alleged epitaph on a churchman's tomb is thought-provoking: "Here lies a man who would have gone to heaven if his church had given him time."

With the ever increasing multiplicity of church organizations and committee meetings, the active church member has little time to enter into the homelife, with the resultant weakening of the home where youth get their bent for life, either in the wrong or right direction. As the church can be no stronger than the home, the church must reappraise its program and squelch all unnecessary time-consuming meetings which contribute little or nothing to the primary business of the church—winning souls and nurturing God's children into Christlikeness.

Told by a pastor

* * *

When Seen from the Inside

How drab and uninspiring are the stained glass windows of the great European cathedrals—some of them dating back to the twelfth century—when seen from the *outside*.

How dazzlingly beautiful and vivified they are when seen from the *inside* with golden sunshine filtering through them.

How precious is the vision we get of the Saviour in the house of God when we unite our hearts with others in extolling Him. It is a foretaste of that blessed time when the redeemed will ceaselessly praise Him in glory!

* * *

Click and Clatter of Church Machinery

Dr. G. Campbell Morgan said, "One of Satan's methods today is to start so many organizations in a church that the members have no time for communion with God. Many Christians are so busy they can hear only the click and clatter of church machinery. Oh, that God would turn us back to unhurried communion with Himself! Oh, that we might take time to sit submissively at Christ's feet and hear His fear-allaying, strength-imparting voice!"

* * *

"Don't Sell Your Birthright"

Will Herberg, a Jewish philosopher and writer, said, "Do not sell your birthright —the great heritage of Christian truth— for a mess of 'modernistic pottage,' no matter how fashionable or attractive it may seem.

"Let me remind you that the church has grown great not by accommodating itself to the changing spirit of the age, but by taking a stand against it. Protestantism has suffered greatly from the erosion produced by the modern temper. The church must be relevant to the times, but relevance means showing that the basic beliefs of the church about God, man and the world have much to say to mankind in our time."

Adapted from *Sunday School Times*

* * *

Turned Out

The Jews of Christ's day dreaded being expelled from the synagogue. There were some who "believed on him; but because of the Pharisees they did not confess him, lest they should be put out of the synagogue" (John 12:42).

There were three steps of excommunication: First, there was rebuke, which lasted from seven to thirty days.

Second, there was thrusting out, which lasted for thirty days, and could be followed by a "second admonition" of thirty days more. The admonition meant execration. People would maintain a prescribed distance from the one thrust out—four cubits, as if he were a leper. In the event of his death, mourning for him was prohibited and stones were thrown on his coffin.

Third, there was final excommunication. This was of indefinite duration. The excluded one was to be considered as dead. Social contacts were forbidden and others could not eat and drink with him.

Which Church?

A minister sat beside a stranger on a bus. The stranger asked, "To which church do you belong?"

The minister replied, "I belong to Christ's body."

"That's a new church. When was it organized and by whom, and where is its headquarters?" asked the stranger.

The minister replied, "All born-again believers belong to this church. It was organized some two thousand years ago by Christ Himself who 'loved the church, and gave himself for it.' Its headquarters is in heaven."

Every Christian, who is a member of the body of Christ, has the privilege of also being an active member of a local church where God's Word is faithfully proclaimed.

Told by HYMAN J. APPELMAN

* * *

The Crucifix

Said Dr. A. W. Tozer, "How enfeebled is any church when it venerates the crucifix and is not vitalized by the Crucified—Christ."

* * *

The Secret

When asked why he succeeded so well in his ministry, Henry Ward Beecher replied, "I have four hundred hearers on Sunday who tell on Monday what I preached."

* * *

Almost a Sin

Before John Wesley followed George Whitefield's example of open-air preaching, he thought that the saving of souls was almost a sin if it was not done in a church.

* * *

Bathtubs

Fishing for souls in the average church is like fishing for fish in our bathtub. They're not there. To catch souls, we must do as Jesus did—go where they are.

* * *

Untouched

Said Stanley High, late editor of the *Reader's Digest*, "Seventy-eight percent of the people of the United States are untouched by the Sunday school."

* * *

The Crime

Dr. David Johnson commented, "The crime of the church is not murder, or adultery, or stealing. It is the sin of sleeping: 'He that sleepeth in harvest . . . causeth shame' (Prov. 10:5). 'Look on the fields; for they are white . . . to harvest' (John 4:35)."

* * *

What to Fear

Billy Graham stated, "I wish the churches were as afraid of imperfection as they are of perfection; of unholiness as of holiness; of sin as of sanctification."

* * *

Politics

Warned John Calvin, "The church has no scriptural authority to speak outside the ecclesiastical field or meddle in politics which are divisive and inimical to the church's success."

* * *

Wanted: Better Men

God is not looking primarily for better methods, but for better men—men of unimpeachable character who know no fear other than the fear of incurring His disfavor: "There was a man sent from God, whose name was John" (John 1:6).

* * *

Not Good if Detached

Someone asked Sir Winston Churchill, "Are you a pillar of the church?"

He quipped, "I am more of a flying buttress: I support it from the outside."

* * *

Schism and Heresy

John Ruskin, English writer and social reformer, said, "I believe that the root of almost every schism and heresy from which the Christian church has ever suffered has been the effort of men to earn, rather than to receive, their salvation."

51

A Contradiction

G. Campbell Morgan stated, "To call a man evangelical who is not evangelistic is an utter contradiction."

* * *

Where Ministers Are Recruited

Commented the *Standard*, "A segment of ministers was polled on the size of church they were reared in. Eighty percent of them said, 'A church of less than one hundred members.' "

* * *

Unfed

John Milton averred, "The hungry sheep look up and are not fed."

* * *

That's Different

To live above with the saints we love,
Ah, that will be glory!
To live below with the saints we know,
Well, that's a different story!

* * *

Travailing

St. Catherine prayed fervently for souls, saying, "Promise me that Thou wilt save them! O give me a token that Thou wilt!"

* * *

One True Church

Dr. Roy O. McClain said, "There is but one true church—the *ecclesia*—those who are 'called out of the world,' the transformed, the reborn, the regenerate ones. But these are in every communion. No one organizational group composes it [the true church], no one race nor creed."

* * *

A Most Beautiful Sight

Holmes said, "The most beautiful sight from the pulpit is a whole family sitting together in a pew. The church service is not a convention to which a family may send merely a delegation or representatives."

How blessed is the family whose head resolutely resolves, "As for me and my house, we will serve the LORD" (Joshua 24:15)!

Transformed Individuals Change Society

After extensively observing the frenzied devotion of U.S. churchmen to social action, a Church of England clergyman said, "It would be tragically ironic if the church, grown skeptical about God's power to redeem society by transforming human nature, were to fall into the same ideological error as Communism and attempt to transform man by altering his environment."

* * *

Spiritual Graveyards

Cape Hatteras is known as the graveyard of the Atlantic. There the bottom of the sea is covered with the skeletons of ships that went to pieces on the shoals. On calm days, when the water is clear and unruffled, some of the old wrecks can be clearly seen from the surface. The famous ship the *Monitor* sank off Cape Hatteras.

In his book *The Hatterasman,* Ben Dixon MacNeill wrote, 'This is the graveyard. It covers about thirty square miles of shoal. In this narrow area, through four centuries, 382 ships have been sunk and drawn down into the grave. No man has seen them or touched them to this day."

David Stick wrote in his book *The Outer Banks of North Carolina,* "More federal warships were sunk by the weather off Cape Hatteras during the Civil War than by all the cannons of the Confederacy."

Churches may become moribund and degrade into spiritual graveyards when they cease loving Christ first: "Thou hast left thy first love" (Rev. 2:4); or they may luxuriate in wantonness and in ease: "Woe to them that are at ease in Zion" (Amos 6:1); they may even lapse into selfishness and become self-congratulatory: "I am rich, and increased with goods, and have need of nothing." They do not realize that they are "wretched, and miserable, and poor, and blind, and naked" (Rev. 3:17).

Aptly the Bible depicts such churches: "Thou hast a name that thou livest, and art dead" (Rev. 3:1).

Unless God's children heed the clarion call, "Awake thou that sleepest, and arise

52

from the dead, and Christ shall give thee light" (Eph. 5:14), the chill of indifference will settle increasingly upon them until they come to that tragic state where they are neither hot nor cold—a condition repugnant to Christ.

* * *

Neglecting Living Center of Belief

Dr. David H. C. Read, minister of New York's Madison Avenue Presbyterian Church, said, "I find there is something incomplete, lopsided, and sometimes even false about the new activism in the churches. Renewal of the church does not come from new forms of social action, however necessary these may be. It begins within. A church that sets out to do the work of God, spreading into every area of life, yet neglecting the living center of belief, is doomed not to renewal but to decay."

* * *

Move Back and Find Your Soul

When addressing the United Presbyterian Board of National Missions, Senator Abraham A. Ribicoff said, "As the cities have deteriorated and the middle class moved to the suburbs, you, too, have moved out with your churches. Move back and you might find your souls. You might not find it as comfortable as it is in the suburbs, though. The problems of the cities will not be solved unless Americans stop looking at programs and begin looking at *people*."

* * *

An Agnostic Converted

An agnostic often expressed the wish that he could live in a more practical world where there were only useful things, minus religion.

One night the agnostic had a dream which awakened his slumbering soul to realism.

In the dream a voice said, "What do you want?"

He replied, "Give me a community without a church; where there is no Lord's Day; where there are no ministers, and no gospel preached."

Such a community seemed to pass in view before his eyes. As it faded, he became distressed. He exclaimed, "What? No church? No Lord's Day? No Ten Commandments? No Bibles? No restraining, religious training for children? No solemnizing of marriages as a sacred relationship? No respect for the laws of man and the laws of God? No promise of immortality and a life of future bliss?"

The man awakened with a piercing shriek. "Such a community would be hell on earth. Give me a community with a house of God and people who live according to the good Book—the Bible," he pleaded.

Told by BISHOP R. J. RENISON

* * *

Majoring in Minor Things

Frederick the Great, king of Prussia, won a strategic battle with comparative ease and with little loss of men. When asked the explanation of his victory over the enemy, he said, "The enemy had seven cooks and one spy, but I had seven spies and one cook."

Perhaps the church's lack of power is traceable to the fact that it majors on minor things and minors on major things.

Evangelical Witness

* * *

Different Assortments

In most churches, there are the following kinds of Christians: (1) *tired* Christians, who work if cajoled and coaxed; (2) *retired* Christians, or has-beens, who usually sit idly by—the victims of donothingism; (3) *rubber-tired* Christians, who go along if the road is smooth; (4) *flat-tired* Christians, whose ego has been punctured and pride wounded. What kind of a Christian are you?

VANCE HAVNER

* * *

She Died of Improvements

A German immigrant was suddenly stricken with illness. She was rushed to a hospital. That night the husband inquired about her condition. "She's improving," he was told. Daily he visited his wife. Daily he inquired how she was getting along. The report was always the same: "She is still improving."

One night the husband was called to the hospital and told that his wife had died. When he met the doctor, he asked, "Well, doctor, what did she die of—improvements?"

Some churches die spiritually of improvements. They become so top-heavy with organizations, so enmeshed in a maze of time-consuming, energy-expending activities that the main purpose for the existence of the church—the salvation of the lost and the building up of God's children in Christian character—is lost sight of.

Many churches need an additional society, namely, a society for the suppression of superfluous societies.

Told by R. E. NEIGHBOUR

The Church Lincoln Would Join

Some speak disparagingly of Abraham Lincoln because he spoke thus of the different churches which claim to be the true church:

"They all claim to be Christian and interpret their several creeds as infallible. I doubt the possibility of settling the religion of Jesus Christ into molds of man-made creeds and dogmas. It was a spirit of life that the Saviour laid stress on and taught. I cannot without reservations assent to long and complicated creeds and catechisms. If a church would ask simply for assent to the Saviour's statement of the substance of the law: 'Thou shalt love the Lord thy God with all thy heart, and with all thy soul, . . . and with all thy mind; and thy neighbour as thyself' [Luke 10:27], I would gladly unite with that church."

CIGARETTES

More about Crippling Cancerettes

Dr. George E. Moore, director of the Rose Park Memorial Institute, New York State's cancer research and treatment center, said, "The filter tips of several brands of cigarettes are ineffective in screening out harmful tars and nicotine. . . . None is really protecting smokers from possible lung cancer, emphysema, cardiovascular diseases and other ailments known to occur more frequently among smokers than among nonsmokers. Cigarette advertisement has given smokers the impression that just because a cigarette is filtered it is helpful in cutting down tars and nicotine. This is simply not true."

* * *

A Preventable Cause of Death

Dr. R. T. Ravenholt, director of the New York State Department's Population Service, said, "A pack of cigarettes a day cuts eight years off a man's life; two packs, sixteen precious years. Cigarette disease is now the foremost preventable cause of death in the United States."

More Lethal than Bullets

Dr. Hollis S. Ingraham, New York State's Commissioner of Health, warned, "Cigarettes are more lethal for Americans than all the bullets, germs and viruses combined. Nothing is as lethal as cigarettes. Nothing kills as slowly and painfully as the cigarette. Educational programs designed to curb smoking among Americans haven't been too successful."

* * *

The Definite Link

The U.S. Health Service Advisory Committee on Smoking Hazards definitely linked cigarette smoking to lung cancer; to cancer of the bladder; to chronic bronchitis and emphysema, a lung condition that impairs breathing; probably to cancer of the esophagus, mouth and tongue; and to coronary disease which causes heart attacks.

* * *

Infanticide

Pediatrician-professor Dr. Neville R. Butler and economist Martin Feldstein

54

compared the statistics of 617 stillborn and neonatal deaths with those of 16,377 live births. They found that pregnant women who are moderate smokers (one to nine cigarettes a day) are 20.8 percent more likely than the average of all pregnant women to bear dead babies or babies who die soon. Heavy smokers (ten cigarettes a day or more), they found, are 25.9 percent more likely to bear stillborn babies.

Time

* * *

The VA Refuses Donations of Cigarettes

The Veterans Administration recently doubled its facilities for treatment of emphysema, a deadly lung disease. With this increase of facilities, it has urged the VA's five thousand doctors to step up efforts to discourage patients from smoking.

The VA said, "Smoking, which provides a specific pollution of the air in the lungs, has been clearly established as one cause of emphysema, a progressive loss of lung function which frequently results in death." In keeping with its efforts to dissuade patients from smoking, the VA refuses donations of cigarettes from the tobacconists.

* * *

Where Air Pollution Is Nil

Lois Mattox Miller said in *Reader's Digest,* "The Royal College of Physicians, London, gave the lung-cancer death rates of smokers and nonsmokers who live in cities, in rural areas and even in countries where air pollution is virtually unknown. Finland, for example, which has the second highest lung-cancer death rate in Europe, is essentially a rural country which has little air pollution but a population of heavy smokers. This suggests that smoking is more of a health hazard by far than air pollution."

* * *

Is Your Health Going up in Smoke?

Dr. Gerald Baum, associate professor of medicine, Western Reserve University, and chief of the pulmonary section, Veterans Administration Hospital, Cleveland, Ohio, said, "Inhalation of tobacco smoke, an act performed by more than fifty million Americans many times each day, is responsible for more human misery and suffering than any other activity man engages in.

"This includes fighting wars, driving cars or making the many items we get from manufacturing plants. As many people will die of lung cancer in a year as will die in automobile accidents. In lung cancer, no doubt exists that cigarette smoking is the most important factor in the cause of the disease. As if cancer were not enough, it is now quite clear that chronic bronchitis is closely related to, if not actually caused by smoking. Filters now available are without influence on the bad effects of smoking.

"Because of the vast financial resources of the cigarette industry, it is able to control so much advertising time and space that the reality of self-destruction associated with cigarette smoking is effectively hidden."

Plain Dealer

* * *

Coupons for Funeral Expenses

Said Dr. Howard S. Van Ordstrand, head of the pulmonary diseases department of Cleveland (Ohio) Clinic, "Coupons good for medical care and funeral expenses should accompany the sale of cigarettes. There is no question but what the most important pollution of the air we breathe is cigarette smoking. It should be entirely avoided."

Plain Dealer

* * *

Guilty as Charged

The Royal College of Physicians, London, recently reported that the dangers to health attributable to cigarette smoking are so great that preventive measures should be taken promptly.

The report states that "cigarette smoking is a cause of lung cancer and bronchitis, and probably contributes to the development of coronary heart disease and various less common diseases. Cigarette smokers have the greatest risk of dying from these diseases, and the risk is greater for the heavier smokers.

55

"During the past forty-five years lung cancer has changed from an infrequent to a major cause of death in many countries. It is necessary to postulate some causative agent to which human lungs have been newly and increasingly exposed during the present century. Cigarette smoke is such an agent and there is now a great deal of evidence that it is an important cause of this disease."

The report stated that the chance of death for a man aged thirty-five who is a heavy smoker is one in twenty-three compared with only one in ninety for a nonsmoker.

LOIS MATTOX MILLER, in
Reader's Digest

* * *

Smoking and Nonsmoking Women

New findings by the American Cancer Society show that death rates from lung cancer and several other diseases are higher among women who smoke cigarettes than among women who don't smoke.

Releasing a report on a survey of the smoking habits of 1,003,229 subjects, including 440,558 men and 562,671 women, the society said: "This is the first time a very large group of women has been traced for the effects of cigarette smoking. Among both men and women smokers, death rates from the following maladies were much higher in cigarette smokers than in nonsmokers: emphysema, a hardening and progressive inefficiency of the lungs; cancer of the lung; cancer of the mouth cavity, pharynx, larynx and esophagus; aortic aneurysm; cancer of the pancreas; and cirrhosis of the liver."

* * *

Crippling Cancerettes

Dr. Alton Ochsner, Professor of Surgery, Tulane School of Medicine, New Orleans, said, "Lung cancer will reach almost epidemic proportions in the United States by 1975 unless something is done about it. When heavy cigarette smokers die of heart disease, they spare themselves death by lung cancer. Had they shot themselves at forty they would have been spared both. A bullet is cheap and quick. Suicide by smoking is long and expensive.

"We have treated more than three thousand of these cases. To see them die from a preventable disease hurts. Some of them tell me that they are willing to lose a lung. But it is not that simple.

"If there were one-tenth the evidence that Brooklyn Bridge was unsafe, it would be closed within an hour. Why the reluctance about cigarettes? *The reason is economic!*

"It frightens me to think what is going to happen in another decade when our present smoking habits catch up with us! There is scarcely a biological process that is not harmed in some way by tobacco. Regardless of whether an ulcer is in the stomach or in the duodenum, I have yet to see a patient get well if he continues to smoke. I flatly refuse to treat an ulcer patient who does not agree to discontinue smoking."

Dr. Ochsner quoted Dr. Linus Pauling, winner of two Nobel prizes, as saying, "Every time a person smokes a cigarette he shortens his life 14.4 minutes."

* * *

A National Catastrophe

Emerson Foote, who heads the National Interagency Council on Smoking and Health, stated, "The annual death rate of smoking might be as high as 300,000. In any case, the number represents a national catastrophe."

* * *

No Safe Level

The U.S. Public Health Service reported, "There is no safe level for smoking, and even moderate smokers run a substantial health risk. At least eighteen million Americans are now ex-cigarette smokers. This shows that the habit can be broken. But progress would be much greater and our work a lot easier if the pressure of cigarette commercials, posters and ads were reduced.

"We hear the charge that once the government starts to enforce health warnings on cigarettes, there is no telling where it will stop. Maybe a warning label on alcoholic beverages or on automobiles, which also kill people, will be next. It is possible to drink moderately and not kill yourself. It is possible that a safe driver will survive to a ripe old age. There is, however, no safe level for smoking, and even moderate smokers run a substantial health risk."

* * *

A Hazardous Risk

Commented the American Cancer Society, "Death caused by cancer of the lung is eight times greater among those who smoke cigarettes than among non-smokers. A longtime addict to cigarettes has about one chance in ten of developing lung cancer. For a nonsmoker odds are about one in two hundred and seventy."

* * *

An All-American Athlete Speaks Out

Otto Graham, All-American football player, head coach at a U.S. service academy, said, "I am firmly convinced that smoking is bad for anybody who engages in competitive sports. As a teenager I was too interested in baseball and football to want to hurt my wind by smoking. Apart from a few experimental puffs that I didn't like, I have never smoked in my life. One of the saddest things to me is to see the large number of teenagers who now smoke."

* * *

Quite Clever, Isn't It?

A heavy smoker commented to a friend, "I'm so disturbed in reading so much about the link between cigarettes and lung cancer that I have decided to do something about it."

The friend asked, "Are you giving up cigarettes?"

"No, I'm giving up reading."

* * *

Why Take the Fatal Risk?

St. Anthony Messenger, the National Catholic Family Magazine, commented,

"In a recent study among 187,783 men whose medical history was traced for an average of forty-four months, the risk of developing lung cancer was at least ten times as great among smokers as non-smokers."

* * *

The Surgeon General Speaks

Surgeon General Luther Terry of the U.S. Health Service said, "I would advise anyone to discontinue smoking cigarettes which are a health hazard of sufficient importance in the United States to warrant appropriate remedial action. Let there be no foot dragging in seeking possible remedial steps.

"There is no longer any question that cigarette smoking produces lung cancer, bronchitis and other diseases. The facts are now in, and no responsible person should dispute that cigarette smoking is a serious health hazard."

* * *

A Greater Danger than Nuclear Fallout

Dr. Linus C. Pauling, two-time Nobel prizewinner, said, "Cigarette smoking presents a far greater danger today than current nuclear fallout. I feel that smoking cigarettes cuts the average life expectancy four years, whereas fallout from six hundred megatons tested to date by the United States, Great Britain and Russia decreased it only one week."

* * *

Earplugs

There's a new cigarette almost ready for the market. It comes with earplugs for those who don't want to hear why they should not smoke.

* * *

Wormy Apples

Dr. David Starr Jordan said, "Boys who smoke cigarettes and drink alcoholic beverages are like wormy apples—they drop before their time."

COMMUNION WITH GOD

"Study to Be Quiet"

Dr. A. W. Tozer averred, "Strong emotion has its place in life and in religion, but the mood in which we find God most real to us is often one of quietness. Only in quiet waters are objects mirrored without distortion, and only in a quiet mind is there a clear perception of truth. The psalmist said, 'Be still, and know that I am God' (Ps. 46:10). Those who have not learned to be quiescent before God miss life's profoundest lessons."

Isaiah said, "In quietness and in confidence shall be your strength" (Isa. 30:15).

* * *

Solitude

Dr. Alexander Maclaren said, "Solitude is 'the mother country of the strong.' The wilderness, with its savage crags, its awful silence, and the unbroken round of its blue heaven, was a better place for Moses to meet God than in the heavy air of a palace or the profitless splendors of a court."

* * *

The First Twenty Minutes

Sir William Osler, famed physician, said, "What one does the first twenty minutes of the day sets the moral tone for the rest of the day."

David said, "My voice shalt thou hear in the morning, O Lord; in the morning will I direct my prayer unto thee, and will look up" (Ps. 5:3).

* * *

A Moment in the Morning

Just take a moment of each morning,
  Ere the cares of the day begin;
And open wide your heart's door,
  To let God's love flow in.

Take that moment of each morning,
  And with God's own Word in hand,
Try to catch a glimpse of heaven,
  Of that precious promised land.

Hurrier and Behinder

Said a Pennsylvania Dutchman, "The hurrier I go the behinder I get."

Ours is a hurry, worry, bury age. We are getting nowhere fast. Quiet, unhurried waiting before God is a prerequisite to the acquisition of spiritual knowledge and spiritual renewal: "Be still, and know that I am God" (Ps. 46:10). "But they that wait upon the Lord shall renew their strength" (Isa. 40:31).

* * *

Waiting upon God

William Wilberforce, the English philanthropist, once wrote to his son, "Let me implore you not to neglect, curtail or hurry over your morning prayer. Of all things, guard against neglecting God in the secret place of prayer. There is nothing more fatal to spirituality. How much better I might serve God if I had cultivated a closer communion with Him."

Haste in prayer means failure in Christian living. Time spent in prayer is time saved. Our Christlike influence in public is always in exact proportion to the depth of our hidden life with God in secret.

Christian Herald

* * *

"Slow Me Down, Lord"

Slow me down, Lord, I'se a-going too fast,
I can't see my brother when he's walkin'
  past;
I miss a lot o' good things, day by day,
I don't know a blessin' when it comes my
  way.

* * *

"I Love Thy Morning"

Lord, I love Thy morning
  When the sun breaks through,
When the birds are glad with singing,
  And the grass is wet with dew;
When all the world is full of living,
  And all nature seems to pray,
"Thou hast kept us through the darkness,
  Father, guide us through the day."

For it will always remind me
It was morning in my soul
On the day I met my Saviour,
When He touched and made me whole.

BARBARA E. CORNET

* * *

Body Outdistancing Soul

An explorer employed a group of natives to attend him on a trek in the wild upper Amazon region. The march was difficult through the tangled jungle.

One morning, after several days of marching, the natives sat silently and sullenly on their haunches, heedless of the command to get going.

"What's the trouble?" demanded the explorer of the leader of the natives.

"We must wait," he said.
"Wait for what? What's there to wait for?" angrily demanded the explorer.
Said the leader, "We have been going too fast. Now we must wait until our souls can catch up with our bodies!"

Because of our restless scattering of our energy over an amazing multiplicity of activities, there is little or no time left for the soul's communion with God.

* * *

Not Too Fast

Be not in such a hurry to *do* that you fail to *be*, so anxious to give out that you fail to take in: "He that believeth shall not make haste" (Isa. 28:16).

* * *

COMMUNISM

The Uncommitted

Vance Havner said, "Peace without victory? It is the vain hope of all appeasers today who think freedom can get along with slavery. Communism is a moral cancer and there is no peaceful coexistence with a cancer—the cancer gets you.

"There are those who try to imagine a third dimension today where one is committed neither way, where black and white are merged into an indefinite gray. They would be 'neither nor' when the issue is 'either or.' A prominent senator speaks of a 'world in which neither good nor evil is absolute.' This is the philosophy of the uncommitted and it is utterly impossible."

* * *

800 Million People Sealed Off

Dr. George W. Peters declared, "Asia, with more than half of the world's population, is where Communism is creating a stronghold for itself. Some 800 million people are sealed off from outside contact and from the gospel light. In Afghanistan at present the death penalty is mandatory for anyone who converts from Islam to any other religion."

A Better Example

Karl Barth said, "Communism cannot be defeated with guns. It must be defeated with a better example of a better humanity. Freedom can be victorious only by showing itself real freedom. America must clean its own house before it can act as a missionary to the world."

* * *

Intrinsically Evil

Said Pope Pius XI in the encyclical *Divini Redemptoris*: "Communism is intrinsically evil, and no one desiring to save Christian civilization may cooperate with it in any undertaking whatever."

* * *

One of Today's Greatest Tragedies

Dr. Arch Campbell, who was for many years a United Presbyterian missionary to Korea, said, "One of today's greatest tragedies is that the once brightest spot in the world missionary picture is now perhaps the blackest. The response to the gospel, and the development of the Christian church in northern Korea, was a phenomenon possibly unmatched in the entire history of the church. Today in North Korea, which is most untruthfully called the People's Democratic Republic of Korea, Christianity and other forms of religion are positively and actively prohibited by law. All church buildings have been destroyed or put to other uses. The Bible is completely banned. Any kind of religious service, even in private homes, is strictly outlawed, and few believers are still alive."

Enslaving, atheistic Communism, with its attendant cruelties and intrigues, is probably the greatest curse in the world today. Wherever its sinister shadow falls, all that God-fearing, freedom-loving people most cherish vanishes.

J. Edgar Hoover said, "We have witnessed the intrusion of a highly malignant cancer—a cancer that threatens to destroy civilization. One-fourth of the world's land surface has been seared and blackened by this cancer—Communism— while one out of every three human beings is caught in its tentacles!"

* * *

A Move Equivalent to Suicide

Dr. Walter H. Judd, former medical missionary to China and congressman from Minnesota, stated, "Some people say that one step toward better relations with China is to admit China to the United Nations. This is the argument of the lady who thinks the way to reform a brute is to marry him. But once she marries him, she has lost her bargaining power. Admitting China would be an overt renunciation of the charter's principles—a move equivalent to suicide."

* * *

International Criminals

Rev. Richard Wurmbrand, a Lutheran minister, was first arrested by Rumania's Communist regime in February, 1948. This was the beginning of more than fourteen years of "relentless interrogation, attempted brainwashing and physical torture." He said this of Communist rulers: "They are criminals on an international scale, and only when the criminal is defeated does he change. . . . I was convinced that the fate of the West was

either to destroy Communism or be destroyed by it!"

* * *

Change of Tactics, Not Heart

Dr. James D. Bales said, "There are those who think that the Communists have undergone a change of heart when they have simply changed their tactics to achieve their goal of world conquest. When Communists enter into agreements with non-Communists, some think that a new day of cooperation has arrived and that the era of brotherhood may not be far away. The fact is that both Communist theory and history show that all sorts of turns, twists and retreats are but a part of their struggle for victory. If a robber seizes two million dollars and returns one million, has he ceased to be a robber? If an aggressor advances one hundred miles and finds that he has overextended himself, has he ceased to be an aggressor because he regroups his forces at the fifty-mile line?

"How long will people be deceived by their wishes and by their ideological illusion? How long will it take them to learn the meaning of the following statement of Lenin: 'To carry on a war for the overthrow of the international bourgeoisie— a war which is a hundred times more difficult, protracted and complicated than the most stubborn of ordinary wars between states—and to refuse beforehand to maneuver, to utilize the conflict of interests (even though temporary) among one's enemies, to refuse to temporize and compromise with possible allies, is not this ridiculous in the extreme? We may have to zigzag, retrace our steps, give up the course once selected and try others.' "

* * *

Morally Confused and Irresolute

In an open letter addressed to Pope Paul VI, Prof. A. Voobus, of the Lutheran School of Theology, Chicago, said in Christianity Today: "On this side of the Atlantic there is no scarcity of those who shout 'Peace, peace, no more war.' Who among decent human beings would not prefer peace? But the situation is not that simple. In the first place, the bloodi-

60

est aggressors want peace, too, to keep their victims in submission and to grab new ones, as they are doing in Vietnam and elsewhere, until finally the rest of the free world, having become morally confused and irresolute, falls into their hands. This is why the Communist *Worker* [No. 76, Oct. 10, 1965] greeted your message with jubilation.

"This state of affairs must be a serious concern for Christians. Furthermore it is alarming that in the West there are so many who want peace for themselves at the expense of the sufferings and sacrifices of others. Our so-called peace is paid for by the anguish, torture and blood of millions of innocent human beings. This, too, must be a serious concern for Christians. This attitude is immoral. It is the very source of the catastrophes which have befallen us."

* * *

Unmasked

In Allen Drury's book *Three Kids in a Cart* the following realistic words should awaken all who love freedom and believe in the God-given dignity of man who was made "a little lower than the angels, and . . . crowned . . . with glory and honour" (Ps. 8:5).

"There has never been any evidence at any hour of any day since the end of World War II, except that which we ourselves have blown out of all proportion with our desperate hopes, to indicate that the Communists have ever had any intention of permitting peace to come to the world or do anything but destroy the free civilization of the West.

"Each little crumb which has fallen from their table has been hailed as ten loaves of bread—*by us*. Each trickily conciliatory gesture, always made with a devious and destructive purpose, has been turned into a hopeful sign—*by us*. And while we have been busily scurrying about telling ourselves we saw good faith where good faith never existed, the patient plan of murder and deceit and our ultimate destruction has gone forward, unchanged to the slightest degree by the self-delusions we have desperately clung to."

A Prophecy

Nearly fifty years ago Lenin said, "In fifty years, armies will no longer have much significance. We shall undermine our enemies to such an extent before war breaks out that it will be impossible to set the war machine in motion in the hour of need!"

* * *

Confessions of a Communist

"There is only one thing about which I am in dead earnest—the Communist cause. It is my life, my business, my religion, my sweetheart and wife, my meat and bread. I work at it in the daytime and dream of it at night. Its hold on me grows, not lessens, as time goes on. I'll be in it the rest of my life. It is my alter ego. I am inseparably bound to it. I can't carry on a friendship, a love affair, or even a conversation without relating it to this force which both drives and guides my life. I evaluate people according to the Communist cause and their attitude toward it."

Throughout the centuries, there have been uncounted numbers of God's children who have been equally as devoted and dedicated to Christ, not counting their lives dear to themselves, that the cause of Christ might prosper. With Paul, they have said, "Christ shall be magnified in my body, whether it be by life, or by death" (Phil. 1:20).

* * *

From Socialism to Communism

Said Nikita Khrushchev, as quoted in *Congressional Record*, "We cannot expect the Americans to jump from capitalism to Communism, but we can assist their elected leaders in giving Americans small doses of socialism until they suddenly awake and find they have Communism."

* * *

The Peace of the Cemetery

J. Edgar Hoover warned, "The peace which the Communists so deceptively and hypocritically talk about is, in reality, the peace of the cemetery, or the peace of the canary that has been swallowed by a

61

cat. How slow many are to learn that the word of a Communist is worthless."

* * *

Youth Will Decide

In their ceaseless effort to communize and dominate the world, Communists are dedicated to this Lenin dictum: "Youth will decide the issue of the entire struggle—the student youth and the working-class youth."

* * *

Lies Are Truths

Walter Winchell stated, "Communists accept the perverted concept that slavery is peace, tyranny is liberty, and lies are truths. They rule by terror and strive to gain objectives by violence. The final irony of Communism is that its leaders are slaves to the Communist ideology. Those who attempt to master the world have been conquered by Lenin and Marx. Our most dangerous enemy is not a Red dictator. It is the Communist doctrine. In the end the Red dictator who vowed to bury us has been buried by Communists."

* * *

For the Minds of Men

Billy Graham cautioned, "Today I see a battle emerging at the university level. We don't find Communism making great inroads with the masses, but with the intellectuals. The struggle for the minds of men is going to be decided in the halls of learning throughout the world."

CONFESSION OF CHRIST

No Recruiting in the Dark

A faithful minister saw the Martin Luther film. He was deeply stirred by the courage of the fearless Reformer. After the film was shown, the chairman of the meeting made this timid appeal: "While all heads are bowed, eyes closed and lights dimmed, just slip up your hand if you want to confess your faith in Christ."

The faithful minister seemed to see Luther facing the Reichstag and the wicked political and religious leaders. In imagination he could hear their threats and maledictions. He seemed to hear Luther's courageous words: "Here I stand!" The vision vanished as the timid voice from the platform said, "Just slip up your hand."

What would the intrepid Reformer say about an eyes-closed-and-lights-dimmed appeal? Must God's warriors be recruited in the dark?

Regardless of any possible consequences, we must openly and fearlessly and self sacrificially say, "Jesus, I my cross have taken." We must say with Paul who paid the supreme sacrifice to fully follow his Lord: "Christ shall be magnified in my body, whether it be by life, or by death" (Phil. 1:20).

Confessed Before the Father

A minister noted for his Christlikeness dreamed that he stood at heaven's gate, knocking for admission. He was conducted to the throne of the Judge of all the earth. There he was asked, "Have you always been forgiving, loving, honest and just?"

"I fear not," was his quavering reply. To other questions He replied, "I have failed in these things, too."

When it seemed that his case was hopeless, the One who sat at the right side of the throne of God stood and said, "Father, it is true that he failed in some things, but he confessed Me as his Saviour, and faithfully stood for Me. Now, I confess him before Thee."

"Whosoever . . . shall confess me before men, him will I confess also before my Father which is in heaven" (Matt. 10:32).

LOUIS BANKS

* * *

Unashamed

Said a Scottish laddie to his mother, "Mither, there's a new mon come to toon to preach. Gang and hear him."

The mother thought it most unusual that her boy should ask her to attend a revival meeting. *If I go, how can I conceal it from my neighbors and escape their jeers?* she thought.

To circumvent ridicule, she took her market basket on her arm when she emerged from her home, seemingly going to market.

Under the power of the gospel, she was convinced of sin and of her need of the Saviour's mercy and forgiveness. She was joyously converted.

With a twinkle in his eye, the evangelist said to her, "You will not need your market basket now."

"For the scripture saith, Whosoever believeth on him shall not be ashamed" (Rom. 10:11).

Told by HARRY A. IRONSIDE

* * *

Either Death or Banishment

A burdened Arab, a man of social prominence in his community, came to a missionary late one night. He said, "I know that Christ is the Son of God and the Saviour."

"That's fine," exclaimed the missionary. "You are ready to publicly confess Him before others."

"If I did that, it would mean either my death or banishment to the hills, like a wild animal. I could endure such a fate for myself, but I feel that I should not bring such suffering to my young son."

The missionary reminded the Arab of the words of Jesus, "He that loveth son or daughter more than me is not worthy of me" (Matt. 10:37).

Later, as the missionary looked out of his window, he saw the Arab agonizing in prayer beneath a tree, asking God for strength to confess Christ before the world, no matter what the cost might be.

Adapted from *Sunday School Times*

A Wac's Question

Two Wacs attended an open-air meeting, conducted by some Christian servicemen. Afterward one of them said, "I am a Christian, but I am not very open about it. Is it not possible to pray in bed?"

The other answered, "Yes, but it is no testimony to others, is it? I haven't confessed Christ yet, but I am interested. There was a girl in my barracks who knelt at her bedside every night, and the first time I saw her do it, I cried myself to sleep."

As they walked along, God spoke to them, and both gave themselves fully to Christ. Both resolved to confess Him anywhere.

Told by an army chaplain

* * *

"I Shall Never Be Ashamed"

A dear lady, long since gone to be forever with her Lord, was an honored member of my church. She was Lady Burgoyne. When she wished to unite with us she said to me, "Dear sir, I cannot go before the church. It is more than I can manage to make a confession of Christ before the members." I told her we could make no exception for anybody.

Lady Burgoyne came bravely and spoke most sweetly for her Lord. When she had confessed her faith in Him, she put both hands on mine and said joyfully, "With all my heart I thank you for this! I shall never be ashamed of Christ now. When aristocratic friends call upon me, I will speak to them of my Lord." She did so constantly. She frequently said to me, "Oh, what a training that was for me! I might have been a timid one all my days if I had not made that confession before the church."

CHARLES H. SPURGEON

CONFESSION OF SIN

His Hunch Was Right

A service station had been burglarized. An officer, standing before a class of junior high students, had no evidence against any of them. He had a hunch, however, and he acted according to his suspicion. He said, "You doubtlessly know about the break-in at the service station. We took fingerprints. All we have to do is to compare them with yours to complete the case."

A thirteen-year-old boy stood and said, "You may have my fingerprints, but they won't prove a thing. I wore gloves."

An unintentional or an excusing confession isn't enough. Pleading no extenuating circumstances, we must say to God, "I have sinned."

Baptist Standard

* * *

Comfort at Portals of Death

Selden the learned scholar said, "I have endeavored to know many things deemed worth knowing among men. But with all my acquisition of knowledge, nothing comforts me now, at the close of my life, except the saying of the apostle Paul, 'Christ Jesus came into the world to save sinners; of whom I am chief' " (I Tim. 1:15).

Nails Digging into Conscience

In a sermon a pastor said, "We cannot get right with God until we confess our sins to Him and to others against whom we have sinned."

A troubled young man said to the pastor at the close of the service, "I build boats. My employer is an unbeliever. I have talked to him about his need of Christ, but he scoffs and ridicules it. In my work I use copper nails. I've been carrying home quantities of them to use on a boat I am building at home. The nails are digging into my conscience. I know that I cannot have peace until I confess my theft of the nails."

"That's right," said the pastor to the young man.

Later he joyfully said to the pastor, "I confessed my sin to my employer, and he looked oddly at me and said, 'I always did think you were a hypocrite. Now I am beginning to believe there's something real in Christianity. If it makes a dishonest workman confess that he has been stealing copper nails and settle for them, it's worth having.' "

"He that covereth his sins shall not prosper: but whoso confesseth and forsaketh them shall have mercy" (Prov. 28:13).

Adapted from *Christian Index*

CONSCIENCE

"Son, Remember"

Ivan the Terrible, czar of the Russians, grew up in a brutal environment. During his reign, his hands were crimsoned with the blood of the slain. He insanely imagined everyone to be against him. He ordered the wholesale execution of the land-owning aristocracy. Deranged and depressed, he struck his son Ivan and killed him! He became progressively engulfed in the agonies of remorse and regret.

In a futile effort to atone for his atrocious crimes, Ivan immured himself from society and became a hermit. Brooding over his crimes, he died.

The conscience never dies. After death, the conscience of the rich man was accusingly alive: "Son, remember" (Luke 16:25).

How blessed are those who have a "conscience void of offence toward God, and toward men" (Acts 24:16).

Adapted from *United Presbyterian*

Conscience and Tradition

One night a hoodlum in Chicago murdered a policeman in a tavern. He was apprehended and put in jail. On the next day, Friday, he was served mutton in his noon meal. Indignantly he said to the guard, "Take that away. Do you think I would eat meat on Friday?"

The hoodlum had no compunction about taking the life of an officer of the law, but he was slavishly observant of a religious tradition.

* * *

Condemned

My conscience hath a thousand several tongues,
And every tongue brings in a several tale,
And every tale condemns me for a villain.
Perjury, perjury, in the highest degree,
Murder, stern murder, in the direst degree,
All several sins, all used in each degree,
Throng to the bar, crying all—Guilty, guilty!

Shakespeare, in *Richard III*

* * *

"Daddy, You Didn't Look Up"

One day in late summer, a father and his little boy were out walking. They chanced to pass a watermelon patch. A wicked thought came to the father. He reasoned, *No one is in sight, and no one will know if I take one of these watermelons.* He told his little boy to sit on the fence and keep close watch in all directions for anyone approaching.

Then the father crept into the watermelon patch. Before he stooped down to get one of the big melons, he looked this way, that way and all around.

The little boy, observing his father's every move, yelled out, "Daddy, there is one direction in which you didn't look. *You didn't look up!* "Conscience-stricken, the father left the watermelon patch.

We may hide in God: "Your life is hid with Christ in God" (Col. 3:3). We cannot hide from God: "Thou God seest me" (Gen. 16:13).

Told by ALICE MARIE KNIGHT

Misdeeds Become Alive on Stage of Memory

Many people hate the desert. They are afraid of it because they are afraid of being alone with themselves. If they were left alone in the middle of the desert for a week, they would crack up mentally. I've seen it happen. I knew a man who sprained his ankle and couldn't travel. The party he was with had to go on, but they left him an ample supply of water, food, matches and wood. All he had to do to recover was to keep quiet for five or six days.

Later, when he rejoined the party, he was almost totally demented. When he was alone, his conscience became alive. The misdeeds of his sinful past stalked unbidden across the stage of memory and terrified him.

Shakespeare said, "To be alone with my conscience is hell enough for me."

Dr. Sadler, a famed psychiatrist, averred, "A clear conscience is a good step toward barricading the mind against neuroticism."

How ill at ease are those who live with an accusing conscience. A conscience "void of offence toward God, and toward men" (Acts 24:16) gives spiritual poise and courage.

DONALD GREY BARNHOUSE

* * *

God's Moral Law Ingrained

The German philosopher Immanuel Kant said, "Two things strike me with awe: the starry heavens above and the moral law within."

As David looked into the star-spangled sky, he exclaimed, "The heavens declare the glory of God; and the firmament sheweth his handywork" (Ps. 19:1).

God's moral law is ingrained in the fiber of mankind: "the law written in their hearts" (Rom. 2:15a). Man intuitively has a sense of right and wrong: "Their conscience . . . bearing witness, and their thoughts the mean while accusing or else excusing one another" (v. 15b).

65

Indelibly Imprinted

An employe in a post office had long been suspected of stealing sheets of stamps. It was difficult, however, to place the theft on him.

Then it happened. Several sheets of postage stamps were found on him. He maintained that he had bought the stamps.

"What! All of these?" the investigator exclaimed, as he swished a moist brush over one of the sheets. As he did so, red words shone forth, saying, "Stolen from the post office."

The chemically treated sheets of stamps revealed the theft.

Indelibly imprinted upon the conscience are our secret sins. God knows how to cause the guilty conscience to reveal its secrets.

Adapted from *Home Messenger*

* * *

"I've Tried My Own Case"

Years ago a young man murdered his employer. In a futile, frantic effort to conceal his crime, he burned the house where the employer's body lay.

His trial was stubbornly fought by the prosecutor and the defending lawyer. At the conclusion, the judge began to give his charge to the jury. Suddenly he became greatly agitated and buried his face in his hands.

The lawyers looked at each other in consternation. Going to the judge, they asked, "What's the matter, Your Honor? Are you ill?"

With great emotion and difficulty, the judge replied, "I've tried my own case! Thirty years ago I murdered my employer and, to hide my crime, I burned down the house where his body lay. If anyone ever suspected me of the terrible deed, I do not know it."

During the years, the judge's conscience had slumbered, but it hadn't died.

Be sure your sin will find you out before the judgment bar of God "when God shall judge the secrets of men by Jesus Christ" (Rom. 2:16).

Told by GEORGE W. TRUETT

* * *

"The Dreadful Interior Verdict"

Arnold Bennett the English novelist said in *The Old Wives' Tale*, "No one can possibly be satisfied, or happy, who feels that in some paramount affair he has failed to take up the challenge of life. For the voice within him, which none else can hear but which he cannot choke, will constantly be murmuring, 'You lacked courage. You ran away.' It is better to be unhappy in the ordinary sense than to have to listen to the end of one's life to that dreadful interior verdict."

* * *

Ghosts of Bygone Crimes

The frightful ghosts of bygone crimes and cruelties stalk unbidden across the stage of memory to accuse and alarm evildoers.

In terror, conscience-stricken Charles IX of France, who had ordered the massacre of the Huguenots, cried, "Awake or asleep, I see the mangled forms of the Huguenots passing before me! What blood! What murders! I am lost!"

Herod, hearing of the mighty miracles wrought by Christ, thought that Christ was John the Baptist risen from the dead. He mumbled, "John . . . is risen from the dead" (Mark 6:16). John the Baptist was dead, but not the accusing conscience of murderous, adulterous Herod.

Told by GEORGE W. TRUETT

66

CONSECRATION

(See also Will of God)

Submission Work

After many years of outstanding work as a missionary and Bible translator in Africa, A. W. Banfield was rendered helpless by a stroke, and was bereft of speech and memory. During the years of his lingering helplessness, Mrs. Banfield wrote a Christian friend, "The Lord is mindful of His own. We rejoice in the Lord. In the will of God, I engaged in foreign mission work. During my husband's illness, I at first engaged in home mission work. Now I am living in *submission* work."

Moody Monthly

* * *

Willing to Go

More than a century ago, a missionary meeting was held in the First Baptist Church, Richmond, Virginia. When the offering for missions was taken, the people gave generously and sacrificially.

When the ushers were counting the offering, they found in one basket a card on which was written the word *Myself.* It was signed, "John Lewis Shuck."

The card was immediately carried to the pastor. With deep feeling he read it to the congregation.

John Lewis Shuck had heard God's call "Whom shall I send, and who will go for us?" and he had responded, "Here am I; send me" (Isa. 6:8). He was the first Southern Baptist missionary to go to China.

The gift which God wants most of all from us is the gift of self: "I seek not yours, but you" (II Cor. 12:14).

* * *

Stay Close to Christ

Dr. Charles Malik, scholar and a past president of the General Assembly of the United Nations, stated, "It is perfectly clear that we could save nobody and nothing if we are not first sure of ourselves. Only those who stay close to Jesus Christ can help others who are far away.

Only those who prefer Him to everything else, even to the call of the needy world, can be used of Him for the need of the world."

* * *

What Makes the Difference

The birds appear to sing more sweetly,
    The sun more brightly shines,
When I give to Jesus love completely,
    Fully assured that He is mine.

The flowers bloom with fragrance new,
    Life's beauties never pall,
God's Spirit descends like morning dew,
    When Jesus has my all.

HARRISON PALMER

* * *

Severing Connections

One day a missionary in New Guinea observed the natives of a village making their way to him. They were carrying fetishes and idols which they had formerly used in idolatrous worship. They were now Christians and knew that they must get rid of these things.

To test their sincerity, the missionary advised, "Be sure of your ground before you destroy these things."

The natives returned to their village. The following week, they again came to the missionary with their fetishes and idols. A spokesman for them said, "Keep your advice to yourself. We know that if we follow Jesus wholly and love Him with all our hearts, we must sever connection with all that formerly held us in bondage and spiritual darkness."

Adapted from *Alliance Witness*

* * *

Giving God First Place

Dr. R. Earl Allen said in *Bible Paradoxes*, "Dr. E. A. Fuller, president of the Southern Baptist Seminary for many years, told his fiancée before they were married that he could not marry her unless she would agree to take second place in his life. He hastened, however, to make

67

plain what he meant. He said, 'God must have first place in my life.' His fiancée graciously replied, 'I would choose to have second place in your life if God is to have first place.' "

When God is enthroned in our hearts and has the first place in our lives, we are better husbands, fathers, Christians and citizens.

Full-orbed blessedness comes when we say, "Christ shall be magnified in my body, whether it be by life, or by death" (Phil. 1:20).

* * *

His Full-Time Occupation

Someone asked a businessman, "What's your occupation?"

"I'm a Christian," was his reply.

"No, no," said the man. "I mean what's your job?"

The reply was the same. "I'm a Christian."

"You don't understand. I mean what do you do for a living?"

"My full-time occupation is to be a Christian, but I am a meat packer to pay expenses," answered the dedicated Christian businessman.

Adapted from *United Methodist*

* * *

Total Commitment

Protestant Action tells of a conversation that ensued between a hen and a pig when they passed a church and observed the sermon topic of the pastor: "How Can We Help the Poor?"

After a moment's reflection, the hen said, "I know what we can do. We can give them a ham-and-egg breakfast!"

The hog protested, saying, "The breakfast would be only a contribution for you, but for me it would mean *total commitment!*"

Any commitment God's children may make to God short of total commitment isn't enough. Joy comes when we love and serve the Lord with all our heart, soul and mind.

"I Dare Not Give Myself"

"I dare not give myself wholly to the Lord for fear He will send me to some faraway place as a missionary," said a young woman to her pastor.

He replied, "Suppose on a snowy, cold morning a little bird came pecking at your window and allowed you to take it in, thereby putting itself entirely in your power. What would you do? Would you crush it, or would you give it food and care?"

Thoughtfully she replied, "I see it now. I'll put myself wholly in the molding, protecting hands of the Lord and be what He wants me to be, and go where He wants me to go."

Told by W. H. Griffith Thomas

* * *

Dedication of Person and Possessions

Early in his life, David Livingstone wrote in his diary: "I will place no value on anything I have or may possess except in relation to the kingdom of Christ. If anything will advance the interests of that kingdom, it shall be given away or kept, only as by the giving or the keeping of it I shall promote the glory of Him to whom I owe all my hopes in time and eternity. May grace and strength sufficient to enable me to adhere faithfully to this resolution be imparted to me so that all my interests may in reality be identified with His cause."

Choice Gleanings Calendar

* * *

Men and Methods

Years ago someone said to Dwight L. Moody, "The world has yet to see what God can do with one man who belongs totally to God."

After silent, prayerful thought, Moody said, "By the grace of God, I'll be that man."

God is seeking not better methods but better men—Spirit-empowered, self-sacrificing men who weep with Christ over perishing souls.

God's ancient quest hasn't changed: "And I sought for a man among them,

68

that should make up the hedge . . . but I found none" (Ezek. 22:30).

Was the cause for the failure of the quest long ago the same as it is today: "For all seek their own, not the things which are Jesus Christ's" (Phil. 2:21)?

A. W. TOZER

* * *

Doing the Difficult Thing

How difficult it is for us to part with things to which we are sentimentally attached, and around which cluster hallowed, cherished memories!

A friend of mine, Mrs. Bertha McHenry, who is one of the most dedicated and Christlike Christians I have ever known, told me, "As I prayed one day, I said, 'Dear Lord, I want to give to You my best, my very best!' The Lord seemed to say to me, 'How about your diamond ring?'

"Momentarily the thought came into mind, *How can I part with the diamond ring which my beloved doctor-husband, who has long since been with You in glory, gave to me?*

"As I waited before the Lord, I wept silently. Presently my sorrow was displaced with the peace of God. Joyously I exclaimed, 'Dear Lord, I have committed myself and all that I have to You. Until I awaken with Your likeness in glory, I want You always to make me willing to fully follow You!' "

Joyfully my friend gave her diamond ring to build a church for the Christian natives in a faraway place where Satan has long held souls in spiritual darkness and fear.

Long ago David said, "Neither will I offer burnt-offerings unto the LORD my God of that which doth cost me nothing" (II Sam. 24:24).

* * *

Make Me Thy Fuel

Give me the love that leads the way,
The faith that nothing can dismay,
The hope no disappointments tire,
The passion that will burn like fire,
Let me not sink to be a clod,
Make me Thy fuel, flame of God.

"Take the Whole of Me"

In utter resignation to God's will for his life, Dr. B. H. Carroll prayed, "Lord, take my hands and let them work for Thee; take my mind and let it think for Thee; take the whole of me, for I belong altogether to Thee."

* * *

I Am Third

On the desk of a Christian businessman was a motto which said, "I am third."

"What's the meaning of the motto?" a caller asked.

He replied, "My mother was a devout Christian. My father was a good Christian, too. They sacrificed greatly to put me through college and start me in business. When I left home for the first time, my mother gave me this motto. I asked her what it meant, and she said, 'Son, no matter how high you may climb or how low you may fall, always remember God is first, others second, and you are third.' "

Florida Baptist Witness

* * *

God Is in the Remnant Business

Some of God's people have a notion today that if we have enough members, enough money, enough effort and enough means, we can win the world. But God doesn't want it that way. God can do more with a dedicated few than with an indifferent host.

I think we have mobilized into an unwieldy multitude. Our size has become our great embarrassment. But we can't reach the goal if we are stumbling over our team.

God is in the remnant business and always has been—Noah and his family, Gideon and his men, Elijah and seven thousand, Isaiah and the small remnant, Ezekiel, Daniel, Ezra and Nehemiah.

Even Jesus Christ did His greatest work not with the many but with a handful.

Let us never forget that, when God is in it, little is much.

VANCE HAVNER

69

God's Ownership

Our stewardship is our acknowledgment of God's ownership: "Ye are not your own . . . ye are bought with a price: . . . glorify God in your body, and in your spirit, which are God's" (I Cor. 6:19-20).

* * *

"Let Me Burn Out for God"

It has been said, "God does not need unusual ability but unreserved availability for His cause."

When Henry Martyn reached India, he knelt and prayed, "I have hitherto lived to little purpose—like a clod upon the earth. Now let me burn out for God."

Martyn translated the New Testament into Hindustani. Then he began a translation of the New Testament into Persian. He truly burned out for God. Weakened by overwork, he contracted tuberculosis and died at the age of thirty-one.

GEORGE W. TRUETT

* * *

What It Isn't

Consecration isn't our giving anything to God. It is our taking our hands off what already belongs to God: "Ye are not your own . . . ye are bought with a price" (I Cor. 6:19-20).

* * *

Ordinary Things

Dean Stanley stated, "The true calling of a Christian is not to do extraordinary things, but to do ordinary things in an extraordinary way."

* * *

I Have Learned

Dr. Paul Carlson, martyred missionary, once said, "I have learned with the apostle Paul, 'For me to live is Christ, and to die is gain!'"

* * *

Full Heads—Empty Hearts

Alan Redpath lamented, "How tragic it is that we have so many full heads and so many empty hearts."

* * *

Those Who Have Never Heard

Robert Moffat, a pioneer missionary to Africa, stated, "If I had a thousand lives and a thousand bodies, I would devote them to no other employment than preaching the gospel to those who have never heard the joyful sound."

* * *

The Whole Man

Said Michelangelo, "Art is a jealous mistress. She demands the whole man." So does God who does not need unusual ability, but unreserved availability for His cause: "I seek not yours, but *you*" (II Cor. 12:14).

* * *

The Dearest Idol

The dearest idol I have known,
    Whate'er that idol be,
Help me to tear it from Thy throne,
    And worship only Thee.

* * *

Only One Passion

Count von Zinzendorf testified, "I have but one passion—it is Christ."

Paul said, "For to me to live is Christ" (Phil. 1:21); "I live; yet not I, but Christ liveth in me" (Gal. 2:20).

CONVERSION

(See also Salvation)

Horace Bushnell's Conversion

One day Horace Bushnell knelt in his dormitory room at Yale University. He thought, *If there is a God, as I rather hope and very dimly believe to be, He must be a right God. Will He not help me to discover Him?* Then he prayed, "Take the dimness of my soul away. Reveal Thyself to me."

God did reveal Himself to young Bushnell. He rose from his knees and felt as if he had received wings. The whole sky was luminous for him. It was sunrise in his soul. Henceforth he had no troublesome doubts about God's reality. He had proved the genuineness of the promise: "And ye shall seek me, and find me, when ye shall search for me with all your heart" (Jer. 29:13).

Told by GEORGE W. TRUETT

* * *

Religion Isn't Enough

Out of curiosity, Dr. David Rowlands attended a Billy Graham meeting in Harringay Arena, London, with no thought of being converted. Having been reared in a church, he felt no need of anything more. Said he, "I went to the meeting armed with a camera and a light meter. But I didn't come away with pictures. I came away with Christ. When I entered the arena, I had a set of beliefs, a moral standard, and a lifetime of religious forms and externals. I came away with a Person pervading me and living in me—Christ!"

Graham said, "His patients observed the change in him. They began to share their spiritual problems with him."

Said Dr. Rowlands, "As a doctor, I'm dealing with people now, not just with bodies."

* * *

"His Eyes Were as a Flame of Fire"

After groping for years in spiritual darkness, the artist Camillo painted a picture of Christ, called *The Man of Sorrows.* The eyes of the Saviour burned into his so searchingly that he veiled the painting.

A friend urged him to unveil it. As the artist looked intently at the face of Jesus, Jesus seemed to say, "Make reparation, as far as you can, to those whom you have wronged. Buy back your paintings which are suggestive of evil and destroy them."

One night Camillo knelt before the painting, confessed his sins to Christ, and asked His forgiveness. Instantly he passed from spiritual darkness into newness of life in Christ.

* * *

Needed: Three Conversions

Said George Ingle in *The Lord's Prayer,* "Every person should have three conversions. A man needs to be *converted to Jesus Christ:* 'Believe on the Lord Jesus Christ, and thou shalt be saved, and thy house' (Acts 16:31); *to the church:* 'Not forsaking the assembling of ourselves together' (Heb. 10:25); and finally *converted back to the world:* 'Go ye into all the world, and preach the gospel to every creature' (Mark 16:15)."

* * *

Instantaneous Conversion

A Christ rejector scoffed at the idea of instantaneous conversion. He asked a Christian neighbor, "Do you really believe that a deathbed repentance can do away with a whole life of sin?"

The Christian replied, "No, of course not. But I do believe that the blood of the Lord Jesus Christ certainly can. Since salvation is totally of grace, the vilest sinner may penitently look to Christ even in death, as did the evildoer long ago and pray, 'Lord, remember me when thou comest into thy kingdom.'"

Self-excusingly the scoffer said, "Well, I can wait until the last countdown, like the penitent thief, and then turn to Christ for mercy and forgiveness, can't I?"

Said the Christian neighbor, "The only time you have is now. Later may be too late. It was too late for the five foolish

71

virgins who pleaded, 'Lord, Lord, open to us.' "

* * *

Christ Lives in Me

How changed is life since now I see,
O blessed truth, Christ lives in me!
His Spirit fills me day by day,
And as I yield, directs my way.

I need not cry in times of strife
For Him to come into my life,
For He is there since I believed,
And Christ's atoning work received.

* * *

A Painting Did It

Years ago Munkacsy's painting *Christ Before Pilate* was on exhibition in Hamilton, Ontario. A godless sailor, in keeping a promise made to his mother, saw the painting. He studied it intently. At intervals he lowered his head in reverence. As he gazed upon the tender face of the sinless Son of God, the features of his face softened. Then tears came. He asked Christ to enter his heart and life. Submissively he said, "Lord, from today I am a changed man. I make Thee my sovereign Lord."

British Weekly

* * *

You Ask Me How? I Do Not Know

You ask me how I gave my heart to
    Christ?
I do not know.
I had a longing for Him in my soul
So long ago.
I found earth's flowers would fade and
    die,
I longed for something that would satisfy,
And then—and then—somehow I seemed
    to dare
To lift my broken heart to Him in prayer.
I do not know,
I cannot tell you how,
I only know
He is my Saviour now.

* * *

Headhunter's Transformation

How thrilling is the story of the conversion of Tariri, chief of the Condoshi in Peru. A Wycliffe Bible Translator, Doris Cox, had the joy of leading him to Christ.

"How do you take Jesus?" asked the chief.

Miss Cox was suddenly aware that this was no ordinary moment. The Scripture verse she had translated had sparked something in Tariri. An overwhelming force seemed to take over the conversation.

"You say, 'I want Him. I love Him.' You let Him come into your heart," she said as she wondered if she was speaking Condoshi clearly. "Do you want to take Jesus?"

"Yes," Tariri answered, "I want Him very much."

"Let's pray then," she said.

"I don't know how," Tariri said.

"Just tell God what you have just told me," she said.

So Tariri bowed his head and prayed. That was all. A moment later he stepped off the porch and went home.

Then Miss Cox heard Tariri speaking inside his house a short distance away. His voice was deeper than usual, as though he were trying to control his emotions. He said, "I just took Jesus. I closed my eyes and prayed, and now I am a child of God."

Later, Tariri said, "I have beheaded at least ten chiefs of my own rank and twenty of their warriors. Now I follow Christ. I no longer hate and kill. I only want to love people and tell them about Jesus."

* * *

"This Is Too Simple!"

Dr. Arthur T. Pierson used to tell of a young Scottish girl who had come to Christ. When she asked for church membership the minister said, "Now tell me all about it."

"I felt the burden of my sins and I knew that Jesus' precious blood was shed to wash them away. So I just came to Him and told Him," she answered.

The minister said, "That sounds good. You will have to come before the elders and tell them what you have told me."

One of the elders said, "Look here, my lassie, when I got converted I had a long

72

time of deep conviction before I was able to enter into peace. How long a time have you had an experience like that?" She answered him as she had stated to the minister.

Then another elder said, "This is too simple. Do ye ken that in the *Pilgrim's Progress*, when the man was on the way to the wicket gate, he fell into the slough? Now how long a time have ye been in the slough?"

"Oh, please, sir," she answered, "I dinna gang that way at all."

"I think the lassie is right," said the minister. "It is only unbelief that puts anybody in the slough. It is doubt. But the soul that goes straight to Jesus, seeking His forgiveness, finds eternal life and peace!"

HARRY A. IRONSIDE

COOPERATION

Pulling with God

Expressing a widely prevalent and increasingly popular view among intellectuals, called existentialism, Jean-Paul Sartre, a French philosopher, said, "Man can count on no one but himself. He is alone, abandoned on earth in the midst of his infinite responsibilities, without help, with no other aim than the one he sets for himself, and with no other destiny than the one he forges for himself on this earth."

How dismal and dark is the outlook if man exists in a purposeless universe and a hostile environment which he ceaselessly and unavailingly strives to overcome by his self-effort or free will.

How bright is the outlook of those who cooperatively work and strive with God in a hostile environment to overcome innate propensities to evil and outward enticements to sin. Triumphantly they can say, "I have set the LORD always before me: because he is at my right hand, I shall not be moved" (Ps. 16:8).

* * *

Working with God

An aged minister, nearing life's setting sun, lamented, "As I look back over the way I have come, I realize that I wore myself down at times unnecessarily working *for* God when I could have worked more effectively *with* God. I am profoundly convinced that one of the gravest perils besetting ministers is a restless scattering of energies over an amazing multiplicity of marginal activities."

"We are labourers together with God" (I Cor. 3:9).

* * *

Togetherness

An aged man prayed, "O Lord, help me to remember that nothing is going to happen to me today that You and me together can't handle."

Paul said, "We are labourers together with God" (I Cor. 3:9).

It is said of God's warriors of old, "So all the men of Israel were gathered against the city, knit together as one man" (Judges 20:11).

Religion is derived from the Latin *religare* which means "to bind or tie back."

God's children are one, not in any earthly organization, but in the Father and the Son: "That they . . . may be one in us" (John 17:21).

* * *

Pulling with God

In World War II, a platoon of soldiers came under fire at Salerno, Italy. All the men, except the chaplain, dove into foxholes. A sergeant yelled, "Chaplain, get in a foxhole!"

The chaplain said, "God will protect me."

The sergeant flashed, "God will protect me, too, but I want Him to see that I'm cooperating with Him."

* * *

Organized Hornets

A man applied for a job as a teamster on a farm. He was eyed critically. Then he was given a long whip called a black-snake. "Do you know how to use this?" the farmer asked.

The man did not reply. He merely snapped the whip and brought down a butterfly which was flitting over some nearby flowers.

The farmer was thrilled. He asked, "Do you see the honeybee on that clover blossom? Can you hit it?"

The applicant snapped the whip again, and the bee disintegrated.

"Now," said the farmer, "I'll test your ability as a driver."

As they jogged along in the farmer's wagon, the farmer saw a hornets' nest on a limb overhanging the road. "Can you bring down that hornets' nest?" he asked.

"No, sir," was the emphatic reply. "I wouldn't touch that. Those hornets are organized."

Told by RALPH W. NEIGHBOUR

* * *

God, You and I

A skilled surgeon was weary and tense after performing several operations in the course of a morning. The last operation scheduled for the day was a little girl whose critical condition demanded the surgeon's best skill. He thought, *I wish this operation could be postponed until tomorrow.*

The patient was brought in and placed on an operating table. "Breathe normally and count slowly," said the anesthetist.

"May I say the Twenty-third Psalm, nurse?" she asked.

Before the nurse could reply, the surgeon said, "Sure thing! Say it! It will do us all good!"

In a quiet, confident voice, the little girl began, "The Lord is my shepherd." As she quoted the psalm to its conclusion, the Lord's quieting, fear-allaying presence was felt by all.

Before his patient was put to sleep, the surgeon, now wholly relaxed, said, "Little girl, God and you and I are going to take care of this little matter."

ALICE MARIE KNIGHT

* * *

Kinks

J. C. Penney, merchant prince, said, "Cooperation is not so much our learning how to get along with others as our taking the kinks out of ourselves so others can get along with us."

* * *

A Beginning

Said Henry Ford, "Coming together is a beginning; keeping together is progress; thinking together is unity; working together is success."

COURAGE

Volunteers for Hardship Wanted

The heading of a six-column newspaper article was arresting: *Volunteers for Hardship Wanted.* How different it was from most appeals today.

The article began: "Wanted—400 young men and women tough enough to endure the hardship of adjusting to life in another country, where the temperature might never drop below 100 degrees, and where Western food is unavailable."

The unusual appeal was not for missionary volunteers. It was an appeal of the Canadian University Service Over-seas, which wanted to have 1,000 young people on the foreign field by 1967.

The appeal concluded thus: "We're seeking young people who are willing to put up with hardships, who can meet any challenge."

Today God is calling for self-sacrificing, ease-renouncing, totally dedicated youths. He wants those who will count no personal sacrifice too dear to make Christ known and give the bread of life to spiritually starving ones far and near.

The ancient call reverberates down the corridors of time: "Whom shall I send, and who will go for us?" (Isa. 6:8).

74

A Soldier—Not a Bartender

Harry Shepler volunteered for service in the signal corps in World War II. One Sunday he was ordered to report for duty at the bar of the canteen. He refused to obey the order.

The sergeant threatened to report him to the officer of the day. "All right," said Shepler, "go ahead. I did not enlist to be a bartender, but a soldier. I will not report at the canteen!"

Shepler was reported to the major, who sent for him. He went with trembling knees but a steady heart, for he knew he was right.

The major said, "Are you the soldier who disobeyed orders?"

"Yes, sir, I am," said Shepler.

"Why did you do it?"

"Because I do not believe it is right to do what I was told to do. I enlisted to be a soldier, not a bartender."

The major arose, extended his hand and said, "I am glad to see a fellow who has the courage of his convictions. You will not be required to report to the bar in the canteen. You are the kind of man we need in the service."

* * *

Die Decently

From the *Kiwanis Magazine* comes the following thrilling story:

"In one hand I have a Bible," said a North Korean prison guard to Salvation Army Commissioner Herbert Lord. "As a Communist I despise your God. Let me see you prove His power. Pray to Him to tell you which hand holds the Bible and which hand holds the gun. If the answer is wrong, I shall shoot!"

Herbert Lord lowered his head silently. Snow-laden wind whipped through the stockade's barbed wire.

"Have you prayed?" asked the Communist.

Lord nodded.

"And has your God told you which hand holds the Bible?"

"I did not ask Him that," said Lord.

"Then what did you pray for?"

Lord's blue eyes were steady as he replied, "For two things. I prayed to God to help me keep my temper, and I asked Him to give me strength to die decently!"

The guard's face twisted with anger. He lowered the pistol. Then, suddenly frustrated, he turned away.

* * *

These Ashes

During the Reformation, numerous "heretics" were burned at the stake. A certain man thus died in his hometown for maintaining his faith in God and His Word. His widow and son knelt beside his charred body. She gathered some ashes from the smoldering fire. Tearfully and reverently she put them in a little bag which she hung around her son's neck. She said, "Son, whenever you see injustice, cruelty, oppression of the weak, intolerance and persecution prevailing, and you cowardly fail to speak out against them, these ashes will burn your heart!"

"Only be thou strong and very courageous" (Joshua 1:7).

* * *

Had He Failed

Recently I visited Worms, Germany, where Martin Luther in 1521 confronted his accusers—the emperor, the imperial council, archbishops, dukes, princes, ambassadors of foreign courts and other dignitaries. I imagined I could see the monk standing solitarily, and I seemed to hear the echo of his courageous affirmation: "Here I stand! I can do no other! God help me!"

When Luther was asked if he would recant what he had taught, he resolutely said, "I will not recant anything unless it can be shown from the Scripture that I have erred."

W.B.K.

* * *

A Devil's Crown

Before the Bohemian martyr John Huss was burned at the stake, a paper crown on which were printed grotesque devils was placed on his head. The bishops said to him, "Now we commend thy soul to the devil!"

Huss said, "My Lord wore a crown of thorns for me. Why should I not, for His sake, wear this ignominious crown?"

Just prior to his martyrdom, the duke of Bavaria asked him to recant his teaching and escape death. Huss resolutely

75

replied, "What I have taught with my lips, I now seal with my blood!"

As the flames began to envelop him, he prayed, "I commit my soul to Thee, O Lord Jesus Christ. Thou hast redeemed me!"

Thus his triumphant soul passed into the presence of his Lord: "Absent from the body . . . present with the Lord" (II Cor. 5:8).

Though love repine and reason chafe,
There comes a voice without reply:
'Tis man's perdition to be safe,
When for the truth he ought to die.

* * *

Relinquishes Brewery Stock

Mrs. Lorraine John Mulberger, the granddaughter of the founder of the Miller Brewing Company, owned 53 percent of the stock in the brewery. In 1956 she was named board chairman.

Recently Mrs. Mulberger sold for about $36 million her controlling interest in the company. She said, "Alcohol and salvation don't mix. I realized that the brewery was not the will of God for me. The Bible says, 'Let . . . no man put a stumbling-block or an occasion to fall in his brother's way' [Rom. 14:13]. This is the reason I got out of the brewery business."

Mrs. Mulberger attends the Waukesha (Wisconsin) Bible Church. Her pastor said of her, "Mrs. Mulberger's decision was based upon her personal convictions and her understanding and acceptance of the Scriptures."

* * *

A Teenager Stood Firm

The daughter of an Arizona Baptist minister refused to offer a prayer at her high school baccalaureate service because she was requested to omit the words "in Christ's name." The senior said, "If I can't say what I believe, I won't say anything at all."

The principal had suggested, "End your prayer with the words 'in God's name,' or something similar. We expect to have some Jewish people attending, and we all pray in God's name."

God has given the command "Be strong and of a good courage: . . . be . . . very courageous" (Joshua 1:6-7).

* * *

Swift Judgment

Some national Christians had gathered on the bank of a river to witness the baptism of several recent believers. Near the water stood a father and his son who had bitterly opposed the gospel. They tried to hinder others from believing it. When the baptismal service began, the father interrupted with vile words and obscene gestures. The pastor remonstrated with him, but to no avail. Finally the father plunged naked into the water and caricatured the baptismal ceremony.

The pastor, who had been a powerful chief before his conversion, looked fearlessly at the disturber and said, 'O full of all subtilty and all mischief, thou child of the devil, thou enemy of all righteousness, wilt thou not cease to pervert the right ways of the Lord?" [Acts 13:10].

The Holy Spirit seemed to come upon the assembly with mighty power. The disturber, suddenly smitten with terror, fled from the water and fell dead upon the ground.

A. J. GORDON

* * *

"Let There Be No Mistake"

Let us not forget that the men who signed the Declaration of Independence were by that act endangering their property and even their lives. When Charles Carroll affixed his signature to the document, someone asked, "How will anyone know which Charles Carroll is meant among all those called by that name in Maryland and elsewhere?"

"Well, let there be no mistake," said the courageous patriot, and he signed in bold letters "Charles Carroll of Carrollton."

BILLY GRAHAM

* * *

"We Will Never Surrender"

There is something magnificent in the words of Winston Churchill during those dark days when it seemed there was no hope for England's survival. Standing

76

before the House of Commons and reviewing the situation, he gave them the decision of Britain's leaders: "We have talked it over. We will go on to the end. We will never surrender."

Is not this the decision a Christian must arrive at if he is going to wage war successfully against sin?

G. FRANKLIN ALLEE

* * *

Stand Up for Jesus

While he was holding special meetings in Philadelphia, Rev. Dudley A. Lyng sustained an injury from which he never recovered. As he neared death, he was asked, "Is there some message you would like to send to your fellow workers?"

Rev. Lyng replied, "Yes. Let's all stand up for Jesus." His challenging words were the inspiration for the song:

Stand up, stand up for Jesus,
The trumpet call obey;
Forth to the mighty conflict,
In this His glorious day.

* * *

What It Takes

It takes a little courage
And a little self-control,
And some grim determination
If you want to reach the goal.
It takes a deal of striving,
And a firm and stern-set chin,
No matter what the battle,
If you're really out to win.

There's no easy path to glory,
There's no rosy path to fame;
Life, however we may view it,
Is no simple parlor game.
But its prizes call for fighting,
For endurance and for grit,
For a rugged disposition
And a don't-know-when-to-quit.

You must take a blow or give one,
You must risk and you must lose,
And expect that in the struggle
You will suffer many a bruise.
But you mustn't whine or falter
If a fight you once begin;
Be a man and face the battle—
That's the only way to win.

Risked His Life for His Buddies

In the U. S. Army, no American soldier is ever knowingly left behind after a battle, whether wounded or dead. Soldiers often risk their lives to bring their fallen comrades back to their lines.

Pfc. Ed Bable, age nineteen, from Beaver Falls, Pennsylvania, and some of his buddies in Vietnam pushed through the jungle and entered a trap set by the Viet Cong. A vicious crossfire caught them. Several of them fell, seriously wounded. Bable escaped and made his way back to safety, but he didn't stay long. Struggling through the muck, he returned to the scene of the ambushment. Quickly he lifted two of his fallen comrades to their feet. Supporting one under each arm, he brought them back to the American zone.

Ed Bable, at real risk to himself, retrieved his buddies who needed to be rescued from the enemy's territory. Are we enough concerned about our loved ones, friends and neighbors to self-forgetfully do all we can to bring them to the safe, sure ground of life in Christ?

* * *

"Don't Pull Back! Don't Pull Back!"

How thrilling are deeds of courageous heroism wherever displayed. American soldiers were on the side of a hill which was being raked by vicious fire from the Viet Cong. It was a military necessity that the hill be maintained. The major who led the Americans was hit in the leg. As he fell, he was hit again. Later Sgt. Michael Boarland reported, "As he died, the Major pleaded, 'Don't pull back! Don't pull back!'"

God's imperative command to His children is "Don't pull back!"

Let us not forget that God's displeasure is upon those who fail to go forward: "If any man draw back, my soul shall have no pleasure in him" (Heb. 10:38).

* * *

He Who Tries

Said David M. Lloyd-Jones, "The man who tries to do something and fails is infinitely better than the man who tries to do nothing and succeeds."

Morale

Adm. Ben Moreell affirmed, "Morale is when your hands and feet keep on working when your head says it can't be done."

* * *

My Best

Life commented, "There are no words in the Eskimo language for *I will.* They just say, 'I'll do my best.' "

* * *

Only God

M. Royden said, "When you have nothing left but God, for the first time you are aware that God is enough."

* * *

Wanted: Trailblazers

C. T. Studd announced, "I will blaze the trail, though my grave be only a stepping-stone that younger men may follow and make Christ known where He is unknown."

* * *

Crooked Rivers and People

The *War Cry* said, "Rivers get crooked by following the line of least resistance. So do people who fall for everything and stand for nothing. God's call is clear: 'Refuse the evil, and choose the good' (Isa. 7:15); 'Be . . . strong and very courageous' " (Joshua 1:7).

* * *

"I'll Remain True to Jesus"

One almost signs his own death warrant when he becomes a true Christian in Communist China.

True Light, a Chinese who graduated from a Chinese university, was the only Christian among 1,700 students. He was openly ridiculed. Often, as he thanked God for food, it was snatched from him.

After graduating in law, he was assigned to work in a court of law in a certain town. His colleagues soon discovered that a Christian was in their midst. They were embarrassed when he bowed his head at meals and thanked God for the food. They warned him, "You cannot succeed in your law career unless you give up your religious faith. If you don't, you will be dismissed from government service and be without work. You will be given a few days in which to choose."

Bravely True Light replied, "There is no need to give me a few days to make up my mind. I have been considering this for several years. I am quite determined to remain true to Jesus Christ!"

Told by DAVID H. ADENEY, in
Sunday School Times

* * *

"In the Name of the King of Kings"

Many thrilling stories have been told about the courageous Covenanters.

A faithful pastor, who had been dispossessed of his church, held a worship service with his followers in a quiet valley. A band of soldiers, led by a fierce persecutor of the Covenanters, closed in upon the worshipers. The leader seized the frail minister. After shaking him roughly, he said, "In the name of the king, I demand you to stop this meeting."

The worshipers were frightened, but not for long. Courage came to them when they heard their fearless pastor say, "And I, sir, in the name of the King of kings, Jesus Christ, bid you take your hands off me and allow us to continue our worship service." Their enemies sullenly withdrew.

Later the Covenanters said, "We felt that we were surrounded by a band of the heavenly hosts." Were they not right? They surely were: "The angel of the LORD encampeth round about them that fear him, and delivereth them" (Ps. 34:7).

Told by MRS. J. SHIELDS

* * *

If I Knew

Martin Luther said, "If I knew the world would come to an end tomorrow, I'd plant my apple seed today."

* * *

Fit to Live

After learning that his son Quentin, a World War I pilot, had been killed, Theodore Roosevelt wrote in tribute: "Only

78

those who do not fear to die are fit to live."

* * *

A Daring Adventure

Helen Keller said, "Avoiding danger is no safer in the long run than outright exposure. Life is either a daring adventure, or nothing."

* * *

The Difference

'Twixt optimist and pessimist
The difference is droll;
The optimist sees the doughnut,
The pessimist sees the hole.

* * *

Hottest Places

Said Dante, "The hottest places in hell are reserved for those who, in time of crisis, preserve their neutrality."

* * *

Eternal Hostility

Thomas Jefferson declared, "I have sworn upon the altar of God eternal hostility against every form of tyranny over the mind of man."

* * *

When Wrong

Peter Marshall, chaplain of the U. S. Senate, prayed, "When I am wrong, make me easy to change and, when I am right, make me easy to get along with."

* * *

I'd Rather Lose

Woodrow Wilson said, "I'd rather lose in a cause that will one day win than win in a cause that will someday lose."

* * *

Courage to Change

Adm. Thomas C. Hart said, "Dear God, give us strength to accept with serenity the things that cannot be changed, and give us courage to change the things that can and should be changed, and give us the wisdom to distinguish one from the other."

* * *

Nothing Earthly

David Livingstone declared, "Nothing earthly will make me give up my work in despair. I encourage myself in the Lord my God and go forward."

"And David was greatly distressed; for the people spake of stoning him . . . but David encouraged himself in the LORD his God" (I Sam. 30:6).

COVETOUSNESS

(*See also* Riches)

Trapped!

In his vivid article "Last Moments of the Pompeians," Amedeo Maiuri tells of events which occurred on the fateful day when the city of Pompeii was inundated by molten rock and ash: "Many of the Pompeians—principally the wealthy—refused to abandon their homes and precious possessions. They took shelter, hoping the horror would pass. The decision cost them their lives. Steadily the tide of rock and ash rose against doors and windows, burying the victims as they huddled in courtyards and cellars. Poisonous volcanic gases seeped in, trapping others on the upper rooftops. Pompeii lay dying!"

Terrible will be the fate also of those who cling tenaciously and selfishly to the perishable things of the world in the time when the waters of death creep over them: "The hail shall sweep away the refuge of lies, and the waters shall overflow the hiding place" (Isa. 28:17).

A Disease of the Soul

Some years ago, an old man died in New Rochelle, New York, at the age of ninety-six. He lived alone in a skimpily furnished room on the third floor of a rickety building. He dressed shabbily and his neighbors thought he was poverty-stricken. Those who knew him best couldn't recall that he ever treated himself to a square meal.

When he died, his room was examined. It was discovered that he had more than a hundred thousand dollars in savings accounts, stocks and bonds.

Covetousness is a disease of the soul. It is a soul-shriveling, heaven-barring disease: "Nor thieves, *nor covetous* . . . shall inherit the kingdom of God" (I Cor. 6:10).

The Saviour warned, "Take heed, and beware of covetousness" (Luke 12:15).

Told by Roy O. McClain

* * *

"I Must Keep It"

During a wealthy man's terminal illness, his daughter pleaded with him to give some money to an orphanage. He assented to the request and asked for a pen and his checkbook. Suddenly he dropped the pen and laid aside the checkbook, saying, "I can't do it. I have had the money too long. I must keep it. I want to help the orphanage, but my will won't let me."

Covetousness is a soul-stultifying sin.

Adapted from The *Florida Baptist Witness*

* * *

"Covetousness, Which Is Idolatry"

Many years ago John Ward, an Englishman, bought a piece of land when it was inundated and cheap. Being a member of the British Parliament, he introduced a bill to drain the land at public expense.

After his death, there was found among his papers this extraordinary, though thoroughly selfish, prayer:

"O Lord, Thou knowest I have mine estates in the city of London, and likewise that I have recently purchased an estate in fee simple in the County of Essex. I beseech Thee to preserve the two Counties of Middlesex and Essex from fire and earthquake, and as I have a mortgage in Hertfordshire, I beg of Thee likewise to have an eye of compassion on that county. For the rest of the counties, Thou mayest deal with them as Thou art pleased."

The miserable miser died in a debtor's prison. How fittingly Jehoram's epitaph applies to that grasping, greedy man: He "departed without being desired" (II Chron. 21:20).

* * *

Little Land Needed

Tolstoy tells of a rich farmer who was never satisfied. He was greedy and grasping, always wanting more. He heard of a chance to acquire some more land. For a thousand rubles, according to the story, he could have all the land he could walk around in a day. He arose early and began to walk. The hours passed. *I must get back where I started walking to claim the land,* he thought. He began to run. Coming within sight of the starting place, the farmer exerted his last ounce of energy. As he plunged over the line, he fell to the ground and collapsed. Blood ran from his mouth as he lay—dead! A peasant took a spade and dug a grave. He made it just long enough and wide enough to bury him. That was all the ground the farmer needed.

"For we brought nothing into this world, and it is certain we can carry nothing out" (I Tim. 6:7).

* * *

The Root of All Evil

Some time ago in Arcadia, Florida, a mother and father were indicted for the fatal poisoning of their seven young children by putting parathion, an extremely potent insecticide, in their food. DeSoto County Sheriff Frank Cline said the dark deed was "motivated by the desire to collect life insurance." Double indemnity insurance policies of one thousand dollars on the life of each child were taken out the night before their death. Ironically, the policies did not take effect because

80

the father had not paid the initial four-dollar premium.

There is no crime depraved man will not commit for money. Covetousness is one of the foul, dehumanizing sins resident in the "desperately wicked" heart of man.

* * *

The Struggle of a Tightwad

A covetous man confessed: "There is nothing more distressing to me than to be in church and realize that I have nothing less than a dollar to give. I had this agonizing experience on a recent Sunday. The collection was about to be taken. What could I do? Should I give a dollar? That would be too much. Should I appear to be in deep devotion, praying silently, and let the collection plate pass me unnoticed?

"As the collection plate came closer to me, I began to hastily search my pockets for a nickel, planning to give it and shield it from the view of others. I was so nervous my wife thought I was ill. As the plate neared me, I closed my eyes, and any onlooker, seeing me, would have been impressed by my devoutness."

May God deliver us from the foul, soul-shriveling sin of "covetousness, which is idolatry" (Col. 3:5).

Told by BRUCE SLACK

* * *

"Nobody Knows—Nobody Cares"

In a church cemetery in Warwickshire, England, the following lines appear on a tombstone:

Here lies a miser who lived for himself,
He cared for nothing but gathering pelf;
Now where he is or how he fares,
Nobody knows and nobody cares.

One of the deadliest and most soul-deadening sins is covetousness, which the Bible calls idolatry. No wonder the Saviour said, "Take heed, and beware of covetousness."

* * *

The Rich Penny Pincher

For twenty-five years Leopold G. Steinbock lived at the Union Gospel Mission in Fort Worth, Texas. He lived on pennies a day, among the city's poverty-stricken.

Steinbock died at the age of eighty-eight. Those who knew him believed that he was penniless and virtually friendless. They were wrong. A preliminary check by officers revealed that he possessed a small fortune, set tentatively at fifty thousand dollars.

In speaking of the penny pincher, Rev. Paul Campbell, director of the mission, said, "Money was his god. One of his friends brought him food from the mission kitchen every day."

* * *

Starved with $274,000 in Closet

"She Starved with $274,000 in Her Closet!" This headline, with the subhead "Find $200,000 More in Banks," lured millions of readers of daily newspapers over the nation to read one of the most bizarre stories about a frail widow who starved to death in her dreary, fire-charred Staten Island, New York, flat.

The widow's name was Mrs. Emma Buhl DeHart. Besides the money discovered in her flat and in banks, she owned hundreds of shares of stock. Her total assets came to about half a million dollars. Her wealth had been largely untouched during her lifetime. She ate skimpily. She saved boxes and wrappings to burn in her stove. It was her habit, in later years, to arise about noon and go to a nearby dime store for a sandwich. She died intestate—without a will. A court fight was precipitated by nephews and nieces, claimants of the estate of the deceased.

81

CROSS

The Embalmer's Initial Incision

Specialist Jacky C. Bayne, of Ft. Mill, South Carolina, was pronounced dead of wounds near Chu Lai. For forty-five minutes doctors attempted to resuscitate him, but failed. His seemingly lifeless body was sent to an Army Graves Registration Section nearby. Later, as an embalmer's knife made its initial incision, the body showed a faint flicker of life!

Bayne was rushed back to a field hospital. Gradually, after massive transfusions of blood, life began to return.

Amazing and *astounding* were words medics at Walter Reed Hospital used to describe the case. "By all accepted criteria, Bayne was dead," said an army doctor. The spark of life was still there, however, and the blood transfusions caused it to glow and thus reversed the ebb of life.

As the physical life inheres in the blood—"The life of the flesh is in the blood" (Lev. 17:11)—the spiritual life inheres in the blood of Christ: "For this is my blood . . . which is shed . . . for the remission of sins" (Matt. 26:28).

> For my pardon this I see,
> Nothing but the blood of Jesus;
> For my cleansing this my plea,
> Nothing but the blood of Jesus.

* * *

How Screams Were Stopped

The Roman author Cicero, who witnessed many crucifixions, records that victims often became raving madmen long before they were mercifully released by death. It was sometimes necessary to cut their tongues to put a stop to their terrible screams and curses.

LOUIS CASSELS, UPI religious writer

* * *

God Did Just That

One evening in Passaic, New Jersey, when the commuter trains were speeding thousands of people to their homes from New York City, a man sat in the switch house overlooking the tracks. With his hand on the lever, he was ready to throw the switch that takes the oncoming trains across the bridge which spans the river.

As he looked at the bridge he saw a little boy walking across the bridge. If he sent the train over the bridge, the boy would be ground beneath the wheels of the train. On the other hand, if he did not throw the switch, hundreds of commuters would die.

A second look revealed the boy to be his own son! He had but seconds to make his decision. He did the only thing he could do—he sacrificed his son for the sake of the hundreds of people.

Our God did just that—He gave His Son, that we might live and have eternal life.

WARREN WIERSBE, in *Moody Monthly*

* * *

Where Hope Returned

Sir Harry Lauder, the famous Scottish singer, said as he stood to sing in an army chapel, "Before I sing, I want to speak of my son, my only child. He was killed in battle two years ago. My heart was crushed and I said I would never sing again. I started down the road of dissipation to kill my grief. Then I decided to travel another road that was to lead me up a hill. I found it rough and rugged, but I traveled it to the end. There I found the grave of my son and a cross. There my burden of sorrow was lifted. I received the impulse to sing again. Now I can sing with more assurance than ever before, for I know that because of the One who died on the cross of Calvary, my son lives! Someday I shall see him again!"

* * *

What to Stress

Years ago Dr. Sherwood Eddy spoke in a Chinese meeting. At the conclusion of his message, a Chinese pastor told him, "I observed that you spent most of your time in emphasizing the character of Christ. May I suggest that you lay primary stress on the *death* and *resurrection* of Christ? This emphasis makes our gospel message *distinctive and different* from all other religions!"

The Lord Jesus was "holy, harmless, undefiled" (Heb. 7:26). He lived a sinless life. However, we are not saved by His flawless life. We are saved by His atoning death and His triumph over death: "Redeemed . . . with the precious blood of Christ" (I Peter 1:18-19); "If thou shalt . . . believe in thine heart that God hath raised him from the dead, thou shalt be saved" (Rom. 10:9).

* * *

Your Cross Is Heavy

An American tourist had just seen the Passion Play at Oberammergau. He asked Mr. Lang, who played the part of Christ, "May I lift the cross and be photographed with you?"

"You may," said Mr. Lang.

The tourist stooped to lift the cross, but he couldn't. Then he exerted all his energy, but he still could not lift it. He said to Mr. Lang, "Your cross is surely heavy!"

Mr. Lang replied, "Sir, I cannot represent Christ with a light cross."

Told by ALAN REDPATH

* * *

Unconcerned

The Roman soldiers shook the dice
As for the stake they vied,
Quite unaware that on the cross
The world's Redeemer died.

But in the circus of our day
We, thoughtless, act the clown,
While God is speeding up His work
To ring time's curtain down.

The Roman soldiers shook the dice,
As for the stake they vied,
Are we as unconcerned as they
That Christ for us has died?

NATHANIEL KRUM in
Watchman-Examiner

* * *

"Is It Nothing to You?"

Sigismund Goetze's great painting, *Despised and Rejected of Men,* was first displayed in the British Royal Academy in 1904. The painting vividly portrays Christ, crowned with thorns and dying in anguish upon His cruel cross. The surging, restless crowd is shown passing by, heedless of the Sufferer's presence. All segments of human society are represented in that unconcerned crowd. Only one person has her face turned toward the One on the cross—a nurse on her way to minister to the sick. For a moment she pauses and looks reverently at the crucified Saviour.

What a representation this is of Christ neglected, unrecognized, despised and dishonored. "Is it nothing to you, all ye that pass by?"

* * *

"Paid with Blood"

A policeman curbed a speeding car. "The speed limit on this boulevard is thirty miles an hour," he said brusquely. "According to our electronic timer, you were traveling forty miles an hour. I will have to give you a ticket, which stipulates a fine of $17.50. You may either pay the fine at city hall or give a pint of blood to the American Red Cross."

Going to the Red Cross headquarters, the offender gave a pint of blood. Then he went to the city hall, and presented a slip of paper which showed that he had made the blood donation. Without question, the clerk wrote with red ink across the ticket which had been given by the traffic cop, "Paid with blood."

Long ago the sinless Son of God paid with His blood our debt for sin. Peter said we are "redeemed . . . with the precious blood of Christ" (I Peter 1:18-19).

Adapted from *Sunday School
Times and Gospel Herald*

* * *

For Whom Christ Died

Years ago several monks found an old man lying helpless in a forest. They brought him to a monastery. He was a pitiable sight—emaciated, ragged and dirty.

Assuming that the old man would not understand what was said, one of the younger monks spoke disparagingly about him in Latin, saying, "What shall we do with this worthless creature?"

The old man did understand. In his earlier years he had been a scholar but he had experienced misfortune. Arousing himself, he exclaimed, "Do not call any man worthless for whom Christ died."

Man possesses an undying soul and, in God's sight, is of inestimable worth. The wealth of the world fades into worthlessness compared with the value of the soul. Jesus said, "For what is a man profited, if he shall gain the whole world, and lose his own soul?" (Matt. 16:26).

* * *

The Shadow of the Cross

In Holman Hunt's painting *The Shadow of Death,* he depicts Christ as a Boy in the carpenter's shop in Nazareth. The westering sun casts its rays through the open door. The young Carpenter, rising from His bench, stretches out His arms. The setting sun shadows His figure on the wall behind Him in the form of a cross. In this way the artist foreshadows Christ's vicarious death on Calvary's cross for the sin of the world.

* * *

"I Am His Forever!"

A Sunday school teacher of a class of working girls showed them a steel engraving of a famous picture of the crucifixion. Three crosses were on the ground. Soldiers were struggling with the two thieves, and forcing them down upon the crosses while spikes were driven through their hands and feet.

Upon the middle cross Christ lay down quietly and extended His quivering palms to receive the spikes.

As the young women looked at the pictire, one sobbed, "Oh, was Christ nailed there alive? I thought that He was dead before He was nailed there!"

The teacher said, "Yes. He was nailed there alive for you."

The girl, weeping, said, "Then I am His forever!"

Alliance Weekly

* * *

The Crimson Cure

Billy Graham said, "There is a crimson cure for the scarlet sin: 'The blood of Jesus Christ . . . cleanseth us from all sin.' "

Zechariah said, "In that day there shall be a fountain opened . . . for sin and uncleanness" (Zech. 13:1).

"I'll Be Your Slave Forever"

Years ago a procession of captives passed before a powerful chief in Africa. Suddenly he observed one who had wronged him years before. He ordered his men to put their arrows to their bowstrings and avenge the wrong with the blood of the captive.

An English officer, seeing what was about to take place, implored the avenging chief to spare the captive's life, offering a sizable sum of money and costly gifts as a ransom.

The chief was adamant. "I don't want gold or costly gifts. I want blood."

As the executioners made ready to send their arrows to the heart of the captive, the Englishman suddenly thrust himself in front of the condemned man. Several arrows pierced his arm. As he removed the arrows, the blood flowed from the wounds. To the astonished chief he said, "Here is blood. I have given it for this helpless captive and I now claim his life."

The chief said, "The white man has bought the captive with his blood. He shall be his."

With tears of gratitude in his eyes, the ransomed captive knelt at the feet of the Englishman and said, "O white man, you have bought me with your blood. I shall be your slave forever and ever."

Peter said of the One who redeemed us with His precious blood, "Ye were . . . redeemed . . . with the precious blood of Christ" (I Peter 1:18-19).

Adapted from *Alliance Weekly*

* * *

"Man's Inhumanity to Man"

"And he bearing his cross went forth into a place called the place of a skull, which is called in the Hebrew Golgotha" (John 19:17).

Luke designated the place where Jesus was crucified as Calvary. The word *Calvary* comes from the Greek word *kranion,* which means a skull.

Calvary was outside the city wall. It was probably along a public highway, for the Romans selected such a place for executions. Being a place of execution, it abounded in skulls, therefore it was called "the place of a skull." Some believe, how-

84

ever, that it is thus designated because of the bald, round, skull-like appearance of the hill. In the picture *Gordon's Calvary,* the hill has a skull-like appearance.

The climax of "man's inhumanity to man" was reached when man devised crucifixion as a mode of putting human beings to death. Stoning, hanging and burning were merciful modes of execution, compared to the lingering, torturous death by crucifixion. The shame and ignominy of crucifixion were surpassed only by the indescribable and seemingly interminable agony of it.

* * *

Not Between Candles in a Cathedral

The cross and its message should never be withdrawn from the marketplace where the irreverent, unanchored, shepherdless multitude mills and mingles.

Jesus was not crucified in a cathedral between two candles, but on a cross between two thieves. He was crucified by a crossroads where the throng was so racially and linguistically diverse that it was necessary to write the title over His cross in Hebrew, Latin and Greek. In this place, vulgar men talked obscenities, thieves cursed and blasphemed, and soldiers gambled. The Saviour died that this sordid, sin-sodden condition might be changed.

Christ's church can fulfill its divinely apportioned mission only by living a crucified life and by ministering to the slaves of sin, greed and lust, whether among the affluent or among the crowd on skid row.

All gradations of mankind need the heart-transforming, character-ennobling message of the cross. There is no substitute for it.

"For I determined not to know any thing among you, save Jesus Christ, and him crucified" (I Cor. 2:2).

* * *

The Cleansing Fountain

A self-righteous woman said to Dr. Harry A. Ironside at the close of a service, "Surely you don't believe what you and the people sang in the service—'There is a fountain filled with blood'—do you?"

Dr. Ironside replied, "I certainly do. Would you fill it with self-righteousness about which the Bible says, 'All our righteousnesses are as filthy rags' [Isa. 64:6]? Would you fill it with human wisdom about which the Bible says, 'God made foolish the wisdom of this world' [I Cor. 1:20]? Would you fill it with morality? Don't forget that Jesus said to a good, moral and religious man, 'Ye must be born again' [John 3:7]."

To these searching questions the woman said, "I don't know."

Said Dr. Ironside, "The world needs cleansing. I believe what that old song says, and I believe what the prophet said long ago: 'In that day there shall be a fountain opened . . . for sin and for uncleanness' [Zech. 13:1]. Experience has taught me that at the cross people find peace, forgiveness and newness of life."

* * *

Our Sacrificial Lamb

In some rivers of South America, small voracious fish, called piranha, abound. They swim in schools, and can devour, in a short time, any man or animal that enters the water. Rarely does either escape when attacked by the vicious piranha.

To circumvent the destruction of their livestock when driven across a river infested with piranha, the farmers first drive into the water a sacrificial sheep to be attacked and devoured by the piranha, while they drive their other animals across the river.

Satan is a voracious, merciless destroyer. To rescue us from danger and eternal death, Christ, our sacrificial Lamb, "interposed His precious blood."

Watchman-Examiner

* * *

How Do You React?

In commenting upon the praiseworthy project to raise funds to help the children of a White House guard who was slain, President Truman said, "You can't imagine just how a man feels when someone else dies for him."

What are your feelings when you think about the One who died a vicarious death for our sins, the One who was "wounded for our transgressions"?

85

But drops of grief can ne'er repay
The debt of love I owe:
Here, Lord, I give myself away,
'Tis all that I can do.

* * *

Paul Agrees with an Unbeliever

An earnest Christian was engaged in conversation with an unbeliever who said, "I do not understand nor do I believe that the blood of Jesus Christ can wash away my sin."

"You and Paul quite agree on that subject," answered the Christian. "Paul said, 'For the preaching of the cross is to them that perish foolishness; but unto us which are saved it is the power of God' [I Cor. 1:18]."

HYMAN J. APPELMAN

* * *

Blest Cross!

Thus far I did come laden with my sin;
Nor could aught cease the grief that I was in
Till I came hither: What a place is this!
Must here be the beginning of my bliss?
Must here the burden fall from off my back?
Must here the strings that bound it to me crack?
Blest cross! blest sepulchre! blest rather be
The Man that there was put to shame for me.

JOHN BUNYAN, in
Pilgrim's Progress

* * *

Needless Suffering

In Mexico City, twenty-seven-year-old Francisco Castellanos nearly bled to death in an attempt to feel the pain which Christ felt as He was pinioned to His cross.

Francisco drove two ten-inch, hand-forged nails through his hands in a hotel room. Then he went to the National Cathedral to pray. He concealed his bleeding hands with bandages.

The nail in his left hand pierced a vein. The hand bled profusely. He lost so much blood that he nearly collapsed. Other worshipers, observing his condition, called an ambulance. He was rushed to a hospital.

Castellanos told policemen about a vow he had made to subject himself to excruciating pain on three successive Good Fridays as an expression of his gratitude for recovering from a skin cancer which doctors had said was incurable.

How grateful we are that God requires no such sacrifices from His children. There are better ways to express gratitude to God for His numberless blessings. David said, "For thou desirest not sacrifice; else would I give it: thou delightest not in burnt offering. The sacrifices of God are a broken spirit: a broken and a contrite heart, O God, thou wilt not despise" (Ps. 51:16-17).

* * *

How Christ Died

In his book *A Doctor at Calvary*, Dr. Pierre Barbet, a noted French surgeon, says, "The physiological cause of Christ's death was asphyxia. Cramps began in the forearms and spread to the arms and throughout the body. To relieve the cramps, the crucified One pulled Himself up on the footrest or on the nails. The cramps spread to the muscles that control breathing. The lungs, which were filled with air, were unable to expel it. The lungs were caught in a state of forced inspiration, and unable to empty themselves, so the normal oxygenation of the circulating blood was unable to take place. Asphyxiation began as thoroughly as if He had been strangled."

Christ also died of a broken heart: "Reproach hath broken my heart; and I am full of heaviness" (Ps. 69:20).

Why Christ died is more important than *how* He died: "But he was wounded for our transgressions, he was bruised for our iniquities" (Isa. 53:5).

* * *

Deliberately Rejected

A Saint Bernard dog, high in the Alps, found and rescued his sixty-ninth man. The effort to help the man cost the dog his life. After digging the man out from under the snow, the dog stretched himself over the man, as he had been trained to

86

do, to impart warmth and revive the flickering spark of life. When the man began to thaw out, he saw the huge dog over him. In his dazed, drowsy condition, he mistook the dog for a wolf intent on devouring him. Quickly he plunged his dagger into the animal's heart! Without a whimper, the noble dog crept away to his master's cabin where he bled to death on the doorstep.

How like that man are those who "crucify . . . the Son of God afresh, and put him to an open shame" (Heb. 6:6), and spurn His offer of eternal life! There is this difference, however: the freezing man was in a semiconscious condition when he rejected his would-be rescuer. Those who reject the Saviour do it deliberately and knowingly.

* * *

The Ultimate in Suffering

Dr. Howard A. Matzke, professor of anatomy at the University of Kansas, has written a monograph in which he tells why crucifixion was the most agonizing death ever devised by man:

"Crucifixion resulted in severe pain because the body was hanging on the nails through the hands. It also placed considerable stretch on the muscles extending from the chest to the arms, muscles which are very important in breathing. Crucifixion thus prevented normal expiration of the breath, for it held the chest expanded.

"Impaired breathing results in a decreased oxygen supply to the muscles. These in turn accumulate an excess amount of lactic acid. Severe tetany follows. These are muscle spasms comparable to cramps.

"To alleviate the pain of severed nerves and the muscle spasms, the victim would try to push himself up by using the nails through his feet as a brace. Within a few minutes, the pain in the feet would become unbearable, and the body would sag again."

* * *

Where Best Read

We read Thee best in Him who came,
To bear for us the cross of shame,
Sent by the Father from on high,
Our life to live, our death to die.

The Unfailing Remedy

Mrs. Theodore C. Bill had a rare blood disease which prevented the blood from coagulating. This resulted in uncontrollable bleeding. She had only a fighting chance for life. During a period of two months, more than 1,600 persons responded to a plea for blood donors. Finally she died.

Long ago a blood donor was needed to cure the universal sickness of mankind—sin. The sinless Son of God volunteered, saying, "Lo, I come. . . . I delight to do thy will, O my God" (Ps. 40:7-8; cf. Heb. 10:7). His atoning blood was shed "for sin and for uncleanness" (Zech. 13:1). An unfailing remedy is available to all who will take it.

* * *

His Own Blood Saved Him

J. R. Banes of Amarillo, Texas, gratefully tells how he saved his own life. He had donated a pint of his type O Rh-negative blood to the Coffee Memorial Blood Center when this rare type of blood was urgently needed to resupply their stock of it.

The day after Banes gave his blood, he was critically injured when a gravel truck backed over him. In surgery, a blood transfusion became necessary. His own blood saved his life!

Physical life inheres in blood: "The life of the flesh is in the blood" (Lev. 17:11). Spiritual life inheres in the precious blood of Christ: "This is my blood . . . which is shed for many for the remission of sins" (Matt. 26:28). Why will men die spiritually and eternally when the remedy for sin is readily available?

* * *

I Crucified the Son of God

In his book *The Teaching of Contempt*, the Jewish historian Jules Isaac maintains that it is not only historically wrong to allege that the Jews crucified the Saviour, but it fosters anti-Semitism.

Although the Jewish leaders clamored for the death of the Son of God, each one of us, both Jew and Gentile, had a part in His suffering and sacrificial death:

87

"But he was wounded for our transgressions" (Isa. 53:5).

'Twas I that shed that precious blood,
I nailed Him to the tree;
I crucified the Son of God,
I joined the mockery!

* * *

The Burning Shame of It

Once Dr. Alexander Whyte dreamed that he saw a soldier cruelly flogging the sinless Son of God. The lash of the lead-studded whip cut deeply in His quivering, blood-spattered back. "Oh, the burning shame of it!" exclaimed the dreamer as he rushed toward the soldier. At that instant the soldier turned. In amazement, Dr. Whyte recognized *himself!*

* * *

The Remedy Spurned

Mrs. Dorothy Sheridan, of Norwich, Massachusetts, a believer in Christian Science, was convicted of involuntary manslaughter because she failed to get medical care for her five-year-old daughter, Lisa, who died of a lung infection. Authorities said the girl would have lived with proper medical care.

Only God knows the number of those who die spiritually through failure to take the unfailing remedy for the universal malady—sin: "There shall be a fountain opened . . . for sin" (Zech. 13:1).

DEATH

(*See also* Resurrection)

"Death, Be Not Proud"

Just before his death, Tennyson said, "Death, be not proud! A short sleep and I will wake again eternally! A short voyage and I will meet my Maker face to face!"

Tennyson envisioned death as being like the narrow strait that separates the Isle of Wight from England. When returning home across the strait, he often saw the setting sun and the evening star. He heard the "moaning of the bar" and listened to the distant vesper bells.

When he was in his eighty-first year, he wrote the poem which has been called his farewell to life. The opening verses are:

Sunset and evening star,
And one clear call for me!
And may there be no moaning of the bar,
When I put out to sea.

But such a tide as moving seems asleep,
Too full for sound and foam,
When that which drew from out the
boundless deep
Turns again home.

Not Alone

Because of complications beyond the medic's help, a young mother lay dying in childbirth. Deliriously she pleaded, "Oh, doctor, I don't want to go alone! Doctor, please! I want to take my baby with me!"

In an effort to allay her fears and say something that would comfort her, the doctor said, "My dear, your baby will have loving care. You need have no fear. The gate through which you must go is only wide enough for *one.*"

The young mother was a member of Dr. G. Campbell Morgan's church. He heard the well-intentioned words of the doctor and said to him, "Tell her, doctor, that the gate is wide enough for *two*— herself and the Saviour!"

The death-conquering Saviour goes with God's children through the portals of death. He accompanies them through the valley to their eternal home where they will be forever with Him.

Told by HADDON W. ROBINSON, in
Psalm Twenty-Three

Waiting for New Uniform

A girl greatly loved her brother who was killed in World War II. One night she dreamed that she found her brother standing with a group of soldiers. She exclaimed, "I thought you were dead!"

"Dead? No! I am not dead!" he said. "I am only waiting for my new uniform! I am going to parade before the King!"

The Christian's full redemption will be consummated when death's Conqueror, Christ, changes "our vile body, that it may be fashioned like unto his glorious body" (Phil. 3:21). "We ourselves . . . [wait] for the redemption of our body" (Rom. 8:23b).

* * *

Two Realities: Death and Eternity

Some time ago Billy Graham spoke to the students of the University of California. The radicals in the audience interrupted parts of his message with boos and catcalls. They were quieted, however, when he spoke of their unresolved problems—death and eternity. He told about a college girl who was fatally injured in a car accident. Her last words to her mother were these: "Mother, you taught me everything I needed to know to get by in college—how to light my cigarette, how to hold my cocktail glass and how to have intercourse safely. But, Mother, you never taught me how to die. You better teach me quickly! Mother, I'm dying!"

Christianity Today

* * *

In the Hollow of His Hand

Donald William Kuester, senior engineer and chief of the acoustics and electronics division, Naval Ordnance Laboratory, White Oak, Maryland, was on the ill-fated U.S.S. *Thresher* when it sank in some 8,400 feet of water in the Atlantic. He and 129 others aboard went down to the ocean depths.

Kuester was a devout Christian. In early childhood he was converted. For years he was superintendent of the Sunday school of the Chillum Heights Assembly, Washington, D.C.

In speaking of his daddy's death, Kuester's little seven-year-old boy, Bruce, said, "Daddy is all right, because the sea is in the hollow of God's hand!"

Was the boy not right? He surely was. Long ago Isaiah said that God "hath measured the waters in the hollow of his hand" (Isa. 40:12).

In a memorial service for Kuester, a chaplain alluded to the comforting words of Bruce and added, "I could not say more, nor could anyone say more. Little Bruce has said the ultimate word."

* * *

The Valiant in Death

Cowards die many times before their
  deaths;
The valiant never taste of death but once.
Of all the wonders that I yet have heard,
It seems to me most strange that men
  should fear,
Seeing that death, a necessary end,
Will come when it will come.

SHAKESPEARE

* * *

"Will Jesus Be There to Meet Me?"

When a devout Christian couple were told by their family physician that their little daughter was incurably ill, they asked, "Shall we tell her? She has accepted Jesus as her Saviour and is ready to go."

After sorrowful heart-searching, they said to their little girl, "Darling, the doctor tells us that you will not get well. We have prayed that God would heal you, but it seems to be His will to take you to heaven to live with Him forever. Soon, darling, God will send His angels to take you to the beautiful place where He is!"

The face of the little girl brightened and she quickly asked, "Will Jesus be there to meet me?"

"You bet He will!" quickly replied the father, adding, "And what's more, Mother and Daddy will be coming soon to join you!"

Death temporarily separates God's children who die in the Lord. Before long, we ardently believe, "The Lord himself shall descend from heaven . . . and the dead in Christ shall rise first: then

89

we which are alive and remain shall be caught up *together with them.* . . . Wherefore comfort one another with these words" (I Thess. 4:16-18).

Told by Roy O. McClain

* * *

Death Sought in Vain

Sometimes evildoers do not get what they ask for, but Jack Kirschke, a suspended deputy district attorney of Los Angeles, did. He was tried for fatally shooting his wife and her lover. A jury of six men and six women sentenced him to die in the gas chamber, in keeping with his request that they sentence him to death rather than send him to prison for life.

Kirschke said, "I would prefer the death penalty to spending the rest of my life in the penitentiary, especially with the nagging thought that the jury was not certain enough of my guilt to order the death penalty."

Judge Kathleen Parker pronounced the death sentence.

In the time of unparalleled anguish during the great tribulation, "those men which have not the seal of God in their foreheads . . . shall . . . seek death, and shall not find it; and shall desire to die, and death shall flee from them" (Rev. 9:4-6).

How wise we are to flee from the coming day of wrath and seek eternal life and refuge now in the enduring rock, Christ Jesus!

* * *

When Is One Dead?

The transplanting of a heart from the body of one supposedly dead involves legal and moral considerations. When and by whom is a heart donor to be adjudged physically dead?

Judge George J. McMonagle said, "So far as legal responsibility goes, there is absolutely none if vital functions of respiration and circulation cease."

Dr. Jerome J. DeCosse, associate professor of surgery, Case Western Reserve University School of Medicine, stated, "The earliest signs of clinical death are not well defined. Cessation of brain

waves, with loss of all spontaneous reflexes and other heart and lung activity, can be called death. The judgment should be made by senior physicians and not those involved in a transplant."

Only God knows when a person irrevocably dies spiritually; when he no longer hears the wooing voice of the Holy Spirit; when he ceases to hear the plaintive plea of God, saying, "Give me thine heart."

Saul lamented, "God is departed from me, and answereth me no more" (I Sam. 28:15); and Esau "found no place of repentance, though he sought it carefully with tears" (Heb. 12:17).

* * *

Just Away!

You cannot say, you must not say
That she is dead. She is just away!
With a cheery smile and a wave of the hand
She has wandered into an unknown land
And left us dreaming how very fair
It needs must be, since she lingers there!
So think of her faring on, as dear
In the love of There as the love of Here,
Think of her still as the same, and say
She is not dead, she is just away!

James Whitcomb Riley

* * *

Known unto God

As of September 30, 1966, there were 1,110,071 persons interred in the 98 national cemeteries. Of this number, the names of 951,521 were known and the names of 158,550 were unknown.

Thousands who fall in battle are unknown to man, but they are known to God.

God knows everything about His children—their joys, their sorrows, their homelife and their business life.

He knows, He loves, He cares,
Nothing this truth can dim;
He does the very best for those
Who leave the choice with Him.

Two Car-Lengths from Death

"Crash Kills Six Teachers from Akron" was the headline of the tragic story of the sudden, simultaneous death of six schoolteachers. They had been returning to Akron after attending a session of the North Eastern Ohio Teachers Association in Cleveland.

The driver of the car just behind the fatal car testified, "I was two car-lengths behind them. All of a sudden I saw a truck coming across the medial line, its bright lights shining in my eyes. I thought, *This is it!* I heard the crash of the impact. Then there was absolute silence. I thought, *How quickly death can come!* I figured that I was just two car-lengths from death!"

How swiftly death can come to any of us! The Bible says, "There is but a step between me and death" (I Sam. 20:3).

Whether death comes suddenly or slowly, we should be ready. Is your house in order? Long ago Isaiah delivered God's message to Hezekiah: "Set thine house in order: for thou shalt die, and not live" (Isa. 38:1).

* * *

A Respectable Exit

Some time ago an old man in Stanstead Abbots, England, purchased an oak casket for twenty-three pounds. Each day he goes to a shed where it is kept and polishes it. He said, "I have even had my picture taken in it. I wanted to see how I will look in death. I am ninety-two years old. I have had a rough life from infancy. I am making sure I will go out respectably, placed in an oak casket with brass handles and everything."

It is right to make some provision for the body. It is the height of folly to make no provision for the soul.

* * *

All Is Well

A splendid example of a serene attitude toward death is found in the last letter that Dr. Edward Wilson, physician, naturalist, artist and Antarctic explorer, wrote to his wife from the icy wastes of the South Pole.

The men in Scott's ill-fated expedition, of which Dr. Wilson was a member, were starving and had no fuel with which to keep warm when he wrote the letter. Later it was found near his ice-sheathed body.

"Don't be unhappy," he wrote. "We are playing a good part in a great scheme arranged by God Himself. We will all meet after death, and death has no terrors. All is for the best to those that love God. All is well!"

FELIX MARTI-IBANEZ

* * *

There's No Dark Valley

Moody said, "I believe Psalm 23 is more often misquoted than any other part of the Bible. I have heard many tell of the dark valley, but the word *dark* isn't there. The psalm says, 'Though I walk through the valley of the shadow of death.' Did you ever see a shadow in the dark? Go down to your basement tonight without a light and you can't see your shadow. All death can do is to throw a shadow, because Christ, the Light, is present. Shadows never hurt anyone. We have nothing to fear!"

* * *

Darrow at Death's Door

In "The Worry Clinic," in *Power for Living*, columnist Dr. George Crane tells of the disclosure made by a clerk in the office of Clarence Darrow, the famed criminal lawyer and self-acclaimed atheist. The clerk said, "As Darrow lay dying, he hastily summoned three clergymen to his room—a Presbyterian minister, a Catholic priest and a Jewish rabbi. He said to them, 'Gentlemen, I have written and spoken many things against God and the churches during my lifetime. Now I wish I hadn't! Now I realize it is entirely possible that I may have been wrong. So I should like to ask as a final favor that each one of you intercede for me with the Almighty.'"

How different things are when people face the grim reaper—death! With God's children, death is merely a transition into the presence of the Lord: "For I am in a strait betwixt two, having a desire to depart, and to be with Christ; which is far

91

better" (Phil. 1:23). With the unsaved, it is separation from the Lord: "Depart from me, ye cursed" (Matt. 25:41).

* * *

A National Problem

Dr. Howard Sudak said, "The problem of suicide is enormous. More people in the United States have died by suicide in the past twenty years than all our servicemen killed in World War II and Korea combined. It has been estimated that the annual number of suicides is well over forty thousand and that there are at least six unsuccessful attempts at suicide for every one which ends in death."

* * *

How Stalin Died

Svetlana, the daughter of Stalin, said of his death, "My father died a difficult and terrible death. God grants an easy death only to the just. At what seemed the very last moment, he suddenly opened his eyes and cast a glance over everyone in the room. It was a terrible glance, insane and perhaps angry and full of fear of death. Then he lifted his left hand as though pointing to something above and bringing down a curse on us all. The gesture was full of menace."

How dismal and dark is the death of Christ-rejecters! To go out into a lost hereafter is irreparable loss.

How luminous is the valley of death for those who, in life, loved and followed Christ, the Conqueror of death. He is with them in the valley.

* * *

Exit via Suicide

According to *Time Essay*, November 25, 1966, "Nevada has the highest suicide rate (22.5 per 100,000) of any state, and the West Coast the highest of any region. Divorced males seem to have a hard time finding a reason for living: 69.4 per 100,000 of them kill themselves in the United States, as opposed to only 18.4 of 100,000 divorced women. Artists, professional men and top executives commit suicide more than any other people—two in every one hundred doctors kill themselves.

More surprising is the high rate of suicide among psychiatrists."

* * *

The Best and Worst Revealed

In times of crises, the basest and the best in human nature are displayed.

During World War I, the *Lusitania* was sunk by a German submarine. There were 1,198 voyagers who went down with the ill-fated vessel. Included was Alfred G. Vanderbilt, a millionaire sportsman, who gave his life preserver to a nursemaid and went down to the ocean's depth. Elbert Hubbard, an actor, also gave his life preserver to a nursemaid. Charles Frohman, a partially crippled producer, gave his life belt to a terrified woman. Just before Frohman sank beneath the dark waters, he said with a smile, "Why fear death? It is the most beautiful adventure of life!"

* * *

"Where Have You Gone?"

At midnight, the quiet of an African village was rent by a wailing cry. Another soul had passed into eternity.

The wailing cry soon became a weeping chant as many joined and voiced the question, "Where have you gone? Oh, tell us, where have you gone?" For three days, the chant continued throughout the village.

God's children know where their loved ones go in death. They go to be forever with the Lord. Paul said, "I am in a strait betwixt two, having a desire to depart, and to be with Christ; which is far better" (Phil. 1:23).

Brethren Missionary Herald

* * *

So Live

So live that when thy summons comes to join
The innumerable caravan which moves
To that mysterious realm, where each shall take
His chamber in the silent halls of death,
Thou go not, like the quarry-slave at night,
Scourged to his dungeon, but, sustained and soothed

92

By an unfaltering trust, approach thy
grave
Like one who wraps the drapery of his
couch
About him, and lies down to pleasant
dreams.

WILLIAM CULLEN BRYANT

* * *

Seemingly a Joyous Occasion

Frankie Miller, twenty-six-year-old
Gypsy prince, died recently in Cleveland,
Ohio. His funeral was seemingly a joy-
ous occasion. A five-piece jazz group
played "When the Saints Go Marching
In" as the hearse entered the cemetery.
When the casket was lowered into the
grave, the band played the prince's favor-
ite songs, including "Hello, Dolly" and
"Days of Wine and Roses."

Friends threw into the grave flowers,
dirt, beer, wine, whiskey and bills in one-,
five- and ten-dollar denominations and an
untold sum in silver. "This was to kill
lingering evil spirits and to buy the
prince's way into heaven," a Gypsy explained.

Death is no joke, however. It ends
one's earthly existence and his opportunity to prepare for the great beyond.
Jesus told of the unavailing plea of a lost
soul in the place of anguish: "Have mercy
on me; . . . I am tormented in this flame"
(Luke 16:24).

The greatest of tragedies is to die without faith in death's Conqueror, the Saviour.

* * *

Separation Only Temporary

Many years ago there was a beautiful
custom in Sicily. When fishermen went
to sea, their wives, children and sweethearts accompanied them to the shore.
As they embarked, all raised their voices
in a hymn of supplication to God for His
protection. This was followed by a hymn
of praise. Those in the receding boats
and those on shore blended their voices in
an antiphony of trust and devotion until
the voices of the fishermen faded away.

As we say good-bye to our loved ones
who have died in the Lord, we are comforted in knowing that the separation is
only temporary. When we awaken with
the likeness of Christ in glory we'll see
them again and be forever with the Lord.

"For the Lord himself shall descend
from heaven . . . and the dead in Christ
shall rise first: then we which are alive
. . . shall be caught up together with
them . . . to meet the Lord in the air"
(I Thess. 4:16-17).

* * *

For Whom the Bell Tolls

In an Indian village in Guatemala,
where my daughter is a Wycliffe Bible
translator, it is the custom to toll the bell
in the Catholic church when death occurs.
The bell tolls slowly when an adult dies.
It tolls rapidly when a child dies. (Fifty
percent of the children die in infancy.)
The daily tolling of the bell brings sadness to my daughter as she thinks of the
spiritual darkness in that village and the
surrounding area where Satan, the prince
of darkness, has held unchallenged sway
through the centuries.

W. B. K.

* * *

At Home with the Lord

A mother was greatly grieved because
of the passing of her baby boy. Little
June, observing her mother's sadness,
asked, "Mommy, why are you sad?"

Mother replied, "My dear, I am sad
because we have lost our dear baby. He
is in heaven with Jesus."

A serious look came on June's face.
She said, "But, Mommy, if you know
where my baby brother is, he isn't lost,
is he?"

All who die in the Lord are with the
Lord. The Bible says that to be absent
from the body is to be present with the
Lord (II Cor. 5:8). "For I am in a strait
betwixt two, having a desire to depart,
and to be with Christ; which is far better" (Phil. 1:23).

ALICE MARIE KNIGHT

* * *

A Thoroughfare

Victor Hugo said, "I feel in myself the
future life. Heaven lights me with the
reflection of an unknown world I cannot

93

see. My soul becomes more luminous when my bodily powers begin to fail. The nearer I approach the end, the plainer I hear around me the immortal symphonies of the world which invites me. The tomb is not a blind alley. It is a thoroughfare. It closes on the twilight. It opens on the dawn."

* * *

Christ's Last Will and Testament

The making of wills and the bequeathing of possessions have been practiced since ancient times. It is now known that wills were made in the early days of Egypt.

Wills have been carved and written in strange places and on strange things. They have been tattooed on backs, carved on barn doors and written on eggshells, doctor's prescription blanks and a nurse's petticoat. Some of them have made dogs and cats richer than many people.

An Akron, Ohio, eccentric died intestate. He left $1,353,000, more than half of which was in cash. Before his death, he expressed the wish that the money be scattered over the ocean for the seagulls and whales.

The last will and testament of Calvin Coolidge was short and simple. It stated: "Not unmindful of my son, John, I give all my property to my wife, Grace Coolidge, in fee simple."

An old adage about an inheritance is both homey and brief: "A little home, well filled; a little land, well tilled; a little wife, well willed—these are the great riches."

Christ had a last will and testament. He bequeathed His peace to all of God's children: "Peace I leave with you, my peace I give unto you" (John 14:27). He bequeathed His mother to John: "Behold thy mother" (19:27). He bequeathed His spirit to His Father: "Father, into thy hands I commend my spirit" (Luke 23:46).

The greatest and most enduring things a parent can bequeath to a child are an untarnished name, an unsullied character and the memory of a life faithfully lived for God and others. "The memory of the just is blessed" (Prov. 10:7).

At Evening Time It Shall Be Light

A snow-rim on my brow,
    But summer in my heart,
My feet are weary now,
    Soon earth and I must part.
But God has made my pathway bright,
And now, at evening time there's light!

A staff of easy grasp
    Supports my yielding limb,
He bids my faith to clasp
    Its hold and trust on Him.
His will and care are my delight,
And lo, at evening time there's light!

Like winter suns that shine,
    E'en through the cloudy rifts,
His love and favor now are mine,
    Rich in my Father's gifts.
I may not fear there is no light,
Behold, at evening time there's light!

My outer vision's dim,
    My inward eye is clear,
My very thought of Him
    Disperses every fear.
I know life's outcome will be right,
For now, at evening time there's light!

Some night or morn or noon,
    Life's journey will be done,
Nor do I fear if soon
    My endless life's begun.
Then, O the bliss of that first sight,
When path and pillow flame with light!

JOHN PARKER

* * *

Irretrievable Loss—Infinite Gain

What dismal, dreadful impressions of death were etched upon my mind as an unsaved boy! All that I saw and heard caused me to believe that death was the greatest of calamities, an irretrievable loss. As funeral processions wended their way to and from the little church in the small Georgia town, the deep-throated bell in the steeple tolled, oh, so mournfully! The women mourners were attired in deep black and their faces were covered with billowy black veils. The sad-faced men mourners wore black-crepe bands on their arms. Before and after the funeral, black-edged letters went forth with the message of unmitigated sorrow. Not an inkling of light shone on the dismal, dark scene.

The Bible is the only source of light in the time of death. To the Christ-rejecter, death is the greatest possible calamity. To the Christian, however, death is infinite gain: "To die is gain" (Phil. 1:21). Death to the Christian means to be "absent from the body, and . . . present with the Lord" (II Cor. 5:8). Hallelujah!

W. B. K.

* * *

If the Heart Is Right

During the Reign of Terror, from April, 1793, to July, 1794, thousands of people in France were brought before revolutionary tribunals, convicted and sent to the guillotine.

In Paris, 2,639 perished. The guillotine occupied a conspicuous place in the square now called *Place de la Concorde*—"the place of peace."

Dr. Joseph Ignace Guillotin asserted that the gadget he had invented was a more humane mode of decapitation than the clumsier block and ax or sword. He was fated to learn by experience if his claim was true, for he himself died on the guillotine sometime later. Other notables to thus perish were King Louis XVI and his queen, Marie Antoinette.

It doesn't matter a great deal how we make our exit from this world—whether death comes with a crawl or a pounce—if our hearts are right in the sight of God. Before his decapitation in the Tower of London, Sir Walter Raleigh said, "It matters not how the head lies if the heart is right."

* * *

A Predeath Funeral

Death is certain: "It is appointed unto men once to die" (Heb. 9:27). Preparation for death is indicative of wisdom: "Prepare to meet thy God" (Amos 4:12).

Recently newspapers over the nation told the story of Gerald McKinney of Portsmouth, Ohio, who meticulously planned for a predeath funeral. He said, "I am going to attend my own funeral. My friends and relatives can come to see me now while I can see them, and they can give me the roses while I live!"

A hearse, carrying a rose-draped casket, was followed by eleven cars which drove to the county fairgrounds, ten miles north of Portsmouth. Slowly the cortege circled the racetrack and then it stopped in front of the grandstand.

Both religious and popular music were played by a half-dozen musical groups. Most of the music was about roses. Roses decorated the platform where six members of the Portsmouth Eagles lodge, attired in white coats, solemnly placed casket. McKinney stood by the casket while the funeral ritual of the lodge was recited. An estimated eight hundred persons watched the proceedings.

After the predeath funeral, a man asked McKinney, "Now that you have had your funeral, what are your plans for your real death?" He replied, "Just a simple graveside service."

Death for God's children is infinite gain: "For to me to live is Christ, and to die is gain" (Phil. 1:21).

Death for the unsaved is irreparable loss: "For what is a man profited, if he shall gain the whole world, and lose his own soul?" (Matt. 16:26).

* * *

God's Angel-in-Waiting

Dr. R. G. Lee said, "Death is simply God's angel-in-waiting, on the threshold of the unseen, to disrobe the soul of its earthly garment preparatory to its passing into the presence of the King of glory."

Paul said that to be absent from the body is to be present with the Lord (II Cor. 5:8).

* * *

"I Am . . . Ready to Die" (Ps. 88:15)

When informed by Dr. Grayson of his approaching death, Woodrow Wilson said, "I am a broken piece of machinery. When the machinery is broken—" There was a pause. Then the President confidently said, "I am ready."

Jesus said, "Be ye also ready: for in such an hour as ye think not the Son of man cometh" (Matt. 24:44).

95

Calories and Coronaries

There is a vital relationship between calories and coronaries. The smaller your waistline is, the longer your lifeline will be. The Bible warns, "Put a knife to thy throat, if thou be a man given to appetite" (Prov. 23:2).

* * *

Lincoln Witnessed His Own Funeral

Though a practical man, Lincoln believed that dreams often revealed future events. One day he related to some friends an ominous, frightful dream he had. He said, "It began with sounds of anguished weeping in the East Room of the White House. There I saw a funeral bier. On it lay a corpse. Guards and mourners stood by it. I asked, 'Who is dead in the White House?' 'The President,' replied a soldier. 'He was killed by an assassin!' A moment later I awoke, realizing with horror that I had witnessed my own funeral!"

A few days later, Lincoln was fatally wounded by John Wilkes Booth.

In old times God revealed future things to His servants. We have in God's Word a full and final revelation of God and of many things pertaining to His plans and purposes for men and nations.

* * *

Scrabble

Dr. R. G. Lee stated, "The death of a Christian is not like an unfinished game of Scrabble, with incomplete words tapering off in all directions."

* * *

Rightly Occupied

Richard Baxter said, "Spend your time in nothing which you might not safely and properly be found doing if death should overtake you."

* * *

Die Well

Someone asked John Wesley the secret of the success of his movement. He replied, "Our people die well."

Smile

Charles Spurgeon said, "When you talk about heaven, do it with a smile on your face."

* * *

A Contrast

When Saul made his ignominious, suicidal exit from life, he said, "I have played the fool" (I Sam. 26:21). When Paul departed to be forever with the Lord, he said, "I have kept the faith" (II Tim. 4:7).

* * *

Bags Packed

Just before his death, Pope John XXIII said, "My bags are packed! I am ready to leave!"

* * *

True Repentance

True repentance is never too late, but seldom is late repentance true repentance.

* * *

One out of One

Said George Bernard Shaw, "One out of one dies."

* * *

Gladness

Just before Adoniram Judson died, he confidently and joyously exclaimed, "I go with the gladness of a boy bounding away from school! I am so free with Christ!"

* * *

No Separation

If we live, Christ will be with us: "Lo, I am with you alway" (Matt. 28:20). If we die, we will be with Him: "I am in a strait betwixt two, having a desire to depart, and to be with Christ; which is far better" (Phil. 1:23).

* * *

Paths of Glory

The boast of heraldry, the pomp of power,
    And all that beauty, all that wealth e'er gave,
Await alike the inevitable hour:
    The paths of glory lead but to the grave.

THOMAS GRAY

DEFEATISM

(See also Victory)

Dim and Dirty

In expressing his feeling of futility and disappointment in life, the cynical poet Byron wrote on his thirty-third birthday:

On life's road so dim and dirty,
I have dragged to three and thirty,
What have these years left for me?
Nothing, except thirty-three.

In expressing his joy in life and his bright hope for life to come, Paul jubilantly said, "For to me to live is Christ, and to die is gain" (Phil. 1:21).

* * *

A Tale Told by an Idiot

Shakespeare defined life thus: "A tale told by an idiot, full of sound and fury, and signifying nothing."

How aptly does his appraisal of life fit a life which is selfishly lived without God, and then passes ignobly into a hereafter without hope.

* * *

A Dirty Trick

Ernest Hemingway, a suicide, said, "Life is just a dirty trick, a short journey from nothingness to nothingness. There is no remedy for anything in life. Man's destiny in the universe is like a colony of ants on a burning log."

* * *

Compiling Satan's Victories

Dr. Robert Smith, chairman of the department of philosophy, Bethel College, St. Paul, Minnesota, stated, "Too frequently we Christians believe we are doing our Lord a service by compiling all the victories of Satan and hell. This leads only to dire pessimism, a sense of futility and a deepening sense of fear."

* * *

"Nothin' Ever Happens"

Some time ago, an interesting cartoon about Abraham Lincoln appeared in a magazine.

In the cartoon, two Kentucky pioneers and their emaciated, mangy dogs met on a cold February morning.

One asked, "What's new out here, neighbor?"

The other replied, "Nothin' at all. Nothin' at all, 'cept for a new baby boy down at Tom Lincoln's. Nothin' ever happens out here."

But something of nationwide significance had happened on that bleak February morning. The emancipator of a race, the preserver of a nation, had been born—Abraham Lincoln!

How like those Kentucky pioneers many of us are. Often we dejectedly and defeatedly say, "Nothing ever happens. God has forgotten to be gracious."

God is often working most mightily in our behalf when there is little or no outward indication of it.

* * *

Flying Too Low

Coming in for landing at the Greater Cincinnati airport, a Trans World Airlines jet with seventy-five passengers and seven crew members aboard crashed one and one-half miles away. Sixty-seven of the eighty-two perished!

Philip Swift, commissioner of the Kentucky Department of Aeronautics, said, "The four-engine Convair was way below normal flight path when it smashed into a hill. It should have been about one thousand feet above the hill at that point."

"Flying too low" are words descriptive of many of God's children who live in the miasmic lowlands of spiritual defeat when they could "mount up with wings as eagles" (Isa. 40:31) and live radiantly with Christ "in heavenly places" (Eph. 1:3).

* * *

Nothing in Life

David W. Ferrie, a suspect in an alleged conspiracy to assassinate John F.

Kennedy, was found dead in his bed in New Orleans. He had apparently committed suicide. A note found in his apartment read: "To leave this life is, for me, a sweet prospect. I find nothing in it that is desirable and, on the other hand, everything that is loathsome."

How worthwhile and radiant is life for those who are totally dedicated to Christ, living to serve Him and bring joy to others! For them life's pathway grows increasingly bright: "The path of the just is as the shining light, that shineth more and more unto the perfect day" (Prov. 4:18).

It's Always Wrong

"This toy looks very complicated for a child," said a mother to a salesman in a store.

"It's an educational toy, designed to adjust a child to live in the world today," the clerk explained. "Any way you put it together, it's wrong."

Many today do not know what to think of life. Any way it's put together, it seems wrong. Thrills do not answer the inner longing of the soul. Things do not satisfy. The theories of man do not meet the inner need.

JOHN M. DRESCHER, in
Sunday Times

DEVIL

A Farm Bequeathed to Satan

Some years ago a Finnish court upheld the will of an atheist who bequeathed his farm to the devil. The court decision read: "In accordance with the findings of the court, the wish of the deceased is to be carried out by leaving this land untouched by human hands and allowing it to revert to wilderness condition."

The malediction "Go to the devil" is often heard. The unregenerate need only to be left alone to do this.

What must man do to be lost? Utterly nothing! What must he do to be saved? Only one thing: turn penitently from sin to the Saviour, who graciously receives all who come to Him: "Him that cometh to me I will in no wise cast out" (John 6:37).

* * *

The Virgin's Kiss

How cruel was the diabolical "Virgin's kiss" used by the judges of the Spanish Inquisition!

The helpless victim was pushed forward and told to kiss the image of the Virgin. As he unsuspectingly did so, the arms of the image enfolded him in a deadly embrace, piercing his body through with concealed knives.

The devil often traps unwary ones with a "Virgin's kiss." Beneath his seemingly harmless devices are hidden death-dealing daggers.

Let us take with utmost seriousness the admonition "Be sober, be vigilant; because your adversary the devil, as a roaring lion, walketh about, seeking whom he may devour" (I Peter 5:8).

* * *

Satan's Beautiful Guises

The bushmaster is a deadly snake of South America. It is large, fatally venomous and aggressive. No antidote for its venom is known. One bitten by the bushmaster lives no longer than twenty minutes.

The bushmaster is a beautiful creature —a sort of animated rainbow. Its irridescent colors glimmer as it glides noiselessly along in the sunlight. Though dazzlingly beautiful, the bushmaster is deadly.

How like the bushmaster is Satan. When it serves his purposes, Satan presents himself to us in beautiful guises, often as "an angel of light" (II Cor. 11:14). He vivifies and glamorizes sin, and many are unwittingly deceived by his artifices.

The Bible warns, "Be . . . vigilant; because your adversary the devil, as a roaring lion, walketh about, seeking whom he may devour" (I Peter 5:8).

98

A Strange Demand

One of the strangest governmental demands was received by Sir Anthony Panizzi.

In 1821 Panizzi was sentenced to death for taking part in a revolutionary plot against his native duchy in Italy. But on the eve of his execution he escaped from prison and fled to England, where he later became the librarian of the British Museum. Some time later he received a demand from Italian government officials that he reimburse the government for two expenditures for which he was responsible —the cost of erecting the gallows to be used for his hanging, and the fee promised and paid to the hangman who was to have hanged him.

How unwilling is the enemy of souls, Satan, to relinquish his viselike grip upon God's children who, before their deliverance from the shackles of sin, were "taken captive by him at his will" (II Tim. 2:26). How free are those who have been delivered from the slavery of sin by Christ: "If the Son shall make you free, ye shall be free indeed" (John 8:36).

DONALD GREY BARNHOUSE

Undecided About the Devil

The Church of England was undecided about whether the devil should be mentioned in their new catechism or not. Formerly the catechism said, "I shall renounce the devil and all his works—the pomp and vanity of this wicked world, and all the sinful lusts of the flesh."

One group, led by the Bishop of Birmingham, favored simply saying, "I would renounce all that is wrong and fight against evil."

To be victorious over sin, it is not enough to declare Satan *persona non grata*. We must also "submit [ourselves] . . . to God" (James 4:7), and "walk in the Spirit." Then we shall not "fulfil the lust of the flesh" (Gal. 5:16).

* * *

Occupied

Martin Luther said, "When Satan knocks at the door of my heart and asks, 'Who lives here?' I reply, 'Martin Luther used to, but he has moved out, and Jesus Christ now lives here.' "

DISAPPOINTMENT

Disillusioned

Harry S. Truman said, on his eighty-first birthday, "It all seems to have been in vain. Memories are short and appetites for power and glory are insatiable. Old tyrants depart. New ones take their place. Old allies become the foe. The recent enemy becomes a friend. It's all very baffling and trying."

The Bible gives the true picture of mankind's trend apart from God's transforming grace. It says, "The heart of the sons of men is fully set in them to do evil" (Eccles. 8:11).

* * *

Futility

Erich Fromm, a psychoanalyst, declared in *McCall's,* "People are getting tired of the sense of meaninglessness of life; of the sense that they are little automatons and really have nothing to say about their own lives; of trying to save time and then kill it; of trying to succeed, and when reaching what they want, of feeling 'So what?' "

Unalloyed satisfaction is not found in the fading glories of the world. "All flesh is as grass, and all the glory of man as the flower of grass" (I Peter 1:24).

Satisfaction cannot be found in the acquisition of things. "A man's life consisteth not in the abundance of the things which he possesseth" (Luke 12:15).

* * *

Dropouts from Life

To many, life is an enigma, and they seek a solution by going the suicide's route. Artists, professional men and top executive commit suicide more than any other segment of people.

An Associated Press dispatch stated, "Doctors, who take the lives of others in their hands, too often do away with their own lives in one last bout with frustration and depression. Psychiatrists are the most prone to suicide of all doctor specialty groups, the annual rate being 70 for each 100,000. Up to the age of 39, one out of four deaths of medical doctors is a suicide."

Among disappointed divorced males, 69.4 in 100,000 commit suicide! Of divorced women, 18.4 per 100,000 take the desperate step, according to *Time*.

DISCOURAGEMENT — ENCOURAGEMENT

I'ze Tired

Honey, I'ze tired!
I'ze tired of sitting,
And I'ze tired of sighing,
I'ze tired of living,
And I wouldn't mind dying—
Honey, I'ze tired!

I'ze tired of chicken,
And I'ze tired of cake,
I even had a chill,
And was too tired to shake—
Honey, I'ze tired!

* * *

"Joy Cometh in the Morning"

In Idaho, there is a national monument which attracts many tourists—the Craters of the Moon. In the center of the park is a mound of dark volcanic ash—an unattractive, depressing sight. Most of the year, this huge mound is unproductive, but in the spring it is covered with exquisitely beautiful white flowers. Growing in riotous profusion, the flowers transform the whole area into magic whiteness. It is said that these flowers grow only here where the soil and moisture combine to produce a scene of dazzling beauty.

Occasionally there are times of trouble and barrenness in our lives when we feel that God has forgotten to be gracious. God never forgets His children: "Can a woman forget her suckling child? . . . They may forget, yet will I not forget thee" (Isa. 49:15).

The feeling of forsakenness and destitution will soon pass and "thou shalt break forth on the right hand and on the left" (Isa. 54:3).

Adapted from *Moody Monthly*

Down in the Mouth

Someone has said, "When you are down in the mouth, remember Jonah. He came out all right. 'Now the LORD had prepared a great fish to swallow up Jonah. . . . And the LORD spake unto the fish, and it vomited out Jonah upon the dry land'" (Jonah 1:17; 2:10).

* * *

It Could Have Been Worse

For of all sad words of tongue or pen, The saddest are these: "It might have been."
Let's add this thought unto this verse: "It might have been a great deal worse."

* * *

Postmortem Praise

Thomas Carlyle paid many pathetic postmortem tributes to his deceased wife whom he sometimes neglected in life. In Carlyle's diary is a sentence that has been said to be the saddest in English literature: "Oh, that I had you yet for five minutes by my side that I might tell you all!"

* * *

The Occupied and Unoccupied Chair

Nostalgic emotions and a feeling of loss grip those who look upon the rocking chair in which President John F. Kennedy often sat.

It is good to cherish and revere the memory of departed loved ones and friends: "Thou shalt be missed, because thy seat will be empty" (I Sam. 20:18). "The memory of the just is blessed" (Prov. 10:7).

It is wrong, however, to major on the vacant chair and minor on the occupied chair.

How tragic it is that so many of us wait until ears are dulled in death before we speak words of praise and encouragement! How valueless is postmortem praise when compared to words of encouragement spoken in the lifetime. "A word fitly spoken is like apples of gold in pictures of silver" (Prov. 25:11).

I'd rather pin a rose on a friend than lay a rose on him.

* * *

God Is Keeping the Record

One year, in making his annual report to the members of his small country church, the elderly minister was manifestly discouraged. He said, "My preaching and praying have accomplished little visible results. In our revival meeting, only one—the little boy, John—made a public confession of faith in Christ."

Discouragement is contagious. The members likewise were gloomy as they went home.

Years later, at a convention in Hutchinson, Kansas, the famous Methodist Episcopal bishop John Vincent was the speaker. He related the incident. Then, with his heart filled with gratitude to God and the minister, he said, "I am that little boy John!"

"Who hath despised the day of small things?" (Zech. 4:10).

God doesn't ask that we succeed. He asks only that we be faithful in His service. Often He is working mightily in hearts when we see little outward results of our "labour of love" (Heb. 6:10). God is keeping the record of what we do. Job said, "My record is on high" (Job 16:19).

* * *

One Sentence Expresses It

Clarence Darrow, the famed criminal lawyer and confessed atheist, stated, "My colleagues say that I'm a success. Many honors have come to me, but in the Bible there is a sentence which expresses the way I feel about my life. The sentence is this: "We have toiled all the night, and have taken nothing" (Luke 5:5).

* * *

Only a Smile

How encouraging and assuring is a smile!

Robert Louis Stevenson told of a ship which was driven by a violent storm toward a rocky coast. The passengers were filled with terror, expecting the ship at any moment to be dashed to pieces on the jagged rocks.

One bold passenger with great difficulty made his way to the pilothouse. There he saw the pilot holding the wheel and veering the ship, inch by inch, away from the rocks and out to sea.

The pilot saw the daring passenger and smiled at him. Returning below, the passenger said, "All's well! I have seen the pilot, and he smiled at me!"

Blessed are those who, in the midst of the storms and stresses of life, can see through the eye of faith the One who long ago quieted the fears of His disciples and brought calm to the raging sea.

* * *

Against Regulations

A minister wrote a letter to a friend. After he sealed it, he wrote, "Be of good cheer" on the address side of the envelope. A postal employee, seeing the words, stamped beneath them "Contrary to postal regulations."

Some are hesitant to speak words of cheer and encouragement as if it were against regulations or against their religion.

Why wait until ears are dulled in death to speak words of praise? How worthless is postmortem praise!

101

DO-NOTHINGISM

"Please Help Me!"

As seventy-six-year-old Mrs. Nettie Koehn started to board a bus in Cleveland, Ohio, a teenage assailant pulled her off. He dragged her several feet along a sidewalk and snatched her purse, which contained seven dollars. She pleaded, "Help! Somebody please help me!" Her frantic cry for help fell on unresponsive ears.

The self-excusing bus driver, who closed the door of the bus and drove away, said, "I saw the boy grab the purse and knock her down. I thought she was having a fit."

Detective Lee Kenney, expressing his disgust, said, "A fine illustrious group of citizens!"

* * *

When Good Men Do Nothing

Edmund Burke declared, "The only thing necessary for the triumph of evil is for good men to do nothing about it."

The Saviour dealt sternly with the sin of do-nothingism: "I . . . hid thy talent in the earth. . . . Cast . . . the unprofitable servant into outer darkness" (Matt. 25:25-30).

One day the nations will be judged for what they did and what they failed to do: "Inasmuch as ye did it not to one of the least of these, ye did it not to me" (Matt. 25:45).

Failure to do what we ought to do is sin. "To him that knoweth to do good, and doeth it not, to him it is sin" (James 4:17).

* * *

Her Plea Was Ignored

Mrs. Josephine Johnson, who couldn't swim, drowned in the Great Miami River at Dayton, Ohio. Frantically she pleaded for help from the bystanders: "I can't swim! Help me! Help me!"

Her car had apparently struck an oil slick in the road and plunged down a twenty-five-foot embankment into twenty feet of water. Somehow she freed herself from the car. For a moment she thrashed about in the murky water calling for help, and then she disappeared.

Her piteous plea for help was ignored by more than a dozen people!

No one has ever called upon God for help and failed to receive it. The promise is unfailing: "Call upon me in the day of trouble: I will deliver thee, and thou shalt glorify me" (Ps. 50:15).

* * *

The Thirty-and-Nine Safely Sat

Dr. L. E. Maxwell told of a bus driver who was beaten to death while thirty-nine passengers watched the tragedy and did nothing to help him. "The thirty-nine safely sat, unwilling to get involved," said Dr. Maxwell.

How culpable we are when we fail to become involved with the needs of others and turn unhearing ears to their piteous plea "Save! We perish!"

There are ninety-and-nine which safely lie
In the shelter of the fold,
But millions are left outside to die,
For the ninety-and-nine are cold!

Away in sin's delusive snare,
Hastening to death and dark despair,
Hastening to death, and few to care,
For the ninety-and-nine are cold!

* * *

Vanishing Nobility

In an accident, the Rev. George J. Kuechie, a retired Lutheran minister, age seventy-eight, and his wife, Marie, age seventy-two, sank beneath the water in a canal near Miami, Florida, trapped in their car. Six men stood on the bank of the canal and watched the car sink out of sight.

In speaking of the tragic accident, highway patrolman Phil Dixon said, "Those cowardly men made no attempt to do anything. When I arrived at the scene, I could see the headlights burning beneath the water. I dropped my gunbelt, re-

102

moved my shoes and plunged into the water, but it was too late to help the aged couple.

"The six men told me that they saw the car go under the water ten minutes before I arrived. I was so angry because they did nothing that I shouted, 'Get away from here, you ———!' "

Are courage, nobility and a willingness to endanger ourselves for imperiled ones on the wane among us?

* * *

Indifferent and Unconcerned

In Cleveland, Ohio, a burly man threatened with an ice pick Miss Gina Arsena, an attractive twenty-three-year-old Cuyahoga County Welfare Department caseworker.

In the midafternoon, as she entered her car, her attacker jumped into the seat beside her and pressed the ice pick to her neck! In terror, she broke her assailant's grip, slid out of her car and fell on the icy street.

The strange and inexplicable thing about the frightful incident was this: five bystanders watched—indifferent and unconcerned.

Miss Arsena said later, "I lay there screaming, and I noticed one woman especially who merely looked on impassively."

Her attacker fled on foot with her purse containing five dollars and seventy-five cents.

Miss Arsena commented later, "When I took the welfare position, I was also considering joining the Peace Corps. I like my position with the Welfare Department, but I don't believe I can go back to it again." Later she resigned.

How calloused and reprehensible were those unconcerned, unpitying bystanders!

How reprehensible are God's children who turn an unhearing ear to the piteous plea of perishing, imperiled ones: "Come . . . and help us" (Acts 16:9).

Spiritual and Physical Deliverance

Kitty Genovese was stabbed to death in a New York borough by a merciless assailant. Her cries for help continued for half an hour. They were heard by more than thirty people, not one of whom came to help her or called a policeman!

How devoid of humaneness were those thirty insensitive and unresponding individuals!

There is One who is ever attentive to the cries of those who call upon Him for help—God. He does not always give His children physical deliverance. He never fails, however, to give them spiritual deliverance and a sufficiency of His sustaining grace.

* * *

"Curse Ye Meroz"

God's curse is upon do-nothingism: "Curse ye Meroz, . . . curse ye bitterly the inhabitants thereof; because they came not to the help of the Lord . . . against the mighty" (Judges 5:23).

It has been said, "The men who try to do something and fail are much better men than those who do nothing and succeed."

* * *

Our Greatest National Sin

Billy Graham told of a tragic incident that happened in Florida. A car carrying seven persons went out of control and hit a telephone pole. With his companions severely injured, the driver tried for seven hours to hail other cars, but no one stopped. No one seemed to care. Six were dead when help finally came. This is an example of our growing indifference and apathy.

We are apathetic about the church and our souls. We have been spoiled by affluence and pampered by federal handouts, and we have adopted a do-nothing attitude about everything that matters.

103

ENEMIES

A Self-inflicted Death

A man had excellent health until his father died. Then he became involved in a prolonged legal dispute with his sister about their father's will. When the case went to court, the sister won.

Thereafter the man thought of little except the lawsuit. His hatred of his sister deepened. He became depressed and succumbed to illness brought on by the deadly virus of hatred. He ultimately died a self-inflicted death, killed by hatred and ill will.

* * *

Potential Murderers

Clarence Darrow, the famous criminal lawyer, once declared, "Everybody is a potential murderer. I have not killed anyone, but I frequently get satisfaction out of obituary notices."

The Bible says, "Whosoever hateth his brother is a murderer" (I John 3:15).

* * *

Inwardly Wicked

One day Walter said, "Larry did a bad, mean thing to me. I feel like knocking his head off." In God's sight, Walter was guilty of hurting Larry though he never did it.

One day Jane said, "Pamela said something about me that was not true. I'll get even with her if it's the last thing I do." Shortly after, Pamela and her family moved to another city. Jane never got even with Pamela, but she was as guilty before God as if she had. It was in her heart to return evil for evil.

Jesus taught that if the desire to do evil is in our hearts, we are as guilty before God as if we had done the evil. John said, "Whosoever hateth his brother is a murderer" (I John 3:15).

ALICE MARIE KNIGHT

* * *

Getting Even

A mother, who had been badly treated by another woman, said, "I'll get even with that person if it's the last thing I do."

How unchristian she was in her attitude. The only people we should try to *get even with* are those who have befriended us. We should pray for those who treat us meanly.

HARRY A. IRONSIDE

* * *

For My Sake

A faithful minister unintentionally made a remark which angered a Christian woman. She led him to the door, pushed him out and shut the door in his face.

As the minister walked home, he became indignant and resentful. The joy of the Lord vanished from his heart. *This won't do,* he thought.

He began to pray, and then Jesus' word came to him: "By this shall all men know that ye are my disciples, if ye have love one to another" (John 13:35). The Saviour seemed to say, "Return immediately to the one whom you offended and show her kindness *for My sake.*" The result was unity and peace instead of division and bitterness.

* * *

Why Joy Had Vanished

A dejected, defeated Christian went to his pastor and said, "I cannot understand it, but it seems as if God has gone out of my life. I am very unhappy."

The pastor asked, "Why?"

He replied, "I think it has been caused by my treatment of my brother. He was very cruel to me concerning our father's will, and I said I would never forgive him. I am sorry I said it, for he has been going from bad to worse. He has lost his wife and child and is now on his deathbed. I cannot go to him because I said I never would."

The pastor said, "My friend, it is better to break a bad vow than keep it. Go immediately and be reconciled to your brother."

The man obeyed and the peace of God which passes understanding—and misunderstanding, too—returned.

* * *

"Grudgeitis"

Physicians and psychologists assert that the person who tries to get even brings emotional stress on himself which often leads to physical disorders. Dr. S. I. McMillen, in his captivating book *None of These Diseases,* refers to a study at one hospital where personal interviews with patients suffering from mucous colitis revealed that resentment was the most prominent personal characteristic, occurring in 96 percent of the victims. He says colitis usually comes from "colliding" with people emotionally and then trying to get even.

In life's frog ponds, perhaps we are able to outcroak our fellows, but it might truthfully be written on many thousands of death certificates that the victims died of "grudgeitis."

ROY B. ZUCK, in *Moody Monthly*

* * *

Resentment Turned into Love

Billy Graham stated, "A certain man had spoken most unkindly of me. Deep down in my heart was a smoldering resentment toward the man. Resentment is sin. I couldn't go on the platform with resentment in my heart. I couldn't ask people to repent if I had sin in my heart.

"I told God that I was going to stay on my knees until He instilled a genuine love in my heart for the man. I asked God to do what I couldn't do as a human being. After considerable time, God answered my prayer. When I stood before the people, I had genuine love for that man. Only God can turn resentment into love."

Adapted from *Log of the Good Ship Grace*

* * *

Self-imposed Invalidism

A Christian farmer who was being sued was fearful that he would lose an acre of his extensive farm. Surveyors gave conflicting opinions, so he employed a lawyer.

The long months of worry and tension exacted a terrible toll on his body.

When the suit went against him, his health failed. He became crippled with arthritis and spent the rest of his life in a wheelchair.

Perhaps his invalidism could have been averted if the scriptural directive had been obeyed: "And if any man will sue thee at the law, and take away thy coat, let him have thy cloke also" (Matt. 5:40).

* * *

Sorrow Unites

During the 1952 presidential campaign, Dwight Eisenhower and Harry Truman spoke harsh words about one another. Their relationship continued cool until President Kennedy's death. When the two men met in Washington for the funeral of the slain President, old animosities vanished. Ike invited Mr. Truman to ride with him to Arlington. After the burial, Mr. Truman invited the Eisenhowers to be his guests at lunch in the Blair House. After lunch, they parted— friends!

An aide said later, "You could see the warmth in their eyes. They remembered only things which they cared about, things which unite hearts in love and understanding."

* * *

Rejoice, Don't Retaliate

A pioneer missionary to China preached God's Word in village after village. There was little or no response to his efforts. He thought, *My ministry seems useless.*

One day a Chinese student said, "Teacher, I have heard your messages. You speak compellingly about the One you call Jesus. I have spiritual hunger. Before I can make any decision about Jesus, I must have the answer to an important question."

"What's your question?" asked the missionary.

"It is this," replied the student as he slapped the missionary on the cheek.

Stunned and dismayed, the missionary asked, "Why did you do that?"

"I wanted to see how you would react to an insult—if you would retaliate," said the student.

"Retaliation would avail nothing," said the missionary. "My Lord and Master has said, 'Blessed are ye, when men shall revile you. . . . Rejoice, and be exceeding glad' [Matt. 5:11-12]."

The student said, "Oh, teacher, I beg your forgiveness. I have *heard* of the revolutionary words of Jesus. But now I have *seen* them obeyed. Life has taught me to beware of words without meaning. You have brought reality to your words. I wish to become a Christian."

How we react when *under fire* either furthers or fetters the gospel.

The Bible says of our Saviour, "Who, when he was reviled, reviled not again; when he suffered, he threatened not" (I Peter 2:23).

* * *

Rejoice! Don't Retaliate

The Latin words *lex talionis* mean "law of retaliation." Love and forgiveness must ever be the Christian's law: "Love your enemies, bless them that curse you" (Matt. 5:44); "Rejoice, and be exceeding glad" (v. 12).

Longfellow said, "If we would read the secret history of our enemies, we would find in each man's life sorrow and suffering enough to disarm all hostility."

How often, for some trivial wrong,
    In anger, we retaliate;
We learn, although it takes us long,
    That life is far too brief to hate.

* * *

"I Never Knew There Was Such a
    Religion!"

During the Armenian atrocities, a young woman and her brother were pursued by a Turkish soldier. The brother was brutally murdered. The sister escaped. Later she became a nurse in a hospital.

One day a critically ill Turkish soldier was brought into the hospital. She recognized him as the soldier who had slain her brother. Any slight inattention would have meant his death. She, however, being a Christian, tenderly cared for him.

When the soldier convalesced, he recognized the young woman. In amazement he asked, "How could you care for me so kindly and nurse me back to health? Why didn't you get revenge for the merciless slaying of your brother and let me die?"

She replied, "I am a follower of Christ, who said, 'Love your enemies and do good to them!' "

For a while, the Turkish soldier was speechless. Then he exclaimed, "I never knew there was such a religion! Tell me more about it! I want it!"

* * *

Try Him—You'll See

Charles Dickens and William Makepeace Thackeray, English novelists, were intimate friends. A misunderstanding occurred. They quarreled so bitterly that their friendship ceased. They would pass each other on the street without speaking.

One day Thackeray chanced to meet Dickens's daughter on the street. He greeted her cordially and said, "It is ridiculous that your father and I should have positive enmity toward one another. Do you think Charles will meet me halfway if I make the approach?"

"Oh, I can answer for him," the daughter joyfully said. "Just try him, and you'll see."

Two days later, Thackeray called upon Dickens and said, "We have been foolish long enough! Let's be friends again!"

Instantly Dickens extended his hand. They joyfully embraced each other. As they parted, they both said, "Thank God! We are friends again!"

Thirteen days later, on Christmas Eve, Thackeray, the peacemaker, died unexpectedly!

ENVY

Dog Killed by Envy

Some children listened quietly as a missionary from Alaska told them about some of his experiences in the land where the Eskimos live. He thrilled them by showing a picture of his dog team.

"This dog always led my team," he said as he pointed to the lead dog. "One day I decided that it would be a good idea to train another dog as a leader, so I would have two lead dogs. If anything happened to my regular lead dog, I would have another dog to take his place.

"So, boys and girls, one day I put this second dog ahead of my regular leader. Can you guess what happened? The regular lead dog, now second in my team, gnawed the harness of the new leader until he was free. This he did again and again. Finally I decided that I would have to take my regular leader out of the team until the new leader was trained. The displaced dog was so envious of the new leader that he refused to eat. He grieved himself to death!"

After the children's shocked reaction had subsided, the missionary said, "Children, envy is a terrible thing. It makes us very unhappy. The Bible says, 'Let us not be desirous of vain glory, provoking one another, envying one another'" (Gal. 5:26).

ALICE MARIE KNIGHT

How to Overcome Envy

Dr. F. B. Meyer was pastor of Westminster Chapel, London; Dr. G. Campbell Morgan was pastor of nearby Christ's Church; and Charles Haddon Spurgeon was pastor of the Metropolitan Tabernacle. Both Dr. Morgan and Mr. Spurgeon often had much larger audiences than Dr. Meyer. He confessed that envy rankled in his heart until he began earnestly to pray for Morgan and Spurgeon.

"When I prayed for their success," said Dr. Meyer, "the result was that God filled their churches so full that the overflow filled mine, and it has been full since."

* * *

The Sure Killer

In South America, there is a parasitic vine called the "matador." The vine starts growing at the foot of a tree. As it grows upward, it clings to the trunk of the tree. It ultimately kills the tree. When it reaches the top, it sends forth a flower to crown itself.

Matador means "killer."

Envy is also a killer. It kills our joy. It kills the finest and best things in us. Envy, like the matador, seems harmless as it begins its upward climb—it is so small.

If envy is allowed to grow, it will harden into hatred. Hatred sometimes leads to murder.

FAITH

"Yes, I Will!"

Some aspirants to scale Mount Everest were examined by a psychologist at Nepal before they began their climb. They were asked, "Will you get to the top?"

They said, "I certainly hope so," or "I'll do my best."

Only Jim Whittaker replied, "Yes, I will!" He made it. He was the first American to reach the summit of Mount Everest.

"Mountain climbing brings out the best in a person," said Whittaker. "It forces him to try to do something normally beyond his reach."

Browning said, "A man's reach should exceed his grasp, or what's a heaven for?"

How greatly God's children need the spirit of unabating perseverance: "I press toward the mark for the prize of the high calling of God in Christ Jesus" (Phil. 3:14).

David Livingstone said, "I'll go anywhere provided it is forward."

There are peaks of holiness and Christian virtues which ever beckon and challenge us in our upward climb. Let's not be content with God's second best. Let's aspire to attain His first best for our lives.

* * *

Slow to Believe God

In *Eternity* magazine, Roger L. Knudson said, "What if man creates life? Man has an amazingly steadfast faith that he will. In 1962, J. Robert Moskin wrote in *Look* magazine, 'In the next twenty-five years, it is likely that man will create life in a test tube. He will transform dead chemicals into living material that can grow and reproduce itself. He will perform an act of God!'

"If only man had such faith in God! It is amazing what man will believe as long as it does not depend on God, but only on man. So many do not believe that God can do extraordinary things— that Jesus could be incarnate God in man, born of the virgin Mary; that He could rise from the dead, and that He can return visibly at the close of the age. . . . They believe such things must be husked away if Christ is to be relevant to modern man."

* * *

He That Believeth

He that believeth shall not make haste,
In useless hurry his strength to waste;
Who walks with God can afford to wait,
For he can never arrive too late.

He that believeth shall not delay,
Who carries the word of the King on its way
Keeps pace with the Saviour's marching tune,
And he can never arrive too soon.

He that believeth shall walk serene,
With ordered steps and leisured mien;
He dwells in the midst of eternities,
And the timeless ages of God are his.

ANNIE JOHNSON FLINT

* * *

Through Faith We Understand

How fantastic is the explanation of the beginning of the solar system given by Dr. Gerard P. Kuiper, director of the Lunar and Planetary Laboratory of the University of Arizona. He theorizes that a thin pancake of gas and dust, which formed around the infant sun more than four billion years ago, gave rise to the planets, including our own earth. All this took place in the darkness of space, since the sun had not yet grown hot enough to shine.

The Bible says, "Through faith we understand that the worlds were formed by the word of God, so that things which are seen were not made of things which do appear" (Heb. 11:3). At His command "Let there be" the heavens and the earth came into being: "For he spake . . . and it stood fast" (Ps. 33:9).

* * *

Sincere but Wrong

An erroneous and scripturally groundless belief is held by many—that if one is sincere in what he believes, God requires nothing more.

In Houston, Texas, a woman died in agony. A laboratory technician had inadvertently given her sodium cyanide instead of a glucose mixture.

The technician was sincere in what he mistakenly did—sincerely wrong.

Paul was sincere and conscientious while persecuting Christians, but he was wrong—sincerely wrong.

* * *

Doubting Absurd

Fear says, "God may fail me."
Faith knows He keeps His word;
"Hitherto the LORD hath helped us,"
Doubting now would be absurd.

* * *

Cornerstone of Wellesley College

The inscription on the flyleaf of a Bible found in a tin box under the cornerstone of Wellesley College read as follows: "This building is humbly dedicated to our heavenly Father with the hope and prayer that He may always be first in everything in this institution—that His Word may be faithfully taught here, and that He will use it as a means of leading precious souls to the Lord Jesus Christ."

JOHN BOLTON, SR., in
Sunday School Times

108

Needless Fear

A traveler crossed a frozen stream
  In trembling fear one day.
Later a teamster drove across
  And whistled all the way.

Great faith and little faith alike
  Were granted safe convoy,
But one had pangs of needless fear,
  The other all the joy.

* * *

The Upward Look

I look to Thee in every need,
  And never look in vain;
I feel Thy touch, Eternal Love,
  And all is well again.
The thought of Thee is mightier far
  Than sin and pain and sorrow are.

* * *

"It Will Change Your Action"

A man said to Dr. Will Houghton, "Sir, the doctrine you preach is absurd. You say that one has only to believe to change the entire course of his life. In my opinion no one will alter his life by simply believing."

Dr. Houghton replied, "Let me make sure that we understand each other. Seemingly you believe that one's actions are not governed by what he believes. Is that right?"

"Yes," replied the man.

"Suppose someone should suddenly cry, 'The house where you are is on fire!' What would you do?" asked Dr. Houghton.

"Why," quickly replied the self-acclaimed unbeliever, "I would dash for the door, or even leap from a window."

"So you see, one's action is inseparably related to what a man believes. When anyone truly believes in Christ, he becomes a new creature in Christ. He shows the genuineness of his faith by openly confessing Christ and by living for Him and others," said Dr. Houghton.

I simply take Him at His word,
I praise Him that my prayer is heard,
I claim my answer from the Lord;
  I take, He undertakes.

Science and Religion Are Sisters

Dr. Wernher von Braun, director of NASA's George C. Marshall Space Flight Center, stated, "Many believe that science and religion are not compatible. Nothing could be further from the truth. Science and religion are not antagonists. On the contrary, they are sisters. Through science, man tries to harness the forces of nature around him. Through religion, he tries to harness the forces of nature within him.

"The materialists of the nineteenth century and their Marxist heirs of the twentieth tried to tell us that, as science gives us more knowledge about the creation, we could live without faith in the Creator. The better we understand the intricacies of the atomic structure, the nature of life or the master plan for the galaxies, the more reason we have found to marvel at the wonder of God's creation."

The Bible says, "Through faith we understand that the worlds were framed by the word of God" (Heb. 11:3).

* * *

Devout Faith Among Scientists

Christianity Today commented that scientists themselves are speaking out as men of devout faith at a time when a host of nonscientists tend to make science the pretext for their unbelief, and thereby show themselves naïve victims of scientism.

* * *

The Silver Thread

Spurgeon said, "Faith is the silver thread upon which the pearls of the graces are strung. Break the thread and the pearls will lie scattered on the ground, nor can you wear them for your own adornment."

Whittier averred, "The steps of faith fall on the seeming void, but find the rock beneath."

Augustine said, "Faith is to believe what we do not see, and the reward of this faith is to see what we believe."

Lord, give us such faith as this,
  And then, whate'er may come,
We'll taste, e'en here, the hallowed bliss
  Of our eternal home.

A Living or a Dead Faith?

Dr. A. W. Tozer said, "If we don't cherish and defend and 'earnestly contend for the faith which was once [for all] delivered unto the saints,' the time is not distant when the living faith of the dead heroes of the faith will become the dead faith of the living deniers of the faith."

Can what was said of believing Abraham be said of us: "He staggered not at the promise of God through unbelief; but was strong in faith, giving glory to God; and being fully persuaded that, what he had promised, he was able also to perform" (Rom. 4:20-21)?

* * *

Left Untried

G. K. Chesterton stated, "The Christian faith has not been tried and found wanting. It has been found difficult and left untried."

* * *

Triumphant

William James declared, "Every sort of energy, endurance, courage and capacity for handling life's evils is set free in those who have religious faith."

* * *

"Lord, I Believe"

On a simple marker on the grave of William Jennings Bryan in Arlington National Cemetery are these words: "Lord, I believe; help thou mine unbelief."

* * *

An Effulgent Glow

Sir Humphrey Davy commented, "I prefer a firm religious faith to every other blessing. It makes life a discipline of goodness, creates new hope when earthly hope vanishes, casts an effulgent glow over our twilight years, and shines brightest as we enter the valley of death."

* * *

Found the Pot of Gold

Dale Evans Rogers said, "I sought the pot of gold at the foot of the rainbow. It eluded me. By simple faith, I found it at the foot of the cross!"

Keep Your Doubts

Geothe the German philosopher stated, "I will listen to anyone's convictions, but pray keep your doubts to yourself. I have doubts enough of my own."

* * *

Ideas Come from God

Though he believed that religious ritual and joining some sectarian group were not needful, the renowned scientist Dr. Albert Einstein had an unshakable faith in God. He said with reverence, "Ideas come from God."

As he pondered the conclusions of his cosmic investigations he would soliloquize, "Could this be the way God created the universe?"

* * *

The Unknown Morrow

Child of my love, fear not the unknown
    morrow,
  Dread not the new demand life makes
    on thee;
Thy ignorance doth hold no cause for
    sorrow,
  Since what thou knowest not is known
    to Me.

* * *

Obstinacy

Henry Drummond said, "Christ distinguished between doubt and unbelief. Doubt says, 'I can't believe.' Unbelief says, 'I won't believe.' Doubt is honest. Unbelief is obstinate."

* * *

God's Challenge

How quickly is unbelief changed into belief when we accept God's challenge: "Prove me now herewith, saith the LORD of hosts" (Mal. 3:10). "O taste and see that the LORD is good: blessed is the man that trusteth in him" (Ps. 34:8).

* * *

Unshrinking Faith

O for a faith that will not shrink,
  Though pressed by every foe,
That will not tremble on the brink
  Of any earthly woe.

FAITHFULNESS, GOD'S

God's Ways and Works Are Perfect

An eccentric old man was fond of boasting, "My watch has kept perfect time for forty years. It is never too slow or too fast."

One morning he was up just before dawn. Glancing at an almanac, he saw the time when the sun would rise that day. Looking toward the east, he held his watch in his hand and waited for the rising of the sun. He became impatient and exclaimed, "If that sun ain't over the hill in one and a half minutes, it will be too late!"

How vain and presumptuous it is for man to try to regulate God and His works by his imperfect standards of measurement! The Bible says, "He doeth according to his will in the army of heaven . . . and none can stay his hand, or say unto him, What doest thou?" (Dan. 4:35). "As for God, his way is perfect" (Ps. 18:30). He is never ahead of time or late.

* * *

God Keeps His Word

When a minister was going through a testing time, his faith began to weaken. He wrote a Christian friend, "I am ill. My faith in God's promises is lessening daily."

The friend replied, "Are you not making the mistake of examining your faith rather than the promises of God, upon which your faith should rest? If you were traveling a new public highway and approached a bridge of whose strength you were not sure, would you stop to examine your faith in the bridge or examine the bridge itself?"

"Let us hold fast the profession of our faith without wavering; for he is faithful that promised" (Heb. 10:23).

* * *

God's Unfailing Laws

"What's the trouble?" a mother asked her boy, whose look revealed deep distress.

"Well, Mother," the boy began gloomily, "I'm thinking about my silkworm eggs. Spring is here, and the silkworms will soon be coming out. I have no food for them. The buds on the mulberry trees are just beginning to swell. It will be a while before the leaves for the silkworms come. I don't know what I will do."

"You silly boy," replied mother. "Do you suppose that God manages His world so badly as that? If the mulberry leaves will be some time yet in appearing, so will the silkworms. Depend on it. They will come together."

So they did, and the boy learned that life is not a game of chance. God's unfailing laws are constantly at work.

Told by F. W. BOREHAM

FAITHFULNESS, OURS

"Hold the Fort—I Am Coming!"

Some years ago a dedicated young woman went to Africa as a missionary. There she married. A year later her husband died. The young woman found herself alone in Africa with their small baby. Her family urged her to come home. Then a cablegram came from her mission board, directing her to return home. What should she do? She knew that God had called her to serve Him in Africa. *Did I not come to this needy field when un-*

married? she thought. She prayed much.

One day, as the young missionary laid her baby on the bed, she said, "How greatly this little one needs me! How greatly the children of Africa need me, too. I am a 'mother' to them. Though I have been directed to leave them, I know that, if God wants me to remain here, He will provide for my needs and take care of me."

Just then, her servant boy came into her home singing,

111

"Hold the fort, for I am coming,
Jesus signals still!"

The song was God's answer to her prayer. She joyfully exclaimed:

"Wave the answer back to heaven:
By Thy grace I will!"

* * *

"He's God's Man! He Can't Quit"

A young man taught a class of boys in a mission Sunday school. He won their hearts by his love and sincere interest. In time, he became discouraged because of criticism from others. He decided to resign as teacher.

Arriving early one Sunday to get his records in shape for his successor, he overheard a conversation by two of the boys of his class.

One said, "I'm not coming anymore because our teacher is going to quit."

The other boy said, "Why, he can't quit. I was the first boy in his class. One Sunday he told us that God sent him to teach us, and he said that God was his boss and he had to do what God said. He's God's man! He can't quit."

The teacher's eyes filled with tears. Silently he thanked God for the encouragement imparted to him by the saying of a trusting boy: "He's God's man! He can't quit."

ALICE MARIE KNIGHT

* * *

"Be Ye Steadfast"

A suave, persuasive Nazi agent was designedly put in a cell next to the cell where Dr. Martin Niemöller was incarcerated, hoping to convert him to totalitarianism. Daily he observed the equipoise of the courageous minister, his unshakable faith in God, and his belief in the ultimate triumph of righteousness. The would-be converter to totalitarianism was himself converted to Christianity. He was instantly removed from his cell.

Can we overestimate the power of the influence of one man who knows no fear other than the fear of incurring God's displeasure?

A Charge to Keep

God gave this command to His ancient people Israel: "Keep the charge of the LORD, that ye die not" (Lev. 8:35). The word *charge* means "command to do one's duty."

This charge inspired Charles Wesley to write the hymn "A Charge to Keep I Have":

A charge to keep I have,
A God to glorify;
A never-dying soul to save,
And fit it for the sky.

* * *

Man's Chief End

Thomas Carlyle said, "The older I grow —and now I stand on the brink of eternity—the more comes back to me the sentence in the catechism which I learned as a child, and the fuller and deeper its meaning becomes: 'What is the chief end of man? To glorify God and enjoy Him forever.'"

* * *

Our Very Best

While fighting his last battle and rallying from his second operation in seventeen days, the old warrior General Douglas MacArthur said, "I am going to do the very best I can."

The words epitomized his life throughout. He was faithfully and totally dedicated to duty, honor and country, and he was a Christian.

God rewards faithfulness: "Be thou faithful unto death, and I will give thee a crown of life" (Rev. 2:10).

* * *

Dog Awarded Victoria Cross

Jack was a mixed breed, a homeless puppy. Imploringly he trotted up to a sentry outside St. James Palace. The ground was covered with snow. The dog was cold and hungry. The sentry picked him up and fed him. The dog became greatly attached to the sentry whose regiment—the Scots Guards—adopted the dog as a mascot. The dog went through the Crimean War with his master, always at his side on the field of battle. When

112

his master fell, mortally wounded, the dog stood faithfully by until both were removed from the battlefield.

Hearing of the splendid service record of the noble dog, Queen Victoria was deeply touched. She had a miniature Victoria Cross made which she placed on the collar of the dog.

God rewards faithfulness: "Be thou faithful unto death, and I will give thee a crown of life" (Rev. 2:10).

ALICE MARIE KNIGHT

FATHERS

(See also Parental Responsibility)

"The Memory of the Just Is Blessed" (Prov. 10:7)

General Douglas MacArthur said, "I don't want my boy to think of me as a general, but as a father who taught him to pray, 'Our Father which art in heaven, Hallowed be thy name.' "

The most enduring blessing parents can bequeath to their children is an untarnished name and an unsullied character: Their "children arise up, and call . . . [them] blessed" (Prov. 31:28).

* * *

Children Remember

One day Gypsy Smith spoke to a Rotary Club. At the close of his message, he held up a well-worn Bible and asked, "How many of you men can recall a saintly mother and a godly father who loved this Book, read it, lived it, and steeped you in it?"

Practically the entire group, with moist eyes, raised their hands.

Then Smith asked this searching question: "With all your well-known influence, how many of you are so living that your children will remember you for your faithfulness to this same Book?"

It was a tense moment, for the children of some of those Rotarians were already in ways of sin.

* * *

Have You?

In discussing the ruling of the Supreme Court against prayer and Bible-reading in the schools, Richard Crane, well-known photographer, asked a father, "What are you doing about it?"

He replied, "What can I do but write to our congressman?"

Crane asked, "Have you ever thought of repeating the Lord's Prayer and reading a portion of the Bible with your children before they go to school?"

"Ah," said the thoughtful father, "I had not given your wise suggestion any thought."

Have *you?*

* * *

"It Might Have Been!"

On the eve of entering a hospital, a father who was the victim of an incurable illness endeavored to give his son some advice: "Wasted hours destroy one's life. I am afraid I haven't given you much religion, not having much myself. I want, however, to give you a Bible before I enter the hospital. Get familiar with it. I came to the Bible, like everything else of lasting worthwhileness, too late. Think of me when you come to the crossroads of life. I took the wrong turns, but I want you to take the right ones."

How freighted with quenchless regret are the ominous words *too late!*

For of all sad words of tongue or pen,
The saddest are these:
"It might have been!"

* * *

A Prayer Concluded in Heaven

"Is anyone here sick of sin?" asked a minister as he closed a searching sermon.

A young man stood and said, "I am sick of sin." The minister prayed for him and he was joyfully saved.

After the service, the minister said,

113

"My boy, write Mom and Dad and tell them of your newfound joy in Christ."

Shortly thereafter, the young man received a letter from his mother which said, "My dear boy, the joy which your letter brought was boundless! When you were saved, your father was on his deathbed. Throughout the day, he unceasingly cried to God, 'Oh, God, save my boy today!' We tried to divert his attention from you, but to no avail. He continued to plead, 'Oh, God, save my boy today!' Just as his soul departed to be forever with his Lord, he said faintly, 'Oh, God, save—' He finished that prayer, I sincerely believe, in the presence of his Lord in glory!"

* * *

Confused

If Junior hears Dad pray like a prophet on Sundays and then sees him lose his temper on weekdays, he is prone to lose faith in Dad's Bible and the church.

WARREN WIERSBE in *Moody Monthly*

* * *

Father's Compliment

A good wife rose and dressed one morn,
  And thought with nervous dread
Of the piles of clothes to be washed, and more
  Than a dozen mouths to be fed.
The meals to get for the men in the field,
  And the children to get away
To school, and the milk to be pasteurized;
  And all to be done that day.

"Mary, what do you think I told Ben Brown?"
  Called her husband from the well;
And a flush crept up to his sunburned brow,
  And his eyes half bashfully fell.
"It was this," he said and, coming near,
  He smiled and, stooping down,
Kissed her cheek. " 'Twas this, that you are the best
  And dearest wife in town!"

The father went back to the field, and his wife
  In a smiling, absent way,
Sang snatches of tender, little songs
  She'd not sung for many a day.

And the worrisome thoughts were gone, and the clothes
Were white as white could be;
Her bread was light, and she cooked with ease,
And she thanked God gratefully.

* * *

United in Shame

A fine Scottish Christian father had only one son, a well-educated young man, who went wrong. The son was arrested for embezzlement, tried and found guilty. During the trial, he appeared to be unconcerned. When he stood to be sentenced, he observed that his aged father also was standing. His father's head was bowed in sorrow and shame as though he himself were being sentenced to prison. Both the father and son wept bitterly.

None can sorrow so deeply as a parent: "And the king was much moved . . . and wept: . . . O my son Absalom, my son, my son Absalom! Would God I had died for thee" (II Sam. 18:33).

Told by HARRY A. IRONSIDE

* * *

MacArthur's Prayer for His Son

Build me a son, O Lord, who will be strong enough to know when he is weak, and brave enough to face himself when he is afraid; one who will be proud and unbending in honest defeat, and humble and gentle in victory.

Build me a son whose wishes will not take the place of deeds; a son who will know Thee—and that to know himself is the foundation stone of knowledge.

Lead him, I pray, not in the path of ease and comfort, but under the stress and spur of difficulties and challenge. Here let him learn to stand up in the storm; here let him learn compassion for those who fail.

Build me a son whose heart will be clean, whose goal will be high, a son who will master himself before he seeks to master other men, one who will reach into the future, yet never forget the past.

And after all these things are his, give him, I pray, enough of a sense of humor so that he may always be serious, yet never take himself too seriously. Give

114

him humility so that he may always remember the simplicity of true greatness, the open mind of true wisdom, and the meekness of true strength.

Then I, his father, will dare to whisper, "I have not lived in vain!"

DOUGLAS MACARTHUR

FEAR

Groundless Fears

How senseless are most of our fears. Those who trust in the provident care of God should never become the victims of fear: "I will trust, and not be afraid" (Isa. 12:2).

Believing that something was wrong with his heart, a young man went to a doctor for a checkup. As the doctor felt the young man's pulse, he glanced at his wristwatch and exclaimed, "There it goes again."

The fearful young man instantly believed that the doctor meant something was seriously wrong with his heart. He was too afraid, however, to ask what was wrong.

Later he learned that there was nothing wrong with his heart. The doctor's words "There it goes again" meant only that his watch had again stopped running.

* * *

'Tis I

Tossed with rough winds, and faint with fear,
Above the tempest soft and clear,
What still, small accents greet mine ear?
'Tis I. Be not afraid.

'Tis I who washed thy spirit white,
'Tis I who gave the blind eyes sight,
'Tis I, thy Lord, thy Life, thy light,
'Tis I. Be not afraid.

These raging winds, this surging sea,
Bear not a breath of wrath to thee,
The storm has all been spent on Me,
'Tis I. Be not afraid.

"The Foundation of God Standeth Sure"

Political wrangling and the Civil War delayed for a long time the completion of the partially constructed Washington Monument. When the work was resumed, the question arose Will the foundation, laid years before, be sufficiently strong to support the enormous weight of 81,120 tons of stone required to complete it?

Strong cords were fastened high up in the incompleted structure with markers tied on the downward ends of the cords. The markers rested lightly on a large pan filled with soft wax. Any movement of the massive structure, or any give in the foundation, would be registered on the soft wax.

Later the wax was examined. It was crisscrossed with markings. "The foundation is giving away!" said the builders.

Upon further investigation, they discovered that an owl had flown into the top of the monument and had gotten tangled in the cords. The flapping of its wings had set the cords in motion and caused the markings on the wax.

Some of God's children today are unduly alarmed. They are fearful for the foundations of God's eternal kingdom and the thwarting of His changeless purposes. How needless are their fears. God is still on the throne. His plans and purposes will triumph: "He doeth according to his will . . . and none can stay his hand" (Dan. 4:35). "The foundation of God standeth sure" (II Tim. 2:19).

Told by GEORGE W. TRUETT

115

FELLOWSHIP

Walking with God

"Walking with God" is the Old Testament way of describing a holy life. Let us always remember this.

Enoch "walked with God" and men at the same time. Walking with God doesn't mean that we walk in pharisaic aloofness from others. Enoch did not leave the earth to walk with God. He did not shut himself out from the activities of men. He simply found God's way in the forest and field, in the market and home, and he took it. He found out where God was, and went with Him. He became God's man. He became God's friend. He shared the peace of God, the joy of God and finally the rest of God.

Wesleyan Methodist

* * *

All Brethren

John Wesley said, "We give the right hand of fellowship to every lover of God." Likewise, Paul said, "Grace be with all them that love our Lord Jesus Christ in sincerity" (Eph. 6:24).

All born-again believers, irrespective of clime, color or condition, are one in Christ, and children of the heavenly Father: "For ye are all the children of God by faith in Christ Jesus" (Gal. 3:26).

* * *

All Equal Before God

After a meeting one night in London, Dr. Harry A. Ironside walked home with the Marquess of Aberdeen and the Lord Bishop of Norwich. Being an American and unaccustomed to titles, Dr. Ironside felt embarrassed, not knowing how to address men of their rank. He expressed his perplexity to the marquess, who said, "My dear brother, just address us as your brethren in Christ. We have no higher honor than that."

In God's great family, all are equal: "One is your Master, even Christ; and all ye are brethren" (Matt. 23:8).

The Uniting Spirit

A mountain stream ran through the land of a farmer. He went into the business of raising ducks. He made stout pens, separated the breeds of ducks, and placed the respective breeds in different pens. The ducks continued to be separated until a flood came. Then the water rose over the pens and the different breeds of ducks began to swim together.

Today God's children are in different denominational pens. Intermittently there are outpourings of God's Spirit upon them and they are lifted above divisive pettiness onto the plane of sweet fellowship and mutual encouragement.

"Grace be with all them who love our Lord Jesus Christ in sincerity" (Eph. 6:24).

* * *

Christian Love Triumphs over Hatred

During World War II, a Japanese soldier captured a young Christian American soldier in a jungle. The Japanese ordered the American to precede him, as he pressed a bayonet to his back. As he trudged along, the American soldier began to whistle a hymn to lessen his fear.

After a while, the Japanese soldier began to whistle along with his captive.

At first the American soldier thought, *Am I hearing an echo?* Then the Japanese came alongside him and said, "I am a Christian. I learned several hymns in a mission school. Let's stop and rest."

After a time of sweet fellowship, the two parted peaceably. The Spirit of Christ and Christian love had triumphed over hatred and murderous desire.

Told by an army chaplain

* * *

Burning Hearts

Professor Thomas Henry Huxley, English biologist, said that deeply buried in the English soil are tropical seeds of almost limitless variety, brought there by migrant birds from distant regions. They

116

lie dormant, waiting for a tropical climate to bring forth their lovely blossoms.

Within God's children lie potential powers which could bring blessings to our needy world. The unleashing of these potential powers requires sustained spiritual glow. We must walk in unbroken fellowship with Christ: "Did not our heart burn within us, while he talked with us by the way, and while he opened to us the scriptures?" (Luke 24:32).

FORGETTING GOD

We Must Catch up Spiritually

Roger Babson, world-renowned statistician, said, "I do not pose as a preacher, but let me tell you that God will not let us advance much further materially until we catch up spiritually. People must get back to God. We must start praying."

* * *

We Must Look to God

An editorial in the *New Jersey Kiwanian* reported: "Social reform has failed to counteract crime. Politics is unmentionably decayed. Legislation is helpless to restore honesty and integrity. Materialism has been tried and found wanting. We must look to God for salvation. Everywhere, among thinking people, the cry is 'Back to God! Back to the church!'"

* * *

The Unseen Hand

In 1812 the mighty army of Napoleon invaded Russia. After suffering hardships and ignominious defeat, Napoleon and his fragmented army retreated. Then they were defeated by Wellington and his army at Waterloo.

The would-be world conqueror was exiled to the Island of St. Helena. In dictating his memoirs, Napoleon said, "There was a hand moving in Europe which I did not see—the hand of God!"

* * *

Drifting

Drifting away from God in thy youth,
Drifting away from mercy and truth,
Drifting to sin in tenderest youth,
  Drifting away from God.

Drifting away on sin's treacherous tide,
Drifting where death and darkness abide,
Drifting from heaven away in your pride,
  Drifting away from God.

Why will you drift on billows of shame,
Spurning His grace again and again?
Soon you'll be lost, in sin to remain,
  Ever away from God.

* * *

Indifferent to Spiritual Things

Gilbert W. Kirby, General Secretary of the Evangelical Alliance, London, said in *Christianity Today:* "England as a whole remains indifferent to spiritual things. Nearly 99 percent of London's teenagers and more than 90 percent of all British people do not regularly attend any place of worship. One can enter churches with a seating capacity of one thousand and find a dozen in attendance."

The ancient question is pertinent: "Why is the house of God forsaken?" (Neh. 13:11).

* * *

Have You Forgotten God?

H. G. Wells said, "Our world is like a convoy lost in darkness on an unknown rocky coast with quarreling pirates in the chart room and savages clambering up the sides of the ship to plunder and do evil as the whim may take them."

Lincoln said, "We have forgotten God. We have forgotten the gracious hand which preserved us in peace and enriched and strengthened us. We have vainly imagined that all things were produced by some superior wisdom and virtue of our own. Intoxicated with unbroken success, we have become too self-sufficient to feel

117

the necessity of redeeming and preserving grace, too proud to pray to the God that made us."

How applicable to us as a nation is the ancient prophet's indictment of God's children of old: "My people have committed two evils; they have forsaken me the fountain of living waters, and hewed them out cisterns, broken cisterns, that can hold no water" (Jer. 2:13).

Oh, for a voice sufficiently Spirit-empowered to call us back to God!

* * *

"Lest We Forget"

What has been designated by some as the greatest recorded disaster in history occurred in 1923 in Japan. It was an earthquake of such violence that every building in Yokohama was leveled. Three-fourths of Tokyo was destroyed by fire. Nearly three hundred thousand died, and two and one-half million were made homeless. Disease and despair prevailed throughout the nation.

The American people, who always respond generously in times of disaster, sent food, clothes and medical supplies to Japan by shiploads. More than two million dollars was collected from Americans anxious to help.

Expressions of gratitude from the stricken nation were spontaneous. "We never will forget," many Japanese said.

But the Japanese warlords forgot. On December 7, 1941, their airplanes rained death and destruction on Pearl Harbor!

Japan is not the only nation whose leaders or people forgot past mercies. God said of His ancient people, "My people have forgotten me days without number" (Jer. 2:32).

There are many in our nation who live for God and faithfully serve Him, but myriads have forgotten Him. Have *you* forgotten God?

* * *

Building Without God

Bertrand Russell, British philosopher, averred, "The whole temple of man's achievements must inevitably be buried under the debris of a universe in ruins." The Bible says of man's vaunted civilization, built without God and with no thought of His glory, "The earth also and the works that are therein shall be burned up" (II Peter 3:10).

Through the centuries, proud, pompous man has arrogated glory to himself, as did King Nebuchadnezzar who said, "Is not this great Babylon, that I have built . . . by the might of my power, and for the honour of my majesty?" (Dan. 4:30).

Only that which is built upon the enduring foundation, Christ, will last: "For other foundation can no man lay than that is laid, which is Jesus Christ" (I Cor. 3:11).

Those who live for Christ's glory and bring others to Him will endure forever: "They that be wise shall shine as the brightness of the firmament; and they that turn many to righteousness as the stars for ever and ever" (Dan. 12:3).

We are all blind until we see
  That in the human plan
Nothing is worth the building,
  Unless it builds the man.

Why build these cities glorious,
  If man unbuilded goes?
In vain we build the world,
  Unless the builder grows.

* * *

Hopeless Robots

Henry J. Kaiser the industrialist said, "The tragedy of this age is that whole races of men seem to have sunk into faithless surrender to a confused despair. Men feel that they have lost control over their own destiny. War and personal bewilderment have swallowed them up and tossed them about like hopeless robots. They follow false prophets of godlessness and materialism."

Material prosperity tends to forgetfulness of God: "And when thy herds and thy flocks multiply, and thy silver and thy gold is multiplied, and all that thou hast is multiplied; then thine heart be lifted up, and thou forget the LORD thy God" (Deut. 8:13-14).

Ill fares the land,
  To hastening ills a prey,
Where wealth accumulates
  And men decay.

118

FORGIVENESS, GOD'S

One Thing God Forgets

A Canadian authority has advocated the destruction of a criminal's record after twelve years of good behavior, in order to encourage the man to begin anew.

How wonderful it is that the vilest and unworthiest of evildoers may turn penitently to God and his past sins will be forgiven and forgotten: "I will be merciful to their unrighteousness, and their sins . . . will I remember no more" (Heb. 8:12).

Told by L. E. MAXWELL

* * *

No Catch to God's Offer

A man who was serving a lifetime sentence in the Oklahoma State Penitentiary escaped. The warden, Jerome J. Waters, offered the fugitive fifteen hundred dollars if he would surrender himself at the gates of the prison.

There was a catch, however, to the offer. The reward was to be earned and saved by the escapee by doing work in the prison. "If he comes we will see that he does not get out again. Justice will prevail," said the warden.

How different is the offer God makes to all the fugitives from divine justice. There is no catch to His offer: "Let the wicked forsake his way . . . and let him return unto the LORD, and he will have mercy upon him; . . . he will abundantly pardon" (Isa. 55:7).

* * *

Doleful Drums for an Outcast

Some time ago a youthful United States marine was court-martialed for larceny. He was found guilty.

The disgrace of public banishment began when a sergeant major read aloud the bad conduct discharge and snapped the order, "Escort this man from the confines of this United States Navy reservation."

After being led from his quarters by a pistol-armed "chaser," the bareheaded, degraded outcast trudged slowly past rows of marines, standing at attention, while the drummers beat the rogue's march, music played in a jeering manner when a soldier is dishonorably discharged from the service. As the disgraced marine passed each platoon, the men turned from him in an about-face.

The stern, merciless custom of "drumming out" offenders from the service dates back to the English army of the seventeenth century. It was used in the Civil War by both the North and the South to punish deserters and shirkers, as a warning to others who might be tending in the direction of a bad-conduct discharge.

Though military discipline must be maintained, we rejoice in the fact that anyone degraded and discharged by man may turn penitently to God for His mercy and forgiveness. God forgives and forgets our guilty past and gives all who will turn from sin to Him the grant of a new beginning, the opportunity of a new start: "I have blotted out, as a thick cloud, thy transgressions, and, as a cloud, thy sins" (Isa. 44:22). "For I will be merciful to their unrighteousness, and their sins . . . will I remember no more" (Heb. 8:12).

* * *

Now I Can Look Up

One day as I was visiting heart patients in Hines V. A. Hospital, I came to the bed of a man who, in health, had been a Christ-rejecter. I spoke to him of the Mender of broken things, Jesus, and prayed with him. Tearfully and penitently he said, "I'm glad that God, in mercy, put me flat on my back that I might look up and ask for His mercy and forgiveness."

No one needs to wait until some calamity befalls him to ask for God's mercy and forgiveness: "Now is the accepted time; . . . now is the day of salvation" (II Cor. 6:2).

W. B. K.

119

The Outstretched Hands

Upon completing the clay statue of Christ which is now in the House of Arts in Italy, the Danish sculptor, Thorvaldsen, put a wet cover over it. Leaving his work, he joined some friends. Later he invited one of them to go with him and see his latest work.

After removing the covering from the statue, he exclaimed with horror, "My work is ruined!" The hands had moved downward and were reaching out toward them.

His feeling of failure and consternation gave place to satisfaction when the friend said, "Look! Christ is stretching His hands toward us as if to say, 'Come to Me!'"

How grateful we are that Christ's hands are outstretched to all mankind! He offers mercy and forgiveness to the penitent.

* * *

"No Fishing Allowed"

"I get worried. Has God really forgiven my past?" asked a patient in Mildmay Hospital, London, of George Woodall, who had had the joy of leading her to Christ.

Woodall replied, "If this keeps worrying you, I am sure I know what the Lord would say to you: 'Why don't you mind your own business? I have made your sins My business. I died for your sins on the cross!' My friend, God has put your sins behind His back. He has dropped them in the depth of the sea and put up the notice: No Fishing Allowed!"

The patient's doubts vanished. Rejoicing, she said, "I see it now! How wonderful God's forgiveness is!"

God's promises are sure: "I have blotted out, as a thick cloud, thy transgressions, and, as a cloud, thy sins" (Isa. 44:22); "Thou wilt cast all their sins into the depths of the sea" (Micah 7:19); "For I will be merciful to their unrighteousness, and their sins . . . will I remember no more" (Heb. 8:12).

Adapted from *London City Mission Magazine*

* * *

Only One Way to God

Across the front entrance of a massive, stately synagogue in Chicago are the words "Seek ye the Lord *where* He may be found."

How misleading are the words. Some who enter that temple believe that *it* is the place where God may be found. God may be found in any place where He is sought penitently and wholeheartedly through the Saviour: "No man cometh unto the Father, but by me" (John 14:6).

* * *

His Greatest Need

Nicolaus Copernicus was a great mathematician. His studies and calculations revolutionized the thinking of mankind about the universe. At death's door he saw himself, not as a great scholar or astronomer, but only as a sinner in need of God's mercy and forgiveness. He chose his own epitaph: "I do not seek a kindness equal to that given to Paul, but the forgiveness which Thou didst grant to the penitent thief. That I earnestly crave."

* * *

Putting God First

An unbelieving student asked a godly woman, "Would your God give me a hundred dollars if I asked Him?"

"I cannot say," replied the woman. "I know that God gave millions of dollars to George Müller, but George Müller belonged to God and served Him faithfully. Your greatest need is not money but forgiveness of sin. After you become a child of God, you may then ask the heavenly Father to supply your needs according to His riches in glory by Christ Jesus, and He will do it."

Adapted from *Our Daily Bread*

* * *

"I Came in on the Other Shoulder!"

Dr. Philpott called to see an unsaved girl who was dying. She asked, "Isn't there a story in the Bible about a sheep that went astray?"

"Yes," said Dr. Philpott as he opened his Bible and read the story of the lost sheep to her. He also read the promise of the good Shepherd to give eternal life to the sheep: "And I give unto them eternal life; and they shall never perish" (John 10:28). Then he knelt and prayed.

After the prayer the girl said, "Oh, it is wonderful! The good Shepherd has found me! I will trust Him and love Him with all my heart!" The next day she went to be forever with the Lord.

Years later a woman said to Dr. Philpott, "I was present that night when the good Shepherd brought Mary on His shoulder into His fold. *I came in on the other shoulder!"*

* * *

"Don't Create Man"

There is an interesting Jewish legend about the creation of man.

On the eve of man's creation, God counseled with the angels about His throne.

"Create him not," said the angel of justice. "He will commit all kinds of cruelties and injustices toward his fellowman."

"Create him not," said the angel of truth. "He will be false to Thee and to others."

"Create him not," said the angel of holiness. "He will indulge in that which is impure in Thy sight, and he will dishonor Thee."

There was silence until the angel of mercy spoke. Said he, "Create him, heavenly Father. When he sins and turns penitently from sin to the path of right, truth and holiness, I will take him tenderly by the hand, speak loving words to him and bring him to Thee for Thy mercy and forgiveness."

"So God created man in his own image, in the image of God created he him . . . and breathed into his nostrils the breath of life; and man became a living soul" (Gen. 1:27; 2:7).

* * *

I Can't, but God Can

One of God's children awakened early one morning. Her past sins and failures stalked unbidden across the stage of memory. She was weighted with a sense of regret and became so depressed she felt she could not face the duties of the day.

She began to pray for courage and strength. Then the words of Pilate came

to her mind: "What I have written I have written."

What can be God's message to me from these words? she thought. *I, like Pilate, cannot blot out what I have written.*

Then God seemed to say to her, "No, you cannot blot out your past sins and failures, but 'I, even I, am he that blotteth out thy transgressions for mine own sake, and will not remember thy sins' " (Isa. 43:25). All her fears subsided as God's peace flooded her soul.

* * *

Past Sins Obliterated

Frank Howard, a member of Parliament from British Columbia since 1957, confessed that he once served sixteen months in a penitentiary for armed robbery. He made the confession as a result of a blackmail threat. His former prison record of some years before had come to light and was held against him.

When God forgives us, all records of past sins are obliterated! We become in His sight as if we had never committed a single sin—"justified freely by his grace through the redemption that is in Christ Jesus" (Rom. 3:24).

Adapted from the *Prairie Overcomer*

* * *

"Who Forgiveth All Thine Iniquities"

The Muslim prays, fasts, gives alms and goes on hazardous pilgrimages. Believing that he thus becomes righteous, he doesn't seek forgiveness.

The Hindu assumes that goodness and unacknowledged sins are related to a future nothingness or to an existence in which he will be at death reincarnated into an insect or an animal. He knows nothing of forgiveness of sin.

The Confucian has a lofty conception of God as a Judge—stern, relentless, cold, capricious and merciless—existing only as a detached Observer.

Christianity is the only religion which offers forgiveness of sin to all who turn penitently from sin to the Saviour: "Neither do I condemn thee: go, and sin no more" (John 8:11). "I have blotted out, as a thick cloud, thy transgressions, and, as a cloud, thy sins" (Isa. 44:22).

"Their sins and their iniquities will I remember no more" (Heb. 8:12).

* * *

The Miracle Divine

The crimson glow of the sunset,
　The blue of the vaulting skies,
The green of the pleasant pastures
　Refresh my weary eyes.

Yet scarlet dress of the poppies,
　The stars of a winter's night,
Are not one-half so gorgeous
　As when God just paints in white.

The white of the ransomed sinner,
　When grace and mercy shine,
Is the masterpiece of beauty,
　The miracle divine.

* * *

Buried and Forgotten

A minister's little boy often said, "I'm going to be a preacher like Dad." One day his cat died. "I'll practice having a funeral," he said.

The boy placed the cat in a shoe box, and cut a hole in the top so the mourners could take a last look at the remains. He left the cat's tail extending from another hole cut in the end of the box. Then he invited his young friends to the funeral.

The "sermon" was given, the remains were viewed and then the box was buried in a hole in the ground. However the cat's tail was left unburied.

Every two or three days the boy would pull a little on the cat's tail to determine the condition of the remains below. After a while, the tail pulled off. Then the cat's body was left undisturbed—buried.

Though God has buried the sins of His children in the ocean of His forgetfulness, some Christians continue to recall their sins and bemoan them. If God has forgiven and forgotten our guilty past, shouldn't we, too, leave it buried and forgotten?

Told by Dr. Walter Wilson

* * *

Blotted Record

Ella Wheeler Wilcox advised, "Waste no tears upon the blotted record of lost years. Turn the page and smile to see the fair white pages that remain!"

"Come now, . . . saith the Lord: though your sins be as scarlet, they shall be as white as snow" (Isa. 1:18).

FORGIVING OTHERS

Recall the Right—Forgive the Wrong

To leave the old with a joyful song,
To recall the right and forgive the wrong,
To forget the thing that binds you fast
To the vain regrets of the year that's past,
To have the strength to let go your hold
Of the worthless things of the days grown
　old,
To bravely go forth with a purpose true,
To the unknown task of the year that's
　new,
To help your brother along the road
To share his sorrows and lift his load,
To add your gift to the world's good cheer,
Is to have and give a happy new year.

Robert Brewster Beattie

It's Love—It's Forgiveness

Years ago in the course of their missionary work, Harold Hestekind and his wife were riding their bicycles on a busy street in Shanghai, China. She was struck by a bus and thrown beneath it. The husband prayed, "O God, stop the wheels!"

Mrs. Hestekind was rushed to a hospital, where a head wound was treated. Then investigating officers said to her, "The driver of the bus was entirely to blame for the accident. If you will sign these papers, we will take him in custody."

"No, no," said she. "I don't want to hold him responsible. Let him go free.

122

And please see that he does not lose his position."

The driver looked in amazement at Mrs. Hestekind. Weeping, he said, "My father, mother, brothers and sisters are all Christians, but I have never before seen its attraction. It is love! It is forgiveness! Now I want to give myself to Christ."

Those who heard what the driver said were astonished.

Later the Hestekinds said, "That was our greatest opportunity to witness for Christ. Others had seen how Christlike Christians love and forgive."

* * *

"Pa Forgave Everybody"

After the death of Abraham Lincoln, Mrs. Lincoln sorrowfully asked John F. Parker, the President's bodyguard, "Why were you not at the door to keep the assassin out?"

Parker bowed his head and said, "I have bitterly repented it. I did not believe anyone would try to kill so good a man. The belief made me careless. I became so interested in the play, I failed to see the assassin enter the presidential box."

"You should have seen him. You had no right to be careless." Having said this, Mrs. Lincoln covered her face with her hands and wept uncontrollably.

Recovering her composure, she said to Parker, "Go now. It's not you I can't forgive. It's the assassin."

Tad Lincoln, who heard his mother, said, "If Pa had lived, he would have forgiven the man who shot him. Pa forgave everybody."

* * *

"It Was Pure Accident"

In *The Lamp Murder* Sir Frederick Treves tells the story of the brutal murder of a poor seamstress in the slum section of Whitechapel. Her enraged, drunken husband hurled two lighted lamps at her.

Horribly burned, she was rushed to a London hospital. There a deposition was taken. In the presence of a magistrate and policeman, who informed her that death was near, her badly swollen lips moved. She uttered four words, "It was pure accident." Then she was gone!

How like the dying words of the One who long ago pleaded for those who nailed Him to the cruel cross: "Father, forgive them."

Told by W. E. Sangster

* * *

The Quick and Powerful Word

An African pastor assigned to the people in his Bible class a verse to be memorized each week.

A woman confessed, "The pastor gave me a very hard verse to learn. As I repeated it, 'Let not the sun go down upon your wrath,' I was pricked in my heart. I remembered a sister in the church with whom I had quarreled some two years before, and to whom I had not spoken since that day. It was easy for me to learn the verse. It was hard for me to do what it said. But I went and became reconciled to my sister."

* * *

For Christ's Sake

A distressed, weeping woman said to her pastor, "I do not suppose you can help me."

"Why not?" asked the pastor. "I'll surely try to help you."

The woman said, "For years I have been unable to pray. There is a woman who has come between me and my husband. I cannot forgive her."

Thoughtfully the pastor said, "You cannot forgive this woman for her own sake, but can you not forgive her for Christ's sake?"

After heart-searching silence, the wounded wife said, "Yes. I can forgive her for Christ's sake and I will."

* * *

Why He Was Not Forgiven

In New York City, policemen found a young man dying in a filthy, vermin-infested room. Sinful living had exacted its inevitable toll upon him.

As he lay on the floor, the young man said over and over, "I want my father's forgiveness! I want my father's forgiveness!"

The officers asked, "Who is your father?"

The young man gave the name of a well-known industrialist who lived in New Jersey, and the officers immediately contacted him by phone. Mentioning the name of the dying youth, they asked, "Is he your son?"

"He *was* my son," came the answer, "but I have long since abandoned and disinherited the worthless wretch. He has brought only grief to me and his mother."

"But, sir, he is dying and he is pleading for your forgiveness."

Hastening to his son, the father heard the faintly spoken plea, "I want my father's forgiveness!"

Weeping, the man said, "My son, I would have forgiven you long ago if you had only asked for forgiveness."

A smile came to the young man's face and he was gone.

* * *

Forgive Us as We Forgive

A minister visited in a London hospital an army officer who the doctors said could not live three months. He was legally separated from his wife, and was bitter and unforgiving toward her. He said to the minister, "Often I pray the Lord's Prayer, giving special thought to the portion of the prayer which says, 'And forgive us . . . as we forgive.' Does not the Lord say that if we do not forgive others, He will not forgive us?"

"That's right," said the minister.

That night the officer asked God for His mercy and forgiveness, promising that he would likewise forgive his divorced wife.

Soon the officer and his wife were reconciled. He bought a new wedding ring, and at his bedside they were again united in marriage.

Forgiveness is the fragrance the violet sheds on the heel that has crushed it.

The sandal tree perfumes, when riven,
The ax that lays it low;
Let man who hopes to be forgiven
Forgive and bless his foe.

A Stripe-washing Service

In a meeting in Orlando, Florida, Dr. T. T. Martin conducted a unique service —a stripe-washing service. Making an earnest plea to God's children, he urged them to go to those present whom they had injured in any way, confess the wrong and humbly ask their forgiveness.

The men and women began to move out of their seats and go to offended, embittered ones present. Weeping, they sought to get right with one another so that they might get right with God.

We need more stripe-washing services. They could vitalize and revolutionize our churches and bring together some of God's estranged children who have allowed hate and ill will to separate them.

Christ said, "Therefore if thou bring thy gift to the altar, and there rememberest that thy brother hath ought against thee; leave there thy gift before the altar, and go thy way; first be reconciled to thy brother, and then come and offer thy gift" (Matt. 5:23-24).

"And he took them the same hour of the night, and washed their stripes" (Acts 16:33).

* * *

My Teacher, Franz Liszt

To provide for the needs of her invalid parents, a German girl gave piano lessons. "I am a pupil of Franz Liszt," she falsely said to prospective pupils.

One day Liszt visited her town. Someone spoke to him about the girl who was one of his pupils. The great pianist and composer thought for a moment and said, "I can't recall her."

Learning that her false claim had become known to Liszt, she went to him in tears, confessed her misrepresentation and pled for his forgiveness.

After chiding her, Liszt asked her to play a number for him. He corrected her mistakes and then said to her, "Now, you are a pupil of Liszt. You will give a recital by yourself. When you play your last number, you will announce, 'The recital will be concluded with a number by my teacher, Franz Liszt!' "

124

How Christlike we are when we forgive others and try to help them to forsake their false, evil ways.

ALICE MARIE KNIGHT

Vicious Minds

Chesterfield averred, "Little, vicious minds abound with anger and revenge and are incapable of feeling the pleasure of forgiving their enemies."

FREEDOM

(See also Patriotism)

Freedom, a Most Dangerous Gift

As a Fourth-of-July orator eulogized our forefathers who had died to give us freedom, a youth in the crowd called out, "Why don't you tell the whole truth? Why don't you say that freedom is the most dangerous gift that anyone can receive and it will destroy us unless we learn how to use it? Our forebears only had to fight for freedom, while we have to live with it."

A so-called *new* morality is burgeoning in the name of freedom. Promiscuity is displacing decency. God's eternal "Thou shalt not" is being changed to "Perhaps I can."

The ancient question is relevant: "If the foundations be destroyed, what can the righteous do?" (Ps. 11:3).

* * *

Why Live as Fugitives?

To escape the tyrannical dominion and fury during the Nazi occupation of Norway, some of the Norwegians hid in remote mountain valleys. After Norway was liberated, these people did not learn for some weeks that the enemy had been driven out and that their beloved country was once more free. They needlessly lived as fugitives when they might have lived in freedom and happiness.

Some today refuse to accept freedom in Christ and remain in Satan's bondage, having been "taken captive by him at his will" (II Tim. 2:26).

* * *

Enslaving Things

Things! Things! Things!
On the tables, on the floor,
Tucked away behind the door,
On the shelves and on the chairs,
Dangerously on the stairs,
Bureaus crammed and closets filled,
Boxes packed and boxes spilled,
Bundles everywhere you go,
Heaps and piles and overflow
Of things, things, things!

Things! Things! Things!
Things that take our precious time,
Hold us from the life sublime,
Things that only gather dust,
Things that rot and things that rust,
Things that mold and things that freeze,
Things that harbor foul disease,
Things that mock and that defy
Till at last we grimly die
Of things, things, things!

Things! Things! Things!
Let me cease to be their fool,
Let me fly their crafty rule,
Let me with unsparing knife
Cut their canker from my life;
Broad and clear and all serene
Let me make my mansion clean,
Now and evermore to be
Calm, unfettered, grandly free
From things, things, things.

AMOS R. WELLS

* * *

Their Passions Forge Their Fetters

Aristotle warned, "Men are qualified for civil liberties in exact proportion to their disposition to put moral chains upon their appetites. Society cannot exist unless a controlling power upon will and appetite be placed somewhere, and the less of it there is within, the more there must be without. It is ordained in the eternal constitution of things that men of

125

intemperate minds cannot be free. Their passions forge their fetters."

* * *

Continual Butchery of Conscience

John Bunyan, who was imprisoned for twelve years for conscience' sake, was offered his freedom in exchange for silence about Christ. Courageously he replied, "I am determined, God being my helper, yet to suffer if frail life may continue so long till the moss shall grow over my eyebrows, rather than violate my faith and make a continual butchery of my conscience."

* * *

American Citizenship

Some time ago Rosalind Elias, a Metropolitan Opera Company mezzo-soprano, ran a half-page advertisement in the *New York Times,* captioned "I Am Not Afraid." It cost her $2,880, according to the Associated Press. In it she said, "Many blessings have come to me, the greatest of which is my American citizenship—a heritage that makes me unafraid. I count my many blessings and the greatest of these is that my parents came from Lebanon to the United States so I could be born an American citizen. My faith in my God and in my country is far too great for me ever to feel anything but strong and secure!"

* * *

Where Freedom Begins

A news correspondent asked J. Edgar Hoover, "Where do you believe freedom has its beginnings?"

Hoover replied, "In religion. Christ championed the sanctity of the individual. There is respect for human dignity only where Christ and the Bible are a way of life. The philosophy of Christ has meant freedom from despair and tyranny throughout history."

"If the Son shall make you free, ye shall be free indeed" (John 8:36).

* * *

Proclaim Liberty

The Liberty Bell at Independence Hall, Philadelphia, was rung on July 4, 1776, to proclaim the independence of the United States. On the bell are these liberating words: "Proclaim liberty throughout all the land unto all the inhabitants thereof" (Lev. 25:10).

* * *

Unfit for Liberty

John Stuart Mill, English philosopher and political economist, declared, "People may prefer a free government, but if, from indolence or carelessness, they are unequal to the exertion necessary to preserve it, they are more or less unfit for liberty."

* * *

What Freedom Is

Freedom is a breath of air,
  Pine-scented, or salty like the sea;
Freedom is a field new-plowed,
  Furrows of democracy.

Freedom is a forest,
  Trees tall and straight as men;
Freedom is a printing press,
  The power of the pen.

Freedom is a country church,
  A cathedral's stately spire;
Freedom is a spirit
  That can set the soul on fire.

Freedom is man's birthright,
  A sacred, living rampart;
A pulsebeat of humanity,
  The throb of a nation's heart.

* * *

"Thank God! I'm Free!"

One day Konrad Schuman, an East German sergeant guarding the Berlin Wall, suddenly broke away from the group of Communist guards. With a submachine gun in his hand, Schuman leaped over the barbed wire entanglement to freedom in West Berlin. As he tore off his Communist uniform, he exclaimed, "Thank God! I'm free!"

* * *

Freedom Bought with Christ's Blood

William Cowper averred, "There is a freedom which is unsung and unpraised by senators; a freedom which monarchs cannot grant, nor all the powers of earth

126

and hell take away; a freedom which persecution, fraud, oppressions, prisons have no power to bind. It is a liberty of heart derived from heaven, bought with Christ's blood, and sealed with the same token."

* * *

Self-inflicted Genocide

In mankind, there is an inborn instinct and desire to be free. Long ago, when God's ancient people were sorely oppressed, "they cried, and their cry came up unto God by reason of the bondage. And God heard their groaning" (Exodus 2:23-24). Centuries later, the Saviour came to "preach deliverance to the captives" (Luke 4:18).

In Colombia's jungle-thick Vaupes province, there is a strange tribe of tall white Indians—the Carijona Indians. The tribe is destroying itself by killing their sick, and limiting almost all procreation in self-inflicted genocide. "They decided to eliminate themselves rather than continue being slaves to white men who exploit the area," said sociologist Gonzalez Villamizar in a report to the Colombian government.

Vaillamizar explained, "Little is known about the Carijonas except that they are different from most Colombian indigenous groups. They are white, tall and peaceful. They are not nomadic like most of their Indian countrymen. No one knows exactly where they came from, either. They

numbered six hundred not too many years ago. Now there are approximately eighty. Nobody—neither the missionaries nor I—can stop them. They have made up their minds to commit tribal suicide."

How appalling is man's inhumanity to man! How long will God withhold His judgment from oppressors who, for greed of gain, traffic in the bodies and souls of men?

* * *

When Divided

Walter Winchell warned, "When free people are divided, liberty is subtracted."

* * *

How About That?

Ralph W. Neighbour commented, "Give some people an inch and they will become a ruler."

* * *

Rotting Souls

Herbert Hoover said of enslaving, atheistic Communism, "It is rotting the souls of two-fifths of mankind today."

* * *

The Veriest Slave

H. Clay Trumbull declared, "The freest man in the world is the man who is a willing servant of Christ. The veriest slave is the man who thinks he is his own master, while he is the slave of his lusts."

FRIENDSHIP

These Friends of Mine

Dear Lord, my friends have been to me
  Interpreters of love divine,
And in their kindness I have seen
  Thine everlasting mercy shine!
And so I pray, on this Thy day,
  That Thou wilt search through gifts of Thine
And choose Thy rarest, fairest ones,
  To shower upon these friends of mine!
          MARTHA SNELL NICHOLSON

Thank God for You

Thank God for you, good friend of mine.
How scarce is friendship such as thine;
How very much I wish to be
As helpful as you've been to me—
  Thank God for you!

When I recall, from time to time,
How you inspire this heart of mine,
I find myself inclined to pray,
God bless my friend this very day—
  Thank God for you!
          JOSEPH CLARK

Among Greatest Blessings

Charles Kingsley said, "It is a blessed thing to have a friend—one who knows the best and worst about us, and who loves us in spite of our faults; one who will speak honestly to us, while others flatter us to our face and demean us behind our back; one who will give counsel and reproof in the day of prosperity, and comfort and encouragement in the day of difficulty and sorrow."

A friend never gets in our way unless we are on the way down.

"A friend loveth at all times" (Prov. 17:17).

* * *

A Definition of a Friend

"What is a friend? I'll tell you. A friend is a person with whom you dare to be yourself. Your soul can go naked with him. He seems to ask you to put on nothing, only to be what you really are. When you are with him, you do not have to be on your guard. You can say what you think, so long as it is genuinely you. He understands those contradictions in your nature that cause others to misjudge you. With him you breathe freely. You can avow your little vanities and envies and absurdities and, in opening them up to him, they are dissolved on the wide ocean of his loyalty. He understands! You may weep with him, laugh with him, pray with him, and, through and underneath it all, he sees, knows and loves you. A friend, I repeat, is one with whom you dare to be yourself!"

* * *

The Love of Friends

Man strives for glory, honor, fame,
That all the world may know his name;
Amasses wealth by brain and hand,
Becomes a power in the land.

But when he nears the end of life,
And looks back o'er the years of strife,
He finds that happiness depends
On none of these, but love of friends.

* * *

Old Friends

There are no friends like old friends,
And none so good and true;
We greet them when we meet them,
As roses greet the dew.

No other friends are dearer,
Though born of kindred mold;
And while we prize the new ones,
We treasure more the old.

And when they smile to gladden,
Or sometimes frown to guide,
We fondly wish those old friends
Were always by our side.

And when our faltering footsteps
Approach the Great Divide,
We'll long to meet the old friends
Who wait on the other side.

* * *

If We Knew

If I knew you and you knew me,
If both of us could clearly see,
And with an inner sight divine,
The meaning of your heart and mine,
I'm sure that we would differ less,
And clasp our hands in friendliness;
Our thoughts would pleasantly agree,
If I knew you and you knew me.

NIXON WATERMAN

GIVING

(*See also* Tithing)

Which Churches Give Most?

In addressing the annual Minnesota School of Missions, Rev. Robert K. Hudnut said, "Members of so-called affluent churches are less generous than are members of poor churches. The Church of the Nazarene and the Church of God, composed largely of the poorer people, are far in front in giving. Presbyterians, who are much wealthier, are sixth in giving—$70 per capita behind the Church of the Naz-

128

arene. Episcopalians are tenth. The United Church of Christ is fourteenth."

Liberality is one of God's most spiritually enriching gifts to His children: "The liberal soul shall be made fat: and he that watereth shall be watered also himself" (Prov. 11:25).

The Bible gives this word of praise of some of God's children who lived long ago: "Their deep poverty abounded unto the riches of their liberality. . . . Beyond their power they were willing of themselves" (II Cor. 8:2-3).

* * *

Singing a Lie

Dr. Peter Marshall, in leading a consecration meeting in a church, selected the hymn "Take My Life, and Let It Be." He said, "I want you to give special attention to the thought of the words 'Take my silver and my gold, Not a mite would I withhold.' If you cannot sing the words sincerely from your hearts, I want you to refrain from singing them."

The request was dramatic in its effect. With organ accompaniment, hundreds of voices sang zestfully up to the specially emphasized words. Then suddenly there was the sound of the organ only. The people were at least honest. Do Christians not lie when they sing something they do not mean?

* * *

Returns

'Mid the losses and the gains,
'Mid the pleasures and the pains,
'Mid the hopings and the fears,
And the restlessness of years,
We repeat the passage o'er,
We believe it more and more:
"Bread upon the waters cast
Shall be gathered at the last."

Soon like dust to you and me
Will our earthly treasure be,
But the loving words and deeds
To a soul in bitterest need,
They will unforgotten be,
They will live eternally:
"Bread upon the waters cast
Shall be gathered at the last."

"Cast thy bread upon the waters: for thou shalt find it after many days" (Eccles. 11:1).

* * *

A Measured Gift from God

We breathe eighteen times a minute, or about twenty-six thousand times a day. Each breath is a measured gift of life from God.

Job said, "In . . . [God's] hand is the soul of every living thing, and the breath of all mankind" (Job 12:10).

Daniel brought this accusation against the pagan ruler Belshazzar: "The God in whose hand thy breath is . . . hast thou not glorified" (Dan. 5:23).

"Let every thing that hath breath praise the LORD. Praise ye the LORD" (Ps. 150:6).

* * *

Applause of Crucified Hands

A large sum of money was urgently needed by Dr. J. H. Jowett's famous church in Carr's Lane. A special money-raising meeting of the church was called.

At the close of the service, the names of all the donors and the amounts they gave were read. There was applause when the names and gifts of the large donors were read.

The last name read was that of a poor woman who sacrificially give sixpence. There was no applause. Dr. Jowett stood quietly and said impressively, "I hear the applause of the crucified hands!"

* * *

How to Give

Give as you would if an angel
Awaited your gift at the door,
Give as you would if tomorrow
Found you where giving is o'er.

Give as you would to the Master
If you met His loving look,
Give as you would of your substance
If His hand the offering took.

* * *

Baptized Billfolds

A pastor entered the baptismal pool with a railway engineer. He was ready

129

to proceed with the baptismal service, when the engineer whispered, "Wait, pastor! I forgot something. I want to return to the robing room and get my billfold. I want it to be baptized with me."

There are too many unbaptized billfolds among God's children.

* * *

But I'm the Captain

A boy was asked the meaning of stewardship. He said, "It means that life is a great ship, loaded with a cargo of many things to be delivered to many people in many places. God is the Owner, but I am the captain of the ship."

* * *

Hilarious Giving

Someone has said, "He gives little who gives much with a frown. He gives much who gives little with a smile."

Paul said, "God loveth a cheerful [hilarious] giver" (II Cor. 9:7).

Is thy cruse of comfort failing?
  Rise and share it with another,
And through all the years of famine
  It shall serve thee and thy brother.
Love divine will fill thy warehouse,
  Or thy handful still renew;
Scanty fare for one will often
  Make a royal feast for two.

* * *

Rain from Heaven

A little girl gave her pastor $4.32 for missions. "How did you get so much money?" he asked.

She said, "I earned it by collecting rainwater and selling it to washerwomen who live on the edge of our town for two cents a bucket. I want to help send the gospel to those who have never heard about Jesus."

The pastor asked, "Shall I say, 'A gift from Mary'?"

"Oh, no," said Mary. "I'd rather no one knew but Jesus. Put it down as rain from heaven."

Told by ALICE MARIE KNIGHT

A Temporary Expedient

The first century Christian sharing was not an effort to establish a permanent economic system. It was a temporary expedient of relief and was not practiced in churches outside Jerusalem. If all had sold their houses and lands when they became Christians, many would ultimately have been on relief with nobody to relieve them.

V. RAYMOND EDMAN

* * *

You Can't Fool the Lord

George was a Christian handyman. One Monday morning, his employer observed that he was dejected. "What's the trouble?" the employer asked.

George replied sadly, "Yesterday when the offering plate was passed, I put a quarter in the collection. That is, I thought I put a quarter in, but when I got home, I discovered that I had put in the five dollar gold piece you gave me at Christmas."

The employer responded, "George, that is no misfortune. After all, that was a good deed. God will reward you."

George said, "But you can't fool the Lord. He knows that in my heart I wanted to give only twenty-five cents."

God sees the motive which prompts our giving. How precious to Him is sacrificial giving: "This poor widow hath cast more in, than all they which have cast into the treasury; . . . she of her want did cast in all she had" (Mark 12:43-44).

* * *

Channels Only

Years ago as Dr. H. C. Morrison, famous Holiness Methodist minister and editor of the *Pentecostal Herald,* walked along a busy street, a man gave him a five dollar bill. "Thank you, friend," Dr. Morrison said as he resumed his walk. Soon he encountered a poor widow. Knowing about her need, he gave her the five dollar bill the man had just given to him.

Within a few blocks, another man pressed a five dollar bill into Dr. Morrison's hand.

130

As he walked along, another needy person was encountered. God seemed to prompt him to give the second five dollar bill which was given to him. Dr. Morrison said later, "I decided to keep it for myself. Strange to say, that was the last gift of five dollars I received that day. I believe God would have continued the chain of money coming to me as I walked along if I had passed it on."

God uses His children as channels through which to send His blessings to needy ones. What joy we miss when the channel becomes blocked by greed and selfishness!

> Be not selfish in thy greed,
> Pass it on!
> Look upon thy brother's need,
> Pass it on!

Told by ROY O. McCLAIN

* * *

If I Had a Million Dollars

Some say, "If I had a million dollars, I would do great things for God and others!"

It is not what we would do with a million dollars which we do not have, but what we do with the dollar we have, that counts.

Little Gail came from Sunday school with a troubled look in her eyes.

Mother asked, "Are you sad about something?"

Gail replied, "Oh, Mother, I wish I had a thousand dollars!"

"What would you do with a thousand dollars?" asked Mother.

"I'd buy food for the starving children our teacher told us about, and I'd buy some pretty dresses and a warm coat for little Ruthie. Her father is poor and sick."

Mother said, "Gail, I'm glad you have such beautiful and unselfish thoughts. You don't have a thousand dollars, but yesterday I gave you a dime, and you spent it on yourself. You could have bought an ice cream cone for little Ruthie. If you learn to share the little you have now with others, you will very likely share the abundance you may have later with needy ones."

Told by ALICE M. KNIGHT

* * *

Free Water but Costly Pipes

Dr. Adam Clarke delivered a message on the text "Let him that is athirst come. And whosoever will, let him take the water of life freely" (Rev. 22:17).

At the conclusion of the message, he announced that a collection would be taken.

As a lady left the church, she asked him, "How can you reconcile the freeness of the water of life with the collection you took at the close of your sermon? Aren't the two things incongruous?"

Dr. Clarke exclaimed, "Not at all! To be sure, God gives the water of life without money and without price. But don't people have to pay for the pipes and waterworks which bring water into our homes? Surely it is all right for us to pay for the conveyance of the water of life to others."

Isaiah said, "Ho, every one that thirsteth, come ye to the waters, . . . come . . . without money and without price" (Isa. 55:1).

Told by R. E. NEIGHBOUR

GOLDEN RULE

What Confucius Said:

A disciple of Confucius asked him: "Is there one word which may serve as a rule of practice for all one's life?"

"Is not *reciprocity* such a word?" asked Confucius. "What you do not want done to yourself, do not to others."

What Epictetus Said:

Speaking from his bitter experience as a slave and cripple, Epictetus said, "What you avoid suffering yourself, seek not to inflict on others."

What Hillel Said:

A man came to Shammai and said, "I am prepared to be received as a proselyte on condition that you teach me the whole law while I stand on one foot." Shammai dismissed him as a trifler.

Later the man went to Hillel, who said to him, "What is hateful to yourself, do to no other. That is the whole law, and the rest is commentary."

What Christ Said:

Ancient teachers gave negatively only one part of the law which Christ gave: "Do not to others what you would not have others do to you." To desist from doing to others what you do not want others to do to you is the less important aspect of Christ's precept. Christ said, "Whatsoever ye would that men should do to you, do ye even so to them: for this is the law and the prophets" (Matt. 7:12).

GOSPEL

Changed Men Change Society

Daniel A. Poling, on his eighty-first birthday, stated his creed thus: "I believe the gospel is first personal and always social. The place of the church is not to change society but to change men and women, who will then do the changing of society."

* * *

The Race-inclusive Gospel

John Wesley prayed, "O Lord, take back my interest in Thy blood unless it flows for the whole race."

The gospel is race-inclusive: "Ho, every one that thirsteth, come ye to the waters . . . without money" (Isa. 55:1). "Whosoever will, let him take the water of life freely" (Rev. 22:17).

* * *

The Noblest Calling

A Johannesburg businessman, on being informed by Mrs. Agnes Fraser that her husband, Dr. Donald Fraser, was a missionary, said in manifest astonishment, "A missionary! Do you mean to tell me that a man of his caliber could not get a better job than that?"

Mrs. Fraser replied, "If he could, you may be sure he would have jumped at it!"

"But, surely," began the businessman. Then he became silent. Slowly it began to dawn on him what she had meant.

Is there a more noble calling than to proclaim the gospel where it is unknown, and where myriads live in spiritual darkness and are enslaved by agelong degrading, dehumanizing customs?

* * *

Booby-trapped Crossings

In a report on "Booby-trapped Crossings," the *National Observer* pointed out the seemingly paradoxical fact that even safety devices may become a hazard.

It cited the case of an Air Force sergeant named Hill who had driven across a certain railroad crossing many times when the red light was flashing and the bell ringing but no train was in sight.

One day the sergeant's car was crowded with his wife and seven of their twelve children. Traffic had backed up at the crossing because the warning signals were on. Sergeant Hill drove his car around the car in front of him and started across the track. Then the accident happened! An oncoming freight train, traveling at sixty miles per hour, smashed into the station wagon, killing all nine occupants!

The National Transportation Safety Board expressed the opinion that this crossing, along with many others, was a booby trap because people were often forced to wait to no purpose, creating the impression that signals cannot be relied upon and may be ignored.

There are booby traps in the proclamation of the gospel. The preacher is not necessarily at fault. When people hear the warning of the gospel frequently, yet persist in doing nothing about it, the feeling that there is nothing to be concerned about is gradually developed in their minds.

God's Word warns, "He, that being often reproved hardeneth his neck, shall suddenly be destroyed, and that without remedy" (Prov. 29:1).

The deadliest of spiritual maladies is to become gospel-hardened!

ROBERT J. LITTLE, in
Moody Monthly

* * *

Turning Backs on Missions

Senator Mark Hatfield wrote, in an article, "The Erosion of the Lordship of Christ," in the *Wesleyan Methodist,* "Those who substitute the gospel of civil rights for the gospel of Jesus Christ in the pulpit are turning their backs on the commission they have been called to perform."

* * *

The Old, Old Story

William Gladstone, a former prime minister of England, once said, "If I were asked what is the remedy for the deeper sorrows of the human heart, I would point to the old, old story, told in an old, old Book, and taught with an old, old teaching—the gospel. This is the greatest and best gift ever given to mankind!"

* * *

The Inward Urge

After reaching Burma, Adoniram Judson yearned to preach the gospel before he learned the language of the natives. One day he embraced a Burmese man and beamed Christlike concern into his eyes.

The national said to a friend, "I have seen an angel."

* * *

The Life Plant

In Jamaica, there is a plant called "the life plant." It is most difficult to destroy any part of it. If a leaf is taken from the plant and suspended by a string from a wire, it will not wilt or die. It sends out threadlike roots which draw sustenance from the air, and new leaves begin to grow.

The gospel is the life plant of the world. Wherever it goes, it takes root and transforms lives. No climate, however surcharged with sin, wrong or superstition, can kill the everlasting gospel.

* * *

A Firm Standing

For years Dr. Joseph Parker faithfully proclaimed the Word of God in the great City Temple in London. Then he began to give much time and thought to modernistic literature. He studied the theories of the day, which were causing some to undervalue the Bible and lose faith in portions of it. He began to question the doctrine of salvation through the atoning death of Christ for the sin of the world.

One day a great sorrow came to Dr. Parker. His wife, to whom he was devoted, was stricken with illness, and in a few hours she was gone. He sat, brokenhearted, alone in his home. He learned that no comfort could be found in the theories which had caused him to question some of the eternal verities of the Bible.

In time, the clouds of sorrow began to lift. Later he testified, "In those hours of darkness and anguish, I thought of the old gospel of redemption only through the blood of Christ—the gospel I had preached in the earlier years. I put my foot down on that, and I found firm standing."

* * *

When Defied

Dr. Arnold Toynbee warned, in a commencement address at Haverford College, "We defy the gospel's precepts at our peril. We never defy them successfully in the long run."

* * *

But One Problem

William Gladstone stated, "There is but one international problem, and that is to get the gospel to every man, woman and child in every nation."

Practicing the Gospel

When the Salvation Army workers first went to India, they identified themselves fully with the downtrodden and sorrowing ones. They emulated the example of Paul, who said, "I am made all things to all men, that I might by all means save some" (I Cor. 9:22).

The Salvationists who worked with the untouchables, the lowest caste, became untouchables. They suffered revilement and ostracism, gladly undergoing hardships. They exemplified the gospel they preached by *practicing* it.

Elizabeth Geirie was a blue-eyed Salvation Army lassie from Dundee. She lived in a tiny hut in a jungle. One day a man was brought to her in great agony. A large thorn had been driven like a nail into his foot. Only a fractional part of the thorn was visible. She had no surgical instruments, but she had strong teeth. Kneeling, she clamped them around the protruding thorn and drew it out.

The native was deeply impressed and grateful. The next day he and his wife sought and found God's forgiveness. They became active Salvationists.

* * *

Traditional Evangelism

Dr. Colin W. Williams, parish and community life director of the National Council of Churches, said, "Billy Graham's traditional evangelism has a method and message which hold the church in conservatism. It encourages the acceptance of conservative attitudes in American culture without subjecting them to critical examination in the light of the gospel."

The only hope for our morally and spiritually confused world, if the Lord should delay His coming, is a return to traditional evangelism, or the old-time religion. The world sorely needs gospel-saturated preaching by God-called, Spirit-endued preachers—men who know no fear other than the fear of incurring God's displeasure.

Let us say with Paul, "I determined not to know any thing . . . save Jesus Christ, and him crucified" (I Cor. 2:2).

What Charles Darwin Said

Years ago a Christian layman wanted to conduct services in Kent, where Charles Darwin lived and had established a reading room. The layman wrote a letter to the naturalist, asking permission to use the room for religious services. Darwin replied, "You ought not to have to write to me for permission to use the reading room. You have far more right to it than we have, for you have done more for the town than all our efforts for many years. We have never been able to reclaim a drunkard, but through your services, I do not know that there is a drunkard left in the town. Now I have the pleasure of turning the reading room over to you."

* * *

Compromising the Gospel

A man was leading his donkey. His son was walking alongside the donkey. When a stranger scolded the son for letting his old father walk, the father mounted the animal. When another stranger scolded the father for riding while his son walked, the father took his son up with him. Finally, when both of them were chided for riding such a small beast, they got off and carried the donkey. Then, while crossing a bridge, they tripped, and the donkey fell into the stream.

Compromising to suit enemies, we lose friends. Compromising to suit friends, we make enemies. Compromising the gospel, we lose it. Sharing the gospel with the have-nots, we keep it.

Prairie Overcomer

* * *

The Gospel in Action

A Muslim servant accompanied a missionary in Africa on a car trip. The missionary tried in vain to explain the truths of the gospel to the Muslim.

When they were stopped by car trouble, they tried frantically to wave down a passing truck carrying two Africans, but to no avail.

After a while, the missionary was able to get his car started again. They had not gone far when they came upon the stalled truck of the two Africans who had failed to respond to their plea for help.

The Muslim chortled gleefully, "Now we can pay those fellows back in kind. They passed us up and now we'll pass them up."

"Oh, no," said the missionary. "We must stop and help these men."

After they had given aid and were on their way again, the boy said solemnly to the missionary, "Sir, now I begin to understand what you have been trying to tell me all along."

The follower of Islam had seen the gospel in action.

Adapted from *World Vision*

* * *

Mankind's Only Hope

How factual and revealing of the futility of getting rid of evils without a change of heart is Hawthorne's story *Earth's Holocaust*. The inhabitants of the earth, burdened with an accumulation of vain, deceptive, paltry things, determined to get rid of them in a general bonfire. Throughout the night, they tossed things they considered sinful on the fire—obscene books, implements of war, liquor, tobacco and various other evils. Late in the night, someone who had watched the procedure with a cynical smile approached and said, "There is one thing that you have failed to throw into the fire without which the rest of the conflagration amounts to nothing, though you may burn the earth itself to cinders."

Someone asked, "And what may that be?"

"*The human heart,*" was the reply. "Unless you devise some method of purifying that foul cavern, there will issue from it all the evils you have consumed to ashes and vastly worse ones."

The heart-transforming gospel of Christ with its application to earth's sins and sorrows is mankind's only hope.

GREATNESS, GOD'S

"Marvelous Are Thy Works"

Mrs. Charles E. Cowman said, "Look through the telescope at the millions of stars and planets whirling through space —myriads of systems in which our little earth is but a single grain of sand in a sandstorm. The One who is responsible for the amazing energy and orderliness of all that dazzling universe is God—a powerful and intelligent God at work.

"Look into a microscope at a cross section of a blade of grass or a snippet of an insect's wing. All is as orderly as the movements of the planets and stars in their infinite spaces, yet incredibly intricate and exquisite. The source of the tiniest forms of life that swarm in billions unseen under one's feet in the grass, or through the woods, or along a country road, is God—the God of all life everywhere."

In wonder and adoration, we exclaim, "How great Thou art!"

Only God Could Have Conceived It

In relating the change in a woman physician's attitude toward God, the *Atlantic Monthly* quoted her thus: "In an anatomy room, a dead body meant nothing at all to me. I could not visualize the man or woman it might have been. Life left few records on the immobile face. For weeks I worked, and each day the wonder grew. Then, one day, I was working on an arm and hand, studying the perfect mechanical arrangements of the muscles and tendons—how the sheaths of certain muscles are split to let tendons of certain muscles through, so that the hand may be delicate and small and yet powerful. I was all alone in the laboratory when the overwhelming belief came: a thing like this is not just chance, but a part of a plan, a plan so big that only God could have conceived it.

"Religion had been to me a matter of form, a thing without conviction, and now

135

everything was an evidence of God—the tendons of the hand, the patterns of the little butterfly's wings—all was a part of a purpose."

The psalmist wrote, "I am fearfully and wonderfully made: marvellous are thy works" (Ps. 139:14).

GROWTH

Unhitch Yourself

A friend of mine preached a searching sermon in which he happened to offend a lady. She afterward said to him, "I want you to know that I have been standing at my post in this church for forty years."

The friend, who at times spoke roughly to people—and possibly justifiably—said, "It's time you unhitched yourself and got going!"

PAUL REES

* * *

Spiritual Exercise

Dr. Herman K. Hellerstein of Western Reserve University, who is one of the world's leading authorities on cardiovascular diseases, reported, "Americans are suffering from hypokinetic disease—a vicious circle of little activity, which produces still greater inability for activity. Mechanization is making us a fat, lazy, indolent, bored society of people who are aging prematurely. It is no joke that after thirty years of age, when men and women need exercise most, they think they are too old for it. Exercise adds many more useful years to life, counteracts mental stress, and induces sleep better than any known tranquilizer. Good muscle tone improves the efficiency of all bodily functions and will help add years to your life."

As bodily exercise is essential to physical health, so is spiritual exercise essential to the spiritual health and well-being of God's children: "Exercise thyself . . . unto godliness. . . . Godliness is profitable unto all things, having promise of the life that now is, and of that which is to come" (I Tim. 4:7-8).

"It Might Have Been"

In the diamond mines of South Africa, there is often found a substance which is half charcoal and half diamond. This substance didn't fulfill its intended purpose. It will never adorn a king's crown.

For some unknown cause, this substance, in its developmental state, failed to become what it might have become.

Some of God's children stop short of what God intends them to be. They fail to "go on unto perfection" (Heb. 6:1).

For of all sad words of tongue or pen,
The saddest are these: "It might have been."

C. LESLIE MILLER

* * *

Renounce Righteous Self

A young minister talked with a humble layman who asked, "What do you consider the greatest hindrance to spiritual growth?"

The minister replied, "A failure to renounce our *sinful self*."

"No, no," quickly replied the layman, "the greatest hindrance to spiritual growth is our failure to renounce our *righteous self*, and acknowledge that all our righteousnesses, apart from Christ, are as filthy rags in His sight."

Pride was the primeval sin and it began in heaven (cf. Isa. 14:12-13).

* * *

"Let Us Go On"

The motto of the French "Foreign Legion" is:

If I falter, push me on;

136

If I stumble, pick me up;
If I retreat, shoot me!

The Bible says that God has no pleasure in them that draw back. God's command to His children is "Let us go on unto perfection" (Heb. 6:1).

* * *

Kindergarten Christians

Dr. Paul S. Rees stated, "Christians of forty years' duration can still be kindergarten Christians, with an appalling exhibition of arrested development. On the other hand, Christians a month old or less can be astonishingly mature if only their wills are wholly surrendered and their personalities possessed by the Spirit of God."

"Let us go on unto perfection" (Heb. 6:1).

* * *

He Died Climbing

"He died climbing" is the simple inscription on a monument erected to an Alpine guide who perished when attempting the ascent of a peak. What a tribute this was to a noble hero!

Like the climber we should always be looking upward and pressing onward: "Let us go on unto perfection" (Heb. 6:1).

"He died climbing" could be said of Alexander Mackay, who was soon cut off in Uganda; of Bishop James Hannington, who reached the border of the same land and was martyred there; of John Patterson, who was slain in Melanesia by islanders who mistook him for a slave-catching captain; and of the five young missionaries—Youdarian, Saint, Elliot, Fleming and McCully—who were killed by the Auca Indians.

"He died climbing" could be said of Henry Martyn, who did not live to see the results of his labor of love; and of Wycliffe, who sent forth the Bible in England, but did not live to see the Reformation.

* * *

I Long to Know Him Better

For some time Frances Havergal yearned to know Christ better and become more rapidly conformed to His image. She confided to a friend, "I long for deeper, fuller teaching. I know I love Jesus but I want to come nearer to Him. I want to know the power of His resurrection. I want to know the depth of His love."

"The people that do know their God shall be strong, and do exploits" (Dan. 11:32).

* * *

Rigor Mortis of the Personality

General Douglas MacArthur averred, "Life is a lively process of becoming. If you haven't added to your interest during the past year; if you are thinking the same thoughts, relating the same personal experiences, having the same predictable reactions—rigor mortis of the personality has set in."

Paul said, "Forgetting those things which are behind, and reaching forth unto those things which are before, I press toward the mark for the prize of the high calling of God in Christ Jesus" (Phil. 3:13-14).

* * *

The Shallows of Purposeless Existence

The challenging command "Launch out into the deep," given by Christ to the luckless fishermen long ago, and the divine command "Dwell deep," given to the inhabitants of Dedan, are God's commands to His children today. Launch out into the depth of God's boundless love. Sever the ties which hold you in the shallows of a purposeless existence.

* * *

"Let Us Go On"

A friend asked Longfellow the secret of his continued interest in life. Pointing to a nearby apple tree, he said, "The purpose of that apple tree is to grow a little new wood each year. That is what I plan to do."

Longfellow also expressed the thought poetically:

Not enjoyment and not sorrow
Is our destined end or way;
But to live that each tomorrow
Finds us further than today.

137

The Christian life must be a continuous progress toward perfection: "Let us cleanse ourselves from all filthiness of the flesh and spirit, perfecting holiness in the fear of God" (II Cor. 7:1).

* * *

An Oak or a Squash

"I don't believe my son will have time to take a four-year course," said a father as he and his son sat in the office of James A. Garfield, president of Hiram College. "Could you provide him with a shorter course?"

"Why, yes," replied Garfield, "I think I can. But it depends on what you want to make of him. When God wants to make an oak, He takes hundreds of years. But when He wants to grow a squash, He takes only three months!"

GUIDANCE

(*See also* Will of God)

If Someone Had Guided Them Right

A certain boy in a Sunday school made things very difficult for his teachers. The last one went to the superintendent and submitted the ultimatum "Either that boy goes or I will go. Take your choice." The superintendent escorted the boy to the door and said, "There's the street. Go! And don't you come back to this Sunday school."

The boy went into a life of crime which has possibly never been paralleled in the history of the nation. He left a trail of blood behind him wherever he went. Fabulous rewards were offered for his capture, either dead or alive. At last, one night, as he emerged from a Chicago theater, a hail of bullets riddled his body!

In one of the Chicago papers a most intriguing picture appeared. It showed only the feet of the criminal. In bold type the caption read: "These are the feet of John Dillinger." It was followed by the searching question "Who knows where these feet might have gone if someone had guided them right?"

Told by C. LESLIE MILLER

* * *

Guided Steps

Child of my love, fear not the unknown
　　morrow,
　　Dread not the new demand life makes
　　　of thee;
Thy ignorance doth hold no cause for sor-
　　row,
　　Since what thou knowest not is known
　　　to Me.

One step thou seest, then go forward
　　boldly,
One step is far enough for faith to see;
Take that, and thy next duty shall be
　　told thee,
　　For step by step the Lord is leading
　　　thee.

"The steps of a good man are ordered by the LORD" (Ps. 37:23)

* * *

Beware of Shortcuts

Dr. William Culbertson said, "God does not always lead His children in the shortest way, but sometimes in the longest way. Israel's experience during the exodus illustrates this fact: 'God led them not through the way . . . that was near; . . . God led the people about, through the way of the wilderness' " (Exodus 13:17-18).

* * *

"I Have Gone Astray"

One wintry night in London, Charles Kingsley was suddenly enveloped in a dense, pea-soup fog. He was lost several times as he groped his way through the murky darkness. He said as he trudged along, "Isn't this like life—a deep fog all around, with a dim light shining through the gloom? We proceed from one light to another. Sometimes we take the wrong way. Sometimes we go astray. Then we turn back and plead, 'I have gone astray like a lost sheep; seek thy servant' (Ps. 119:176), but we reach the heavenly home at last: 'He bringeth them unto their desired haven' (107:30)."

138

Pea-Soup Fog

Early one morning I received an urgent call to go to a distant hospital. During the night, a pea-soup fog had blanketed Chicago's South Side. When I went to the garage for my car, I became alarmed as I thought of the shadowy, half-hidden dangers I would encounter on the drive to the hospital. With cautious apprehension, I backed my car into the street. As I drove slowly along, I soon observed that the indistinct, distant objects became clearly visible when I reached them. My fears subsided.

I thought, *How like the will of God! As we move forward, often going under sealed orders, God's directing guideposts become clearly visible. The indistinct, unknown ones radiate when we come to them.*

Our steps—and our stops, too—are ordered of the Lord.

W. B. K.

* * *

Let's Go to Church and Sunday School

J. Edgar Hoover said, in *The Message of the Cross,* "Shall I force my child to go to Sunday school and church? Yes! And with no further discussion about that matter. Are you startled? Why?

"How do you answer Junior when he comes to the breakfast table Monday morning and says rebelliously, 'I'm not going to school today'? You know Junior goes. How do you answer when Junior comes in very much besmudged and says, 'I'm not going to take a bath'? You know Junior bathes. How do you answer when Junior, threatened with illness, says, 'I'm not going to take medicine'? You know he takes it.

"Why all this timidity, then, in the matter of his spiritual guidance and growth? Are you afraid he'll succumb to the old wives' tale about too much religion when he was young? This story is demonstrably and obviously false despite its currency. Do you suppose that because you insist over Junior's protests that he take a bath tonight he will refuse to bathe when he becomes twenty-one?

"What shall we say when Junior announces he doesn't like Sunday school or church? That's an easy one. Just be consistent. Just say, 'Junior, in our home we all attend Sunday school and church, and that includes you.' Your firmness and example will furnish a bridge over which youthful rebellion may travel into rich and satisfying experiences in personal Christian living.

"The parents of America can strike a most effective blow against the forces which contribute to juvenile delinquency if our fathers and mothers will *take their children to Sunday school and church regularly.*"

* * *

Steps and Stops

There is a Chinese proverb which says "A journey of a thousand miles begins with the first step."

How bright our path is when our steps and our stops are directed by God: "The path of the just is as the shining light, that shineth more and more unto the perfect day" (Prov. 4:18).

Guide me, O Thou great Jehovah,
  Pilgrim through this barren land;
I am weak, but Thou art mighty,
  Hold me with Thy powerful hand.

* * *

Trackless Ways

"Where is the road?" asked a missionary of an African guide when they came to the trackless desert sands where there was no path of any kind.

With a reproving glance, the guide proudly replied, "I am the road."

Sometimes God's children travel along a trackless way. They do not know which way to go. How assuring are the words of the One who said, "I am the way" (John 14:6). He leads His followers when they cannot see the way.

Adapted from *King's Business*

* * *

I Need Thee

I need Thee, loving Shepherd,
  I need Thy constant care,
So guide me on life's journey,
  And all the way prepare.

I need Thine arms around me,
  To hold me lest I fall;
O more and more I need Thee,
  My only hope, my all.

139

More than Guided Missiles

Dr. W. B. Criswell commented, "We have learned to split the atom but not unite the haman family. To be better off is not to be better. Guided men and women are more urgently needed than guided missiles. Beneath all our boasted attainments, there must be the sure foundation of spiritual values. Without them, our nation will decay and go the way which the mighty nations of the past went."

HEALING

The Great Physician

Dr. A. B. Simpson once reported, "I visited a man during what I believed to be his dying moments. Simply I explained to him the way of eternal life in Christ. Joyfully the man accepted Christ. Seldom have I witnessed a more joyful conversion. The glory of heaven shone upon his face. He began to sing the songs of Zion which, I believed, would soon be sung by him in heaven.

" 'I'll be seeing you in glory by and by,' I said as I left the man. But to the amazement of his physicians, God willed otherwise. The next morning the man was decidedly improved. In a few days he was entirely well. The joy of the Lord became his strength. His merry heart and great faith in the healing power of the great physician, Jesus, wrought wondrously."

* * *

Spiritually Healthy

Plato warned, "Neither ought you to attempt to cure the body without the soul. The part can never be well without the whole."

Spiritual health is conducive to physical health: "A merry heart doeth good like a medicine: but a broken spirit drieth the bones" (Prov. 17:22).

* * *

A Funeral That Didn't Materialize

Dr. V. Raymond Edman testified, "I am a witness of God's healing power to raise one from imminent death. There was the day and hour when, as a missionary in Ecuador, I was given up for dead because of typhus fever. The American doctor had stated that he could detect very little evidence of life, and had urged that the chairman of the mission immediately secure a coffin, and make preparation for the funeral service.

"In the tropics one must be buried within a matter of hours. A coffin was purchased, and the elders of the little church were called to be the pallbearers. Mrs. Edman dyed her wedding dress black for the funeral service.

"Then the Spirit of God put intercession upon a group of Christians meeting in a Bible conference in Massachusetts. They had no knowledge of my need. God gave them believing prayer. I have met many in New England who have told me that, should they live one hundred years, they will never forget that all-day prayer meeting when intercession with tears and deep feeling was made for me.

"As a result of that prayer, there was no funeral service in Ecuador. The coffin was sold, and friend wife used the pieces of the wedding dress, then black, for other purposes. I have had more than thirty-five years of 'borrowed time' since then. The Lord is good."

* * *

Religious Outlook Necessary

Dr. Carl Jung, famed psychologist, said, "Among all my patients, in the long run, none has been really healed who did not regain his religious outlook."

140

HEAVEN

The Last Run

Recently a city newspaper showed the picture of a railroad engineer descending the steps of his engine after his last run. He had made many friends along his run. Many years of faithful service lay behind him. He was held in high esteem by his employers. They spoke glowing words of commendation to him, and gave him a gold watch as a token of their appreciation for faithful service rendered. His joy and satisfaction far outweighed any sorrow he felt because his work had ended. His last run was crowned with glory and honor.

Shouldn't it be the same with us when we make our last run and bid farewell to friends and loved ones? Shouldn't we so run life's race and fight life's battles that when we come to our journey's end, we can say, "I have fought a good fight, I have finished my course, I have kept the faith" (II Tim. 4:7)?

When we make our last earthly run, we may have little of this world's goods. The world may not speak words of commendation. We may even be bereft of friends and loved ones. Still we can rejoice. Think of meeting the Lord and the dear ones who died in the Lord!

* * *

My House Is Waiting

A missionary visiting a Pygmy village in Africa recognized a man to whom he had previously given a Bible. "Have you received God's Word into your heart?" he asked.

"Yes, I have, and my people have received it, too. Every night we meet for prayer. We sing 'Jesus Loves Me' and 'What Can Wash Away My Sins?' Then we ask God to protect us through the night."

"That's fine," said the missionary. Then he asked, "If you should die, would you go to heaven?"

The Pygmy stood at attention, saluted smartly and replied, "When I die, I will go straight to God's village. I will salute Him and say, 'Greetings, God! I have come to my house in Your village!' When God asks me what right I have to enter, I will tell Him that His Son, Jesus Christ, died for me and that I have received Him as my Saviour. Then God will say to me, 'Enter into the joys of your Lord! Your house is waiting for you!' "

* * *

"I've Been Within the Gates!"

A few hours before Dwight L. Moody triumphantly departed to be forever with the Lord, he, like Stephen, got a glimpse of the Homeland: "I see the heavens opened, and the Son of man standing on the right hand of God" (Acts 7:56).

Moody exclaimed, "Earth recedes! Heaven opens before me! If this is death, it is sweet! There is no valley here. God is calling and I must go!"

"No!" said a son at his bedside. "You are dreaming, Father."

Moody replied, "I am not dreaming. I have been within the gates, and I have seen the children's faces. This is my triumph! This is my coronation day! It is glorious!"

* * *

Toward the Sunrise

How thrilling and awe-inspiring it is to fly over the ocean into the sunrise! Boarding a plane in Toronto near midnight and flying toward London, we met the rising sun over the ocean two and a half hours later. It cast a golden glow on the sky, the plane and the clouds below. I sat in reverential silence, thinking about the greatness of God and the marvels of His creation.

God's children are journeying toward the sunrise. For His children, the best is yet to be: "Eye hath not seen, nor ear heard . . . the things which God hath prepared for them that love him" (I Cor. 2:9).

* * *

Looking for the Sunrise

I'm not looking for the sunset,
  As the swift years come and go;
I am looking for the sunrise,
  And the golden morning glow,

Where the light of heaven's glory
  Will break forth upon my sight
In the land that knows no sunset,
  Nor the darkness of the night.

I'm not going down the pathway
  Toward the setting of the sun,
Where the shadows ever deepen
  When the day at last is done;
I am walking up the hillside
  Where the sunshine lights the way
To the glory of the sunrise
  Of God's never-ending day.

I'm not going down, but upward,
  And the path is never dim,
For the day grows ever brighter
  As I journey on with Him.
So my eyes are on the hilltops,
  Waiting for the sun to rise,
Waiting for His invitation
  To the home beyond the skies.

ALBERT SIMPSON REITZ, in
Moody Monthly

* * *

Hallelujah to the Lamb!

Shortly before his tragic death, P. P. Bliss wrote the praiseful song "Hallelujah! What a Saviour!"

Man of sorrows! What a name
For the Son of God who came
Ruined sinners to reclaim!
Hallelujah! What a Saviour!

In commenting on the hymn, Ira D. Sankey said, "It seems as though God prepared it for the great jubilee of heaven when His children shall gather to sing 'Hallelujah to the Lamb!'"

* * *

Jesus Is Our Dragoman

Often in the deserts of the Near East, long trains of camels are seen plodding through the trackless sands and burning heat. Preceding the camels and their drivers is the dragoman, or professional guide for travelers. He is often an advance man, and arranges for a resting place for the oncoming tired, hungry and thirsty caravan. When the resting place is reached, food, drink and lodging have been arranged by the dragoman.

Weymouth translates the "many mansions" Jesus spoke of as "many resting places." Jesus is our Dragoman, who has gone before us to make provision for us. When we reach our eternal abode, our resting place will be awaiting us: "There remaineth therefore a rest to the people of God" (Heb. 4:9). He awaits us in glory to receive us unto Himself, "and so shall we ever be with the Lord!"

* * *

Broad-mindedness

Said Billy Graham, "We often hear the plea for broad-mindedness. There is no room for broad-mindedness in the chemical laboratory. Water is composed of two parts hydrogen and one part oxygen. The slightest deviation from the formula is forbidden. There is no room for broad-mindedness in music. There can be only eight notes in an octave. The skilled director will not permit his first violin to play even so much as one-half of a note off the written note, chord and key. There is no room for broad-mindedness in mathematics. Neither geometry, calculus nor trigonometry allows any variation from exact accuracy.

"There is no room for broad-mindedness in morals or religion. There is but one way to heaven: 'I am the way: . . . no man cometh unto the Father, but by me'" (John 14:6).

* * *

"Out of the Mouth of Babes"

A mother was greatly grieved because of the death of her baby boy. Little June, observing her sadness, asked, "Mommy, why are you sad?"

Her mother replied, "My dear little girl, I am sad because I have lost my dear baby. He is in heaven with Jesus."

A serious look came over June's face. She said, "But, Mommy, if you know where he is, he isn't lost, is he?"

ALICE MARIE KNIGHT

* * *

From a Loved One in Heaven

I would not have you grieve for me today
  Nor weep beside my vacant chair;

142

Could you but know my daily portion
  here
  You would not, could not, wish me
    there.

I know now why He said, "Ear hath not
    heard!"
  I have no words, no alphabet,
Or even if I had I dare not tell,
  Because you could not bear it yet.

So, only this—I am the same, though
    changed,
  Like Him! A joy more rich and strong
Than I had dreamed that any heart
    could hold,
  And all my life is one glad song.

Sometimes when you are talking to our
    Lord
  He turns and speaks to me. . . . Dear
    heart,
In that rare moment you and I are just
  The distance of a word apart!

And so, my loved ones, do not grieve for
    me
  Around the family board today;
Instead rejoice, for we are one in Him,
  And so I am not far away!

MARTHA SNELL NICHOLSON

* * *

Money Put in Lifeless Hands

Gypsy king Alex Mitchell died recently at age sixty-three. More than one thousand of his "subjects," relatives and friends from twenty-five states attended his funeral. They were regaled in colorful garments, some with rings in their ears.

The king's body was interred in Bedford, Ohio. At the wake in the funeral home, on the night before his burial, more than three hundred Gypsies sang boisterously, told stories and drank liquor. They were not disorderly, however. Weeping was observed only when the casket was closed for the last time.

Before the casket was closed, the king's friends and relatives stuffed it with coins and currency. They placed one hundred dollars in bills in his hands. "The money will buy the king's entry into heaven," the Gypsies said. They refused the mortician's offer to write a check for the money and bury the check with the body instead of the money.

Money cannot buy one's entry into heaven. There is only one way to enter into heaven. Jesus said, "I am the way: . . . no man cometh unto the Father, but by me" (John 14:6).

  Nothing in my hand I bring:
  Simply to Thy cross I cling.

* * *

An Enduring Repository

An unusual story was told in newspapers across the nation. Charles H. Manning died a millionaire, though he had worked only one month as a stock clerk. Little is known about him. He died in a retirement home in St. Louis, Missouri. His fortune went to his only known relative, a cousin, William E. Haren. Haren said Manning's wealth probably came from wise investments made by his mother.

After we die, others will become the recipients of all our earthly possessions: "For we brought nothing into this world, and it is certain we can carry nothing out" (I Tim. 6:7).

The safest and only enduring repository for riches is heaven. How wise are those who obey the command of the Saviour: "Lay not up . . . treasures upon earth: . . . but lay up for yourselves treasures in heaven" (Matt. 6:19-20).

In death, the unsaved *leave* their riches. In death, God's children *go to* their riches.

* * *

Homesick for Heaven

In the quiet of the evening
  As I lay me down to rest,
My soul went out in longing
  For the homeland of the blest.

And I almost saw the city
  With the loved ones waiting there,
And the burdens of life grew lighter,
  As I breathed my evening prayer.

JOHN M. BAKER

"God's Tomorrow"

On Rally Day, as A. H. Ackley stood before a large audience to deliver a carefully planned message, the words "God's tomorrow! God's tomorrow!" began to flash through his mind, obliterating all thought of his prepared address. The words so fully filled his thoughts that he spoke to the Rally Day audience on heaven.

After the service, Mr. Ackley went to the parsonage next door. Later he told what happened: "The beautiful words 'God's tomorrow' were ringing like a sweet bell in my soul! I sat down at the piano and the melody and the words of the hymn 'God's Tomorrow' came spontaneously."

God's tomorrow is a day of gladness,
And its joys shall never fade;
No more weeping, no more sense of sadness,
No more foes to make afraid.

God's tomorrow is a day of greeting:
We shall see the Saviour's face;
And our longing hearts await the meeting
In that holy, happy place!

* * *

Property Fire Can't Touch

A Christian family lost all their possessions in a disastrous fire. The family was visited by John Newton. His words of greeting were unusual. "I give you joy," he said.

The mother replied, "What? Joy when all our earthly belongings are gone?"

Newton said, "Oh, no, but joy that you have so much enduring property that fire cannot touch."

God's children have enduring riches in heaven "where neither moth nor rust doth corrupt, and where thieves do not break through nor steal" (Matt. 6:20).

* * *

What He Saw and Felt at Death's Door

David Snell has given an account of his thoughts and feelings as death, because of an anaphylactic shock, began in his toes and fingers and crept upward through his legs and arms, then into his abdomen and chest.

There is order and system in death, as in all that is life. I must try to control the progression, to save the brain for last, so that I may know, he thought.

Just before a shot of adrenalin reversed death's encroachment, he felt and experienced ineffable joy, and saw things of indescribable beauty. He says, "There was something I felt or experienced, at the very last instant. It was there, opening before me, something more beautiful, more gentle, more loving than the mind or imagination of a living creature could ever conceive!"

Could it be that Snell saw and heard what Dwight L. Moody saw and heard as he entered the valley of death? Moody exclaimed, "Earth is receding, heaven is opening. God is calling!"

In relating one of his wonderful experiences, Paul said, "I knew a man in Christ . . . (whether in the body . . . or whether out of the body, I cannot tell: God knoweth;) such an one [was] caught up to the third heaven . . . and heard unspeakable words, which it is not lawful for a man to utter" (II Cor. 12:2-4).

Great and indescribably glorious things await God's children when they pass from this life: "Eye hath not seen, nor ear heard, neither have entered into the heart of man, the things which God hath prepared for them that love him" (I Cor. 2:9).

* * *

Bells Chimed for Him

Dion de Marbelle lived a checkered life. He was a sailor in the United States Navy and a soldier in the Mexican and Civil wars. For a while, he was associated with James Anthony Bailey of the Barnum and Bailey Circus. He also toured America as a singer with an opera company, a magician, and a ventriloquist.

When beyond sixty years of age, Marbelle became a circus clown. A newspaper commented, "He could make people laugh and he laughed with them." Later he teamed up with Colonel William Cody, who was better known as "Buffalo Bill."

In time, the tables turned adversely for Marbelle. He lost everything except his faith in God which enabled him to survive every shock.

144

When a year short of seventy, Marbelle did something which immortalized his memory. He wrote the hymn "When They Ring Those Golden Bells."

There's a land beyond the river,
That we call the sweet forever,
And we only reach that shore by faith's decree;
One by one we'll gain the portals,
There to dwell with the immortals,
When they ring those golden bells for you and me.

During the last three years of his life, Marbelle lived in obscurity and poverty. He would have died of starvation if kind neighbors had not brought him food. As he neared death's portals, he seemed to hear heaven's bells chiming for him:

Don't you hear the bells now ringing?
Don't you hear the angels singing?
'Tis the glory hallelujah jubilee,
In that far-off sweet forever,
Just beyond the shining river,
When they ring those golden bells for you and me.

* * *

Here and There

Here we labor, here we pray,
Here we wrestle night and day,
Here the battle rages sore,
Here the tempter ne'er gives o'er;

There we rest from toil and pain,
There all losses turn to gain,
There we lay our burdens down,
There we wear the victor's crown.

J. C. MACAULAY

* * *

I'll See You Soon

Little four-year-old Kathy Sansovini of Minneapolis was stricken with a rare muscular disease called *dermatomyositis*. The story of her faith and courage went into the homes and hearts of many people throughout the midwest. The *Minneapolis Morning Tribune* carried a front-page feature story about her and also her picture.

Kathy prayed that the Lord would heal her, but the Lord in infinite wisdom took her to heaven to be with Him. Two days before her passing, she said to her father, "Daddy, I'm going to heaven. I'm going to be with Jesus!"

He asked, "How do you know, Kathy?"

She replied, "The Lord seemed to tell me so last night."

Kathy's two-year-old brother, looking into the starlit sky one evening shortly after Kathy's death, said, "Hi, Kathy! See you pretty soon!"

* * *

"Walking Steadily into the Sunrise"

An aged Methodist minister gave a heart-touching testimony in a conference. He concluded with this confident statement: "The end of my days here is not sunset for me, but sunrise! The end of this life is not death, but resurrection unto eternal life. When God calls me home, it will be only a transition—the continuation of life eternal. I am walking steadily into the sunrise!"

The aged minister's testimony so impressed and inspired William C. Poole that he wrote the song "Sunrise." B. D. Ackley composed the music for the words:

When I shall come to the end of my way,
When I shall rest at the close of life's day,
When "Welcome Home" I shall hear Jesus say,
Oh, that will be sunrise for me!

* * *

Forever with the Lord

As one of God's servants neared the sunset gate of life, a friend, wanting to cheer and comfort him, said, "I want to read you the sweetest verse in the Bible." Then he read, "In my Father's house are many mansions: if it were not so, I would have told you" (John 14:2).

The dying man said, "Though that verse abounds in comfort, it isn't the sweetest verse. The next verse is the one I most cherish. It fills my heart with joyful anticipation and confident hope: 'And if I go and prepare a place for you, I will come again, and receive you unto myself; that where I am, there ye may be also.' Soon I shall awaken with Jesus' likeness in glory and be forever with my Lord!"

Paul said, "We are . . . willing . . . to be absent from the body, and to be present with the Lord" (II Cor. 5:8).

Prairie Overcomer

* * *

The Set of the Sail

I stood on the shore beside the sea,
The wind from the west blew fresh and free,
While past the rocks at the harbor's mouth,
The ships went north and the ships went south.
And some sailed out on an unknown quest,
And some sailed in to the harbor's rest,
Yet ever the wind blew out of the west.

I said to one who had sailed the sea
That this was a marvel unto me,
For how can the ships go safely forth,
Some to the south and some to the north,
Far out to sea on their golden quest,
Or in to the harbor's calm and rest,
And ever the wind blew out of the west?

The sailor smiled as he answered me,
"Go where you will when you're on the sea,
Though head winds baffle and squalls delay,
You can keep the course by night and day;
Drive with the breeze or against the gale,
It will not matter what winds prevail,
For all depends on the set of the sail."

Oh, set your sail to the heavenly gale,
And then, no matter what winds prevail,
No reef shall wreck you, nor calm delay,
No mist shall hinder, no storm shall stay;
Though far you wander and long you roam,
Through salt sea spray and o'er white sea foam,
No wind that can blow but shall speed you Home.

* * *

Will You Be There?

"When the Roll Is Called up Yonder" is a favorite revival hymn. It was written by J. M. Black.

Mr. Black was the leader of a youth group. One evening the youths responded to the roll call by quoting verses of Scripture. All quoted a verse except a young woman. Mr. Black was greatly impressed with the thought of how sad it would be if any of the teenagers should not be present to respond to their name when called in heaven.

He said to them, "When your name is called in heaven, will you be there to respond to it?"

As he walked home, he longed for a hymn to express the thought of the question he had asked the youths: "When your name is called in heaven, will you be there to respond to it?"

Upon reaching his home, he wrote:

When the trumpet of the Lord shall sound and time shall be no more,
And the morning breaks, eternal, bright and fair;
When the saved of earth shall gather over on the other shore,
And the roll is called up yonder,
I'll be there!

* * *

Strangers and Pilgrims

In late afternoon, as we sped wearily along a highway, yearning to reach our destination after traveling all day, we observed a tantalizing sign in front of a cozy home which read: "If you lived here, you'd be at home now!"

This world is not the Christian's permanent home: "Here we have no continuing city, but we seek one to come" (Heb. 13:14). Here we are "strangers and pilgrims" (Heb. 11:13). This world is the land of the *dying:* "In Adam all die" (I Cor. 15:22). Heaven is the land of the *living:* "And there shall be no more death" (Rev. 21:4).

How wise we are in obeying the scriptural directives: "Lay up for yourselves treasures in heaven" (Matt. 6:20); "Seek those things which are above. . . . Set your affection on things above, where Christ sitteth on the right hand of God" (Col. 3:1-2).

Joyful obedience to these injunctions makes us better Christians, better fathers and mothers, better brothers and sisters, better neighbors and citizens.

This world is not my home,
I'm just apassing through,
My treasures are laid up
Somewhere beyond the blue!

HOLY SPIRIT

(See also Power)

Noisy Sensationalism

A. W. Tozer said, "God's great works are carried on silently. The planets move noiselessly in their orbits. The dewdrops form themselves quietly on the summer grass. The light of the morning breaks softly over the earth. The sun rises without sound.

"Let us have more confidence in spiritual movements which are undemonstrative but constant, and different from noisy sensationalism. Let's put more faith in the still small voice of the Spirit than in the earthquake."

"In quietness and in confidence shall be thy strength" (Isa. 30:15).

* * *

Miracles of Grace

Spurgeon said, "Miracles of grace must be the seals of our ministry. Who can bestow them but the Spirit of God? Failure to recognize the power of the Holy Spirit lies at the root of many useless ministries. A very important part of our lives consists in praying in the Holy Spirit."

* * *

Wholly Unable to Understand

William Wilberforce was a great Christian statesman. He did much to abolish slavery throughout the British Empire.

At one time Wilberforce became greatly interested in the spiritual welfare of his friend William Pitt, who was the prime minister of England. He induced Pitt to attend with him a meeting in which Lord Cecil was preaching. After the meeting, Wilberforce asked, "What did you think of the sermon?"

Pitt replied, "To tell the truth, I gave that man my most careful attention from start to finish, but I was wholly unable to understand what he was talking about."

The Bible says, "But the natural man receiveth not the things of the Spirit of God: . . . neither can he know them, because they are spiritually discerned" (I Cor. 2:14).

Why God Used Him

Prayer and utter dependence upon God are the explanation of the work of David Brainerd, missionary to the Indians. In the depths of the forest, he spent whole days in prayer.

Brainerd was unable to speak the language of the savages, so he sought for someone who could interpret his messages to the Indians. One day he preached through an interpreter who was so intoxicated that he could hardly stand up. Yet some of the Indians were convicted through Brainerd's Bible-centered, Spirit-empowered message.

Is anything too hard for God to do in us and through us when we depend totally upon His help and are endued with power from on high?

* * *

The Reason for Spiritual Dwarfage

A minister sent one of his helpers to counsel with a young woman who had been defeated and dwarfed in her Christian life. The counselor silently asked God for wisdom in dealing with the young woman. She soon confessed, "I am a Christian, but have made little or no progress in my Christian life. I lapse into worldly ways so easily. God has revealed to me the reason for my defeat and lack of joy. I have never known anything about the keeping and sustaining power of the Holy Spirit in my life. Do please help me and tell me everything you can that will enable me to be the kind of Christian God wants me to be."

Hudson Taylor said, "The Holy Spirit enters, in His fullness, the heart that can boast of nothing but an aching void."

"And to know the love of Christ, which passeth knowledge, that ye might be filled with all the fulness of God" (Eph. 3:19).

* * *

Spiritual Crisis

My father was a doctor in the horse-and-buggy days, long before the discovery of the wonder drugs, the antibiotics. Often

147

he would wait at the bedside of a patient until the crisis had passed. Reminiscent of such scenes is Luke Field's painting of a doctor, absorbed and patient, sitting at the bedside of a critically ill child. In the shadows stand a solicitous father and mother—hoping and praying.

There is a spiritual crisis in the life of each one—a time when the soul hovers between spiritual life and spiritual death, a time when the Holy Spirit convicts us of sin. It is hazardous for us to suppress His wooing: "My Spirit shall not always strive with man" (Gen. 6:3).

* * *

Spirit of the Living God

O Spirit of the living God,
  In all Thy plentitude of grace,
Where'er the foot of man hath trod,
  Descend on our apostate race.

Give tongues of fire and hearts of love,
  To preach the reconciling word,
Give power and unction from above,
  Where'er the joyful sound is heard.

O Spirit of the Lord, prepare
  All the round earth her God to meet,
Breathe Thou abroad like morning air,
  Till hearts of stone begin to beat.

JAMES MONTGOMERY

* * *

A Present Reality

At the opening of the Second Vatican Council in Rome, Pope John XXIII intoned the first notes of the ninth century hymn *"Veni Creator Spiritus"* (Come, Holy Ghost).

On the day of Pentecost, the Holy Spirit did come: "And they were all filled with the Holy Ghost" (Acts 2:4).

* * *

One Bestial—One Noble

Jean Baptiste Carpeaux, French sculptor, worked on a block of marble and made two emerging figures. One was bestial, fierce and heartless. The other was noble, kind and gracious.

Within us are two natures. Which nature emerges victorious depends upon the degree of our yieldedness to the Holy Spirit: "Walk in the Spirit, and ye shall not fulfil the lust of the flesh" (Gal. 5:16).

* * *

All Understood

When the Persian ruler Ahasuerus wanted to send an imperial decree to his subjects in the one hundred and twenty-seven provinces of his domain, he sent letters to every people within his empire in their own language (Esther 1:22).

When the Holy Spirit gave utterance to the disciples at Pentecost, everyone present from the far-flung corners of the Roman Empire heard them speaking in his own language: "Every man heard them speak in his own language" (Acts 2:6).

How wondrous are God's ways!

G. HENRY WATERMAN

* * *

Full Heads and Empty Hearts

A. W. Tozer said, "Some fundamentalists know much about the *doctrine* of the Holy Spirit and too little about the *dynamic* of the Holy Spirit. Though every believer has the Holy Spirit, the Holy Spirit does not have every believer. In steering clear of 'wild fire' fanaticism, many of God's children have only the 'no fire' of formalism."

* * *

Our Nsenga-Mukwashi

For some time, a missionary in Africa sought for the proper word to translate the word *comforter* into the language of the people among whom he worked.

One day he attended a court in an African village. During the proceedings the name *Nsenga-Mukwashi* was used.

At the close of the session, the missionary asked the old chief, "Is there someone in the court by the name of Nsenga-Mukwashi?"

"No," the chief said. "It is the title of an official whose duty it is to interest himself in all my people and stand by them when they are in trouble, and plead their cause. He is the comforting helper."

Silently the missionary thanked God for the exact word to describe the relationship the Holy Spirit sustains to God's children. Here is how he rendered these

148

verses: "If I go not away, the *Nsenga-Mukwashi* will not come unto you" (John 16:7); "If any man sin, we have a *Nsenga-Mukwashi* with the Father, Jesus Christ the righteous" (I John 2:1).

* * *

"Be Still and Know"

F. B. Meyer remarked, "The flesh loves excitement. It is always ready to jump up and run somewhere. It hurries us into action. The Holy Spirit does not. Satan rushes men. God leads them: 'And when he putteth forth his own sheep, he goeth before them' (John 10:4). Never act in panic, nor allow man to dictate to you. Calm yourself and be still. Enter into the quiet of thy closet until the pulse beats normally. When you are most eager to act is the time when you will make the most pitiable mistakes. Do not say what you will or will not do, but wait upon God until He makes known His way. So long as that way is unrevealed by the Holy Spirit, there is no need for action."

* * *

Baptized by the Spirit

The presuppositions in I Corinthians 12:13 are important. The *en heni pneumati* (by one Spirit) reveals that the Holy Spirit is the Agent which places us into the body of Christ. The *eis hen soma* (into one body) states the extent or end of the action. If a man is not baptized by the Spirit he is not in the body of Christ, hence, not a Christian.

ANDRE BUSTANOBY

* * *

The Divine Companion

How thrilling is what Sir Ernest Shackleton said about the presence of his divine Companion—the Holy Spirit—during his trek over trackless snow and ice in Antarctica! He commented, "When I look back upon those days with all their anxiety and peril, I cannot doubt that our party was divinely guided, both over the snowfields and across the storm-swept sea. During the long and trackless march of thirty-six hours over the unnamed mountains and glaciers of South Georgia, it seemed to me often that we were not three but four. I said nothing to my two companions of my feeling of the divine Companion, but afterwards Worsley said to me, 'Boss, I had a curious feeling on the march that there was another Person with us!' I asked, 'Not three but four?' Worsley replied, 'Yes, another Person.' "

* * *

A Fresh Pentecost

G. Campbell Morgan remarked, "Every church service should be a fresh Pentecost. God's resources are inexhaustible. They are the same today as yesterday."

Moody stated, "I believe that the moment our hearts are emptied of pride, self-seeking, and all that is contrary to God's Word, the Holy Spirit will come and fill every corner of our hearts."

* * *

Ninety Percent Organization

A leader of a major evangelical denomination was quoted in the *Changing Continent* as saying, "If it were possible for the Holy Spirit to withdraw from us, we would hardly miss Him. We are 90 percent organization. Only 10 percent remains for the Spirit of God to do! This enfeebling tragic situation is true of other denominations, too."

* * *

Touched to Death

Naturalists tell us of a little plant called the "sensitive plant." If you touch the plant, it quivers in every stem and leaf. If the plant is touched repeatedly, it quivers less and less with each successive touch, until it ceases to respond to the touch. It becomes unresponsive to external stimuli, because it has been "touched to death."

The Holy Spirit speaks to man's sensitive soul in a still, small voice. When man turns an unhearing, unresponding ear to the Spirit's wooings, His voice becomes fainter and fainter. Long ago Saul came to the place where he no longer heard God's voice and lamented, "God is departed from me, and answereth me no more" (I Sam. 28:15).

149

Settled in Time

In a sermon, Dr. George W. Truett said, "When one is convicted of sin by the Holy Spirit, it is hazardous to procrastinate in accepting Christ." When the closing hymn was sung, a young man walked down the aisle and publicly surrendered himself to Christ.

At work next day, an explosion occurred. The young man was fatally injured. As his life ebbed away, he said, "Isn't it wonderful that I settled it last night?" Then he went to be forever with his Lord.

* * *

Convicted and Converted

One night during his meetings in London, D. L. Moody preached to an audience of more than five thousand men, many of whom were professed atheists, agnostics and freethinkers. Moody, empowered by the Spirit of God, preached with fervency and conviction.

Later he related what occurred: "In an instant, the Holy Spirit moved upon those enemies of Jesus Christ. More than five hundred of them stood. Tearfully they cried out, 'I will! I will come to Christ!' Quickly the meeting was closed for personal work to begin. From that night until the end of the week nearly two thousand men were won from the ranks of Satan into the army of the Lord. The enduring character of what took place was evinced by the discontinuance of their atheistic clubs!"

Many of God's children today are praying for more God-sent, Spirit-empowered men—men who have compassionate concern for the unsaved. God isn't looking primarily for better methods. He is looking for better men. G. Campbell Morgan said, "God's best method is always a man: 'There was a man sent from God, whose name was John' [John 1:6]."

HOME

"Stick to One Model"

A reporter asked Henry Ford when he celebrated his golden wedding anniversary, "To what do you attribute your fifty years of successful married life?"

Ford replied, "The formula is the same I've used in the making of cars—*stick to one model!*"

"Until death do you part" is the formula to which God's children must adhere.

God looks with abhorrence on the sundering of the marital tie: "Let none deal treacherously against the wife of his youth. For the LORD . . . hateth putting away" (Mal. 2:15-16).

* * *

Disillusioned

Clark Blackburn, general director of the Family Service Association of America, declared, "There is no question that a tragically high percentage of the young married couples who remain married are disillusioned and dissatisfied with their marriage to the point where it has become a bore, a mockery, a burden and a failure."

* * *

The Most Sacred Relation

Peter Marshall remarked, "The marriage relation is the most delightful and the most sacred and solemn of human relations. It is the blending of lives and the union of hearts that two may walk together up the hill of life to meet the dawn —together bearing life's burdens and sharing its joys and sorrows. It is more than moonlight and roses. It will ever remain in the sight of God an eternal union: 'Wherefore they are no more twain, but one flesh. What therefore God hath joined together, let not man put asunder' (Matt. 19:6)."

* * *

Broken Wedding Vows

Roughly 400,000 U.S. couples are divorced each year. About 40 percent of them are childless. The rest have some

150

500,000 children, two-thirds of them under the age of ten. More than six million Americans are now divorced or separated. Increasingly, the divorce problem is a problem of the young. Forty-six percent of all divorces involve girls who marry in their teens, and 74 percent are those who marry under twenty-five. Conversely, it is estimated that 85 percent of Americans who marry at the age of twenty-five or over stay married.

Time Essay, February 11, 1966

* * *

What He Couldn't Forget

John G. Paton, missionary to the New Hebrides, related, "If everything else were by some accident blotted out from memory, my soul would go back to those days in my boyhood home when my father kept up the practice of family prayer. No day passed without it. Neither business, friends, sorrow nor trouble ever prevented us from kneeling around the family altar where father offered himself and his children to God."

LESLIE D. WEATHERHEAD

* * *

Where Recruited

Many of the famous Christians were recruited from the family altar. As a lad, Charles Sheldon lived in a log cabin in Kansas. Daily he knelt with his family in prayer. Growing to manhood, he wrote one of the most widely read books of modern times—*In His Steps.*

Conversely, evildoers are recruited from prayerless, godless homes. J. Edgar Hoover warned, "Criminals are not born —they are home-grown."

* * *

Husbands Left Alone

John D. Jess stated in *The Prayer That Saves Marriages,* "I have known Christian wives to hike off to a church function night after night, leaving their husbands alone. . . . I am all for faithful church membership, but I believe a compatible marriage is more important, especially when children are involved."

Richest Memories

Among the richest memories of my childhood is that of daily family worship. We read the Bible every day, and children, as well as parents, offered prayer in the family circle, usually before breakfast. We were taught that food could wait, and that the Lord should be honored first.

LT. GEN. WILLIAM K. HARRISON, JR.

* * *

Unseen Realities

Dr. Rufus M. Jones testified of the parental example in the godly home of his boyhood, "We had very few things, but we were rich in invisible, enduring wealth. Our home was permeated with the dew of religious devotion from morning till night. We never ate a meal which did not begin with a prayer of thanksgiving. We never began a day without a family gathering at which mother read a chapter from the Bible. There was work waiting to be done. Yet we sat there hushed until someone would talk with God simply and quietly. When I first began to think of God, I thought of Him, not as some far-off being, but as an ever present Friend and Helper. In those simple ways, the roots of my faith in unseen realities reached down far below my childish surface thinking."

* * *

Divorce Always a Tragedy

Dr. Lawrence S. Kubie, clinical professor of psychiatry at the University of Maryland, said, "Divorce is always a tragedy no matter how civilized the handling of it may be. It is always a confession of human failure, even when it is the sorry better of sorry alternatives."

* * *

Affection and Understanding

For several months during the Antarctic winter night of 1934, Rear Admiral Richard E. Byrd hovered between life and death, alone in a tiny shack buried in the ice and snow on the Ross Ice Barrier. Outside the winter darkness prevailed. During the long and seemingly endless weeks, he suffered indescribable agony.

151

What were his thoughts as he held tenaciously to his flickering life? He tells us in his book *Alone:*

"I did what had to be done piecemeal, doling out my strength in miserable driblets, creeping rather than walking. During those long hours of bitterness, I saw my whole life pass in review. I realized how wrong my sense of values had been and how I had failed to see that the simple, homely, unpretentious things of life are the most important. In the end, only two things really matter to a man: the affection and understanding of his family. So convinced was I that the end was near, my only conscious resolve was to write a message to my wife. After I finished the letter, I thought of the last entry in Captain Scott's diary: 'For God's sake, look after our people.' I understood what Scott meant."

* * *

"Until Death Do You Part"

In the CBS report "The Divorce Dilemma," Walter Cronkite said, "The United States has the highest divorce rate of any nation. It is six times greater than our neighbor to the north, Canada. One out of every four marriages ends in a divorce court. Ninety-five percent of divorces are uncontested."

On the telecast, a judge gave this sage saying: "Divorce and embalming are two processes which should not be resorted to too soon!"

"Until the divorce court do you part" does not abrogate the binding marital dictum "until death do you part" or change the teaching of the Saviour: "And they twain shall be one flesh: so then they are no more twain, but one flesh. What therefore God hath joined together, let not man put asunder" (Mark 10:8-9).

* * *

A Lonely, Homesick Man

On a gray day in October, 1822, in Paris, a lonely, homesick man, far from his family and friends, sat in a cheerless hotel room. Scenes of his happy childhood days in Long Island, New York, raced through his mind. From his window he looked down upon boys and girls, men and women, laughing and happily greeting each other, as they hurried to their families and loved ones.

Suddenly he thought, *Home, sweet home. A man may travel the world over, live in a palace, make new friends, and find new pleasures, but there's no place like home!*

That homesick man—John Howard Payne—sat down and began to write a song that finds a responsive chord in the heart of all mankind: "Home, Sweet Home."

* * *

Why Did This Happen?

Cardigan is a little village in Wales. A century ago, nineteen out of the eighty inhabitants of the village became leaders in British life. Why did this happen? In the early days of the village, the people talked at home about God, what God wanted and expected of man, and man's accountability to God. Their children absorbed the character-molding truths they constantly heard. They grew up and went forth to make their mark for God and the right in their generation.

Obedience to God's ancient directive would do more to solve juvenile delinquency and teenage frustration than all human expedients combined: "And these words, which I command thee this day, shall be in thy heart: and thou shalt teach them diligently unto thy children, and shalt talk of them when thou sittest in thine house" (Deut. 6:6-7).

* * *

Marriage on Approval

In a paper presented to the American Psychological Association, Mrs. Virginia Satir, psychiatric social worker, proposed that marriages should be made on a five-year renewable contract. She reasoned, "If it succeeds, the couple could renew it for additional five-year periods. If it fails, it could be dissolved without undue stress or social stigma."

The social worker made no reference to children who might be born during the five-year marriage.

Children in broken homes are robbed of parental love and care, and they suffer irreparable loss. "Till death do us part"

152

should be the vow made by Christians entering into the divinely ordained marital relationship.

* * *

"Try the Home"

Richard Baxter was a mighty man of God. For three years he preached in a wealthy parish in England. His messages were characterized by zeal and power. There were little or no visible results, however. He became discouraged.

One day he pleaded, "O God, You must do something with these people or I'll die!"

God seemed to say to him, "You've put forth your best efforts in the wrong place. You've expected a revival to come through the church. *Try the home.*"

Baxter began systematically and regularly to call in the homes of the people. He often spent entire evenings in their homes. He helped parents to start family worship with their children. Before long, revival fires began to burn in the church.

We are slow to learn that it is more essential to ring doorbells than church bells. Only the going-out church will survive in our day when the overwhelming majority of the people never attend any church.

* * *

The Wives Know

Dr. George B. Duncan said, "One said with a touch of cynicism that it might be a good thing if, instead of the preachers standing on the platform and preaching, the preachers' wives were invited to stand and tell how it works out in the home."

* * *

A Pathetically Tragic Situation

Don Murray wrote in the *Saturday Evening Post,* "In every American town, on almost every green, shaded street, live housewives who are desperately ill but who do not seek the treatments which are available. They remain prisoners in their homes, isolated by their own guilt and hidden by their family's shame. These lonely, terrified women all suffer the same sickness—alcoholism.

"The woman drunk is protected by her husband, her parents, her children and her family physician. She is treated by her family physician for 'female troubles,' and admitted to a private hospital for a 'nervous disorder.' When the woman alcoholic dies, there is rarely an autopsy. The cause of death is listed delicately as 'heart failure.' "

Alcoholism is different from other diseases in that it is self-imposed and, unlike other physical ailments, often leads to the committing of horrible crimes.

Let us deal lovingly and understandingly with all who need the liberating power and touch of the great Physician, Jesus.

* * *

Home—A Garden of the Lord

Why is the home such a fine and precious thing? Because it is a garden of the Lord, a nursery for human lives to grow in. Its seclusion, its shelter, its wise and careful culture are invaluable to growing souls. Nothing can make up for the lack of them. The home is the God-appointed educator of mankind where the real lessons of life are learned. There we learn the lofty lessons of self-control, self-sacrifice, sublime faith. There is no training to be had in schools or anywhere in the world which can take the place of the discipline of the home. Every true Christian home is a university, fully equipped, amply endowed and able to give the highest education available in this world.

Baltimore Sun

* * *

Too Scared

Dr. A. Whitney Griswold, president of Yale University, commented, "The family has become too scared of its children; the children too insecure in their remoteness from their parents; and the church too much of a social welfare organization for the good of the family or society."

* * *

A Prayer

God give us homes!
Homes where the Bible is honored and
    taught,
Homes with the Spirit of Christ in their
    thought,

153

Homes that a likeness to heaven have
caught—
God give us homes!

* * *

"Except They Be Agreed"

A young man went to Jonathan Edwards to ask for his daughter in marriage.
"You can't have her," said the great preacher.
"But I love her and she loves me. I am abundantly able to support her. Why can't I have her? What have you against me?" asked the young man.
"I have nothing against you. You are a good fellow—too good for my daughter. She has a violent temper, though she is a Christian. You wouldn't be happy with Emily." Then the honest preacher added, "Young man, before you have lived as long as I have, you'll learn that there are some people that the God of all grace can live with, but you can't."
"Can two walk together, except they be agreed?" (Amos 3:3).

* * *

A Reappraisal Needed

A layman has charged that the over-abundance of meetings in the church program militate greatly against Christian home life. He said, "Take a look at this church bulletin. It lists thirty-five different meetings and 'opportunities for service' in a one-week period. And this, observe well, was during Christian Home Week when the emphasis was on family living in the home."
The church needs to reappraise its program and avoid time-consuming, unnecessary meetings which contribute little or nothing to the *primary business* of the church—winning souls, growing God's children into Christlikeness, and giving the gospel to all the world.

* * *

When the Home Is Christian

Chief Inspector Reginald Norris, of London, reported, "I listened to a lecture at the Police College by one of Her Majesty's prison commissioners on the subject 'Juvenile Delinquency.' I asked after the lecture, 'What is your experience with young delinquents who have been trained in Christian homes and who have consistently attended Sunday school?' 'We do not have them,' he replied.
"That answer confirmed my own experience. I have arrested hundreds of criminals, including many juveniles. Very rarely indeed have I been called upon to act in a Christian home."
J. Edgar Hoover, warned, "Criminals are not born—they are home-grown."

* * *

Shortchanged

A teacher asked her class of junior boys to write an essay on "Religion in the Home."
A boy raised his hand. The teacher asked, "What is it?"
The boy squawked, "Teacher, we ain't got no religion in our home."
Children are greatly shortchanged when reared in a prayerless and Christless home. How poorly prepared they are to fight the battles of life.

Told by ALICE MARIE KNIGHT

* * *

What Makes a Home Christian?

Where family prayer is daily said,
God's Word is regularly read,
And faith in Christ is never dead,
    That is a Christian home.

Where father, mother, sister, brother,
All have love for one another,
And no one ever hates the other,
    That is a Christian home.

Where Jesus Christ is Host and Guest,
Through whom we have eternal rest,
And in Him are forever blest,
    That is a Christian home.
"But as for me and my house, we will serve the LORD" (Joshua 24:15).

* * *

Two Wishes

An old farmhouse with meadows wide,
And sweet with clover on each side;
A bright-eyed boy who looks from out
The door with roses wreathed about,
And wishes this one thought all day:
    "Oh, if I could just fly away
    From this dull spot, the world to see,
    How happy, happy, happy I would be!"

154

Amid the city's constant din,
A man who round the world has been,
Who, mid the rushing, hectic throng,
Is thinking, wishing, all day long:
  "Oh, could I only walk once more
    The old path to the farmhouse door,
    The woods and meadow could I see,
  How happy, happy, happy I would be!"
                    ANNIE D. GREEN

* * *

Open and Shut Eyes

Benjamin Franklin wisely said, "Success in marriage consists not only in the right mate, but also in being the right mate. Keep the eyes wide open before marriage, and half shut afterward."

* * *

As the Cord

As the cord unto the bow is,
So unto the man is woman.
Though she bends him, she obeys him,
Though she leads him, yet she follows,
Useless each without the other.
                    LONGFELLOW

* * *

Divorce Dissolves, Seldom Solves

Said Billy Graham, "A broken home is never good for children, or for anyone else. All a divorce does is to dissolve the marriage. It rarely solves the problem. It usually creates more problems. It is frustrating to the children. It makes them feel insecure. It goes against the words of Jesus: 'What . . . God hath joined together, let not man put asunder' [Matt. 19:6].

"I know a man who was on the verge of divorce. He was converted to Christ, and God gave him a new love for his wife and children.

"I am convinced that many marital problems have a spiritual basis—marital unfaithfulness, selfishness and quarreling."

* * *

"I Missed God in the Home"

A Japanese girl in an American college was invited to spend the Christmas holidays with a classmate. Afterward she was asked how she enjoyed the holidays. "Very well," she replied, "but I missed God in the home. I have seen you worship your God in your church. In my country we have a god-shelf so we can worship our gods in our homes. Do not Americans worship their God in their homes?"

* * *

Something Precious Brought into the Home

One Sunday a deacon heard a stirring, heart-gripping message on the family altar. He resolved, "I'm going home and begin to have family prayers and read God's Word."

After dinner the deacon got his Bible. He had never prayed before in the presence of his two children, aged nine and eleven. He read the Bible with little difficulty. Then he tried to pray, but without success. Words would not come to him. His children began to giggle. The mother smiled. He, wanting to be a good sport, smiled too. Beneath the forced smile, however, was an aching heart. Going to his room, he knelt and asked God to forgive him for his failure.

After dinner the next night, the deacon again opened his Bible and began to read. Then he prayed. There was no laughing —only a sense of God's presence and peace. At the conclusion of the prayer, his children put their arms around his neck and affectionately kissed him. He had brought something abidingly precious into his home.

"But as for me and my house, we will serve the LORD" (Joshua 24:15).
                    Told by ROY O. MCCLAIN

* * *

Homespun Advice

Chief Justice Emeritus Samuel H. Silbert of the Common Pleas Court, Cleveland, Ohio, presided at the severance of more than five thousand divorce cases.

Judge Silbert advised, "Marriages need more solemnity and dignity. They should take place in a church if it is at all possible. Certainly elopements and running into a city hall for a quick ceremony should be forbidden. I advocate a six months' cooling-off period before either marriage or divorce. Before marriage, the girl should learn how to cook and keep a clean house. The boy should find a steady job. No one should marry before twenty-one. I think the most horrible thing parents can do to their children is to allow them to date steady early."

What does God say about the breaking of the marital tie? "The LORD hath been witness between thee and the wife of thy youth, against whom thou hast dealt treacherously: yet is she thy companion, and the wife of thy covenant. And did not he make one? . . . For the LORD . . . hateth putting away" (Mal. 2:14-16).

* * *

Happiness

Goethe, German poet and dramatist, averred, "He is happiest, be he king or peasant, who finds peace in his home."

* * *

Successful Marriage

Mignon McLaughlin commented, "A successful marriage requires falling in love many times—always with the *same* person."

Divorce and Embalming

Divorce and embalming are two processes which should not be resorted to too soon.

* * *

Virtues of Mothers

Charles Dickens said, "I think it must be written somewhere that the virtues of the mothers shall be visited on their children, as well as the sins of the fathers."

* * *

Heart's Attitude

Some murmur when their sky is clear
  And wholly bright to view,
If one small speck of dark appears
  In their great heaven of blue.
And some with thankful love are filled
  If but one streak of light,
One ray of God's good mercy, gilds
  The darkness of their night.

In mansions there are hearts that ask
  In discontent and pride
Why life is such a dreary task,
  And good things are denied.
And hearts in poorest homes admire
  How love has in their aid
(God's love that never seems to tire)
  Such rich provision made.

RICHARD C. TRENCH

HONESTY—DISHONESTY

Now They Are a Memory

Recently in Cleveland, Ohio, a jewelry store—the Webb C. Ball Company—closed its doors forever after ninety-three years of honest dealing with the public. There were some prospective buyers but their offers were declined.

The day after the store closed, the old company put a large paid advertisement in the newspaper. It said, "Our old store key has been put away forever. How delightful it is to recall those ninety-three golden years! Now they are a memory. Our highest hope is that our name will inspire happy memories in your heart and mind for years to come."

The Honest Prayer

Caroline Fry, author of *Christ Our Example,* was a woman of wealth and beauty. She enjoyed many of the ephemeral gaieties of life until she became weary of life. Then she sought comfort in religion. Coming to the end of herself, she confessed her true condition, praying, "O God, if Thou art a God, I do not love Thee; I do not seek Thee. I do not believe there is any happiness in Thee. But I am miserable as I am. Give me what I do not seek and do not want. If Thou canst, make me happy. I am tired of this world. If there is anything better, give it to me."

The honest prayer was answered. She was immediately saved!

156

Man's bankrupt soul should lead him to look up and discover heaven's open door and God's pardoning grace.

"O taste and see that the LORD is good: blessed is the man that trusteth in him" (Ps. 34:8).

Adapted from *Prairie Overcomer*

* * *

There's a Difference

A Jewish lawyer attended a meeting in a Christian church and heard several testify. One of those who testified was well known to the lawyer. He knew the man was careless in meeting honest obligations and often did questionable, shady things.

In commenting on the service later, the lawyer said, "To me there is a vast difference between testimony and evidence."

* * *

"Tell Him I'm Out"

An errand boy entered the office of his employer and said, "Sir, Mr. Carmichael would like to see you."

The employer frowned and said, "Tell him I'm out."

"But, sir," the boy replied, "he said he had a special reason for wanting to see you."

Commanded the employer gruffly, "Do what I tell you. Tell him I'm out."

Bravely the boy said, "But, sir, I can't do that because it is not true. I may lose my job, but I will not lie."

ALICE MARIE KNIGHT

* * *

How to Improve Business

A Christian businessman turned down a shady deal which would have brought him a large sum of money. The person offering him the dishonest deal asked why he did it.

The Christian said, "My concern does business on Christian principles."

"Surely you don't try to mix two good things like business and religion?" asked the would-be shady dealer.

The Christian replied, "I have discovered that when we mix business and religion, we prove our religion, and we improve our business."

An Honorable Zero

John was a high school student. One day he cheated on an examination. Shortly thereafter he received Christ as his Saviour.

"Now I belong to Christ," he thought. "I must do all I can to make right the sinful, dishonest things I did before becoming a Christian."

Going to his history teacher, he said, "I deserve a zero in my recent history test because I cheated. I have received Christ as my Saviour and Lord, and I must now do all I can to make amends for past misdeeds."

Looking with admiration at John, the teacher said, "I will give you a zero, but it will be a noble, honorable zero! By your confessing that you cheated you have demonstrated the genuineness of your change of heart and life. I know your influence will be great upon your fellow students."

ALICE MARIE KNIGHT

* * *

This Above All

This above all: to thine own self be true,
And it must follow, as the night the day,
Thou canst not then be false to any man.

SHAKESPEARE

* * *

Losing Honestly

Billy's team lost the game to a team which played unfairly and dishonestly. Dejected, Billy said to his mother, "God was on the side of the opposing team. They cheated and won the game."

When Billy's father came home, the mother told him what Billy had said. He went immediately to Billy's room and cheerfully said, "Hi, Billy! I heard your team won today!"

Billy replied, "You heard wrong, because we didn't."

"Son," said his father, "I heard there were *two* contests. It is true that your team was outscored by the opposing dishonest team, but your team won *morally* because your team didn't resort to any unfair or dishonest tactics and you didn't become angry and use obscene language.

157

Congratulations, Billy! Your team won and I'm proud of you!"

Whenever anyone wins unfairly and dishonestly, he is in reality the loser.

ALICE MARIE KNIGHT

* * *

Moral Suicide

In a sermon, the dean of Boston University's Marsh Chapel said, "Forty to eighty percent of college students cheat—some more and some less."

Robert H. Hamill stated, "When college students see public officials grafting from public funds, citizens cheating on income taxes, loose law enforcement, they conclude they must train themselves for sophisticated skulduggery in the future, and the campus seems a good place to practice."

Dishonesty is moral suicide, a disintegration of the moral self.

Christianity Today

* * *

Why Timothy Died

The failure of an eight-year-old boy to tell the truth cost him his life, as reported in the *Chicago Tribune*.

Timothy Bates of Brentwood, New Jersey, had eaten tranquilizing pills. The stomachs of the two younger Bates children, who had also eaten the pills, were pumped out. Timothy steadfastly affirmed that he had not eaten any of the pills. He was not treated.

The mother put the three children to bed. The next morning she went to see if they were all right. The two younger children were fine. *Timothy was dead!*

Truth and honesty, as taught in God's Word, cannot be instilled in children too early.

* * *

Anxious to Employ

The world is anxious to employ
Not just one, but every boy
Whose heart and brain will e'er be true
To work his hands shall find to do.
Honest, faithful, earnest, kind,
To good awake, to evil blind,
Heart of gold, without alloy—
Wanted—the world wants such a boy.

Weasel Words—Juggled Figures

A professed Christian contractor in Chicago was adept in the use of weasel words in contracts and juggled figures—always to his advantage and to the disadvantage of unsuspecting workmen. One day, however, the scheming contractor received from a workman a stinging and deserved rebuke. The laboring man, after he had read carefully a contract handed to him for his signature, said, "If I sign this contract I will be deprived of a week's wages. You are a professed Christian. I am an atheist. Now you know why I am an atheist!'

* * *

Abundantly Rewarded

Some years ago Fred Skinner of London, England, found a bag containing $2,800. He was greatly tempted to say nothing about his find. However, he returned it to the owner who gave him $280 as a reward.

Today Skinner is richer by $84,000. The man who lost the money died and left him half of his estate.

Cleveland Press

* * *

Bravo!

A public utilities concern was seeking a franchise in a large city. An unscrupulous representative of the company was sent to interview a key city official whose approval of the franchise was needed.

The dishonest representative said, "Think of the money your approval can bring to you. It's the bargain of a lifetime. You'll never have another chance to make on the QT so much easy money."

"So easy?" flashed the honest official. "No one ever got a bargain by chicanery or dishonesty. You are wrong when you tell me that all I have to do is to vote 'right.' If I bartered my honor, I would have to carry the consciousness of my dishonesty to the grave. My vote is not for sale."

* * *

The Hole in the Ceiling

Two brothers ran a store in a country town. They became perplexed when they discovered that many small items on their

158

shelves were disappearing. A check showed that the items had not been sold. The brothers came to the same conclusion and began to seek for a solution to their problem. Finally one of them hit upon a plan. He climbed up into the attic above the store and bored a hole in the ceiling.

Then each brother took his turn watching through the hole, while the other waited on the trade. What they discov-ered about some of the townspeople was amazing! However, no accusations were made. Instead, they simply dropped the gentle hint that there was a hole in the ceiling. Almost immediately the pilfering ceased. Occasionally, however, the brothers noticed with amusement some conscience-stricken shopper strolling about the store and glancing furtively toward the ceiling.

HOPE

A Hopeless Hereafter

Robert, age forty-seven, and his wife Paula, age fifty-one, were found shot to death in their suburban home in Philadelphia. They were socially prominent and lived in affluence. Paula phoned a state trooper and said, "My husband begged me to kill him. I did it. I shot him, and now I am going to kill myself!" The trooper tried to keep her talking while he radioed a patrol car to go to the scene of the tragedy. Sensing his purpose, she said, "You're not going to keep me on the phone until someone interferes. We made this agreement, and I'm going to keep it."

Ten minutes later the officers entered the home where murder and suicide had just occurred. They found a note which contained these forlorn words: "We have no hope for the future."

How hopeless are those who go out into a Christless hereafter!

Told by HYMAN J. APPELMAN

* * *

Without Hope

Expressing a widely prevalent and increasingly popular belief among the intellectuals—negative existentialism—Jean-Paul Sartre said, "Man can count on no one but himself. He is alone, abandoned on earth in the midst of his infinite responsibilities, without hope, with no other aim than the one he sets for himself, with no other destiny than the one he forges for himself on this earth."

How hopeless and purposeless is life for those who embrace this negative be-lief! How worthy and satisfying is life for those who live for Christ and others!

* * *

"There Is Utterly No Hope"

A brilliant university student from a wealthy family sought to find the solution to the enigmas of life in death. He leaped from a window of his dormitory room and died horribly on the pavement below!

Why did this darksome termination of the young man's life occur? He had wealth, friends, and a devoted father and mother. He didn't, however, have the One who is the answer to life's enigmas—Christ. A suicide note was found in his room. Its message was brief, but sufficient to disclose the cause of his self-destruction. It read: "There is utterly no hope."

The power-imparting Christ brings hope to despondent ones, "which hope we have as an anchor of the soul, both sure and steadfast" (Heb. 6:19).

* * *

Dimmed Vision

Sir Winston Churchill stated, "I am an old man. I have lived a long time. I have never seen days like these. I am tired of it all. I see no hope for the future. Our problems are beyond us."

How dark and dismal the future seems when we fail to reckon with God and cherish "that blessed hope, and the glorious appearing of the great God and our Saviour Jesus Christ" (Titus 2:13).

159

Better to hope, though the clouds hang low,
    And keep the eyes still lifted;
For the sweet, blue skies will soon peep through,
    When the ominous clouds are rifted.
There was never a night without a day,
    Nor an evening without a morning;
And the darkest hour, as the proverb goes,
    Is the hour before the dawning.

HUMILITY

The Loveliest Crown

When she was nine years old, Princess Elizabeth II went shopping with her grandmother, Queen Mary, in one of London's leading stores. Crowds gathered outside the store, waiting for a glimpse of the princess. Little Elizabeth became very impatient with her grandmother for spending so much time in making purchases. She pleaded, "Please hurry, Grandmother. I want to go out and let all those people see me."

Sorrowfully Queen Mary led little Elizabeth to the rear exit of the store. They returned to Buckingham Palace in a roundabout way. She said to Elizabeth, "England must never see one of its princesses when she is full of foolish conceit, my child. England loves its rulers because they *serve,* not because they rule. Never forget that, Elizabeth. Your loveliest crown is not made of gold and precious stones, but of humility."

"Be clothed with humility: for God resisteth the proud, and giveth grace to the humble" (I Peter 5:5).

Adapted from *American Holiness Journal*

* * *

Branded by Humility

Editorialized *Moody Monthly,* "Paul was branded by humility. Moths could not corrupt this God-given robe. He never fished for praise with humility's bait. And in the long line of sinners, he put himself first. An old Welsh divine said that if you know Hebrew, Greek and Latin, do not put them where Pilate did—at the head of Christ, but put them at His feet. 'What things were gain to me,' said Paul, 'those I counted loss for Christ.'"

Unconscious of Any Goodness

Truly great people are usually humble people who are not aware of their humility: "Moses wist not that the skin of his face shone while he talked with . . . [God]" (Exodus 34:29b).

How revealing of greatness it is to be unconscious of any goodness or ascribed greatness. How praiseworthy it is to ascribe all glory to God for any attainment, saying, "By the grace of God I am what I am" (I Cor. 15:10).

* * *

To God Be the Glory

Johann Sebastian Bach averred, "The sole object of all music should be the glory of God and pleasant recreation."

On many of his scores he scribbled these dedicatory words: "To God alone be the glory!"

* * *

The Violet

Down in the green and shady bed
    A modest violet grew.
Its stalk was bent, it hung its head,
    As if to hide from view.

And yet it was a lovely flower,
    Its color bright and fair.
It might have graced a rosy bower,
    Instead of hiding there.

Yet there it was content to bloom,
    In modest tints arrayed,
And there it spreads its sweet perfume
    Within the silent shade.

Then let me to the valley go,
    This pretty flower to see,
That I may also learn to grow
    In sweet humility.

JANE TAYLOR

160

Cutting Down to Size

The naturalist William Beebe told of visits he made to Theodore Roosevelt at Sagamore Hill. Often, after an evening's talk, the two men would stroll over the wide-spreading lawn and look up into the night sky. They would see who could first find the pale bit of light near the upper left-hand corner of the Great Square of Pegasus.

Then either Beebe or Roosevelt would exclaim, "That is the spiral galaxy of Andromeda. It is as large as our Milky Way. It is one of a hundred million galaxies. It is two and a half million light-years away. It consists of one hundred billion suns, many of them larger than our own sun!"

After a moment of awesome silence, Roosevelt would grin and say, "Now I think we are small enough. Let's go to bed!"

Adapted from *Reader's Digest*

* * *

Preparation for Enrichment

Flavel said, "When God intends to fill a soul, He first makes it empty. When He intends to enrich a soul, He first makes it poor. When He intends to exalt a soul, He first makes it sensible to its own miseries, wants and nothingness."

Charles Fox, in writing of God's army, stipulated the following requisites for service in His army: "Foolish enough to depend on God for wisdom; weak enough to have no honor but God's honor; despised enough to be kept in the dust at His feet; and being nothing enough for God to be everything."

* * *

Condemned Without Cause

"It is a mark of deepest and truest humility," said Alexander Whyte, "to see ourselves condemned without cause and remain silent. To be quiet during insult and wrong is a noble imitation of our Lord 'who, when he was reviled, reviled not again' (I Peter 2:23). When I remember in how many ways He suffered and didn't deserve it, I know not where my senses are when I am in such haste to defend and excuse myself."

The Queen Stood

Soon after Queen Victoria ascended her throne, she attended a concert in which the *Messiah* was rendered. She was told, "Your Majesty, it is customary for royalty not to stand when the 'Hallelujah Chorus' is rendered."

When the orchestra and chorus came to the part where they proclaimed Christ as King of kings and Lord of lords, the queen stood and bowed her head in worship and adoration!

* * *

Dwell Deep

A. B. Simpson stated, "The heart that knows the heights of God reaches them from the depths of nothingness and self-abasement. Dwell deep in the hidden life of God. The cedar grows more beneath the ground than above it. Dwell deep in the peace of God. As in the ocean's depth the surges never swell, so in the heart of God there is a place where the peace of God passeth all understanding."

There is a place of quiet rest,
Near to the heart of God;
A place where sin cannot molest,
Near to the heart of God.

* * *

Silence About Ourselves

Bishop Wilberforce advised, "Think as little as possible about yourself. Turn your eyes resolutely from any view of your influence, your success, your following. Above all speak as little as possible about yourself. Guard especially against those little tricks by which a vain man seeks to bring around the conversation to himself and gain the praise or notice which his thirsty ears drink in so greedily. Let the Master's words ever ring in your ears: 'How can ye believe, which receive honour one of another, and seek not the honour that cometh from God only?' [John 5:44]."

* * *

Not Big Enough

So few of us are big enough to become little enough to be used of God: "When thou wast little in thine own sight, wast

161

thou not made head of the tribes of Israel?" (I Sam. 15:17).

* * *

They That Know

John Flavel commented, "They that know God will be humble, and they that know themselves cannot be proud."

He That Is Down

John Bunyan said, "He that is down needs fear no fall; he that is low, no pride; he that is humble ever shall have God to be his guide."

* * *

Out of the Devil's Reach

Jonathan Edwards stated, "Nothing sets a person so much out of the devil's reach as humility."

HYPOCRISY

The Judas Tree

In some regions of the world there grows a tree which is appropriately called the Judas tree because of its deceitfulness. At times, the Judas tree abounds in beautiful, crimson blossoms. Their flaming beauty attracts innumerable, unsuspecting insects, including the busy bees, ever on the lookout for nectar. As the insects suck the fatal secretion from the blossoms, the ground below is strewn with their lifeless bodies!

* * *

Our Children Tell on Us

A pastor called at the home of a church family. It was his custom to read a chapter from the Bible and pray at the conclusion of his visit, so he asked for a Bible.

The mother, with a great show of piety, said to her little three-year-old girl, "Darling, go and bring Mother the Book she loves best."

The little girl dashed away. Presently she returned, carrying the large catalog of a mail-order concern!

ALICE MARIE KNIGHT

* * *

"Their In-front Words"

In many tribal languages, the word *hypocrisy* is not found. The Wycliffe Bible Translators, therefore, adopt descriptive phrases to convey the meaning of the word to the natives. In the Huitoto language of Peru, the words *their hypocrisy,* referring to the hypocrisy of the Pharisees, is translated thus: "their in-front words were good."

INFLUENCE

(*See also* Christian Example)

Not Sure They're Dead

It has been said, "The reward of great men is that, long after they have died, one is not quite sure that they are dead."

Of Abel's postmortem influence the Bible says, "By faith Abel offered unto God a more excellent sacrifice than Cain ... and by it he being dead yet speaketh" (Heb. 11:4).

Lives of great men all remind us
We can make our lives sublime,
And, departing, leave behind us
Footprints on the sands of time.

LONGFELLOW

If I Could See a Christian

A Hindu student said to Billy Graham in Madras, "I would become a Christian if I could *see* one!"

Later Graham said, "And when he said that, he was looking at me! That was one of the greatest sermons ever preached to me!"

* * *

Never Tiresome

An Indian student said to a missionary, "We sometimes get tired of hearing about Christ, Christ, Christ. But, sir, we never get tired of seeing Christ in a Christlike person!"

* * *

"Odour of a Sweet Smell"

The Bible says, "Ointment and perfume rejoice the heart" (Prov. 27:9). Millions of people have found this to be true.

As unbelievable as it may seem, New York City cab drivers spend a whopping $15 million on colognes annually. Alexander the Great wore perfumed tunics. Napoleon emptied close to sixty bottles of eau de cologne over himself in a month.

The word *perfume* is derived from the Latin *per* and *fuma* which, roughly translated, mean "through smoke." The word referred to the incense burned by the ancient Greeks and Romans in their religious ceremonies.

In Exodus 30 two formulas are given—one for the anointing oil and the other for a perfume—both to be used solely for religious purposes and only by the tabernacle priests.

From each life there emanates an influence which is either odorous or malodorous, either magnetic or repellent.

In speaking of the influence of God's children, Paul said, "For we are unto God a sweet savour of Christ, in them that are saved, and in them that perish" (II Cor. 2:15).

* * *

Pleasant Street

The folks who live on Pleasant Street
Are just the kind you like to meet:
Smiling lips and twinkling eyes
That make you think of sunny skies.

They always have a word to say
That sends you happy on your way.

It gives new zest to merely meet
The kind that live on Pleasant Street.
Their dispositions are serene;
You know the people that I mean!
The kind one always likes to meet;
I wish more lived on Pleasant Street.

* * *

"What Silly Sheep!"

One wintry day when Joe was sliding on the pond, the ice broke! He struggled out of the water and went home wet and bedraggled.

"Why did you slide on the ice?" asked Aunt Jane.

" 'Cause all the other boys did," said Joe.

Aunt Jane gave him dry clothes and a hot drink. Then she told him a story:

"When I was a little girl, Joe, my father had a great flock of sheep. One day a big ram jumped through a gap in the fence. He was followed by the other sheep. When the ram tumbled into the bottom of an old well where father used to throw rubbish, the next sheep never stopped to see what had become of him. He jumped in right after the ram, and so did the next one and the next. The sheep kept jumping into the well until it was full. Then father pulled them out as best he could. The sheep at the bottom of the well were almost smothered to death."

"My, what silly sheep!" exclaimed Joe. Then he looked at his aunt and smiled. He had gotten the point of the story.

The Bible says, "Enter not into the path of the wicked, and go not in the way of evil men" (Prov. 4:14).

Told by ALICE MARIE KNIGHT

* * *

Reflected Glory

A college student who had heard Dr. A. J. Gordon preach said, "That man's face would convert me to a belief in Christ."

Sinew and blood
  Are a thin veil of lace;
What you wear in your heart,
  You wear on your face.

163

If your life is unselfish,
    If for others you live,
For not what you get
    But how much you give,
If you live close to God
    In His infinite grace,
You don't have to tell it
    It shows on your face.

* * *

A Blight or a Blessing, Which?

In every solid block of metal there are atoms. They move in keeping with their respective laws. You may put a block of pure gold against a block of silver and then separate them. No change is discernible. A change has occurred, however, as metallurgists attest. When in contact with each other some of the invisible atoms of gold moved into the silver block, and some of the atoms of silver moved into the block of gold.

How illustrative of the silent influence which emanates from the daily life of each one of us—an influence which either blights or blesses others. Of Jehoram long ago it was said, "He . . . departed without being desired" (II Chron. 21:20).

* * *

Enduring Monuments

There lived long ago in Arabia two brothers—Ahmed and Omar. Each wished to perpetuate his own memory. Omar proudly had an imposing obelisk erected at the crossroads of a much-traveled caravan route. On it were carved his name and some of his alleged great accomplishments. There it stood for decades, of no worth to mankind.

Ahmed chose a different and worthier way to perpetuate his memory. He had a well dug beside a desert highway and planted date palm trees beside it. There weary, thirsty and hungry travelers found rest and refreshment. They blessed Ahmed's name and called him Ahmed the Good.

How precious and enduring is the memory of those who have lived for God and others. Their monuments are erected in glowing, grateful hearts: "The memory of the just is blessed" (Prov. 10:7).

After monuments of stone and bronze have crumbled into dust, the deeds of love and kindness rendered in the name of Christ will live enduringly: "Let her alone; . . . She hath done what she could. . . . Wheresoever this gospel shall be preached throughout the whole world, this also that she [Mary of Bethany] hath done shall be spoken of for a memorial of her" (Mark 14:6, 8-9).

Told by ALICE MARIE KNIGHT

* * *

My Daddy Drinks

The Sunday school lesson was on temperance and the teacher spoke simply about the evils of alcoholic beverages. She quoted the verse "Wine is a mocker . . .: whosoever is deceived thereby is not wise" (Prov. 20:1).

"But, teacher," interrupted Freddie, "a drink once in a while does no harm. *My daddy drinks!*"

* * *

Transferred Fragrance

A press correspondent entered a small restaurant in a French village. Soon a group of men entered for the noonday meal. Immediately a delicate odor permeated the room.

When the men left, the correspondent asked the waiter, "Who were those men?"

He replied, "They are workmen from a nearby perfume factory. They bring the perfume with them."

Shouldn't God's children "manifest the savour of his [Christ's] knowledge . . . in every place" (II Cor. 2:14)?

Like the vase in which roses
    Have once been distilled,
You may break, you may shatter
    The vase if you will,
But the scent of the roses
    Will cling to it still.

164

INTERCESSION

(*See also* Prayer)

Prayer Helpers

"It is queer that missionaries don't seem to be what they used to be," bemoaned a speaker. "Take William Carey, for instance. He changed the history of India. We don't have missionaries like that today."

The speaker then spoke of Carey's sister who lay paralyzed in bed for fifty years and could not even articulate her words most of the time. Propped up in bed, she wrote lengthy letters of encouragement to Carey and prayed continuously for him.

If we do not have missionaries like Carey today, it may be because they do not have prayer helpers like Carey's sister.

Adapted from *His* magazine

* * *

Jesus Talked to the Father

One morning Dr. C. I. Scofield was downcast and depressed. A cloud seemed to come between him and the heavenly Father, and he was unable to pray. As he thought upon the Saviour, the cloud lifted. Joy came.

Later he said to a friend, "I was very depressed this morning. You must have prayed for me."

"No," said the friend, "but I know your great High Priest and Intercessor, the Lord Jesus, talked to the Father about you."

"He ever liveth to make intercession for them" (Heb. 7:25).

* * *

Our Heavenly Intercessor

Dr. H. C. Morrison's parents died when he was an infant. As a boy he got into trouble. He was arrested and arraigned. He could not look at the judge, because he was guilty.

"Has this boy anyone to represent him?" the judge asked the clerk of the court. "No, Your Honor," said the clerk. Then the judge said to a lawyer present,

"I appoint you to take this boy's case."

Going to the boy, the lawyer asked, "Are you guilty?"

"Yes, sir, I am guilty."

"Don't you think we had better confess the guilt and ask for the mercy of the court?"

"Yes, sir," Morrison replied.

"Please, Your Honor," said the lawyer, "I have observed that when the ends of justice can be secured and society can be protected, it is Your Honor's custom to show mercy. I stand with this trembling orphan to beg Your Honor's mercy. He confesses his sin and pleads for forgiveness."

Then the lawyer, forgetful of court amenities, added, *"Father,* I'll sponsor this boy and give him an education. I believe he will become an upright, useful citizen!"

The judge had appointed *his own son* to represent young Morrison!

The heavenly Father has appointed His Son to plead for us! Christ has "entered . . . into heaven . . . now to appear in the presence of God for us" (Heb. 9:24).

* * *

Prayer Immersed with Tears

For years a Christian woman was greatly abused by her cruel, unsaved husband. She prayed earnestly for his salvation. There was no change in him, and she said in discouragement, "I'll continue to pray for him for another six months, and if he isn't converted then, I'll cease to pray for him."

On the last day of the six months, the woman felt that she had failed, and wept. A few moments later her husband came in. He was deeply dejected and refused to eat.

"What's the trouble?" she asked.

"I am a miserable, lost sinner," he said. "What hope is there for me? Could you ever forgive me for all the mean things I have done to you?"

With tears of joy in her eyes, she said, "I forgive everything. Now let us kneel and ask God to forgive you and make you one of His children."

God heard their cry. A lost one passed from spiritual death into spiritual life in Christ.

Told by JOHN R. RICE

* * *

When a Day Was Misspent

John Welch, a Scottish preacher, felt that a day was misspent if he did not spend from eight to ten hours in prayer. Asked why he spent so much time in prayer, he said, "I have the souls of three thousand to answer for before the judgment seat of Christ, and I know not how it is with many of them."

HYMAN J. APPELMAN

JESUS

"I Am the Way"

One foggy night in London, a little boy lost his way. He began to cry. A bobby asked, "Are you lost, my boy?"

"Yes, I am," whimpered the boy.

"Where do you live?"

The boy told him. Then the bobby said, "Go down the street one-half mile and cross the bridge. Then turn to your right and follow the river a little way. You'll see then where you are."

Bewildered and chilled, the boy said, "I can't find the way in the dark."

Just then a kind man who had been standing nearby said, "My boy, just come with me, and I'll take you right to your home."

The bobby *told* the way. The kind man *became* the way. Jesus not only tells us the way to our heavenly home, but He is the way: "I am the way: . . . no man cometh unto the Father, but by me" (John 14:6).

ALICE MARIE KNIGHT

* * *

"I Want Someone with a Face"

One night when Mommy put her to bed, little Jane said, "I want a light."

Mommy said, "You are getting bigger, Jane, and you don't need a light. You are quite safe. God's angels will take care of you."

Little Jane said, "But, Mommy, I don't want angels. I want someone with a face!"

For many years, the people on earth wanted a God whom they could see. Then "when the fulness of the time was come, God sent forth his Son" (Gal. 4:4). When Jesus came, the people saw God "with a face." Jesus was God "manifest in the flesh" (I Tim. 3:16).

ALICE MARIE KNIGHT

* * *

What Is He to You?

One time Dr. William Evans and others stood reverently in Chicago's Marshall Field department store before the life-size painting of *Christ Before Pilate*. The picture showed the cruel, hardhearted Roman soldiers on one side. On the other side were the Jews. In the center of the scene Christ serenely and silently stood alone before Pilate. There was a solemn hush as the group gazed upon the painting.

Dr. Evans said softly to the man standing beside him, "My friend, what is He to *you*?"

The man replied, "What do you mean?"

Dr. Evans replied, "What is He to you—the lonely figure?"

The stranger retorted, "Well, what is He to *you*?"

Dr. Evans replied by quoting words he was sure he would say when he stood before his Lord in glory: "My Lord and my God!"

Told in *Moody Monthly*

166

Familiar Things

He talked of grass, and wind, and rain,
Of fig trees and fair weather,
And made it His delight to bring
Heaven and earth together.

He spoke of lilies, vines, and corn,
The sparrow and the raven;
And words so natural, yet so wise,
Were on men's hearts engraven.

Of yeast, with bread, and flax, and cloth,
Of eggs, and fish, and candles;
See how the whole familiar world
He most divinely handles.

T. T. LYNCH

* * *

A Sinless Incarnation

A missionary in India asked Lakhan Singh, a street preacher, who, before his conversion, went on innumerable pilgrimages to so-called holy shrines seeking peace, "How were you first drawn to Christ?"

Lakhan Singh replied, "One day I stopped to listen to a street preacher in Shahjahanpur who declared that the Lord Jesus was a sinless incarnation. He said, 'There are many incarnations in the Hindu religion. Some of them are cruel, capricious and murderous; but none of them are sinless.' I was deeply impressed when I heard that and I continued to think about it. I had no peace of mind until I accepted the sinless Son of God as my Saviour. For forty years I have been joyfully preaching Him!"

Only of Christ can it be said, "who knew no sin," "who did no sin," "in him is no sin."

Guilty, vile and helpless we:
Spotless Lamb of God was He:
"Full atonement!" Can it be?
Hallelujah! What a Saviour!

* * *

Myriads Emancipated

Said Dr. Kenneth Scott Latourette, professor emeritus of missions and Oriental history, Yale University, "In this world of men appeared Jesus Christ. To most of His contemporaries who knew Him, He seemed a failure. Yet from that brief life has flowed a more powerful force for the triumphant waging of man's long battle than any other ever known by the human race. Through it millions have had their inner conflicts resolved in progressive victory over their baser impulses. By it millions have been sustained in the greatest tragedies of life and have come through radiant. It has done more to allay the physical ills of disease and famine than any other impulse known to man. It has emancipated millions from chattel slavery and millions of others from thralldom of vice. It has protected tens of millions from exploitation by their fellows."

* * *

"Thou Remainest"

While visiting many cathedrals and castles in Europe, some dating back to the twelfth century, I observed how time had exacted its inevitable toll. Only a little of the former glory was left of the works of the world's masters.

In Westminster Abbey, where some of England's illustrious dead are interred beneath the floor, I observed that the endless tread of sightseers over the slabs atop the graves had effaced epitaphs which once extolled the dead. Not one letter was discernible on some slabs.

Amidst scenes of change and decay, my mind reverted to the One who is "the same yesterday, and to day, and for ever" (Heb. 13:8)—the changeless Christ.

W. B. KNIGHT

* * *

Jesus Understands

Joseph Mallord Turner, English painter, invited Charles Kingsley to his studio to see a picture of a storm at sea. In rapt admiration, Kingsley exclaimed, "It's wonderful! It's so realistic! How did you do it?"

The artist replied, "I went to the coast of Holland and engaged a fisherman to take me out to sea in the next storm. Entering his boat as a storm was brewing, I asked him to bind me to the mast. Then he steered his boat into the teeth of the storm.

"The storm raged with such fury that

167

at times I longed to be in the bottom of the boat where the waves would blow over me. I could not, however. I was bound to the mast. Not only did I see the storm in its raging fury. *I felt it!* It blew into me, as it were, until I became a part of it. After this terrible ordeal, I returned to my studio and painted the picture."

It is written of the Saviour, "For in that he himself hath suffered being tempted, he is able to succour them that are tempted" (Heb. 2:18).

Told by BISHOP SLATTERY

* * *

"The Image of the Invisible God"

A little girl asked, "Daddy, what color is God's hair?"

The father replied, "Honey, God is a Spirit. He doesn't have any hair."

But the little girl insisted, "My Sunday school teacher said He looks like us."

Said the father, "You must have misunderstood your teacher. The Bible says we are made in God's image and likeness. But that doesn't mean that God looks like us. It means that in some ways we are like God. It means that God thinks, and He made us so we can think. God loves, and He made us so we can love. Jesus came to show us what God is like. Jesus said to one of His helpers, 'He that hath seen me hath seen the Father'" (John 14:9).

The little girl's face lit up. "I get it, Daddy. God is like us on the inside, not on the outside."

Told by ALICE MARIE KNIGHT

* * *

"That I May Know Him"

In the first large bequest given to what is now Harvard University, John Harvard stipulated, "Let every student be plainly instructed and earnestly pressed to consider well the main end of his life and studies; to know God and Jesus Christ, which is eternal life, and to lay Christ in the bottom as the only foundation of knowledge and learning, and see the Lord as the Giver of all wisdom. Let everyone seriously set himself by prayer in secret to see Christ as the Lord and Master."

Fingertip Facts

* * *

The Saviour's Hands

What wealth to meet the world's
    demands
Is found engraved on Jesus' hands;
Hands with the chisel and saw so sure
For Nazareth homes made furniture,
Ploughs for the farmers, for the oxen a
    yoke;
So doing He mingled with ordinary
    folk—
  Precious hands, which in God's plan,
  Were the ready hands of a working
  Man.

Talented hands at the carpenter's bench,
Hands so strong to twist and to wrench,
But naught could e'er their beauty spoil;
And though oft stained with daily toil,
His hands were never marred by sin
For He Himself was pure within—
  Hands, which since the world began,
  Were the hands of a sinless Man.

Sympathetic hands were they,
Touching all who came His way;
The blind, the lame found life anew,
For His were the hands of a Healer, too.
The dead were raised, the lepers cured;
One touch of His hand, and health was
    assured—
  Power to heal, to help and to bless,
  Hands of infinite tenderness.

NELL HAWKINS

* * *

I Know a Name

I know of lands that are sunk in shame,
  Of hearts that faint and tire;
But I know of a name, a precious name,
  That can set those lands on fire!

I know a soul that is steeped in sin,
  That no man's art can cure;
But I know a name, a precious name,
  That can make that soul all pure!

So listen, my heart, an angel speaks
  To save thy life from dross;
Christ Jesus is that precious name:
  He saves by way of the cross!

Baptist Observer

What Josephus Said

Flavius Josephus was born in A.D. 37, some four years after the crucifixion of Jesus. In referring to events that occurred within four years of his own birth, he said:

"At the same time there appeared in Judea an extraordinary Person called Jesus, if it be lawful to call Him a man. He was a famous Worker of miracles and a Teacher of those who were desirous of receiving the truth in simplicity, and brought over to Him many disciples, both Jews and Gentiles.

"This was the Christ whom Pilate, at the accusation of the princes and great men of the nation, delivered up to the ignominious punishment of the cross, notwithstanding which those who first loved Him did not forsake Him.

"He appeared to them alive again the third day after His crucifixion, which the divine prophets had foretold together with numberless other wonders concerning Him. And thence to this day there is a set of people who bear the name of Christian, as owning Him for their Head, Lord and Master."

Antiquities, chapter 4, paragraph 3

* * *

He Didn't Seek Popularity

When Jesus, God's Son, was on earth, He did not seek popularity—He spurned it: "When Jesus . . . perceived that they would come and take him by force, to make him a king, he departed again into a mountain himself alone" (John 6:15).

According to the biblical record, He was never very popular with some of the populace. He ate and mingled with the publicans and sinners. He helped the lepers, demoniacs and beggars.

Much of Jesus' ministry caused Him to be unpopular with the scribes and Pharisees—cleansing the temple, mingling with publicans and sinners, and healing on the Sabbath. His life ended with His ignominious death upon a cross where He died for the sins of all people.

During His earth life, however, Jesus' heavenly Father praised Him: "This is my beloved Son, in whom I am well pleased" (Matt. 3:17), and so did those who experienced His saving and healing power.

* * *

What Christ Is

What the hand is to the lute,
What the breath is to the flute,
What the fragrance to the smell,
What the spring is to the well,
What the flower is to the bee,
That is Jesus Christ to me.

What the mother to the child,
What the guide in pathless wild,
What is oil to troubled wave,
What is ransom to the slave,
What is water to the sea,
That is Jesus Christ to me.

CHARLES H. SPURGEON

* * *

Empty Boxes

Some clever thieves in Illinois broke into a shoe store and stole over five hundred dollars' worth of shoes. They removed the shoes from the boxes and put the empty boxes back on the shelves. Imagine the owner's bewilderment when he pulled box after box from the shelves in waiting on a customer and found the boxes empty.

How like those shoe boxes is life without Christ—empty and disappointing.

* * *

"His Name Shall Be Called"

Dr. Hyman J. Appelman once noted: "Christ is the *Shiloh* of Genesis; the *I Am* of Exodus; the *Star and Sceptre* in Numbers; the *Rock* in Deuteronomy; the *Captain of the Lord's Host* in Joshua; and the *Redeemer* in Job; the *Lord* and *Shepherd* in the Psalms; the *Beloved* in the Song of Songs; and *Wonderful, Counsellor*, the *Mighty God* and the *Prince of Peace* in Isaiah. In Jeremiah, He is the *Lord Our Righteousness*; in Daniel, He is the *Messiah*; in Zechariah, the *Branch*; in Haggai, He is the *Desire of All Nations*; in Malachi, He is the *Messenger of the Covenant* and the *Sun of Righteousness*; in Revelation, He is the *Alpha* and the *Omega,* and the *Morning Star.*"

What is Christ to you?

What Christ Meant to Tennyson

Lord Tennyson was a humble believer in Christ. To him, Christ was a living reality. One day while out walking with his niece he said, "Christ is walking with us now, just as truly as He was with the two disciples on the road to Emmaus long ago. To feel that He is by my side now as much as you are, fills my heart with joy! There is not a flower beside our pathway that owes as much to the sun as I do to Jesus Christ."

* * *

"That Which Satisfieth Not"

Naturalists tell us of a plant called the *nardoo* plant, which grows in India. Its spores and seed are made into bread or porridge which is very pleasing to the taste. It is eaten with gusto and delight, but it possesses no nutriment for the body. One could gorge himself with the pleasant-tasting bread or porridge and die of starvation.

We may endeavor to satisfy our spiritual hunger by partaking of sinful pleasures, but our soul will shrivel. How sad it is that so many, like the prodigal son, long for worldly husks when Jesus, the bread of life, may be had for the asking.

Told by GEORGE W. TRUETT

* * *

"I Thought Only of Christ"

In a sermon, Spurgeon preached on the lordship of Christ. As a visitor was leaving the church, a friend asked him, "What do you think of Spurgeon?"

He replied, "I didn't think of Spurgeon as he preached. I thought only of Christ."

* * *

The Only Way to Take

Captain Mitsuo Fuchida, who commanded the first air fleet of the Japanese Imperial Navy, consisting of 360 planes, in the devastating attack on Pearl Harbor, became a Christian eleven years later. Said he, "Little did I dream that my view of life would be so revolutionized. Japan today is standing at the crossroads. Communism is working strongly on the left hand. The old Shinto imperialism seems to be coming back again on the right. Now, since I have found Christ, I am convinced that the way for Japan is neither left with Communism nor right with imperialism. I believe that the *only way* to take is Jesus Christ!"

* * *

Tender but Not Weak

Thomas Watson, an early leader among the Puritans, gave this glowing appraisal of Jesus: "He was tender without being weak, strong without being coarse, lowly without being servile. He had conviction without intolerance, enthusiasm without fanaticism, holiness without pharisaism, passion without prejudice. He alone never made a false step and never struck a jarring note. His life alone moved on those high levels where local limitations are transcended and the absolute law of moral beauty prevails!"

* * *

The Messiah Has Already Come

During World War II, a Jewish soldier became greatly interested in Christianity. He diligently read the New Testament. He was impressed by the life and character of Jesus.

One day he said to his rabbi, "Christians say that the Messiah has already come. You believe and teach that the long-promised Messiah is yet to come."

"That's right," said the rabbi.

Thoughtfully the soldier asked, "Rabbi, when our Messiah comes, what will he have over the Messiah who has already come?"

"That," said the rabbi, "we do not know." What else could he say?

Long ago, Jesus engaged a woman in conversation at Jacob's well. She said to Him, "I know that Messias cometh, which is called Christ: when he is come, he will tell us all things."

Jesus said to her, "I that speak unto thee am he" (John 4:26).

At the first coming of Jesus, many Old Testament prophecies were literally fulfilled. When He comes as King of kings and Lord of lords, other prophecies will be fulfilled to the letter.

Adapted from *Moody Monthly*

170

Still Vibrant in Human Relations

In a Christmas editorial, the journalist Spencer D. Irwin wrote, "The Christ Child grew to preach a philosophy that men can best be governed by love, not hate and fear. He showed that goodwill and kindness had more force over the minds and hearts of men than the legions of Rome. These truths, for which man had been groping through the ages, conquered. The power of Augustus and the Caesars vanished into the limbo of history. Still vibrant in human relations are the teachings of the Bethlehem Babe!"

* * *

"We See Jesus"

In an antique shop was a skillfully engraved copperplate picture. When looked at closely, it appeared to be only writing. When viewed from a distance, it revealed the face of George Washington. The face was depicted distinctly in the shading of the letters. A close view revealed only letters; a distant view revealed a person.

When we read God's Word meditatively, we see not mere words, but a Person —Jesus. Long ago He said, "Search the scriptures, for . . . they are they which testify of me" (John 5:39).

* * *

The All-sufficient Saviour

A frail Irish boy lay in a hospital bed. His thin face and emaciated body aroused the deepest sympathy of a lady missionary. She spoke kindly to him and won his confidence.

The missionary told him about Jesus, the sinner's all-sufficient Saviour. In turn, he spoke about penance and the confessional and the sacraments of his church, being careful not to omit the atoning death of Jesus for the sin of the world.

When the missionary called again on the boy, she found him aglow with newfound joy! Now fully assured of his salvation through Jesus Christ alone, he said to the missionary, "Oh, missus, I always knew that Jesus was necessary, but I never knew till yesterday that He was enough!"

HARRY A. IRONSIDE

Heaven Vibrant with His Praise

'Tis the Church triumphant singing,
　Worthy the Lamb!
Heaven throughout with praise is ringing,
　Worthy the Lamb!
Thrones and powers before Him bending,
Odors sweet with voices blending,
Swell the chorus, never ending,
　Worthy the Lamb!

* * *

"Never Man Spake Like This Man"

Often the enemies of Jesus asked Him subtle questions, "tempting him, that they might have to accuse him" (John 8:6).

Jesus was never in a dilemma or quandary. He answered their questions instantly and with consummate wisdom.

One time some scribes and Pharisees brought to Jesus a woman who was allegedly guilty of a capital offense under the Mosaic law—adultery. They cited Moses as ground for the condemnation of the woman and then asked Jesus, "but what sayest thou?" (v. 5).

Would Jesus go against Moses? Would He condemn the woman? He did neither. He pronounced the death sentence prescribed by Moses, but He framed it in such a way that it would be impossible to carry it out for lack of a qualified executioner: "He that is without sin, let him first cast a stone at her" (v. 7). Not one of the woman's accusers could meet the qualifying condition: "For all have sinned, and come short of the glory of God" (Rom. 3:23). Conscience-stricken, they slunk away like varmints going to their lair at daybreak.

Turning to the woman, Jesus gave her the opportunity of a new start, saying, "Neither do I condemn thee: go, and sin no more" (John 8:11).

* * *

Praise Him!

In London's Royal Albert Hall, one of God's servants attended a magnificent rendering of Handel's *Messiah* by a choir of several hundred voices. The friend who accompanied him was an aged saint, then in his seventies.

When the "Hallelujah Chorus" reached its climax with the words "King of kings and Lord of lords," the aged friend could hardly restrain himself. With tears in his eyes, he whispered, "That is *my* Saviour they are singing about!" His companion never forgot the meaning he put into *my*.

Abundant life, in full-orbed blessedness, begins with God's children when they say with Thomas, "My Lord and my God" (John 20:28).

* * *

"Give Me Thine Heart"

Said a Hindu, "No one else is seriously bidding for the *heart* of the world except Jesus Christ."

* * *

Jesus Whispers Peace

O that the world might hear Him speak
The word of comfort that men seek;
To all the lowly, and unto the meek,
Jesus whispers peace.

* * *

When Handel Wept

Handel wept uncontrollably as he read the verse "He is despised and rejected of men; a man of sorrows, and acquainted with grief" (Isa. 53:3).

* * *

Our Small Hearts

H. G. Wells asked, "Is it any wonder that to this day this Galilean, Jesus, is too much for our small hearts?"

* * *

The Thing That Counts

Bobby Richardson, former infielder with the New York Yankees, declared, "It matters not our profession or our field—the thing that counts for eternity is our personal relationship with the Lord Jesus Christ."

* * *

Plowed into History

Emerson is quoted thus: "The name of Jesus is not so much written into history as it is plowed into history."

* * *

The Cornerstone

Joseph Ernest Renan, French historian, said, "Jesus is the cornerstone of humanity. If He were taken away, it would shake the world to its foundations."

* * *

Thou Hast Conquered

The Roman Emperor Julian, "the Apostate," did everything he could to crush Christianity, but he failed.

As he lay dying on a battlefield, he lifted his face heavenward and defeatedly said, "O Galilean, Thou hast conquered!"

JEW

After 2,000 Years

In June, 1967, the Israeli troops, while battling the Jordanian soldiers, reached the Wailing Wall—the western remnant of Herod's wall around the temple area and the object of Jewish pilgrimages for centuries. In uniforms and still carrying weapons, they wept and prayed. Their chaplain, Rabbi Shlomo Goren, came and brought with him a shofar (ram's horn) and a Torah, a parchment scroll on which are written the first five books of the Old Testament. "We are now realizing the dreams of the Jews for two thousand years," he proclaimed. "We are entering the Messianic era. We shall never leave this place!"

Someday penitent Israel will have mingled joy and sorrow when God pours "upon the house of David, and upon the inhabitants of Jerusalem, the spirit of grace and of supplications: and [when] they shall look upon . . . [Him] whom they have pierced" (Zech. 12:10).

172

Planned Destruction

Rabbi Israel Miller of New York City claimed, "The Jews of the Soviet Union are victims of a policy to weaken the fabric of their lives as Jews by systematically destroying Jewry's unique threads.

"The doors of hundreds of Jewish synagogues are closed. Rabbis and teachers are growing old and there are no functioning institutions for training successors. Jewish printing presses are virtually at a standstill. Jewish children are cut off from their heritage and Jewish youth is denied its birthright—the pride and dignity of belonging to the Jewish people."

The Jew is indestructible. The Bible says, "Thus saith the LORD, which giveth the sun for a light by day, . . . the moon and . . . stars for a light by night. . . . If those ordinances depart from before me, saith the LORD, then the seed of Israel also shall cease from being a nation before me for ever" (Jer. 31:35-36).

* * *

Close to the End of the Age

Dr. Wilbur M. Smith, in *Comments on Mid-East Crisis*, stated, "For the first time since 597 B.C., the Jews have sovereignty over the old city of Jerusalem. If they can keep it, we are very close to the end of the age.

"It is an interesting fact that the city of Jerusalem is the city of peace, for *salem* is 'peace.' This city, however, has had more war and bloodshed than any other great city in the world. It has changed hands twenty-six times. It has been destroyed five times. But the Word still holds."

* * *

"That's My Favorite Verse!"

One day I visited a Jewess in Mercy Hospital, Chicago. She was a woman of affluence and culture. At her bedside stood two Jews, manifestly men of means.

I was kindly received. It is my custom in visiting sick people to pray and include John 3:16 in my prayer. I thought, *If I quote the verse, I might offend these Jewish people.* God seemed to say to me, "What are you here for if not to speak for the One who saves from sin and who is the *only way* to God?"

In my prayer, I quoted the verse.

Imagine my joy and surprise when the Jewess said, "That verse you quoted comforts me. It has become my favorite verse!"

"Ye that make mention of the LORD, keep not silence" (Isa. 62:6).

W. B. K.

* * *

When a Jew Ceases to Be a Jew

The Supreme Court of Israel ruled that a Roman Catholic cannot be a Jew. Father Daniel is a Polish-born Jew. He became a Catholic. He claimed Israeli citizenship under stipulations of the country's Law of Return.

Speaking for the court, Judge Moshe Silberg said, "The Law of Return is secular legislation and must be interpreted according to secular principles. The question is What is the ordinary Jewish meaning of the term Jew? Does it include an apostate? From the extreme Orthodox Jew to freethinkers, there is one thing common to all people who dwell in Zion—we do not sever ourselves from the historic past and we do not deny the heritage of our forefathers. There are some differences of nuance and approach, but the lowest common denominator is that no one can regard an apostate as belonging to the Jewish people."

A change in one's religion today costs little in comparison to what Paul suffered when he accepted Jesus as the true Messiah. Paul "suffered the loss of all things" to champion Christ's cause and follow Him.

* * *

Slowly Strangled

Russia's three million Jews are being subjected to a systematic, shocking and shameful persecution. The Jew has no religious articles, like the prayer shawl or phylacteries. He is permitted no publications. No Hebrew Bible has been published for Jews since 1917. The study of Hebrew has been outlawed, even for religious purposes. The Jew has no central organization nor nationwide federations and he is vilified in the rigidly controlled Soviet press. Jews are not being slaughtered in mass pogroms as once was the style there. But they are being slowly strangled.

ABRAHAM A. RIBICOFF

* * *

A Searching Question

David Ben-Gurion, a former prime minister of Israel, said to William L. Hull, a missionary: "The New Testament teaching and standards are wonderful, but where are those who live up to them? Are there any folk in the world who do? Are there any living the Christian life? Can this Book really produce that which it sets forth?"

Mr. Hull replied, "God has saved me and made me a new creature in Christ."

"But are there others like you?" asked the prime minister.

"Yes, millions," he replied.

"Where are they then? Why do they let conditions exist as they are in the world today?" asked Ben-Gurion.

Much is expected of Christians. The question persists: "What do ye more than others?" (Matt. 5:47).

* * *

The True Messiah

A Hebrew Christian engaged a Jewish friend in conversation. "I want to read to you a portion of the Bible," he said, "and when I have finished, I want you to tell me what part of the Bible I have read." Then he began to read Isaiah 53. When he had finished, he asked, "From what part of the Bible did I read?"

Without hesitation, the Jewish friend replied, "From the New Testament."

"And to whom does the passage refer?"

"To Jesus of Nazareth," was the reply. Then the Hebrew Christian said,

"Your first answer was incorrect. Your last answer was correct. The scripture I read was from the book of Isaiah, and it contains several remarkable prophecies about Jesus Christ, the true Messiah."

Jesus said, "Search the scriptures; for . . . they are they which testify of me" (John 5:39).

* * *

The Indestructible Jew

William Gladstone was asked to tell his reason for believing in the inspiration of the Bible. He replied, "The Jew."

There are in the world today 12,000,000 Jews. They trace their genealogy back nearly four thousand years to Abraham, a Middle East nomad.

Their continuance through forty centuries as a self-conscious entity, unassimilated into other races, makes the Jews a unique people.

Through the centuries, the Jews have been savagely persecuted and great numbers of them have been liquidated. Heartless tyrants have sought their extirpation from the earth. Genocide, or their racial destruction, was the avowed fiendish purpose of Hitler when six million of them perished in his incinerators.

Still, the Jew lives. He is indestructible. The Bible says, "Thus saith the LORD, which giveth the sun for a light by day, and the ordinances of the moon and of the stars for a light by night, which divideth the sea when the waves thereof roar; The LORD of hosts is his name: If those ordinances depart from before me, saith the LORD, then the seed of Israel also shall cease from being a nation before me for ever" (Jer. 31:35-36).

As a race, the Jew has placed an ineradicable mark on human history, especially in the moral and religious life of mankind. From the Jew came the world's great theistic religions—Judaism and Christianity.

174

JOY

Where May Joy Be Found?

Dr. Peter Rossi, a sociologist at the University of Chicago, said, "All it takes to be happy is youth, money, success, good health and a wife. Possessing these requisites, one has found a wellspring of happiness."

We do not speak disparagingly of these blessings, but it is possible to have all of them and lack happiness, not to mention the deeper, lasting joy. Sometimes the most wretched persons are those who have them.

Nero, emperor of the Roman Empire, lived only for the ephemeral glories and pleasures of the world. He died a suicide. He grew so weary of passing pleasures that he offered rich rewards to those devising new ones. His crown was worth a half million dollars. A thousand chariots accompanied him when he traveled. He never wore the same garment twice. Still he was peevish, gloomy and miserable.

King Solomon, too, had a superabundance of the things Dr. Rossi equated with happiness. Solomon said, "Whatsoever mine eyes desired I kept not from them, I withheld not my heart from any joy" (Eccles. 2:10). He tried wine, women, wealth, works and wisdom.

Did they bring abiding joy? The contrary was true. Solomon said, "I hated life; . . . for all is vanity and vexation of spirit" (Eccles. 2:17).

Where, then, may unalloyed joy be found? It can be found only in the Lord, who bequeathed to all of God's children peace: "Peace I leave with you, my peace I give unto you" (John 14:27).

* * *

How Can I Keep from Singing?

My life flows on in endless song;
　Above earth's lamentation
I catch the sweet, tho' far-off, hymn
　That hails a new creation!
Thro' all the tumult and the strife
　I hear the music ringing;
It finds an echo in my soul—
　How can I keep from singing?

What tho' my joys and comfort die?
　The Lord my Saviour liveth.
What tho' the darkness gather round?
　Songs in the night He giveth!
No storm can shake my inmost calm,
　While to that refuge clinging;
Since Christ is Lord of heaven and earth,
　How can I keep from singing?

I lift my eyes—the cloud grows thin,
　I see the blue above it;
And day by day this pathway smooths,
　Since first I learned to love it!
The peace of Christ makes glad my heart,
　A fountain ever springing;
All things are mine since I am His—
　How can I keep from singing?

ROBERT LOWERY, in *United Presbyterian*

* * *

The Secret Disclosed

Actor Zero Mostel was asked about the secret of his happiness. He replied, "Getting lost—being involved in something you can't understand. Mystery is the main thing in life. Why should you have to understand everything?"

* * *

No Reason to Look Glum

One Christmas Eve, as late Christmas shoppers hurried along the street, a crippled newsboy stood on his crutches offering his papers to the passersby. He looked happy and his crutches were decorated with evergreens.

One man greeted him with a cheerful smile. "My boy, you surely have the Christmas spirit."

The boy replied, "What's the use of putting on a sour face? Sure, I'm poor and lame but that's no reason for looking glum. I won't get a lot of presents, like other boys get at Christmas; but I can have fun, too. So I decorated my crutches just to make them seem special for Christmas."

If we go out to seek joy, it will elude

us. If we go out to impart joy, we will find it.

Told by ALICE MARIE KNIGHT

* * *

Mr. Glory-Face

The face of Adoniram Judson was so aglow with the love of God that the Burmese called him Mr. Glory-Face.

The face of Stephen also shone with heavenly radiance: "And all that sat in the council . . . saw his face as it had been the face of an angel" (Acts 6:15).

* * *

Scatter Sunshine

Years ago a Boston daily commented thus on the weather: "The day opened cloudy and cheerless but about noon Phillips Brooks came downtown and everything brightened up."

Jesus said, "Ye are the light of the world. . . . Let your light so shine before men . . . and glorify your Father" (Matt. 5:14-16).

* * *

Impart Joy

Laugh, and the world laughs with you;
    Weep, and you weep alone;
For the sad old earth must borrow its
        mirth,
    But has trouble enough of its own.

Sing, and the hills will answer;
    Sigh, it is lost on the air;
The echoes bound to a joyful sound,
    But shrink from voicing care.

Rejoice, and men will seek you;
    Grieve, and they turn and go;
They want full measure of all your
        pleasure,
    But they do not need your woe.

ELLA WHEELER WILCOX

* * *

Cheer Up!

"Cheer up!" the sparrow chirpeth,
    "Thy Father feedeth me;
Think how much more He careth,
    O lonely child, for thee!

"Then don't you trouble trouble
    Till trouble troubles you;
You'll only double trouble,
    And trouble others, too."

* * *

The Happiest People

Dr. George Gallup took a poll of a representative group to ascertain which people are happiest. He said, "Our survey showed that the happiest people are those who have had a real religious experience. The most unhappy people are those who frequent taverns."

* * *

Radiant Faces

Robert Murray McCheyne, saintly Church of Scotland divine, exclaimed, "Oh, for the holy shining of the face and the holy unawareness of the shining: 'Moses wist not that the skin of his face shone' [Exodus 34:29]."

A biographer said of Henry Martyn, famed English missionary to India and Persia, "His features were not regular, but his facial expression was so luminous, so intellectual, so affectionate, so beaming with divine love as to hold the attention of every onlooker."

Long ago when Stephen stood before his enraged accusers, they "saw his face as it had been the face of an angel" (Acts 6:15).

The upward vision causes the heart to rejoice and the face to shine: "They looked unto him [God], and were lightened [cheered]: and their faces were not ashamed" (Ps. 34:5).

* * *

Shining Serenity

A contemporary of John Wesley said of him, "He thought prayer to be more his business than anything else. I have seen him come out of his closet with a serenity of face next to shining."

It is said of Jesus, "And as he prayed, the fashion of his countenance was altered" (Luke 9:29).

176

JUDGMENT

A Weeping Judge

Ray H. Lane, Jr., murdered a policeman. When the jury returned its verdict —guilty—no recommendation for mercy accompanied it. The death sentence, therefore, was mandatory.

When Superior Court Judge Wayne Millington pronounced the death sentence and concluded it with the words "And may God have mercy on your soul," he broke down and wept. He left immediately and locked himself in his chambers. Later he emerged to talk with newsmen. "When I went out there," he said, "I had no thought that this would happen. Then all of a sudden—bang! It was a very unpleasant situation, but we judges have to meet them."

Does God, the Judge of all mankind, take pleasure in passing sentence upon the wicked who spurn His offers of mercy and forgiveness? "As I live, saith the Lord GOD, I have no pleasure in the death of the wicked" (Ezek. 33:11).

* * *

Look First into Your Own Heart

John Hyde, also known as Praying Hyde, underwent a transforming experience as he prayed for a certain pastor whose spirituality he judged to be very low. Entering his "inner chamber," he began his prayer thus: "O God, Thou knowest how cold the brother is." That's as far as he got. God's hand seemed to be laid on his lips, and a voice said rebukingly to him, "Before you judge another, look well into your own heart for coldness."

A feeling of horror and self-loathing came over him. He was humbled before God, who revealed to him that he must first get right with God before he could pray rightly and prevailingly for anyone. As he searched his own heart, he began to thank and praise God for the brother whom he later learned had a deeper spiritual experience because of Hyde's prayer for him.

An American Indian chief often prayed, "Great Spirit, don't let me criticize my brother until I have walked a mile in his moccasins."

* * *

The Day of Wrath

The day of wrath, that dreadful day,
When heaven and earth shall pass away!
What power shall be the sinner's stay?
How shall he meet that dreadful day?

When, shivering like a parched scroll,
The flaming heavens together roll,
And louder yet, and yet more dread,
Swells the high trump that wakes the
    dead!

O on that day, that wrathful day,
When man to judgment wakes from clay;
Be Thou, O Christ, the sinner's stay,
Though heaven and earth shall pass
    away.

SIR WALTER SCOTT

* * *

Judge Not

In men whom men condemn as ill
I find so much of goodness still,
In men whom men pronounce divine
I find so much of sin and blot,
I do not dare to draw a line
Between the two, where God has not.

JOAQUIN MILLER

* * *

Business as Usual

"In the death of a great civilization, the masses are always unaware of their tragedy," said Bishop Fulton J. Sheen.

In the midst of a morally and spiritually confused world, there exists a business-as-usual attitude.

"Awake thou that sleepest." It is later dispensationally than we think it is. As we scan world horizons through the telescope of the "sure word of prophecy," we are constrained to say, "The coming of the Lord draweth nigh!" (James 5:8).

Bow in Grace or Judgment

In executing his political enemies—those who have refused to bow in submission to him and his Communistic regime—Fidel Castro has the firing squad shoot them first in the legs. Thus they are forced to bow in death.

Those who do not voluntarily bow to Christ in grace will bow to Him in judgment, "and . . . confess that Jesus Christ is Lord, to the glory of God the Father" (Phil. 2:11).

Why not bow in grace now and acclaim Him as "my Lord and my God," as Thomas did (John 20:28)?

* * *

With Whom He Disagreed

A minister preached a searching sermon on the judgment.

The next day a young man said to him, "I heard your sermon yesterday, and I don't believe what you preached."

"Let's talk it over," said the minister.

The young man said, "I don't believe, as you said, that the wicked go into eternal punishment."

"Oh," said the minister, "your disagreement is not with me. It is with the Lord Jesus Christ. He said long ago, 'And these shall go away into everlasting punishment: but the righteous into life eternal' [Matt. 25:46]. I would urge you to turn to Christ immediately and try to harmonize your differences."

Adapted from *Evangelist*

* * *

"Will Jesus Understand?"

As one of God's children neared the close of his life, he was in great distress. His pastor spoke comfortingly and assuringly to him. The man listened as if in a trance. Then he said, "I am saved. I have no fear of dying. But what can I say at the judgment seat of Christ about the wasted years of my life? Will He understand?"

* * *

"God Hath Appointed a Day"

A disastrous explosion and fire occurred in Boston. Two hotels were wrecked and at least thirteen persons were killed and more than fifty were injured.

In describing what occurred, William Terrenzi, district fire chief, said, "The explosion lifted up the floor of a cocktail lounge and dumped it right down below!"

A survivor said, "There were about thirty or thirty-five people in the bar at the time. Everybody began to scream and holler as the ceiling fell and the floor caved in!"

How suggestive this tragedy is of God's coming judgment, for then the flimsy foundation of people's self-righteousness will crumble beneath them, and every false way will be destroyed. "Them . . . that obey not the gospel of our Lord Jesus Christ . . . shall be punished with everlasting destruction" (II Thess. 1:8-9).

* * *

Two Guiding Stimuli

Dr. Wernher Von Braun, development operations director, Army Ballistic Missile Agency, has stated, "Two stimuli are necessary to make man endeavor to conform with the accepted ethical standards: belief in an ultimate judgment and belief in the immortality of the soul. Belief in God and in immortality gives us the moral strength and ethical guidance we need for virtually every action in our daily lives."

JUSTICE

An Ironic Occurrence

Harry Glick, an inmate of the Ohio Penitentiary, designed an electric chair, but it did not work. At the suggestion of Charles Justice, a fellow prisoner, he designed another chair with arm and leg clamps, and it proved to be satisfactory.

Charles Justice was pardoned. Later he committed murder, was arraigned, tried and sentenced to death. On October

27, 1911, he died in the electric chair he had helped to design for the death of others.

The incident is reminiscent of wicked Haman, who was "hanged . . . on the gallows he had prepared for Mordecai" (Esther 7:10).

* * *

Given What Was Asked For

Judge Kaufman presided at the trial of the Russian spies, the Rosenbergs. They were charged and convicted of treason against the United States, and sentenced to death.

The trial was long and bitter. Judge Kaufman was harassed and insulted.

In his summation at the end of the long trial, the lawyer for the Rosenbergs said animatedly, "Your Honor, what my clients ask is for justice!"

Judge Kaufman replied calmly, "The court has given you what you ask for—justice! What you really want is mercy. But that is something this court has no right to give."

Each of us has sinned against the Judge of all the earth—God. If God gave us justice, our case would be hopeless: "If thou, LORD, shouldest mark iniquities, O LORD, who shall stand?" (Ps. 130:3).

We are grateful that "the LORD is merciful and gracious" (Ps. 103:8), and that "it is of the LORD's mercies that we are not consumed" (Lam. 3:22).

Because of the vicarious death of Christ, who paid the penalty for our sins, God acts in mercy toward those who penitently turn from sin to Him.

* * *

The Wrong Man Hanged

The plea of Timothy Evans was as old as justice itself. "You have the wrong man," he said when he was indicted for murdering his wife and infant daughter. "The real killer is the prosecution's star witness, John Christie."

Neither the judge nor the jury was impressed. In 1950, Evans was hanged in a London prison.

Three years later some startling new evidence was brought to light. In the garden and wall of Christie's rundown,

ratty place, police found the bodies of seven women. Among them was the corpse of Evans' wife!

Sixteen years after his execution, Timothy Evans was given a posthumous pardon by Queen Elizabeth. This cleared his name of the horrible crime for which he was innocently executed.

In this life, glaring and irreparable miscarriage of justice often occurs. However, the sins and crimes of evildoers will surely find them out, either in this life or in the life to come.

Men's sins find them out before the bar of conscience: "It is John, whom I beheaded: he is risen from the dead" (Mark 6:16).

Their sins often find them out in their posterity: "Our fathers have sinned, and are not; and we have borne their iniquities" (Lam. 5:7).

And their sins find them out before God's bar of justice: "God shall judge the secrets of men by Jesus Christ" (Rom. 2:16).

* * *

Distorted Justice

A glaring miscarriage of justice took place because of a ruling of the U.S. Supreme Court that an accused person must be advised of his right to counsel at the time of his arrest.

Judge John M. Manos of the Common Pleas Court, Cleveland, Ohio, freed two ex-convicts because they had not been advised of their right to counsel at the time of their arrest, though they had been involved in 274 crimes of larceny, housebreaking and burglary since 1964.

In freeing them, the judge said, "I know of no greater travesty of justice than to release two men like you. Neither of you is worthy of the protective features of the law. The pity of it is that the police were following existing rules at the time of their investigation."

The Bible says, "And judgment is turned away backward, and justice standeth afar off: for truth is fallen in the street, and equity cannot enter" (Isa. 59:14).

* * *

Swift Justice

Sometimes justice overtakes evildoers

179

swiftly and summarily. An eighteen-year-old youth was fatally burned in Sandusky, Ohio, while setting fire to the building of his father's competitor.

Long ago swift justice was meted out to Ananias and his wife Sapphira for lying: "Thou hast not lied unto men, but unto God" (Acts 5:4). What a thriving business morticians would do if all evildoers were thus speedily dealt with!

* * *

Unjust Recompense

George E. Robison was freed from the Ohio Penitentiary after serving a prison term of twelve extra years by mistake. He had committed a crime whose penalty called for a maximum sentence of two years. How this mistake occurred is not known.

Asked about the offense for which he was sent to prison, Robison said, "I pled guilty because I was told I'd get only one to two years. I am now fifty-three years old, and the twelve years I mistakenly spent in prison might otherwise have been the best years of my life."

Injustices often occur. Sometimes evildoers escape detection. There are occasions when the penalty imposed on them is severer than the crime justifies. Sometimes the penalty is far short of just and deserved punishment.

In reference to God's punishment of evildoers, the Bible says: "Every transgression and disobedience received a just recompense of reward" (Heb. 2:2), and "God . . . hath appointed a day, in the which he will judge the world in righteousness by that man [Jesus] whom he hath ordained" (Acts 17:30-31).

KINDNESS

Late-ripening Fruit

Many years ago, a lonely traveler stopped one Sunday morning for the worship service at the Andersonville Methodist Church in Georgia. At the close of the service, he was warmly greeted by the people. Then he left and was never seen again.

Recently in Washington, New Jersey, Robert B. Brown, age ninety, died. Some commented, "He was a thrifty man who kept to himself."

Mr. Brown bequeathed his entire estate to the Andersonville Methodist Church! His estate consisted of 2,100 shares of American Telephone and Telegraph Company stock and 740 shares of Continental Can Company stock. At the time of Mr. Brown's death, the stocks were worth $178,302.50. The dividends from them will bring about $5,000 annually to the Andersonville church.

The decedent's attorney, Martin B. Bry-Nildsen, informing the church of the bequest, wrote: "My client told me that on a Sunday morning years ago, when he was traveling through Georgia, he felt

sad and lonely. He stopped at your church. A friendly welcome was accorded him. He never forgot the kindness you showed him. He did not have any church affiliation and said, 'I want to give what I have to that little church!' "

The lawyer added this personal comment: "This is a good example of the parable of the mustard seed. Just look at the fruit borne by a tiny seed of kindness, sown long ago!"

How surprised were Rev. W. J. Stanford and the members of the Andersonville Methodist Church! No one could recall Mr. Brown's visit to the church.

Constitution State News Service

* * *

Love Killed by Kindness

Is it possible to kill love by kindness? One incident where this occurred was told in a newspaper article under the caption "Kindness Makes Her Heart Grow Harder." Here are the salient features:

Leona P. Jeske, age sixty, asked for a divorce from her husband, Carl, age sixty-eight, on the ground of mental cruelty.

In the Superior Court at Oakland, California, she complained, "He never would let me wash the dishes or do the washing and ironing. When I was baking, he would jump up and take the pan from me as I was removing it from the oven, saying, 'I'm afraid you'll burn yourself.' At night, he would insist on tucking me into bed.

"At first, I went along with his attentiveness. In time, I began to feel that he was treating me like a child. I became nervous and upset. His actions caused me grievous mental suffering."

Lyle E. Cooke, the presiding judge, commented, "This is one of the strangest forms of mental cruelty I have ever come across. Some men just can't win."

Mr. Jeske's excessive kindness was actually depriving his wife of the joy of creative work and of being his helpmeet. Her life had lost purpose and fulfillment.

The perfect loving-kindness of God inspires love and provides even more joy and satisfaction than life itself. "Because thy lovingkindness is better than life, my lips shall praise thee" (Ps. 63:3).

* * *

Christ Often Unrecognized

In an orphanage, the superintendent usually gave thanks at dinnertime, saying, "Come, Lord Jesus, be our Guest, and bless the food which Thou hast provided."

One evening a little orphan boy remarked, "You always ask Jesus to come, but He never does. Will He ever come?"

"Oh, yes," said the superintendent, "if we really want Him to, He will come."

"I want Him to come," said the little boy. "I'll put a chair beside me tonight to be ready for Jesus when He comes."

As the orphans were eating, there was a knock at the door. Standing there was an old man who was cold, hungry and poorly clothed.

"Come in and warm yourself," said the kind superintendent. Then he added, "And join us at our meal. There is an empty chair waiting for you!"

The old man sat down beside the boy. Later the boy exclaimed, "I see it now! Jesus wasn't able to come Himself tonight, so He sent the poor man in His place! Isn't that it?"

"That is it," said the superintendent. "Often Jesus comes to us in the persons of those who need our help and encouragement. When we help them in His name, it is the same as helping Jesus Himself. Jesus said, 'Inasmuch as ye have done it unto one of the least of these my brethren, ye have done it unto me' [Matt. 25:40]."

Told by ALICE MARIE KNIGHT

* * *

Risked Life by Helping a White Man

Roy A. Harrell, Jr., in Lenten Guideposts, related the following experience. "In October, 1960, I was on a flight to Brazzaville, Congo. The plane was grounded because of engine trouble. I was cautioned to stay away from the city itself, but I left the airport on foot, determined to find a way to reach my destination. Ahead of me was a group of soldiers, talking angrily. As I approached them, one of them grabbed me. I shook him off, but another knocked me flat.

"Later, I hired a car and driver to take me to Leopoldville. Some Kasavubu soldiers rushed out of a home and dragged us both from the car. One of them knocked me down with the butt of his gun. Another guard pulled me to my feet and told me to leave.

"As I stood dazed and hesitant on a street corner, an African woman spoke to me, asking what happened. I told her. She took me over to a water hydrant and bathed the cuts on my face. I said to the woman, 'You had better not let the Force Publique see you helping a white man.'

" 'Monsieur, I don't care if you are white or not. It is my Christian duty to help you,' she said simply. Then she led me to the safety of the American Embassy and said, 'As children of God, we must have faith in the Lord, and in His mercy, that all things happen for the best. Through misfortune we often become better Christians.'

"I would like to forget the entire experience, but I can't forget that gentle Congolese woman who practiced her

181

Christian belief in the face of mob violence."

* * *

General Patton Did It

During World War II some soldiers were stationed in the California desert for final maneuvers before being shipped overseas. The men were granted weekend passes, but the one train passing through the small community didn't stop. How dejected and disappointed the servicemen were as they stood on the platform.

The commanding general, George S. Patton, heard what had occurred. The following weekend, he stood alone on the station platform, in full-dress uniform. The servicemen kept themselves out of sight.

Seeing the general, the engineer brought his train to a grinding stop. From their hiding places, the soldiers came running and boarded the train.

As the train pulled out, the soldiers waved gratefully from every window to General Patton, still standing on the platform, smiling.

Told by an army chaplain

* * *

The Greatest Pleasure

Charles Lamb is quoted as saying, "The greatest pleasure I know is to do a good deed by *stealth* and have it found out by *accident*."

* * *

Things Left Undone

It isn't the thing you do, dear,
 It's the thing you leave undone
Which gives you the bitter heartache
 At the setting of the sun;
The tender word unspoken,
 The letter you did not write,
The flower you might have sent, dear,
 Are your haunting ghosts at night.

The stone you might have lifted
 Out of your brother's way,
The bit of heartsome counsel
 You were hurried too much to say,
The loving touch of the hand, dear,
 The gentle and winsome tone,
That you had no time or thought for,
 With troubles enough of your own.

* * *

"Never Mind"

Sometimes, when nothing goes just right
 And worry reigns supreme,
When heartache fills the eyes with mist,
 And all things useless seem,
There's just one thing can drive away
 The tears that scald and blind—
Someone to slip a strong arm 'round
 And whisper, "Never mind."

No one has ever told just why
 Those words much comfort bring,
Nor why that whisper makes our cares
 Depart on hurried wing;
Yet troubles say a quick "Good-day,"
 We leave them far behind,
When someone slips an arm around
 And whispers, "Never mind."

But love must prompt that soft caress,
 That love must, aye, be true;
Or at that tender, clinging touch
 No heartease comes to you;
But if the arm be moved by love,
 Sweet comfort you will find,
When someone slips an arm around
 And whispers, "Never mind."

Evangelical Visitor

LAW

When One Link Breaks

On December 15, 1967, the Silver Bridge, which spanned the Ohio River at Point Pleasant, West Virginia, collapsed. The awesome tragedy occurred during the rush hour when the structure was loaded with traffic. Cars and trucks plunged into the dark, murky water, and many perished. Forty-two bodies were recovered; four were not found.

182

Dr. Thomas Stelson, head of the civil engineering department of Carnegie-Mellon University in Pittsburgh, said, "The bridge was probably subjected to the greatest load it had ever been under. It was the first bridge in the United States to be constructed with heat-treated I-bars holding up the roadway instead of woven wire strands. The I-bars are like chains and a chain is only as strong as its weakest link. The I-bar linkage to one of the supporting piers on the upstream side failed. This threw the full weight of the roadway on the other side, which couldn't hold it either."

Long ago God welded a chain of ten links—the Ten Commandments. Its "thou shalts" and "thou shalt nots" were designed for mankind's highest and enduring good. They are as binding, in their moral implications, as when they were first thundered from Sinai's rocky crags. When one link, or commandment, is broken, man is adjudged a lost sinner by God—guilty of breaking all of them: "For whosoever shall keep the whole law, and yet offend in one point, he is guilty of all" (James 2:10).

* * *

Divinely Placed Barriers

Speeding over the Pennsylvania Turnpike at a death-defying eighty-five miles per hour, four teenagers died horribly in a head-on crash with another car occupied by the driver, his wife and their three-year-old daughter. The husband was instantly killed, and the wife and daughter were critically hurt.

The tragic accident occurred when the car of the joyriding teenagers hurtled over the three-foot metal road divider and smashed into the oncoming car.

Along life's highway, God in goodness has placed barriers to keep us from going on the downward way to destruction. One such barrier is the Ten Commandments. Their "thou shalts" and "thou shalt nots" were designed for man's protection and

good. When man hurls himself against this adamant barrier, he breaks not the barrier but himself: "The word of the Lord endureth for ever" (I Peter 1:25).

* * *

The Unchanging Moral Law

The Ten Commandments are as up-to-date and urgently needed today as when they were thundered from Sinai's crags.

The Union of Orthodox Jewish Congregations of America urged a White House conference on public morals to help "strengthen and elevate moral standards of American society and ask Americans to affirm the immutability of the moral law established by the Creator and revealed to man on Sinai, and reject the notion that the mores of a society can substitute, or change, the moral norm."

Who is so undiscerning as to deny the widespread moral decay?

Human cures are futile to change man's desperately wicked heart: "Can the Ethiopian change his skin? . . . then may ye also do good, that are accustomed to do evil" (Jer. 13:23).

* * *

The Law's Limitation

C. H. Mackintosh has stated, "If I stand before a mirror with disheveled hair and a smudged face, it shows me my disarrayed hair and soiled face, but it does not straighten my hair or clean my face. If I measure a crooked wall with a perfect plumb line, the plumb line reveals the crookedness of the wall, but it does not straighten it. If I take a lantern out on a dark night, it reveals to me the objects over which I could stumble, but it does not remove them. The mirror and the plumb line and the lantern do not create the evils or remove them. They only reveal them. So it is with the law of God. It does not create the evil in the heart of man or remove it. It only reveals it."

183

Paul said, "By the law is the knowledge of sin" (Rom. 3:20).

* * *

Lawful Things Unlawfully Used

Unlawful things have ruined thousands. Lawful things, unlawfully used, have ruined tens of thousands. The existence of bodily appetites presupposes the lawfulness of their gratification. Hunger is satisfied by partaking of food, but only in moderation—not gluttonously. Warningly the Bible says, "And put a knife to thy throat, if thou be a man given to appetite" (Prov. 23:2).

"Enlawed" Inexorably to Christ

Dr. A. W. Tozer explained, "Freedom from the law means to be 'enlawed' inexorably to Christ. The Mosaic law deals primarily with outward misdeeds—overt acts. Jesus gets to the root of the matter and emphasizes the inward thoughts, moods and dispositions which prompt the outward sin: 'Ye have heard that it was said by them of old time, Thou shalt not commit adultery: but I say unto you, That whosoever looketh on a woman to lust after her hath committed adultery with her already in his heart' [Matt. 5:27-28]."

LAWLESSNESS

I Can't Sleep at Night

Having been robbed ten times, Charles Vargo, the owner of a service station in Cleveland, Ohio, closed his business after years of honest service to a large clientele.

Charles complained, "I hate to close my gas station. I've built up a good business, but I'm afraid somebody's going to get killed. I can't sleep at night anymore."

How shameful it is that a law-abiding, hardworking man is forced out of business by the lawless element of our society!

* * *

Anyone Is a Potential Criminal

Editorialized *Christianity Today*, "The President's Commission on Law Enforcement and Administration of Justice fails to recognize godlessness as a basic cause of crime, and religion as a basic cure. None of the experts in government, sociology and education say that man commits crime because he is a sinner and rebels against God. The root of sin in a person's life makes anyone a potential criminal."

It is either Christ or crime.

"I Will Never Forget It"

Two youths of Cleveland, Ohio, were found guilty of first-degree murder. They had robbed and murdered a gas station attendant during a crime spree. They were sentenced to prison for life. The three judges who presided at the trial decreed that the boys be placed in solitary confinement February 12-23 each year, the time of their crime spree.

"I don't need solitary confinement to remind me of the shooting," one boy said. "I will never forget it. I am very sorry."

The other boy confided, "I tried to be a grown man. I would listen to their talk, smoke cigarettes and drink liquor with them. I wanted to show off."

The remorse and regret of the two boys could not restore the murdered man to his family.

* * *

Criminals Get the Break

It is becoming increasingly difficult for officers of the law to arrest and convict criminals. Obviously the criminals often get the break instead of law-abiding citizens.

When apprehending one who is guilty or suspected of crime, the arresting officer must present to him a card which reads, "You do not have to make a statement. If you do make a statement, anything you say will be used against you. You are entitled to the advice of an attorney. If you cannot afford an attorney, one will be appointed for you."

The Bible says, "Because sentence against an evil work is not executed speedily . . . the heart of the sons of men is fully set in them to do evil" (Eccles. 8:11).

* * *

Calling Evil Good

After a horrible crime had been committed against a young girl by six teenage boys, the policeman said this about the youthful criminals: "They are not really evil but are basically good."

How utterly at variance with the officer's appraisal is the ancient prophets' depiction of the wickedness of human hearts: "The heart is deceitful above all things, and desperately wicked: who can know it?" (Jer. 17:9); "The whole head is sick, and the whole heart faint. From the sole of the foot even unto the head there is no soundness in it; but wounds, and bruises, and putrifying sores" (Isa. 1:5-6).

For confirmation of these divine appraisals of the unregenerate heart of man, read your daily newspaper.

* * *

Perpetuity of Nation Threatened

J. Edgar Hoover said, "Crime is of such magnitude as to threaten the very perpetuity of our nation. Our daily crime bill is $60 million. Our streets are as fraught with danger as jungle trails. Crime has doubled in the last ten years. One-half to two-thirds of the crimes are committed by youths less than eighteen years old."

* * *

Crime Pays

Richard Starnes, news columnist, reported, "Ever since a purloined apple caused the tenants of the Garden of Eden to be evicted, moralists, policemen, parents and teachers have been preaching that crime does not pay. By any sensible yardstick, however, that hoary bromide is false. Crime, by a conservative estimate of the FBI, is an annual $27 billion business in the United States!"

In the ultimate analysis, ill-gotten gain does not prosper evildoers. A time of reaping is inevitable. Evildoers and their progeny reap a dire harvest: "Be not deceived . . . whatsoever a man soweth, that shall he also reap" (Gal. 6:7); "Our fathers have sinned, and are not; and we have borne their iniquities" (Lam. 5:7).

* * *

Growing Six Times Faster than Population

Cartha Dekle DeLoach, the probable successor to FBI director J. Edgar Hoover, in addressing the American Farm Bureau Federation convention, gave these statistics: "The volume of crime in the U. S. has risen 58 percent since 1958 and is growing six times as fast as the population. More than 2.6 million serious offenses—an all-time high record—were reported to U. S. police departments in 1964. Americans in the ten-to-seventeen age group comprise 15 percent of the population but were charged with 43 percent of all crimes against property in 1964."

* * *

Flout with Impunity

Earl F. Morris, president of the American Bar Association, said, "An ordered society cannot survive—and ours, strong as it is, will not survive—if each individual may determine which laws he will obey, and may with impunity flout those which he finds distasteful."

* * *

A Grave Problem

J. Edgar Hoover made this statement: "To every man and every nation there comes a time when decisions must be made about grave problems. Further delay can bring disaster. That time has come for the United States. We must now face realistically the startling fact that since 1958 crime has increased six times faster than the population growth; that youths are now involved in nearly three-quarters of the crimes committed.

185

The moral strength of our nation has decreased alarmingly. We must return to the teachings of God if we are to cure this sickness!"

Let the people of our nation personally and penitently acknowledge the fact that to us "belongeth confusion of face . . . because we have sinned against . . . [God]" (Dan. 9:8).

"O LORD, revive thy work in the midst of the years . . . ; in wrath remember mercy" (Hab. 3:2).

* * *

Pampered or Punished, Which?

In the field of crime and social justice the doctrine is rapidly becoming fashionable to believe that the real victim is the criminal whose actions are conditioned by heredity and environment and irresistible impulses for which he is not responsible. He must therefore be pampered and not punished. This doctrine encourages the criminal in the illusion that resistance to temptation is useless!

Christianity Today

* * *

Bleeding-heart Judges

Bishop Fulton J. Sheen said, "A federal judge in Washington assailed the unfortunate trend of judicial decisions which strain and stretch to give the guilty not the same but vastly more protection than the law-abiding citizen.

"Bleeding-heart judges are so concerned for criminals and terrorists that today the good citizens are considered off the reservation, as the new compassion exalts the guilty and condemns the innocent.

"What is the cause of this reversal of judgment? The loss of a moral sense. Dostoevski wrote that in the future day men would say there is no crime, no sin, no guilt."

Long ago God's prophet pronounced woe upon such self-deluded men who "call evil good, and good evil; who put darkness for light, and light for darkness" (Isa. 5:20).

* * *

Our Survival Threatened

Justice Charles E. Whittaker of the U. S. Supreme Court warned, "Can any thoughtful person reasonably believe that a disorderly society can survive? In all recorded history, none ever has. History shows that every society which became lawless soon succumbed, and that the first evidences of each society's decay appeared in the toleration of disobedience of its laws and the judgments of its courts."

* * *

Misplaced Blame

"We are not presuming to condemn a race or a color, but only the small minority of criminal elements which takes to the streets and spreads fire, violence and theft throughout the community, while the appalled majority—black and white —is forced to stand by helplessly.

"Our burning cities are the reward for indulgence. We are lectured by the Kerner Commission on Civil Disorders that 'white racism is especially responsible' for the revolt against civil order. That is not only silly but contemptible. White racism exists, but black racism demonstrably exists, too. . . . There are immoral white people. So are there immoral colored people. It is this fringe which is the common enemy. This is what the Kerner commission ignored. The commission put the blame everywhere but where it belongs—everywhere, that is, except upon the rioters."

Chicago Daily Tribune

* * *

Fifty-year-old Delinquents

Supreme Court Justice William O. Douglas remarked, "The juvenile delinquents I have known are mostly over fifty years of age."

LIGHT

"More Light"

Some years ago, a young Texas circuit rider was given the oversight of three rural Methodist churches.

At one of the churches, the chairman of the board of trustees—a tall, gaunt cattleman—greeted the circuit rider and said, "Pastor, we sure are glad to have you preach to us. We want to help with the work. Is there anything you can see which needs improvement?"

The pastor's gaze lingered on the single small light bulb which hung from the ceiling, and then shifted to the bronzed face of the lay leader. "I think that a chandelier would be most helpful" was his modest suggestion.

Weeks later, he mentioned it again.

"Well, pastor," drawled the chairman, "we hit a little snag on that request. In the first place, none of us could spell it, so we couldn't order it. Furthermore, nobody here can play one. Besides that, we all decided that the first thing this church needs is more light."

And the trustees needed light on the subject of chandeliers!

Do not all of us and our churches need spiritual illumination: "God is light. . . . If we walk in the light, as he is in the light, we have fellowship one with another" (I John 1:5-7).

Told by HOWARD H. HAMLIN,
medical missionary in
Swaziland, Africa

* * *

The Unfailing Light

Every foggy night a light in the window of a little cottage between Falkirk and Slamannan, Scotland, shines over the moor.

Some years ago a boy named Robert lived in the cottage. He attended school in Falkirk, and on foggy afternoons, when he was returning from school, his mother lit a lamp and put it in a window to guide him safely home.

After Robert grew to manhood, World War II came and he was called into the army.

Before he went away, his mother said, "Robert, I'll keep the light burning in the window. Then if you come home on a foggy night, it will guide you safely over the moor."

But Robert never came home! He fell in battle. The noble mother, however, unfailingly keeps the lamp shining over the moor on foggy nights.

Many are groping in the darkness of sin. If God's children are not faithful in reflecting the heavenly light, the lost will continue in the dark way of sin and spiritual death.

"Let your light so shine before men, that they may see your good works, and glorify your Father which is in heaven" (Matt. 5:16).

* * *

"More Light!"

There are two kinds of light in the world: natural light and spiritual light.

Scientists have tried to explain natural light. Newton conjectured that light is a stream of tiny particles, emanating in all directions from a body of light. His successors theorized that light is concentric waves, rippling out from a luminous source like wavelets when a pebble is dropped into a pool. Recent theories say that light is distributed in separate packages of energy called quanta, or photons.

Man needs spiritual light as well as natural light. As Geothe the German philosopher entered the valley of death, his famous last words were "Mehr Licht! (More Light)!"

Spiritual light emanates from Jesus Christ who said, "I am the light of the world: he that followeth me shall not walk in darkness, but shall have the light of life" (John 8:12).

How luminous and increasingly bright is the path of those who follow the light of the world, Jesus: "But the path of the just is as the shining light, that shineth more and more unto the perfect day" (Prov. 4:18).

The Bible says, "The god of this world [age] hath blinded the minds of them

187

that believe not" (II Cor. 4:4). A spiritually blind man is incapable of discerning spiritual light: "But the natural man receiveth not the things of the Spirit of God: for they are foolishness unto him: neither can he know them, because they are spiritually discerned" (I Cor. 2:14).

* * *

Life-bringing or Death-bringing Light

Long ago there shone a light that turned night into day: "The people that walked in darkness [saw] a great light" (Isa. 9:2). The Saviour—the sun of righteousness—arose with healing in His wings. In the effulgent glow of the light, the heavenly host chorused their message of peace and goodwill. The heavenly light was a manifestation of the heavenly Father's love for all mankind.

Suddenly the skies over the Pacific and Siberia were luminous with light and heat equivalent to a thousand suns! A war-weary, fear-craven world contemplated this light from the explosion of a hydrogen bomb with horror and fear because it potentially betokened the end of civilization and life on the earth unless goodwill through the Prince of peace, the Saviour, rules in hearts and among nations.

* * *

Shadows

He who keeps his face toward the sun cannot observe the shadows that fall behind him.

LORD'S DAY

Use Screws

One Sunday an aged Scotsman went to his barn to mend a barrow.

His wife heard him hammering and yelled, "Donald, Donald, what are you doing on the Sabbath?"

He replied, "I must mend this barrow."

"You must not," she said peremptorily. "What will the neighbors think?" Then she added softly, "Donald, if you do it, you must use screws! It's the Lord's Day."

* * *

A Sure Way to Lessen Sunday Work

Bill usually attended church regularly, so when he had been absent for several Sundays his pastor was deeply concerned. He went to see Bill and said, "I haven't seen you in church lately. Is there any reason for your absence?"

"Yes, there is a reason," said Bill. "As you know, I handle perishable commodities. Someone must handle them even on Sundays, though I greatly miss the fellowship of God's people in His house. But, pastor, since I am doing this necessary work on the Lord's Day, I am going to give to the church all the money I make on the Lord's time."

Sunday work would be greatly lessened if all workers had to follow Bill's example.

* * *

"Mule, You Must Have Religion"

One Sunday morning Tommy and Grandpa sat in the living room waiting for the rest of the family to get ready for Sunday school. Tommy began to whistle.

Grandpa said, "Be quiet, Tommy. Don't you know this is Sunday?"

Tommy was quiet for a few minutes. Then he put a record on the record player.

Grandpa ordered, "Tommy, turn that off. Didn't I tell you this is Sunday? You must be quiet."

Tommy turned the record player off. Then he tiptoed out of the room. He went outdoors. Near the fence he saw an old mule. The mule stood almost motionless with his ears hanging low and with a sad expression on his long face. Tommy walked over close to the mule and said, "Mule, you must have religion. You look just like Grandpa!"

The Lord's Day should be the most joyous day of the week. "This is the day which the LORD hath made; we will rejoice and be glad in it" (Ps. 118:24).

ALICE MARIE KNIGHT

* * *

The Last Sunday

One Monday, as the father of a pastor worked among his flowers, he passed away suddenly to be forever with his Lord. On the previous day, Sunday, he had said to his daughter, "I am not feeling well, but I'm going to Sunday school and church. One of these Sundays is going to be my last, and I want to be in church that Sunday."

Not knowing about his father's words, the son had included this quotation in the church bulletin for that last Sunday: "It is a poor preparation for one's first Sunday in eternity to have misspent one's last Sunday on earth!"

* * *

Accounts Settled in the Judgment

Said an unbeliever to a minister, "I never attend church. I spend Sundays settling my accounts."

The minister replied solemnly, "Then you will find, sir, that the day of judgment will be spent in the same manner."

Christian Herald

* * *

The Rat Race Temporarily Stopped

Dr. Victor Frankl, brilliant psychoanalyst, in *The Doctor and the Soul*, noted, "In any city, Sunday is the saddest day of the week. It is on Sunday, when the tempo of the working week is suspended, that the poverty of meaning in everyday, urban life is exposed. . . . These people who have no goal in life are running the course of life at the highest possible speed so that they will not notice the aimlessness of it. They are at the same time trying to run away from themselves, but in vain. On Sunday, when the frantic race pauses for twenty-four hours, all the aimlessness, meaninglessness and emptiness of their existence rises up before them once more."

* * *

A Day of Gladness

An aged Scot who was visiting Edinburgh attended church on the Lord's Day. There he saw many happy faces and radiant smiles. The manifested joy of the worshipers was contrary to his notion about the Lord's Day. He believed it was a sad, somber day and that it was wicked for people to be joyful on it.

The Lord's Day should be a day of gladness. 'Twas on the Lord's Day, the first day of the week, that a gloom-dispelling, hope-kindling event occurred long ago—the resurrection of Christ from the dead!

* * *

Jane Was Right

Jane was trying to learn the Ten Commandments.

"Write them down, dear," said her mother, "and that will help you to learn them more quickly."

Jane carefully wrote them and brought them to her mother for inspection.

Mother observed with amusement that Jane had written the fourth commandment thus: "Remember the sabbath day, to keep it *wholly*." She said, "Dear, you misspelled a word. The word here should be *h-o-l-y-*, not *w-h-ol-l-y*."

Grandmother, who sat nearby, said, "Maybe the child has not made a mistake. At least her idea of 'holy' is preferable to that of many people who think they keep the Lord's Day holy if they go to church in the morning and spend the rest of the day selfishly."

Told by ALICE MARIE KNIGHT

* * *

Nature's Law

Daniel Webster is quoted thus: "Observance of Sunday is nature's law as well as God's. No individual or nation habitually disregarding Sunday has failed to experience disaster and grief. The longer I live, the more highly do I esteem the Christian Sabbath, and the more grateful do I feel to those who impress its importance on the community."

* * *

Result of Misuse

Henry Ford rued his misuse of Sunday. "We would have had our Model A car in production six months earlier if I had forbidden my engineers to work on Sunday."

LOST

He Almost Made It

A father, his twin sons, and a neighbor's boy drowned when their boat overturned and sank in Lake Erie. The body of one of the boys was found a few feet from the shore, perhaps indicating that he *almost* reached safety.

Many come near to God's kingdom, but do not enter it. They are like the scribe to whom Jesus said, "Thou art not far from the kingdom of God" (Mark 12:34).

* * *

Unheeded Entreaties

A man climbed to the seventh floor ledge of the rotunda in the U.S. courthouse in Chicago. He stood there for some time, ignoring all entreaties to desist from leaping to his death. Hundreds of horrified spectators saw the man, Jerry Hollins, take the fateful plunge.

Those who wanted to divert him from suicide were powerless to do so because he would not heed their pleadings.

The Lord is long-suffering toward us and not willing that any should perish. However, myriads perish despite His entreaty: "Turn ye, turn ye from your evil ways; for why will ye die?" (Ezek. 33:11).

* * *

Sentence Must Be Pronounced

In Cleveland, Ohio, sixteen-year-old Fred Esherick, Jr., was found guilty of the murder of his father. The verdict of the jury read: "This jury finds the defendant guilty of murder in the first degree." The imposing of the death sentence was mandatory.

Shock, anguish and sorrow filled the courtroom. The face of presiding judge John F. Clair, Jr., darkened. He slipped into his chambers. Court officers observed him apprehensively, for they knew of his heart condition. At his desk, he slumped into a chair and covered his face with his hands as tears filled his eyes. He whispered, "I have never had to pronounce such a sentence—never, never!"

God, the Judge of all mankind, has no pleasure in the death of the wicked: "As I live, saith the LORD God, I have no pleasure in the death of the wicked" (Ezek. 33:11). Plaintively He asks, "Why will ye die?"

In mercy, God has placed athwart man's downward path the cross of Christ. He has done all He could do to divert man from death and destruction.

* * *

What Then?

An unbeliever asked an aged Christian, "Suppose you discover after death that there is no such place as heaven and that through the years you have been laboring under a delusion. What then?"

"Well," the Christian replied, "I would still be the gainer, for I have had a most wonderful and joyous time getting there! Suppose you, on the other hand, make the discovery after death that there is a hell. *What then?*"

* * *

Suddenly Destroyed

Some years ago a truck carrying a load of TNT on a highway in Tennessee caught fire. Both drivers leaped from the truck and ran in opposite directions, frantically waving their arms to halt approaching cars. Soon a car was seen in which were a man, his wife and children. The man must have thought that the one waving his arms so frantically was either drunk or demented. He pressed his foot on the accelerator and sped by. Just as he neared the burning truck there was a blinding explosion.

When the truck drivers returned to the scene of the blast, all they could see was a crater twenty feet deep. Not a trace of the car and the people could be found!

The man in the car was like millions who are heedless of God's warnings of sure destruction and doom to all who "obey not the gospel of our Lord Jesus Christ: who shall be punished with everlasting destruction from the presence of the Lord" (II Thess. 1:8-9).

Told by W. WOODWARD HENRY

*   *   *

Out-of-Date Punishment

Once, when Dr. Donald Grey Barnhouse preached a sermon on eternal punishment, an unbeliever said to him, "Your preaching is out-of-date. It smacks of the Middle Ages."

"What epoch of history do you consider the Middle Ages?" asked Dr. Barnhouse.

"Oh, the tenth to the thirteenth centuries, more or less," answered the critic.

Dr. Barnhouse said, "Man, you are ten to thirteen centuries wrong about my preaching, for it is not of the Middle Ages but the first century. It comes from the Word of God. The question is not whether you agree with it, but whether the Bible teaches it."

*   *   *

The Up-and-outs Need Christ, Too

Dr. G. Campbell Morgan said, "There was a time in my evangelistic work when I feared to talk to people of high position and culture in the inquiry room. Then one night I knelt beside an old man whom sin had all but wrecked. I spoke to him of the cleansing blood of Christ and of the possibility of his becoming a new creature in Christ. Presently someone asked, 'Please speak to the other man kneeling beside you.' I turned and recognized the mayor of the city, who six weeks before had sentenced the oldster to a month's hard labor. Both men were equally lost. Both accepted Christ. The mayor joyfully shook hands with the old man and said, 'Well, we didn't meet here the last time!'

"The old man recognized the mayor and said, 'No, and we will never meet again as we did the last time! I'm a new man in Christ, and we are now brothers.'

"That scene lingers with me yet. It removed my fear to speak to anyone about Christ."

*   *   *

God's Search

Religion is man's search for God, but Christianity is God's search for man. After man's fall, God began a quest which has continued through the centuries: "Adam . . . , Where art thou?" (Gen. 3:9). The Saviour came "to seek and to save that which was lost" (Luke 19:10).

A Christian worker asked a Chinese, "Have you found Jesus?"

"No, no," he instantly replied. "Jesus not lost. I lost. Jesus find me."

*   *   *

Tired of Life

"Tired of life, a Chicago co-ed and her school girl friend inhaled gas in a wine-celebrated suicide pact that left one dead and the other in critical condition." Thus began the tragic newspaper account of two nineteen-year-old university students. In the gas-filled apartment were two half-gallon wine bottles, one empty and the other half empty. "Today I die," began one of the suicide notes. "I die simply enough, because I haven't enough life in me to maintain life through long, long years."

"Tired of life" is the condition of millions today who do not know the One who came that we might have abundant life through faith in His all-sufficient name.

*   *   *

"If Ye Will Not Hearken"

Early one morning a rockslide occurred near the summit of Snoqualmie Pass in the state of Washington. Boulders crashed thunderously down a mountain, splintering trees on their downward, destructive plunge. They swept over a highway, demolishing two huge trucks and trailers.

When the rumbling was first heard, a flagman stopped both trucks and shouted, "Don't go farther! Run for your lives!" One driver heeded the warning and ran, and he barely escaped with his life.

The other driver remained in his cab, just to see what would happen. Hours later his crushed body was removed from the demolished cab by workmen using large jacks, pry bars and shovels to remove the debris and boulders.

How like that heedless truck driver are many today who, heedless of God's warnings, go on in the downward way to death and destruction! God warns, "They would none of my counsel: they despised all my reproof. Therefore shall they eat of the fruit of their own way" (Prov. 1:30-31).

* * *

Satanic Sweetness

One day a minister stopped to talk with a young preacher affiliated with one of the most Bible-distorting cults of our day. At first the young man displayed satanic sweetness and graciousness.

Then the minister asked, "Have you ever seen yourself as a lost sinner?"

Instantly the young man jerked off the mask, as it were, and disclosed his unbelief in future retribution and the need of the new birth.

The minister again pressed the question: "Have you ever seen yourself as a lost sinner who needs the Saviour and His forgiveness?'

Then the young man began to speak abusively of all ministers and churches.

* * *

"I Will Pour out My Fury"

A young woman who had been reared in a Christian home often heard God's call, "Give me thine heart," but continued to reject Christ. God's call to her gradually became fainter and fainter. In time she went recklessly into sinful ways. Her mother continued to plead with her to come to Christ, but she refused. Finally she contracted a fatal illness.

One night the young woman awoke and said, "Mother, I just had a most vivid dream. There seemed to be an angel in my room who said solemnly, 'Read Ezekiel 7:8-9.' Will you please read it to me?"

Opening her Bible to the reference, the mother read, " 'Now will I shortly pour out my fury upon thee, and I will judge thee according to thy ways. . . . I am the LORD that smiteth.'" Shortly afterward the girl, who had so often refused God's calls, passed into the hereafter.

Told by JOHN R. RICE

* * *

A Successful Failure

Some years ago a well-known businessman in the Northwest died. Shortly before his death, he said to his son who was holding his hand, "Son, you are holding the hand of the greatest failure in the Northwest!"

"No, no, father. You have been a most successful man. You have amassed a great fortune, and the business world holds you in high esteem," said the son.

"That may be true, my son, but I have lived as though this world were all. Now I am dying and I'll go out into a Christless hereafter—unprepared! All is dark! I am a monstrous failure, having lived only for the perishing things of this world."

"So is he that layeth up treasure for himself, and is not rich toward God" (Luke 12:21).

Adapted from *Baptist Standard*

* * *

A Single Soul

The Talmud of Sanhedrin says, "Whosoever destroys a single soul, Scripture imputes guilt to him as though he had destroyed a complete world; and whosoever preserves a single soul, Scripture ascribes merit to him as though he had preserved a complete world."

RABBI JULES LIPSCHUTZ

* * *

Without Remedy

In the coal mining town of Mount Carmel, Pennsylvania, a tragic thing oc-

192

curred one morning. A Christian mother, who for long had been burdened for the salvation of her son, opened her well-worn Bible at the breakfast table. In a gentle voice she said, "Harry, I don't know the meaning of it, but this morning I am more burdened for your soul's salvation than I have ever been."

Angrily the son got up and said, "Why don't you leave me alone? I don't want your religion." Raging with fury, he left the house and started down the walk. On his person were sticks of dynamite which he intended to use in his mining work that day. For some unknown reason, the dynamite suddenly exploded.

Miraculously the son was not killed instantly, but every part of his body was bruised and broken. He was rushed to a hospital.

The mother's pastor hurried there to plead with him to look to the Saviour for mercy and forgiveness. While he was talking, the son breathed his last. He went out, so far as was known, into a lost eternity.

As the pastor left the hospital, this warning from the Bible came to his mind: "He, that being often reproved hardeneth his neck, shall suddenly be destroyed, and that without remedy" (Prov. 29:1).

Told by C. Leslie Miller

* * *

Some Fixed Things

One of the symptoms of Parkinson's disease is rigidity of the muscles. The face of the patient gradually assumes a set, masklike expression. The rigidity of the facial muscles hinders changes of expression such as grimaces, frowns, stares or smiles. The fixed expression is suggestive of a Halloween mask.

The Bible tells us of some fixed things in this life and in the hereafter.

Some decisions are fixed, or irrevocable. No regret or remorse can change them: "He found no place of repentance, though he sought it carefully with tears" (Heb. 12:17).

One's destiny is fixed this side of the grave. Death solidifies it. Between the saved and the unsaved in the hereafter there "is a great gulf fixed," which is im-passable: "They which would pass from hence to you cannot; neither can they pass to us, that would come from thence" (Luke 16:26).

"Unto God the Lord belong the issues from death" (Ps. 68:20).

* * *

"Why Will Ye Die?"

Early one June morning, when nearly eleven hundred guests were asleep, a fire started in the twenty-two-story Hotel LaSalle, Chicago. The fire raged for three hours. Many of the guests panicked. Over two hundred persons were injured, some seriously. Sixty lost their lives. Two leaped to their death. Fire Commissioner Michael J. Corrigan said, "Many of the deaths were tragically unnecessary!"

There are millions who unnecessarily die spiritually when God, in mercy, has provided a way of escape for them. Pleading, God asks, "Why will ye die?" (Ezek. 18:31).

* * *

The Worst Part of Him

A wife who was burdened for the salvation of her husband said to Moody, "Do please pray for my husband. He is unsaved, but he has a good heart."

Moody flashed, "Why, woman, that's the worst part of him! Have you never read what the Bible says about the human heart which has never been changed by God's grace? 'The heart is deceitful above all things, and desperately wicked: who can know it?' [Jer. 17:9]."

* * *

God Kept His Part of the Bargain

A granddaughter of Aaron Burr gave her heart to Christ in an evangelistic meeting. That evening she went to her grandfather and said, "I wish you were a Christian, too."

Her grandfather told her, "When I was a young man, I went to an evangelistic service. I felt my need of God's mercy and forgiveness, and knew that I should give my heart to Christ, but I walked out without doing it. I stood under the stars and looked up toward the heavens and said, 'God, if You don't

193

bother me anymore, I'll never bother You.'

"Honey, God has kept His part of that bargain. He has never bothered me. Now it is *too late* for me to bother Him."

For of all sad words of tongue or pen,
The saddest are these: "It might have been!"

A misspent life, filled with chicanery and treason against the United States, followed Aaron Burr's fateful decision.

* * *

Not Far from the Kingdom

When the Northwest was being settled, a young couple built a small house several miles from the nearest settlement. One morning the husband went to the trading post to get supplies. "I'll be back in the evening," he said to his wife.

In the afternoon, the snow began to fall. It piled up deeper and deeper. Night came. The husband hadn't returned. The wife became distressed. Her distress deepened into despair. Through the hours of the night, she stood in anguish by the cabin door, swinging a lantern, hoping that her husband would see the light and find his way home.

At daybreak the wife began to make her way through the deep snow. A few hundred yards from the house she stumbled over the body of her husband— frozen to death! Weeping, she said, "Oh, he perished within sight of home!"

How many there are today who, like that pioneer, perish eternally after coming close to the kingdom of God!

O weary soul, the gate is near;
In sin why still abide?
Both peace and rest are waiting here,
And you are just outside.

Told by RALPH W. NEIGHBOUR

* * *

Too Late!

A faithful Sunday school teacher became greatly burdened for the salvation of a certain young man in her class. She earnestly spoke to him about his soul.

The young man said, "I'm going west to make a fortune. When I return, I'll consider giving my life to Christ."

Shortly thereafter he succumbed to illness. Once more the teacher pleaded with him to penitently turn from sin to Christ. Again he procrastinated, saying, "Please don't speak to me anymore about this matter." The teacher went away with a sad heart.

Progressively the young man's condition worsened. He asked, "Send for my Sunday school teacher."

Going to his bedside, the teacher saw the young man staring vacantly toward the ceiling and muttering, "Too late! Too late! Too late!" Those were his last words!

Told by GEORGE W. TRUETT

* * *

Have You Counted the Cost?

A. B. Bond, M.D., said, "When I was a medical student forty years ago, our teacher in anatomy said in his first lecture, "Man has a soul and a body. That's enough for the soul. For the next four years I shall be talking about the body."

The soul is of incalculable worth. Jesus asked, "For what is a man profited, if he shall gain the whole world, and lose his own soul?" (Matt. 16:26).

* * *

"Later but Not Now"

It was a foggy Monday morning in the section of Florida where the tragedy occurred. The aged driver of a school bus was making the rounds, gathering the boys and girls to take them to school. The last child he usually picked up lived in an orange grove across the railroad track. As he neared the track, the driver saw through a fog the dim light of an oncoming fruit train. *I can easily cross the track ahead of that approaching freight,* he reasoned.

But he misjudged the distance of the train. Only half of the bus, loaded with happy boys and girls, cleared the track. The train's engine ploughed through the rear of the bus, and more than twenty children, including four of a widow, were instantly killed. Others were horribly injured and died later.

The aged bus driver, who himself was badly injured, had taken a chance and lost.

194

Many people today are running a losing race in life. They gamble with their souls and take a chance. They do not deliberately plan to go out into a lost hereafter without God and without hope; but, when they are almost persuaded to accept the Saviour, they say, "Later but not now."

> Almost cannot avail,
> Almost is but to fail;
> Sad, sad, the bitter wail,
> Almost but lost.

LOVE, GOD'S

There's More

We can only see a little of the ocean,
    Just a few miles distant from the rocky
      shore;
But out there, far beyond our eyes'
      horizon,
    There's more, immeasurably more.

We can only see a little of God's loving,
    A few rich treasures from His mighty
      store;
But out there, far beyond our eyes'
      horizon,
    There's more, there's infinitely more!

* * *

"I Know You Love Jesus"

A sad, distressed little girl told her pastor, "I want to love Jesus, but I can't do it."

The pastor said, "My dear little girl, stop thinking about your not being able to love Jesus. Just keep saying, 'Jesus loves me!' Say it to yourself many times every day."

Later the little girl returned to the pastor with a happy smile on her face. The pastor said, "I know you love Jesus. Your happy face tells me that you do!"

ALICE MARIE KNIGHT

* * *

Many Have Yet to Hear

Carolyn Griswold, a Christian and Missionary Alliance missionary to Vietnam, wrote just before her martyrdom by the Viet Cong, "Pray with us that the Lord will keep the doors to this country open! There are so many who have yet to hear for the first time the story of God's love! It is true that we do not know what the future holds; but we know the One who holds the future, and that is enough."

* * *

"I Have Loved Thee"

D. L. Moody said, "I know of no truth in the whole Bible that ought to come home to us with such power and tenderness as that of the love of God. The enemy of souls, Satan, tries to persuade men that God does not love them."

How changeless is God's love: "I have loved thee with an everlasting love" (Jer. 31:3).

> Do you know the world is dying
> For a little bit of love?
> Everywhere we hear them sighing,
> For a little bit of love.

* * *

Inseparably Linked to Christ

Many newspapers across the nation carried a drawing of the five-chamber heart that the seventeen-day-old Pantaleon Siamese twins shared. Cardiologists said that the babies could not be separated without causing the death of one of them. Because of this fact, the Roman Catholic church opposed the separation.

To be separated from God by sin is to die spiritually: "For the wages of sin is death; but the gift of God is eternal life through Jesus Christ our Lord" (Rom. 6:23).

To be inseparably linked to Christ by love is triumphant life: "Neither death, nor life . . . shall . . . separate us from the love of God, which is in Christ Jesus our Lord" (Rom. 8:38-39).

195

"To the Memory of an Undying Love"

Standing on the banks of the Jumna River at Agra, in India, is the Taj Mahal, the tribute of the love of Shah Jahan to Princess Arjamand, his wife, whom he called Mumtaz Mahal, the "exalted of the palace." She was a woman loved as few women ever have been loved.

Shah Jahan had promised his wife a palace more magnificent than any which man had ever built. Eight times Mumtaz Mahal hazarded her life for motherhood; the eighth time the baby alone survived.

As Shah Jahan sat, bowed in irreparable grief by the side of his lifeless mate, he cried, "O my Mumtaz Mahal, you shall have the palace I promised you although it must be your tomb!"

He employed over twenty thousand men for almost twenty years and spent more than $20 million in building the marvelous mausoleum. It is one of the most beautiful structures in the world, and has been called "frozen poetry." Engraved upon the tomb is the inscription "To the memory of an undying love."

There is One who, in His undying love for all mankind, triumphed over death at the cost of infinite suffering. What monument have we built to Him? May it be a monument, not in perishable marble, but in a life pure and undefiled, lived in unselfish loyalty to Him who loved us and gave Himself for us.

WILLIAM EDWARD BIEDERWOLF

* * *

A Problem

One evening Dr. A. T. Pierson preached on the verse "As it is written, Jacob have I loved, but Esau have I hated" (Rom. 9:13).

At the close of his message, a man said, "Dr. Pierson, I have great difficulty to understand the last part of that verse: 'Esau have I hated.' "

Dr. Pierson said, "I also have a problem with that verse. My problem is the first part: 'Jacob have I loved.' "

As we think upon what we were before Christ saved us—"dead in trespasses and sins" (Eph. 2:1), we are amazed that He could have loved us.

I stand amazed in the presence
Of Jesus the Nazarene,
And wonder how He could love me,
A sinner condemned, unclean.

* * *

Beyond Description

In beauty indescribable
In thought or tongue or pen,
The mountains rise against the skies—
God's power displayed to men.

'Midst anguish indescribable
In thought or tongue or pen,
A cross did rise against the skies—
God's love displayed to men.

In glory indescribable
In thought or tongue or pen,
Our Lord did rise through radiant skies,
And soon He will come again.

In wonder indescribable,
In thought or tongue or pen,
I, too, shall rise through those skies,
When Jesus comes again.

ESTHER ARCHIBALD in
Gospel Herald

* * *

Sowing Precious Seed

"You don't know me," said a gnarled and badly stooped old Chinese woman to Mrs. E. Weller, of the China Inland Mission (now the Overseas Missionary Fellowship).

"I don't believe I do," replied Mrs. Weller.

The old lady stood, supporting herself with a cane, as she related this touching story:

"Twenty years ago, in this very place, a foreign young woman who couldn't speak many of our words taught me the first two lines of 'Jesus Loves Me.' My daughter and I say them every night. We worship Jesus and pray to Him about everything. We've had no idols in our home since that young woman taught me those lines."

Mrs. Weller sat beside the old woman and told her more about her wonderful Saviour.

Years later, Mrs. Weller said, "That old lady probably has long since seen her

Saviour face to face and has greeted the unknown young lady who told her about the love of Jesus!"

Told by Mrs. Howard Taylor

* * *

Not Humanitarian Sentiments

An English businessman visited a mission hospital for lepers in India. He was deeply impressed by the nurse's loving care of the suffering and repulsive-looking patients.

"Your humanitarian sentiment and sacrificial service for these outcasts are praiseworthy indeed," he said.

"I can assure you, sir, that if my continuance here was based only on humanitarian sentiments, I would not have the will to carry on. I would leave before nightfall. The constraining love of Christ enables me to carry on day by day."

LOVE FOR GOD

A Boy Defines an Idol

A minister asked a Scottish laddie, "Angus, how would you define an idol?"

The boy thought for a moment and then said, "I used to think idols were what the heathen worshiped, until I had one. It was my collie dog. I loved him too much. I used to go on long tramps with him on Sundays when I was supposed to be in church. When I trusted Jesus as my Saviour, I learned that anything I love more than I love Him is an idol."

Told by Mrs. J. Shields

* * *

Inseparably Related

Long ago a Pharisee questioned the Saviour: "Master, which is the great commandment in the law?" Jesus answered him, "Thou shalt love the Lord thy God with all thy heart, and with all thy soul, and with all thy mind. . . . Thou shalt love thy neighbour as thyself" (Matt. 22:37-39).

It is not possible to truly love God and hate or wrongfully treat others: "Love worketh no ill to his neighbour: therefore love is the fulfilling of the law" (Rom. 13:10).

Whenever we detect any ill will toward others rankling in our heart, let us plead:

"More love to Thee, O Christ,
More love to Thee."

* * *

What's Our Answer?

Charles H. Spurgeon once said, "Brother, you may take up theological problems and labor to solve this difficulty or expound that text, till the heart grows as dry as the pages of the books you have read. Remember, the bookworm may eat at your soul as well as at paper. It is, therefore, a healthy thing for the Lord to come into the study, close the book and say to us, 'Lovest thou me?'"

LOVE FOR OTHERS

Quenchless Love

Throughout the nation the press carried the story of a young woman who was married a few days before having her right leg amputated to prevent the spread of cancer. Everyone at the wedding knew the operation was coming, except the joyful bride. How happy she was as she exchanged marital vows with a Korean War veteran! He knew that she faced the ordeal, and he had secured an emergency furlough.

A few days after the wedding, the bride was told by a physician that the operation must be. "You're kidding me," she said to the doctor.

The bridegroom told of his decision: "During our grade school days, we were sweethearts. We hadn't planned to be married until after my tour of duty was over. Then this thing came up, and I decided we ought to be married right away."

"Many water cannot quench love, neither can the floods drown it" (Song of Sol. 8:7).

* * *

Thirst for Bloody Sacrifice

In Albany, New York, a mentally unbalanced youth of nineteen years climbed out on the top ledge of an eleven-story hotel building and threatened to plunge to his death.

One observer among the spectators below called to the youth, "Jump!" The crowd took up the chant, "Jump!" They waited expectantly until firemen finally rescued the youth.

Did the crowd applaud the brave firemen who hazarded their lives to rescue the demented youth? No. They booed! They were disappointed in not witnessing a bloody sacrifice, just as were the ancient Romans who called for the kill with the thumbs-down signal in the uncivilized rites of the Roman Coliseum. Has all compassion vanished from human hearts?

Let us pray for the compassion and tenderness of Christ in this tragic hour of the world's sorrow and suffering. Then we will look with love and pity upon distressed, distraught ones and enter feelingly and helpfully into their heartaches and heartbreaks.

* * *

Individual Forgotten

An editorial in the *Moody Monthly* warned, "Somehow we have lost our concern for the individual. We think of masses, not of individuals. This is traceable to the curse of Communism and socialism. These ideologies try to obliterate the importance and influence of individuals. We convene in conferences, form societies, issue manuals, and pass resolutions dealing with people en masse. But while we are here and there, the individual is forgotten. We need a baptism of love for souls—a love to win them one by one for the Master.

* * *

"You Go First"

The noblest in human nature is often displayed in times of peril, stress and strain.

Near midnight on April 14, 1912, the allegedly unsinkable ship, the *Titanic,* struck an iceberg and began to sink. Edith Evans and Mrs. John Murray Brown reached the last overcrowded lifeboat at 2 A.M. Said Miss Evans, "You go first. You have children waiting for you at home!" Those were her last words.

Jesus said, "Greater love hath no man than this, that a man lay down his life for his friends" (John 15:13).

* * *

The Strongest Argument

Lord, try us, lest our holy creed
We hold in word, but not in deed,
Or hold mere forms of godliness
Without a Christlike holiness.

Lord, halt us, lest with roughshod tread
We live a name and yet are dead;
Or lest, in fighting error's pen,
We smirch, not heresy, but men.

Lord, keep us true but ever kind,
With Thine own gentleness of mind,
With Thine own wisdom from above,
Whose strongest argument is love.

* * *

Wanted: People, Not Things

A church society sent a lonely old lady a Christmas box of good things plus a tempting dinner on a decorated tray. The lady expressed her thanks for the gracious act. But she tearfully said, "Tell the kind ladies I am deeply grateful, and also tell them that I want people more than things."

* * *

"I Will Never Give You Up"

A Christian couple were engaged to be

married. When World War II came, the young man enlisted. Letters telling of their ardent love were written daily. Then weeks passed without the young woman hearing from her fiancé. In distress, she wrote the War Department in Washington. While she waited for a reply, she received a letter which said: "There has been another terrible battle, and I have lost both of my arms. My chaplain is writing this letter for me. Because of what has happened to me, I tearfully release you from our engagement."

The noble girl didn't write an answer. She immediately flew to the distant hospital to see her fiancé. A most touching scene took place at his bedside when she said, "I love you devotedly. I will never give you up. We will face life together and live for God and for each other."

The Bible says, "Love is strong as death. . . . Many waters cannot quench love" (Song of Sol. 8:6-7).

Told by an army chaplain

* * *

The Essential Thing

Henry Drummond said, "You can take nothing greater to the mission field than the reflection of the love of God in your own character. Real love is the universal language—understood by all. You may have every accomplishment or give your body to be burned; but, if love is lacking, all this will profit you and the cause of Christ nothing."

* * *

Enduring Monuments

On the tomb of Sir Christopher Wren in St. Paul's Cathedral, London, which he designed, are these words, "If you would see his monument, look around you!"

Enduring monuments are built, not with mortar and stone, but with Christlike deeds of love and kindness, erected in human hearts. The gnawing teeth of time crumble into dust the mortar and stone cathedrals, but deeds motivated by the constraining love of Christ for all mankind will endure.

Love Through Me

Love through me, love of God,
  There is no love in me;
O fire of love, light Thou the love
  That burns perpetually.

Flow through me, peace of God,
  Calm river flow until
No wind can blow, no current stir
  A ripple of self-will.

AMY CARMICHAEL

* * *

The Neighbor Test

Farmer Brown lived in the country near a crossroad. He was friendly to everybody. One day a wagon loaded with furniture passed his gate.

"Hi, friends," said Farmer Brown cheerily. "Where are you moving from and where are you moving to?"

"We are from Jamestown and are moving to Johnstown. What kind of neighbors will we find in Johnstown?"

"What kind did you leave in Jamestown?"

"The worst, the very worst. They were mean, snoopy and gossipy!"

"You'll find the same kind of neighbors in Johnstown," said Farmer Brown.

The next day another wagon loaded with household effects passed Farmer Brown's house.

"Hi, friends," said Farmer Brown cordially. "Where are you moving from and where are you moving to?"

"We are moving from Jamestown to Johnstown. Can you tell us what kind of folks we will find in Johnstown?"

"What kind of folks did you have in Jamestown?" asked Farmer Brown.

"The best, the very best! They were kind and friendly. How we hated to leave them!" replied the stranger.

Farmer Brown smiled. "You'll find the same kind of folks in Johnstown!"

For life is the mirror of king and slave,
  'Tis just what you are and do;
Then give to the world the best you have,
  And the best will come back to you.

Told by ALICE MARIE KNIGHT

199

MIRACLES

"We Can Do Nothing for You"

Charles E. Fennell now drives a cab in Athens, Tennessee. Some years ago he had become blind. Doctors said, "We can do nothing for you. You must learn to live with blindness and have faith in God. If you ever regain your sight, it will be a miracle."

How revealing of his faith was the fact that Fennell continued to wear his wristwatch in spite of his blindness.

When he awakened one morning, he looked at his watch and at the objects in his room. He jumped out of bed, exclaiming, "I can see! I can see!"

Now he sees perfectly, without the glasses he formerly wore.

The only explanation he gives is to quote the words of the doctor. "It's a miracle!"

* * *

Be a Miracle!

We may not be able to work miracles. John the Baptist didn't: "John did no miracle" (John 10:41). But each one of us can be a miracle of God's transforming grace, a product of His saving and sanctifying power.

Luther said, "Miracles happen, not because they are performed, but because they are believed."

* * *

"God's Fool"

Before the Communists took over China, John Ting, who has been called God's fool, did a mighty work for God. He was a member of the Little Flock evangelists. He had utter faith in God, as the following thrilling incident attests.

One day Ting and his companions were being pursued by bandits. They came to a river which was overflowing its banks. The water was deep. The situation was humanly hopeless, but Ting said, "Our God is a mighty God, and He can open a way for us through the river." He prayed, "O Lord, hold back the waters, and make a way of escape from our enemies."

Stepping into the water which swirled about his knees, Ting motioned to the others to cross as he bowed his head and silently prayed. For a moment, his companions hesitated. Then, to their amazement, they saw that the water was steadily dropping. In a short while all crossed the river safely.

The God who divided the Red Sea and rolled back the water of the Jordan River so that His people might pass through safely still lives. His challenging promise has not been rescinded: "Call unto me, and I will answer thee, and shew thee great and mighty things, which thou knowest not" (Jer. 33:3).

* * *

"Clothed and in His Right Mind"

In the *Alliance Weekly*, Rev. Carl Volstad related the story of Ruperto Varas, a Chilean Christian, whose weird actions paralleled the actions of those who were demon-possessed in Christ's day.

"Seemingly a voice was speaking to him constantly," said Rev. Volstad, "a voice which he obeyed without questioning. He emptied his house of its contents, including food, in obeying the voice. His sleepless nights were spent wandering over the hills. At times he would sit silent and unblinking for hours. At times he seemed to see visions. Since the man was supposed to be an evangelical Christian, great harm was done to the cause I represented. I prayed for God's direction as to what I should do. Confidence in His power 'to do exceeding abundantly above all that we ask or think' (Eph. 3:20) brought fear-allaying assurance. I announced a meeting. People came in large numbers to see what I would do with the demon-possessed man. I preached on the demoniac of Gadara and told how Christ delivered him from the destroying demons which had all but wrecked his life. Then I prayed. A miracle occurred: the formerly demented, demon-controlled man was completely healed!"

200

Like God's children of old, we limit "the Holy One of Israel" (Ps. 78:41) and because of unbelief minimize His liberating power: Christ "did not many mighty works there because of their unbelief" (Matt. 13:58); "If thou canst believe, all things are possible to him that believeth" (Mark 9:23).

MISSIONS

Lengthening Bread Lines

Prime Minister Indira Gandhi of India said, "One-seventh of the human race lives in India in an area less than one-third the size of the United States. More than one-half of India's 500 million people live in the bread line on four dollars a month, and there are one million more new mouths to feed every month."

* * *

One of the World's Greatest

A New York minister has said that New York is one of the world's greatest mission fields. There are more Jews than in all of Palestine, more Italians than in Rome, more Irishmen than in Dublin, more Spaniards than in Madrid, more Puerto Ricans than in San Juan. It has more Negroes than any other city.

J. WILBUR SMITH

* * *

What a Waste of Life!

About one hundred fifty years ago, a young man went as a missionary to India. His family, friends and church tried to dissuade him, but to no avail. After a short while on the field, he succumbed to sickness and died.

"What a waste of life!" some said. Not so, however, for his story was read by Dr. John Scudder, a New York physician, who decided to become a medical missionary in India. Dr. Scudder was the father of the famous Scudder missionary family. He had seven sons, two daughters and ten grandchildren who have given many years of faithful service as missionaries in India.

Where Christ Is Unknown

When Amy Carmichael went to India, she did not know that many beautiful and intelligent little girls in that land were taken from their homes and trained to become temple women to satisfy the lusts of men in the degrading worship of the Hindu gods. Later Miss Carmichael said, "What a little girl, who had escaped from a temple, told me darkened the sunlight!" Her heart became deeply burdened to save these girls from moral ruin and bring them to Christ.

How dark are the vast regions of earth where Christ is unknown. How dark, too, are hearts and homes where He is excluded.

* * *

A Missionary Now

I may not go to India,
    To China or Japan,
To work for Jesus. Here at home,
    I'll do the best I can.

I'll tell of His great love to me,
    And how I love Him, too.
And, better far, I'll show my love
    In all that I may do.

I'll pray for those who cross the sea.
    My offering, too, I'll send,
And all within my power I'll do,
    This great, sad world to mend.

Olive Plants

* * *

Because You Prayed

Because you prayed,
God touched our weary bodies with His power,

201

And gave us strength for many a trying hour,
In which we might have faltered, had not you,
Our intercessors, faithful been and true.

Because you prayed,
The dwellers in the dark have found the Light,
The glad good news has banished heathen night,
The message of the cross, so long delayed,
Has brought them life at last, because you prayed.

* * *

A Romance Nipped in the Bud

In 1910 a girl in Apsley Guise, Bedfordshire, England, mailed a postcard to her sweetheart in Clifton, fifteen miles away. The postcard recently arrived there, but her sweetheart had died in 1929. "Fifty-six years for the delivery of this lost mail is a record for the post office," said a postal official.

Quipped a news columnist, "Perhaps an Edwardian romance may have been nipped in the bud."

Centuries ago the Saviour gave His church the command to proclaim the good news of the gospel to all the world. How slow some of God's children have been to deliver the message to all mankind!

* * *

The Black Man's Resurrection

Canon Taylor Smith, a missionary to Africa, testified, "If I had ten more lives, I would gladly lay them down for Christ in the white man's grave—Africa—to gain, by the grace of God, the black man's resurrection."

* * *

O-missionary Christians

Dr. A. J. Gordon stated, "Forget not that your first and principal business as a disciple of Christ is to give the gospel to those who have it not. He who is not a missionary Christian will be a missing Christian when the great day of bestowal of rewards for service comes."

Bought with Blood

Bishop James Hannington died a martyr's death in Uganda. In his early years he said, "I dread my ordination to the ministry. Humanly speaking, I recoil when I think of the hardships and privations which lie ahead as I serve my God in some faraway place as a missionary. When I am tempted to draw back, the words of the Saviour burn their message into my heart: 'No man, having put his hand to the plough, and looking back, is fit for the kingdom of God.' "

What a straight furrow he plowed! When he was dying, he said, "Go and tell my brethren that I have bought the road to Uganda with my blood!"

* * *

Why They Didn't Jest

During the last century, it was the custom of students in universities in Scotland to make jesting remarks about the recipients of honorary degrees.

When the heroic and faithful missionary, David Livingstone, was home on furlough from Africa, he was chosen to receive an honorary degree. Some wondered what the students would say when he stood to receive his degree.

As Livingstone stood before them, the students saw his arm hanging limply from the shoulder. The arm had been mangled when Livingstone was attacked by a lion in Africa. Thinking of his life of sacrifice and unselfish service for God and others, the students involuntarily stood en masse—silently, reverently and admiringly.

* * *

"Was Jesus a Black Man?"

A little African boy asked a missionary, "Was Jesus a black Man?" "No, my boy," said the missionary.

A look of disappointment clouded the little boy's face. As he turned away, he said sadly, "The white people have all the good things!'

Then the missionary said, "Jesus lived in the Middle East. He probably had a complexion between yours and mine."

A smile lit up the boy's face as he

202

joyfully said, "Then Jesus belongs to both of us, doesn't He?"

"That's right," said the missionary. "Jesus belongs to all people. All around the world there are those who love Him and serve Him. The Bible says, 'God is no respecter of persons.'"

* * *

The Undelivered Message

Queen Elizabeth I was greatly admired by Robert Devereux, the earl of Essex. If she loved any man, it was he. She gave him a ring and said, "If ever you are in trouble, send this ring to me and your request will be granted."

In time, they quarreled. In anger she struck his ear. Soon after, he left England.

When the earl returned, he was arrested, charged with treason and sentenced to death. At first he was too proud to ask the queen for mercy. But when the time for his execution drew near, he sent the ring to her by a countess, asking for mercy. For unknown reasons, the countess failed to deliver the ring and tell his request. The earl of Essex was executed!

"We've a story to tell to the nations." Let us not be remiss in telling it.

* * *

Knowing the Language

Noted the *Wall Street Journal,* "Missionaries must know the national languages. The nationals are wide open to you if you speak their own tongue. You can get down to basic facts with them and find out what they are thinking about. Without the language, they consider you an enemy instead of a friend."

"And they were all amazed and marvelled, saying . . . how hear we every man in our own tongue, wherein we were born" (Acts 2:7-8).

* * *

"You've Never Seen Heathenism"

Someone asked multimillionaire William Borden, a Yale University student who was deeply involved in God's service, "Why should you throw your life away in missionary work?"

Borden replied, "You have never seen heathenism!"

When Borden died, at the age of twenty-five, he bequeathed more to missions than any other man had ever done before.

* * *

"We Preach Christ"

Shortly after World War II, four Russian Baptist leaders were permitted to visit the United States. A news correspondent asked one of them, "Since you are a Christian, I am sure you cannot concur in all that the Soviets believe and practice. How do you oppose these things?"

His answer was brief: "We preach Christ!" That was what the first century church did.

* * *

The Mother Tongue

Dr. Kenneth Pike of Wycliffe Bible Translators said, "We have learned that only through his mother tongue does a person respond quickly and deeply to the most crucial issues of life. With a scalpel, test tube and telescope, the scientist can get across to the pattern of a fish, hexamethylenetetramine or the Milky Way. But only through his language can a man gain access to love, joy, peace, faith and hope in himself, his wife or God. Here, then, is the driving scientific axiom lying behind our translation work."

On the day of Pentecost, the startled multitude exclaimed, "We do hear them speak in our tongues the wonderful works of God" (Acts 2:11).

When Tariri, chief of the Condoshi in Peru, heard for the first time a Scripture verse translated into his language, he joyfully exclaimed, "My heart understands with a leap!"

* * *

Reaching the Moon—Losing the Earth

Clay Cooper warned, "While we are striving for the moon, we could be losing the earth. Let us not deceive ourselves. Are we going to be guilty of spending billions to send a man to the moon and mites to send Christ's heart-transforming gospel to the millions of earth?"

"He That Goeth Forth and Weepeth"

When visiting a little-known island in the Pacific, Dr. John G. Paton was amazed to find the natives observing the Lord's Day. Two old men kept track of the days. On the first day of the week, all work ceased. The two oldsters put on their calico shirts, which were kept especially for Sunday wear. They told as many as would listen all that they could remember of what a stranger had told them about Jesus many years previously.

Dr. Paton asked them, "From whom did you learn the things you are telling others about Jesus?"

They said, "Long, long ago someone came to our island, gave each of us a calico shirt, and told us the story of Jesus."

"Do you remember his name?" asked Dr. Paton.

"Oh yes," they said. "His name was Paton!"

Dr. Paton recalled that thirty-three years before, he had stopped at this island for a few days. The calico shirts were well worn, but having been used only on Sundays, they were in fairly good condition.

How challenging is the promise "He that goeth forth and weepeth, bearing precious seed, shall doubtless come again with rejoicing, bringing his sheaves with him" (Ps. 126:6).

* * *

Population Explosion

James Reston, a journalist, said, "World population is now increasing by almost 63 million a year. Of the present world population of about 3.3 billion, 10 to 15 percent are undernourished."

We've a Saviour to show to the nations
  Who the path of sorrow hath trod,
That all of the world's great peoples
  Might come to the truth of God.

* * *

If I Had a Thousand Lives

Richard Cameron was martyred by some infuriated, demon-propelled natives. As he died, he said, "If I had a thousand lives, I would willingly lay them all down, one after the other, for Christ."

Paul said, "Christ shall be magnified in my body, whether it be by life, or by death" (Phil. 1:20).

* * *

The Countdown Is Not Yet

Whatever the hour may be on God's clock, the countdown has not come yet. There is much work to do for God, and so few to do it: "The harvest truly is plenteous, but the labourers are few; pray . . . the Lord . . . that he will send forth labourers into his harvest" (Matt. 9:37-38).

* * *

Rich America and a Starving World

Sir Charles Percy Snow, British scientist, author and philosopher, said, "You cannot maintain a rich America in the center of a famine-ridden world. We cannot live on a cloud when people are starving at our door."

* * *

Where Most Needed

Said Count von Zinzendorf, "That land which most needs the gospel is henceforth my country."

* * *

Shall We?

Shall we whose souls are lighted
  With wisdom from on high,
Shall we to men benighted
  The lamp of life deny?

* * *

Only One Son

David Livingstone stated, "God had only one Son and He was a missionary. The morning stars sang together when they saw the first place a missionary was to fill."

* * *

Fourth Class

Someone asked Hudson Taylor, founder of China Inland Mission, "Why do you travel fourth-class?"

He replied, "Because there is no fifth class."

On Livingstone's Tomb

On the tomb of David Livingstone in Westminster Abbey, London, are these words: "And other sheep I have, which are not of this fold: them also I must bring" (John 10:16).

* * *

His Parish

John Wesley prayed, "The world is my parish. Take back my interest in Thy blood unless it flows for the whole human race."

* * *

More Than Two Billion

H. H. Lippincott said in *Christianity Today,* "More than two billion of the earth's inhabitants are either pagan, atheistic or nonchristian."

* * *

Not for a King's Throne

Adoniram Judson said in Burma, "I do not know that I shall live to see a single convert, but I would not leave my present field of labor to be made king of the greatest empire on the globe."

* * *

One of Us Is Dead

In his farewell address to the Church Missionary Society, William Mackay said, "Within six months you will probably hear that one of us new missionaries is dead. When the news comes, do not be cast down, but send someone else immediately to take the vacant place."

10|28

Where Christ Is Leading

Robert E. Speer stated, "If you want to follow Jesus Christ, you must follow Him to the ends of the earth, for that is where He is leading."

* * *

In God's Way

J. Hudson Taylor averred, "God's work done in God's way will never perish."

* * *

Faith or Love, Which?

A friend asked Judson, "Was it faith or love that influenced you most to go to Burma?"

He replied, "There was little of either in me at the time. 'Twas Christ's command, 'Go . . . preach the gospel to every creature.' "

* * *

Make Christian Circle Larger

A boy listened attentively as his Sunday school teacher drew two circles on a chart to show the number of Christians and the number of non-Christians in the world. The circle of non-Christians was much larger.

When the boy prayed that night, he said, "Dear Jesus, when I grow up and become a man, help me to make the Christian circle larger and the non-Christian circle smaller."

Shouldn't this be the earnest prayer of every Christian?

ALICE MARIE KNIGHT

* * *

Out and On

John Wesley said, "When God takes the world out of your heart, He puts the world on your heart."

MOTHERS

(*See also* Parental Responsibility)

They Died Together

At the trial of World War II war criminals, Dr. Otto Wolken, a Viennese physician at Auschwitz prison, weepingly testified, "Children were automatically sent to the gas chambers. Mothers preferred to die with their children clasped to their breasts than to live, so guards finally decided to send them all to their deaths!"

True love is boundless and self-sacrificing: "Many waters cannot quench love, neither can the floods drown it" (Song of Sol. 8:7).

* * *

Only One Explanation

Dr. John Scudder was asked the explanation of the early conversion and consecration of his nine children to God's work. He replied, "The only explanation I can give is that the children were prayed into God's kingdom by their mother. She spent the birthday of each child in all-day prayer for that one."

* * *

A Frightful Dream

A mother said to me, "Pastor, I had a most realistic dream last night. I dreamed that I went to heaven and made the heartbreaking discovery that not one of my five sons was there! Then I awoke, weeping bitterly!"

Seldom had I known a mother who displayed so little concern for the spiritual welfare and eternal destinies of her sons. I felt that I should speak some searching words to her. I said kindly, "Madam, God, in goodness, may have given you this dream to give you a sleepless concern for the salvation of your unsaved sons. The dream could be an *actuality* if you do not earnestly pray for their salvation and do your best to bring them to the Saviour."

W. B. K.

* * *

Mother Let Me Down

When nineteen years old, a youth joined the navy. For three years, during World War II, much happened to his ship. It was bombed several times. It was frequently the target for submarines. It was hit twice by enemy planes. The youth saw men suffer and die. He learned the meaning of loyalty and devotion.

When discharged from the service at the close of the war, he was no longer a boy. He was a man.

One day, as he related some of his experiences, including close brushes with death, he said, "Mother, you let me down!"

"Why, what do you mean, Bob?" she asked in astonishment.

He replied, "Though you have been a good mother to me, you let me grow up without going to Sunday school and church where I could have learned about God and my need of His mercy and forgiveness. I didn't miss these things until I became involved in the dangers and horrors of war."

Adapted from *Biblical Recorder*

* * *

The Outstretched Arms

Excavators among the ruins of Pompeii came upon the body of a child with outstretched arms. Exclaimed one, "There is a mother here somewhere!" Excavating in the direction of the outstretched arms, they found the mother's body.

* * *

Gentle Jesus, Meek and Mild

Some years ago when I was young,
Of many songs my mother sung,
There's one that often stirred my breast
More often than all the rest;
A prayer I learned beside her knee,
How oft its strains come back to me—
    Gentle Jesus, meek and mild,
    Look upon a little child.

The words, of course, are doubly dear
Because I somehow seem to hear
Through all their simple chords and tones
The heaven-gone voice my mother owns—
    Gentle Jesus, meek and mild,
    Look upon a little child.

The prayer she taught me Jesus heard
And now I live and tell His Word,
And you who pray this little prayer,
Never forget that He is there,
Concerned for you who really long
To be His children, meek yet strong—
    Gentle Jesus, meek and mild,
    Look upon a little child.

BRANFORD CLARKE

* * *

"I Even Forgot Her Face"

Billy Sunday said, "I stretched the

bonds of my mother's love until I thought they would break. I went so far in the dark, downward way that I ceased to hear her prayers and pleadings for me. I even forgot her face. Finally I yielded to the tender memories of my mother, and I was drawn away from the yawning abyss.

"One memorable day in Chicago, I groped my way out of darkness into the arms of Jesus Christ! I fell on my knees and cried, 'God be merciful to me a sinner.' "

* * *

Shining Gold

They say that mothers have no pay,
But Linda smiled at me today,
And Karen stopped and hugged me tight
As I went in to say good night.

Dear God, please help me on my way,
To be more faithful every day,
And thank You for the shining gold
I have, as these small lives I mold.

* * *

The One Who Knows

When I'm tired as tired can be,
My mother takes me on her knee;
She knows where all my aches belong,
And holds me there, so kind and strong.

And when I'm just so full of play,
I want to run and romp all day,
She laughs and plays around with me,
Because she understands, you see.

When I'm so hungry I could cry,
And dinnertime is nowhere nigh,
She gives me bread and currant jam,
She sees exactly how I am.

I don't see what a boy would do
Without his mother, all day through,
For mothers understand things so,
They don't have to be told—they know!

* * *

Just a Housewife

"Just a housewife," she told the census taker, with a half-apologetic smile.

Just a housewife? Oh, no! Such a tiny little bit of her was that. She was an artist—an expert in color, atmosphere and design. Three hundred and sixty-five paintings she finished every year. Many

of them would hang in the halls of memory long after she was gone. There had been some dark, tragic days, but she made each one a miniature of courage and framed it with hope. High moments of praise and devotion also found their place in her gallery of days.

Just a housewife? She was a poet. A glass of plum jelly on a sunlit windowsill was a sonnet of beauty. Clean, fresh curtains, stirring in a gentle breeze, whispered a poem of love. Crisp loaves of bread effused a folk song to be remembered; a child kneeling in prayer was a hymn of praise.

Just a housewife? She was a builder, an architect with visions and plans for a better tomorrow. Her foundation was laid on essential goodness. Her walls were squared with gracious living. The windows opened wide to love and understanding. A roof of faith made the house safe from the storms. A fence of contentment kept away strife, prejudice and ill will. It was not a house alone that she built—it was a home where the heart could rest.

BEULAH G. SQUIRES, in
Sunshine Magazine

* * *

A Mother's Dying Prayer

Both the mother and father of Dr. C. I. Scofield were Christians. His mother died in childbirth. From her dying lips came a prayer, heard by the husband and other members of the family, that the new arrival would become a minister of the gospel.

When Scofield grew into manhood, he became an alcoholic. Later he not only was saved and delivered from strong drink, but he also became a minister of the gospel and the editor of the Scofield Reference Bible. His mother's dying prayer was not made known to Scofield until he became a true Christian, and was called of God to devote his life to the Christian ministry.

* * *

Christian Character Revealed

A mother and her little daughter sat together in a church service. In his sermon, the minister said, "Christian character is revealed by the manner in which we attend to the small duties of everyday life. Many parents neglect their spiritual duties in the home. They fail to ask God to watch over them. They fail to thank God for His blessings and seek His protection and guidance."

The little girl listened attentively, and whispered to her mother, "Is the minister talking about you?"

* * *

"You Can't Go, Mother"

"But you just can't go, Mother. We can't get along without you," said Jane, who was the oldest girl in a large family. Mother had been suddenly called away on a necessary mission.

Mother replied, "Dear, every day I will write and encourage you. I will give you instructions for the care of the smaller children."

Mother kept her promise. Daily a letter came from her. How valuable were the suggestions she made from time to time:

"Forget the wrinkles in Johnnie's shirts, but be sure to kiss him and encourage him when he leaves for school. Don't forget Sally's birthday. Have a surprise party for her. Her love is not secure like yours, and she needs more care and attention!"

When Jane knelt to pray one night, she said, "Thank you, dear Lord, for taking Mother away from us for a while. I would never have known about her beautiful thoughts about us. I know now

that You used her absence to teach me lessons in kindness and helpfulness for others—especially the weaker ones!"

Adapted from a family experience

* * *

Housecleaning Heart and Mind

A new mother was propped up in her hospital bed, writing. Smiling, she said to a visiting minister: "I'm housecleaning and I want your help. Ever since I was a little girl, I hated restraint. I wanted to be free. When I finished high school, I took a business course and got a job, not because I needed the money, but I wanted to be on my own. Before Joe and I married, we agreed not to be slaves to each other. Therefore our apartment became headquarters for a crowd like us. We did just what we pleased."

Continuing, the young mother said, "God didn't mean much to us. We ignored Him. And now that I am a mother, I am afraid. Well, things are different now. I'm not free anymore and I don't want to be. The first thing I must do is to clean house. That's my list! You see, when I take Betty home from the hospital, our apartment will be her home, not just mine and Joe's. It isn't fit for her now. Certain things will have to go for Betty's sake. I've got to houseclean my *heart and mind*. I'm not just myself. I'm Betty's mother, and that means I need God. I can't do my job without Him. Won't you pray for Betty, Joe and me and for our new home?"

CATHERINE MARSHALL

NATURE

Forget-me-nots of the Angels

As Catherine Louise Nichla looked in wonder at the evening sky, she exclaimed, "Silently one by one, in the infinite meadows of heaven, blossomed the lovely stars, the forget-me-nots of the angels."

David said, "The heavens declare the glory of God; and the firmament sheweth his handywork" (Ps. 19:1).

Out in the Fields with God

The little cares that fretted me,
  I lost them yesterday,
Among the fields above the sea,
  Among the winds at play,
Among the lowing of the herds,
  The rustling of the trees,
Among the singing of the birds,
  The humming of the bees.

The foolish fears of what might pass,
    I cast them all away,
Among the clover-scented grass,
    Among the new-mown hay,
Among the rustling of the corn,
    Where drowsy poppies nod,
Where ill thoughts die and good are born,
    Out in the fields with God!
                ELIZABETH BARRETT BROWNING

* * *

Autumn

With the ever changing seasons
    We have beauty near divine,
Winter snow and springtime blossoms
    Summer fruit on tree and vine.
But the trees of bronze and crimson,
    The gay meadowlark's clear call,
And the goldenrod's bright color
    Make the autumn best of all.

* * *

The Lord God Made Them All

All things bright and beautiful,
    All creatures great and small,
All things wise and wonderful,
    The Lord God made them all.

He gave us eyes to see them,
    And lips that we might tell
How great is God Almighty,
    Who has made all things well.
                CECIL FRANCES ALEXANDER

* * *

The Unbought Good

What would our land be worth to us,
    The land we sell and buy,
And fence about, and call our own,
    Without God's open sky
To hold the sunset's rose and gold,
    The white clouds floating high?

What would our fields bring forth for us
    Without the gifts He sends,
Without the sunshine and the rain
    On which our bread depends,
His little waterbrooks to flow,
    His birds to be our friends?

Oh, as the land without the sky
    That ever bends above,
So barren and so desolate

Our lives without His love;
The blessings that no gold can buy
    Our greatest riches prove.
                ANNIE JOHNSON FLINT

* * *

The Capstone of the Year

The capstone of the year has come,
    The brightest of them all!
With the accumulation poured
    From summer into fall.
The blue and gold of autumn tints
    Are mingled with the green,
And everywhere the eye can look
    God's handiwork is seen.
We've had the flowers of May and June,
    And been knee-deep in clover,
But none can rival for one hour
    Our month of bright October.

* * *

Heralds of Spring

The first robin now arrives,
    The grass is faintly green,
The first crocus lifts its head,
    The signs are plainly seen.

The turtledove is in the land,
    With others on the wing,
Proclaiming nature's chorus,
    Heralding the spring!

"For, lo, the winter is past, the rain is
over and gone; the flowers appear on the
earth; the time of the singing of birds is
come, and the voice of the turtle is heard
in our land" (Song of Sol. 2:11-12).

* * *

Why?

I cannot say just why 'tis so,
    That spring returns again;
But God is faithful, this I know,
    While day and night remain.

I cannot say why buds appear,
    Upon the maple tree;
But this I know: my Lord is near,
    The finished leaf I'll see.

I cannot say why birds return,
    From far, exotic climes;
But surely God has helped them learn
    Their clear, melodic chimes.

209

I cannot say why flowers sweet
  Should bloom along my way;
But, with their fragrance, they repeat
  God's glory every day.

MARIAN BULEY

* * *

It Isn't Raining Rain

It isn't raining rain to me,
  It's raining daffodils,
In every dimpled drop I see
  Wild flowers on the hills,

The clouds of gray engulf the day,
  And overwhelm the town,
It isn't raining rain to me,
  It's raining roses down!

It isn't raining rain to me,
  But fields of clover bloom,
Where every buccaneering bee
  May find a bed and room.
A health unto the happy,
  A prayer for him who frets,
It isn't raining rain to me,
  It's raining violets!

ROBERT LOVERMAN

NEGLECT — INDIFFERENCE

"Poor Kid! She Never Had a Chance!"

On hearing of the tragic death of Marilyn Monroe, a woman remarked, "Poor kid! She never had a chance!"

Two weeks prior to Miss Monroe's death, Billy Graham awakened in his hotel room in Seattle with a burden on his heart to pray for her conversion. Later, when Graham was in Los Angeles, one of his associates contacted Miss Monroe through her agent, indicating the evangelist's desire to have a visit with her. The reply was "Not now. Maybe two weeks from now."

It is wisdom to obey the command "Seek ye the LORD while he may be found, call ye upon him while he is near: . . . he will abundantly pardon" (Isa. 55:6-7).

In life, Marilyn Monroe's physical beauty was exploited for monetary gain. What a waste of life!

For of all sad words of tongue or pen,
The saddest are these, "It might have
  been!"

* * *

He Took a Chance

Three Cleveland (Ohio) men en route to their work were killed by a train at a railway crossing.

In explaining to policemen how the tragic accident occurred, E. J. Herris, the fireman on the locomotive, said, "I saw the auto approaching the grade crossing.

The driver of the car slowed down about thirty-five feet from the tracks, then speeded up. The locomotive struck the car broadside."

Three men were killed, two women widowed and four children orphaned because the driver took a chance. He thought that he had time to clear the crossing ahead of the oncoming train.

Many go into a lost hereafter thinking that there is still time enough to settle the all-important question Where will I spend eternity?

Freighted with the greatest consequence is the moment when we hear in our hearts God's beseeching plea "Give me thine heart."

* * *

"I'll Never Forgive Myself!"

During a lax time, a workman began to repair the cesspool in his backyard. Before he completed the job, he was called back to work. He placed boards over the open cesspool, and told his wife not to let their little girl go near it.

His wife said, "It is dangerous to leave the cesspool with only boards across the top of it. Make it safer and do it without delay." He promised he would but neglected to do it.

One day the little girl was missing. After frantic search, her dead body was found at the bottom of the cesspool.

Weeping uncontrollably, the father said, "I intended to make the cesspool safe, but I neglected to do so. I will never forgive myself. How could I have been so neglectful?"

Told by JOHN A. MACARTHUR

* * *

I Drifted Along

Andrew Duncannon said, "When I was a boy, I heard Moody preach from the text 'Seek ye first the kingdom of God.' It seemed to me that the kingdom of heaven stood wide open to me. I knew the Holy Spirit was wooing me to enter. I meant to do it, but somehow I didn't. I drifted along with the crowd. Fifty years later I became a Christian. My life can never be what it might have been if I had done what I meant to do that night."

Oh, the tragedy of having a saved soul and an ill-spent life!

* * *

Drifting

Many years ago the captain of a whaling vessel in the North Atlantic saw through his binoculars an indistinct hulk in the distance, surrounded by icebergs. As his ship came near, he called, "Ship ahoy! Ship ahoy!" There was no answer. Going aboard the vessel, he found a frozen captain and a frozen crew. The captain was fully dressed and sat before a desk with the logbook open before him. The last entry revealed that the vessel had been in those northern waters, far removed from the usual flow of oceangoing traffic, for nearly ten years. It was a floating sepulcher, tossed by wind and waves, drifting from no port to no port.

Many men and women are like that derelict—unmoored and adrift, without chart, compass and captain, "having eyes full of adultery, and that cannot cease from sin" (II Peter 2:14).

Told by RALPH W. NEIGHBOUR

* * *

Lost Canyons of Cities

Msgr. Francis J. Lally, editor of the Boston Pilot, said, "The world is wounded seriously in many ways. Favored nations have everything they want, while one-half of the children in many underdeveloped countries die before they are fifteen, and one-half in Latin America before they are four. Most cities put a line around the problem. As we speed along the expressways, we never see the poor sections—the lost canyons of the cities or the blighted fields of Appalachia."

* * *

At Ease in Zion

The eagle is a stately bird, noted for its sharp eye and powerful wings. It is shown on the national emblem of the United States.

With his binoculars, an ornithologist watched two eagles building their nest high up on a rocky crag. They made it of sticks, branches and twigs, covering them with soft leaves. The nest became a comfortable home where the mother eagle could hatch the young eaglets.

The comfortable nest was not destined to remain the permanent home of the eaglets. The time would come when the mother eagle would "stir up" the nest to discomfort the eaglets and force them to learn to fly and forsake their life of ease.

In his song of praise, Moses referred to this custom of the mother eagle: "As an eagle stirreth up her nest, fluttereth over her young, spreadeth abroad her wings, taketh them, beareth them on her wings: so the LORD alone did lead" (Deut. 32:11-12).

How prone are God's children to lapse into an existence of ease, thus incurring God's displeasure and necessitating His discomforting them: "Woe to them that are at ease in Zion" (Amos 6:1).

Told by ALICE M. KNIGHT

* * *

Reason for Alarm

Thomas Guthrie said in the Alliance Weekly, "If you find yourself loving any pleasure better than your prayers, any book better than the Bible, any house better than the house of the Lord, any table better than the Lord's table, any persons better than Christ, or any indulgence better than the hope of heaven —be alarmed."

A Tragedy Which Might Have Been Averted

According to the findings of a reviewing board which met for ten weeks, deficient engineering, shoddy workmanship, faulty inspection and overall sloppiness and carelessness were the cause of the tragic deaths of the American astronauts Grissom, White and Chaffee aboard the ill-fated *Apollo* spacecraft.

Friends, loved ones and the nation were overwhelmed with sorrow because of the tragedy which might have been averted.

To do God's work sloppily or negligently or halfheartedly incurs God's displeasure. The Bible says, "Cursed be he that doeth the work of the LORD deceitfully [remissly, negligently]" (Jer. 48: 10).

"Whatsoever thy hand findeth to do, do it with thy might" (Eccles. 9:10).

* * *

Ursus Horribilis

In the summer of 1967, five carefree young people were on their way at dusk to a back-trail campsite in Montana's Glacier National Park. They passed a group of campers who warningly told them that they had just been chased by a bear. The young people went on, however.

Reaching the campsite at dark, they built a fire as a protection against an attack. As the campers lay around the fire in their sleeping bags, a huge grizzly bear was seen through the smoke! Closer and closer he came! Feigning death, the youths lay motionless and hid their heads in blankets. Snuffling at the bags, the bear began to rip them apart. As the beast reared to its full height, four of the campers bolted for trees. The fifth one, Michele Koons, age nineteen, was caught in her sleeping bag and dragged away, screaming, "He's ripping my arm! My God, I'm dead!"

Those in the trees looked helplessly upon the horrible scene!

Later the bear was killed. Human blood was on its fur and bits of human flesh were in its claws.

The bear lived up to his Latin name— *Ursus horribilis.*

The night of indescribable horror and death might have been averted if the young campers had heeded the warning.

Multitudes, in failing to heed the warnings of God's Word, have brought upon themselves and others sorrow and suffering which could have been averted.

The Bible warns, "He, that being often reproved hardeneth his neck, shall suddenly be destroyed, and that without remedy" (Prov. 29:1).

* * *

"If Only I Had!"

Many years ago a tragic and needless accident occurred at a railway drawbridge. One day the shrill whistle of a steamboat blew for the bridge to open. The watchman reasoned, *It's almost time for the express train, but I'm sure that I have ample time to open and close the bridge before it speeds past."* He took the miscalculated chance and opened the bridge. As he began to draw it closed, he heard in the distance the mournful whistle of the oncoming express train with its cargo of human freight. Though he made a frantic effort to close the bridge in time, he failed. On came the train and crashed into the river below!

Many perished that fateful day. The keeper of the bridge became deranged. The cries of the dying so preyed upon his mind that he completely lost his reason. He was committed to an asylum. During the wakeful hours of the day and night he mumbled incessantly, "If only I had! If only I had! If only I had!"

To "neglect so great salvation" and go out remorsefully and self-accusingly into a lost hereafter is the *supreme* tragedy.

Told by R. E. NEIGHBOUR

* * *

"I Left Him Asleep"

In a sermon Martin Luther said, "Satan held a great conclave in which his emissaries reported the results of their several missions.

" 'I let loose the wild beasts of the field on a caravan of Christians and their bones are now bleaching on the sands,' said one.

212

" 'What of that?' parried the devil. 'Their souls were all saved.'

" 'I drove the east wind against a ship freighted with Christians, and they were all drowned,' said another.

" 'What of that?' questioned the devil. 'Their souls were all saved.'

Another said, " 'For ten years I tried to get a single Christian asleep, and I succeeded, and I left him asleep.'

"Then the devil shouted gleefully, and all hell became vibrant with joy."

"Awake thou that sleepest, and arise from the dead, and Christ shall give thee light" (Eph. 5:14).

* * *

Fiddling

Editorialized *Christianity Today*: "We are like Nero who fiddled to the tune of Rome's crackling fire. We have been living in a make-believe pink cloud of $100,000 quiz shows, higher tail fins, brighter chrome, crunchier crumbles and dewier lips."

Paul said, "Awake thou that sleepest . . . and Christ shall give thee light" (Eph. 5:14).

* * *

Guess My Name

I am more deadly than bullets, and I have wrecked more homes than the mightiest of siege guns.

I steal in the United States alone over $300,000,000 each year.

I spare no one and find my victims among the rich and poor alike, the young and the old, the strong and the weak. Widows and orphans know me.

I massacre thousands upon thousands of wage earners in a year.

I am relentless. I am everywhere—in the home, on the street, in the factory, at railroad crossings and on the sea.

I bring sickness, degradation and death, yet few seek to avoid me.

I destroy, crush and maim. I give nothing, but take all.

I lurk in unseen places and do most of my work silently. You are warned against me, but you heed not.

I am your worst enemy.

I am *carelessness*.

Grand Rapids News

Spiritually Hibernating

Dr. R. W. Chaffee, of the University of Missouri's space science research center, believes that new experiments with hibernating hamsters raise hope for eventually inducing temporary hibernating power in man for long space voyages. He says, "In space travel, prolonged hibernation could make a month seem like a day, if the traveler were asleep."

Spiritually, many of God's children are hibernating—sleeping the sleep of deadly unconcern and indifference. They have long since ceased loving Christ first.

Spiritual somnambulism is exacting a terrible toll. Dispensationally, it is later than most Christians realize: "The night is far spent" (Rom. 13:12). The harvest is plenteous, and "he that sleepeth in harvest . . . causeth shame" (Prov. 10:5).

The clarion call comes: "Awake thou that sleepest, and arise from the dead, and Christ shall give thee light" (Eph. 5:14).

* * *

Pigs and Kids

The night was cold. The time was past midnight. Husband and wife were sleeping soundly. Then a sick child's whimpering cries were heard by her mother. Awakening her husband, the wife said, "Mary must be ill. Go and see what the trouble is."

The husband mumbled something and said, "You go." Shortly he was again sleeping soundly.

About that time, a pig out in the barnyard began to squeal distressingly. Instantly the husband awakened and sprang out of bed. As he hastily dressed, his wife said to him, "Do you know the difference between you and the daddy of that squealing pig?" Before he could reply, she gave this deserved and rebuking answer to her question: "He is a thoroughbred, and you are not!"

Told by BILLY SUNDAY

* * *

A Mountain of Ice

A friend said to William Lloyd Garrison, the antislavery crusader, "William, cool off! Moderate your imagination. You are on fire."

Garrison replied, "I have to be on fire. There is a mountain of ice about me."

Burning zeal for souls is greatly needed among God's children today. Moody said, "I would rather have zeal without knowledge than knowledge without zeal."

Slow Leaks

Paul E. Little commented, "Collapse in the Christian life is seldom a blowout. It is usually a slow leak."

OBEDIENCE — DISOBEDIENCE

Instant Obedience

Charles Stalker was a noted Quaker evangelist. At a railway station in a small town, he asked the station agent, "What time does the next train come through?"

The agent replied, "You just got off the train. Why didn't you stay on?"

Stalker replied, "Some distance from here, I had a deep impression to get off the train which has just gone through and take the next train. I felt that I would have been disobeying the prompting of the Holy Spirit if I had failed to do as I have done."

At that moment, the agent's telegraphic transmitter began to click out a message. The agent said, "The train you just got off has been wrecked with the loss of several lives!"

In speaking of the incident later, Stalker said, "I have long since learned that when God speaks I must obey His voice. The impression came as definitely as though an audible voice spoke to me. Had I disobeyed I might have been among those who were killed."

* * *

A Sine Qua Non

Anne Sullivan, who tutored young Helen Keller, said, "I saw clearly that it was useless to try to teach her language or anything else until she learned to obey me. I have thought about it a great deal, and the more I think the more certain I am that obedience is the gateway through which knowledge, yes, and love, too, enter the mind of a child."

I Blocked Him

When I stand at the judgment seat of Christ
And He shows me His plan for me,
The plan of my life as it might have been
Had He had His way, and I see

How I blocked Him here, and I checked Him there,
And I would not yield my will,
Will there be grief in my Saviour's eyes,
Grief, though He loves me still?

He would have me rich, and I stand there poor,
Stripped of all but His grace,
While memory runs like a hunted thing
Down the paths I cannot retrace.

Then my desolate heart will well-nigh break
With tears that I cannot shed;
I shall cover my face with my empty hands,
I shall bow my uncrowned head.

Lord of the years that are left to me,
I give them to Thy hand;
Take me and break me, mold me now
To the pattern Thou hast planned!

MARTHA SNELL NICHOLSON

* * *

The Responsibility Is His

On a quiet Sunday morning, Hudson Taylor took a step of faith in response to a simple spiritual principle he had just discovered.

"How long this fear-allaying truth evaded me!" he joyfully exclaimed. "If we are obeying the Lord, the responsibility rests with Him, not with us."

Then Hudson Taylor prayed, "Thou, Lord, Thou shalt have all the burden. At Thy bidding, I go forward, leaving results with Thee."

"Thus saith the LORD, . . . the battle is not yours, but God's" (II Chron. 20:15).

* * *

Backward About Going Forward

A little boy wrote an essay on the mule: "The mule is a stronger bird than the goose or turkey, and different. He has two wings on the sides of his head. He has two feet to walk with, and two more to kick with, and is awful backward about going forward."

How like that mule are stubborn people. Long ago stubbornness was punishable by death (cf. Deut. 21:18-23).

ALICE MARIE KNIGHT

* * *

A Ruler or a Scavenger

John Newton said, "If two angels were to receive at the same time a commission from God—one to go and rule earth's grandest empire, and the other to go and sweep the streets of its filthiest village, it would be a matter of entire indifference to each angel which service fell to his lot—the work of ruler or the work of scavenger. The joy of the angels lies only in obedience to God's will. With equal joy, they would lift a Lazarus in his rags to Abraham's bosom or be a chariot of fire to carry an Elijah home."

* * *

The Unoccupied Niche

In a stone quarry at Baalbec lies a magnificent column, the largest stone column upon which any sculptor ever worked. In the nearby crumbling Temple of the Sun is a niche which for centuries has waited to be occupied by the magnificent column.

How like that unused column are some of God's children who, through disobedience, have failed to occupy the niche which God designed for them. Each one of God's children is His "workmanship, created in Christ Jesus unto good works, which God hath . . . ordained that . . . [they] should walk in them" (Eph. 2:10).

* * *

"I Listened Right Away"

"I want to follow Jesus," said a boy in a mission school in Africa.

"Have you felt for some time that Jesus has been calling you?" asked the teacher.

"Oh, no," replied the boy. "I heard His call just a moment ago, and I listened right away!"

* * *

Doers of the Word

"What he preached he lived," said a friend of a faithful pastor whose daily life had exemplified his sermons.

A neighbor asked a friend who was on her way home from church, "Is the sermon done?"

"No," she replied. "It is all said, but now it must be done, or obeyed."

James said, "Be ye doers of the word, and not hearers only, deceiving your own selves" (James 1:22).

It is better not to know than to know and not do: "For it had been better for them not to have known the way of righteousness, than, after they have known it, to turn from the holy commandment delivered unto them" (II Peter 2:21).

* * *

Practical Obedience

A teacher in a mission school said to a minister who visited her class, "I believe the children know the Ten Commandments."

The minister asked, "Do they obey them?"

The teacher said, "Let's find out."

She called on a little boy to repeat the fifth commandment, "Honour thy father and thy mother." The teacher asked, "What does the commandment mean?"

The boy replied, "Yesterday I showed a strange man the way over the mountain. The sharp stones cut my feet. The man gave me some money to buy shoes. I gave the money to my mother. She

215

needed shoes, too. I thought I could go barefooted better than she could."

The boy obeyed the commandment in a most practical and unselfish way.

ALICE MARIE KNIGHT

* * *

Delayed Obedience

During a miners' strike in Scotland, there was widespread unemployment among the membership of a certain congregation. On two consecutive nights, as the minister prayed, God seemed to tell him to go and help a certain family, but he didn't go. On the third night, the minister couldn't sleep, so he said to his wife, "I must get up and take some money to a needy family."

It was near midnight, so the minister quietly dropped the money through the letter slot in the door and went away. A half hour later he heard a knock at his door. Answering the knock, he saw the man at whose door he had left the money.

"I'm almost a murderer!" said the man. "My children—five of them—and my wife and I have been without food for three days. God seemed to have forsaken us. I couldn't stand to see my children without food any longer, so I decided to kill them and my wife and myself if God hadn't answered our prayers and supplied our needs before the midnight hour. I held an open razor and walked back and forth in the room. Suddenly I heard footsteps. Then I heard something drop on the floor through the mail slot. There I found the three pounds. When I opened the door I recognized you as you disappeared. I was almost a murderer!"

That experience changed the whole ministry of Dr. David Laurie, former Director of Carrubber's Close Mission, Edinburgh. He was the minister who had delayed to obey God's voice until it was almost too late.

* * *

When Not to Obey

A teenage girl was converted. Her glowing heart was filled with joy! Going home from church, she broke the glad news to her mother.

Her mother became enraged. She telephoned the minister in whose church the daughter was saved, speaking contemptuously of what she called the girl's emotional upset.

The daughter held fast to her profession of faith in Christ.

Shortly after, the mother went to the daughter's room. She saw her daughter on her knees with the open Bible on her bed. She snatched the Bible and demanded that the daughter change her peculiar ways.

The teenager was deeply distressed. She bared her heart to the minister, calling attention to the command "Children, obey your parents in the Lord: for this is right" (Eph. 6:1).

The minister yearned to be a true friend to the noble girl. He said, "Let us look closely at that verse. It says, 'Children, obey your parents *in the Lord.*' If a parent demands of a child anything which goes counter to the Word of God, the child is to obey God and not the parent, remembering that the Bible says, 'We ought to obey God rather than men.' "

Told by C. LESLIE MILLER

* * *

Cooperating with God

God has pointed out a way that will keep His children triumphant and blessed with peace. Going counter to God's way brings defeat and disquiet.

When I was beginning my ministry in one of my former churches, there was an oldster in the community who was an annoyance to me. Though not a member of my church, he arrogated to himself the right to speak critically and disparagingly of the members and of the policies of the church. Weekly he wrote me an abusive letter. When I read the missives, I became discouraged. A feeling of futility held me momentarily in its viselike grip.

As I prayed and looked to the Lord for help, He seemed to say to me, "You are going counter to My directive, given to keep My children in peace and triumphant: 'Whatsoever things are true, . . . honest, . . . just, . . . pure, . . . lovely,

. . . [and] of good report; . . . think on these things'" (Phil. 4:8).

I acknowledged my failure to obey God's directive. After that, when I received the weekly letter from the self-appointed critic, I didn't read it. I went to the furnace and consigned the letter to the flames!

W. B. K.

* * *

Trust and Obey

In one of Moody's meetings, a man stood and testified, "I am not sure of all the doctrines, and I do not know the Bible very well. There is one thing, however, I am determined to do: I'm going to trust and obey!"

The man's resolution greatly appealed to D. B. Towner who was conducting the music. Later he mentioned it to Rev. J. H. Sammis, a Presbyterian minister.

"Why, that's the heart of Christian living!" Rev. Sammis exclaimed. Before long, he wrote the verses of the greatly loved and often sung hymn "Trust and Obey." Towner composed the music.

* * *

"If Only They Had Obeyed"

Two Boy Scouts who were brothers were killed by a cave-in near Denver, Colorado. Their troop leader, Willard Shaner, had warned them, saying, "Stay off the ledges. The soil is insubstantial and dangerous."

The boys, John and Robert, didn't heed the warning and this resulted in their deaths.

Their sorrowing father lamented, "If only they had done what they were told to do, this tragedy would have been averted."

It is hazardous for God's children to go in forbidden paths, heedless of God's warning. The Bible asks, "What shall the end be of them that obey not the gospel of God?" (I Peter 4:17).

Church Mission

* * *

Pupil of John Philip Sousa

One summer evening, as John Philip Sousa sat in his hotel room, he heard an organ-grinder in the street below play-ing his famed march "The Stars and Stripes Forever." He dashed to the street and jerked the organ away from the lazy organ-grinder. "Here! Here! This is the way to play that march," he said as he turned the handle of the organ vigorously. The music came forth spirited, snappy and inspiring. The organ-grinder listened intently. Then he bowed low, smiled and profusely thanked Sousa.

The next night, Sousa again heard the organ. His favorite composition was being played animatedly in the right tempo. Looking out of his hotel window, he saw a large crowd gathered around the organ-grinder. Over the organ was a sizable placard which read Pupil of John Philip Sousa.

The organ-grinder was quick to obey the instruction of Sousa, his benefactor.

How filled with melody our hearts would be if we were quick to obey the directives of God.

* * *

Give All

Years ago, as Sister Abigail sat in a church service, God seemed to say to her, "Give all."

She thought, *But, Lord, I have only three dollars and that is at home.*

God seemed to say, *Go home and get that three dollars.*

She said in her heart, *Yes, Lord. I will obey Thy voice, but I don't understand the meaning of it.*

Quietly Sister Abigail left the service. As she returned to the church, she saw an old woman shivering in a doorway. A troubled look was on the woman's face.

"Why are you out on such a cold day? Are you ill?" asked Sister Abigail.

The woman replied, "I have been sick, but I am better now. As I waited for my bus, I came into this doorway to pray. Recently my husband died. My daughter, who lives in a distant city, wants me to come and live with her. I am poor. After I sold the few things I had, I found that I am short three dollars of the price of the railway ticket to my daughter's home. As I stood here in the doorway, I asked God to somehow supply the need."

217

Now Sister Abigail knew why God had called her out of the church service. She gladly gave the woman her three dollars.

What wonderful opportunities for service God reveals to us when we are sufficiently close to Him to hear His voice speaking to us in our hearts.

Told by ROY O. MCCLAIN

* * *

"There Is a Sin unto Death"

A missionary in Africa told this story about her brother, who began the Christian life with joy and great promise. God had called him to preach.

Then the brother enlisted in the navy. While in the service, he got into sinful ways. Before long, he succumbed to a fatal illness—an inoperable brain tumor. Shortly before his death, he imploringly said to his sister: "Don't let anything or anyone keep you from doing what God wants you to do. With deep regret, I confess that I did!"

In commenting upon the early death of her brother, the missionary said, "I feel that his death was God's judgment upon him for getting into sinful ways and failing to go on with the Lord. Let us never forget that 'there is a sin unto death' [I John 5:16]."

"God's Word warns that some may be delivered 'unto Satan for the destruction of the flesh, that the spirit may be saved in the day of the Lord Jesus' (I Cor. 5:5)."

* * *

Unquestioning Obedience

Someone gave a little girl a box of paper dolls. She ran to show them to her father who sat before an open fire. "They're pretty, dear, but I want you to throw them in the fire! I won't compel you to do it, but if you can trust me, do as I tell you." She obeyed.

Enfolding her in his arms, the father said, "I asked you to do a hard thing because I want to teach you to trust and obey your heavenly Father. He may require you to do seemingly hard and difficult things. If you will trust and obey Him, as you have me, you will find that His way is always the best way."

The next day the father rewarded the little girl for her obedience by giving her an unusually beautiful doll.

ALICE MARIE KNIGHT

* * *

Choosing the Wrong World

John and Charles were brothers in a home in New York State. Upon reaching manhood, Charles decided on a business career involving both of them, but John's interest lay in another direction. One day he said, "Charles, I feel that God is calling me to be a preacher. I must answer God's call."

Charles answered, "Perish the thought. Let's start a business concern together, amass riches, and make a name for ourselves." He did his best to dissuade John from becoming a minister, but to no avail.

John became a preacher, and Charles moved to the Pacific Northwest and began a business.

As the years passed by, Charles did amass riches. He and his family lived in affluence and for the passing pleasures of the world.

One Christmas he sent railway tickets to John and his family and invited them to spend the Christmas holidays with him and his family.

One night, as the two brothers sat alone in the living room before a cheerful fire, they reminisced. Charles said, "John, what a fool you were to become a poor preacher and give up the enjoyment of the many pleasures and good things of life."

A look of sadness came on the face of John as he thought of the spiritual blindness of his brother who wanted the unsatisfying things of this world more than spiritual riches.

Told by R. E. NEIGHBOUR

* * *

A Senator Speaks

Sen. Mark Hatfield stated, "We are witnessing today an undermining of the Scriptures, the authority of Christ and the authority of the church."

A Sociologist Speaks

Will Durant warned, "We are in a revolt, so to speak, in all areas of society: man against the state, child against parent, student against teacher. Today anything which is a symbol of authority is to be shunned or overthrown."

* * *

A Condemned Criminal Speaks

Louis Blanc said shortly before his execution: "When I was an infant, I rebelled against my nurse. When I was a child, I rebelled against my teachers. When I was a young man, I rebelled against my father and mother. When I reached mature age, I rebelled against the state. When I die, if there are a heaven and a God, I'll rebel against them!"

God Has Spoken

Long ago God's Word foretold the coming of the time when restraints would be cast away: "The kings of the earth set themselves . . . against the LORD, . . . saying, Let us break their bands asunder, and cast away their cords from us" (Ps. 2:2-3).

History is repeating itself. Long ago "every man did that which was right in his own eyes" (Judges 17:6).

* * *

Marching Orders

A young minister asked the duke of Wellington, "Do you not deem it useless to attempt to convert India?"

The duke flashed, "Sir, what are your marching orders?"

OLD AGE

Planning in Advance

On his fifty-fifth birthday, Thomas Edison attended a party given in his honor. "What plans do you have for the future?" he was asked.

"From now until I am seventy-five, I will be occupied with my work," he replied. "At seventy-five, I expect to take up golf. Coming up to eighty and beyond, I am going to gossip with the ladies."

"And at ninety?" he was asked.

"I never plan more than thirty years in advance," said Edison.

* * *

No Time for Retirement

Dr. E. H. Lines, a medical examiner of the New York Life Insurance Company, warned, "Men who retire don't live long. They're not prepared for leisure. It's too great a shock for them."

Mrs. Robert W. Stewart said on her eighty-fourth birthday, "Don't slow down and Father Time won't catch you." She bakes and sews and is an active member of her church.

Said Dr. William Lyon Phelps, who lived to seventy-eight years old, "I live every day as if this were the first day I had ever lived and the last day I should ever live."

* * *

An Inviting Future

Shortly before his death, David Livingstone celebrated his sixtieth birthday. A national commented, "You are getting old."

Radiantly Livingstone replied, "I am not old. No man ever had a brighter prospect or a more inviting future."

With God's children, the best is yet to be: "Eye hath not seen . . . the things which God hath prepared for them that love him" (I Cor. 2:9).

* * *

"You Are Younger than You Think"

Said Dr. Martin Gumpert, in his book *You Are Younger Than You Think*, "Idleness is the greatest enemy of the aged and presents them with their ticket to death. Michelangelo was writing poetry and designing buildings up to the time of his death at ninety. Gladstone, prime minister of England, at eighty-three fought the greatest battle of his life—the passage of a home-rule bill.

Goethe completed *Faust*, his greatest work, at eighty-one. Titian finished his painting *The Last Supper* at eighty. *You* are younger than you think you are."

* * *

As Young as Your Faith

Gen. Douglas MacArthur said, "You are as young as your faith, as old as your doubts, as young as your self-confidence, as old as your fear, as young as your hope, as old as your despair.

"In the central place of your heart there is a wireless station. So long as it receives messages of beauty, hope, cheer, courage, grandeur . . . and power from the Infinite, just so long, and no longer, are you young.

"When the wires are all down and your heart is covered with the snows of pessimism and the ice of cynicism, then, and then only, are you old."

* * *

I Live in Memories

Fritz Kreisler, the world-renowned violinist, died at the age of eighty-six. For twelve years prior to his death, his violin lay mute—a faded echo of his genius.

In his last years, Kreisler thought regretfully about a society whose major emphasis was now upon the materialistic, not the artistic. "I live in memories," he said.

How enchanting are one's memories if, in the winter of old age, he can say, "I have lived in all good conscience before God until this day" (Acts 23:1).

* * *

Uphill

Does the road wind uphill all the way?
    Yes, to the very end.
Will the journey take the whole long
        day?
    From morn to night, my friend.

But is there for the night a resting place?
    Yes, shelter when the slow, dark hours
        begin.
Might not the darkness hide it from my
        face?
    You cannot miss that inn.

Shall I meet other travelers at night?
    Yes, those who've gone before.
Then must I knock, or call when just in
        sight?
    They will not keep you standing at
        that door.

Shall I find comfort, travel-sore and
        weak?
    Tenderness and joy are in that Home.
Will there be place for me and all who
        seek?
    Place for all in Christ who come.

                CHRISTINA G. ROSSETTI

* * *

Down Memory Lane

I'd like to stroll down memory's lane
    Together, you and I,
And sing the songs we used to sing
    In happy days gone by.
Our thoughts will bloom like flowers,
    And we'll gather every one;
We'll laugh at things we used to do,
    The joyous things we've done;
And then, someday, if God permits,
    Perhaps beneath the sky—
Hand in hand we'll stroll once more
    Together, you and I.

* * *

Then You Are Old

Truly, age is a quality of mind—
If you have left your dreams behind,
    If hope is cold,
If you no longer look ahead,
If ambition's fires are dead—
    Then you are old.

But if from life you take the best,
    And if in life you keep the zest,
    If love you hold—
No matter how the years roll by,
No matter how the birthdays fly—
    You are not old.

* * *

Morning Is in My Heart

On his eighty-sixth birthday, Judge Mulock, of Ontario, wrote. "I am still at work with my hand to the plow and my face to the future. The shadows of evening lengthen about me but morning is in my heart. The testimony that I bear is this: the castle of enchantment is not yet behind me—it is before me still. Daily I catch glimpses of its battlement and towers. The rich treasures of memory are mine. Mine, too, are the precious things of today—books, flowers, pictures, nature. The best thing of all is friendship. The best of life is always farther on—its lure hidden somewhere beyond the hills of time."

With God's children, the best is yet to be: "Eye hath not seen, nor ear heard, neither have entered into the heart of man, the things which God hath prepared for them that love him" (I Cor. 2:9).

* * *

What Makes Old Age Hard

W. Somerset Maugham, a novelist and an avowed agnostic, said, "What makes old age hard to bear is the burden of one's memories. When I look back on my life it seems to me strangely lacking in reality. It may be that my heart, having found rest nowhere, had some deep ancestral craving for God and immortality which my reason would have no dealing with."

* * *

"It Is Ridiculous"

Dr. Paul Dudley White, world-renowned heart specialist, stated, "It is ridiculous to think that one must retire at middle age. Work should extend to seventy or perhaps even longer. Many intelligent leaders in every walk of life think nothing of continuing in their seventies to row, climb mountains or walk many miles daily."

* * *

"I See No Reason Why"

On Sir Winston Churchill's eightieth birthday, a news photographer jokingly said, "I shall photograph you on your one hundredth birthday."

Churchill quipped, "I see no reason why you shouldn't, young man. You look healthy enough!"

* * *

The Fag End of Life

When eighty years old, an outstanding citizen of Dallas, Texas, sought and found Christ's forgiveness. He regretfully told Dr. George W. Truett, his pastor, "My life has been almost a total loss. I didn't come to Christ till the fag end of my life. In mercy, Christ saved me, but, oh, how sorry I am that I gave nearly all my life to the wrong side!"

* * *

What Life's For

Eleanor Roosevelt said on her seventy-seventh birthday, "I think I have a good deal of my Uncle Theodore in me because I could not, at any age, be content to take my place in a corner by the fireside and simply look on. Life was meant to be lived. One must never, for whatever reason, turn his back on life."

* * *

Arbitrarily Ending Man's Work

In addressing the American Medical Association, Dr. Irving S. Wright, of Cornell University Medical College, said, "Today there are some 20 million Americans above the age of sixty-five, and some 12,000 above one hundred. If medical science finds an answer to the artery-clogging disease of arteriosclerosis, there may be as many as 150 million over sixty-five by the year 2000. Medical science must find a way to measure biological age, rather than merely totaling up a man's years. For many of today's sixty-five-year-olds, society and science have created an artificial and painful dilemma. Science has extended life and man's potential usefulness. But society, the company, the union and the retirement plan have arbitrarily ended a man's working days when he reaches sixty-five. The company, the economy and the individual suffer both financially and psychologically."

* * *

Viewpoint and Ideas

Sen. Everett M. Dirksen said on his seventieth birthday, "I may be seventy timewise, but in viewpoint and ideas I'm still fifty, or even less."

A Foolscap

The Bible says, "The hoary head is a crown of glory, if found in the way of righteousness" (Prov. 16:31). The hoary head is a foolscap if found in way of unrighteousness.

More Hopeful

Oliver Wendell Holmes said, "To be seventy years young is sometimes far more cheerful and hopeful than to be forty years old."

PARENTAL RESPONSIBILITY

(See also Children, Fathers, Mothers)

"Please Stop Hurting Us Kids"

The following pathetic letter was sent to a newspaper columnist: "My letter is a simple plea to the parents of teenagers to please consider what their excessive drinking does to their children. My father is an alcoholic. If he only knew how many times he has made me ashamed to be his daughter. If he only knew the times my girl friends have come over and seen him dead drunk—and how I shudder when boys come to take me out and I must rush to meet them on the front steps so they won't get inside the house.

"I hate to come home because I never know what I will find there. My father is downstairs now, sick as a dog, but tomorrow night he will go out and do the same thing over again.

"I beg of parents—please stop hurting us kids."

* * *

"Am I Alone Responsible?"

"Have you anything to say before I sentence you?" sternly asked a Canadian judge of a seventeen-year-old youth who had committed murder and who was soon to hear the death sentence pronounced.

"Yes, Your Honor, I have something to say. Am I alone responsible for the crime I committed? My father put the first bottle of liquor in my hand. My parents taught me that there is nothing to religion. I never saw a Bible in our home. I never heard my parents pray. May God have mercy on their souls and mine!"

Left to Shift

J. Edgar Hoover stated, "There are 17,000,000 teenage boys and girls in the United States who have not as yet been reached and perhaps will never be reached for Christ because their parents have left them to shift for themselves without the influence of the gospel or the church."

* * *

A Teenager's Plaintive Plea

A discouraged, disillusioned fifteen-year-old boy addressed the following pathetic plea to his parents:

"Dear Parents: Do you know how much you hurt your children when you argue and fight in front of them? Lately I have been crying myself to sleep to the noise of your fighting. I can't think straight in school because I worry about whether you will really get the divorce you threaten each other with. I am afraid to come to you with problems I want to talk to you about because you are always in such a bad mood. Why can't you love each other like you did when you got married? We didn't ask to be born. Now that we are here, why don't you try to get along so we can have a happy home? If you have something to argue about, why don't you do it sometime when your children don't hear you? I try hard to be a good, obedient and happy son. Won't you please try to be better parents?"

A Tragic Lack

The Cuyahoga County Grand Jury, Cleveland, Ohio, ended a recent session by deploring the lack of parental authority: "Never has there been a greater need for parental concern, guidance and courageous counsel for growing children. Ironically and regrettably, never, by the same token, has there been either greater or more convincing evidence of unprecedented and conspicuous lack of parental counsel or guidance than at the present."

How essential it is for parents to rear children in the way they should go and to go that way themselves.

* * *

Earliest Memory

A visiting friend found a young mother sitting with her baby on her lap and holding her Bible in her hand. She asked, "Are you reading the Bible to your baby?"

The mother replied, "Yes."

The visitor said, "Surely you do not think he understands it?"

"No," said the mother. "He does not understand it now, but I want his earliest memory to be that of seeing and hearing God's Word."

* * *

Delinquent Parents

Some teenage boys, guilty of serious offenses, were arraigned in juvenile court, Cleveland, Ohio. They were intoxicated when they were arrested.

Before passing sentence upon the youths, Judge Walter G. Whitlach sternly reprimanded the parents who were present. He said, "These boys know the difference between right and wrong, but you have not cared about their being out at four o'clock in the morning. Two fathers are alcoholics. One father is not here because he deserted his family and his responsibilities. As fathers and mothers, *you are failures.* These youngsters are in a typical pattern."

* * *

Why the Judge Hated Parents

A judge of a juvenile court in New York said, "When I retire, I am going to write a book and call it *Why I Hate Parents.*"

Asked why he hated parents, he replied, "Because of my disgust with their failure to assume their primary job—the care of their children."

A youth who lives in Chicago's South Side and has already been in trouble with the law stated, "The only reason I know what my mother's face looks like is because my family gets together on Thursday evenings for one hour—from 7 to 8 P.M. The rest of the week, my mom and dad are running in a thousand directions."

No activity, however worthy, which robs the children of parental care and companionship can atone for the neglect of the boys and girls.

* * *

His First Bible

My little boy's first Bible
　Is the greatest thrill he's known.
There's a sweet, unique excitement
　In a Bible all his own!

And yet my heart is smitten
　At this touching sight I see.
Has this reverence for that Bible
　Depended much on me?

As I see him with his Bible,
　I bow my head and pray;
May he always love that Bible
　The way he does today.

Then I hear a voice within me
　Speak in solemn words and true:
"How he cherishes that Bible
　Will depend a lot on you!"

I love my Bible better
　Since I've seen the beaming joy
This wonderful possession
　Has afforded to my boy.

May I seek to give mine daily
　A devotion he can see,
For the love he bears his Bible
　Will depend a lot on me.

United Presbyterian

* * *

Heaven-sent Little Ones

Children are gifts from God: "For this child I prayed; and the LORD hath given

223

me my petition" (I Sam. 1:27). How great is parental responsibility for their eternal destinies!

A mother became greatly burdened for the conversion of her boy as she listened to a sermon on the text "How shall I go up to my father, and the lad be not with me?" (Gen. 44:34).

She thought, *How can I go up to my heavenly Father and my boy is not with me?*

Quietly she left the church, hurried home, and said to her boy, "I am a Christian, but I have never asked you to receive Christ as your Saviour. Do forgive me for my terrible neglect! Won't you ask Him to come into your heart?"

After earnest discussion and prayer, she had the joy of leading her boy to the Saviour.

* * *

"It's All My Fault"

A sixteen-year-old boy, who stole $9,000 in cash from his parents and paid an eighteen-year-old neighbor $1,500 to ransack his home to make it appear that the theft was burglary, was sentenced to the Fairfield School for Boys.

Upon hearing the sentence pronounced by juvenile court judge Angelo J. Gagliardo, the boy's mother sobbed bitterly and pleaded with the judge not to send her boy away. "It's all my fault," she said. "I put temptation there for him. O dear God, let me be punished! Let me be punished!" So overcome was she that she had to be assisted from the courtroom.

Great will be the accountability to God of parents who fail to set the right Christian example before their children.

* * *

Be a Pal to the Lad

A distant cousin, passing through a city, called at the home of her relatives. She was greeted at the door by the young son, whom she had never met. Introducing herself she said, "How are you? I am your third cousin on your father's side."

"Well," drawled the lad, "I can tell you right now—you're on the wrong side."

We can only surmise what caused the boy to speak disparagingly of his father, but we know that, if a dad fails to be a pal and confidant to his son, he has failed in his most important, God-given responsibility and privilege.

* * *

"God? Who's That?"

The following letter from a grief-stricken mother appeared in the Warsaw, Indiana, *Times-Union:*
"DEAR SIR:

"Three months ago, I sat in a courtroom and heard a judge say, 'Twenty years!' He was pronouncing punishment on my twenty-one-year-old son, a penalty for drinking, gambling and robbery which ended in the almost-fatal shooting of a man.

"The sentence might have been less but my son had a sneering, defiant attitude all through the trial. The crowning, shocking climax came when the judge sternly asked, 'Young man, don't you believe in God?'

"My son laughed loud and long as he answered, 'God? Who's that?' Every eye in the courtroom turned to look at me.

"I went to Sunday school when I was small and learned about God. After I married I decided to go again and take my children. I went regularly for a year. Then I skipped a Sunday. Soon I skipped two or three. Then we went only on special days.

"If I only had those years to live over! Night after night, I've paced the floor with the words 'God? Who's that?' echoing in my ears.

"I am sick with shame. So many say they do not believe in making a child go to church if he doesn't want to, but how many children would go to school if they weren't made to? Ask any child that question."

224

PATRIOTISM

(See also Freedom)

Gravely Endangered

Dr. Wernher von Braun, famed scientist, warned, "In our constitutionally guaranteed pursuit of happiness, many Americans refuse to look at the dark clouds which are rapidly moving up. I fear it is later than we think. Our position in the world is gravely endangered."

* * *

A Marked Change Needed

Dr. Albert Hyma, professor of history, University of Michigan, warned, "Unless a marked change takes place in the United States, it is doomed, just as surely as was ancient Babylonia!"

* * *

Nationalism Is a Religion

Arnold J. Toynbee, historian and philosopher, said, "Nationalism is the common religion of the people of the world, on both sides of the iron curtain. It is an offense against both God and men. It is the worship of men instead of God, and is idolatry. The worship of one's own nation is also an offense against the human race. When we worship our own nation, we treat the rest of the human race as if it were not fully human."

* * *

"I've Never Known a Time Like This"

George Gallup said, "I think the mood of America today is one of great confusion. I've never known a time like this when people were so disillusioned and cynical. The public wants desperately to find a way to resolve international problems without going to war."

* * *

Critical Internal Danger

Sen. John L. McClellan warned, "Mounting crime—murder, rape, robbery, rioting and civil disobedience—has reached a level and momentum that borders on open rebellion and insurrection and is the most critical internal danger confronting the nation."

* * *

Statesmanship

Harold Wilson, British prime minister, said, "The hardest part of statesmanship is to show restraint in the face of understandable demands for action which, however immediately satisfying, could have incalculable effects—effects indeed for the whole world."

* * *

Individuals

In a prayer in the U.S. Senate, Peter Marshall, the chaplain, said, "Our heavenly Father, we are beginning to understand at last that the things that are wrong with the world are the sum total of all the things that are wrong with us as individuals."

* * *

Necessary Fundamentals

Herbert Hoover averred, "The whole of the inspiration of our civilization springs from the teaching of Christ and the lessons of the prophets. To read the Bible for these fundamentals is a necessity of American life."

Andrew Jackson stated, "The Bible, sir, is the foundation upon which the Republic stands."

The question is relevant: "If the foundations be destroyed, what can the righteous do?" (Ps. 11:3).

* * *

The Most Essential Things

Col. Charles A. Lindbergh said, "In my youth science was more important to me than either man or God. I worshiped science. Its advance had surpassed man's wildest dreams. It took many years for me to discover that science, with all its brilliance, lights only a middle chapter of creation.

"I saw the aircraft I loved destroying the civilization I expected it to save. Now

225

I understand that spiritual truth is more essential to a nation than the mortar in its cities' walls. For when the actions of a people are undergirded by spiritual truths, there is safety. When spiritual truths are rejected, it is only a matter of time before civilization will collapse. We must understand spiritual truths and apply them to our modern life. We must draw strength from the almost forgotten virtues of simplicity, humility, contemplation and prayer. It requires a dedication beyond science, beyond self, but the rewards are great and it is our *only* hope."

* * *

Not Immune from God's Judgment

Sen. Strom Thurmond warned, "Our nation today stands in our gravest time of peril from the standpoint of survival. For our nation to come through this dangerous time, we must be strong spiritually and seek the guidance of God. We must be sure, as Lincoln so aptly said a century ago, not only that God is on our side but, more importantly, that we are on God's side. Our nation is not immune from God's judgment."

* * *

No Misgivings About Gettysburg

After the epochal, decisive Battle of Gettysburg, Gen. Daniel E. Sickles asked President Lincoln, "Why were you so confident of victory when the Army of the Potomac had suffered many reverses?"

Lincoln replied, "When Lee crossed the Potomac and entered Pennsylvania followed by our army, I felt that the crisis had come. I knew that defeat in a great battle on northern soil involved the loss of Washington. I went to my room and got down on my knees in prayer. Never before did I pray with so much earnestness. I felt that I must put all my trust in almighty God. He gave our people the best country ever given to man. He alone could save it from destruction. I prayed that He would not let the nation perish. I felt that my prayer was answered. I had no misgivings about the result of Gettysburg."

V. RAYMOND EDMAN

On the Brink

In December, 1967, the National Committee for an Effective Congress analyzed the political situation, saying, "Malaise, frustration, alienation, identity are now becoming part of the professional political vocabulary. At all levels of American life, people share similar fears, insecurities and gnawing doubts to such an intense degree that the country may be on the brink of . . . a depression of the national spirit."

* * *

"A Splendid Misery"

John Adams said of the presidency of the United States, "No man who ever held the office of President would congratulate a friend on obtaining it. He will make one man ungrateful and a hundred men his enemies for every office he can bestow."

President Jefferson described the presidency as "a splendid misery."

James Buchanan wrote to his successor, Abraham Lincoln, "If you are as happy on entering this house [the White House] as I am in leaving it and returning home, you are the happiest man in this country."

* * *

When Tyrants Forge Their Chains

Patrick Henry said, "Bad men cannot make good citizens. It is impossible that a nation of infidels or idolaters should be a nation of freemen. It is when a people forget God that tyrants forge their chains. A vitiated state of morals, a corrupted public conscience, are incompatible with freedom."

* * *

Moral Deterioration

Gen. Dwight Eisenhower commented, "I do not believe that one out of every hundred prospective draftees expresses the belief that we owe anything to our country. I get so upset that we don't feel more obligation to our country. There seems to be some kind of moral deterioration and we should all be fighting this."

226

Men Who Stand

Not gold, but only men can make
   A nation great and strong,
Men who for truth and honor's sake
   Stand fast and suffer long.

Brave men who work while others sleep,
   Who dare while others shy—
They build a nation's pillars deep,
   And lift them to the sky.

              RALPH WALDO EMERSON

* * *

Memorial Day

At the close of the Civil War, a group of women in Columbus, Mississippi, honored both Confederate and Union dead by placing flowers on their graves. When the news of this act of compassion reached the North, it helped to heal the recent wounds the young nation had suffered.

In 1868 Gen. John A. Logan, national commander of the Grand Army of the Republic, issued his historic order to all chapters of the Grand Army of the Republic to set aside May 30 as Decoration Day (now called Memorial Day) to decorate the graves of the heroic dead.

          American Legion Advance

* * *

Our Modern Despair

Prof. Edward P. Coleson, Spring Arbor College, said, "No less than twenty-two major civilizations have risen and flourished through the centuries, but only seven still survive. I am not a pessimist but I am deeply distressed with most of our modern despair—often lightly disguised with shallow optimism and giddy gaiety braced up with cocktails and tranquilizers."

* * *

"I Kissed the Free Soil!"

A contingent of Cubans, arriving in Miami, knelt and prayed tearfully, thanking God for their new home.

Sixty-year-old Felipa Moya said, "I am so happy to be here that I kissed the free soil!"

Renato Rodriguez stated, "I feel like I'm getting out of jail!"

Few of us are sufficiently grateful to God for the numberless blessings which He has showered upon us as a nation.

* * *

Duty, Honor, Country

Gen. Douglas MacArthur stated, "Duty, honor and country—these three hallowed words reverently dictate what you ought to be, what you can be, and what you will be. They are your rallying point to build courage when courage seems to fail, to regain faith when there seems little cause for faith, to create hope when hope becomes forlorn."

* * *

As Seen Through Foreign Eyes

An Austrian visited America for six months. Here are some of her impressions of our country:

"America is the most prosperous country in the world. Its spaciousness is overwhelming. Its beauty is awesome! I love every inch of it. But something is wrong with the people. They are friendly and helpful, but appear to be unhappy. They hurry a great deal and are afraid of quiet —afraid to think. As one listens to much of the social conversation, it is apparent that they do not think. They repeat only what they heard on the radio or TV. May God bless all Americans and may they find the true joy that things or passing pleasure cannot bring."

* * *

Needed: Old-fashioned Morality

Sen. John L. McClellan stated in the *Omaha World-Herald*, "Our nation is in desperate need of a resurgence of old-fashioned morality. Apathy must go. It needs to be replaced by the outraged righteousness of a people who rose to greatness through the spiritual values that their forefathers wrote into the Declaration of Independence and the Constitution of the United States. There is no better way to stop the advance of crime which permeates every structure of our society."

"Righteousness exalteth a nation: but sin is a reproach to any people" (Prov. 14:34).

The Breath of Self-respect

When an American says that he loves his country, he means not only that he loves the New England hills, the prairies glistening in the sun, the wide and rising plains, the great mountains and the sea. He means that he loves an inner air, an inner light in which freedom lives and in which a man can draw the breath of self-respect.

ADLAI STEVENSON

* * *

If America Goes Down

Dr. Raymond B. Wilbur said, "I firmly believe that if America goes down, it will not be under the impact of megaton missiles, but the final collapse of that inner moral structure that makes a nation great. There should be no mistaking what is at stake."

* * *

The Inevitable Cycle

Commented the *News Letter* of the Aaron Post of the American Legion, "The average age of the world's great civilizations has been two hundred years. They passed through this sequence: from bondage to spiritual faith; from spiritual faith to courageous action; from courageous action to liberty; from liberty to abundance; from abundance to self-indulgence; from self-indulgence to complacency; from complacency to apathy; from apathy to dependency; from dependency back again to bondage."

In less than a decade, the United States will be two hundred years old. Increasingly existent in our land are all the corrosive ills and sin-diseases which wrought havoc in the mighty nations of the yesteryears and brought about their decay and disintegration.

The only cure, should the Lord delay His coming, is a spiritual revival with resultant sorrow for sin and a turning from sin to God.

Dr. William Culbertson, president of Moody Bible Institute, said, "Frankly I see no way out of this spiritual and moral torpidity and actual turpitude apart from either the Spirit of God or the coming of the Son of God."

Our Sorry Record

Editorialized the *Chicago Tribune:* "The decay of a people's moral fiber has, through history, always been the prelude to the collapse of a civilized society. It was so in imperial Rome. The collapse has always been heralded by the example of the nation's leaders. If some future Gibbon should come to write *The Decline and Fall of the American Republic,* would he ponder our sorry record?"

* * *

The Way Out

J. Edgar Hoover stated, "The banners of Christ can lead the way to the moral and spiritual rebirth of our great nation. In the forefront of His standard-bearers are the Sunday schools. There is only one ray of hope—God."

* * *

Patriotism Dying

Dr. William P. Saunders, who for twenty-one years was an examining physician and a member of Draft Board 21, Cleveland, Ohio, said, "Young people today don't have patriotism as formerly. I don't know where it has gone. We're fighting for our country, but we don't seem to appreciate it all."

* * *

"Is Life So Dear?"

Standing in his pew in St. John's Episcopal Church, Richmond, Virginia, Patrick Henry spoke in "torrents of sublime eloquence," saying, "Is life so dear, or peace so sweet, as to be purchased at the price of chains and slavery? Forbid it, Almighty God! I know not what course others will take; but as for me, give me liberty or give me death!"

As he spoke, the atmosphere of the church became vibrant with two of the noblest of sentiments—patriotism and freedom!

George Washington and Thomas Jefferson sat in nearby pews as Patrick Henry delivered his courageous appeal.

228

Patriotism Is Not Enough

Edith Cavell, an English nurse in World War I, helped some two hundred English, French and Belgian soldiers to escape to England during the occupation of Belgium. She was court-martialed by the Germans and sentenced to death as a spy.

On the eve of her execution, she said to an English chaplain who visited her, "I have no fear of death. I willingly give my life for my country. But, standing as I do, viewing God and eternity, I realize that patriotism is not enough. I must have no hatred or bitterness toward anyone."

The chaplain described what took place then: "We partook of the holy communion together. I quoted the verse 'Abide with us: for it is toward evening, and the day is far spent' [Luke 24:29]. Then we softly sang the hymn 'Abide with me.'

"When I said good-bye, she smiled and said, 'We shall meet again in heaven!' "

* * *

A Dying Civilization

Said the historian Arnold Toynbee, "The first heralds of the gospel brought a living faith to a dying civilization."

Rome did not seem to be dying. Her ironhanded rule encompassed the known world. Her legions were triumphant everywhere. Rome lacked, however, spiritual power and the redemptive ministry of Christ. Hence, her vaunted civilization was a dying civilization. The seeds of lust, cruelty and violence were in it.

Ill fares the land,
To hastening ill a prey,
Where wealth accumulates
And men decay!

* * *

Decline and Fall of America

May Craig, a Washington correspondent, said, "Unless there is a change deep down in the American people, a genuine crusade against self-indulgence and immorality, public and private, then we are witnesses to the decline and fall of the American republic."

The Bible says, "Righteousness exalteth a nation: but sin is a reproach to any people" (Prov. 14:34).

Planned Lawlessness

Associate Justice Charles E. Whittaker of the U.S. Supreme Court said, "Can any thoughtful person reasonably believe that a disorderly society can survive? In all recorded history, none ever has. On the contrary, history shows that every society which became lawless soon succumbed. The first evidence of each society's decay appeared in the toleration of disobedience of its laws and the judgments of its courts. These are ancient and universal lessons. In recent times all of us have daily seen with unmistakable clarity the rapid spread of planned lawlessness in our land that threatens seriously to get out of hand."

* * *

Chaotic

Dr. Roger L. Shinn, Dean of Instruction at Union Theological Seminary, recently said, "In the twenty-five years that I've been studying theology, I've never seen the situation so chaotic."

The situation could be changed if we as a nation would penitently confess to God that "to us belongeth confusion of face . . . because we have sinned against thee" (Dan. 9:8), and seek His mercy and forgiveness.

* * *

A Spiritual Underpinning

J. Edgar Hoover, Director of the Federal Bureau of Investigation, stated, "The modern age has achieved miracles. Twentieth century man is the beneficiary of a world so marvelous, staggering and overwhelming that it would have been unbelievable two decades ago. This is the heritage of man's victory over his physical world. Endlessly his mind is attempting to produce new devices which will lessen human pain and provide greater material comfort. If man's needs could be measured in terms of physical well-being alone, American civilization could be deemed highly successful. Unfortunately this is not true, for man does not live by bread alone. He has a much deeper need, a spiritual need, a spiritual underpinning of life. This is the crying need of society. Giant fissures of immorality, criminal deeds and glaring wrong abound."

Isaiah's indictment of Judah aptly depicts our nation today: "Ah sinful nation, a people laden with iniquity: . . . the whole head is sick, and the whole heart faint" (Isa. 1:4-5).

A plea: "O LORD, revive thy work; . . . in wrath remember mercy" (Hab. 3:2).

* * *

"I'm Worried"

Kate Smith, radio and TV star, commented, "I tell you, I'm worried about the future of America, because I'm meeting more atheists every day. If you don't believe in God, how can you believe in a country like ours? When you lose God, forget the whole thing. Every other value has got to go, sooner or later. You can destroy a country just as fast by taking away the things it stands for, like respect for God and the flag, as you can by adding elements that are against everything it stands for, like Communists. When we were kids, we said prayers in school and saluted the flag every day before we started lessons. With that kind of upbringing, you have a feeling in your heart about your country. It just seems that people don't want to hear the truth anymore. They don't want to admit they're proud of their country. They drink more. That's just to escape thinking. You walk into somebody's house and the first thing they say, no matter what time of day, is 'What are you drinking?' I tell you I'm very proud to stand up and say, 'Nothing, thanks. I don't indulge!' It makes me feel important and different!"

* * *

I Am the Nation

I was born on July 4, 1776, and the Declaration of Independence is my birth certificate. The bloodlines of the world run in my veins, because I offered freedom to the oppressed. I am many things and many people. *I am the nation.*

I am 195 million living souls, and the ghosts of millions who have lived and died for me.

I remember the Alamo, the *Maine* and Pearl Harbor. When freedom called I answered and stayed until it was over—

over there. I left my heroic dead in Flanders fields, on the rock of Corregidor, on the bleak slopes of Korea and in the steaming jungles of Vietnam.

Yes, I am the nation, and these are the things I am. I was conceived in freedom and, God willing, in freedom I will spend the rest of my days.

May I possess always the integrity, the courage and the strength to keep myself unshackled, to remain a citadel of freedom and a beacon of hope to the world.

* * *

An Urgent Need

Great is the need of our nation to rediscover courage and selfless patriotism. These qualities characterized the framers of the Declaration of Independence. They expressed this in its closing words: "For the support of this Declaration, with a firm reliance on the protection of divine Providence, we mutually pledge to each other our Lives, our Fortunes and our sacred Honor."

* * *

My Native Land!

Breathes there the man with soul so dead,
Who never to himself hath said,
"This is my own, my native land!"

SIR WALTER SCOTT

* * *

The Greatest Threat

Lawrence Gould, geologist and Arctic expert, said, "I don't think that the greatest threat to our future is from bombs or guided missiles. I don't think our civilization will die that way. I think it will die when the spiritual forces that make us wish to be right and noble die in the hearts of men."

Arnold Toynbee, English historian, said, "Nineteen of the past twenty-one notable civilizations have died from *within,* not by conquest from without. It happened slowly when no one was aware of it."

* * *

The Roman Empire and Us

"Relatively few members of our Western society realize the complexity, the intensity and the universality of the crisis in which mankind finds itself today.

There is nothing comparable to it in history—neither the age of the Renaissance nor the Reformation. If we can liken it to any period of upheaval and change, it would be to that of the fall of the Roman Empire, when a whole world order collapsed—religion, culture, morals, manners, and a highly developed, world-embracing legal and political system. That fall was a debacle of such magnitude that we can hardly comprehend it. Nothing remained except ruins.

"There is a striking similarity between the time before the fall of the Roman Empire and our own age. Again all areas of life are being shaken, all values and traditions questioned, whether they be cultural, religious, political or moral."

JOHN BOLTON, SR.

* * *

What Is Your Reaction?

What is your reaction when you look upon our beautiful flag, rippling in the gentle breeze; or when you look upon the Statue of Liberty, the emblem of freedom to the oppressed, enslaved ones everywhere? Are you thrilled when you hear our national anthem played? While acknowledging that glaring wrongs and corroding evils are alarmingly existent in America, do you thank God for the pricelessly precious freedoms we have and for the material and spiritual blessings He has so bountifully bestowed upon us?

A displaced person from Europe came to America. She was given work in the home of a minister. One day her face showed that she had been crying. The minister asked whether something was wrong. She answered quickly, "Anything wrong? No, sir, everything is right in this good America! I have been praising God for allowing me to come here! I am so grateful to Him! I love this land. It puzzles me that your people aren't more grateful and joyful and continually praising God. As for me, my big desire is to serve the Lord and America."

Let this be our daily prayer:

Long may our land be bright
    With freedom's holy light.
Protect us by Thy might,
    Great God our King!

Worthless Friendships

Congressman William E. Minshall warned of the nation's futile efforts to make friends through financial giveaways. He said, "With Americans hard pressed to meet their tax obligations and buy meat and potatoes, this is no time to give away money we don't have to people who are getting along without it. The United States is the most vilified nation on the face of the globe today because it has pursued the misguided policy of trying to buy friends."

How worthless in time of need are bought friendships!

* * *

"Wealth Accumulates—Men Decay"

Dean Rusk, former secretary of state, commented, "The economic growth and power of the United States are almost beyond comprehension. The current total output is ten times that of Communist China or all of Latin America. It is twice that of the Soviet Union, and the gap continues to widen. It is equal to that of all fourteen other North Atlantic treaty allies plus Japan. The gross national product is at present about 764.3 billion dollars a year."

* * *

Americanitis

At a railway station, a lady had only five minutes to make connection with an outgoing train. As she ran toward the train, a porter waved her to slow down and said: "Lady, you better take it easy or you'll come down with Americanitis!"

"What's that?" gasped the lady.

"I can't tell you what it is, but I can tell you how it acts—Americanitis is running up an escalator!" said the porter.

* * *

Shocked Foreigners

As ever, shocked foreigners seem to overlook conditions elsewhere. U.S. violence has never matched the Japanese rape of Nanking or the massacre of

231

400,000 Communists in Indonesia. Watts and Detroit were tea parties compared with assorted mass slaughters in India, Nigeria and Red China. What country has the world's highest homicidal rate? El Salvador, with 30.1 deaths per 100,000 people. In comparison, the U.S. rate stands around 5 per 100,000 people.

Time, April 19, 1968

* * *

How They Respond

Sir Winston Churchill said of Americans, "No people respond more spontaneously to fair play. If you treat them well, they always want to treat you better."

* * *

A Moral Bust

Said Ralph W. Neighbour, "America seems to be on a religious boom and a moral bust."

* * *

The Panic Button

Billy Graham said, "Some people may think that in my sermons I am constantly pushing the panic button. But I see a great nation going the way of twenty-one fallen civilizations of history, and I cannot keep still."

* * *

Power Corrupts

Lord Acton stated, "Power tends to corrupt. Absolute power corrupts absolutely."

* * *

The Test

Lincoln said, "If you want to test a man's character, give him power."

* * *

It Adds Up

Said one U. S. senator to another, "You spend a billion here, a billion there, and the first thing you know, it adds up."

* * *

Remember

Sen. Gerald Ford warned, "We must remember that a government big enough to give us everything we want is big enough to take away everything we have."

* * *

Promises

Bernard Baruch commented, "Vote for the man who promises least. He'll be the least disappointing."

* * *

Calamity

Emerson stated, "No greater calamity can befall a nation than the loss of worship."

* * *

Hats Off

Our hats off to the past; our coats off to the future.

* * *

Do-nothingism

Edmund Burke, an English statesman, averred, "The only thing necessary for the triumph of evil is for good men to do nothing."

* * *

Peace

Thomas à Kempis said, "All men desire peace, but very few desire those things that make for peace."

* * *

God or Tyrants

William Penn warned, "Men must be governed by God or they will be ruled by tyrants."

* * *

Invaluable

Saavedra de Cervantes said, "Liberty is one of the most valuable blessings that heaven has bestowed upon mankind."

* * *

Disgrace

Theodore Roosevelt stated, "Shame and disgrace will be ours if in our eyes the light of high resolve is dimmed, if we trail in the dust the golden hopes of man."

* * *

God's Opportunity

If a nation's extremity is God's opportunity, we say with the psalmist, "It is time for thee, LORD, to work: for they have made void thy law" (Ps. 119:126).

232

Roots

Henry David Thoreau commented, "There are thousands striking at the branches of evil and few striking at the roots."

* * *

Irresistible

Victor Hugo averred, "No army can withstand the strength of an idea whose time has come."

Brute Force

Napoleon Bonaparte said, "The more I study the world, the more I am convinced of the inability of brute force to produce anything durable."

* * *

Lodestar

Gen. Omar Bradley commented, "The time has come to chart our course by the distant stars and not by the lights of each passing ship."

PEACE

Peace Doesn't Come in Capsules

Said S. I. McMillen, M.D., "Peace does not come in capsules. It is regrettable because medical science recognizes that emotions such as fear, sorrow, envy, resentment and hatred are responsible for the majority of our sicknesses—over 60 percent."

There is nothing so conducive to spiritual and physical health as to be at peace with God and man: "In quietness and in confidence shall be your strength" (Isa. 30:15).

Unconfessed and unjudged sin causes physical and spiritual unwellness: "When I kept silence, my bones waxed old through my roaring all the day long" (Ps. 32:3).

* * *

"My House Is in Order"

An aged country doctor was preparing to leave his office at the close of the day. He said to a late patient, "As you know, I am living on borrowed time. My little ticker could cease throbbing at any moment. But my house is in order. I am at peace with God, and at peace with my fellowman."

Long ago God said to Hezekiah, "Set thine house in order: for thou shalt die, and not live" (Isa. 38:1).

Drop Thy Still Dews

Drop Thy still dews of quietness,
Till all our strivings cease;
Take from our souls the strain and stress,
And let our ordered lives confess
The beauty of Thy peace.
                    JOHN GREENLEAF WHITTIER

* * *

When Peace Vanished

Dr. J. C. Massey told of a young medical doctor whom God called to go as a medical missionary. While preparing to go, the young doctor met and fell in love with an attractive Christian girl. They became engaged, and he went to her father and asked his approval of their marriage. The father gave his consent on the condition that they remain in America. For days there was a struggle in the doctor's soul. Then he acquiesced to the father's condition and married the girl.

The young couple remained in America. The doctor prospered in his profession and lived in affluence. But, in later years, he confided to a close friend, "From the day I gave my consent to remain in America, God's peace went out of my heart, never to return as I once felt it."

* * *

No Peace Left

When we give people a piece of our minds, we have no peace of mind left.

PERSECUTION

No Scars?

Hast thou no scar?
No hidden scar on foot, or side, or hand?
I hear thee sung as mighty in the land,
I hear them hail thy bright ascendant
star.
Hast thou no scar?

No wound? No scar?
Yet, as the Master shall the servant be,
And pierced are the feet that follow Me,
But thine are whole. Can he have
followed far
Who hath no wound nor scar?

* * *

"Jesus, Lover of My Soul"

When Charles Wesley was preaching in an open-air meeting near Killyleagh, Ireland, he was assaulted by a frenzied mob. Unable to withstand his assailants, he fled for his life. Jane Moore, the kindhearted wife of a farmer, hid him in the milk house.

Soon Wesley's pursuers arrived. Wanting to divert their attention, Mrs. Moore said, "May I go to the milk house and get some refreshing milk for you?"

Reaching the milk house, she whispered, "Quickly go through the rear window. Hide under the hedge!" Wesley climbed through the window. A little brook flowing beside the hedge and overhanging branches afforded him a cool and safe hiding place.

While the mob unsuccessfully searched for him, Wesley wrote on a scrap of paper the words of the universally loved hymn "Jesus, Lover of My Soul."

* * *

How to React to Insults

The men in basic training with Dave Stowell knew that prior to his enlistment in the army he had been pastor of a small church, and they gave him a rough time. He was often ridiculed. He was purposely assigned by his superior to the detail of cleaning latrines.

Dave cheerfully and dutifully accepted the assignment. He did his work well.

He showed no resentment or sign of breaking under the treatment he was receiving. His attitude during severe provocation made an impression on the men. They began to come to him with their troubles. He had the joy of winning some of them to Christ.

How we react when wrongly treated reveals our Christian character: "Being reviled, we bless; . . . being defamed, we intreat: we are made as the filth of the world" (I Cor. 4:12-13).

* * *

Through Bloody Seas

Vance Havner said, "The pioneers of the gospel trod the way of blood and tears. Of the three hundred and eighteen delegates to the Council of Nice there were not more than a dozen who had not lost an eye or a hand, or who did not limp upon a leg shrunk in its sinews by the burning iron of torture. They remembered that their Lord invited men to self-denial and a cross."

Must I be carried to the skies
On flowery beds of ease,
While others fought to win the prize,
And sailed through bloody seas?

* * *

Crucified Head Down

Lactantius, an early church Father, wrote, "Execrable and noxious tyrant as he was, Nero determined to destroy the heavenly church and to abolish righteousness. He crucified Peter and slew Paul."

The violent death of Peter must have been envisioned by Jesus when He said, "When thou wast young, thou . . . walkedst whither thou wouldest: but when thou shalt be old, . . . another shall . . . carry thee whither thou wouldest not" (John 21:18).

Tradition says that Peter's dying request was "Crucify me with my head down. My Master was crucified for me with His head upward. I am not worthy to die as He did!"

234

PERSEVERANCE

Stick-to-itiveness

In an article entitled "Here's Why There'll Always Be an England," the Cleveland, Ohio, *Plain Dealer* said, "During a recent marriage ceremony in Bournemouth, the bridegroom fainted at the altar steps. No sooner had the bride gotten him on his feet again than the best man slumped down. A bridesmaid collapsed in the aisle. Before the service was completed, four guests were carried out. But finally the bridegroom, Alan Farwell, was married by Rev. William Stedmond to Gillian Seare.

"The vicar attributed the fallout to sheer nerves, although guests mentioned the extreme heat. The point is that probably only in England would the ceremony have been carried to a successful finish. A less stouthearted bride would have decided, after both the groom and the best man fainted, that she could do better elsewhere and would have called off the marriage. But in England, the home of the bulldog and Winston Churchill, one muddles through. One faints only to rise again to exalted deeds. There'll always be an England."

* * *

Bright Prospects

For seven years, Adoniram Judson labored in Burma without winning one convert. When he and his wife observed the Lord's Supper, they would say, "We are Christ's church in Burma."

Someone asked Judson, "What are the prospects of winning Burmese to Christ?"

He replied, "Prospects? They are as bright as the unfailing promises of God. I do not know that I shall live to see a single Burmese won to Christ. Notwithstanding, I would not leave my present situation to be made a king!'"

* * *

Trial and Error

Thomas A. Edison tried more than eleven hundred experiments which turned out to be failures. A friend commented, "Thomas, you have wasted your time."

Edison replied, "Oh, no. I found out eleven hundred ways how not to do things."

* * *

The Tide Will Turn

Said Harriet Beecher Stowe, "When you get into a difficult place and everything goes against you until it seems you cannot hold on another minute, never give up then, for that is just the place when the tide will turn."

God's command to His children is this: "Hold that fast which thou hast, that no man take thy crown" (Rev. 3:11).

* * *

When a Stamp Gets a Licking

When a stamp gets a licking, it doesn't give up. It holds on tightly. Trials, testings and temptations are sure to come. When they do, cling closely to the One whose grace is sufficient.

If the day looks kinder gloomy
An' your chance is kinder slim,
If the situation's puzzlin'
An' the prospect's awful grim,
An' perplexities keep pressin'
Till all hope is nearly gone,
Jus' bristle up, and grit your teeth,
An' keep on keepin' on.

* * *

Carry On

When he was a young minister, Nathan Bangs became discouraged because there were no apparent results from his labor of love. When he was almost ready to give up, he had a dream in which he worked hard trying to break a huge rock with a pickax. Blow after blow left the rock undented. At last he flung the pickax away and in discouragement said, "Useless."

Then a stranger appeared and asked, "You will work no more?"

"No more," he forlornly said.

"Did you not determine at the beginning to cleave the rock?"

"Yes," he replied.

"Why are you stopping then?" asked the stranger.

"It is useless to try any more. I have made no impression on it."

"What is that to you?" asked the stranger. "The work of using the pickax is in your own hands. The result is not."

In the dream, Nathan Bangs resumed his task. The very first blow broke the rock in two.

Many times we are nearer the goal than we think. If we will continue unwearied in welldoing, God will reward our faithfulness. The tide will turn, and our seemingly lost efforts will be crowned with success.

Told by HAROLD R. CROSSER

POWER

(See also Holy Spirit)

Straw Driven Through Telephone Pole

Some years ago in *Life* appeared a full-page picture of the devastation wrought by a midwestern tornado. In the center of the picture was a telephone pole with a straw driven through it. It seemed incredible! How could a flimsy, insubstantial straw be thrust through a rugged, seasoned telephone pole? Here's the answer: the straw was utterly surrendered to the tornado and its awesome power.

The weakest of God's children, when utterly surrendered to the Spirit of God, can bring to pass things which are humanly impossible.

In our morally and spiritually confused world, many are asking—often mutely—the question "Where is the LORD God of Elijah?" (II Kings 2:14). He lives! He is still "able to do exceeding abundantly above all that we ask or think" in and through His children who are fully surrendered to Him.

* * *

"As Thy Days"

God's still small voice I heard today,
For in the Word I read,
And then when I knelt down to pray,
His Spirit softly said:
"Go forth, My child, in service free,
And as thy days, thy strength shall be."

Help of the Helpless

A huntsman heard the baying of his hounds in the distance. Closer and closer they came. In a moment a little fawn leaped wearily and exhaustedly over a fence and fell at the huntsman's feet. The imploring eyes of the helpless creature seemed to say, "You won't let the hounds kill me, will you?"

In relating the incident later, the huntsman said, "I stood there for some two minutes, fighting off the dogs. How could I allow them to harm that helpless creature when it, in its helplessness, appealed to my strength?"

Our weakness, not our imagined strength, moves the heart and hand of God in our behalf: "He giveth power to the faint; and to them that have no might he increaseth strength" (Isa. 40:29).

* * *

Doomsday for Civilization

Brig. Gen. Thomas Farrel witnessed the first explosion of the atom bomb in New Mexico in July, 1945, from a vantage point several miles distant. He said, "Thirty seconds after I saw the dazzling flash of light, the explosion came. The air-blast pressed hard against people and things. This was followed almost immediately by the strong, sustained, awesome roar which warned of

236

doomsday. It made us puny beings feel that we were most blasphemous to dare to tamper with the forces hitherto reserved to the almighty God!"

Man has harnessed sufficient power to efface all living things from the earth and reduce to rubble his vaunted civilization. How bereft of spiritual power is man, because of his failure to relate himself to the One in whose mighty hands reposes "all power . . . in heaven and in earth" (Matt. 28:18).

* * *

Disqualifying Infirmities

J. S. Stewart said, "It is thrilling to discover that it is upon human weakness and humiliation—not human strength and confidence—that God chooses to build His kingdom. He uses us, not merely in spite of our disqualifying infirmities, but precisely because of them. Nothing can defeat us when we take, not our strength, but our weakness and offer it to God to be His weapon: 'He giveth power to the faint' [Isa. 40:29]; 'When I am weak, then am I strong' [II Cor. 12:10].

"It was the way of Francis Xavier, William Carey and Paul. This is the strategy to which there is no retort. This is the victory which overcomes the world."

Adapted from Moody Monthly

God's Mightiness

Pictures of the devastation wrought by the 1964 Alaskan earthquake revealed its awesome power. According to seismologists, it was about ten million times mightier than the atomic bomb which fell on Hiroshima in 1945. Such force released above the earth's surface could have destroyed the world. The power of the first atomic bomb was puny in comparison with the Alaskan earthquake.

In comparing mankind's weakness with God's mightiness, Isaiah said, "It is he [God] that sitteth upon the circle of the earth, and the inhabitants thereof are as grasshoppers" (Isa. 40:22).

* * *

Back of the Sun

And back of the sun is the Voice that spoke
Unto the light, and the light awoke;
From the dateless dawning of time it rings,
From the dim, forgotten beginning of things;
And back of the Voice is the Word;
And the formless void heard
And the face of the deep was stirred.
And back of the Word is omnipotent Thought,
Omniscient Spirit, in power that wrought,
Infinite, Triune Creator, who brought
Light from the darkness and life from the clod;
In the beginning, God.

ANNIE JOHNSON FLINT

PRAYER

(See also Intercession)

God Accepted His Challenge

For thirty-seven years a man lived in atheistic darkness. His wife was a devout Christian. Daily she implored God to save her husband. One night he entered a church and sat on a back seat. In spite of himself, he listened to the earnest plea of the minister for unsaved ones to come forward and accept Christ. He responded. As he knelt at the altar, he prayed, "If there be a God, make me to know it, and I will accept Him." God accepted his challenge, revealed Himself to the suppliant, and he was joyfully saved!

Later the man testified, "I went home that night rejoicing in my Saviour." For years he was an elder in the Presbyterian church and a teacher of adult classes. When ninety years old, he said, "God

237

called my wife home when she was nearly eighty-nine years old. It was her prayers for me that brought me to God."

Told by WILLIAM EVANS.

* * *

There's a Difference

There's a difference between a cry and a call. When my daughter Alice was a toddler, she stood uncertainly one day at the top of the stairway. I was sitting in the front room downstairs. Suddenly I heard her anguished cry, "Oh, Daddy!"

I sprinted two-thirds of the way up the steps and caught Alice just as she began to tumble down the steps. Her anguished cry brought instant help.

When we cry to our heavenly Father, He instantly responds to our cry: "Thou shalt cry, and he shall say, Here I am" (Isa. 58:9).

W. B. K.

* * *

"Jesus, Jimmy's Here"

Jimmy, a Scottish lad, worked in a shipyard. At noon every day he entered a nearby church and silently prayed.

One day the minister asked, "What do you pray about, my boy?"

Shyly Jimmy replied, "Nothing, sir. I just say, 'Jesus, this is Jimmy.'"

Jimmy didn't tell Jesus what to do. He just reported to Jesus and listened to hear Jesus' voice in his heart.

Prayer isn't a monologue. It is a dialogue—our talking to God and God talking to us. The psalmist said, "I will hear what God the LORD will speak" (Ps. 85:8).

ALICE MARIE KNIGHT

* * *

To Whom Can I Go?

Little Jackie often did naughty things. He was headstrong and sometimes disobedient. Sometimes he got hurt. When hurt, he always ran to his mother.

One day Mother asked, "Why do you run to me when you get hurt doing things I told you not to do?"

With tears in his big, blue eyes, Jackie answered, "Mommy, who can I go to but you when I get hurt?"

Mother drew him close to her heart and kissed the hurt place and said, "My darling boy, you can always come to me when you are hurt, or when you need help!"

Then she thought, *Lord, to whom can I go but to Thee with my heartaches and troubles?*

ALICE MARIE KNIGHT

* * *

Praying in Outer Space

In speaking to Congress, Astronaut L. Gordon Cooper said, "I am not too much of a preacher, but while on the flight on the seventeenth orbit I felt so inclined to put a small prayer on the tape recorder in the spacecraft. I was over the middle of the Indian Ocean at midnight. Everything had been working perfectly. I prayed, 'Father, I thank You for letting me fly this flight and behold many startling things You have created. Direct all of us that we may shape our lives to be much better Christians and work with one another. Be with our families. Give them guidance and encouragement. Amen.' "

* * *

Lost in Good Works

Samuel Chadwick said, "Satan dreads nothing in the church so much as prayer. The Laodicean church that had ceased loving Christ first was full of good works. Church activities are multiplied, organizations increased, so that prayer has no chance. Souls may be lost in good works as surely as in evil works."

* * *

Imbalance

Andrew Murray warned, "Little of the Word with little prayer is death to spiritual life. Much of the Word with little prayer gives a sickly spiritual life. Much prayer with little of the Word trends toward unbridled emotionalism. A full measure of the Word and prayer each day gives healthy and powerful spiritual life."

238

"Pray Without Ceasing"

Gen. Stonewall Jackson testified, "I live in the spirit of prayer. I pray as I walk, when I lie down, and when I arise. When I am persuaded that a desired thing is right, I continue to pray for it until the answer comes. I never seal a letter without putting a word of prayer under the seal."

* * *

You Don't Tell God—You Ask Him

A little boy and his sister were playing "doctor." The "patient" was the little girl's doll. "Your child will not get well," said the little boy to his sister.

She replied, "You aren't a good doctor. I'm going to get another doctor."

The little boy said, "There isn't any other doctor. So what will you do now?"

The little girl thought and said, "I'll tell God to make her well."

"All right, lady," said the little boy, "but you don't *tell* God. You *ask* Him."

"And this is the confidence that we have in him, that, if we ask any thing according to his will, he heareth us" (I John 5:14).

Told by ALICE MARIE KNIGHT

* * *

The Soul's Sincere Desire

Prayer is the soul's sincere desire,
 Uttered or unexpressed,
The motion of a hidden fire
 That trembles in the breast.

Prayer is the burden of a sigh,
 The falling of a tear,
The upward glancing of an eye,
 When none but God is near.

* * *

Futile, Isn't It?

The lamas of Tibet, wishing to help weary travelers who have no horses, cut out horses in paper. Then they ascend high mountains, pray, and fling the paper horses in the air. The wind carries them in all directions. They believe that Buddha changes the paper horses into living horses for weary travelers to use.

Futile, isn't it? How like the misguided lamas are those who pray only for God to help others and do little or nothing in a practical way to effectuate the answer to their prayers.

* * *

A Doctor Appraises Prayer

Dr. Alexis Carrel, famous physician and research genius, stated, "The results of prayer can be measured in terms of increased physical buoyancy, greater intellectual vigor, moral stamina and deeper understanding of the realities underlying physical relationships. How does prayer fortify us with such dynamic power? When we pray, we link ourselves with the inexhaustible power that spins the universe. We ask that a part of this power be apportioned to our needs. Even in asking, our human deficiencies are filled. We arise strengthened and repaired."

* * *

Putting Shoe Leather to Your Prayers

The Latin expression *laborare est orare* means "to work is to pray."

The Bible teaches that to pray is to work: "Epaphras, . . . a servant of Christ, . . . always labouring fervently for you in prayer, that ye might stand perfect and complete in all the will of God" (Col. 4:12).

To pray prevailingly, it is often necessary for us to add this postscript to our prayers: "Lord, I'm Your servant and amenable to Your directive. I am willing for You to use me to effectuate the answer to my petition."

* * *

What Makes the Difference

If the way seems rough and rugged,
 And your burdens hard to bear,
It will make a heap of difference
 To begin the day in prayer.
The sun will shine much brighter,
 You will know less pain and care,
If you take some time each morning
 To begin your day in prayer.

ALMA B. THURBER, a shut-in

* * *

In His Way

He answered prayer!
Not in the way I sought,

239

Not in the way that I had thought He
  ought,
But in His own good way, and I could
  see
He answered in the fashion best for me!
And I was glad that I had such a share
In His parental love and gracious care,
  That thus He answered prayer.

He answered prayer!
But not in my brief hour;
I looked to see the fruit ere yet the flower
Had shed its gales of sweetness o'er my
  path!
But I have learned that slowest blossoms
  yield
The choicest fruit; and so I leave them
  there
Upon the boughs, assured that they will
  bear
In time my answered prayer.

* * *

"A Great While Before Day"

In the villages, towns and cities where
Islam is the religion, the call to prayer
is sounded from the minaret just before
dawn. The set time for the Muslims to
pray is when they can first distinguish
the difference between a black and a
white thread in the early dawn light.

Surely Christians should begin each
day in prayer, alone with God in the
secret place: "And Abraham gat up early
in the morning to the place where he
stood before the LORD" (Gen. 19:27).

I met God in the morning,
  When the day was at its best,
And His presence came like sunrise.
  Like a glory in my breast.

It is written of our Saviour "And in
the morning, rising up a great while
before day, he went out . . . into a solitary place, and there prayed" (Mark
1:35).

* * *

When We Mean Business with God

Dorothy Howard prayed, "God, I must
know tonight if You are real. Life is
empty, and I must find a reason for living. Please answer now, for I am at the
end of my rope, and will not ask again."

God did hear her earnest plea. A whole
new life opened to a woman whose world,
until then, consisted only of that which
could be known through the five senses.
Christ stepped out of history and became
her life.

Eternity

* * *

"What Things Soever Ye Desire"

William Carey said, "Attempt great
things for God, and expect great things
from God."

Thou art coming to a King,
Large petitions with thee bring;
For His grace and power are such,
None can ever ask too much.

* * *

"Only a Miracle Can Save Us"

Earnestness and definiteness are elements in prevailing prayer: "O our God,
wilt thou not judge them? . . . our eyes
are upon thee" (II Chron. 20:12); "What
wilt thou that I should do unto thee? . . .
Lord, that I might receive my sight"
(Mark 10:51).

After a fierce battle, the Viet Cong
soldiers strode among the fallen dead
and wounded soldiers of the lost American infantry platoon, firing bullets into
those who showed any sign of life.

Lying among the fallen ones was a
medic, Melvin W. Schultz, who in the
previous three hours had seen all his
buddies mowed down by the vicious fire
of the enemy. He whispered to a nearby
fallen comrade, "Pray! Pray! Only a
miracle can save us now. God will help
us. He must save us."

God worked a miracle. Sixteen hours
later, the two were rescued. The medic
said, "The enemy thought we were dead.
One of them sat on my shoulders and went
through my pockets as I lay motionless
with my face in the mud. He took my
wallet and snatched my watch from my
wrist."

God's promise is sure: "Call upon me
in the day of trouble: I will deliver thee,
and thou shalt glorify me" (Ps. 50:15).

240

Praying Troublemakers out of Church

In a church there was a family that caused endless trouble and confusion. What a diseased appendix is to the human body, that family was to the church. Hardheartedness seemed to characterize each member of the family.

In time, the family incurred the deadly hatred and enmity of another family of the church. After futile efforts to placate the two feuding families, the pastor and other Christians prayed that God would either remove them from the church or save them. God answered the cries of His children. Both families soon withdrew from the church.

Told by F. B. MEYER

* * *

In Christ's Presence

One day the five-year-old son of D. L. Moody went into the study where his father sat writing. Wanting no interruptions, Mr. Moody gruffly asked, "Well, what do you want?"

"Nothing, Daddy," the boy replied. "I just wanted to be where you are." Sitting on the floor he began to quietly amuse himself. He desired only companionship.

G. Campbell Morgan said, "This little incident, told by Mr. Moody, helped me greatly to understand the true meaning of prayer. To pray is to be where Jesus is. When we are in His presence, we need nothing more to pray prevailingly."

In the secret of His presence
How my soul delights to hide!
Oh, how precious are the lessons
Which I learn at Jesus' side!

Adapted from *British Weekly*

* * *

The Greatest Source of Help

Capt. Eddie Rickenbacker testified, "Prayer has been the greatest source of help in my life. I never go to sleep at night without saying the simple prayers I learned at my mother's knee. During the day I ask God's help about my business problems, my friends, my family and my country."

God at His Elbow

It was said of Praying Hyde, missionary to India, "He prayed as if God were at his elbow."

The feeblest cry of God's children brings Him preciously near to them: "Then shalt thou call, and the LORD shall answer; thou shalt cry, and he shall say, Here I am" (Isa. 58:9).

* * *

An Answer from the Word

Ben Wilcox, a fine Christian layman of Cleveland, Ohio, was close to death's door. Peritonitis had set in. After being told that immediate surgery was necessary, he began to pray, "Lord, You know I love You. My chiefest joy has been to tell others about You. Now, Lord, give me some assurance from Your Word that I will come through this ordeal to praise You and continue to tell others that the day of miracles hasn't passed."

The Lord brought to his mind this verse: "And call upon me in the day of trouble: I will deliver thee, and thou shalt glorify me" (Ps. 50:15).

Quietly Ben said, "Thank You, Lord. Your grace is now sustaining me. I have no fear."

The operation lasted for four and one-half hours. "There is only a slim chance that he will recover," the surgeon said to the waiting loved ones.

After seven days in the hospital, Ben emerged. Today he is an active, practicing Christian. His life exemplifies a portion of the verse that God gave to him: "And thou shalt glorify me."

* * *

A Mother's Cry

A grief-stricken mother entered a heathen temple in India. Weeping, she knelt before an idol with her sickly, deformed child in her arms. A lady standing nearby heard her anguished plea, "Grant that my child may be strong and well like other children."

As she went away, the lady asked, "Friend, to whom did you pray?"

With a look of bewilderment, she replied, "I don't know, but surely there must be someone somewhere to hear a

241

mother's cry and keep a mother's heart from breaking!"

Thank God, there is Someone who always hears the faintest cry of His children. Myriads have proved the genuineness of God's unfailing promise: "Call upon me in the day of trouble: I will deliver thee, and thou shalt glorify me" (Ps. 50:15).

* * *

A Prayer for a Recipient:

Dear letter, go upon your way
O'er mountain, plain or sea;
God bless all who speed your flight
Where I wish you to be.

And bless all those beneath the roof
Where I would bid you rest,
But specially bless the one to whom
This letter is addressed.

* * *

"Give Me a Plateful of Food!"

One day, during family worship in a Christian home, all said together the prayer Jesus taught His disciples to pray. When they came to the words "Give us this day our daily bread," little Stephen misquoted the words, saying, "Give me this day a plateful of food." Though he said the words reverently and sincerely, his brothers and sisters laughed. Mother and father, however, did not laugh.

During breakfast, mother gave little Stephen a plateful of food. Was not this what he asked for in his prayer? As she passed the plate to him, the wise mother said, "Son, as you grow up, continue to ask God to supply all your needs. Do not be ashamed. Others may laugh, but God will not."

"Ye have not, because ye ask not" (James 4:2).

Told by ALICE MARIE KNIGHT

* * *

Read and Blush

Vernon W. Patterson said, "The Supreme Court, on the same day it declared praying in the schools unconstitutional in the state of New York, endorsed sending homosexual literature through the mails."

"O God, Drive Them Home"

During Colonial days, when an enemy fleet was sailing toward New England, the governor of Massachusetts called for a day of fasting and prayer. In Boston's Old South Church, the pastor, Thomas Prince, stood and prayed earnestly, "O God, deliver us from the enemy! Scatter the ships of our tormentors! Drive them home!"

While he prayed, black clouds began to scud across the sky and a strong wind began to blow. It swept through the church steeple and rang the bell twice.

Looking heavenward through tear-filled eyes, Thomas Prince said, "Thine be the glory, Lord!" A violent storm came upon the Atlantic and destroyed most of the enemy ships.

* * *

Sheep

When at night you cannot sleep, talk to the Shepherd—stop counting sheep.

* * *

Don't Instruct God

Said Dr. John Short, "I believe in prayer, but I remember that once, when my mother heard me pray, she said, 'Son, don't bother to give God instructions; just report for duty.'"

* * *

Feet in Another's Shoes

An Indian brave prayed, "Great Spirit, help me not to judge or criticize my neighbor until I have walked a mile in his moccasins."

* * *

Prayer Is a Dialogue

Fénelon said, "How rare it is to find a soul quiet enough to hear God speak."

* * *

A Dialogue

Prayer is a dialogue. It is our talking to God and God talking to us: "I will hear what God the LORD will speak" (Ps. 85:8); "Be still, and know that I am God" (46:10).

242

Syntax

Leonard Ravenhill said, "Prayer has its own syntax. Its punctuation differs from the grammarians'. Often it is punctuated by sobs, and it may have groans for its periods."

* * *

Only One Thing

Nothing lies beyond the reach of prayer except that which lies outside the will of God: "No good thing will he withhold from them that walk uprightly" (Ps. 84:11).

* * *

Fragile

Life is fragile—handle it with prayer: "It is even a vapour, that appeareth for a little time, and then vanisheth away" (James 4:14).

* * *

Just in Case

In a Detroit school, a believer in prayer put this notice on the bulletin board: "In case of atomic attack, the ruling against prayers in this school will be temporarily suspended."

Mingled

Happy are those who mingle prayer and toil till God responds to the former and rewards the latter.

* * *

Work and Prayer

General Booth advised, "Work as if everything depended upon work, and pray as if everything depended upon prayer."

* * *

Only Three

Remember when you pray to God
  The answers are but three:
Yes, or No, or Wait a while;
  Accept what it may be.

* * *

Vainly Spent

Were half our breath that's vainly spent
To heaven in supplication sent,
Our words of praise would more often be:
Hear what the Lord hath done for me.

PREACHERS

"Line upon Line"

An outstanding lawyer said to Dr. Len G. Broughton, the founder of the Baptist Tabernacle, Atlanta, Georgia, "Preachers often fail to make themselves understood by not repeating enough. When I address a jury, I always repeat the points of my argument at least twice to impress them upon the minds of the jury. I have, upon occasion, repeated things as many times as there were jurymen before me. If I failed to repeat, I would fail to win the verdict I wanted."

"For precept must be upon precept, . . . line upon line, . . . here a little, and there a little" (Isa. 28:10).

* * *

Politicking Preachers

The religious editor of a city daily affirmed that the new breed of clerics have donned an activist role in the community. The clergyman might "ring your doorbell, ask not about your spiritual state, but . . . ask you to vote for their man for president."

In commenting on the editor's statement, Rev. Carl J. Schuette, a Lutheran minister, said, "Be it hereby known that I am advising my parishioners to push such a clergyman off the porch. Hopefully he will fall on his head and get religion. The movement of the activist is led by clergymen of the new breed variety who have come out of seminaries in the last ten years. They get into politics as 'saviors' of their country. I hope they know more about politics than many of them seem to know about religion. Ask some clergymen who have had them as associates or assistants. You will learn how they can louse up a good congregation. All denominations are 'blessed' with them. I submit that churches have enough troubles without their 'shepherds' getting into politics."

* * *

"Preach the Word"

Some years ago in Buffalo, New York, two young men broke into a photographic studio on a Sunday night. The aged owner was there. The youths murdered him and then robbed the studio.

Headlines of the crime were front-paged in Monday morning's papers. The two youths were apprehended and charged with murder. Their names seemed familiar to a secretary of one of the local churches, who always wrote letters to those whose names were written in the visitor's book. The names of the two murderers were found in the book.

The young men were in church on Sunday morning, and murdered on Sunday night. The pastor's sermon subject in the morning service was "An Educated Ministry." Only God knows what might have happened if the minister had preached Christ and told of Christ's power to change desperately wicked hearts.

How urgent is the need for pastors and teachers to "preach the word."

* * *

"At Evening Time It Shall Be Light"

For seventy summers I have seen
The rolling hills, the meadows green,
And now, although my eyes grow dim,
I will not cease my praise to Him.
I marvel at His matchless grace,
As He renews my strength to face
The coming dark—as light grows dim
He gives anew a light within,
Enabling me to see afar
A brighter Light, a shining Star—
Dayspring of hope forevermore,
A light that shines on yonder shore.

As blindness comes with its gray day,
And light fast fades without a ray,
The spark of faith will ne'er grow dim,
For faith, I know, is light from Him.
And though my path becomes obscure
When sight has fled, of this be sure,
That faith has taught me to behold
My way to walk toward streets of gold.
For I can see with sightless eyes
The sunrise of celestial skies.
'Neath them one day I'll walk with Him,
And light shall nevermore grow dim.

WHITNEY E. WARD, a retired pastor
for whom reading was a
vital part of daily life

His Greatest Wish

One day as G. Campbell Morgan prayed, the Lord seemed to say to him, "Which do you want to be—a servant of Mine or a great preacher?"

Morgan replied, "May I not be both, Lord?"

A spiritual struggle ensued as he thought, *God may want me to be an unknown minister in an obscure place.*

Then Morgan submissively prayed, "O Lord, my greatest wish is to be a *servant* of Thine!" The Lord responded by making him one of the greatest preachers of modern times.

"Seekest thou great things for thyself? Seek them not" (Jer. 45:5).

* * *

Taking One's Own Medicine

Dr. A. T. Pierson called on a minister who had been hospitalized for six months. He said to the patient, "My brother, you have been a very busy man. It may be that God has wanted to say something to you, but you have been too busy to listen. So God, in goodness and infinite wisdom, has put you on your back so you may hear His voice and receive His message."

As Dr. Pierson left the hospital, the Lord seemed to say to him, "You, too, have been very active *for* Me and have not taken enough time to be occupied *with* Me."

Dr. Pierson said, "At that time, I resolved to *practice* what I preached. At the close of each day, I sit for an hour in the quiet of my study, not to speak to the Lord, but to listen to what the Lord has to say to me, and to lay the day's life and work open for His penetrating gaze and appraisal."

"Be silent, O all flesh, before the LORD" (Zech. 2:13).

* * *

Not Far Enough Back

A critic told Billy Graham, "Your preaching has put Christianity back one hundred years."

Graham replied, "That's not back far enough. We must go back to the cross of Christ and to the 'faith which was once delivered to the saints.' "

Christ in the Pulpit, Too

In Boston, near the church where he preached for years, there is a statue of Phillips Brooks. In the statue his left hand rests upon the Bible, and just above and behind him the fingers of His Lord rest upon his shoulder. The two are in the same pulpit.

A news correspondent related this interesting story about the statue: "Saint-Gaudens, the sculptor, was an irreligious man when he started to work on the statue. As he read a book on the life and work of Phillips Brooks, he thought he would put an angel with the mighty preacher. Later he asked for a copy of the Gospels. Having read them carefully, he came to the conclusion that instead of putting an angel in the statue, he would put the image of Christ. Shortly after the completion of the statue, he died a Christian, converted through the production of the marble representation of one of God's servants who lived to bring men to his Lord, and by the heart-transforming power of the gospel of Christ."

Still "the gospel of Christ . . . is the power of God unto salvation" (Rom. 1:16).

* * *

Preach to Broken Hearts

R. W. Dale made this response to a young English preacher who insisted that it is essential for ministers to preach relevantly—to the times: "Young man, don't preach to the times. Go and preach to broken hearts and you will preach relevantly and to the eternities."

* * *

Censured

The grand jury in Cuyahoga County (Ohio) censured the participation of the clergy in the ever increasing demonstrations in the streets and buildings:

"It is of grave concern to us when we learn that members of the clergy are going to great lengths to aid and assist these men who would tear down the very foundations of our government.

"If an investigation were made of some of these leaders, their purposes ascertained, their vicious goals uncovered and their illegal and unlawful assemblies dis-covered by those [the clergy] who should be more careful before becoming sponsors and supporters of these evildoers, our society would be safer, our property more secure, and the rights of all more adequately protected."

* * *

Whitefield Believed It

David Hume the philosopher and skeptic often attended the services of George Whitefield.

A friend asked him, "You surely do not believe what Whitefield preaches, do you?"

Hume replied, "No, I don't, but Whitefield does."

* * *

What a Sermon Reaches

Evangelist Leonard Ravenhill stated, "A sermon born in the head reaches only the head; a sermon born in the emotions reaches only the emotions; a sermon full of imagination reaches only the imagination. But a sermon born of the Spirit of God captivates the heart of listening ones."

* * *

Pauca Verba

The day after Lincoln delivered his famed address at Gettysburg, Edward Everett, who also spoke, wrote a letter to President Lincoln in which he said, "I should be glad if I could flatter myself that I came as near to the central idea of the occasion in two hours as you did in two minutes!"

* * *

Food for Thought

A friend spoke thus of an aged minister: "The older he grew, the *less* he spoke and the *more* he said."

As a minister stood to speak, he ineptly said, "Before I begin to preach, I want to say something."

Someone has given this advice to young ministers: "Stand up; speak up; shut up."

Paul admonished, "Let your speech [words] be alway with grace, seasoned with salt" (Col. 4:6).

Knowing How to Preach

Dr. Charles E. Jefferson said, "It is surprising how stoutly and stubbornly churches insist upon preachers knowing how to preach. They will overlook almost anything else, but they will not overlook inability to preach. They have a wholesome reverence for learning, but they would rather have a man with no diplomas who can preach than a man with two diplomas who cannot preach.

"The world judges Christianity largely from sermons. If sermons are dull, then religion seems dull also."

* * *

Where They Mended

Two pastors' wives sat mending the trousers of their husbands. One said dejectedly, "My husband is so discouraged. His people are unfaithful in attending church, and they are behind with his salary. He is so blue that he does not like to visit them anymore. So he sits around the house much of the time."

Said the other wife, "My husband is getting along fine! He spends much of his time visiting and helping people. The attendance at our church is good, and best of all, souls are being saved and the people are growing in grace and Christlikeness."

The wife of the prospering pastor was mending the *knees* of her husband's trousers. The wife of the dejected pastor was mending the *seat* of her husband's trousers.

What a day is ours in which to put shoe leather to our prayers!

* * *

Contemporizing Preaching

Dr. Donald G. Miller, in *Fire in Thy Mouth*, wrote, "True preaching is an extension of the incarnation into the contemporary moment, the transfiguration of the cross, and the resurrection from ancient facts of a remote past into the living realities of the present."

Someone else has said, "Authentic preaching is not a repetition of Calvary—that is impossible—but a contemporizing of it."

Speak to Me, Lord

Lord, speak to me, that I may speak
In living echoes of Thy tone;
As Thou hast sought, so let me seek
Thy erring children lost and lone.

O teach me, Lord, that I may teach
The precious things Thou dost impart;
And wing my words, that they may reach
The hidden depths of many a heart.

O fill me with Thy fulness, Lord,
Until my very heart o'erflows
In kindling thought and glowing word,
Thy love to tell, Thy praise to show.

FRANCES RIDLEY HAVERGAL

* * *

With Motherly Affection

Said Fénelon, "I would have every minister of the gospel address his audience with the zeal of a friend, the generous energy of a father, and the exuberant affection of a mother."

* * *

Whom Do They Represent?

In February, 1966, the General Board of the National Council of Churches recommended that U.N. membership and diplomatic recognition be accorded Peking. Congress has voted unanimously against admission of Red China to the U.N. and against recognition of the Peking regime.

Many people wondered if the recommendation of the General Board of the National Council of Churches represented the opinion of the Protestant clergy throughout the nation.

A nationwide poll, taken by the Rev. Daniel A. Poling of *Christian Herald* magazine, cleared up the confusion. Of more than 30,000 clergymen, chosen at random, 72 percent voted against the seating of China in the U.N.; 71 percent voted against diplomatic recognition; and 94 percent voted against expulsion of Nationalist China from the U.N. to make room for the Red delegation.

Adapted from *Plain Dealer,*
Cleveland, Ohio

Offered Only Chunks of Clouds

Dr. Robert G. Lee commented, "Multitudes of church members today are being offered a chunk of cloud bank buttered with the night wind instead of Christianity's vital, life-giving bread. There is no gospel if the atoning blood of Christ is omitted, the virgin birth denied, Christ's resurrection eliminated and justification by faith not proclaimed."

* * *

Spreading Ourselves Ineffectively Thin

John H. Jowett stated, "I am profoundly convinced that one of the greatest perils which besets ministers is a restless scattering of our energies over an amazing multiplicity of activities which leaves little time for absorbing communion with God."

Activity *for* Christ will not compensate for communion *with* Christ: "They that wait upon the LORD shall renew their strength" (Isa. 40:31).

* * *

We're Ambassadors—Not Diplomats

Craig Skinner said in *Christianity Today*, "We are in the business of publishing, proclaiming and preaching the good news of God, the gospel. This means that we are ambassadors and not diplomats. The ambassador's responsibility is to declare policy, not debate it."

* * *

What Made the Change?

"Sweet are the uses of adversity," declared the Bard of Stratford on Avon. The turning point in the life of Thomas Chalmers was a prolonged illness. Up to that time, his preaching was not Christ-exalting nor Bible-centered, but a proclamation of morality.

Chalmers' illness took him from his pulpit for almost a year. During this time, he did much heart-searching. His merely ethical view of Christianity brought him little or no consolation when his life hung in the balance.

He emerged from that sickness a changed man, totally consecrated to God and lifted onto a high plane of fellowship with God. He began to proclaim the gospel in the power of the Holy Spirit. Truly he could say with the psalmist, "It is good for me that I have been afflicted; that I might learn thy statutes" (Ps. 119:71).

* * *

"Ugh! Canned White Man!"

Some years ago Bishop Rowe of Alaska visited a tribe of Indians who lived where civilized man had seldom gone. Only a few of the tribe had ever seen a white man. A member of Bishop Rowe's party had a phonograph with him. He began to play it. The Indians listened incredulously. They examined the gadget from every direction. The old chief got down on his knees and peered into it. He stood, flung his arms out in a sweeping gesture, and exclaimed, "Ugh! Canned white man!"

How uninspiring are "canned" sermons unfeelingly and mechanically delivered, sermons devoid of fervor and spiritual power.

* * *

Wanted: Better Men

John Wesley did a wonderful work among the miners of Cornwall. Whole villages were changed. Scores of evildoers were transformed.

Wesley's picture was on the wall in many homes. He was greatly loved and revered by the people. One day a stranger entered a miner's home. Observing Wesley's picture, he asked, "Whose picture is that?"

The aged miner reverently said, "There was a man sent from God, whose name was John."

How great is the need for God-sent, Spirit-empowered men who know no fear other than the fear of incurring God's displeasure. God is not looking primarily for better methods. He is looking for better men. Said G. Campbell Morgan, "God's method is always a man."

* * *

Customs Change

A dignified bishop "sounded off" ineptly about the ladies' use of cosmetics. Said he, "I don't like any of this makeup. Especially abhorrent is the lipstick ladies wear. Why, the more I come in contact with it the worse I like it."

Styles and customs change from generation to generation. Principles and the eternal verities of God's Word never change.

To His children, God has given this directive: "Whose adorning . . . let it be the hidden man of the heart, . . . a meek and quiet spirit, which is in the sight of God of great price" (I Peter 3:3-4).

* * *

Waning Popularity

A poll by Lou Harris and Associates of the views of two thousand Americans showed that clergymen are down in public esteem and confidence to a rating below that of doctors, bankers, scientists, military leaders, educators, corporation heads, psychiatrists and even local retailers.

If the main reason for ministers' decline in popularity was their bold proclamation of the revelation of God—a proclamation that brought down the cutting edge of God's Word and exposed man's corruption and his need of divine rescue —that would perpetuate biblical loyalties. Ecclesiastics who have emerged as sacred specialists in political, economic and military strategy have unfortunately scarred the image of the clergy.

Christianity Today

* * *

Protest Not Against Ancient Ghosts

On Reformation Sunday a faithful pastor spoke these timely words: "I think that if Luther and Zwingli were to rise from their graves, they would drive us from our churches and say to us, 'We know you not. You are not Protestants at all. You only commemorate our protests. Do you not see that what we said in our times to a decadent church must be said today—not in the same words but in the same spirit? What we said must be thunderously reiterated to a morally corrupt society. Repent and turn to God. Put off your lukewarmness. Protest again, not against ancient ghosts, but against the enemies who dominate your age!' "

The plea of the ancient prophet is relevant: "Cry aloud, spare not, lift up thy voice like a trumpet, and shew my people their transgression, and . . . their sins" (Isa. 58:1).

* * *

Unnecessary Wearing Down

As an aged minister neared life's setting sun, he lamented, "I realize now that I wore myself down at times unnecessarily working *for* God when I could have worked more effectively *with* God."

One of the gravest dangers besetting ministers is a restless scattering of energies over an amazing multiplicity of fleshly energized activities.

"For we are labourers together with God" (I Cor. 3:9).

* * *

How Not to Leave a Church

The following letter from a discouraged pastor was printed in a religious publication:

"I have been in ——— for three years. Fifteen pastors have come and gone. Now my number is up. I have been forced out of my pulpit by some D.D.'s— diabolical deacons. I recently called on three pastors who resigned their churches about the time I did, and I could ditto everyone's story. Right now I have no desire to candidate, even though three churches have contacted me. I'm not a youngster anymore. With four pastorates behind me and four heartaches with them, how many more can I take?"

There are no perfect churches. The only church which approximated perfection long ago was the church at Ephesus. That church, however, had ceased loving Christ first.

It is true that the descendants of Diotrephes, "who loveth to have the preeminence among" God's children, are still with us. But through grace, pastors may be radiant and triumphant. The greatest need among God's children is Christlikeness. He was despised and rejected of men. Jesus said, "Remember the word that I said . . . , The servant is not greater than his lord" (John 15:20). Of Christ it is written, "Who, when he was reviled, reviled not again;

248

when he suffered, he threatened not; but committed himself to him that judgeth righteously" (I Peter 2:23).

There is an adage which says "Leave the feast when it is merriest!" When a pastor severs the pastoral relationship with a church, it should be on the high plane of Christian love, and done with thanksgiving that God in goodness gave him the opportunity to engage in a labor of love.

* * *

Results of One Sermon

Early in his ministry, Dr. Lyman Beecher exchanged pulpits one Sunday with the pastor of a small country church. It was in midwinter. Snow was piled up along the road, and traveling was almost impossible. Dr. Beecher urged his horse to go through the deep snow. Arriving at the church, he discovered that he was the only one present.

When the time for the service arrived, Dr. Beecher entered the pulpit. There he sat prayerfully and silently. Finally one man entered the church. Then Dr. Beecher brought an earnest message, preaching to an audience of one as his Lord often did. At the conclusion of the sermon, he went to the door to greet the lone worshiper. Before he could do so, however, the man had gone.

Twenty years passed. Then one day a pleasant-looking man greeted Dr. Beecher as he got off a train. He asked, "Do you remember me, Dr. Beecher?"

"I don't believe I do," he replied.

Said the stranger, "Do you remember preaching twenty years ago in a small country church to an audience of one man?"

"Yes, sir, I do, and if you are the man, I have been wishing to see you ever since."

"I am the man, and the sermon you preached that Sunday morning brought me to God and made a minister of me. Yonder is my church. The converts from that sermon, sir, are all over the country!"

* * *

Reading the Name Plates

When Mrs. McIntyre was a young girl, she often went with her father, Dr. An-

drew Bonar, into his great church in Glasgow, Scotland, on weekdays when the church was empty. He would place her in a pew in the rear of the church. Then he would sit silently in the different pews, after carefully reading the name plates to see if he was in the desired pew. She sensed that he was praying for those who usually occupied the pews on the Lord's Day—those who were making little or no progress in the Christian life.

The little daughter at the time did not understand the meaning of her noble father's deep and prayerful concern for his flock. However, as she grew into womanhood, she observed the growth in Christlikeness of those for whom her father earnestly had prayed.

* * *

Nostrums

Vance Havner said, "Multitudes follow preachers who hawk formulas for banishing worry, fear and tension while the prophets of God, with their painful requirement of heartrending repentance, with resultant forsaking of sin, go unheeded."

* * *

A Glib Tongue

Commented *Zion's Herald*, "The Christian pulpit needs to be on guard against the snare of words. One of the greatest curses that can come to a young preacher is a glib tongue. It means almost certain ruin. How futile, no matter how pleasing, are the efforts of a mere ministerial rhetorician."

* * *

Every Christian an Evangelist

The word *evangelist* means "a publisher of good news." Its verb form signifies "make known the gospel; bring under the influence of the gospel truths."

Each Christian is commanded to "go . . . tell . . . how great things the Lord hath done for . . . [him]" (Mark 5:19).

* * *

An Active Membership

Clyde R. Hoey, a former governor of North Carolina, often told with a chuckle in his political campaigns of a conversation he had with a country pastor in the western part of the state.

The governor asked, "How many members do you have?"

The pastor replied, "Fifty."

"How many of them are active?" asked the governor.

"Fifty," was the prompt reply.

"My!" exclaimed the governor. "You must be an unusual preacher to have a 100 percent active membership."

"Well," admitted the pastor, "twenty-five are active for me, and twenty-five are active against me."

Told by BILLY GRAHAM

* * *

Image Changed

Melvin G. Williams stated, "During the twentieth century the image of the clergyman in fiction has changed. Once a crusader, he has become a doubter. Once a comforter, he is now an accommodator."

* * *

His Life Tells

William Cecil, an English statesman, said, "The world looks at ministers out of the pulpit to know what they mean when in it."

* * *

The Best Sermon

Frances Hodgson, American novelist, commented, "The best sermon is not the one which causes the hearers to go away praising the speaker, but the one which makes them go away thoughtful and serious, and hastening to be alone."

* * *

Preaching

Bernard Manning said, "Preaching is a manifestation of the incarnate Word, from the written Word, by the spoken word."

* * *

Too Much Runway

How important it is, with an audience's progressively shortened attention span, that the preacher get airborne without having to use too much runway.

Example

Charles Kingsley averred, "Nothing is so infectious as example."

* * *

Be Brief

Robert Southey, English poet, advised, "Be brief, for words are like sunbeams— the more they are condensed, the deeper they burn."

* * *

A Poor Sermon

George Whitefield stated, "It is a poor sermon that gives no offense, that neither makes the hearer displeased with himself nor with the preacher."

* * *

The Difference

Louis XIV commented, "I don't know why it is, but when I hear other chaplains I admire them, but when I hear Massillon, I go away displeased with myself."

* * *

A Pope Within

Martin Luther said, "I am more afraid of my own heart than of the pope and all his cardinals. I have within me the great pope—*Self*."

* * *

Only God Knows

Gen. William K. Harrison said, "The major part of the present visible religious revival is superficial rather than deep, spurious rather than sincere."

* * *

Only Two Thoughts

Jonathan Edwards testified, "I preach with two thoughts in mind: Every person ought to give his life to Christ; and whether or not anyone else gives Christ his life, I will give Him mine."

* * *

Why They Fail

R. A. Torrey stated, "I believe more promising Christian workers have failed through self-sufficiency and self-esteem than through any other cause."

250

Luther said, "When I preach, I regard neither doctors nor magistrates, of whom I have above forty in my congregation. My eyes are on the servant maids and the children."

The More I See

Evangeline Booth stated, "The more I see of the darkness of this world, the more I want to tell about Jesus, the light of the world."

PREJUDICE

"I Know How You Feel"

Years ago, in a Kansas town, a young man eighteen years old was cordially greeted by Dr. Forrester, who said, "I expected you to look as pleased as punch. Why are you sad? Not every boy gets to be the captain of his football team."

The young man replied, "Sir, I was proud when the fellows elected me captain, but something came up. We've got a big game scheduled with Carlton High School and the team has refused to go through with it because one of the Carlton players is a Negro."

"I know how you feel," said Dr. Forrester.

"I've decided to have it out with the team this afternoon," said the young man.

That afternoon the young captain entered the dressing room. Speaking to the assembled team he said, "I'm ashamed of you, pretending you believe in fair play and justice and then calling off a game because a player is black. Get yourself another captain. I'm through!" He walked out of the room.

The boys stood motionless. Then the quarterback said, "How about it, fellows? Let's call him back." The others nodded assent.

Opening the door, they shouted, "Captain, come back. We're all with you!"

You ask the name of that young man? Dwight Eisenhower.

The Bible says, "God is no respecter of persons: but in every nation he that feareth him, and worketh righteousness, is accepted with him" (Acts 10:34-35).

* * *

One Man's Example

One Sunday morning, shortly after the close of the Civil War, a lone Negro entered a church in Richmond, Virginia, to worship God.

It was communion Sunday. The Negro knelt at the altar to receive the emblems of Christ's blood and broken body. There was momentary resentment by some until a distinguished layman walked erectly down the aisle and knelt beside the Negro. Captured by his spirit, others followed.

Who was that layman? Gen. Robert E. Lee.

* * *

Gandhi's Rebuff

As a young man, Mahatma Gandhi went forth in quest of the truth. He sought to discover the religion which would emancipate India from the wicked caste system. Diligently he examined various religions. He came to the conclusion that Christianity held the right answer to India's divisive, degrading problems.

One Sunday Gandhi went to a Christian church. An usher coldly confronted him at the door and said, "Sir, this church is only for Europeans." Deeply disillusioned, Gandhi walked silently away from the church. The racially exclusive attitude he had encountered caused him to turn away from Christianity and dedicate himself to the spreading of Hinduism to India's millions. How different India's history might have been if Christlikeness had been displayed by that usher!

* * *

No Unity of Brotherhood

Said the columnist Nora Bixler, "No matter what politicians or diplomats say at the United Nations, there is no unity of brotherhood among the world's nonwhites. Most of Africa today is divided

251

into independent, nonwhite nations. Yet tribe oppresses tribe within the same nation, black men fight and die at the hands of other black men.

"Asia is little different. Pakistan and India live under an armed truce. Burma has sent away her Indians. Indonesian youths have started a new drive against the islands' Chinese. Filipino Muslims struggle against Filipino Christians."

Only when the love of God is regnant in our hearts can we live in peace and show goodwill to all people.

PRESENCE, GOD'S

Unseen Ones Present

A church in a small community voted to discontinue the midweek prayer service. There was one woman who had never failed to attend the prayer meeting, and she said, "I will continue to come at the usual time for the prayer service."

The following Wednesday night she sat alone in the prayer room. Next day, a church member jestingly asked her, "Did you have a prayer meeting last night?"

She replied cheerfully, "That we did."

"How many were present?"

She replied, "Four."

"Four?" the inquirer asked in astonishment. "I heard that you were there all alone."

"No, no," protested the brave woman. "I was the only one *visibly* present. The Father, the Son and the Holy Spirit were invisibly present, and we all were agreed in prayer."

* * *

"Jesus . . . Went with Them"

In his book *The Last Hundred Days*, John Toland tells of a thrilling incident which occurred in World War II when Gen. Dwight D. Eisenhower was with the soldiers of the 30th Infantry Division.

As the general moved among the soldiers, preparatory to the crossing of the Rhine into Germany, he encountered one who was manifestly nervous and frightened.

"How are you feeling?" the general asked.

"General, I'm awful nervous. I was wounded two months ago, and I just got back yesterday from the hospital. I don't feel good."

"Well," said General Eisenhower, "I'm nervous, too. We've planned this crossing into Germany for a long time, and we've got all the planes, guns and airborne troops we can use. Maybe if we walked together to the river, it would be good for both of us."

Deeply moved and encouraged by the general's offer, the soldier said, "I meant I *was* nervous. But I'm not nervous anymore. I guess it isn't so bad around here after all."

As God's children fight the battles of life, it is encouraging to know that there is One on the road with them: "While they communed together and reasoned, Jesus himself drew near, and went with them" (Luke 24:15). How reassuring is His sure promise: "Lo, I am with you alway" (Matt. 28:20).

* * *

"Just Jesus and Me, Sir"

Many years ago, a Methodist circuit rider came unexpectedly to a broken-down cabin in a clearing. In the doorway of the cabin stood an aged Negro woman. Her hair was white, her face deeply furrowed with wrinkles, and her hands rough from years of toil and drudgery. Her eyes were bright and her face shone with the glory of God.

"Good morning," said the itinerant minister. "Do you live here alone?" he asked.

Cheerfully the woman replied, "Just Jesus and me, sir."

Later the minister said, "The very atmosphere of that broken-down cabin seemed to be surcharged with God's presence. In vision, I saw standing beside that aged saint Someone whose face was like the Son of God!"

God's children are never unattended: "Lo, I am with you alway, even unto the end of the world" (Matt. 28:20).

* * *

A Sustaining Fact

The everywhereness of God is a precious and sustaining fact to God's children: "If I take the wings of the morning, and dwell in the uttermost parts of the sea; even there shall thy hand lead me, and thy right hand shall hold me" (Ps. 139:9-10).

Madame Guyon, a French mystic, was imprisoned in the Bastille for eight years. The thought of God's unfailing presence with her lifted her spirit onto a plain of joy and triumph. She wrote:

To me remains neither place nor time,
My country is in every clime;
I can be calm and free from care
On any shore since God is there.

* * *

Immanuel: God with Us

In the high and holy place
Dwelt the Father of all grace,
Yet, with men of low degree,
Condescended in love to be.

Christ, the Lord of heaven and earth,
Came with unpretentious birth;
He, whose love was measureless,
Poor became, the poor to bless.

* * *

The Indwelling Christ

A minister had an ungovernable temper. For a long time he struggle to conquer the sin, but to no avail.

One day as he sat wearily in his study, he fell asleep and had a dream. He saw a most gracious Person approaching the study, which was in disarray. The Visitor stood at the door, knocking.

Recognizing the Visitor as the Lord Jesus, the minister became greatly distressed. Thinking, *I cannot allow Him to enter such an untidy place,* he began to sweep the floor and dust the desk and books. The more he tried to clean things up, the dirtier they became. Defeated and dejected, he said, "I can do no more Come, if Thou wilt, into this unkept, dirty place."

The Lord Jesus entered and instantly, as if under the wave of a magic wand, the study became bright and clean.

The minister cried, "O Master, Your presence within accomplished instantly what all my self-effort utterly failed to accomplish." Then he awoke, a changed man.

* * *

Illumined Dungeons

Strong are the walls around me
That hold me all the day,
But they who thus have bound me
Cannot keep God away:
My very dungeon walls are dear,
Because the God I love is here.

They know, who thus oppress me,
'Tis hard to be alone,
But know not One can bless me,
Who comes through bars and stone:
He makes my dungeon's darkness bright,
And fills my bosom with delight.

MADAME GUYON

* * *

Three Persons Present

A friend asked Lord Moynihan, a former president of the Royal College of Surgeons and one of the greatest surgeons of all times, "How can you operate before groups of distinguished fellow surgeons?"

Lord Moynihan smiled and replied, "There are just three persons present when I operate—the patient and myself."

"Who is the third?" questioned the friend. "You mentioned only two."

Reverently the great surgeon replied, "God."

* * *

His Pervasive Presence

Dr. John Baillie said to his class in Edinburgh University, "Gentlemen, in discussing God we cannot talk without His hearing every word we say. We may talk about our fellows behind their backs, but we cannot do that with God. He is everywhere. He is in this classroom. We must be aware of His infinite presence when we talk about Him."

Big Enough and Small Enough

One Sunday morning an atheistic neighbor asked a Christian, "Where are you going?"

The Christian replied, "I am going to church to worship God."

Sarcastically the atheist asked, "Is your God great or small?"

"He is both, sir."

"That's impossible," said the atheist. "He can't be both."

The believer replied, "He is so great that the heaven cannot contain Him: 'The heaven and heaven of heavens cannot contain him' [II Chron. 2:6], and so small that He can dwell in my soul: 'If a man love me, he will keep my words: and my Father will love him, and we will come . . . and make our abode with him' [John 14:23]."

Later the atheist confessed that the simple answer affected him more than all the books about God he had read.

* * *

Good, Better, Best

God is *for us*—that is good: "If God be for us, who can be against us?" (Rom. 8:31).

God is *with us*—that is better: "Fear thou not; for I am with thee" (Isa. 41:10).

God is *in us*—that is best: "That they all may be one; as thou, Father, art in me, and I in thee, that they also may be one in us" (John 17:21).

Precious and indissoluble is the relationship which Christ sustains to His children: "Unto you . . . which believe he is precious" (I Peter 2:7); "For I am persuaded, that neither death, nor life . . . shall be able to separate us from the love of God, which is in Christ Jesus our Lord" (Rom. 8:38-39).

* * *

Not Alone

Alone, yet not alone!
No, not alone. That cannot be,
For I, thy Lord, am still with thee
Nor ever will forsake.
I know thy sorrow, feel thy care,
And all thy lonely grief I share;
My love makes no mistake.

Trailed Through the Storm

A blizzard was raging in the little village in which Jack lived. He looked in wonderment at the swirling snow. He longed to walk in it and go see Larry who lived a quarter of a mile away. He pleaded, "Daddy, let me go out in the snow. Let me go see Larry."

Daddy refused at first, but finally he yielded to Jack's plea.

Jack was overjoyed! He quickly put on his warmest clothes and boots and ran out into the swirling snow. The driving snow made it difficult for him to see. The drifts were deep. Finally he reached Larry's house.

As Jack rang the doorbell, he looked around and saw the retreating figure of his father. His father, fearful of Jack's safety, had followed him and watched him every step of the way.

How comforting it is to know that our heavenly Father always watches over His children. He never sleeps. Before we close our eyes in sleep at night, we should trustingly say, "I will both lay me down in peace, and sleep: for thou, LORD, only makest me dwell in safety" (Ps. 4:8).

Told by ALICE MARIE KNIGHT

* * *

God Is in the Dark

Little Gloria was afraid of being alone in the dark. Her mother, learning of her fear, told her that God, her heavenly Father, was as loving as her own daddy and more powerful than her daddy. "Our heavenly Father takes care of His children in the dark as well as in the light," said her mother.

Later Mother sent little Gloria on an errand to the sewing room. It was getting dark and the room was not lighted. "I'm afraid of the dark, Mommy," said Gloria.

Taking the little girl into her arms, Mother said assuringly, "It isn't very dark in there, and don't forget that God is in the dark as well as in the light."

The words encouraged Gloria. Going into the dark room, she said, "God, O God, I'm comin'." She went alone—yet not alone.

ALICE MARIE KNIGHT

254

PRIDE

His Fading Fame

Napoleon epitomized his fading fame thus: "I am doing now what will fill thousands of volumes in this generation. In the next, one volume will contain it all. In the third, a paragraph, and in the fourth, a single line."

How ephemeral is earthly glory: "For all flesh is as grass, and all the glory of man as the flower of grass" (I Peter 1:24).

The boast of heraldry, the pomp of power,
  And all that beauty, all that wealth e'er gave,
Await the inevitable hour:
  The paths of glory lead but to the grave.

* * *

Why Mirrors Were Removed

As Queen Elizabeth I advanced in years, her many wrinkles deepened. The hapless master of the mint incurred the Queen's disfavor and was dismissed because he produced a faithful likeness of her on a shilling. The die was destroyed and only one mutilated specimen of those coins is now in existence. The queen's maids of honor, wishing to please her, removed all mirrors from the palace. A journalist wrote, "The Queen has not had the heart to look herself in the face for the last twenty years."

* * *

Too Proud to Accept Help

Too proud to accept their neighbors' help, an aged couple died from starvation and exposure, according to Dr. Thomas F. Corriden, the coroner. When neighbors found the aged couple, they rushed them to Cooley Dickinson Hospital, Northampton, Massachusetts.

Neighbors said, "We did our best to help them, but we were turned away from the door by the proud husband. When we finally gained admission to the home, we found the couple unconscious."

Justifiable Pride

F. B. Meyer said, "I should take more pride in my work for the Lord. When I speak, my words should be my choicest. When I plan, I should be ambitious, prudent, courageous. I must not allow my secular work to be better done than my religious work. Let my work for God be perfect and praiseworthy."

* * *

Give Somebody Else a Chance

A socially prominent, self-important woman said to Abraham Lincoln: "Mr. President, you must give my son a colonel's commission. I request it, not as a favor, but as a right."

Proudly she continued, "My grandfather fought at Lexington, my uncle was the only soldier who did not run at Blandensberg, and my husband was killed at Monterey."

After a moment's silence, Lincoln said softly, "Perhaps, Madam, your family has done enough for our country. It is time to give somebody else a chance."

* * *

"How Are the Mighty Fallen"

When Gen. Charles DeGaulle was informed of the fall of Krushchev, he exclaimed, *"Sic transit gloria mundi"* which means "Thus passes away the glory of the world."

Peter said, "All flesh is as grass, and all the glory of man as the flower of grass" (I Peter 1:24).

How quickly a "Who's Who" becomes a "Who Was"!

* * *

Spiritual Pride

One of the deadliest of sins is spiritual pride: "I am rich . . . and have need of nothing" (Rev. 3:17); "The wicked, through the pride of his countenance, will not seek after God: God is not in all his thoughts" (Ps. 10:4).

Remonstrated Shakespeare, "But man, proud man! drest in a little authority plays such fantastic tricks before high heaven as to make angels weep."

God's Word warns, "Pride goeth before destruction, and a haughty spirit before a fall" (Prov. 16:18); "Let him that thinketh he standeth take heed lest he fall" (I Cor. 10:12).

Beware of Peter's boastful words,
Nor confidently say,
"I never will deny Thee, Lord,
But grant I never may."

* * *

"I Hae Me Doots o' Ye, Laddie"

James McDougall, a young Scot, was a candidate for the ministry. Proudly and self-confidently he entered the pulpit to deliver a trial sermon. He felt that it was a good one. He had studied diligently in its preparation. He had a good voice and an excellent personal appearance. He was sure he could make a good impression.

Observing his proud, self-inflated manner upon entering the pulpit, the old sexton mused, *I hae me doots o' ye, laddie.*

James McDougall made a miserable failure in the pulpit that day. Upon the conclusion of his poorly delivered trial sermon, he walked slowly and dejectedly from the pulpit. His head was bowed and his heart humbled.

The old sexton thought to himself, *Aye, laddie, if ye had gone up as ye come doon, ye hae come doon as ye went up.*

The queenliest of the Christian graces is humility. God waits patiently for His children to obey the command "Humble yourselves . . . under the mighty hand of God" (I Peter 5:6). When they refuse to do this, He, in love, often humiliates them.

Told by HARRY A. IRONSIDE

* * *

Convoluted Verbosity

Said Will Rogers, "I always like to hear a man talk about himself, because then I never hear anything but good."

PRINTED PAGE

The Pen and the Sword

In November, 1862, Abraham Lincoln received a visitor at the White House— a small, middle-aged lady. He greeted her heartily and exclaimed, "So this is the little lady who made this big war!"

The lady was Harriet Beecher Stowe, author of *Uncle Tom's Cabin.* When her book was started on its long and history-making journey, neither she nor anyone else knew the mighty torrent it would unleash, or that it would end at Gettysburg and Appomattox. She thought of the story as a messenger of peace, not of war. She said, "The Lord Himself gave it to me. I was merely His amanuensis!"

In commenting upon the book, Kirk Monroe, noted New York critic, said, "The abolition of slavery was not, and

could not, be accomplished by any one person. It was the result of united efforts. But the greatest and most far-reaching of all these influences was *Uncle Tom's Cabin.*"

* * *

Dragons' Teeth

As Johann Gutenberg worked on his invention of movable type in the fifteenth century, he seemed to hear warning voices telling him that his discovery would be used by wicked men to sow dragons' teeth and disseminate evil by the printed page.

When he lifted a hammer to smash his type, he seemed to hear another voice— God's voice—encouraging him to perfect his invention and make the printed page a perennial fountain of immeasurable blessing to all mankind.

More Powerful than Bombs

Said Dr. V. Raymond Edman in *Heartbeat*, "Who can measure the impact of Gutenberg's invention of the printing press? The first crude printing press of the fifteenth century and the use of movable type made possible the expansion of knowledge beyond our power to comprehend. . . . Gutenberg's first product was the Bible—the beginning of a worldwide flood of God's Word. To be sure, wicked men have likewise learned the value of the printed page. The press, like atomic energy, has infinitely vast potential power for good and, likewise, for destruction.

"The future of the world lies far more with books than with bombs. . . . The pen is mightier than the sword. The call of the hour for God's people is the Spirit-anointed heart and head, with ready hands and feet, to use the printing press to get God's Word to our bewildered generation."

* * *

Communist Missionaries

Joe Weatherly, vice-president of Overseas Gospel Films, said in *Child Evangelism*, "It has been only forty-six years since Nikolai Lenin wrote *The State in Revolution*. Yet in those forty-six years, his writings have been translated into more than one thousand living languages. Communist missionaries across the world follow a clear commission: 'Go into all the world and conquer it in the name of Communism.' "

What a challenge this situation should be to God's children to redouble their efforts to "preach good tidings . . . [and] liberty to the captives" (Isa. 61:1). The hour is late: "The night is far spent" (Rom. 13:12); "The coming of the Lord draweth nigh" (James 5:8).

* * *

Good and Evil Books

Who can overestimate the power of an evil book or a good book?

In 1883 Karl Marx, the German revolutionist, was interred in Highgate Cemetery, London. A small group attended the solemnities. In eulogizing the decedent, Friedrich Engels said, "Humanity has lost its greatest thinker."

Engels and Marx were cofounders of scientific socialism, or modern Communism.

Today the teaching of Karl Marx is basic in the philosophy and thinking of two-fifths of the world's population. Their creed is given in his treatise on economics, *Das Kapital*.

Mein Kampf, a book written by Adolph Hitler while in prison in 1924, setting forth his political beliefs and outlining a plan for the domination of Europe by Germany, was a potent factor in engulfing the world in World War II.

* * *

If Truth Is Not Diffused

Daniel Webster warned, "If truth be not diffused, error will be. If God and His Word are not known and received, the devil and his works will gain the ascendancy. If evangelical volumes do not reach every hamlet, corrupt and licentious literature will. If the power of the gospel is not felt throughout the length and breadth of the land, anarchy and misrule, degradation and misery, corruption and darkness will reign without mitigation or end."

* * *

"If I Had a Hundred Million Dollars"

Dr. Frank Laubach said, in speaking to the Canadian branch of the British and Foreign Bible Society, "If I had one hundred million dollars to spend, I would invest every cent of it in the dissemination of Christian literature, so convinced am I of the power resident in the printed page to bring enlightenment to the nations that still sit in darkness and the shadow of death."

* * *

A Great Potential—Minds Won by Printer's Ink

G. Christian Weiss said, in the Christian Literature Crusade's *Floodtide*, "About 80 million books and 85 million copies of their two magazines, *Watchtower* and *Awake*, are printed annually by Jehovah Witness. The Seventh-Day

257

Adventists are the next most aggressive group in the literature field. This body spends more than $15 million annually for literature. A third group which resorts strongly to literature is Christian Science. Their sizable magazine, *Christian Science Sentinel,* is widely distributed in public places everywhere. The Latter-Day Saints, or Mormons, have vast literature programs. Wherever their missionaries go, they leave their literature.

"The battle for men's minds will be won by printer's ink! Make no mistake about that."

* * *

Age of Exploding Literacy

In addressing a Southern Baptist foreign missions conference, Dr. John H. McCombe, Jr., an official of the American Bible Society, said, "The Soviet Union is spending yearly $1.5 billion for literature outside Russia—all of it atheistic. Christian churches spend annually $15 million for translation, production and distribution of the Bible. How can $15,000,000 stand up against $1,500,000,-000 in an age of exploding literacy?"

* * *

How to Counteract Evil

A vender of candy, books and papers walked down the aisle of a railway coach, saying, "Here you are, ladies and gentlemen—Ingersoll on hell!"

Dwight L. Moody was a passenger on that coach. He grabbed the boy, thrust a book in his hand and said, "Here, boy, is Moody on heaven. Offer the passengers this book, too."

The quick-witted boy said, "Yes, sir." Off he went through the coaches, calling, "Ingersoll on hell and Moody on heaven."

* * *

How to Revive God's Work

John Wesley was in the prime of his work as David Brainerd lay dying of tuberculosis. Said Wesley, "What can be done to revive the work of the Lord where it has decayed? This can be done: let every preacher read carefully the life of David Brainerd."

LEONARD RAVENHILL

Mental Health Undermined

Dr. Max Levin, New York City psychiatrist, stated, "I am convinced that pornography is undermining the mental health of countless youngsters. Unscrupulous publishers cater to their sex hunger. Their lurid books are hot numbers on the newsstands where teenagers gather."

* * *

A Direct Relationship

Dr. Benjamin Karpman, chief psychotherapist at St. Elizabeth's Hospital, Washington, D.C., commented, "There is a direct relationship between juvenile delinquency and pornographic literature."

J. Edgar Hoover said, "Sex-mad magazines are creating criminals faster than jails can be built to house them."

* * *

A Primary Problem

O. W. Wilson, former Chicago police superintendent, warned, "Obscene literature is a primary problem in the United States today. Sexual arousals from obscene literature have been responsible for criminal behavior from vicious assaults to homicide."

* * *

What a Tract Did

Years ago a young physician in Philadelphia, Dr. John Scudder, chanced to pick up a tract in the home of one of his patients. He read the tract and was deeply touched by its message. As a result, he gave up his lucrative practice, and he and his wife went as missionaries to India. In time all of their nine children became missionaries!

* * *

A Burning Shame

The disclosure by Senate investigators of a $500,000,000 yearly traffic in pornography in this country presents a shameful target for those who make and those who enforce the law.

The investigators' report states: "The quantity and quality of this material beggars description. It is wanton, depraved, nauseating, despicable, demoralizing, de-

258

structive and capable of poisoning any mind of any age!"

This is indeed a serious indictment against those who are so enslaved by the desire for monetary profit that they will stoop to any form of degradation for the sake of a dollar.

Adapted from *Christianity Today*

* * *

Beetles and Human Beings

Some years ago a horrible crime was committed in Chicago—the murder of little Bobby Franks. The youthful thrill killers, Richard Leob and Nathan Leopold, were defended by the famed criminal lawyer Clarence Darrow. It was one of the most publicized court cases of all time.

In his plea for their lives, Darrow said, "In the university where these young men are students, you can find copies of a book written by Nietzsche, who taught that it is no more harm to impale a human being upon a needle than a beetle in the interest of scientific investigation. Philosophers like him are more to blame for this crime than these youths. Your Honor, it is hardly fair to execute them because they took seriously what was taught them."

How hardening and devoid of consideration of human life are those who believe bestial philosophies! It is generally conceded that Nietzsche's doctrines—the survival of the fittest, the ruthless destruction of the weaker ones, the emergence of the superman and superior race—greatly influenced the philosophy and propaganda of National Socialism in the German Third Reich, and precipitated World War II.

Though Leob and Leopold were totally without any excuse for the horrible crime they committed, Darrow spoke of a danger which calls for serious thought in our day when faith-undermining, Bible-ridiculing philosophies are being widely taught.

Who is sufficiently wise to appraise the havoc an evil book can work? Conversely, who can compute the blessings a good book can impart?

* * *

Crowns Spurned

Said François Fénelon, "If the crowns of all the kingdoms of the world were laid down at my feet in exchange for my books and my love of reading, I would spurn them all."

* * *

One Communist Tract

Book Club Chatter stated, "It was a communistic tract given to Lee Oswald that led him into Communism."

* * *

The Greatest Potential

Christian Life Missions affirmed, "One of the greatest potentials in the history of missions is the 80 million people who have learned to read in recent years."

PROPHECY

Prewritten History

Dr. Harry A. Ironside said, "Prophecy is history prewritten. The prophetic scriptures are as trustworthy as any other scripture. Prophecies occur throughout the Bible. Sixteen books of the Old Testament and one book of the New Testament are wholly prophetic in character. Nearly one-fourth of the Bible was predictive when it was written. It is most reasonable to conclude, since every Bible prediction concerning the past has been fulfilled in the minutest detail, that we may expect all the remaining unfulfilled prophecies to be just as literally fulfilled."

* * *

Russell and John Agree

Bertrand Russell, a skeptic, gloomily prophesied, "Utter and unrelieved gloom awaits us! It is likely that during this

259

present generation all our large cities in every part of the world will be destroyed!"

Centuries before Russell wrote those direful words, John envisioned God's impending judgment and said, "And the cities of the nations fell; and great Babylon came in remembrance before God, to give unto her the cup of the wine of the fierceness of his wrath" (Rev. 16:19).

* * *

The Unfailing Light

Said Sun Tzu, a sixth century B.C. Chinese military theorist, "What enables the wise sovereign and the good general to strike and conquer and achieve things beyond the reach of ordinary men is foreknowledge."

God's children have the "sure word of prophecy . . . that shineth in a dark place, until the day dawn" (II Peter 1:19). With this unfailing light, they know God's future plan for His children and the nations. With this foreknowledge, they can live radiantly and without fear.

Of some of God's children who lived long ago it is written, "And of the children of Issachar . . . were men that had

understanding of the times, to know what Israel ought to do" (I Chron. 12:32).

* * *

Perhaps the Stage Is Being Set

The famed historian Arnold Toynbee said, "By forcing on mankind more and more lethal weapons, and at the same time making the world more independent economically, technology has brought mankind to such a degree of distress that we are ripe for the deifying of any new Caesar who might succeed in giving the world unity and peace."

Many believe that the stage is being set for the revelation of the Antichrist of whom the Bible says, "[He] opposeth and exalteth himself above . . . God . . . so that he as God sitteth in the temple of God, shewing himself that he is God" (II Thess. 2:4); "And through his policy . . . he shall cause craft to prosper; . . . he shall magnify himself, . . . and by peace shall destroy many" (Dan. 8:25).

"And when these things begin to come to pass, then look up, and lift up your heads; for your redemption draweth nigh" (Luke 21:28).

PROTECTION, GOD'S

In the Hollow of His Hand

Most people act differently in times when death seems inevitable. There are no atheists in foxholes.

Recently the survivors of an American airliner that was ditched in the ocean sang hymns and recited together the Lord's Prayer as ten-foot waves tossed their raft about like a chip on the ocean for five hours. Then they were rescued by the Swiss freighter *Celerina*. The survivors came ashore thanking God, the captain of the freighter, their pilot and their navigator for the rescue.

The captain of the ill-fated plane, John D. Murphy, of Oyster Bay, New York, said, "God had His hand on the controls to help me make such a magnificent landing in rough weather!"

What a difference it makes with us when God's hand is on us in blessing: "If I . . . dwell in the uttermost parts of the sea; even there shall thy hand lead me, and thy right hand shall hold me" (Ps. 139:9-10).

* * *

"I Will Defend This City"

During World War I, Jerusalem was occupied by the Turks until taken by the British soldiers. Its capture was most interesting. The appearance of allied planes overhead frightened the Turks. They fled from the city. Could it be that the planes overhead fulfilled this prophecy: "As birds flying, so will the LORD of hosts defend Jerusalem; defending also he will deliver it; and passing over he will pre-

260

serve it" (Isa. 31:5)? No bombs were dropped. Not a shot was fired by General Allenby's advancing army.

In commemoration of the miraculous, bloodless occupancy of Jerusalem, the Allenby Bridge was built, spanning the Jordan River.

When a little boy, General Allenby was taught to close his prayer with a special plea for Israel: "Forget not Thine ancient people. Hasten the day when they shall be restored to Thy favor and to their land."

At a reception honoring him in London, he said, "I never knew that God would give me the privilege of helping to answer my own childhood prayer!"

* * *

God at the Center

Someone had explained simply the law of gravity to a little girl. One night her mother observed that she was deep in thought. "What are you thinking about?" she asked.

The little girl replied, "I was thinking about gravity, and I've decided that gravity is God at the center of the world, protecting and keeping His children right side up when the world is upside down!"

ALICE MARIE KNIGHT

* * *

Our Wakeful, Watchful Protector

Years ago bandits were reported to be on their way to a village in China. The Wongs were the only Christian family in the village—the only ones able to pray for God's protection in the time of danger. At their evening prayer time, they read, "If ye have faith as a grain of mustard seed, ye shall say unto this mountain, Remove to yonder place; and it shall remove; and nothing shall be impossible unto you" (Matt. 17:20).

With implicit trust in God, they prayed, "O Lord, put a mountain in front of our door so the bandits won't be able to find us."

During the night it snowed. The snow drifted and covered the door of the Wong home!

Next morning the bandits came. All homes in the village were looted except the Wong home.

After the robbers had gone, neighbors cleared away the snow which had obscured the Wong home. When they entered the home, the Wongs told them about claiming God's promise for protection and care in the time of danger.

How great is our wakeful, watchful Keeper, God!

Adapted from a China Inland
Mission leaflet

* * *

"O God, Scatter the Ships"

During the Revolutionary War, an enemy fleet was sailing toward New England. The governor of Massachusetts called for a day of fasting and prayer. In Boston's Old South Church, the pastor, Thomas Prince, stood and importuned, "O God, deliver us from the enemy. Scatter the ships of our tormentors. Drive them home."

As he prayed, black clouds began to scud across the darkened skies. A strong wind swept through the church steeple and rang the bell twice. As Thomas Prince looked skyward through tearful eyes, he said, "Thine be the glory, Lord."

A violent storm swept the Atlantic and destroyed most of the enemy ships.

* * *

In His Hands

In an effort to get Martin Luther to renounce his beliefs and return to the Catholic church, a cardinal was sent to him.

When he confronted Luther, he said contemptuously, "Do you think the pope cares about the opinion of a German boor? Do you expect your princes to take up arms and defend a wretched worm like you? I tell you, No! And where will you be then?"

Luther replied, "Where I am now—in the hands of the almighty God!"

* * *

"No Kill Them"

In 1777 a little group of Friends assembled to worship in their meetinghouse in Easton, New York.

261

Suddenly thirteen Indians came in noiselessly. They were intent on killing the worshipers, and had poison arrows ready to fly at the signal of their chief.

The chief's piercing eyes searched every corner and nook for weapons. Seeing none, he signaled to his warriors, and they placed their arrows back in their quivers and stacked them with their bows against the wall.

The braves peered into the calm, blue eyes of Zebulon Hoxie, leader of the meeting. There they saw reflected only love and friendship. Then they sat down around their chief.

The silent worship went on. The atmosphere was surcharged with the very presence of God.

When the hour's worship ended, Zebulon Hoxie advanced and shook hands with the Indian chief, who said, "Indians came to kill white people. Indians find no guns, no arrows, no knives. White people worship Great Spirit. Great Spirit say to Indian, 'No kill them.'"

As the chief left with his braves, he placed a white feather from his arrow over the doorway. It was a sign of peace between the Indians and the Quakers. A New York historical marker commemorates the incident.

RACIAL PROBLEMS

Man's Inhumanity

Many and sharp the numerous ills
  Interwoven in our frame;
More poignant still we make ourselves
  Regret, remorse and shame;
And man's heaven-erected face
  The smiles of love adorn;
Man's inhumanity to man
  Makes countless thousands mourn.

ROBERT BURNS

* * *

You Called Me Brother

When a famous writer entered a cathedral, a beggar asked him for alms. The writer searched his pockets and then said apologetically, "I am sorry, my brother, but I have nothing to give you."

The beggar said, "I thank you."

"But I said I had nothing to give you," the writer replied.

"Ah," said the beggar, "you gave me something better than money. You called me 'brother'!"

Adapted from *Sunshine Magazine*

* * *

Groundless Prejudices

How devoid of foundation are many of our prejudices.

A boy used to come home from school very hungry. One day he saw on the kitchen table what he thought was a hunk of cheese. He took a big bite of it and discovered that it was a bar of yellow soap. To this day he has a prejudice against bars of yellow soap.

God's children should have only one attitude toward all people of all races, namely: "Grace be with all them that love our Lord Jesus Christ in sincerity" (Eph. 6:24).

* * *

Our Basic Problems

Editorialized *Moody Monthly,* "Our basic problems cannot be traced to any of the captions we see in newspaper headlines. Men are out of line with the will of God because of sin, and this puts them out of harmony with one another at virtually every point of contact. Though there is a cure, the disease, for the most part, is overlooked while we vainly treat the symptoms."

* * *

No Excuse for Rioting

Sen. Robert Byrd of West Virginia, who throughout his youth was acquainted with the poverty of coal mining communities, said, "We hear the usual excuse for riots. The ghettos are blamed. Yet people of all races have lived in ghettos in the past, and they didn't riot. Poverty-stricken white people outnumber poverty-

262

stricken Negroes in America. There are millions of poor but upstanding Negro citizens who deplore violence and disorder, and do not condone riots.

"If living in poverty reposes in one a duty or a right to riot, then Abraham Lincoln would have been the Stokely Carmichael of his day."

Jesus said, "Cleanse first that which is within . . . that the outside . . . may be clean also" (Matt. 23:26).

* * *

We Desperately Need Jesus Christ

John Whitnah, branch chief in the division of biology and medicine of the Atomic Energy Commission, commented, "It seems to me that we need very desperately to keep Jesus Christ in the center of our thinking. Christ can bring peace not only to individuals who are groping for the way in their own lives but also to those involved in human relations, whether in communities or in the world. We cannot afford to continue the trend toward moving God and Jesus Christ out of our national affairs."

* * *

Political Activists

Billy Graham stated, "Man's greatest need is spiritual. Church leaders have become politicians, social engineers and political activists, and have quit preaching the Bible and conversion. The church, while trying to become relevant through social activism, is becoming irrelevant by losing touch with the needs of people."

When Paul entered morally corrupt Corinth, he "determined not to know any thing among . . . [them], save Jesus Christ, and him crucified" (I Cor. 2:2). His preaching effected an inward change in lives which no outward restraint could work: "Know ye not that . . . neither . . . thieves, . . . nor drunkards, nor revilers, nor extortioners, shall inherit the kingdom of God. *And such were some of you:* but ye are washed, . . . sanctified, . . . justified in the name of the Lord Jesus, and by the Spirit of our God" (6:9-11).

Education Is Not Enough

Dr. John Broger, director of education and information for the United States Armed Forces, declared, "Many people say that our problems will be solved if we will just make people literate. Educate them, and good will come automatically. This is not always true. Japan and Germany were two of the most literate nations in the world prior to World War II. Education in itself is not the answer. There has to be a change first in the heart of man, and enough change in enough hearts to make society move in the direction that's basically for the good of all. I think General MacArthur recognized this in Japan after World War II when he said the problem is basically spiritual and theological."

* * *

Time Is Running Out

Arthur Glasser said in *East Asia Millions,* "I do not know of any nation in the world today that does not have a racial problem of some sort. I believe the racial issue is going to be far more determinative in the world tomorrow than it is in the world today. For this reason, I do not believe that time is on the side of the evangelical church. . . . It must come to terms with its uneasy conscience and downright disobedience to biblical injunctions, and *do so in a hurry.*"

* * *

The Nation's Largest Ghetto

In *America's Mistake* Tom Tiede said: "Window Rock, Arizona, a dusty and dismal village, is the gateway to the nation's largest ghetto—the Navajo Indian Reservation. It is 25,000 square miles of privation. It is sixteen million acres of despair. It is 100,000 faces of poverty. The median income of a family of five is $580 a year. One Indian described it thus: 'This is the place God and the government forgot.'

"Our government hasn't forgotten the reservation moneywise. With its 22,000 employees, the Bureau of Indian Affairs yearly gives fifty million dollars to the reservation for public health, schooling, housing, old age assistance, care of de-

263

pendent children and social security. One government official said, 'In the past six years, we've spent over $1,500,000,000 on the Indians. Tell me, what more do they want?' "

There are government programs in abundance, but there is little or no progress in changing this Indian ghetto. In the century since the Navajos were herded into the reservation, they have retrograded in some aspects of their living. They have in many incidents been treated so unjustly that inertia, sloth and hopelessness characterize most of them. Aspiration has been displaced by alcoholism. Six hundred Navajos are arrested for drunkenness each month.

The pathetic plight of the Navajos is a striking example of the fact that material things do not effectuate the inward change needed in hopeless, oppressed ghetto dwellers. Significant outward changes occur only when man is changed inwardly by God's transforming grace.

* * *

Not Skin but Sin

Said Samuel Dalton in the *Watchman-Examiner*, "I am a Negro who never clamored for civil rights, knowing 'that the law is not made for a righteous man, but for the lawless and disobedient' (I Tim. 1:9). Now that the Civil Rights Bill is passed, where do we go from here? With demonstrations getting out of hand, it is evident that the stringent laws of men have not the answer to the perplexing problems of our day. Yet there is cause for rejoicing that love, which is of God, is the answer. No matter how many enforcers of the law, how much money is spent, what good intentions, or even how many may lay down their lives for such, it is all in vain unless the law of love reigns in our heart.

"Many make the issue skin. The real issue is sin. Only Jesus Christ, God's beloved Son, and His love prevailing in the hearts of people of every race and color will end the hatred so prevalent. Apart from Him there is no hope."

A Practical Suggestion

In commenting upon the racial demonstrations in the streets, Rev. Henry Mitchell, a Negro minister and pastor of the North Star Missionary Baptist Church, Chicago, said, "The marches don't represent the mass of the Negro people, who prefer to live in their community. I propose that marchers march to the West Side slums with rakes, brooms and grass seed to spruce up the area."

* * *

Negative Approaches

Dr. Joseph H. Jackson, president of the National Baptist Convention composed of five and one-half million Negro members, said, "Civil disobedience and economic boycotts are negative approaches which may call attention to racial problems, but cannot solve them. We must go from protest to production. I feel that education, not 'gate-crashing,' puts the Negro in a better economic and political position to demand equal rights. Any man who forces his way into church membership is just as guilty as the one who would keep him out. The same applies to segregation. We should obey the laws."

From an Associated Press dispatch

* * *

The Better Way

Donald Warden, a Negro attorney and chairman of the Afro-American Association, told United Press International, "What the Negro needs is the same pride that helped the Chinese, Jews and Irish to overcome prejudice."

He urged his followers to "throw away your bleaching creams and your hair straighteners, quit dropping out of school, quit flunking out, and get off welfare. If you won't accept the challenge to improve yourself, then admit that you are inferior. It may cost a million dollars to desegregate a lunch counter; and, if successful, this will create maybe a dozen jobs. The Negro would be smarter to spend that million on a factory which might employ one thousand Negroes. The majority of Negroes need to improve their lot through education and self-respect."

264

Changed Individuals Change Society

In his book *Where Do We Go from Here: Chaos or Community?* Martin Luther King epitomized his belief concerning social justice in the following statement: "If the society changes its concepts by placing the responsibility on its system, not on the individual, and guarantees secure employment or a minimum income, dignity will come within the reach of all."

In appraising this "cure" for the ills of our society, C. Ralston Smith said in *Christianity Today*, "Like all other panaceas, this one is too simple. And it runs contrary to the character of man as he was intended when created in the image of the Almighty. Little or nothing is said in the book about acquiring industry or accepting responsibility, or about the baseness of human nature and its need of regeneration."

The basic need of man is a changed heart and attitude. The Saviour, who "knew what was in man" (John 2:25), dealt with man's basic need when He said, "Ye must be born again" (3:7).

The heart of mankind is "deceitful above all things, and desperately wicked" (Jer. 17:9). For confirmation read your daily newspaper. Only transformed individuals can change society and produce amicable relationships among all people.

Clement Attlee said in the House of Commons, "The problem with the world is not with the bomb. The problem of the world is man."

* * *

A Kindergartner Speaks Wisdom

A five-year-old kindergartner said to his mother when he came home from school, "I have a new friend on the big yellow school bus. I like him."

"That's fine," said mother. "And why do you like him?"

"I like him because he treats me like I'm a people!" said the boy.

Shouldn't everyone be treated thus— the old, the young, the rich, the poor, the black and the white?

Mutual respect for each other is fundamental in right human relationships.

ALICE MARIE KNIGHT

Inward Love for Mankind

Commented *New York Times Service*, "There is severe and widespread discrimination in England against people with dark skins—West Indian Negroes, Indians and Pakistanis—who make up 2 percent of British population."

Mankind the world over will continue to practice cruelties and injustices until goodwill and Christlikeness enter the heart of man and change his nature and attitude. God's love in our hearts with concomitant love for all mankind is infinitely more powerful than all outward constraints.

"He that loveth not his brother whom he hath seen, how can he love God whom he hath not seen?" (I John 4:20).

* * *

"We Will Not Hate You"

In expressing his attitude toward those who unjustly mistreat or wrong Negroes, Dr. Martin Luther King said, "We will match your capacity to inflict suffering with our capacity to endure suffering. We will meet your physical force with soul force. We will not hate you. . . . We will soon wear you down by our capacity to suffer. And in winning our freedom, we will so appeal to your heart and conscience that we will win you in the process."

The Lord Jesus Christ left a very specific command for Christians when He said, "Love your enemies, bless them that curse you, do good to them that hate you, and pray for them which despitefully use you, and persecute you" (Matt. 5:44). He also said, "Resist not evil: but whosoever shall smite thee on thy right cheek, turn to him the other also" (v. 39).

* * *

Light at the End of the Tunnel

Said Eric Severeid, "Totally oppressed people, in America or in Africa, do not go into action. It is when the chains have been loosened, or when they see some light at the end of the tunnel when hope is aroused, that oppressed people arouse themselves."

265

It Is Time

Gov. Ronald Reagan stated, "It is time for us to stop being our brother's keeper and be his brother, and perhaps we'll find out he can keep himself."

RESURRECTION

(*See also* Death)

Changed!

Simple markers are set up on the graves in the churchyard at Oberhofen, Switzerland. One person, who was too poor to purchase a marker, printed on a board the name of a departed loved one and the dates of birth and death, then placed it upon the grave. Over this marker he put a little protective roof. In time a caterpillar fastened itself on the underside of the roof. There it passed through the deathlike state of a chrysalis and ultimately emerged as a beautiful butterfly, leaving its former tomblike abode behind.

What a beautiful picture of the resurrection when Christ at His second coming "shall change our vile body, that it may be fashioned like unto his glorious body" (Phil. 3:21).

* * *

Science Has a Surprise

Dr. Wernher von Braun said, "Some people think that science has made religious ideas passé. Science has a real surprise for the skeptics. Science, for instance, tells us that nothing in nature, not even the tiniest particle, can disappear without a trace. Nature does not know extinction, only transformation. If God applies this fundamental principle to the most minute parts of His universe, doesn't it make sense to assume that He applies it also to the soul of man? Everything that science has taught me strengthens my belief in the continuity of our spiritual existence after death."

* * *

A Joyous Meeting

As C. Austin Miles sat alone meditating on the meeting of the death-conquering Saviour with Mary in the garden, the scene became so realistic that he seemed to be a part of it.

He said later, "I seemed to be transported by inspiration to the entrance of the garden. I saw Mary. Her head was bowed. Her hand was clasping her throat, as if to choke back her sobs. Coming to the tomb, she wept. As she turned, she saw Jesus. He said, 'Mary!' She joyously exclaimed, 'Rabboni . . . Master!'

"Mary!" just one word;
'Twas all He need employ
To turn a woman's sorrowing heart
Into a well of joy!

"Under the inspiration of that vision, I effortlessly wrote the poem 'In the Garden' exactly as it has since appeared. That night I wrote the music."

I come to the garden alone,
While the dew is still on the roses;
And the voice I hear, falling on my ear,
The Son of God discloses.

* * *

"I Know I Shall Meet"

Said Louis Pasteur, "I am a scientist and accustomed to reason, and to think as a scientist. But in this matter, the death of my daughter, I am going to believe what I wish to believe. *I know* I shall meet that immortal spirit again!"

* * *

Not a Blind Alley

Victor Hugo stated, "When I go down to the grave, I can say I have finished my day's work. But my day's work will begin the next morning. The tomb is not a blind alley—it closes in the twilight to open with the dawn!"

The Foundation of Christian Faith

When his oldest child died, Sir James Simpson, a Scottish physician, had an obelisk erected on the grave. On it were carved these words: "Nevertheless, I live!" Chiseled above the words was a butterfly, which had emerged from a chrysalis into the freedom of life with wings.

How meaningless would have been the words and the emblem if Christ had not risen from the dead.

The Bible says, "And if Christ be not raised, your faith is vain. . . . Then they also which are fallen asleep in Christ are perished. If in this life only we have hope in Christ, we are . . . most miserable" (I Cor. 15:17-19).

* * *

"They Must Not Rise!"

Robert Moffat, a pioneer missionary to Africa, won the confidence and respect of Makaba, a powerful native chief. One day, as Moffat visited with the chief, he said, "I have come to tell you good news: The dead will rise again!"

"What! The dead will rise again?" the chief asked, unable to comprehend the truth. "Will my father and those I have slain in battle arise?"

"Yes," replied Moffat.

A look of fear and anguish came to the face of the chief as he thought of the cruel, heartless things he had done. In a quavering voice he said, "I do not wish to hear again about the dead rising. The dead must not rise. I have slain thousands! They must not rise!"

The resurrection is an integral part of God's changeless plan and purpose: "The hour is coming, in the which all that are in the graves shall hear his [Christ's] voice, and shall come forth; they that have done good, unto the resurrection of life; and they that have done evil, unto the resurrection of damnation" (John 5:28-29).

* * *

"Abide with Us"

During World War II, a battle was fought between the Turks and the English army near Emmaus. A lad of nineteen who was greatly liked by the men of his outfit and by his commanding officer, Major Gilbert, was mortally wounded.

Major Gilbert visited the wounded lad in a hospital. The major was a Christian and knew his Bible. He told the lad the story of Jesus' two discouraged, disconsolate disciples going to Emmaus long ago.

The major recounted how the risen Christ drew near the two disciples as they trudged along the dusty road and reprimanded them for their unbelief. Then He told them what the Scriptures taught concerning Him. When they reached Emmaus, the two disciples said to Jesus, "Abide with us: for it is toward evening, and the day is far spent" (Luke 24:29).

When the story was finished, the light of the setting sun shone through the window upon the soldier's face. He exclaimed, "Thank you for telling me that wonderful story about what happened in Emmaus long ago! 'Abide with Me' was my mother's favorite hymn. Thank God for the living Saviour! I can go to sleep now. God bless you, sir!"

Next morning there was an empty cot in the hospital at Emmaus, waiting for the next occupant.

* * *

Emptied Graves

In a futile effort to cast doubt on the raising of Lazarus from the dead, Ingersoll, an agnostic, asked an audience, "Can anyone tell me why Jesus said, 'Lazarus, come forth'?"

An elderly man stood and said, "Sir, I can tell you! If my Lord had not said, 'Lazarus, come forth,' every grave in that Bethany cemetery would have been emptied!"

Someday "all that are in the graves shall hear his voice, and shall come forth; they that have done good, unto the resurrection of life; and they that have done evil, unto the resurrection of damnation" (John 5:28-29).

Today, as long ago, "some . . . will say, How are the dead raised? And with what body do they come?" (I Cor. 15:35). Here's how: "It [the body] is sown a natural body; it is raised a spiritual

267

body" (v. 44). When the believer's mortal body puts on immortality, his spiritual body will be like the glorified body of his Lord: "We know that, when he shall appear, we shall be like him; for we shall see him as he is" (I John 3:2).

Joyously we exclaim, "Death is swallowed up in victory" (I Cor. 15:54).

* * *

He Is Not Here

In a Spanish cemetery there is a monument with a unique and happy design. It is a marble coffin with the lid open, revealing the place where a body *had lain.* A Bible and a cross are shown in the vacated place. Inside the raised lid are engraved these triumphant words: *Non est hic, sed resurrexit!* Translated, the words mean "He is not here, but is risen!"

* * *

The Strife Is Over!

The strife is o'er, the battle done;
The victory of life is won;
The song of triumph has begun.
                    Alleluiah!

The powers of death have done their worst,
But Christ their legions hath dispersed;
Let shouts of holy joy outburst.
                    Alleluiah!

The three sad days have quickly sped:
He rises glorious from the dead;
All glory to our risen Head!
                    Alleluiah!

He brake the bonds of death and hell;
The bars from heaven's high portals fell;
Let hymns of praise His triumph tell.
                    Alleluiah!

Lord, by the stripes which wounded Thee,
From death's dread sting Thy servants free,
That we may live, and sing to Thee.
                    Alleluiah!
                    F. POTT

* * *

Strike Your Harps!

Strike your harps, ye saints on high,
With your anthems fill the sky!

Ye who sang a Saviour born,
Hail His resurrection morn!

Jesus lives the world to save.
Where thy triumph, boasting grave?
Death is vanquished, bound in chains.
Christ our Lord forever reigns!

On this bright and glorious day,
When the faithful meet to pray,
Bring the Easter lilies fair,
Nature's gems of beauty rare!

Let the organ's lofty strain
Thrill our raptured souls again.
Christ hath risen from the tomb,
Clothed in heaven's immortal bloom!
                    FANNY CROSBY

* * *

Dormant for Three Thousand Years

A sealed vase containing some peas was found in the tomb of a mummy in Egypt. The peas were wrinkled and hard as stones, but were planted under a glass. At the end of thirty days, they sprang into life, although they had lain dormant in the dust of a tomb for almost three thousand years.

The Bible says, "And many of them that sleep in the dust of the earth shall awake" (Dan. 12:2).

* * *

Resurgam!

A great conflagration, referred to as the Great Fire, occurred in London in 1666. Afterward, when the site of St. Paul's Cathedral was being cleared, a stone was found in the debris on which was carved the word *resurgam,* meaning "I shall rise again."

The stone was given to Sir Christopher Wren, the renowned architect. *This is a good omen,* he thought. The stone was placed over the south transept door of the new building.

How filled with cheer and comfort for God's children is the word *resurgam!* Because of Christ's triumph over death, they have been "begotten . . . again unto a lively [living] hope by the resurrection of Jesus Christ from the dead" (I Peter 1:3). Because Christ lives, they, too, will live everlastingly!

Deepfreezing Corpses

R. C. W. Ettinger, in his book *The Prospect of Immortality*, presents the theory of cryogenic interment, or the deepfreezing of corpses. He surmises that scientists may devise a freezing method which will not injure body organs so the dead may later be reanimated and rehabilitated. He affirms, however, that it may be some two centuries before science can devise a method to revive, or bring to life again, the frozen corpses! He estimates the cost of deepfreezing a body at about $8,500.

The fertile imagination of man often soars into the realm of fanciful vagaries and macabre speculations. How utterly futile are many of the ephemeral and nonsensical ideas.

How hope-bringing and comforting are the factual disclosures of God's Word in reference to the death of God's children and the resurrection of their bodies at the second coming of Christ: "In Christ shall all be made alive" (I Cor. 15:22); "It [the body] is sown a natural body; it is raised a spiritual body" (v. 44).

The time may be nearer than we think when "the Lord himself shall descend from heaven with a shout . . . and the dead in Christ shall rise" (I Thess. 4:16).

* * *

There's Irrefutable, Evidential Proof

A student of science asked a Christian professor, "Can you prove to me that Jesus Christ rose from the dead?"

"I believe I can," said the professor. "There is unimpeachable, irrefutable, evidential proof. After His triumph, Christ was seen by eyewitnesses. Regarding their testimony, Simon Greenleaf, a Jewish lawyer, said, 'If human evidence is capable of proving anything, then the resurrection of Christ has been proven beyond a shadow of doubt.' Yes, I can prove to you that Christ's victory over death is a historic *fact*, but it will be far better for you if you will ask Him to prove to you that He lives. Pray and ask Christ to reveal Himself to you."

"There Is But One Hope"

Dr. Otto Dibelius, bishop of the Protestant United Church of Berlin—both East and West, kept the flame of Christian hope alive for his people under Nazism and Communism. He was asked, "Do you face the future with pessimism or with optimism?"

Dr. Dibelius replied, "Pessimism and optimism are secular terms. The world is doomed to die! *There is no hope but the risen Christ.* Should the time ever come when I could no longer say, 'The risen Christ is triumphant,' I would lapse into hopelessness!"

* * *

Intellectual Assent Not Enough

A warm friendship developed between a brilliant unsaved lawyer and a prominent minister of New York City. The attorney did not believe in Christ's resurrection.

One day the lawyer asked the minister, "Do you really believe that Christ rose from the dead?"

The minister replied, "I certainly do!" Then he related certain irrefutable proofs of Christ's victory over death, including the testimony of eyewitnesses.

For some time the lawyer, who was accustomed to pondering the validity of evidence, studied the proofs carefully. Relating his conclusion to the minister, he said, "Having weighed carefully and impartially the varied evidence attesting to the resurrection of Christ, I am convinced that He really did rise from the dead. But I am no nearer being a Christian than I was before. I thought the difficulty was in my head. I find that it is really in my *heart*."

A mere intellectual assent to the truths of the gospel is powerless to save us: "For with the heart man believeth unto righteousness" (Rom. 10:10).

Told by WILLIAM EVANS

* * *

"He Is Not Here"

The angel rolled away the stone from Jesus' tomb, not to let the death-conquering Lord emerge, but to let outsiders

269

enter: "He is not here. . . . Come, see the place where the Lord lay" (Matt. 28:6).

Mary wept because Jesus' tomb was empty. Well might she have wept if the tomb had not been empty: "And if Christ be not raised, your faith is vain; ye are yet in your sins" (I Cor. 15:17).

* * *

"If in This Life Only"

William James said, "The great use of a life is to spend it for something that outlasts it."

Count Bismarck stated, "Without the hope of eternal life, this life is not worth the effort of getting dressed in the morning."

Paul said, "If in this life only we have hope in Christ, we are of all men most miserable" (I Cor. 15:19).

* * *

Longings for Immortality

"God never made a fish with fins until He made an ocean for it to swim in. God never made a bird until He made an atmosphere for it to fly in. And God never put the longings for immortality in a soul until He made a heaven to satisfy those longings."

The psalmist said, "My soul thirsteth for God, for the living God; when shall I come and appear before God?" (Ps. 42:2).

* * *

"Wake up, Mommy"

Some time ago in Cleveland, Ohio, newspapers ran the picture of a sad-faced four-year-old girl who was the only witness to the slaying of her mother.

In their effort to apprehend the one who committed the horrible crime, detectives questioned little Donna. She mumbled only a few phrases.

Neighbors found Donna and her one-year-old brother David crying beside their dead mother. Donna was saying, "Wake up, Mommy."

The only One who is sufficiently powerful to bring the dead back to life is Christ who Himself triumphed over death. He has given this word of assurance to all those who enter the portals of death trusting in Him: "Because I live, ye shall live also" (John 14:19).

* * *

Deepfreeze Corpses

Members of the Cryogenic Society of California recently froze the body of a man who had died of lung cancer.

Robert Nelson, president of the cryogenic group, said of the cancer victim, "It was his hope to contribute to scientific experimentation. He hoped that his body could be revived with future techniques at a time when a cure for cancer is available."

It is infinitely better to die with faith in the living Saviour who triumphed over death, and has "begotten us again to a lively hope by . . . [His] resurrection" (I Peter 1:3).

When He comes again "all that are in the graves shall hear his voice, and shall come forth" (John 5:28-29).

* * *

"I Am He That Liveth!"

Renan, a French skeptic, wrote a story of the life of Christ. He ended the story with Christ's death on the cross. There he wrote the word *Finis!* On the flyleaf of the published story was a picture of the dead Christ on the cross. Beneath it was the dismal word *Finis*.

Christ's death was only a passing episode. He rose and "abolished death, and . . . brought life and immortality to light" (II Tim. 1:10).

* * *

Glory Light

Morning light!
Very early in the dawn,
On that resurrection morn,
Hope was dead, but joy was born.
O the light!

"Mary" was the name He said.
"Master!" Gone was all her dread;
He was living, and not dead.
Glory light!

270

Sorry About Your God

Over the entrance of the Wealthy Street Baptist Church, Grand Rapids, Michigan, are these words of special significance to the God-is-dead cultists: "Our God is alive! Sorry about yours."

How radiant and triumphant are those who say with full assurance: "I know that my Redeemer liveth!"

* * *

Variously Supported

Bishop Brooke Foss Westcott said, "Taking all the evidence together, it is not too much to say that there is no single historic incident better or more variously supported than the resurrection of Christ."

Alive! 4/9?

As Dr. Robert W. Dale was preparing his Easter message, the fact of Christ's resurrection thrilled him. He joyously exclaimed, "Christ is alive! He is the great 'I AM' and not the great 'I was'!"

* * *

Nothing Disintegrates

Dr. Wernher von Braun stated, "I believe in an immortal soul. Science has proved that nothing disintegrates into nothingness. Life and soul, therefore, cannot disintegrate into nothingness, and we are immortal."

* * *

The Reason

Dr. Donald G. Barnhouse commented, "The angel rolled away the stone from Jesus' tomb, not to let the living Lord out, but to let unconvinced outsiders in."

REVIVAL

"O God, Do It Again!"

In Nottingham, England, is the Wesleyan chapel where William Booth, founder of the Salvation Army, was converted. A memorial tablet marks the spot where the friend of the friendless was endued with power from on high. Salvation Army leaders from over the world go to visit that sacred place.

One day a Negro, dressed in the uniform of the Salvation Army, entered the chapel and asked the caretaker, "Can a man say his prayers here?"

"Of course he can," was the reply.

The Negro knelt and poured out his heart to God in prayer, saying, "O God, do it again! O God, do it again! Revive Your work in the midst of the years. In wrath remember mercy!"

* * *

A Great Revival Predicted

J. Hudson Taylor, founder of the China Inland Mission, which is now the Overseas Missionary Fellowship, said, "I am convinced that there will be a great spiritual awakening, which will usher in the second coming of Christ!"

Alexander Whyte said, "I may not live to see it, but the day will come when there will be a great revival in the whole world!"

* * *

Crowded Churches and Penitentiaries

Two ministers were commenting on the strange anomaly that, although many of the churches throughout America are crowded, the penitentiaries are crowded also.

Said one, "What America gravely needs today is a resurgence of old-fashioned, heart-transforming, Holy Spirit-convicting and converting religion—a spiritual awakening such as the present generation has not seen."

The other expressed wholehearted agreement, asserting, "Despite our great inventions and our amazing technological

271

and educational advances, the indubitable fact remains that success or failure, sweetness or bitterness, depends entirely on the reaction of our hearts—whether destructive or constructive."

* * *

Needed: A Spiritual Bath

The Cuyahoga County Grand Jury, Cleveland, Ohio, pinpointed the basic cause of general lawlessness throughout the nation in its concluding statements in a recent report:

"We believe in the elevation of moral and ethical standards and conduct, including those in high places in government and in business and in the professions—a general reappraisal of our entire pattern of national life and values.

"What this country and this community need . . . is not so much a blood bath, but a good, cleansing, spiritual bath."

Long ago the prophet Isaiah also spoke of spiritual cleansing, saying, "Come now, and let us reason together, saith the LORD: though your sins be as scarlet, they shall be as white as snow; though they be red like crimson, they shall be as wool" (Isa. 1:18).

A heart-transforming spiritual awakening would do more to heal the ills of our nation than all the politically motivated ideas which fail to reckon with man's basic need—a change of heart and attitude.

* * *

Needed: A Spiritual Renaissance

Sen. Mark O. Hatfield stated, "Only if we can experience a spiritual renaissance in which man sees his need for regeneration through Jesus Christ and not mere reformation through human agencies can we justifiably hope that our plans for peace can be fulfilled."

* * *

It Functioned Without Techniques

Dr. Richard Halverson said, "Evangelism never seemed to be an issue in the New Testament. That is to say, one does not find the apostles urging, exhorting, scolding and organizing for evangelistic programs. It was assumed and it functioned without special techniques. Evangelism happened!"

* * *

The Watershed of British History

In his book *Faith and Freedom*, J. W. Bradley, Canadian historian, said, "In an age when skepticism was dominating the intellectual life, and when the slave trade was poisoning the economic life, John Wesley saved the Anglo-Saxon civilization from moral and spiritual collapse. England after Wesley became a vastly different country from the England before Wesley. The spiritual awakening, of which Wesley was the center, marks the watershed of British and American social history. Had there been no Wesley and no spiritual awakening, it is more than doubtful if there would have been a British Commonwealth of Nations. They would have likely perished as did the old classic civilizations of Greece and Rome through moral decay."

"O LORD, revive thy work in the midst of the years; . . . in wrath remember mercy" (Hab. 3:2).

REWARDS

God Will Not Forget

Though God's children do not serve for reward, it is challenging to know that "God is not unrighteous to forget . . . [their] work and labour of love" (Heb. 6:10). After they become God's children, they are rewarded for service faithfully rendered.

> I will not work my soul to save,
> For that the Lord has done;
> But I will work like any slave,
> For the love of God's dear Son.

Promoted for Service Above

When William Booth died at eighty-three years of age, a placard was placed in the window of the international headquarters of the Salvation Army in London. It read: "The General has laid down his sword!"

Servant of God, well done;
Thy glorious warfare is past.
The battle is fought, the race is run,
And thou art crowned at last!

A good soldier of Jesus Christ had fought valiantly and had entered into the presence of the Captain of his salvation to hear His commendation and receive the crown of life!

* * *

When Our Efforts Seem Futile

A woman who was a great lover of flowers planted a rare vine at the base of a stone wall. It grew rapidly, but there were no blossoms. Though she did her best to coax the vine to blossom, her efforts seemed futile.

One morning her neighbor, who lived on the other side of the wall, said to her, "You can't imagine how much I have been enjoying the gorgeous blooms of the vine you planted!"

The vine had crept through the crevices, and had flowered luxuriantly on the other side of the stone wall.

Often, when we see little or no evidence of our labor of love, God is working silently in the hearts and lives of others and blessing our efforts to help them.

The promise is sure: "He that goeth forth and weepeth, bearing precious seed, shall doubtless come again with rejoicing, bringing his sheaves with him" (Ps. 126:6).

Adapted from *Forward*

* * *

"Just Show Him Your Hands"

A pastor stood by the bedside of a dying, elderly Christian lady who, through the years, had worked hard in a factory. She was uneducated and poor, but she loved Christ and others with all her heart. Through the years, she visited the poor and sick. She often did their washing and ironing at night. In time, her strength failed and her hands became gnarled and twisted with crippling arthritis.

Weeping, the lady said to her pastor, "I have never been able to do much for my Lord, or to give much money for His work. I am afraid that when I appear before the judgment seat of Christ, I will have very little to show Him."

The minister grasped her crippled, gnarled hands and said assuringly, "When you stand before your Lord, just show Him your hands."

* * *

The Unoccupied Niche

In a museum in New York there are niches in which are enshrined busts of illustrious personages, including heroes of the Revolutionary War.

One unoccupied niche never fails to get the quizzical gaze of sightseers. They often inquire, "Why is this niche vacant? For whom is it intended?"

"Oh," responds the guide, "that niche was for Benedict Arnold, but he betrayed his country. His traitorous act is perpetuated in this unique way."

God's children, because of unfaithfulness, may forfeit heavenly rewards and Christ's commendation.

"Hold that fast which thou hast, that no man take thy crown" (Rev. 3:11).

* * *

Approved or Disapproved

During my chaplaincy at the U.S. Northeastern Penitentiary, Lewisburg, Pennsylvania, the inmates would come to me in the chaplain's office every Friday for help with their burdens and problems. Sometimes those whose applications for parole had been approved would come joyfully. Others whose applications had been disapproved would come dejectedly.

Paul had a fear of being disapproved. He said, "I . . . so run, not as uncertainly. . . . I keep under my body, and bring it into subjection: lest that by any means . . . I myself should be a castaway [disapproved]" (I Cor. 9:26-27).

Each one of God's children must appear before the judgment seat of Christ, where his works for Him will be appraised. Will you hear there His words of approbation, "Well done, good and faithful servant," or will you be disapproved, though saved "so as by fire"

(I Cor. 3:15)? Oh, the tragedy of a saved soul and a squandered life!

W. B. K.

* * *

In Eternity

Said John Wesley, "The real value of a thing is the price it will bring in eternity."

RICHES

(*See also* Covetousness)

How Does God Measure a Man?

David Lloyd George, prime minister of England, once spoke in a meeting in South Wales. The chairman of the meeting, who had never met him before, said in presenting him, "I have heard so much about him that I naturally expected him to be a big man. But you can see for yourselves that he is small in stature."

The prime minister said in reply, "I am grieved that your chairman is disappointed in my size, but this is because of his way of measuring a man. In North Wales we measure a man from his *chin up*, but evidently your chairman measures a man from his *chin down*."

How does God measure a man? Not by his wealth: "Let not the rich man glory in his riches" (Jer. 9:23); not by his boastful appraisal of himself: "God, I thank thee that I am not as other men are" (Luke 18:11).

Those who serve God and others unselfishly and sacrificially are adjudged great by God. They emulate the example of their Lord who said: "Even . . . the Son of man came not to be ministered unto, but to minister" (Matt. 20:28).

* * *

Where Their Folly Lay

Many thrilling stories have been told about the Klondike gold rush. This one is most impressive.

One day a prospecting party, penetrating far into the Klondike, came upon a miner's hut. Entering the hut, they found the frozen bodies of two men and a large quantity of gold. On a table there was a letter which told of the successful search for the precious ore. In their eagerness to mine the gold, the miners had neglected to make provision for the coming of winter.

Each day the two men found gold in abundance. One morning they awoke and saw that a blizzard had come. For days the tempest raged. All hope of escape left when their little store of food was gone. They wrote the letter and lay down to die in the midst of abounding gold!

The miners' folly was not in finding and gathering gold, but in neglecting to provide for the coming of winter. How like them are those who make no provision for the coming winter of death.

* * *

If I Could

If I could know, when each day dies,
    I had brought joy to tired eyes;
If I could know, when falls each night,
    I'd helped to make some child's life bright;
If I could know, at set of sun,
    The fruit of some good deed I'd done;
I'd count my life of grander mold
    Than if I'd simply gathered gold.

EDWIN CARLILE

* * *

The Things I Valued Most

One by one He took them from me,
    All the things I valued most,
Until I was empty-handed,
    Every glittering toy was lost.
And I walked earth's highways, grieving,
    In my rags and poverty,

274

Till I heard His voice inviting,
  "Lift your empty hands to Me!"

So I held my hands toward heaven,
  And He filled them with His store
Of His own transcendent riches
  Until my hands could hold no more.
And at last I comprehended
  With my mind so slow and dull
That God could not pour His riches
  Into hands already full.

MARTHA SNELL NICHOLSON

* * *

The Greatest Riches

After a disastrous fire, a man's business lay in smoldering ruins. In the midst of the charred debris he placed a large placard with these words: "Everything lost except wife, children, hope, and faith in God. Business will be resumed as usual soon."

* * *

Defeating Trivialities

When a man was taking some currency from his wallet to pay for a purchase in a store in Indianapolis, two pennies fell to the floor. Stooping to pick up the pennies, he unintentionally left his wallet on the counter. When he arose, the wallet containing more than fifty dollars was gone.

Often the trivialities of life so preempt our time that we miss the abiding, abundant riches which God bestows upon His obedient children: "The blessing of the LORD, it maketh rich, and he addeth no sorrow" (Prov. 10:22).

* * *

"Blessed with All Spiritual Blessings"

Dr. F. B. Meyer said, "Always distinguish between the words *attain* and *obtain*. We can never attain or earn God's gracious help by prayer or service, but we can obtain, appropriate and take it. Learn to put your hand on all spiritual blessings in Christ and say, 'Mine.'"

How spiritually rich are God's obedient and submissive children: "Heirs of God, and joint-heirs with Christ; if so be that we suffer with him" (Rom. 8:17).

Spiritually Dead

A wealthy financier said to Dr. George W. Truett, "You think I have won in life's race, don't you?"

Dr. Truett replied, "Yes, in a way, you have."

With an anguished look on his face, the financier said, "The world says that I have won and am a business success." Then, after a moment of tense silence, he forlornly said, "I would give every dollar I have if I could weep about my spiritual condition like I did when I was a boy. But I have so completely given myself to accumulating a fortune that I have neglected my soul. Now I seem to be dead to spiritual things."

"A man's life consisteth not in the abundance of the things which he possesseth" (Luke 12:15).

He always said he would retire
  When he had made a million clear;
So he toiled from dusk to dusk,
  From day to day, from year to year.

At last he put his ledgers up
  And laid stock reports aside;
But when he started out to live,
  He found out he had already died.

* * *

An Old Man's Lament

When David Livingstone died in Africa, his body was brought back to London. The funeral cortege wended its way through the streets of London. Thousands of spectators stood silently and reverently as the procession passed.

One old man wept uncontrollably. A bystander said, "Sir, you seem completely brokenhearted. Was Dr. Livingstone your relative?"

The old man replied, "No, but he was a friend. He and I finished college together. We were both equally prepared. He gave himself to God to serve Him as a missionary in Africa. I decided to use my abilities to become rich and famous. I amassed wealth and succeeded in my profession. Wouldn't it break your heart if you had lived only for the empty, passing glory of this world, as I have done?"

Pocketless Shrouds

Some time ago, in Chicago, a hoard of cash was found in the rear bedroom of a dead policy wheel operator's home. It totaled $763,223.30. Weary policemen worked in shifts for nearly eighteen hours counting the thick stacks of bills. A high-speed change counter was brought in to count the mounds of coins.

Lawrence Wakefield, age sixty-eight, who had amassed the fortune and stashed it away, died suddenly of a heart attack. Said one of the investigating officers, "The money was everywhere—scattered all over the room—on the floor, on the bed, in shopping bags, wrapped in rolls, and loose."

The windows of the house were covered with wire mesh and five watchdogs were kept inside.

Material riches are left behind in death: "For we brought nothing into this world, and it is certain we can carry nothing out" (I Tim. 6:7). God's children lay up their riches in heaven by using them for God and others.

* * *

God or Gold, Which?

How revealing and interpretative of character is George Frederick Watts' painting of the rich young ruler to whom Christ said, "If thou wilt be perfect, go and sell that thou hast, and give to the poor, and thou shalt have treasure in heaven; and come and follow me" (Matt. 19:21).

In the painting, the rich young ruler's head is bowed, depicting thought. The back of his right arm and hand is shown clearly. The fingers are bedecked with costly rings. The hand is half open and half closed, indicative of conflicting desires to give up his wealth and obey Jesus' command, "Follow me," or to selfishly cling to his riches.

Refusing to meet Jesus' terms of discipleship, the rich young ruler retreated from the Saviour with sorrow. He loved gold more than he loved God. He made a disastrous choice.

How different it was with Moses of whom the Bible says, "By faith Moses . . . refused to be called the son of Phar-aoh's daughter; . . . esteeming the reproach of Christ greater riches than the treasures in Egypt" (Heb. 11:24-26).

* * *

Of Royal Lineage

In one of his essays, Charles Lamb tells of an aged, indigent couple who always walked with courtly dignity. Those who saw them wondered what could be the explanation of their mien. Were their ancestors members of the nobility?

The explanation of the courtly manner and dignified bearing of the couple was that they were lineal descendants of a member of the nobility. That's why they held their heads high through adversity.

God's children are members of heavenly royalty—"heirs of God, and joint-heirs with Christ" (Rom. 8:17).

What a privilege it is to be the sons and daughters of the most high God! How rich they are!

Told by HARRY A. IRONSIDE

* * *

Go Easy

Dr. John R. Rice stated, "My little girls often came to me and told me about their needs—clothes, shoes, money for music lessons, and many other things. At times I was compelled to say, 'Go easy! I'm not made out of money. We'll just have to get what we can afford and go without the rest.'

"God never says, 'Go easy! I can't give you as much as you ask.' We don't ask enough."

Thou art coming to a King;
Large petitions with thee bring,
For His grace and power are such,
None can ever ask too much.

* * *

Money Talks Back

"They do me an injustice who say that I am the cause of all the woes in the world. I am an obedient servant, running on whatever errands I am sent. I am always under orders. Give me an opportunity and I will build the highways of peace by which humanity may enter the kingdom of God. Loose me and let me go, and I will carry healing to the suffering victims of hate and malice around the world. Open the doors for me, and I will build hospitals, train nurses, care for little children, comfort the aged, and provide food for hungry multitudes. I know no color lines. I serve all men with equal fidelity. Give me a chance, and I will train youths in the highest and holiest ideals of Christian living.

"Just a little of me is necessary to build churches and schools and orphanages. Much of me is necessary if invested in police courts and penal institutions. Make me an ally of righteousness, and I will do much to impart joy and bring in the kingdom of God.

"I am power. I am waiting to be either your servant or enslave you. Be wise—hold your dollars in trust for God."

Religious Telescope

* * *

All Things Are Mine

Oh, matchless mercy that rates me
   Joint-heir with the sinless Son!
Oh, golden glory that awaits me
   When tempests and clouds are done!

All things are mine, for I am His,
   Oh, infinite gifts divine!
He gave His Son, His only one,
   And all that He has is mine!

ANNIE JOHNSON FLINT

* * *

He Left the Methodist Church

When John Wesley died, he left few material things: a silver teapot, two silver spoons, and a well-worn frock coat. He left, however, a great spiritual heritage—the Methodist church.

* * *

No Time to Make Money

Professor Agassiz, famed naturalist, said, "I have no time to make money. Life is not sufficiently long to enable a man to get rich and do his duty to his fellowmen."

Pope Paul IV said of John Calvin, "What made the strength of this heretic has been that money could never reach him."

Riches of No Worth

It is said that Mrs. Owen Robertson Cheatham and her husband own $5,000,000 worth of Salvador Dali jewelry. The collection consists of thirty-six pieces. The fabulous jewels bear revealing names such as "living flower," "honeycomb heart," "the bleeding world," "eye of time" and "the persistence of memory." When the jewels are not being displayed for charity, they are kept in a New York bank vault.

Asked if she ever wears any of the jewels, Mrs. Cheatham said, "Goodness gracious no! I never wear them."

Though these jewels are dazzlingly beautiful and of great value, they are perishable, and will be of no worth to their owners after they enter the valley of death.

* * *

The Safest Repository

The warehouse of two young businessmen in California burned. Forgetful of their safety, they dashed into the burning building to retrieve money and some important papers from the open vault. They entered the vault and closed the door behind them to keep out the smoke and heat.

Gathering up the currency and papers, they tried to push open the door, but they couldn't. The heat had expanded the iron door and it could not be budged. No one outside could reach them through the flames. They perished. When they were later reached, they held in their lifeless hands the currency and valuable papers.

How worthless are riches in death. The safest repository for our riches is in heaven, where we may lay them up by investing them for God here.

* * *

While a Beggar Starved

How tragic it is for people to forget their accountability to God as did the rich man of old who was "clothed in purple and fine linen, and fared sumptuously every day" (Luke 16:19), while a beggar starved at his door. One-half of the world goes to bed hungry every night.

"How Unsearchable Are His . . . Ways"

When Amy Carmichael went to India in 1895, she did not realize that for fifty-five years India would be her home and the children of India her beloved family. Nor did she know then that many beautiful, intelligent little girls in India were taken from their homes and trained to become temple women to satisfy the lusts of men in the degrading worship of the Hindu gods. She first learned of the horrible custom in 1901 when a seven-year-old girl who had escaped from the temple was brought to her house. "What she told me darkened the sunlight," said Miss Carmichael.

From that day, the Lord laid upon her heart the burden to save these girls from moral ruin and train them to do the will of her heavenly Father.

In 1931 Miss Carmichael slipped into a pit, broke her leg and dislocated her ankle. For nearly twenty years, she was an invalid and rarely left her room.

On the morning of the accident, she had submissively prayed, "Do anything, Lord, that will fit me to serve Thee and help these beloved children."

In her confinement she wrote thirteen books. The most challenging and faith-strengthening of them were *Gold by Moonlight, Rose from Brier* and *If.*

* * *

Not an Accident, but an Incident

A minister was seriously injured in an automobile accident. Hours later, he regained consciousness as he lay on a hospital bed. He asked, "Nurse, why am I here?"

She whispered, "Be very quiet! You have had an accident."

Later, during his convalescence, the minister said, "That wasn't an accident! It was only an *incident!*"

My Father's ways may twist and turn,
  My heart may throb and ache,
But in my soul I'm glad to know
  He maketh no mistake!

God's Dawn

Hilaire Belloc and a friend were once crossing the Pyrenees into Spain. Late one evening they reached a point high up on the mountains, erected a small tent, and went to sleep. Presently they were awakened by a terrific storm. Their tent was blown down, stones were hurled down the mountainside, and they managed to stay where they were only by digging their hands and feet in the scrub.

Belloc's friend whispered, "I believe it is the end of the world!"

Belloc, who had been there before, replied in a joyful tone, "Oh, no, this is how the dawn comes to the Pyrenees."

God's dawn sometimes comes to His children, as the dawn comes to the Pyrenees, with a fearful and shattering experience—sorrow, suffering and the seeming miscarriage of cherished plans. The dawn will come, however. This is certain: "As for God, his way is perfect" (Ps. 18:30).

Told by Rita F. Snowden

* * *

The Veiled Future

If we could push ajar the gates of life
  And stand within and all God's working see,
We might interpret all the doubt and strife,
  And for each mystery would find a key.

But not today. Then be content, dear heart:
  God's plans, like lilies, pure and white unfold.
We must not tear the close-shut petals apart;
  Time will reveal the calyxes of gold.

And when through patient toil we reach the land
  Where tired feet, with sandals loosed, may rest,
When we shall clearly know and understand,
  We'll rejoicingly say that God knew best.

278

"Past Finding Out"

One dark, stormy night many years ago, a train carrying hundreds of passengers suddenly plunged into the raging waters which flowed under a weakened bridge! Many bodies were washed out to sea and were never recovered.

On that ill-fated train, one of the passengers went on the rear platform of the train as it stopped on approaching the trestle. His hat was blown off. He quickly leaped from the platform to recover it. The train moved on, and he was left standing in the tempest. As the taillights of the receding train disappeared into the darkness, he raged furiously. Then he sought cover in the darkness. It was not until the next morning that he learned that he alone of all the passengers had survived!

Why was only one man saved? Only God knows the answer. Some of God's ways are inscrutable. In wonder we exclaim, "O the depth of the riches both of the wisdom and knowledge of God! how unsearchable are his judgments, and his ways past finding out!" (Rom. 11:33).

Adapted from *Senior Bible Teacher*

* * *

Some Soul Is Glad

Whichever way the wind doth blow,
Some soul is glad to have it so;
Then blow it east, or blow it west,
The wind that blows that wind is best.

SACRIFICE

The Mangled Arm

During the nineteenth century, it was the custom of students in universities in Scotland to make jesting remarks about the recipients of honorary degrees.

When the self-sacrificing missionary, David Livingstone, was home on furlough, he was chosen to receive an honorary degree. Some wondered what the students would say when he stood to receive the degree.

As Livingstone stood before the student body, they observed his arm hanging limply from the shoulder. The arm had been mangled when Livingstone was attacked by a lion in Africa. The students involuntarily stood en masse—silently, reverently and admiringly.

* * *

She Couldn't Save Herself

In the early spring of 1919, a country school near Center, North Dakota, was dismissed early because of a raging blizzard. Hazel Miner, one of the older pupils, started home in a buggy with her two little brothers. In the raging tempest, the buggy turned over and the horse got loose. Hazel wrapped her little brothers in blankets. They got beneath the overturned buggy. As night came on, the blizzard raged. The cold became more intense. The noble girl removed her coat and spread it and herself over the boys.

When rescued the next day, the boys were living. The sister had frozen to death!

How noble and enduring is self-sacrificial love for others! In saving others, Hazel could not save herself, neither could the Saviour who died a vicarious death for the sin of the world.

* * *

Count No Sacrifice Too Costly

During a raging blizzard in Strasburg, North Dakota, farmer Eugene Welk, a distant relative of Lawrence Welk, pushed his way through snow twelve feet deep in search of his six-year-old daughter. The blizzard was said to be the worst in the Dakotas in the past half century. After hours of searching, Mr. Welk found his daughter's frozen body standing upright.

How commendable was that noble father who hazarded his own life in his search of his daughter! How praiseworthy also are those who count no sacrifice too dear to find the spiritually lost and bring them to the good Shepherd's fold! Each one of God's children is needed for this important and rewarding endeavor.

The Bible says that Paul and Barnabas "hazarded their lives for the name of our Lord Jesus Christ" (Acts 15:26). Should we do less?

* * *

Perish the Thought

David Livingstone said, "I have suffered severe attacks of fever no fewer than twenty-seven times in the space of two and one-half years. These sicknesses, I beg you to observe, are not mentioned as if I considered them in the light of sacrifice. Perish the thought! I think the word *sacrifice* ought never to be mentioned in reference to anything we can do for Christ who, though He was rich, yet for our sake became poor."

* * *

Risky and Dangerous

At the entrance of a driveway leading to a church is a sign which reads Enter at Your Own Risk.

How intriguing is the sign! Though placed there for a different purpose, it could proclaim the fact that church affiliation, if it means what it ought to mean—separation from sin and utter dedication to God—could be risky and dangerous. Discipleship costs something. Many have hazarded their lives to follow Christ: "Men that have hazarded their lives for the name of our Lord Jesus Christ" (Acts 15:26). Some have forfeited their lives to follow Him: "They loved not their lives unto the death" (Rev. 12:11).

She Gave Her Best

As a missionary spoke to a congregation in a Kurdish village, he was fascinated by the faces of a poor washerwoman and her son, an intelligent and outstanding boy.

At the close of the service, the missionary asked the mother, "Do you love Christ?"

She replied, "Oh, missionary, I have little. Yet all I earn I give to Christ, save for food for myself and my little boy."

The missionary questioned her further. "Would you give your little boy to Christ?"

She replied, "He is my all—my life!"

As he left, the missionary said, "Think seriously about it tonight and pray."

The following day the missionary returned to the village. During the day, he was very busy. When he mounted his horse to leave, he observed a most wonderful sight. The mother came, leading her boy by the hand. She placed a little bundle of the boy's clothing, on which she had worked all night, at the missionary's feet and said, as she pointed upward, only two words, "Thomas, Christos!" She meant, "I give him to Christ." Then she turned to go back to her lonely life.

At the mission school, Thomas studied hard. He soon led his class. When he graduated, he returned to the Kurdish mountains and to his mother who had prayed and waited for him.

The natives called him the prophet of Kurdistan. His mother's sacrifice bore much fruit as Thomas preached the gospel and helped hundreds of orphans and widows.

Condensed from *Youth's Companion*

SALVATION

Things Cannot Satisfy

Eleanor Searle Whitney, a woman of culture, refinement and wealth, had many things—riding stables, yachts, summer homes, apartments, hunting and fishing lodges, and an exciting social life. She enjoyed the distinction of being one of the best-dressed women in the nation.

She was active in humanitarian causes, lived a moral life and was a regular attendant at church services.

One day she made the discovery that mere things cannot satisfy or fill the spiritual emptiness of the heart. She knew that she was spiritually poverty-stricken.

She began to attend a Billy Graham crusade in New York City. One night Graham gave an invitation to unsaved ones to confess Christ. A struggle ensued in her soul. She thought, *What will my friends think if I go forward? How ridiculous it all seems!*

Later she did go forward, and Christ came into her life. She joyfully said, "Imagine being able to go to the Bible and hear God say, 'I will never leave you nor forsake you. . . . Lo, I am with you always. . . . My strength cometh from the Lord!' I hung onto God and found He was enough!"

Today Eleanor Whitney is a radiant Christian. She speaks to many different audiences—to liberals, conservatives and the nonreligious. In all of them she tells the story of her personal conversion and of God's offer of salvation to all who will believe. News correspondents describe her thus: "She is a fireball, an evangelist and a lovely lady." One said, "Her story is so convincing I found myself forgetting to describe what she was wearing, and jotted down Ephesians 2:8-9 and John 3:16."

Told by GLADYS M. HUNT

* * *

"A New Heart Will I Give You"

In December, 1967, the first successful heart transplant occurred in Groote Schuur Hospital in South Africa. Louis Washkansky, a fifty-five-year-old Jewish man, was dying because his heart was damaged beyond repair. Medics gave him only a few days to live. The well heart of Denise Ann Darvall, age twenty-four, was quickly removed from her body after her death from an automobile accident. The damaged heart of Washkansky was removed and her heart was placed in his chest.

The transplanted heart was started beating by an electric shock. "It was like turning the ignition switch of a car," said Dr. Jan H. Louw, the hospital's chief surgeon.

Through the redemptive work of Christ, God gives new hearts to all who trust in the Saviour. How wonderful is the promise He gave long ago: "A new heart . . . will I give you. . . . I will take away the stony heart out of your flesh. . . . I will put my spirit within you" (Ezek. 36:26-27).

Washkansky lived for eighteen days with the transplanted heart. When God gives penitent ones a new heart, they live eternally. Said death's Conqueror, Jesus, "I give unto them eternal life; and they shall never perish" (John 10:28).

* * *

"I Want to Live!"

For two years Grisha Sikalenko, a Ukrainian who deserted the Russian army, existed under a dung heap. Then one day he rushed forth, malodorous and emaciated, crying, "I want to live! I want to live!"

The first night in army camp, Grisha had deserted. He had sneaked home to the strange hiding place his parents had devised for him—the manure pile at the back of the goat shed! His mother said to him, "Don't mind the goats and the dung. At least you'll survive." He did— for two years in this horrible hiding place.

Astonished neighbors reported the almost unbelievable story to the Soviet newspaper *Izvestia,* and Grisha was apprehended. All his village had thought he died a hero's death fighting the Germans.

Long ago David said, "They are all together become filthy" (Ps. 14:3). Each one of us needs cleansing. In God's sight the moral sinner and the immoral sinner are equally defiled. Thank God for the cleansing fount!

* * *

Chemical Salvation

Prof. B. F. Skinner of Harvard University said, "We are entering the age of the chemical control of human behavior. The motivational and emotional conditions of normal daily life will probably be maintained in any desired state through the use of drugs."

Until man's "deceitful and desperately wicked" heart is changed by God's grace, he will continue in his sinful way.

Popular Pastor Is Revitalized

Years ago a well-known minister in England was called late one night to visit a dying woman in one of the poorest sections of London. After reaching her wretched apartment, he sat beside her bed and sought to comfort her by speaking of hope, courage, patience and good deeds—things which had been the substance of his preaching for some time.

The dying woman interrupted him, saying, "All you say is true, but it is of little or no help to me now. I'm a dying woman and I'm not ready to die. Just tell me how a poor sinner can get into heaven."

In his earlier years, the minister had preached Christ as the only way to eternal life. Simply he told the dying woman the story of the cross. Later, in relating the incident, the minister said, "She saw the light. She accepted Christ as her only hope of eternal life. Now I see the folly of preaching anything less than Christ crucified. He is the sinner's only hope of salvation!"

Told by HARRY A. IRONSIDE

* * *

Jesus Came to Save Cinders

In the Pacific Garden Mission, a man who had almost made shipwreck of his life stood and unintentionally misquoted this verse: "This is a faithful saying, and worthy of all acceptation, that Christ Jesus came into the world to save *cinders; of whom I am chief*" (I Tim. 1:15).

How grateful we are that the Saviour did come to save blasted, burned-out lives. He came to give "beauty for ashes" (Isa. 61:3).

* * *

Spiritual Euphoria

In a futile effort to circumvent the changeless scriptural requirement of conversion, some today have advanced the idea that certain drugs can bring about an inward or spiritual change, producing a feeling of euphoria, or well-being. They assert that a more vivid and profound spiritual change can be produced by chemical means than by the biblical means of having sorrow for sin and trusting in the Saviour.

What vagaries the spiritually darkened mind of man can conjure up! How aptly and accurately the Bible speaks of the spiritually darkened heart and mind: "They . . . became vain in their imaginations, and their foolish heart was darkened" (Rom. 1:21).

Truly "the god of this . . . [age] hath blinded the minds of them which believe not, lest the light of the glorious gospel of Christ . . . should shine unto them" (II Cor. 4:4).

Apart from the transforming grace of God, the heart of man will continue to be "deceitful above all things, and desperately wicked" (Jer. 17:9). For confirmation of this fact, read your daily newspaper.

* * *

"I'll Exchange You"

An aged Scot told how he was converted: "When I was sixty years old, the Lord Jesus said to me, 'Sandy, I'll exchange you!' Then he took my misspent life and gave me a new life."

* * *

"It's Supernatural"

A girl from a Christless home attended a Bible class and was converted. Her unbelieving parents ridiculed her. "It is not natural for a young girl like you to be religious," they said.

The girl replied, "The change of heart I have experienced is not natural—it's supernatural! It is altogether from God. By His help I'll never go back to my former life."

Time passed. Her parents, observing the wonderful change which had taken place in her life, said, "Mary's experience must be real. She is so different now. She even gets up early every morning to pray and study her Bible before going to school. Formerly she was lazy and we had trouble getting her out of bed for school."

* * *

Physical and Spiritual Life

Newspapers over the nation publicized the spectacular accomplishment of Drs. Arthur Kornberg, Robert L. Sinscheimer and Mehran Goulian, California biochemists, in moving closer to the creation of life in a test tube and opening the way to speedier advances in man's quest to solve the mysteries of life, disease and death.

God gives physical and spiritual life. How filled with mystery is the beginning of physical life! When God created man, He "breathed into his nostrils the breath of life; and man became a living soul" (Gen. 2:7). Equally wonderful and mysterious is the beginning of spiritual life!

* * *

"God Must Do It or Else"

In striving to achieve enlightenment, self-knowledge and perfection, Stephen Shlafer, a twenty-five-year-old Jew in Saigon, became a Buddhist monk. He said, "It's hard work. Half the time during the ritual I kept on worrying that my inner robe would fall off."

Shlafer's day begins with a vitamin pill to supplement his Vietnamese diet of rice and soup.

Since the beginning of time, man has sought to improve by self-effort, self-mortification and self-imposed tortures. Martin Luther fasted, scourged himself and underwent great privation. He became emaciated in body and broken in health. Then the light broke upon his darkened soul, and he exclaimed, "He that made the heavens must do this, or it will remain forever undone." God revealed to him the soul-liberating truth that "the just shall live by his faith" (Hab. 2:4) and be justified before God.

* * *

What Is Mud?

Said John Ruskin in *Ethics of Dust,* "What can mud become when God takes it in hand? What is mud? Mud is clay and sand, and usually soot, and a little water. When God takes it in hand He transforms the clay into a sapphire, for a sapphire is just that. He transforms the sand into an opal, for that is the analysis of an opal. He transforms the soot into a diamond, for a diamond is just carbon which has been transformed by God. He transforms the muddy water into a bright snow crystal, for that is what the crystals are when God takes the soiled water up into heaven and sends it back again."

God transforms sin-soiled souls by His marvelous grace.

* * *

"If I Could Be Born Again"

A friend of a minister's wife came to her deeply disturbed. After relating her story of failure and frustration, she tearfully said, "If only I could be born again!"

The new birth, thank God, can be realized by anyone who will penitently turn from sin to the Saviour, and thus become a new creature in Christ.

* * *

"I Tried to Save Her!"

During the World War II blitz in London, a woman stood by an open window in the top story of a blazing building. An escape ladder was quickly run up. A brave fireman made his way to the top. He leaned with outstretched arms to take the woman to safety, but she retreated in terror. The flames enveloped her, and the noble fireman returned without her. Weeping, he said, "I tried to save her, but she wouldn't let me."

If you are eternally lost, it won't be because God failed to make provision for your eternal safety and salvation in Christ.

HYMAN J. APPELMAN

* * *

God Works from the Inside

A little boy asked, "Why is it that when I open a marigold it dies, but if God does it, it's so beautiful?"

Before the question could be answered, the boy said, "I know! It's because God always works from the *inside.*"

That is the way God works with men— from the inside. Men with "deceitful and desperately wicked" hearts cannot be changed by outward reformation.

The basic need of sinful man is inward cleansing. Isn't it significant that Jesus said to a religious, moral man, "Ye must be born again" (John 3:7)?

Society will be Christianized in proportion to the conversion of individuals.

"I'm Looking for God"

A missionary in Thailand asked a national who came to his home, "Do you want medicine?"

"No," the man replied.

"Are you looking for the doctor?" he asked.

"No, I'm looking for God!" was the cry from the native's heart.

How easy it is for the sincere seeker to find God: "And ye shall seek me, and find me, when ye shall search for me with all your heart" (Jer. 29:13).

* * *

Christ Must Be Born in Us

Though Christ a thousand times
  In Bethlehem be born,
If He's not born in thee,
  Thy soul is still forlorn.

ANGELIUS SILESIUS

* * *

Mr. Chandranondnaiwinit

A candidate for a master's degree in pharmacy at the University of Oklahoma claimed the distinction of having the longest name ever to go on a diploma at the university: Winita Chandranondnaiwinit. He was from Bangkok, Thailand.

In the nomenclature of the Bible, the student's name is reduced to the inclusive word used for all mankind in God's wondrous offer of salvation and eternal life—*whosoever:* "And whosoever will, let him take the water of life freely" (Rev. 22:17).

* * *

"I Dare You to Go Forward"

Two boys sat together in church during a revival meeting. When the invitation was given to the unsaved to confess Christ, one of the boys said to the other, "I dare you to go forward." It is hard for a boy not to take a dare. So the boy went forward. Later he was baptized. He did not experience any change of heart, however.

In his teens, the boy decided to enter full-time Christian service. Yet in his heart he knew that he had never experienced the miracle of regeneration. God's Spirit seemed to say to him, "You have not done the main thing."

When nineteen years of age, the boy returned to the church during another revival meeting and sat in the same pew where he had sat as a lad of nine. There he was convicted of sin and was gloriously saved.

Told by GEORGE W. TRUETT

* * *

The Most Comforting Word

Richard Baxter said, "The word *whosoever* is the most comforting word in the Bible to me. If God had said there was mercy for Richard Baxter, I am so great a sinner that I would have thought He meant some other person with the same name. But when God says 'whosoever,' I know that He included me, the worst of all Richard Baxters."

* * *

"Then Jesus Came"

Dr. Oswald Smith was present when A. H. Ackley and Homer Rodeheaver discussed a sermon Dr. Harry Rimmer delivered on "Then Jesus Came."

With the words glowing in his heart, Dr. Smith went to his office and wrote the words of the hope-kindling hymn "Then Jesus Came." Homer Rodeheaver wrote the music. As long as time lasts, the hymn will bring its message of deliverance to sin-shackled ones.

One sat alone beside the highway begging,
  His eyes were blind, the light he could not see;
He clutched his rags and shivered in the shadows,
  Then Jesus came and bade his darkness flee!

So men today have found the Saviour able,
  They could not conquer passion, lust and sin;
Their broken hearts had left them sad and lonely,
  Then Jesus came and dwelt Himself within!

Great changes occur in hearts and homes when Jesus enters them!

284

A Transformed Society

L. Nelson Bell, in *Christianity Today,* stated, "People whose lives have been transformed would do more to right the ills of the world than all the hosts of unregenerate people whose efforts are directed toward a reformed society rather than a transformed society."

* * *

Lopping off Twigs and Branches

Thoreau said, "There are thousands striking at the branches of evil and few striking at the roots."

John said, "And now also the axe is laid unto the root of the trees" (Luke 3:9).

Jesus said, "Either make the tree good, and his fruit good; or else make the tree corrupt, and his fruit corrupt: for the tree is known by his fruit" (Matt. 12:33).

* * *

God Tailors the Man

God does not tailor the robe of righteousness to fit the man. He remakes the man to fit the robe: "If any man be in Christ, he is a new creature: old things are passed away; behold, all things are become new" (II Cor. 5:17).

The most righteous thing an unregenerate man can do apart from the righteousness of Christ is, in God's sight, as filthy rags: "But we are all as an unclean thing, and all our righteousnesses are as filthy rags" (Isa. 64:6).

* * *

A Cesspool of Iniquity

How factual and revealing of the futility of getting rid of evils without a change of heart is Hawthorne's story *Earth's Holocaust.*

The inhabitants of the earth, overburdened with an accumulation of vain, deceptive, paltry things, determined to get rid of them in a general bonfire. Throughout the night they tossed things they considered sinful on the fire—obscene books, implements of war, liquor, tobacco and various other evils.

Late in the night, one who had watched the procedure with a cynical smile approached and said, "There is one thing that you have failed to throw into the fire, without which all the rest of the conflagration amounts to nothing, though you may burn the earth itself to cinders."

He was asked, "And what may that be?"

"The human heart," was the reply. "Unless you devise some method of purifying that foul cavern, there will issue from it all the evils you have consumed to ashes and vastly worse ones!"

What a cesspool of iniquity is the unchanged heart—"deceitful above all things, and desperately wicked" (Jer. 17:9). For confirmation, read your daily newspaper.

Until the heart of man is changed, human relationships will worsen. Application of outward restraints will fail, and glaring inequalities and agelong wrongs will go unrectified.

When the love of God is in our heart, we will practice goodwill and show unfeigned love toward all people.

The heart-transforming, character-strengthening gospel of Christ is mankind's "last, best hope!"

* * *

"Wilt Thou Be Made Whole?"

This question was the text of a minister who spoke one night in the Pacific Garden Mission. A man who had all but wrecked his life by drink was present. He had many times resolved to do better, but to no avail. He thought, *I've been putting on patch after patch—making good resolves and turning over a new leaf —but the patches all fell off.*

That night the man sought and found the Saviour. He was made perfectly whole and became a new creature in Christ: "If any man be in Christ, he is a new creature" (II Cor. 5:17).

* * *

A Close-up of the Human Heart

A naval officer testified, "I was brought up in a Christian home. The Bible was read and prayer was offered daily. The home atmosphere worked no spiritual change in me.

"Later I entered business. My work

took me to the Orient. There I was employed as a photographer, taking pictures of objects in nature. I met a Chinese who was also a photographer. I spoke to him in Chinese. He replied in perfect English. He asked, 'Have you ever taken a close-up of the human heart?'

" 'No,' I replied.

" 'Oh,' he said, 'let me show you one.'

"Opening his Bible, he read, 'The heart is deceitful above all things, and desperately wicked' [Jer. 17:9].

"For the first time, I realized my need of Christ and His cleansing blood. I sought Him, and His peace came to me."

* * *

"O Taste and See!"

A grateful patient who had been brought through a serious illness asked the physician, who was a Christian, to write in her autograph album.

"May I write a prescription?" cheerfully asked the physician.

"Write what you wish," said the patient.

He wrote, "O taste and see that the LORD is good: blessed is the man that trusteth in him" (Ps. 34:8).

* * *

Religion Is Not Enough

A minister pleaded with a young man to accept Christ. The young man said, "I've tried religion for the past five years. It hasn't worked and I've given it up."

To the astonishment of the young man, the minister said, "I tried religion for fifteen years, and it did nothing for me. Discouraged, I gave it up."

"Then why are you a minister?" the young man asked.

The minister replied, "After dismally failing with mere religion, I tried Christ. He fully met my spiritual yearnings. Now I can testify, 'For me to live is Christ.' "

Told by HENRIETTA MEARS

* * *

A Terrifying Trap

In quest of parasitic plants one summer, two college students—Jack Pickett and Fred Stahl—entered the low swampy land south of Florida's Lake Okeechobee. As they walked along the sandbank of a small stream, Pickett, who was ahead, suddenly cried, "It's soft here! Stay back!"

What seemed to be sunbaked sand was quicksand! Pickett sank up to his ankles. He struggled forward a few more steps in an effort to get onto firm ground. With each step, however, he sank deeper. The sand rose to his knees. He shouted, "It's quicksand! Help me!"

Stahl knew if he plunged into the quicksand, both of them would be trapped. Quickly he searched for a tree branch. Pickett continued to struggle to extricate himself from the ghastly trap, but to no avail. Slowly he toppled forward!

Finding a branch, Stahl raced back to his imperiled companion. "Grab the branch!" Stahl shouted. Pickett made a frantic effort to extricate his hands from the down-pulling sand, but he couldn't. Horrified and powerless to help, Stahl buried his face in his hands and wept. When he looked up again, he saw nothing but a stretch of level sand!

Long ago the psalmist testified, "He brought me up also out of an horrible pit, out of the miry clay, and set my feet upon a rock" (Ps. 40:2).

In loving kindness Jesus came,
My soul in mercy to reclaim,
And from the depths of sin and shame,
Through grace He lifted me.

* * *

Confused

When David Brainerd was seventeen years old, he was confused about the plan of salvation. He knew that the New Testament told him to come to Christ, but he didn't know how to come. He said, "I thought I would gladly come to Jesus, but I had no directions as to getting through."

As he prayed, David thought, When a mother tells her child to come to her, she does not tell him how to come. He may come with a run, a jump, a skip or a bound. He may come laughing or shouting or singing. It doesn't matter how he comes, so long as he comes.

286

Cannibals Prefer Long Pig—Man

In *New Guinea, the Land That Time Forgot,* Lowell Thomas wrote, "In many parts of Australian-controlled New Guinea an unwary stranger still runs the risk of being speared by a headhunter, brained by a stone ax, or winding up as a menu item for cannibals who have a fondness for 'long pig'—man!"

How greedy and piglike man is before his nature is changed by the transforming grace of God!

* * *

Merely Ask for It

The bodies of two men were found in an Arabian desert. Beside their bodies lay the carcass of a camel, whose stomach had been cut open to get what water it contained to quench the agonizing thirst of the travelers. In their money bags was found an assortment of most valuable jewels. How gladly would those thirst-crazed men have given their jewels for a few drops of water!

The living water which Jesus gives to thirsty ones is available to all who will merely ask for it: "If thou knewest the gift of God . . . thou wouldest have asked of him, and he would have given thee living water" (John 4:10); "Ho, every one that thirsteth, . . . come . . . without money and without price" (Isa. 55:1).

Told by JACKSON WRAY

* * *

"Made . . . to Be Sin for Us"

After God revealed to Martin Luther that the just live by faith, totally apart from any alleged meritorious works, he pleaded with another monk, "Dear brother, learn Christ and Him crucified. Sing to Him, and, despairing of thyself, say to Him, 'Thou art my righteousness. I am Thy sin. Thou hast taken me upon Thyself, and given to me what is Thine. Thou hast taken on Thee what Thou wast not —sin—and hast made me what I was not, a child of God!' "

Impact

Benjamin Franklin said, "He who introduces into public affairs the principles of primitive Christianity will change the face of the world."

* * *

"Have You Counted the Cost?"

The thrilling story of the rescue of Morris Baetzold from a rocky cave in Hinckley, Ohio, was told in newspapers throughout the nation. The boy's seemingly hopeless entrapment brought to Hinckley members of the National Capital Cave Rescue team, members of the National Speleological Society, and an expert rescue team from the U.S. Bureau of Mines in Cave City, Kentucky, near Mammoth Cave. Cave experts were flown in from Washington and a lot of rescue equipment was brought.

In commenting on the great expenditure of time and money to rescue the boy, Fire Chief Paul Chodera said, "Our services and the voluntary services of the rescue squads were free. After all, what is a life actually worth? I estimate the total cost of the rescue of the boy was around $250,000."

After twenty-five and a half hours, Morris was brought up from what would have been his tomb without the heroic and sacrificial efforts of many volunteer helpers.

We are powerless to estimate the value of one soul. It is of incalculable worth. Jesus asked, "For what is a man profited, if he shall gain the whole world, and lose his own soul? Or what shall a man give in exchange for his soul?" (Matt. 16:26).

* * *

Why Needlessly Perish?

In Huron, Ohio, three small children, clustered helplessly near a window, died in a fire that swept their three-room apartment. They had been left alone. Heroic firemen did their best to rescue the children but were beaten back by the flames.

Dr. Richard Blackman, coroner, said,

287

"Had there been a fire escape from the second-story apartment instead of only an inside stairway, the children might have been rescued."

God in mercy has provided for mankind a sure way to escape from spiritual death. Through neglect many needlessly perish: "How shall we escape, if we neglect so great salvation?" (Heb. 2:3).

* * *

The Plank of God's Free Grace

As one of God's aged servants lay dying, a friend said to him, "Soon you will depart from this life to be forever with the Lord. What are your thoughts now?"

The dying man feebly replied, "I have just been thinking of my sins and failures. I have tied them up in a bundle and thrown them into a pit. I have collected all my good works—my sermons, visits, prayers and gifts. I have tied them, too, in a bundle and cast them into the pit. Now I am going to heaven on the plank of God's free grace, singing, 'In my hand no price I bring, simply to Thy cross I cling!' "

Told by DONALD GREY BARNHOUSE

* * *

Hope for the Humanly Hopeless

In a sermon Whitefield said, "There may be someone in my audience who is drink-ridden, lust-sodden, and demon-possessed. If such a person is present, Christ can deliver you from Satan's shackles."

A man, deeply convicted of sin, stood and said, "I am that man! Sin has all but ruined my life. I am miserable. Is there any hope for me? Can your Christ save me?"

Whitefield answered, "Yes, He can! God's promise is sure: 'Look unto me, and be ye saved!' The Saviour came to seek and to save lost ones. Trust Him to do it, and you will instantly become a new man in Him!"

Long ago the question was asked, "Is any thing too hard for the LORD?" (Gen. 18:14). Absolutely nothing: "With God all things are possible" (Matt. 19:26).

Until a Catholic Is Converted

In a Central American parish which is staffed by three priests and two nuns from the United States, Bible study groups in homes have been started. The aim of the staff is the regeneration of the individual. In answering a question about the effect of this effort on sinful personal living—dishonesty, immorality, drunkenness, illegitimacy—one of the priests replied, "Until a Catholic is converted, no amount of church or government pressure changes him. We try to expose him to the Word of God, so that he wants to be born again."

Adapted from *Sunday School Times*

* * *

Came with Bankrupt Soul

Burdened with his sins, a sadhu wearily trudged over eight hundred miles to ask Gandhi, India's great leader, two questions: "How can I get rid of my sins?" and "How can I find God?"

After the interview with Gandhi, the seeker for forgiveness and for God went to Dr. E. Stanley Jones, a missionary, and asked the same questions. The missionary, knowing that he had sought help from Gandhi, asked, "Before I answer your questions, would you mind telling me what Gandhi said?"

"Not at all," the sadhu replied. "He told me to sit down in one place and not roam about as the sadhus do, but stay in one place until I had conquered my senses and passions and worn them out. Then I might find relief."

"Was there no offer of immediate relief?" asked the missionary.

"Oh, no. Gandhi said it would take a long, long time. Now what do you say?"

Dr. Jones replied, "My yearning was once exactly like your yearning. I needed to get rid of my sin, and I wanted to know God. But I did not have to stay in one place until I had worn out my passions. I simply turned over my bankrupt soul to Jesus Christ and prayed, 'God, be merciful to me a sinner.' Instantly I became a new creature in Christ!"

A Mild Case

Dr. William Culbertson said, "Some people want to be vaccinated with a mild case of Christianity so as to be protected from the real thing."

* * *

Deliverance

William Temple stated, "We need to be delivered from the freedom which is absolute bondage into the bondage which is perfect freedom: 'If the Son . . . shall make you free, ye shall be free indeed' " (John 8:36).

* * *

No Peace

People who try to live without God cannot long live in peace with one another or with themselves.

* * *

Nightcaps

Said Dr. Vance Havner, "Salvation is a helmet—not a nightcap."

* * *

Clever

No man can at the same time give the impression that he himself is clever and that Jesus Christ is mighty to save.

* * *

Still Unimproved

Said Laurence Oliphant, Australia's top atomic scientist, in an address to the Royal Society, "I can find no evidence whatever that the morality of mankind has improved over the five thousand years or so of recorded history."

* * *

Enter God

Robert Louis Stevenson said, "No man can truly say that he has made a success of life unless he has written at the top of his life journal 'Enter God.' "

He's No Fool

Jim Elliot, one of the five missionaries martyred by the Aucas, wrote in his diary, "He is no fool who gives up what he cannot keep to gain what he cannot lose."

"I give unto them eternal life; and they shall never perish" (John 10:28).

* * *

Standing Tall

Said Dr. Roy O. McClain, "No man stands so tall as when he kneels and asks God to set the record straight."

* * *

Use a Mirror

When looking for faults, use a mirror not a telescope, and plead, "Create in me a clean heart, O God; and renew a right spirit within me" (Ps. 51:10).

* * *

Greatest Miracle

Samuel Rutherford said, "When I think of my guilt, I see that my salvation is one of our Saviour's greatest miracles."

* * *

His Greatest Discovery

Someone asked Lord Kelvin, "Which one of your discoveries do you consider the most valuable?"

He replied, "To me the most valuable was when I discovered my Saviour, Jesus Christ."

* * *

Rest

Said Augustine, "Thou hast made us for Thyself, O God, and the heart never rests until it finds its rest in Thee."

* * *

Utmost Felicity

Adam Clarke said, "The soul was made for God. He who is saved from sin possesses the utmost felicity that the soul can enjoy, in this or the coming world."

The Change It Worked for Them

Dr. R. A. Torrey testified, "A study of the Lord's second coming broke the power which worldly ambition held over me and filled my life with the most radiant optimism even under most discouraging circumstances!"

Dr. James M. Gray said, "There are at least five things which the blessed hope of Christ's return effected in my life: it awakened a real love and enthusiasm for the study of every part of God's Word; it quickened my zeal for Christian service, especially in foreign missions; it delivered my mind from an overweening ambition for worldly success and the praise of man; it developed patience and quietness in the face of unjust treatment; and it broke the bands of covetousness and set me free to give my substance to the Lord."

* * *

A Memorable Experience

On a gray Monday morning, years ago, I enrolled as a student at the Moody Bible Institute. The air was oppressive and muggy, and a dismal drizzle fell.

As I neared the old Moody Church where the students had assembled for the morning chapel service, I heard them sing:

"Jesus is coming to earth again,
What if it were today?
Coming in power and love to reign,
What if it were today?"

Just as I entered the church, the sun burst through the leaden skies. I thought, *What a day it will be for our sin-sodden, war-torn world when Jesus, the Sun of righteousness, comes again in power and great glory to reign as King of kings and Lord of lords!*

W. B. K.

* * *

Prerequisites for Christ's Return

Norman Grubb stated, "There are three prerequisites for Christ's return: the return of the Jews to Palestine in unbelief; world evangelization; and the worldwide outpouring of the Spirit. The first two are being completed before our eyes, and there are signs of the last. May we be instruments of the Holy Spirit in His last great preparation for the return of Jesus, our King."

* * *

The Coming King

He shall come, the King victorious,
David's Branch and Jesse's Rod,
He shall come, the Lord all-glorious,
Mighty conquering Son of God.

Peace shall then extend her borders,
None shall hurt, and none destroy,
He, the Prince, shall issue orders,
"Sword and spear no more employ."

Field and farm their tribute bringing,
In the wild shall roses grow,
Sorrow shall be turned to singing,
And the earth its Savior know.

FREDERICK H. STERNE

* * *

God Must Intervene

Dr. Merrill C. Tenney said, "The converging trends of universal government, universal culture, centralization of economic power in fewer and fewer hands, the increasing ability of man to destroy himself and his world by the powers of nature which he has harnessed—all point to the climactic focus at which God must intervene if the world is to survive at all. Nothing but the advent of the King of kings and Lord of lords can save mankind."

"And when these things begin to come to pass, then look up . . . for your redemption draweth nigh" (Luke 21:28).

* * *

The Full Number of God's Elect

Said D. L. Moody, "I never preach a sermon without thinking that possibly the Lord may use that sermon to call the last of the saints who should go to make up the full number of God's elect and to bring about the Lord's coming!"

290

"The Night Is Far Spent"

In 1937 H. G. Wells glowingly wrote of man and his achievements: "Can we doubt that presently our race will more than realize our boldest imaginations; that it will achieve unity and peace; that it will live in a world made more splendid and lovely than any palace or garden that we know, going on from strength to strength in an ever-widening circle of adventure and achievement? What man has done—the little triumphs of his present state—are but the prelude to the things that man has yet to do."

At the outbreak of World War II, Wells gloomily wrote of man: "Homo sapiens, as man has been pleased to call himself, is played out."

This is eminently man's day. Everywhere we see man high and lifted up and his triumphs are thrilling the people. Expo 67 in Montreal was devoted almost exclusively to the display of man's brilliant achievements. It exalted man as the lord of the earth.

We do not speak disparagingly of the magnificent achievements of man, but it is tragic shortsightedness for an individual or a nation to build without God and fail to ascribe glory and honor to Him.

The day of the Lord is sure to come, perhaps sooner than we think: "The night is far spent, the day is at hand" (Rom. 13:12). Then man's vaunted civilization "shall pass away . . . and the works that are therein shall be burned up" (II Peter 3:10).

Only those who become the children of God through the miracle of regeneration shall abide *in perpetuum*—forever: "And the world passeth away, and the lust thereof: but he that doeth the will of God abideth for ever" (I John 2:17). They "shall shine as the brightness of the firmament . . . for ever and ever" (Dan. 12:3).

* * *

No Peace Until

There can be no peace until the Prince of peace comes at the second advent. As a revelation of His wrath over human rebellion against Himself, God has given men up to those moral evils that cause war and the other troubles of society (Rom. 1:18-32). Apart from God's intervention, there can be no lasting peace. Wars will continue until man's rebellion runs its full course, terminating in the wars of the great tribulation. Only the second coming of the Lord Jesus Christ, as so often foretold in the Bible, will end conflict and bring an age of peace and prosperity (Matt. 24; Isa. 2:1-5).

Adapted from LT. GEN. W. K. HARRISON (U.S. Army, Retired) in *Christianity Today*

* * *

A Purifying Hope

Dr. R. A. Torrey stated, "The imminent return of our Lord is the great Bible argument for a pure, unselfish, devoted, unworldly, active life of service: 'And every man that hath this hope in him purifieth himself, even as he is pure' [I John 3:3]. Be momentarily ready for His coming: 'For in such an hour as ye think not the Son of man cometh' [Matt. 24:44]."

* * *

The Telescope

As we scan world horizons through the telescope of the "sure word of prophecy," we are constrained to say, "The coming of the Lord draweth nigh" (James 5:8).

* * *

The Great Apostasy

Dr. H. C. Morrison said, "We are now living in the twilight of the great apostasy, and perilous times are gathering like the hurrying regiments of a mobilizing army: 'In the last days perilous [dangerous, fierce] times shall come' [II Tim. 3:1]."

* * *

Try the Uplook

When the outlook is dark, try the uplook: "When these things begin to come to pass . . . look up . . . for your redemption draweth nigh" (Luke 21:28).

* * *

The Only Remedy

Said Lord Shaftesbury, "The only remedy for all this mass of misery is the return of our Lord Jesus Christ. Why do we not plead for it every time we hear the clock strike?"

Christ's Last Recorded Words

"Surely I come quickly" are Christ's last recorded words. The earnest response of many of God's children around the world is "Amen. Even so, come, Lord Jesus" (Rev. 22:20).

* * *

380 Verses

Dr. Robert G. Lee said, "About three hundred eighty verses in the New Testament refer to Christ's second coming."

Since A.D. 70

Christianity Today stated, "The Jews have won control of the entire city of Jerusalem for the first time since A.D. 70."

* * *

Scars, Not Medals

When we appear before the judgment seat of Christ, He will not look for medals, but for scars. Paul said, "I bear in my body the marks of the Lord Jesus" (Gal. 6:17).

SELF-CONTROL

Heated Arguments

The ancient peripatetic (itinerant) Greek scholars became so heated in debate over minor points of logic that they often exchanged fistic blows. Before the close of the day, however, they affectionately embraced, lest the day close with ill will toward each other.

Paul said, "Be ye angry, and sin not: let not the sun go down upon your wrath" (Eph. 4:26).

* * *

If Men Are Mean

In his preface to the play *Caesar and Cleopatra*, George Bernard Shaw said, "Of what avail are great machines, if the men who mind them are mean? Man's increased command of nature is paltry if it be not accompanied by an increased control of himself."

* * *

The Kinks in Ourselves

J. C. Penney observed, "It is not so much learning how to get along with others as taking the kinks out of ourselves so that others can get along with us."

Jesus said, "First cast out the beam out of thine own eye; and then shalt thou see clearly to cast out the mote out of thy brother's eye" (Matt. 7:5).

Tantrums

Little Charles often got very angry and had tantrums. His parents did not correct him. As he grew older, he became more and more uncontrollable.

When Charles became a young man, he was usually pleasant, but when he became angry he was a terror. One time, in a fit of anger, he beat up his younger brother. His parents excused him, saying, "Anger is Charles's weakness. He can't help it."

One day Charles asked his uncle for some money. The uncle refused to give it to him. Charles became angry and struck his uncle several times on the head. The old man fell on the floor. Then Charles became alarmed. He was sorry about his anger, but it was *too late!* His uncle was dead!

The Bible says, "He that hath no rule over his own spirit is like a city that is broken down, and without walls" (Prov. 25:28).

ALICE MARIE KNIGHT

* * *

The Most Dangerous Period

Adlai Stevenson said, "When I visited Dr. Albert Schweitzer in his primitive jungle hospital in French Equatorial Africa, he told me he considered this the most dangerous period in all human history. Why? Because, he said, heretofore nature has controlled man, but now man has learned to control nature's elemental forces before he has learned to control himself."

* * *

Disciplining Ourselves

Dr. Charles Mayo, world-famed surgeon, entered a patient's room at the Mayo Clinic dragging one of his legs clumsily. The patient asked him about it. He replied, "There is a passage in the Bible which says, 'They made me the keeper of the vineyards; but mine own vineyard have I not kept.' I saw this condition coming on, but I would not pay heed."

The famed doctor had not disciplined himself to follow the advice he had given to many others.

Some of God's children are dragging themselves lamely through life, slaves to health-undermining habits because of their failure to discipline themselves and seek divine deliverance from them.

* * *

Keeping the Soul on Top

"What did you learn in Sunday school today?" asked a mother of her little boy when he returned home.

He replied, "Mommy, I learned that I should always keep my soul on top. Teacher said so and she read us a verse about it."

A puzzled look came on his mother's face. She said, "I can't remember a verse like that."

The boy said, "I can't remember it either, Mommy, but that is what it means anyway."

His mother's curiosity was aroused. She thought long. Finally it flashed into her mind that the verse probably was this: "But I keep under my body, and bring it into subjection" (I Cor. 9:27). Tears came to her eyes as she thought, *My little boy has gotten the larger meaning of a truth which so many Christians never learn.*

ALICE MARIE KNIGHT

* * *

Inwardly Boiling, Outwardly Calm

Abigail Gray, a Quakeress, always displayed calm and self-control. Once a shopkeeper spoke roughly to her, but her peaceful countenance showed no anger.

As she left the shop with her niece, the niece said, "Aunt Abigail, how could you remain calm and unresentful when that man spoke so roughly to you? I was inwardly boiling, but you spoke so serenely not one of the ruffles on your cap stirred."

Smiling, Aunt Abigail replied, "If thee could have seen beyond the cap ruffles, thee would have seen that I, too, was boiling, but without steam, my dear."

When we give a piece of our mind to those who mistreat us, we have no peace of mind left.

* * *

"Lock Me Up!"

An eleven-year-old boy in juvenile court, Cleveland, Ohio, pleaded to Judge Albert A. Woldman, "Lock me up before I do something real bad. I can't control myself. I need help!"

The boy had snatched several purses, stolen an automobile and broken into a supermarket.

Judge Woldman said, "If the boy is like this at eleven, I dread to think what he will be like when he is older."

SELFISHNESS — UNSELFISHNESS

Stretching the Soul

One spring day a farmer, accompanied by his little boy, left a hoe and a rake to be repaired at Tussel's Blacksmith Shop in a little town in Alabama. The smith did a splendid job.

Later, the boy related what occurred when his father called for the implements:

"Father handed the blacksmith a silver dollar for the repair job. The smith wouldn't take it. He said, 'No, there's no charge for that little job.' Father insisted that he take the money, but Mr. Tussel refused. I'll never forget what he said: 'Neighbor, can't you let a man do something now and then to stretch his soul?'

"Since then, I've heard many eloquent sermons, but the saying of that noble, unselfish, neighbor-loving blacksmith surpasses all of them. It has caused me to find again and again the joy and satisfaction which come by 'stretching the soul a little,' by helping and bringing happiness to others."

Adapted from *Alabama Baptist*

* * *

Seeing Oneself

As I walked through the Gallery of Mirrors in the palace at Versailles, I was greatly impressed with the fact that wherever I looked, I saw myself reflected in a mirror. I thought, *How vain it is in life to see only oneself. How unlike Christ we are when self is exalted.*

"Seekest thou great things for thyself? Seek them not" (Jer. 45:5).

W. B. K.

* * *

A Boy's Self-Denial

Rev. O. L. King, a Pilgrim Holiness missionary, gave this testimony:

"When a poor lad of eight, I had my first taste of coconut. How good it was! It whetted my appetite for more. When I was twelve years old, my grandfather gave me the first dime I ever had. My first thought was to buy a coconut which cost ten cents. As I longingly looked at it, God seemed to say to me, 'Don't buy it.' After a struggle, I walked over to the drugstore. In the window, I saw a little New Testament which was marked ten cents. God seemed to say to me, 'Buy it.' As I went home, I made the acquaintance of another poor boy about eight years old. God seemed to say to me, 'Give the New Testament to him.' That boy was eventually converted and became a minister.

"Years later God called me to be a missionary in a land where coconuts abound. He placed me in the middle of a forty-acre grove of stately, waving coco-

nut palms! How richly God rewarded my first act of self-denial when a poor boy!"

Told by ALICE MARIE KNIGHT

* * *

Immured

Herman Idle, an eighty-nine-year-old recluse, died sometime ago in Narberth, Wales. He lived and dressed like a pauper. The dingy house where he lived was crammed with rubbish. As local officials poked among the junk and dusty furniture, they found five violins bearing the name of the master violin maker—Antonius Stradivarius! If genuine, the violins would be worth $280,000, but they had lain mute and tuneless for decades.

How like the violins are some of God's children who are immured from a sorrowing, suffering world, and fail to bring blessing to others.

* * *

True Nobility

"Are you a preacher?" asked a porter of Dr. James H. Franklin, who was traveling by train across the continent.

"Yes," replied Dr. Franklin, "but how did you guess it?"

"Oh, I saw the Bible lying next to you on the seat," he said.

Then the porter confided in Dr. Franklin, saying, "I once planned on becoming a preacher myself, feeling that God had called me."

"Why did you give up the thought?" asked Dr. Franklin.

"Well, it was like this: I've got a young brother, and when I told him that I wanted to be a preacher, he looked longingly at me and told me that this was also the greatest desire of his heart. We prayed and talked it over. Then I decided that he should go ahead to college while I worked on the railroad to pay his way. After preparation, he became a preacher. Perhaps you have heard of him. He went to Africa. They call him Bishop Scott."

"Bishop Scott!" exclaimed Dr. Franklin in amazement. "Why, he is the first Negro the Methodist Episcopal Church advanced to that office. He is doing a great work among his people!"

Later Dr. Franklin had the privilege of

meeting Bishop Scott. Greeting him cordially, he asked, "Have you a relative who is a porter?"

"Yes," replied Bishop Scott as tears flowed down his cheeks. "He's my brother. I owe everything to him!"

* * *

Giving Our Very Best

Della and Jim were characters in one of the short stories written by O. Henry, the master of short stories.

Della and Jim, who had recently been married, were very poor. Each, however, had one unique and cherished possession —Della, her beautiful long hair, which almost enveloped her when let down; Jim, a beautiful gold watch to which he was sentimentally attached because it was a gift from his father.

As Christmas approached, each greatly desired to present the other a gift expressive of their deep love for each other.

Della had only one dollar and eighty-seven cents to buy Jim a present. Feeling that this was too little, she decided to sell her hair for twenty dollars. With the money, she bought a beautiful platinum fob for Jim's treasured watch.

When Jim saw Della without her beautiful long hair, he gasped—not because she had ceased to be beautiful to him nor because his love for her had lessened. To him she was as lovely as ever.

Slowly he handed Della her gift—a set of expensive tortoiseshell combs set with jewels for her lovely hair. He had sold his prized watch to buy them for her!

The lovers had given to each other all they had to give—their very best.

When we love the Lord with all of our heart, soul and mind, we give Him our best in service and devotion. Like Mary of old, we give to Him joyfully and sacrificially.

Told by R. E. NEIGHBOUR

* * *

Get All You Can—Can All You Get

Aesop tells of a dog who stole a piece of meat which he held firmly in his mouth as he ran away with it. He came to a stream which was bridged over by a log. When he got midway on the log, he saw in the clear water below what he thought was another dog holding a piece of meat in his mouth. Greedily he opened his mouth and lowered his head to grab the other dog's meat. He lost his piece of meat. The "dog" seen in the water was the greedy dog's shadow. Sad and hungry, the dog went his way.

Many people are like that greedy dog. They are never satisfied with what they have. They want what others have, too. Their motto is "Get all you can and can all you get."

ALICE MARIE KNIGHT

SERVICE

Unpoetic Service

Frederick Faber the hymn writer said, "The colored sunsets and starry heavens; the beautiful mountains and the shining seas; the fragrant woods and painted flowers are not half so beautiful as the life that is serving Jesus because of love for Him and others, serving in the wear and tear of common, unpoetic life."

* * *

Only One Life

Two little lines I heard one day,
As I plodded in my usual way;

They rang in my ears again and again,
Repeating in solemn, sweet refrain:
"Only one life, 'twill soon be past,
Only what's done for Christ will last!"

Only one life, the still, small voice
Gently allures to the better choice,
Bidding me never let selfish aims
Overshadow my Saviour's claims!

Give me, Saviour, a purpose deep,
In joy or sorrow Thy trust to keep;
And so through trouble, care, and strife,
Glorify Thee in my daily life.
"Only one life, 'twill soon be past,
Only what's done for Christ will last!"

Play with Your Hearts

In rehearsals Toscanini often said to the members of his orchestra, "Play with your hearts, not your instruments."

During concerts, when there was a lack of depth of feeling, the great maestro would put his hand over his heart.

When he was pleased, though he never smiled, his pleasure was shown to all by his facial expression.

Sidney Lanier, a southern poet, said, "The world needs heart, not head." The world needs both. How enduring and blessed will be our service if both our head and heart are in it!

* * *

God's Service Star

Late one wintry afternoon during World War II, a Scottish father was out walking with his little son. The boy was especially interested in the little star-centered service flags in the windows of homes from which sons had gone into the armed forces.

"There is a star in that window!" he would exclaim excitedly when he saw a service flag.

Looking up toward the western sky, the boy saw the evening star shining brightly. He exclaimed, "Look, Daddy! God has a son in the service, too!"

Yes, God had one Son. He sent Him to the earth to serve. Jesus said, "Even the Son of man came not to be ministered unto, but to minister, and to give his life a ransom for many" (Matt. 20:28).

ALICE MARIE KNIGHT

* * *

We Are Generals

Two boys, wearing soldiers' uniforms, were playing war.

Their father asked, "What are you doing, boys?"

They replied, "Oh, we're playing war."

"But," said the father, "I don't hear any firing of guns, nor do I see any chasing of the enemy."

"But, Dad," said the boys, "we're both generals."

In the Lord's army, too many want to be generals who occupy places of honor and ease. Too few want to be alert, active, humble soldiers.

ALICE MARIE KNIGHT

Untie Christ's Hands

Jacob Epstein, a sculptor, carved a statue of Christ which was twice the normal size of a man. He gave this title to the statue: *Ecce Homo*, the Latin version of the words spoken by Pilate when he presented Jesus to the people before His crucifixion: "Behold the man!" (John 19:5). The statue portrays the sinless Son of God at His scourging and trial. Serenity and strength of character radiate from His face. Stout ropes bind His hands. As an aged woman gazed fixedly and tearfully upon the statue, she exclaimed, "Oh, let us untie His hands!"

Are Christ's hands tied now? He uses the hands of those who love Him to disseminate His blessings to needy ones far and near.

"Let him labour, working with his hands the thing which is good, that he may have to give to him that needeth" (Eph. 4:28).

* * *

"I've Done So Little"

There was a humble, obscure Christian housewife who was faithful in her sphere of service. She set a good example before her children. One day she said, "I'm so discouraged. I've done so little for Jesus. I have wanted to do great things for Him."

I said to her, "You have done great things for Him. You have faithfully served Him. Your reward in heaven may be even greater than that of others whose names and exploits are known to the world. Remember, Jesus will reward us, not for the *quantity* of service rendered, but for its *quality*: 'And the fire shall try every man's work of what *sort* it is.'"

C. LESLIE MILLER

* * *

"I Am an Ambassador"

A French diplomat refused to let a missionary ride with him in the same railway car from Pahlevi to Tehran, saying, "I am a diplomat."

The missionary could have felt squelched, but he didn't. He thought, *But I am an ambassador.*

296

Such he was and such are all of God's children: "Now then we are ambassadors for Christ" (II Cor. 5:20).

* * *

How She Served

A humble servant girl applied for membership in Dr. John H. Jowett's church. "What are you doing for the Lord?" asked Dr. Jowett.

She replied, "My hours are long, and I seldom have time off to attend church, but I always take a daily paper with me to my bedroom at night. I turn to the births, marriages and deaths. I pray for the little babies that they will early come to Jesus. I pray for the newlyweds that they will be true to God and to each other. I pray for the bereaved ones, commending them to the Healer of broken things—Jesus."

"What a great work you are doing for God!" exclaimed Dr. Jowett.

* * *

Expendable

Soon after the death of Phillips Brooks, his oldest brother said to a friend, "Phillips might have saved himself and so prolonged his life. Others do that, but he was always giving himself to anyone who needed and wanted him."

The friend replied, "Yes, he might have saved himself, but in so doing he would not have been Phillips Brooks. The glory of his life was that he did not save himself!"

* * *

The Joy of Service

A prominent judge was asked by his pastor to teach a class of junior boys in the Sunday school. He declined, saying, "I'm too busy." Later he accepted the responsibility and said to the pastor, "It was sheer pride that made me refuse. I thought I was too great a man to teach a class of boys. I have tried to play the distinguished Christian gentleman role, and I have been worthless to God's kingdom."

After a year, the judge said, "Teaching those boys has been the greatest thing that ever happened to me! I never knew the joy of service before!"

ALICE MARIE KNIGHT

Conditioned for Service

One morning before Amy Carmichael the missionary to India left her room, she submissively prayed, "Do anything, Lord, that will fit me to serve Thee and glorify Thy name."

That day she fell into a pit, broke her leg, and dislocated her ankle. The accident invalided her for nearly twenty years. During her confinement, she wrote thirteen books, including *Gold in Moonlight, Rose from Brier* and *If*, which have enriched countless lives.

God's ways are inscrutable: "O the depth of the riches both of the wisdom and knowledge of God! How unsearchable are his judgments, and his ways past finding out!" (Rom. 11:33). However, we know that "as for God, his way is perfect" (Ps. 18:30).

* * *

Greatest Joy and Greatest Grief

William Grimshawe said, "When I die, I shall then have my greatest grief and my greatest joy—my greatest grief that I have done so little for Jesus, and my greatest joy that Jesus has done so much for me."

With joy God's children can testify, "The LORD hath done great things for us; whereof we are glad" (Ps. 126:3).

We should aspire to do our best for Him, even if we seemingly fail in the effort.

Before God's footstool to confess,
A poor soul knelt, and bowed his head:
"I failed!" he cried. The Master said,
"Thou didst thy best—that is success."

* * *

Being Wanted

A depressed, discouraged man quietly entered his pastor's study in Aurora, Illinois. Said he, "I'm a little at loose ends, and would like some employment or some place of service around the church that will give to me a sense of being wanted and accomplishing something."

The pastor thought and then said, "There is no opening at the moment, but I'll surely keep you in mind and help you all I can."

The man stood, thanked the pastor, and went home and hanged himself!

Then the pastor thought with sorrow about the quiet man who had confided in him and sought to find a place where he could render constructive service.

Let us be alert to the needs of others, especially the distressed and discouraged ones. Let us strive to enter feelingly into their heartaches.

"They helped every one his neighbour; and every one said to his brother, Be of good courage" (Isa. 41:6).

* * *

Our Hands Are Needed

During World War II, a church in Strasbourg, Germany, was destroyed. Seemingly nothing remained but a heap of rubble. When the rubble was cleared away, a statue of Christ, standing erect, was found. It was unharmed except that both hands were missing.

In time, the rebuilding of the church began. A sculptor, on observing the missing hands of the statue of Christ, said, "I'll carve a new statue of Christ with hands."

The church officials met to consider the sculptor's friendly gesture. His offer was not accepted. The consensus of the board was "Our broken statue will serve to remind us that Christ touches the spirits of men, but He has no hands to minister to the needy or feed the hungry or enrich the poor except our hands!"

Adapted from *Friendship Book*

* * *

Heavenly-minded

Said Dr. Vance Havner, "Some people are so heavenly-minded that they are of no earthly use."

* * *

The Impossible

Dr. F. B. Meyer said, "We never test God's resources until we undertake the impossible."

* * *

Results

Amy Carmichael wrote, "Our Master has not promised us success. He only asks that we obey Him and be faithful. The results are His concern, not ours."

"The Shrimp Became a Whale!"

William Wilberforce was a great Christian reformer. He was the weak human instrument which God used to free slaves throughout the British Empire.

When James Boswell heard Wilberforce speak in advocacy of his cause, he said, "I saw what seemed to me a shrimp mounted on a table, but as I listened he grew and grew until the shrimp became a whale!"

* * *

God Chooses Human Weakness

J. S. Stewart said, "It is thrilling to discover that God chooses human weakness and humiliation—not human strength and confidence—to accomplish His purposes in the world. He can use us, not merely in spite of our ordinariness and helplessness and disqualifying infirmities, but precisely because of them. Nothing can defeat those who offer to God, not their strength, but their weakness to be His weapon."

"But God hath chosen . . . the weak things of the world to confound the things which are mighty . . . that no flesh should glory in his presence" (I Cor. 1:27-29).

* * *

Our Best

Queen Mary usually visited Scotland during the summer. There she often strolled unattended. One afternoon, as she was out walking, dark clouds overcast the skies. Her Majesty went hastily to a nearby house and asked to borrow an umbrella. "I'll return it tomorrow," she said.

The lady was hesitant to lend her good umbrella to a stranger. Thinking fast, she recalled that she had a cast-off umbrella in the attic. This one she loaned to the stranger.

The next day, there was a knock at the door. A man in a uniform with gold braid handed the woman the old umbrella, saying, "The Queen sent me to thank you personally for the use of the umbrella."

For a moment, the woman was stunned. Then she burst into tears. "Oh, what an opportunity I missed when I didn't give her my *best!*"

SIN

All Could Qualify

Sometime ago a letter came to the post office in a small town, addressed to "Any Sinner."

All the residents could have qualified as claimants: "For all have sinned, and come short of the glory of God" (Rom. 3:23); "If we say that we have no sin, we deceive ourselves, and the truth is not in us" (I John 1:8).

The post office held the unclaimed letter for thirty days, and then sent it to the dead-letter office.

Because of pride, many refuse to acknowledge that they are "dead in trespasses and sins" (Eph. 2:1). Both the religious and the irreligious sinner, the moral and the immoral sinner, need God's mercy and forgiveness, "for there is no difference" (Rom. 3:22).

* * *

"Your Iniquities Have Separated"

After I had spoken in a university on the west coast, a professor of science came to me and said, "You are going to be amazed at the ultimate question I am here to ask you."

First the scientist related the story of his long inward spiritual and intellectual struggle, and confessed, "More and more, I have come to realize that my problem with Christianity is really not intellectual at all. *It is moral!* I have not been willing to meet the moral requirements of Christianity." Then he asked, "This is my question: What can I do to receive Jesus Christ?"

BILLY GRAHAM

* * *

Come, Chain and All

"I would like to come to Jesus Christ," said a man in a meeting, "but I am chained to sinful habits. I cannot break the chain!"

A redeemed man sitting near him urged, "Come to Christ, chain and all!"

Cobwebs and Cables

Samuel Johnson said, "The chains of habit are generally too small to be felt until they are too strong to be broken. Habits are first like cobwebs—at last, cables."

* * *

Too Late

A little banyan seed implored a stately palm tree, "I am weary of being tossed about by the wind. Let me stay awhile among your leaves."

The palm tree replied, "Certainly! Stay as long as you like."

The little seed was not idle. It sent its tiny roots around the trunk and under the bark and into the heart of its host.

One day the stately palm tree cried out, "What is this you are doing?"

The banyan replied, "I am only the little seed you allowed to rest among your leaves."

"Leave me now," pleaded the palm tree. "You have grown too large and strong."

"I cannot leave you now," argued the banyan. "We have grown together. I will kill you if I tear myself away!"

The palm tree tried to shake the banyan off, but could not. Little by little the palm tree withered and its trunk shriveled until only the banyan could be seen.

Beware of little sins!

Told by ALICE MARIE KNIGHT

* * *

Detest Utterly

One afternoon in Florida, as I was going on my customary hike along a country road, I saw a graceful diamondback rattlesnake wriggling across the road just ahead of me. I watched the deadly reptile with fear, reacting as the Bible says God's children should react to evil—with abhorrence: "Abhor that which is evil" (Rom. 12:9). The word *abhor* in the Greek means "to detest utterly."

W. B. K.

299

Why People Are Slaves to Sin

A minister was walking with an atheistic barber through a slum section of Chicago's South Side. Poverty, filth and sin were in evidence on every side. The barber said, "If there's a God of love, how can there be so much poverty, privation and slavery to vile habits?"

The minister didn't reply until they passed a stumbling bum with unsightly stubble on his face and with unkempt hair. Then he said, "You can't be a very good barber, or there wouldn't be men like that fellow we just passed."

The barber indignantly replied, "I can't help it if that man goes unshaven and lets his hair grow wild. He has never given me a chance to change his appearance."

"Ah," said the minister, "there is but one reason why people are slaves to sin. They won't come to Christ and trust Him to transform them."

* * *

Biological Dynamite

Near Mesa, Arizona, is an insectarium where various entomological specimens are collected. One day a visitor presented to the keeper of the insectarium two giant *Achatina fulica* snails, native to the east coast of Africa. He had brought them from Hawaii. He thought they were harmless, but they were biological dynamite.

These snails range in size from six to nine inches. They have a shell as large as a man's fist. Each snail can produce up to three hundred eggs at a time. It is estimated that two snails can produce a progeny of twenty-two billion twice a year!

Fortunately the identity of the two snails left at the insectarium was detected by Dr. Albert R. Mead, zoologist of the University of Arizona, and they were destroyed.

An entomologist in India described a scourge of these voracious destroyers in that country. Said he, "They were seen everywhere, literally millions of them, crawling over the ground, climbing walls and poles, and clustered on tree trunks! Their appetite is insatiable. They feed on anything green—fruits, vegetables and flowers."

God's children greatly need the help of the indwelling Holy Spirit to detect evil readily. They must be alert and unflagging in their warfare against sin, which is often popularized and glamorized. They must be unremitting in their attitude toward sin.

* * *

What Sin Did for Christ

C. H. Spurgeon said, "Sin is no little thing. It girded the Redeemer's head with thorns, and pierced His heart! Could you weigh the least sin in the scales of eternity, you would fly from it as from a deadly serpent. Look upon all sin as that which crucified the Saviour, and you will see it to be 'exceeding sinful.' "

* * *

The Neglected Emphasis

Said Henry C. Link, psychologist, "The emphasis on sin has largely disappeared from the teachings of religion at the very time when psychology has discovered its importance and extended its meaning."

* * *

Which Works More Havoc?

The Bible differentiates between two kinds of sins—sins of the flesh and sins of the spirit or disposition: "Let us cleanse ourselves from all filthiness of the flesh and spirit" (II Cor. 7:1).

When will we stop giving a clean bill of health to the elder brothers who are in our midst and condemning the prodigal sons? Which work more divisively and destructively in our homes and churches —the prodigal sons or the elder brothers? The almost unanimous verdict of pastors is the latter.

* * *

Sin Pays Wages

"Schoolgirl, sixteen, found dead in hotel room" was the boldface headline across the front page of the *Chicago Daily News*. Adjoining the tragic story was the picture of a sorrowing father, leaning over a still form in the county morgue, identifying the body of his daughter. Empty liquor bottles in the hotel room indicated that a drinking party preceded the girl's tragic death.

"Sin, when it is finished, bringeth forth death" (James 1:15).

* * *

A Drift Toward Nothingness

Dr. Charles Malik, past president of United Nations General Assembly, stated, "The Judeo-Christian thrust alienates the world from God because the world wants to be left alone, wallowing in its own corruption and left in its own inherent drift toward nothingness. Those who love Christ must fight against the forces of evil with all their strength."

* * *

"You Are Missing So Much"

A dissipated young man said to a fellow employee who was a devout Christian, "I can't see what you get out of life. You are missing a lot."

The Christmas holidays came and passed. When work was resumed, the Christian's critic didn't report for work. Officers went to his room. The door was locked. They forced it open and found his body sprawled on the floor amid empty liquor bottles.

When informed of the death of the young man, the Christian thought, *Yes, I'm missing a lot!*

* * *

An Immunizing Virus

In 1927 the Rockefeller Foundation yellow fever laboratory in Lagos, West Africa, took a blood specimen from an African named Asibi. That original strain was cultured and from that virus has come all the yellow fever vaccine which has been produced since that time, it is reported. It has given immunity against yellow fever to millions of people in many countries.

When Adam sinned, the virus of sin entered the bloodstream of mankind and brought universal defilement. Isaiah said, "The whole head is sick, and the whole heart faint. From the sole of the foot even unto the head there is no sound-ness in it; but wounds, and bruises, and putrifying sores" (Isa. 1:5-6).

How thankful we are that the blood which the sinless Son of God shed on the cross has provided an efficacious, never failing cure for the virus of sin. In speaking of that sure remedy, the prophet Zechariah said, "In that day there shall be a fountain opened . . . for sin and uncleanness" (Zech. 13:1).

Adapted from *Christian Digest*

* * *

Nothing Casual About It

Brooks Robinson, one of the recent world champion Baltimore Orioles, said in *Christian Athlete,* "When I commit sin, there is nothing casual about how I feel. I am not simply violating a self-created code of honor. I know that I am sinning against the One who gave His life for me on the cross."

David said, "Against thee [God], thee only, have I sinned, and done this evil in thy sight" (Ps. 51:4).

* * *

All Is Now Changed

Some babies are born with a disorder of body chemistry and become mentally retarded. Formerly it was impossible to diagnose this condition. The victims were doomed to live abnormally.

This is now changed. Medical science has devised an inexpensive test that may be given shortly after the birth of a baby. If the test reveals the phenylketonuria (PKU) chemical disorder, a corrective diet enables the baby to grow and develop normally. But the test and diet must be employed before brain damage occurs.

God, in goodness, has provided a sure cure for an inborn, universal malady—sin. This remedy must be taken in time—the sooner the better. Failure to take it ultimates in disaster and irreparable loss: "In that day there shall be a fountain opened to the house of David . . . for sin and uncleanness" (Zech. 13:1).

* * *

Arrogant Revolt Against Ethical Standards

The vaunted "situational ethics" being championed in our age would assign to

301

the present moment and the passing whim greater authority for the individual than the cumulative wisdom of the ages and the authority of eternal God. It makes gratification of primal desires more to be sought after than ability of character. It is man's arrogant revolt against ethical standards and moral absolutes. Indeed, it bows to no absolutes save personal will and cynical self-interest.

Such a rootless philosophy of life produces anarchic opportunism in personal relationships and threatens our most cherished institutions. It prostitutes liberty into libertinism, and hides blatant self-indulgence under the mask of freedom. In short, the exponents of "situational ethics" would deify situations which compromise human dignity and offer the spurious coin of moral individualism for the pure gold of Christian character. It is a dire threat to the survival of the values that form the warp and woof of the home and all other cherished institutions.

THOMAS B. McDORMAND, president, Eastern Baptist Theological Seminary

* * *

A Human Vegetable

Albert DeSalvo, a self-confessed rapist who killed thirteen women in Massachusetts, was recently tried in Cambridge, Massachusetts.

In his defense of DeSalvo, the famed criminal lawyer F. Lee Bailey said, "He is a completely uncontrollable vegetable walking around in a human body."

Satan-driven, lust-craven man goes to the depth of depravity. Resident in his "desperately wicked" heart is every conceivable evil: "For from within, out of the heart of men, proceed . . . adulteries, fornications, murders" (Mark 7:21).

* * *

The Greatest Destroyer

An avalanche of snow is one of nature's most destructive forces, often surpassing in power tornadoes, earthquakes and floods. Sometimes avalanches occur in mountain fastnesses where no one lives. Sometimes they strike populated areas with awesome destructiveness. When millions of tons of snow crash down a mountainside, gathering earth, trees and boulders in their downward sweep, houses are smashed like matchboxes. Railroads, highways, steel and concrete bridges are obliterated.

One Peruvian avalanche of snow obliterated nine villages, burying hundreds of victims in its great depths. No medicines, nurses, doctors, ambulances or morticians were needed. Death brooded over the tragic scene.

Avalanches of wet snow are comparatively slow. Avalanches of dry snow whistle down steep slopes at breathtaking speed. On March 6, 1898, an avalanche streaked down the Vorder-Glarnisch in Switzerland at an estimated speed of two hundred eighty miles an hour! It swept across a valley some two miles wide and roared on up the opposite mountain.

Avalanches of dry snow drive columns of compressed air ahead of them and create a vacuum in their wake. The blast of air splinters trees. An Austrian avalanche blew eight freight cars off their rails.

The worst avalanche on record occurred on December 13, 1916, during World War I on the Austrian-Italian front. Thousands were buried alive!

It is said that the slightest vibration—a pistol shot or the crack of a whip—may start an avalanche on its downward, destructive plunge. There is a Swiss legend which says that the dulcet tones of a cello once triggered a major slide.

Avalanches are surpassed in destructiveness by sin and evil: "The wages of sin is death" (Rom. 6:23). Myriads topple and fall before sin's onslaughts, sinking helplessly in the maelstrom of vice.

Without Christ we are powerless to cope with sin:

Did we in our own strength confide,
 Our striving would be losing;
Were not the right Man on our side,
 The man of God's own choosing.

The promise is unfailing: "When the enemy shall come in like a flood, the Spirit of the LORD shall lift up a standard against him" (Isa. 59:19).

302

The Unfailing Remedy

In 1665 a plague struck the little village of Eyam, one hundred and sixty miles north of London. The grim reaper reigned for more than a year in the little village, reducing its three hundred fifty inhabitants to ninety-one.

The killing scourge was brought from London in some tailor's samples. Finding the samples damp, the tailor spread them out in front of the fireplace to dry. Shortly he was stricken with illness. He died within a few days.

During that perilous year, the Christians of the village faithfully met for worship, sitting a distance from each other to avert the spread of the killing disease.

Long ago a deadly universal scourge entered the world—sin: "By one man sin entered into the world, and death by sin; and so death passed upon all men, for that all have sinned" (Rom. 5:12).

God, in goodness, has provided a never failing remedy for sin: "a fountain opened . . . for sin and uncleanness" (Zech. 13:1).

* * *

Sexual Cripples

In Cleveland, Ohio, a Unitarian minister said in a sermon, "There is no meaning or value in condemning sex offenders as criminals, moral offenders or social pariahs, any more than there would be in criticizing or punishing a tubercular or a cripple. What is a sex offender but an emotional cripple?"

Failure to deal realistically with the factors of sin and man's need of a Saviour ultimates inevitably in the ruin of individuals and the downfall of nations. Unregenerate evildoers will continue in their dark, downward way until transformed by grace divine: "The heart of the sons of men is fully set in them to do evil" (Eccles. 8:11).

* * *

Sinless Anger

The Puritan John Trapp stated, "He that will be angry and sin not, let him be angry at nothing but sin."

Paul said, "Be ye angry, and sin not" (Eph. 4:26).

It is written of the sinless Son of God, "And . . . he . . . looked round about on them with anger, being grieved for the hardness of their hearts" (Mark 3:5).

* * *

"Some Deficiency in My Makeup"

A professor of sociology was convicted of burglary in Santa Barbara, California. The testimony of the women from whom he stole valuable rugs and other household furnishings convicted him.

He said, "I wish I could explain the motive that drove me to burglarize wealthy homes, but I don't think I can. Apparently it was some deep-seated impulse in me and a deficiency in my makeup that I can't trace."

The thieving professor did not realize that the impulse to steal was resident in his "deceitful . . . and desperately wicked" heart (Jer. 17:9). The deficiency in his makeup lay in his failure to receive Christ as his Saviour from sin.

Ironically, the defending attorney asked the court to put the professor on probation so he could do something creative in the line in which he had been trained—sociology and crime prevention.

Thus the world attempts to have its sick cure its sickness.

Adapted from *Eternity*

* * *

You Can Do Something About It

Dr. Henry Brandt, psychologist, said in his book *The Struggle for Peace,* "You cannot erase the past. You cannot decide what your marriage partner will do. You cannot control the conduct of your associates or the turn of world events. But you can do something about your sin which cuts you off from personal peace. It is not someone else's wrongs that cause your anxieties and tensions. It is your own sin. If you want to, you can do something about it."

David pleaded, "Search me, O God, and know my heart: try me, and know my thoughts: and see if there be any wicked way in me" (Ps. 139:23-24).

303

Don't Judge Sin Superficially

It is said that only about one-eighth of an iceberg is visible above the waterline. Let us not judge sin superficially and leniently, but remember that sin is like an iceberg—the greater part is out of sight, in deceitful and desperately wicked hearts.

* * *

A Very Bad Heart

The chest of an allegedly poor woman was X-rayed in a hospital clinic free of charge. "I am unable to pay anything," she said.

The X ray revealed a concealed purse stuffed with sizable bills.

Said the X-ray technician, "Madam, you have a very bad heart. You lied when you said you were very poor."

We may succeed for a while in hiding our sins from others, but we can never hide them from God: "Thou hast set our iniquities before thee, our secret sins in the light of thy countenance" (Ps. 90:8).

Baptist Standard

* * *

Crouching in the Dark Corners

Dr. Carl Jung, famed psychiatrist, stated, "All the old primitive sins are not dead but are crouching in the dark corners of our modern hearts—still there, and still as ghastly as ever."

Jesus said, "For from within, out of the heart of men, proceed evil thoughts, adulteries, fornications, murders" (Mark 7:21).

* * *

Missing the Mark

The word usually used in the New Testament for iniquity is *hamartia,* which means "missing the mark."

Failure to measure up to the mark, or standard, that God has given is missing the mark.

The worst kind of sin is no consciousness of sin.

John said, "If we say that we have no sin, we deceive ourselves, and the truth is not in us" (I John 1:8).

Alike in Only One Way

Each person is different. Dermatoglyphics affirms the fact that each one has a unique thumbprint. Job expressed this fact when he spoke of the seal on the hand of each one: "He sealeth up the hand of every man" (Job 37:7). The word *seal* comes from a root word which means "to close up or seal up." The sealing up of the hand refers to the thumbprint, the unique and unmistakable identification of each individual.

We are all different except in one respect: "For *all* have sinned, and come short of the glory of God" (Rom. 3:23).

* * *

Found Out

Three safecrackers were suspected in Menlo Park, California, when the lid of their car trunk flew up. The headlights of a police car revealed a small safe, whose jimmied door swung back and forth as the car rounded a corner.

Observing that they were being followed, the burglars speeded up to ninety miles an hour. They were overtaken in Redwood City and arrested. Burglary charges were placed against them.

Often evildoers are successful in escaping detection by officers of the law. There is One, however, from whom they cannot hide—God: "All things are naked and opened unto the eyes of him" (Heb. 4:13).

BRUCE SLACK

* * *

Giving Sin a Foothold

There is a fable which teaches a profound lesson: "Beware of giving sin a foothold."

An Arab sat comfortably in his tent one cold night. Outside, his camel was shivering from the cold.

Looking through the canvas flap, the camel pleaded, "Let me put my head inside."

Hesitantly the Arab consented.

How good the warmth of the tent felt. Said the camel, "My nose is quite warm, but my shoulders are so cold. Do please let me put my shoulders and forelegs inside."

304

Reluctantly the camel's master gave permission.

Little by little, the Arab yielded to the continued pleas of the camel, until the camel was completely inside the tent.

Looking at his master, the camel said, "This tent is too small for both of us. You had better get out."

Satan, the enemy of souls, is too shrewd to ask a man to descend precipitously into the depths of sin. His method is to lure the man on, one step at a time, finally bringing him to the point of no return, where he is bound body and soul.

ALICE MARIE KNIGHT

* * *

Found Out

For decades the stately, imposing buildings of Paris have had a casket-gray drabness. Since 1959, however, workmen have ascended scaffoldings to sandblast and wash the soot and grime from the ancient structures. Visitors to Paris now see a city they have never seen before, a city which De Balzac called the color of cream. Parisian skies are still gray, but there is sunshine in the stones, restored to their initial glory by the cleansing process.

The cleansing of some of the buildings brought to light things that had long been hidden. For instance, it was discovered that some of the columns of the famed Hôtel Crillon were made of wood, cleverly painted to simulate stone. The façade of the Hôtel des Invalides, where Napoleon lies buried, revealed another embarrassing surprise. Pockmarked by gunfire during the liberation of Paris, it had been cheaply repaired with cement.

We may be seemingly successful in covering up our sins, but there will come a time when they will surely be uncovered "in the day when God shall judge the secrets of men by Jesus Christ" (Rom. 2:16).

* * *

Her Deformed Baby

We read of the documented case of a baby born with severe deformities because her mother, age nineteen, took enough LSD four times during pregnancy to succumb to hallucinations. Her baby's right leg is shorter than the left leg and attached to the hip at an odd angle. The baby's right foot also is short and has only three toes. Dr. Hans Zellweger and his associates at the University of Iowa described the case in the *Lancet,* a British medical journal.

How tragic it is that parental sins are reaped by innocent ones!

* * *

A Catching Advertisement

A tourist agency publicized a Holy Land tour thus: "Our Holy Land tour will fulfill your dreams of being a crusader. Once you have seen Gordon's Calvary, the victorious Christian life will become an everyday experience. Think of sharing the missionary task of the church by covering your shoes with the dust from the very roads on which Paul sped forward with the gospel!"

How utterly misleading was the catchy advertisement! One could live on Gordon's Calvary and die in his sin. One could be covered with dust from the roads Paul trod and not be missionary-minded.

* * *

Right and Wrong

William Penn said, "Right is right even if everyone is against it, and wrong is wrong even if everyone is for it."

* * *

The Scars Remain

John B. Gough was a humanly hopeless and helpless alcoholic. As he lay drunk one Sunday morning in the doorway of an abandoned building, someone put a clean handkerchief over his face. Sobering, he removed the handkerchief and said, "Somebody cared enough for me to place this clean handkerchief over my face."

His slumbering conscience began to awaken. He called to God for mercy and deliverance. Gough became a mighty power for God and the cause of temperance. He could give to God, however, only the fag end of his life. This was his deepest regret. He said self-accusingly, "The scars remain. I have been snatched as a brand from the burning, but the scars remain."

The *Chicago Tribune* editorialized, "Moral values are at the lowest level since the decadence of Rome. Moral values are scoffed at and ignored. Drug addiction among the youth is so widespread that we are treated to the spectacle at great universities of faculty-student committees solemnly decreeing that this is no longer a matter of correction under law. At countless universities the doors of dormitories are open to mixed company, with no supervision. We are knee-deep in marijuana, LSD, and the other hallucinogens. We do not need any of these. We are self-doped to the point where our standards are lost."

SINGING

Cover My Defenseless Head

After the close of the Civil War, Col. J. J. Phillips of the 9th Virginia Regiment spoke at a banquet that was attended by veterans of the Union and Confederate armies. He told a touching incident of how the singing of "Jesus, Lover of My Soul" saved a soldier's life. He said, "The point of attack had been selected. The awaited dark night had arrived. My command was to fire when General Pickett signaled the order. There was that dread, indescribable stillness. Suddenly the awesome silence was broken by a deep, full voice singing in the darkness, directly in line with our guns—

'Jesus, Lover of my soul,
Let me to Thy bosom fly.'

"I had heard that grand old hymn sung under circumstances which intensified its impressiveness, but never had it seemed so solemn as when it broke the stillness in which we waited for the order to fire. Just as the order was given the words rang out:

'Cover my defenseless head
With the shadow of Thy wing!'

"I gave the command, 'Ready, aim to the left, boys! Fire!'

"The guns were shifted. The volley that blazed out went to the left and that defenseless head was covered with the shadow of His wing!"

At the conclusion of the thrilling story, a veteran of the Union Army approached the colonel and said, "Sir, I remember that night! That midnight attack killed many of my comrades. *I was the singer!*"

Swept Along on Wings of Song

Centuries ago the Protestant Reformation was swept along on the wings of song —both martial and devotional hymns. One of the greatest of the militant Reformation hymns—"A Mighty Fortress Is Our God"—was written by Martin Luther. It is often called the battle hymn of the Reformation. Luther's inspiration for this hymn was the verse "God is our refuge and strength, a very present help in trouble" (Ps. 46:1).

Dr. Samuel Taylor Coleridge the poet said, "Luther did as much for the Reformation with his hymns as he did with his translation of the Bible."

Luther's hymn of triumph brought strength to the Christian martyrs who refused to surrender their faith, even in the face of death.

* * *

Abide with Me

When shadows begin to gather in the evening of life or when sorrow overwhelms them, Christians find consolation and comfort in the meaningful words of the hymn "Abide with Me."

For twenty-five years, Dr. H. F. Lyte, the author of "Abide with Me," was pastor of a little parish in Lower Brixham, Devonshire, England. He was an indefatigable worker. It was he who said, "It is better to wear out than to rust out."

Because of poor health, Dr. Lyte resigned from his church. The final service was a memorable one, concluded by the observance of the Lord's Supper.

Before the service Dr. Fyte took a long walk. As he returned to his study, he watched a glorious sunset which filled his soul with thoughts of the greatness and goodness of God. Darkness came as he entered his study. Within an hour he had written the words of the hymn "Abide with Me."

* * *

Sweet By and By

"What's the matter?" asked S. F. Bennett of his depressed friend, Joseph P. Webster.

"No matter," replied Webster, "it will be all right by and by."

"By and by," repeated Bennett. "In the sweet by and by. Why, Webster, that would make a good song!"

The hymn "Sweet By and By" came into being because of the chance saying of Webster. Within thirty minutes, Bennett wrote the verses of the hymn, and Webster composed the tune. Then Webster and Bennett sang it together.

Told by PHIL MARQUART

* * *

Singing and Making Melody

The Christian religion is a singing religion. Hope and triumph are dominant in the music that tells of the unique doctrines of Christianity. Most of the Christian hymns are written in the major mode, expressing joy and victory.

In contrast, the minor mode, which is so expressive of futility, sadness and death, is used in the music of heathen religions.

The music of Hinduism is monotonous and weird, and is in the minor mode. Sadness and helplessness are dominant throughout.

The limited music of Confucianism is in the minor mode—sad and doleful.

The music of Muhammadanism, which is based on ancient Arabian melodies, is also in the minor mode. It is little more than a monotone and lacks finality. The singsong call to prayer, intoned from a minaret, is in the minor and abruptly ends in incompleteness. With Muhammad, music was taboo. He said, "Music and singing cause hypocrisy to grow in the heart."

Only Memories of Past Glories

More than two hundred years ago, George Frederick Handel, forlorn and dejected, walked nightly along London's fog-shrouded streets. Only memories of past glories remained. Kings and queens had lavished praise and honor on him, but now he felt that the creative spark within him had died.

Early one wintry morning in 1741, after hours of aimless wandering, Handel entered his shabby room. On the table he saw a package. It contained a libretto written by the famed librettist Charles Jennens. Numbed by cold and hunger, Handel began to shift the pages. The smoldering embers of creativity began to glow and burn within him as he read the Messianic scriptural passages: "Comfort ye, comfort ye, my people, saith your God," "Behold, a virgin shall conceive, and bear a son, and shall call his name Emmanuel," and others.

Going to the piano, he began to compose the music of his great oratorio the *Messiah*. For three weeks he was so completely absorbed with the task that he ate and slept little.

* * *

"Singing . . . unto the Lord"

Gypsy Smith explained the difference between the singing of many white people and Negroes thus: "The whites sing the music, but the music sings the Negroes."

Heaven is vibrant with song: "And they sing the song of Moses . . . and the song of the Lamb, saying, Great and marvellous are thy works, Lord God Almighty; just and true are thy ways, thou King of saints" (Rev. 15:3).

* * *

The Universal Language

Mozart remarked to Franz Joseph Haydn, "Oh, you have no education to reach the wide world, and you speak so few languages."

Haydn countered, "But my language [music] is understood all over the world!"

Hope Rekindled by a Hymn

After suffering great financial losses, J. C. Penney, the famed merchant prince, lay in a sanatorium, suffering from a nervous breakdown. Discouraged and despondent, he felt that he could not live out the night and wrote a farewell letter.

Next morning some patients held a prayer meeting in a nearby room. They sang softly the hymn "God Will Take Care of You." This song brought courage and hope to Penney. He resigned himself completely to God, regained his health, recouped his fortune, and became a glowing testimony to the power of God.

* * *

The Nation's Music

John Philip Sousa said, "I care not who writes my country's laws if I may write its music."

* * *

He Keeps Me Singing

Luther Bridges was a zealous young evangelist. On the last night of a series of meetings, he retired to his room. About 2 A.M. he was awakened to answer a long-distance telephone call. The caller said, "I am so sorry to tell you, but your home burned to the ground and your wife and children perished in the flames!"

Bridges wept bitterly. After recovering from the shock, he knelt and prayed, "Lord, I have preached Your gospel to others, and told them that it would comfort and sustain them in the time of sorrow. Grant that this same gospel will comfort me."

Returning to the place where his home had stood, and where he had last seen his loved ones, Bridges could still sing the song he had written: "He Keeps Me Singing." Shortly thereafter he added the fourth verse:

Though sometimes He leads through
   shadows deep,
Trials fall across the way,
Though sometimes the path seems rough
   and steep,
See His footprints all the way.

Sometime later, Bridges and a friend one night occupied the same room in a hotel. The friend was suddenly awakened when Bridges, half awake, sobbed out, "Yes, Sally! I'm coming!" Then, in the darkness of the room, he prayed, "I can't understand it, but don't let me fail You, Jesus. People are watching me. Help me to be true."

Still later, Bridges added the chorus to his song:

Jesus, Jesus, Jesus,
   Sweetest name I know,
Fills my every longing,
   Keeps me singing as I go.

* * *

Song Prevented Suicide

The song of a plowman working in his field kept the mother of Grattan Guinness from committing suicide. Dr. Guinness often said, "All that I am for God I owe to the humble Christian plowman who sang praises to God as he did his lowly task."

* * *

Old Glory Face

For years Ed Card was the superintendent of the Sunshine Mission in St. Louis, Missouri. He was a radiant, joyous Christian, familiarly called Old Glory Face. Often his cup of joy overflowed and he said, "Glory!" All who heard him knew that his gratitude came from a glowing heart, totally dedicated to God. He always ended his prayer with the triumphant words "And that will be glory for me!"

These words were the inspiration for the "Glory Song," written by Charles H. Gabriel. It is universally loved and sung.

Old Glory Face lived long enough to sing the song. Then he was promoted for service on high where he and myriads of saved ones ceaselessly praise the One who redeemed them by His precious blood.

* * *

Arid Sands of Speculation

Said Ferguson, "Without giving a voice to the throngs it touched, Methodism might have spent itself in the arid sands of speculation. It needed the transforming influence of song to become more than a body of doctrine. And that was what Charles Wesley gave it."

* * *

Making Melody in Your Hearts

Long ago it was the Christians' psalm-singing that first alerted the Roman Empire to the new revolutionary force in its midst. When the pleasure-bent populace saw the martyrs go into a den of hungry, ravenous lions joyfully singing psalms, they were filled with amazement.

Both Christianity and Judaism are singing religions. Atheism is songless. It has nothing to sing about.

As the cross cast its dark shadow before the Saviour, He joined with His disciples in singing a psalm.

When defeat seems inevitable, sing: "And when they began to sing and to praise, the LORD set ambushments against the children of Ammon, Moab, and mount Seir" (II Chron. 20:22).

When suffering unjustly, sing: "And at midnight Paul and Silas prayed, and sang praises unto God" (Acts 16:25).

* * *

The Fiercest Grief Charmed

Music the fiercest grief can charm,
And fate's severest rage disarm;
Music can soften pain to ease,
And make despair and madness please;
Our joys below it can improve,
And antedate the bliss above.

ALEXANDER POPE

SMALL THINGS

Nothing Trivial

Henry Ward Beecher advised, "Be inspired to nobleness of life in the least things. Set such sacredness upon every part of your life that nothing shall be trivial, nothing unimportant, and nothing dull in the daily life."

* * *

Life's Components

Said Horatius Bonar, "A holy life is made up of a multitude of small things—little things of the hour, and not the great things of the age. The avoidance of little evils, little inconsistencies, little weaknesses, little follies, little indulgences, little outbreaks of temper—the avoidance of such little things makes a beautiful and holy life."

* * *

If God Is in It

Little is much when God is in it,
Man's busiest day's not worth
God's minute.
Much is little everywhere,
If God the labor does not share;
So work with God and nothing's lost.
Who works with Him does best and most:
Work on! Work on!

The Rutty Road of Drudgery

John H. Jowett said, "I think that Christians who are faithful in that which is least will wear radiant crowns. They are the people who are great in little tasks. They are scrupulous in the rutty roads of drudgery. They win their triumphs amid small irritations. They finish the obscurest bit of work as though it were to be displayed before an assembly in heaven by Him who is the Lord of glory."

* * *

Little Foxes and Spoiled Vines

What havoc small and seemingly inconsequential things can work!

A plastic dust cover, no larger than a nickel, and worth two cents, was unintentionally left in a rocket. It could have halted both of the attempts to put into orbit *Gemini 6* if it had not been discovered and removed. An electric plug, valued at $108, became loose and halted the first attempt to launch the $15 million rocket with its $30 million spacecraft on top. When the loose plug was being located, the plastic dust cover was found.

Beware of so-called little sins: "Take . . . the foxes, the little foxes, that spoil the vines" (Song of Sol. 2:15).

Thankful for Little Things

I thank You, Lord, for little things,
  The things of every day:
A birdsong clear, a blossom sweet,
The green grass growing at my feet,
  A little child at play.

I thank You, Lord, for little things:
  The handclasp of a friend,

A happy smile, a cheering word,
A bit of song or verse I've heard,
  All these and more You send.

These gifts You give are precious gifts;
  I thank You for each one.
But far above all else You gave
Stands Calvary's cross, an empty grave,
  The gift of Christ, Your Son!

SORROW

The Splashed Painting

Sir Joshua Reynolds was a renowned English painter. One day he was high on a scaffold in St. Paul's Cathedral, London, putting the finishing touches on a great painting. As he looked at it, his face became radiant with joy and satisfaction. Unconsciously, he began to step backward as he gazed on the painting. Seeing Reynolds' imminent danger, a helper threw a wet brush at the painting! The paint splashed the treasure of art and marred it. Instantly Reynolds stepped forward toward the painting and his life was saved. When the situation was explained to him, he sincerely thanked the helper.

Sometimes it becomes necessary for God to resort to jolting expedients to turn our steps from the ways of death and destruction. When we wake with His likeness, how we shall praise Him for thus dealing with us!

* * *

Despise Not the Desert

Dr. R. A. Torrey said, "Despise not the desert. There is where God polishes His brightest gems. There Moses had bleached out all self-assertiveness and impetuousness."

Job said, "But he knoweth the way that I take: when he hath tried me, I shall come forth as gold" (Job 23:10).

Said Dr. V. Raymond Edman, "The Christian graces are displayed, not in the protected precincts of the monastery, but in the arena of struggle and opposition."

Not Down but Through

When thou passest through the waters,
  Deep the waves may be and cold,
But Jehovah is our refuge,
  And His promise is our hold,
For the Lord Himself hath said it,
  He, the faithful God and true:
"When thou comest to the waters
  Thou shalt not go down, but through."

Seas of sorrow, seas of trial,
  Bitterest anguish, fiercest pain,
Rolling surges of temptation
  Sweeping over heart and brain—
They shall never overflow us,
  For we know His Word is true;
All His waves and all His billows
  He will lead us safely through.

ANNIE JOHNSON FLINT

* * *

Come, Ye Disconsolate

Many of the great hymns of the church were born in times of sorrow.

Thomas Moore was an Irish poet. His warm, generous spirit early began to express itself in poetry. The death of his eldest daughter brought deep sorrow to him. Later his younger daughter also succumbed to illness. He wept in the arms of his wife as they watched her die. "Oh, Bessie, I can't bear it!" he sobbed.

Moore sought solace in solitude. Alone with God, he proved the genuineness of the promise "The LORD is nigh unto them that are of a broken heart" (Ps. 34:18). He found comfort and consolation as he thought of heaven where sorrow is forever banished. The hymn he wrote at that time has brought a healing message to countless sorrowing hearts around the world:

Come, ye disconsolate, where'er ye languish,
   Come to the mercy seat, fervently kneel;
Here bring your wounded hearts, here tell your anguish;
   Earth has no sorrow that heaven cannot heal.

* * *

Send Us Trouble

An Ethiopian prayed the following prayer:

"Dear God, from the depth of my heart, I plead with Thee to send us trouble. When our king was exiled we were in much trouble with foreign rulers. We had to worship in secret, and were in constant danger of our lives. Then we worked in harmony with our fellow Christians.

"Many a night, after I had gone to bed weary from a day's long journey of preaching and teaching, many knocked persistently. They wanted to be baptized.

"I told them that if they were baptized they would be put in prison and beaten. But they said that they had seen the Christians' joy and they, too, wanted the Jesus religion. Every night, more and more came. We read Thy Word, talked about it and prayed through the nights. We shared our joy in the Lord. We had only one desire—to preach and teach the gospel.

"Then, Lord, our king came back. The foreign rulers were forced to leave our country. We have peace in our land. We baptize in the daytime. We are not beaten. We meet and pray, but we are beginning to grow careless in our zeal for Thee. Jealousies creep in and spoil the harmony. Petty troubles take on large meanings. We are selfish and ambitious.

"Dear Lord, send us more trouble, I pray Thee, that we may forget ourselves and be so dependent on Thee that we have no time to become selfish and jealous of our fellow Christians. For Jesus' sake. Amen."

Moody Monthly

Storms and Rainbows

How beautiful are the delicate colors of the rainbow, seen through the storm!

A rainbow is produced by the refraction of rays of sunlight shining through raindrops. Without the storm, there could be no rainbow.

God's love, shining through a sorrowing heart and tearful eyes, beautifies our character and enriches our lives.

The psalmist said, "Before I was afflicted I went astray: but now have I kept thy word" (Ps. 119:67).

* * *

A Troubled World

Sure, this world is full of trouble,
   I ain't said it ain't;
Lord, I've had enough, an' double,
   Reason for complaint.
Rain an' storm have come to fret me,
   Skies are often gray;
Thorns an' brambles have beset me
   On the road—but say,
   Ain't it fine today?

It's today that I am livin',
   Not a month ago;
Havin', losin', takin', givin',
   As God wills it so.
Yesterday a cloud of sorrow
   Fell across the way;
It may rain again tomorrow,
   It may rain—but say,
   Ain't it fine today?

* * *

Clouds and the Cross

Overlooking San José, Costa Rica, is a mountain range with many lofty peaks. On one of the highest of them is a large steel cross which is visible for miles away. It can be seen, however, only when clouds rest over the mountains in the background. On clear days, the cross is there, but it takes the clouds to make it visible.

It often takes clouds of sorrow to make the cross of Christ visible to us and draw us closer to the One who died on the cross.

311

A Loving Heavenly Father

When we cry to God in times of sorrow and suffering, we are not importuning an impassive Buddha whose arms are folded and whose eyes are closed in contemplation. We are calling upon a loving heavenly Father of whom we can say:

He knows, He loves, He cares,
Nothing this truth can dim;
He gives the very best to those
Who leave the choice with Him.

* * *

Physical Weaklings—Spiritual Giants

Many of the greatest hymns of the Christian church were written by those who suffered much. Some had lifelong physical weakness, including Sarah Flower Adams, who wrote "Nearer, My God, to Thee"; W. B. Bradbury, who wrote "He Leadeth Me"; Augustus Toplady, who wrote "Rock of Ages"; and Philip Doddridge, who wrote "O Happy Day." Tuberculosis cut short the lives of each one of these songwriters.

Isaac Watts had a frail body, and much of the time he was an acute sufferer. Among his many hymns are these favorites: "Am I a Soldier of the Cross?" "Alas, and Did My Saviour Bleed?" "When I Survey the Wondrous Cross," "Jesus Shall Reign," "Marching to Zion" and "Joy to the World!"

Though physically weak, all of these sufferers were spiritual giants. They will continue to speak through their hymns as long as time lasts.

* * *

Out of Sorrow's Crucible

Some of our most meaningful hymns were born in the crucible of sorrow.

Joseph Scriven was born in Ireland in 1820. Adversity and sorrow dogged his life. But for the fact that he had a Friend who is always with the children of God, he might have failed mentally.

Scriven fell deeply in love with a beautiful girl. They became engaged and then his fiancée accidentally drowned. Overwhelmed with sorrow, he left Ireland and settled in Canada.

Late one night in 1855, burdened with loneliness and despondency, he poured out his heart to God, asking Him to take away his burden and promising that he would dedicate his life anew to the service of Jesus Christ. God heard his prayer and lifted his burden. Expressing his newly discovered joy, he quickly wrote a poem which later became a hymn: "What a Friend We Have in Jesus." This hymn will cheer and inspire God's children as long as time lasts.

* * *

The Saddest Thought

We look before and after,
And pine for what is not;
Our sincerest laughter
With some pain is fraught;
Our sweetest songs are those
That tell the saddest thought.

PERCY BYSSHE SHELLEY

* * *

His Suffering Spared Her

In *The Doctor and the Soul*, Viktor Frankl, the Viennese psychiatrist, tells of an elderly physician who came to him as a patient. The doctor had lost his wife some months before. They had been very close and his life had been bound up in happiness with her. Now he felt useless and shattered. He could find no interest in going on.

Dr. Frankl did not try to tell his patient that things were not so bad as they seemed. Nor did he exhort him to bear his grief bravely. Instead he asked him a question, "Tell me, what would have happened if you had died first and your wife had survived you?"

"That would have been terrible," replied the physician. "How she would have suffered."

He saw then that his own suffering served to spare his wife from sorrowing and suffering. By bearing his grief courageously, he was doing something for her, he reasoned.

Although crushed by seemingly irrational and meaningless blows, we can carry incredible burdens when we do so for a reason and with hope.

Adapted from *Christianity Today*

312

Our Better Home

How wisely God our cup has filled
  With mingled joy and grief,
To teach our hearts that mortal things,
  Though bright, are only brief.

Had earth no thorns among the flowers,
  And life no fount of tears,
We might forget our better Home
  Beyond this vale of tears.

* * *

Not the Scrap Heap

A Christian blacksmith was passing through deep waters of sorrow and suffering. An unbeliever tauntingly asked him, "If God loves you, why does He send sorrow and suffering to you?"

The tested one replied, "Possibly I cannot answer your question to your satisfaction, but I can to my own satisfaction. I often take a piece of iron and bring it to a white heat. Then I plunge it into water. Then I put it on the anvil and hammer it several times to see if it will take temper or be brought to the desired texture of hardness. I repeat the operation several times. If I discover it cannot take temper, I throw it onto the scrap heap. I believe my heavenly Father is testing me to see if He can make of me what He wants. I will bear my sorrow and suffering patiently, and daily pray, 'Lord, put me in the fire if You will. Do anything You please, but don't throw me onto the scrap heap! Make me usable in Your service!' I can trustingly say with His ancient servant, 'He knoweth the way that I take: when he hath tried me, I shall come forth as gold' [Job 23:10]."

Adapted from *Baptist Standard*

* * *

Smiling Through Tears

It is easy enough to be pleasant
  When life flows by like a song;
But the man worthwhile is one who'll smile
  When everything goes dead wrong.

For the test of the heart is trouble,
  And it always comes with the years;
And the smile that is worth the praise of earth
  Is the smile that shines through tears.

Help of the Helpless

As the bodies of astronauts Grissom, White and Chaffee were placed in hearses at Cape Kennedy, the U. S. Marine Band played "Abide with Me."

In times of sorrow, mankind turns instinctively to the changeless One—Christ —for solace, strength and light: "Jesus Christ the same yesterday, and to day, and for ever" (Heb. 13:8).

How helpless we are without divine help!

* * *

Does Jesus Care?

When Rev. Frank E. Graeff went through sorrow and suffering, he began to feel that God had forgotten to be gracious. In his extremity, his thoughts turned to the Saviour. Instantly his burdens became lighter. Emerging triumphantly into full-orbed knowledge of Christ's entrance into his sorrows, he exclaimed, "Oh yes, He cares, I know He cares!" The words of the sorrow-assuaging song came to him as if by divine revelation:

Does Jesus care when my heart is pained
  Too deeply for mirth or song,
As the burdens press, and the cares distress,
  And the way grows weary and long?

Oh yes, He cares, I know He cares;
  His heart is touched with my grief.

* * *

Good Night—Good Morning

A great sorrow came to Mrs. Lizzie De-Armond—the loss of one of her lovely daughters. She was deeply grieved.

She confided to a friend, "When God called my girl to be with Him, it left an aching void in my heart. The question 'My God, why?' came persistently. While I wrestled with the question, my health was affected and my faith clouded.

"One night these words came to me, as if spoken from heaven: 'Christians do not sorrow without hope. They do say good night to loved ones here, but they have the glorious hope of saying good morning to them over there!' My grief subsided. God's peace filled my soul. Im-

313

mediately I wrote the words of the hymn 'Good Night and Good Morning.' "

When comes to the weary a blessed release,
When upward we pass to His kingdom of peace,
When free from the woes that on earth we must bear,
We'll say "good night" here but "good morning" up there!

* * *

What God Hath Promised

God hath not promised skies always blue,
Flower-strewn pathways, all our lives through;
God hath not promised sun without rain,
Joy without sorrow, peace without pain.

God hath not promised we shall not know
Toil and temptation, trouble and woe;
He hath not told us we shall not bear
Many a burden, many a care.

God hath not promised smooth roads and wide;
Swift, easy travel, needing no guide;

Never a mountain, rocky and steep;
Never a river turbid and deep.

But God hath promised strength for the day,
Rest for the labor, light for the way,
Grace for the trials, help from above,
Unfailing sympathy, undying love.

ANNIE JOHNSON FLINT

* * *

Tea Bags

Said Eleanor Whitney, "Christians are like tea bags. You never know what kind you are until you are in hot water."

* * *

His Greatest Work

Handel had lost his health. His right side was paralyzed. His money was gone. His creditors threatened to imprison him. He was so discouraged that he almost lost faith and despaired. He came through the ordeal, however, and composed his greatest work, *Messiah*, which reaches its apex in the "Hallelujah Chorus."

Job said, "When he hath tried me, I shall come forth as gold" (Job 23:10).

SOUL-WINNING — PERSONAL WORK

Melting the Saints

During the reign of Oliver Cromwell, there was a shortage of silver coinage. Cromwell sent some soldiers to a cathedral in search of silver. They reported, "The only silver we can find is in the statues of the saints standing in the corners."

"Good!" exclaimed Cromwell. "We'll melt the saints and put them into circulation!"

Oh, that revival fires would glow again and melt the living saints and put them into circulation, with their hearts aflame with Christ's love for perishing souls!

"O LORD, revive thy work in the midst of the years, . . . in wrath remember mercy" (Hab. 3:2).

What Would Happen If—

A three-year-old boy, Kenneth Vanderleest of Drayton Valley, Alberta, strayed from his home. He was lost for four days. Helicopters, airplanes, motorcycles, horses, tracking dogs and eight hundred volunteers combed one hundred square miles in their search for the child. When found, Kenneth was alive—hungry, insect-bitten, and badly slashed by briers and thorns.

How commendable it is that no effort was spared to find the lost child!

What would happen if all of God's children were helping the good Shepherd, Jesus, find lost and straying sheep—sin-sick, bruised, baffled souls, without God and without hope.

Adapted from *Prairie Overcomer*

314

Searching Words

A lady closed a letter to a sailor with the Bible verse "Here we have no continuing city" (Heb. 13:14). Then she added, "Can you say, 'I seek one to come'?"

Shortly she received a letter from the sailor in which he said, "Thank you so much for those searching words. I am an orphan, and no one has spoken to me like that since my mother died."

* * *

The Right Answer

Bishop John Taylor Smith, Chaplain General of the British army in World War I, adopted a simple method to determine the fitness of those seeking to enter the chaplaincy. He asked each one, "What would you say to a dying soldier who said, 'I have but one minute to live. What must I do to be saved?'"

If the volunteer for the chaplaincy said, "Believe on the Lord Jesus Christ, and thou shalt be saved," or words to that effect, he was accepted. If a candidate gave an evasive or erroneous answer, he was rejected.

* * *

The Wesley of Norway

Hans Nielsen Hauge is called the Wesley of Norway. When he was a workman on his father's farm, God called him to preach the gospel to his countrymen and win souls in a time of spiritual darkness. God gave him a yearning desire to speak personally to others about their soul's salvation.

Hauge's parents doubted whether a peasant's son should preach. He said, "Well, unlearned fishermen did it for Christ long ago. If a farmer may not fish as well as they, he can still sow the seed of God's kingdom."

Hauge's confidence and steadfastness of purpose were contagious. Other laymen in the Norwegian church were challenged. They in turn invigorated Christianity and transmitted it to the Norwegian people.

To each one of God's children is given the command "Go home to thy friends, and tell them how great things the Lord hath done for thee" (Mark 5:19).

Not Tigers, but Souls

Old Kim, a native African, hunted tigers for many years. His face and body were terribly scarred by his many encounters with them. One day old Kim heard the gospel. He gladly accepted Christ as his Saviour and Lord.

Later the missionary met Kim on a trail carrying a little bag. "What do you have in that bag?" asked the missionary.

"Ammunition," old Kim said as he opened the bag.

The missionary saw only a New Testament and a hymnal in it, and he said, "You can't hunt tigers with those things."

"That's right," said old Kim, "but I'm hunting for souls now!"

ALICE MARIE KNIGHT

* * *

The Greatest Thing

Henry Ward Beecher stated, "The greatest thing is not to be a great scientist, important as that is, nor a great statesman, as vitally important as that is, nor even a theologian, which is immeasurably important. But the greatest thing in life is to bring others to Jesus Christ."

Daniel said, "They that be wise shall shine as the brightness of the firmament; and they that turn many to righteousness as the stars for ever and ever" (Dan. 12:3).

* * *

Stir Me Up

A Christian layman sat beside a seventy-eight-year-old man on a park bench. The Christian, who was a stranger to the oldster, spoke to him about his soul and eternal destiny. After the Christian had quoted and explained some verses from the Bible, the old man said, "I have known for a long time that Christianity was the right thing. I only needed someone to stir me up."

* * *

Lassitude and Laziness

God's children, who are so prone to lapse into lassitude and laziness, need to be stirred up constantly. Paul said to the young man Timothy, "Stir up the gift of God, which is in thee" (II Tim. 1:6).

Pleading with the Queen

Queen Victoria often visited the poor in their humble homes. One day she visited a woman who was a joyous believer in the Lord Jesus, and a faithful witness for Him.

At the conclusion of her visit, the queen asked, "Is there anything I can do for you?"

The woman replied, "Thank you, your gracious Majesty, but I have all I need."

"But I should like to do something for you," insisted the queen.

Again the woman replied, "I have all I need. But I am grateful to Your Majesty for your offer. If Your Majesty would promise me one thing, I would be very glad."

"I shall do that if I can," replied Victoria.

"Oh, Your Majesty, just promise to meet me in heaven."

Humbly and joyfully the queen replied, "I shall do that by virtue of the blood of the Lord Jesus Christ."

Adapted from *King's Business*

* * *

How William Booth Differed

William Booth once had an audience with King Edward VII of England. His Majesty highly commended the Salvationist for his unflagging zeal and wonderful work among the poor.

How revealing was Booth's reply to the king's glowing words. He said, "Your Majesty, some men's passion is for gold. Some men's passion is for art. Some men's passion is for fame. My passion is for souls!"

* * *

Lost—a Lamb

One evening General Garibaldi, the Italian patriot, met a Sardinian shepherd who was weeping uncontrollably over the loss of a lamb.

At once Garibaldi organized a search party. Lanterns were lit and the seekers for the lost lamb went over the mountain and into the ravines. Their search was in vain, so the party disbanded.

The next morning, after sunrise, a servant found Garibaldi asleep. When awakened, the general gently took from under his covering the lost lamb. He had searched through the night until he found it.

That is what the shepherd did in the story that Jesus told. He left the ninety-and-nine safe in the fold and went to search for the lost sheep, not giving up until the lost one was found. Jesus Himself is our seeking Shepherd.

Told by HAROLD R. GROSSER

* * *

One Lone Christian

One lone Christian won her neighbor true,
Brought her to church, and then there were two;
Two earnest Christians each won one more,
That doubled their number, so then there were four;
Four sincere Christians worked very late,
And each won another, so then there were eight.

Evangelical Friend

* * *

Swiping Fish

Dr. Kermit Long, president of the Methodist Council on Evangelism, said in *Christianity Today*, "We no longer are fishers of men but keepers of an aquarium. Among our churches it has become a matter of 'you swipe from my fishbowl and I'll swipe from yours.'"

* * *

The Firmament of the Redeemed

Have you ever heard of John Livingstone? He was the brother of David Livingstone, the pioneer missionary to Africa. John died one of the richest men in Ontario.

The brothers grew up together in a simple Scottish home. Both received the same parental instruction.

In time, the brothers made decisions which affected their subsequent years. David decided to forsake all and follow Christ. John decided to amass a fortune instead. David died in a hut in Africa. John lived in affluence and died a wealthy man.

When John died, a notice in the obituary column of a newspaper said, among other things, that he was the brother of David Livingstone, the famed missionary to Africa.

In evaluating the lives of the Livingstone brothers, let us remember this Bible verse: "They that be wise shall shine as the brightness of the firmament; and they that turn many to righteousness as the stars for ever and ever" (Dan. 12:3).

Told by L. E. MAXWELL

* * *

Waiting Fish

Spurgeon said, "We would do better if we went further afield. We are fools to waste time in the shallows of our churches, when the deep outside teems with waiting fish. Invite the often-invited, certainly, but do not forget that those who have never been invited as yet have not been hardened by refusals."

* * *

A Welcome in Heaven Awaits You!

"Many and precious have been my experiences for fourteen years as a missionary in Africa," said Miss Mary Baker. "The following incident will always be cherished and treasured:

"Guirifard was an aged African witch doctor. Often he went into the bushes and forest and mumbled his dark incantations. I became greatly burdened for him, for soon I was to leave his territory. I prayed much for his deliverance from the power of darkness and Satan. The Holy Spirit worked mightily in his sin-darkened heart. Having planted the seed of God's Word, I claimed the unfailing promise 'So shall my word be that goeth forth out of my mouth: it shall not return unto me void' [Isa. 55:11].

"Guirifard was gloriously saved. Sometime later I returned to his territory. A native came running to me and said, 'Mlle Baker, during your absence Guirifard died. A great change occurred in his life after he accepted Christ. Here's a letter he wrote to you.'

"In the letter Guirifard said, 'I will be waiting for you at heaven's gate. I want to have the joy and honor of presenting you to our Saviour and telling Him that it was you who brought me to Him.'"

What joy will be ours if even one soul greets us in heaven with the glad words "It was you who brought me to the Saviour!"

* * *

Passing the Message

Out in the mountains of India, one can hear in the twilight hour a call from the ridge below. Through the stillness comes the call. From the ridge above comes the response. Then a faint call comes from a far ridge beyond, sounding like a distant echo.

The man close above passes the word from the man below to the man beyond. The man below could never reach the one beyond except for the man who stands on the middle ridge and passes the message on.

To each one whom Christ saves comes the command "Go . . . tell . . . how great things the Lord hath done for thee, and hath had compassion on thee" (Mark 5:19).

* * *

At Rope's End

Billy Graham stated, "When I was entertained in the mansion of one of our state governors, we engaged in heart-searching conversation. One day he conducted me into a back room and locked the door. I could see that deep emotion was surging within his soul. Regaining his composure, he said to me, 'I am at the end of my rope! I need God! Can you tell me how to find Him?'

"What joy it was to point him to the Lamb of God 'who taketh away the sin of the world!' "

* * *

Jesus Is the Answer

Vonda Kay Van Dyke, Miss America of 1965, said in *That Girl in Your Mirror,* "Jesus is the answer to the restlessness many people feel. Don't put off receiving Him until some other time in your life."

* * *

Where One Man Is the Congregation

Dr. Jitsuo Marikawa, secretary of evangelism for the American Baptist Convention, said, "Contemporary evan-

317

gelism is moving away from winning souls one by one to the evangelism of the structures of society."

Henry Ward Beecher commented, "The longer I live, the more confidence I have in those sermons preached where one man is the congregation; where one man is the minister; where there is no question as to who is meant when the preacher says, 'Thou art the man!'"

* * *

Where Responsibility Ends

Said Dr. A. T. Pierson, "We are not responsible for conversion, but we are responsible for contact. We cannot compel any man to decide for Christ, but we may entreat every man to decide one way or the other. We may so bring to others the gospel message that the responsibility is transferred from us to them. God will take care of the results if we do our part: 'He that goeth forth and weepeth, bearing precious seed, shall doubtless come again with rejoicing, bringing his sheaves with him' [Ps. 126:6]."

* * *

Make Christ Known

Oh, that in the last remnant of time, before we hear the shout of our descending Lord, we might come back with holiness of heart to our mission!

Let us leave the government of the world till the King comes. Let us leave the civilizing of the world to be an incidental effect of the presence there of the gospel of Christ. Let us give our time, our strength, our money, our days to make Christ known to every creature.

C. I. SCOFIELD

* * *

Potential Living Stones

One day John Mihok entered the shop of a Chicago expert in precious stones. Removing from his pocket a rough, red stone, Mihok said, "I want you to cut and polish this stone."

The lapidary asked, "Where did you get it?"

Mihok replied nonchalantly, "Oh, my father picked it up in Hungary some fifty years ago. He thought it was a pretty stone. When I came to America, I found it in my suitcase. It has been lying around the house ever since. My children have often played with it. Come to think of it, my last baby cut his teeth on it. One night I dreamed that it might be a diamond and worth a lot of money."

The expert exclaimed, "No, it is not a diamond. It is a pigeon's-blood red ruby!"

"What might it be worth?" asked Mihok.

"I would say that it is worth many thousands of dollars!"

The stone was cut to a flawless ruby of twenty-three and nine-tenths carats. It is believed to be the largest ruby in the world.

Oh, for the vision to see in our unsaved friends potential "living stones" (I Peter 2:5), priceless gems! If we discover them and bring them to the Saviour, great will be our rejoicing "in that day when . . . [He makes] up . . . [His] jewels" (Mal. 3:17).

Adapted from *Moody Monthly*

* * *

African Diamonds

The center of much of South Africa's history is Kimberley, a town strewn with diamonds. There one looks with awe into the Big Hole—the original Kimberley mine.

In 1860, Johannes Nicholas DeBeer bought a farm for about $150. Diamonds were discovered on the farm. He was harrassed incessantly by those wanting to pan for the bright pebbles. Finally he sold the farm for about $19,000. He moved to a quieter spot where he could farm in peace.

Between then and 1914, 25 million tons of ore were processed and 14,504,566 carats of diamonds were discovered, the equivalent of three tons of diamonds.

At first the mining was from the open surface of the pit, and the tailings were spread over a wide area of what is now the town of Kimberley. Even now the backyards and alleyways of Kimberley are again being processed through many makeshift rigs, and lone prospectors find payable amounts of the glitter.

The daily production of one of the ultramodern DeBeer mines and processing plants amounts to 4,500 carats (two pounds). These are recovered from 15,000 tons of ore mined and treated. Simple arithmetic reveals the fact that 15 million pounds of ore must be mined and sifted to recover one pound of diamonds. Fifteen million to one—what a ratio!

One gazes in amazement at the perfect glass replicas of the world's famous diamonds on display in a showroom: the 971-carat Excelsior; the 634-carat Reitz; the Koh-i-noor, now one of the British crown jewels; the Star of India; and the Hope.

As I thought on the fact that 15,000,000 pounds of ore must be mined and treated to yield one pound of diamonds, I said, "There's a sermon here!"

I realized that God had brought me to Africa to mine "black diamonds" for the kingdom of God. I felt rebuked at our inordinate preoccupation with numbers, and at our tendency to become discouraged because of the seeming unconcern of the mass of nationals over the exciting news of the gospel. Then the comforting thought came to me: *Our average is better than the fifteen million-to-one ratio of the diamond industry. In fact, I've known some Swazi saints that will someday, in the firmament of the redeemed, outglitter the total output of Kimberley's mines.*

The promise is sure and challenging: "They that be wise shall shine as the brightness of the firmament; and they that turn many to righteousness as the stars for ever and ever" (Dan. 12:3).

What a day of revelation and rejoicing it will be when the Saviour comes to make up His jewels!

He will gather, He will gather
The gems for His kingdom,
All the pure ones, all the bright ones,
His loved and His own.

Like the stars of the morning,
His bright crown adorning,
They shall shine in their beauty,
Bright gems for His crown.

Told by DR. HOWARD H. HAMLIN,
medical missionary in
Swaziland, Africa

Tragic Silence!

It was the Lord's Day. Two business partners were sitting together on a bus. One was going to a golf course. The other was going to church.

Before they parted, the golfer said to the churchman: "I am unable to believe that your religion and church connection mean anything vital to you!"

"Why?" asked the bewildered churchman.

"This is why. For twelve years, we have been business associates. We have met and talked together almost every day. You know quite well that I make no profession of faith in God, yet you have been silent about it, and have shown no interest in helping me to be different from what I am."

Great will be our accountability to God if we fail to speak for Him to our unsaved friends and loved ones, and to exemplify what we say in our daily life.

Paul said, "Now then we are ambassadors for Christ, as though God did beseech you by us: we pray you in Christ's stead, be ye reconciled to God" (II Cor. 5:20).

Told by BILLY GRAHAM

* * *

Try Tears

In Latin America an evangelist spoke lovingly and sincerely to a young woman, who was hardened in sin, about her soul. In anger the young woman turned away, saying, "I will have nothing to do with your Jesus. You cannot pray for me."

Distressed and wounded, the evangelist began to weep. The young woman chanced to look back. When she saw his tears, she returned and said, "You are the first person who has ever cared enough about me to weep for me. Do pray for me."

Oh, that more of us were weeping with Christ over a lost world! Oh, that more of us were solicitously concerned for the salvation of perishing souls and were so burdened for their conversion that we would spare no effort to bring them to Christ!

Told by L. NELSON BELL

The Most Effective Method

Bishop Jesse Peck stated, "If my eternal salvation depended on winning a thousand souls to Christ within the next ten years, I would not attempt to do it from the pulpit. I would come right down and go personally after souls."

* * *

Years of Preaching Failed

Dr. Courtland Myers said to a young man as he left the church one Sunday, "I hope you are a Christian."

Dr. Myers was amazed at the young man's reply: "No, I am not a Christian, but I know you and have heard you preach for seven years."

Taking the young man aside, Dr. Myers had a heart-to-heart talk with him and had the joy of winning him to Christ.

Dr. Myers said later, "What seven years of preaching Sunday after Sunday had failed to do, was accomplished by a few minutes of personal contact."

* * *

Sharing Jesus

Bill Glass, defensive end of the Cleveland Browns, stated, "Too many people simply know *about* Jesus, but don't really know Him. Until you really know Him you can't get excited about sharing Him with anyone."

* * *

"I Watch Faces"

Joe Baronci is a taxicab driver in New York City. As a fare enters his cab, Joe genially says, "My name's Joe Baronci. Where to, sir?" When the passenger leaves his cab, Joe asks, "Would you mind if I gave you a copy of God's Word?"

One day a fare asked, "Why do you do this?"

Joe replied, "Because the gospel has brought new joy and hope into my life!"

The glove compartment of Joe's cab is always filled with scripture portions and gospel tracts. He also places tracts on the rear seat of his cab. Said he, "From my mirror, I watch faces. Most people seem troubled and in a hurry. Some of them are so tense they can't relax while they are seated." Often Joe gives tracts to distraught ones and says, "Slow down, friend, and take along a share of God's comfort."

Adapted from *Church Herald*

* * *

A Soul-winning Judge

Two condemned men stood before Judge A. C. Saunders to be sentenced. The judge declared, "The retribution for your crime is settled by the law of the land. On me reposes the solemn duty of carrying it into effect. May I remind you that you will appear before another Judge, God? Before you pass into His presence, may I, in all sincerity, urge you to prepare for that great day? The way is through repentance for your sins, confession of them, and embracing Christ's forgiveness which is assured you through His blood. I beseech you to accept Christ now so you may be with Him through eternity."

* * *

Face-to-Face Confrontation

Dr. George W. Truett stated, "One evening, as I sat on the platform with the pastor of a prominent church, an influential citizen entered the church. The pastor whispered to me, 'For twelve years I have tried to win that man to Christ. I have preached to him so long that I find myself doing it almost unconsciously.'

"'How many times have you gone to him and lovingly said, "I want you to become a Christian?"'

"The pastor replied, 'I must confess that I have never spoken to him personally concerning his salvation.'

"'Then,'" I said, "'a loving personal appeal may be all that is needed to bring him to the Saviour.'

"At the close of the service, the pastor personally pleaded with the man to receive Christ as his Saviour. The next night that man was among the first to come forward to confess Christ as his Saviour."

Good News for Everybody

A minister visiting in a hospital came to a patient who said, "You've come to the wrong patient. I'm waiting for the priest."

The minister replied kindly, "I don't think I have come to the wrong patient. You are the patient I want to speak to." Then in a quiet, friendly way, he added, "I hold in my hand a New Testament. In it are the words of the Saviour, 'Go ye into all the world and preach the gospel to every creature.' It isn't possible for me to go to the wrong person when I tell of the One who came that all might have eternal life."

The patient replied, "If you look at it that way, you have come to the right person. Tell me more about the Saviour."

* * *

How Far Shall I Go?

How far shall I go, for the way is wild,
    And rough is the rocky steep?
My Shepherd replied, "Go as far, My child,
    As wanders My straying sheep."

All the way, all the way,
    And nothing less will do,
To save the lost, count not the cost,
    'Twas the way of your Lord for you.

* * *

God Hasn't Reached That Altitude

Julia Ward Howe wrote a senator in behalf of a man whom she felt was suffering unjustly. The senator replied, "I am so much taken up with plans for the benefit of the race that I have no time for individuals."

The great woman commented, "God hasn't reached that altitude."

Although our Lord was "moved with compassion" for the shepherdless multitudes, He never failed to minister to the individual.

* * *

The Rare Adventure

Professor Kyle M. Yates said, "If you would become a champion in the rare adventure of soul-winning, you must want them, walk with them, warn them and woo them. Then you'll win them."

* * *

Nothing Else Important

David Brainerd stated, "There was nothing of any importance to me but holiness of heart and life, and the conversion of the Indians to God."

* * *

Presidential Nominations

William Jennings Bryan testified, "There is more happiness in bringing souls to God than in three presidential nominations!"

* * *

One Hungry Beggar

Paul Devanandam, an Indian writer, averred, "Soul-winning is simply one hungry beggar telling another hungry beggar where to find food."

* * *

Through Him

Phillips Brooks commented, "I do not believe any man ever yet sincerely gave himself to Christ without another finding Christ through him."

* * *

My One Ambition

Dr. R. A. Torrey stated, "My one ambition in life is to win as many souls as I possibly can. It is the most worthwhile thing in life."

TESTIMONY

What Scientists Say

As a scientist who discovered the Christian message when an adult, I can testify to the profundity and appeal of the Christian explanation of these facts: that man is estranged from God and that his life is empty and incomplete until he returns to God through His Son, Jesus Christ. Further, I know of no scientific facts which contradict this view.

DR. JOHN A. MCINTYRE,
professor of physics,
Texas A. and M. University

* * *

I see no incompatibility in outlook between the scientist and the Christian. A Christian can be a scientist in the strictest sense of the word while believing in God the Creator and in the divinity of Christ, in whose person God projected Himself into the existence of our world in space and time.

DR. CLAUDE RIMINGTON, PH.D., Sc.D.,
professor of chemical pathology,
University of London

* * *

Some nonbelievers today argue that if they could actually see something supernatural or miraculous, they would believe in God. I cannot but doubt this. If they saw, they would probably run and see a psychiatrist, showing they believe neither in God nor in themselves. I believe in Jesus Christ. I accept the truth as it stands, and with gladness of heart.

DR. YAJIRO MORITA, associate
professor at the Tokyo
Institute of Technology

* * *

My relationship to God is a highly personal affair. When I am troubled or afraid; when I am deeply concerned for those I love; when I listen to the hymns that go back to the best memories of my childhood, then God is to me a directly comforting God, a protecting Father. And when I am trying to work out within myself a problem of right and wrong, then God is a clear and unambiguous voice, an unfailing source of moral guidance. I cannot think of a single instance in my life when I asked what was the right thing to do and the answer was not forthcoming.

DR. WARREN WEAVER,
distinguished mathematician
and author of several books
on science

* * *

For myself, faith begins with a realization that a supreme intelligence brought the universe into being and created man. It is not difficult for me to have this faith, for it is incontrovertible that where there is a plan there is intelligence. An orderly, unfolding universe testifies to the truth of the most majestic statement ever uttered: "In the beginning God created the heaven and the earth.

DR. ARTHUR COMPTON, Nobel
prize winner in physics

* * *

Anyone who says he can't accept Christianity on an intellectual basis is simply making an excuse for his lack of faith. There may be some real stumbling blocks in this area for students, but in most cases, it's an excuse. In a recent survey of scientists, the question was asked, "Do you think that science negates the idea of a personal God as revealed in Christ?" Only twenty-six thought so. One hundred and one did not.

DR. GORDON C. MILLS, professor
of biochemistry, University of
Texas, Medical Branch,
Galveston, Texas

* * *

Science is like trying to follow God's thoughts or participate in the Creator's plan. It is an exciting human adventure. There are many practical human problems that science helps to solve. I like to see Christians have a part in solving them. I'm better at science than preaching. My work puts me in a position to witness where I couldn't as a preacher.

322

· In my life, ultimate personal questions find their solution in my relationship to God through the person of Jesus Christ. We Christians believe that we can come into such direct contact with our Maker and Redeemer that His wisdom can be applied to our deepest problems and His love can be applied to our deepest problems and flow through us to touch others as well.

DR. WALTER R. HEARN,
associate professor of biochemistry,
Iowa State University

* * *

The evangelical church has never really attempted to reach the highly educated. Both uneducated and educated need to be saved, but the church has usually gone out of its way to reach the uneducated. Hardly ever has it gone out of the way to reach the highly educated.

DR. A. KURT WEISS, professor of physiology, University of Oklahoma Medical Center

* * *

When I observe the amazing organization of the universe in its microcosm and its macrocosm, and when I confront the vast unknown and perhaps unknowable, I join the psalmist in affirming that "the heavens declare the glory of God; and the firmament sheweth his handywork."

DR. ROBERT MILLIKAN, winner of a Nobel prize in physics

* * *

I deplore the attitude that scientific enlightenment and religious belief are incompatible. I consider it one of the greatest tragedies of our times that this is so widely believed.

DR. WERNHER VON BRAUN, director of NASA's George C. Marshall Space Flight Center, Huntsville, Alabama

* * *

I can find nothing in science that prevents me from believing that Jesus Christ is the Son of God or that He is my Saviour and the Saviour of the world. When one knows God and has experienced faith in Christ, all the world is open to him. I am thankful that God has made Himself known to me in Christ, and that He has given me His grace to live in this world as a Christian.

"Let the redeemed of the LORD say so, whom he hath redeemed from the hand of the enemy" (Ps. 107:2).

DR. GORDON VAN WYLEN,
chairman of the department of
mechanical engineering,
University of Michigan

* * *

Faith in the omnipotence of science . . . makes man no more than a thinking machine. Without religion, right and wrong are meaningless—terms only of relative convenience. Without God, man is alone in the universe, and without Him man cannot conceive of his own nature and destiny. I seek to be a practicing Christian, convinced personally as well as mentally of the authority of the Bible, because I believe that only in Jesus Christ can genuine, authentic manhood be seen and realized. To me, Jesus Christ is the norm of humanity, and to know and love Him is to know and love God personally.

DR. JAMES M. HOUSTON, fellow of Hertford College and lecturer at Oxford University

* * *

I have come to know God in an ever expanding way through Jesus Christ, and it is my privilege to share in the study of His marvelous creation.

DR. DAVID H. IVES, assistant professor, department of agricultural biochemistry, Ohio State University

* * *

I believe that one's belief in God and in Jesus Christ is a fundamental decision on which all human destiny turns. Will people become nonreligious and pseudoreligious materialists or will they become practical, practicing Christians?

DR. ELBERT H. HADLEY,
professor of chemistry,
Southern Illinois University

Judaism and Christianity bear witness to a God who is at least personal. This God has spoken to men and continues to speak in the dimension of man's personal life as well as in history. As a man who works in science, I do not find Christianity in any sense outmoded. On the contrary, my experience is that a personal relationship to Jesus Christ as God incarnate in man, a relationship of trust and love, is both possible in and relevant to daily life.

PROFESSOR THORSON of
Massachusetts Institute
of Technology

* * *

Some scientists have adopted an impersonal view toward the universe. Others, like myself, find satisfaction in the belief that a Supreme Being not only is responsible for our existence, but also takes an interest in our activities. Faith in a personal God and in the redeeming work of Christ is a decision that can only be made by the individual, scientist and nonscientist alike.

DR. GEORGE W. ANDREWS, geologist
with the United States
Department of the Interior

* * *

The moral and human values intended for man by his Creator are revealed for man in many ways, but the highest revelation is in Jesus Christ. The future direction of our world turns upon our individual, pertinent and personal commitment to Jesus Christ.

DR. RICHARD D. CAMPBELL,
associate professor of chemistry,
University of Iowa

* * *

In this age, when nuclear experiments threaten the world with final destruction, the only hope for humanity lies in Christianity. Our Bible does not teach scientific theory, but theological and eternal truths. God who created man also created science. I believe that no man of science has a proper reason for not becoming a Christian on the grounds of his science. The gospel terms cannot be lessened, cheapened or altered. If a scientist comes to God, he must come the same way as any other man. He must repent, confess his sin to God, and believe in Jesus Christ with all his heart.

DR. PHILIP SABER SAIF,
Egyptian researcher in the
ministry of education in Cairo

* * *

For over forty years, I have been engaged in scientific research and teaching at the advanced level in Cambridge University, and I have found no reason to think that there is any incompatibility between science and Christianity. Many of the greatest scientists have been Christian believers, and I should judge that there is now in this country about the same proportion of such believers among scientists as among nonscientists.

MALCOLM DIXON, PH.D., SC.D.,
British scientist and reader
in enzyme biochemistry,
Cambridge University

* * *

No standards for morals, no universal concern for one's neighbor, no satisfaction for the yearning human heart can spring from any amoral, impersonal body of knowledge. Science has no answer to man's dilemma. For me, the answer is a personal relationship with God freely given by Him in response to faith in and commitment to the claims of Jesus Christ. Science can never displace Jehovah God of the Bible as Lawgiver and Jesus Christ, His Son, as Saviour and Mediator between God and sinful man.

DR. JAMES H. SHAW, associate
professor of biological chemistry,
Harvard School of Dental Medicine

* * *

I believe in the God of the Bible as a Person, and faith in Him to me means commitment to Jesus as the Christ. Actual communication with Him changes man's life from within. It is here that the answer is waiting.

DR. BODO VOLKMAN, professor of
mathematics, Institute of
Technology, Stuttgart, Germany

The theories established in one generation are often contradicted by another. After more than thirty years of teaching, I have had no occasion to change my view of the spiritual realm or of the mission of Jesus Christ. I have come to the settled conviction that no established fact of science contradicts the Bible.

PROF. H. ENOCK, retired head
of the department of zoology,
University of Madras

* * *

In my own life ultimate personal questions find their solution in my relationship to God through the person of Jesus Christ. . . . His love can be applied to our deepest problems and His love can flow through us to touch others as well.

DR. WALTER R. HEARN,
associate professor of biochemistry,
Iowa State Univeristy

* * *

Jesus Christ, the Son of God, died upon the cross to bear the guilt and penalty of my sin, and because of His finished work, I received eternal life when, at seventeen, I chose Him to be my Lord and Saviour. I am a better man, a better scientist, a better husband, a better father and a better citizen because I know Him.

DR. ROBERT H. CAMERON,
professor of mathematics,
University of Minnesota

* * *

Science and technology have greatly enriched mankind in material things, not least in agriculture, where more and more food can be grown by the efforts of fewer and fewer workers. For these material blessings we should be devoutly thankful. But they have not helped us to solve the great and pressing problem of our race— how to find peace with God. To this I can find only one answer, given by Christ Himself: "I am the way, the truth, and the life: no man cometh unto the Father, but by me."

DR. HENRY S. DARLING,
director of the Institute
of Agricultural Research,
Ahmadu Bello University,
Northern Nigeria

Believe Me

And must I wait till science gives
  All doubts a full reply?
Nay, rather, while the sea of doubt
Is raging wildly round about,
  Questioning of life and death and sin,
  Let me but creep within
Thy fold, O Christ, and at Thy feet
  Take but the lowest seat,
And hear Thy assuring voice repeat
In gentlest accents, heavenly sweet,
  "Come unto Me and rest,
  Believe Me and be blest!"

ELISABETH EDMUNDS

* * *

Psychiatrists Could Close Office

Dr. Smiley Blanton, a well-known psychiatrist, told about a new patient who entered his office. Seeing a Bible on his desk, the patient asked, "Do you, a psychiatrist, read the Bible?"

Said Dr. Blanton, "I not only read it, I study it. It's the greatest textbook on human behavior ever put together. If people would just absorb its message, a lot of us psychiatrists could close our offices and go fishing."

"You are talking about the Ten Commandments and the Golden Rule?" the patient asked.

"Certainly, but more, too. There are dozens of other insights that have profound psychiatric value. Take your own case. For the past hour you've been telling me how you've done this, tried that, all to no avail. It's pretty obvious that you're worrying yourself into a state of acute anxiety, isn't it?" asked Dr. Blanton.

"That is why I'm here," the patient acknowledged.

Said Dr. Blanton, "For more than three thousand years, the Bible has been a help in time of trouble to any person wise enough to use it."

Reader's Digest,
used by permission.

* * *

A Governor's Discovery

Sen. Mark O. Hatfield testified, "I discovered that real Christianity is not a re-

325

lationship to an organization—the church —but a relationship to Jesus Christ. I discovered what all can discover if they will only look: 'But as many as received him, to them gave he power to become the sons of God, even to them that believe on his name' [John 1:12]."

* * *

Hero of World Series Accepts God's Gift

Bobby Richardson, second baseman for the New York Yankees, who was chosen as 1964 All Major League second baseman, testified, "We must have a purpose in life—to know God, love Him and walk with Him in our daily lives. Salvation does not come by 'doing good,' but by faith in Jesus Christ. God's forgiveness comes to us freely. We don't deserve it. We can do nothing to earn it: 'It is the gift of God: not of works, lest any man should boast' [Eph. 2:8-9]."

* * *

Hidden Hunger

David C. Morley, M.D., declared, "If we do not eat a diet containing sufficient vitamins and minerals, our tissue cells may become deficient in these important items, resulting in improper function of the cells, and adversely affecting our body as a whole. This condition is called hidden hunger by a manufacturer of vitamin products.

"When I was assured of forgiveness of sin and eternal life in Christ, I accepted His gracious challenge in John 7:17: 'If any man will do his will, he shall know of the doctrine, whether it be of God, or whether I speak of myself.' From that moment, joy and peace filled my soul. The Lord Jesus became 'my light, and my salvation.' My hidden hunger disappeared. I found this spiritual experience to be the most important thing in my life!"

* * *

Preaching Without Preaching

Dr. Russell H. Conwell, the author of *Acres of Diamonds,* stated, "The faithful and silent witnessing of John Ring saved me from a life of folly to a life of faith in Christ. He was my orderly during the Civil War. On his first night in my tent he read the Bible and knelt and prayed. I was an agnostic and ridiculed him. Thereafter he went outside to read his Bible and pray. One day he was mortally wounded. 'Twas then I surrendered myself to Jesus Christ."

* * *

"Christ Is My Personal Saviour"

Gov. Carl E. Sanders of Georgia, said, "Christ is not only the Saviour of the world, but my personal Saviour. I do not think anyone can be a real man—a whole person—without knowing Him. I do not see how anyone can go through life, in the sense of really living, without accepting Christ and then following Him. When I was ten years old, I accepted Him as my Saviour. 'O taste and see that the LORD is good: blessed is the man that trusteth in him' [Ps. 34:8]."

* * *

When Effective

An Indian pastor said, "When I preach something ahead of what I am, I only irritate people. But when I preach what I have experienced, I inspire and challenge the people."

Paul said, "For I will not dare to speak of any of those things which Christ hath not wrought by me" (Rom. 15:18).

To be effective, our testimony must be in keeping with our experience of God's saving, sustaining and sanctifying grace.

* * *

Be Ready to Give an Answer

Dr. Charles Malik, a former president of the United Nations General Assembly, unequivocally affirmed his faith in the heart-transforming and changeless truths of the Bible. He said, "Peter, after admonishing us to sanctify the Lord God in our hearts, added, 'Be ready always to give an answer to every man that asketh you a reason of the hope that is in you with meekness and fear.' I believe in the authority of the Bible, which I love most dearly, the more I read it. Increasingly it means everything to me."

He also spoke of the unbelief which is so prevalent today, saying, "Today God is denied, or watered down. Creation is denied, or at least conceived as self-creative. Jesus has become a 'stalwart young man.' His claims about Himself are either denied outright or passed by in frigid silence. His cross is denied and His resurrection is said to be a myth. Who would speak today of His second coming, or of the Holy Spirit, without ridicule?"

* * *

Nothing Second-Class About Christian Life

Bill Glass, star defensive end for the Cleveland (Ohio) Browns, testified, "It is easy for any of us to let our lives slip into a rut—into a path of least resistance. Sometimes we don't even realize it has happened. That was the case with me during my senior year in college. When I sense myself wanting to let down, I only need to remind myself that through Christ I can be used in a more dynamic way, and through Him I am free and obligated to do everything with my whole heart. In this way I best witness to others that there is nothing second-class about the Christian life which is dedicated to Christ."

* * *

A Buffer in Times of Storm

Irene Jordan, famed operatic singer, stated, "Religion has been the mainstay of my life, and a great buffer against the storms of a career. I have never forgotten that I owe my voice to my Creator. One's happiness should not be dependent upon one's success in a career. Success will not make one happy. I know many good and famous singers who are unhappy. I would advise young people to 'seek first the kingdom of heaven,' and everything else will take its rightful place."

THANKSGIVING

"Thank You"

The owner of a large department store offered a prize of $5,000 to the one giving the best answer to the question "How can my business be most speedily and surely improved?"

Many students of economics submitted different lengthy answers. Roy McCardell received a check for $5,000 for simply writing on a postcard, "Tell your clerks to say 'Thank you!' "

* * *

Have You Ever Told Her?

Two men were discussing individuals who had meant much to them in molding their characters and shaping their destinies. Said one, "There was a schoolteacher who greatly enriched my life. I owe more to her than I can possibly say."

"Have you ever told her, or written her a letter expressing your gratitude for her good influence?" asked the other.

"No, I've never taken the time to write her a letter, because I thought she would receive so many letters of appreciation that a letter from me would mean little to her," was the reply.

Later, the man thought further upon the conversation. He decided to write his former schoolteacher, and express gratitude for her painstaking efforts with him.

Several days later, he received a letter from her which said, "I can't tell you how much your letter meant to me! I am in my eighties, and I live alone. I am lonely, and, like the last leaf of fall, I linger and cling to the fragile spark of life. As you know, I taught school for fifty years, and your letter is the first and only note of appreciation I have ever received. It came on a cold, gray morning, and it brought cheer and comfort to me as nothing has in years."

* * *

A Daily Load

One day Dr. R. C. Chapman said to a friend, "I have such a load burdening me."

Sympathizing, the friend replied, "I am very sorry. Is there anything I can do to lighten your burden?"

Dr. Chapman answered, "But wait till you hear what my burden is: He 'daily loadeth . . . [me] with benefits, even the God of . . . [my] salvation' [Ps. 68:19]."

Hush, Child

After church one Sunday, a father took his family to a cafeteria for dinner. As they sat at a table, little Margie bowed her head and waited for the usual prayer of thanks before the meal, but her father began to eat.

She whispered, "Mom, Daddy has started to eat, and we haven't said grace."

"Hush, child," whispered her father. "People don't say their prayers in a place like this."

A questioning look came on Margie's face. She asked, "Why don't they? Doesn't God go to cafeterias?"

Told by ALICE MARIE KNIGHT

* * *

An Expression of Genuine Interest

James A. Farley said, "I like to thank the people who make my world run smoothly—waitresses, elevator operators, taxi drivers, anyone—not with just a casual word, but with an expression that shows genuine interest in them. Expressed gratitude is the fairest bloom which springs from a grateful heart."

* * *

"I Came to Say thank you!"

During the fearful days of Dunkirk, a vicar in the southeast of England entered his church one evening. He was surprised to see a small boy kneeling before the altar. Presently the boy stood, turned and hurried toward the door.

In the foyer, the vicar smiled and asked the boy, "What have you been doing here?"

"Oh," he replied, "I've been coming here every evening this week, sir. You see, I was afraid my daddy might be left on Dunkirk beach, so I came to ask God to bring him safely home. God did so. I came this time just to say, 'Thank You, Lord!' "

Not for Granted

Toward the close of his long and useful life, G. K. Chesterton the English writer was asked what was the most important lesson he had learned. He replied, "It was to take things with *gratitude* and not take them for *granted.*"

* * *

The Greater Love

When a torpedo ripped open the side of the transport ship the *Dorchester,* the vessel began to sink within minutes and there was panic on the slippery icy decks. The ship was a hundred miles off the Greenland coast, and no one could live long in those icy waters.

Four chaplains were aboard the sinking ship—two Protestants, a Jew and a Catholic. Making their way among the frightened men and speaking encouragingly to them, they went to the forward deck and began to give out the life preservers. Soon there were none left, but there were still outstretched hands. Silently each chaplain removed his life preserver and gave it to another man. Suddenly the *Dorchester* shuddered, lurched and sank! The four chaplains linked their arms and raised their voices in prayer until the waters covered their heads!

Thus was enacted one of the noblest episodes of World War II. Only 229 of the 906 men aboard the *Dorchester* survived. The survivors have never ceased to tell the story America will always cherish.

Who and where are the four men to whom the heroic chaplains gave their own life preservers? We don't know. But whoever they are, wherever they are, they must be daily giving thanks for their benefactors!

TIME

Upward—Onward

New occasions teach new duties;
 Time makes ancient good uncouth;
They must upward still, and onward,
 Who would keep abreast to Truth;
Lo, before us gleam her campfires!
We ourselves must Pilgrims be,
Launch our Mayflower, and steer boldly
 Through the desperate winter sea,
Nor attempt the Future's portal
 With the Past's blood-rusted key.

JAMES RUSSELL LOWELL

* * *

Too Late

When Arthur Arch of Coventry, England, celebrated his ninety-fifth birthday, he said, "The world is moving too fast—twenty minutes too fast to be precise."

For more than four decades, Mr. Arch lived twenty minutes behind the British time.

Asked for an explanation, he said, "It's very simple. In 1922 the clocks in England were changed twenty minutes. I never accepted this. Nobody was going to take twenty minutes off my life. So I just kept my watch set at the old time. It has never stopped since. It is twenty minutes behind the fool time that everybody else keeps."

Over the years, Arch lost six positions for being late to work. He was always twenty minutes late for appointments, and he missed a lot of trains. "But," he said, "they won't beat me. I am going to die twenty minutes late, and show them I was right."

One is blameworthy if he is habitually late for work or appointments, but he is guilty of ultimate folly if he too long delays accepting God's offer of forgiveness and eternal life.

* * *

Beyond Sanguine Dreams

Said William E. Gladstone, "Believe me when I tell you that thrift of time will repay you beyond your most sanguine dreams, and that waste of time will make

you dwindle in intellectual and moral stature beyond your darkest reckoning."

"See then that ye walk . . . as wise, redeeming [buying up; rescuing from loss] the time, because the days are evil" (Eph. 5:15-16).

* * *

Do It Now

If you have hard work to do,
 Do it now.
Today the skies are clear and blue,
Tomorrow clouds may come in view,
Yesterday is not for you,
 Do it now.

If you have a song to sing,
 Sing it now.
Let the notes of gladness ring,
Clear as song of bird in spring,
Let every day some music bring,
 Sing it now.

If you have kind words to say,
 Say them now.
Tomorrow may not come your way,
Do a kindness while you may,
Loved ones will not always stay,
 Say it now.

* * *

The Time Element

Over the entrance of an imposing Jewish temple in Chicago are these words, chiseled in stone: "Seek ye the Lord *where* He may be found." God may be found there, or anywhere, if those seeking Him seek Him penitently and wholeheartedly through the Saviour who came to "seek and to save that which was lost" (Luke 19:10). Not the place element, but the time factor is of paramount importance.

"For this shall every one that is godly pray unto thee in a time when thou mayest be found: surely in the floods of great waters they shall not come nigh unto him" (Ps. 32:6).

* * *

God Keeps the Key

Life is a story in volumes three,
The past and present and yet to be,

The first is written and laid away,
The second we are writing every day,
The third and the last of the volumes
    three
Is locked from sight—God keeps the key.

* * *

Time's Running Out

Beneath a newspaper picture of a beautiful, laughing three-year-old girl were the ominous words "Time's running out for pretty Peggy!" Peggy was held on the lap of her mother who was smiling, though there was deep inward sorrow.

Peggy walked when she was six months old and began talking soon afterward. Grandpa called her Dynamite because she was so full of life and energy. He also called her Princess because of her genial, sunny disposition and way of bringing happiness to others.

Then Peggy underwent brain surgery. The doctors discovered a malignant tumor.

Peggy didn't know what her parents and the doctors knew—that time was running out and that she would die in two months or possibly a year.

Time, too, is running out for the unsaved: "My Spirit shall not always strive with man" (Gen. 6:3); "He, that being often reproved hardeneth his neck, shall suddenly be destroyed, and that without remedy" (Prov. 29:1).

The cup of man's iniquity is brimming over: "Thrust in thy sickle, and reap . . . for the harvest of the earth is ripe [for judgment]" (Rev. 14:15).

* * *

The Future Walks Toward Us

Kermit Shelby said in the *War Cry*, "The future walks toward us. As we meet it, it blends into the present. We are given another golden moment called 'now' to shape as a blacksmith shapes a piece of glowing hot metal, or as a sculptor molds his clay. Then, shaped by our mind, words and deeds, we let the present moment leave our hands forever as it fades into the unchangeable past.

"We can ignore the present moment by daydreaming it idly away, or we can grasp it eagerly and weld it into a golden deed which will shine down through the centuries. This new and present moment is God's generous gift to us.

"Let us joyously meet the future which comes so challengingly toward us: 'As we have . . . opportunity, let us do good unto all men, especially unto them who are of the household of faith' [Gal. 6:10]."

* * *

There Is a Tide

There is a tide in the affairs of men
Which, taken at the flood, leads on to
    fortune;
Omitted, all the voyage of their life
Is bound in the shallows and in miseries.

SHAKESPEARE

* * *

About Time

A United Air Lines flight magazine said: "Modern passenger planes are time-machines that can make you lose a Christmas day or have two Halloweens in a row. They can lull you to sleep on your twentieth birthday, and jolt you awake when you are still nineteen years old. They can fly forward into tomorrow or backward into yesterday. Whenever you're in them, your watch won't work. Whatever time you think it is, it isn't.

"Michael Sanderson took his wife across the Pacific Ocean on the eve of their wedding anniversary and landed in Tokyo when the anniversary was all over. She never knew whether he forgot the day or simply lost it. On their return trip, she had her revenge: she left Tokyo on her fiftieth birthday, landed in Honolulu while she was still forty-nine years old, and celebrated her birthday all over again on Waikiki Beach.

"The best advice is this: If you are asked the time of day, say 'I don't know,' and change the subject. If you are asked the day of the week, do what an Australian friend does whenever he crosses the date line. He replies soberly that it is either half-past Monday or twenty-five minutes to Saturday night, adding, 'People who fly in time-machines shouldn't be clock watchers.' Then he fastens his seat belt for another journey into yesterday."

330

The world's twenty-four time zones are confusing to many, but there is one point of time that we can be sure of: "Behold, now is the accepted time; behold, now is the day of salvation" (II Cor. 6:2).

* * *

Plant My Apple Seed

Martin Luther stated, "If I thought the world was coming to an end tomorrow, I would plant my apple seed today."

* * *

Success

Lord Nelson said, "I owe all my success in life to having been always a quarter of an hour beforehand."

* * *

Crime

Greatly begin
Though thou hast time but for a line;
Not failure, but low aim is crime.

JAMES RUSSELL LOWELL

Before Sunset

Amy Carmichael commented, "We have all eternity to celebrate the victories, but only a few hours before sunset to win them."

* * *

A Good Time

Said Emerson, "This time, like all times, is a very good one if we know what to do with it."

* * *

Invincible

Victor Hugo wrote, "No army can withstand the strength of an idea when its time is come."

TITHING

(*See also* Giving)

A Common Thievery

A gunman entered the Joshua Baptist Church in Indianapolis while the pastor was reading the Scriptures. He flourished his pistol, saying, "I am sorry to disturb you, but this is a holdup! All of you throw your wallets into the aisle. Don't anybody move! I've already killed one man!" Hastily he gathered up his booty and backed out of the church, warning the people not to use the telephone.

That was a most unusual occurrence in a church, far less frequent than another kind of robbery in which no firearms are flourished. Malachi tells of this common thievery: "Will a man rob God? Yet ye have robbed me . . . in tithes and offerings. Ye are cursed . . . for ye have robbed me" (Mal. 3:8-9).

Adapted from *Prairie Overcomer*

Don't Shortchange God

In a sermon on tithing, Dr. Oswald Smith said, "You can't beat God at giving. If you will deal honorably with God in money matters, obeying the command 'Bring ye all the tithes into the storehouse,' God will prosper you spiritually and materially."

In the audience was a dejected Christian man. He had lost his job. He was in financial difficulty. Somehow he was challenged by Dr. Smith's message. He resolved to give to God's work a tenth of future earnings.

To his joy, the man secured a position within a short time. He was steadily advanced in his work, with an increase in salary with each promotion.

He said to Dr. Smith, "I owe much to you and your challenging message on tithing. I have proven God's faithfulness to do exactly what He says: 'I will . . . pour you out a blessing, that there shall not be room enough to receive it.' "

* * *

"God Runs My Business"

The depression of the late twenties left Robert LeTourneau broke and heavily in debt. Previously he had made a sizable monetary pledge to the Christian and Missionary Alliance church which he attended. What would he do about the pledge? A struggle ensued. The question persisted: "Shall I pay my creditors first, as I am able to do it, or shall I pay my pledge to God first?" The Lord seemed to say to him, "Trust Me fully. Pay first your pledge to Me."

From that moment, God took over the management of LeTourneau's business. Years later, he wrote his autobiography, *God Runs My Business.*

For years, the profits of his globe-encircling business have gone to God's work throughout the world, the LeTourneau family retaining only enough to live on.

The one-tenth of his income which Le-Tourneau initially pledged to give to God eventually became 90 percent or more for God's service.

Told by ROY O. McCLAIN

* * *

We Can't Outgive God

God endows some of His children with the talent to make money: "It is . . . [God] that giveth thee power to get wealth" (Deut. 8:18).

Henry Crowell, the founder of the Quaker Oats Company, was a Christian industrialist. He was known as the Autocrat of the Breakfast Table. As a young man, he accepted Christ as his Saviour and Lord. When he began his business career in a little factory in Ohio, he, like Jacob of old, entered into a solemn agreement with the Lord: "Of all that thou shalt give me I will surely give the tenth unto thee" (Gen. 28:22).

God's smile of approval was upon him. Prosperity marked his every move. As his business grew, he increased his giving.

After decades of faithful stewardship, Mr. Crowell testified, "For over forty years I have given 60 or 70 percent of my income to God, but I've never gotten ahead of God. He has always been ahead of me in giving."

God's command has never been rescinded: "Bring ye all the tithes into the storehouse . . . and prove me now herewith" (Mal. 3:10a). Nor has His promise been abrogated: "I will . . . open you the windows of heaven, and pour you out a blessing, that there shall not be room enough to receive it" (v. 10b).

* * *

"Jesus Can Use It Somehow!"

A little girl earned fifty cents. Her Christian parents had taught her to tithe. As she sat by them in church, she joyfully placed her offering in the collection plate.

After service, the little girl asked, "Mommy, how much is one-tenth of fifty cents?"

"Five cents, dear," said the mother.

A surprised look came on the little girl's face. She said, "Oh, Mommy, I thought it was twenty-five cents, and I put that much into the envelope. But that's all right. Jesus can use it somehow."

Told by ALICE M. KNIGHT

* * *

Two Valuable God-given Gifts

Bishop Joseph S. Key said, "Note the literal identity of two divine statutes, the holy Sabbath and the holy tithe: 'Remember the sabbath day, to keep it holy' [Exodus 20:8]; 'The tenth shall be holy unto the LORD' [Lev. 27:32]. Two of the most valuable gifts of God to man are time and money: 'My times are in thy hand' [Ps. 31:15]; 'It is [God] that giveth thee power to get wealth' [Deut. 8:18]. Both time and money are sacred trusts. Both should be used for God."

* * *

Unexcelled Education

Dr. A. J. Gordon commented, "The best kind of education for the church is the training of Christians to set apart one-tenth of their income to the treasury of the Lord."

A Condition for Church Membership

Dr. Joseph Parker stated, "I would not allow any man to become a member of my church until he pledged to give one-tenth of his income to Christ. This might reduce the church roll, but it would increase the power and fervor of the church."

* * *

Dishonest with God

Spurgeon said, "We cannot expect to prosper if we are dishonest with God. He can easily give back to us as we give out to Him. Happy are they who, having been saved by grace, bring to Him their tithes. Peace and prosperity shall be their portion."

* * *

It's Unthinkable

Dr. J. B. Gambrell said, "It is not thinkable from the standpoint of the cross that anyone would give less under grace than the Jews gave under law."

It has been said of the tithe that Abraham commenced it, Jacob continued it, Moses confirmed it, Malachi commanded it, and Christ commended it.

TONGUE

They Couldn't Qualify

As a minister was being shaved in a barber shop, five young men entered. The minister knew them by their voices, but they did not recognize him with his face covered with lather. They sat down and began to tell off-color stories, punctuating them with profanity.

When the barber removed the towel from the cleanly shaven face of the minister, the embarrassed youths recognized him.

When the barber chair was vacant, the barber called, "Next gentleman, please. Next gentleman."

The pastor said to the barber, "John, it isn't a bit of use. There isn't a man here that has the effrontery to answer to the name of gentleman!"

* * *

A Prayer for Clean Language

Lord, help me by Thy grace divine
To guard from sin these lips of mine
From lurid words and filthy phrase,
From foolish cursing that displays
A tragic lack of self-control
And shameful poverty of soul.
From vulgar slang, from tales obscene,
Christ, by Thy mercy, keep me clean.

ROBERT BARR

Doing Our Best

Lincoln said, "If I were to read, much less answer, all the attacks made on me, this shop might as well be closed for any other business. I do the very best I know how—the very best I can. I mean to keep doing so until the end. If the end brings me out all right, what is said against me won't mean anything. If the end brings me out wrong, ten angels swearing I was right would make no difference."

Nothing is easier than faultfinding. No talent, self-denial, brains or character is required to set up in the grumbling business. Often the sin of criticism is greater than the sin that is criticized. When looking for faults use a mirror not a telescope.

* * *

Before It's Too Late

If you've a tender message
Or a loving word to say,
Don't wait till you forget it,
But whisper it today.
The tender words unspoken,
The letter never sent,
The long-forgotten messages,
The wealth of love unspent:
For these some hearts are breaking,
For these some loved ones wait;
Then give them what they're needing
Before it is too late.

333

Too Late!

Thomas Carlyle paid many postmortem tributes to his deceased wife whom he sometimes neglected in life. In his diary occurs what has been said to be the saddest sentence in English literature: "Oh, that I had you yet for five minutes by my side, that I might tell you all!"

How lamentable it is that many of us wait until ears are dulled in death to speak words of praise and commendation.

* * *

"I Have an Unhappy Mouth"

"I want to see the doctor," said an elderly Chinese woman as she entered a missionary hospital. The doctor was called.

Approaching her, he asked, "What can I do for you?"

She said, "The mayor of our town has lately been a patient here. He used to be a very bad man. He was cruel to his children. He wasted his money gambling. He did not provide for his family. He had a foul mouth, and all the water in the world could not have made it clean. But since he has been with you, the tiger has been changed into a lamb. His wife is full of joy. He no longer speaks unhandsome words to her. They live together in peace."

"That is good news indeed!" exclaimed the Christian doctor. "But what do you wish?"

Said the woman, "You are to tell nobody, but I, too, have an unhappy mouth, and I am afraid my daughter-in-law finds it none too easy to live with me. I have come to beg you to give me some of the medicine that cured our mayor."

How glad the doctor was to tell her the story of Jesus, and of His tongue-controlling, character-sweetening power!

* * *

My Name Is Gossip

Morgan Blake, sportswriter for the *Atlanta Journal,* wrote: "I am more deadly than the screaming shell from the howitzer. I ruin without killing. I tear down homes, break hearts and wreck lives. I travel on the wings of the wind. No innocence is strong enough to intimidate me, no purity pure enough to daunt me. I have no regard for truth, no respect for justice, no mercy for the defenseless. My victims are as numerous as the sands of the sea, and often as innocent. I never forget and seldom forgive. My name is Gossip."

* * *

"And Satan Came Also"

One day when I entered a doctor's office, my attention was drawn to a unique picture. It showed a hideous, repulsive human skull! As I went closer to the picture, I realized that the picture was actually of a group of women gossiping, with their heads together. An expression of fiendish delight pervaded their faces as they indulged in their favorite though wicked pastime, gossip!

How revealing and appropriate was the verse beneath the picture: "And Satan came also among them" (Job 1:6).

Possibly no command is more frequently and flagrantly violated by Christians than this one: "Speak evil of no man" (Titus 3:2).

Spiritual maturity should be aimed at in the realm of speech, in the right use of our tongues: "If any man offend not in word, the same is a perfect man, and able also to bridle the whole body" (James 3:2).

Unless we yield our tongues as instruments of righteousness for God, Satan will use them to his advantage and to our spiritual impoverishment.

W. B. K.

* * *

"I'll Never Forgive Myself"

Billy Graham said, "After a meeting in one of America's greatest cities, a man who had come forward to commit his life to Christ told me, 'Billy, I know that God has forgiven my sins, but I can never forgive myself. A few years ago, when a neighbor of mine was being gossiped about unjustly, I failed to speak out in his defense. Ruined in reputation, he later committed suicide! I'll carry the guilt of my cowardice to my grave.'"

* * *

Plain Yellow

There are times when silence is golden:

334

"In the multitude of words there wanteth not sin: but he that refraineth his lips is wise" (Prov. 10:19).

There are times, however, when silence is yellow: "Among the chief rulers . . . many believed on him; but because of the Pharisees they did not confess him" (John 12:42).

* * *

How You Say It

It's not so much what you say
As the manner in which you say it.
It's not so much the language you use
As the tone in which you convey it.
"Come here," I sharply said,
And the child cowered and wept;
"Come here," I gently said.
He looked and smiled,
And straight to my lap he crept.

* * *

Needed: A Spiritual Glossectomy

Glossectomy is the total or partial removal of the tongue by surgery.

Jesus taught that spiritual surgery is sometimes necessary: "And if thy right eye offend thee, pluck it out. . . . And if thy right hand offend thee, cut it off" (Matt. 5:29-30).

A critical, faultfinding woman didn't like the length of John Wesley's coat. She told him, "Your coat is too long."

Wesley turned the criticism to good advantage. Said he, "If it is too long, take these shears and cut it off to your liking."

The woman, embarrassed, said, "Well, I didn't—"

"Woman," said Wesley, "your tongue is too long. It needs to be shortened."

* * *

Glossolalia

In recent years, Christians of different denominations have had renewed interest in glossolalia—the gift of tongues, or speaking in an unknown tongue. Interest in this phenomenon was deemed sufficiently widespread to cause the U.S. Department of Health, Education and Welfare to award the Lutheran Medical Center, Brooklyn, New York, a grant for a psychological and linguistic study of glossolalia.

Whatever our belief may be in reference to glossolalia, there is one tongue which all Christians should seek—the *kind* tongue: "In her tongue is the law of kindness" (Prov. 31:26).

Too many possess a cutting, caustic, critical tongue. Too few possess a kind, encouraging tongue.

* * *

Forked Lightning

Said Dr. A. B. Simpson, "I would rather play with forked lightning than speak a reckless word against any servant of Christ or idly repeat the slanderous words which thousands of Christians hurl at others to their own spiritual impoverishment and injury of others."

The Bible says, "Touch not mine anointed, and do my prophets no harm" (I Chron. 16:22).

* * *

A False Report Wrecks a Home

A woman, weeping uncontrollably, went to her pastor. She was filled with remorse and regret. She had spoken untruthfully about a young woman whom she disliked, and caused a home to be wrecked and a marital tie to be broken. "Oh," she lamented, "I didn't dream that the report I started would work such havoc! Now it is too late to undo the terrible thing I have done!"

Of the unkind, unbridled tongue the Bible says, "Death and life are in the power of the tongue" (Prov. 18:21).

Told by C. LESLIE MILLER

* * *

Busybodies

In a small town there was an obnoxious busybody who made life miserable for her neighbors by constantly prying into their affairs. She was the cause of much ill will and grief in the one church of the town, which most of the people attended.

What a problem she was to the pastor! He finally tried to show her the harm she was doing. Defensively she said, "What I do isn't half as bad as what Mrs.———— does. She gets high at cocktail parties."

After expressing his disapproval of cocktail parties, the pastor courageously said, "God's Word classes one who constantly meddles in the lives of others with a murderer and a thief: 'But let none of you suffer as a murderer, or as a thief, or as a busybody in other men's matters' [I Peter 4:15]."

* * *

A Deserved Rebuke

One day a southern client entered the New York office of a Christian who dealt in investments. The client was a multimillionaire. During the conversation he repeatedly used the Lord's name flippantly and irreverently—like slang.

The broker finally said, "Please, sir, the name you just used is the most precious name I know. I don't like to hear His name used so irreverently. I am a Christian."

"I, too, am a Christian," the client said. "I teach a Sunday school class down south."

The Christian broker replied, "Well, I never would have guessed it."

After the Southerner left, the broker thought, *Possibly I will lose that man's business.* He didn't, however.

Some months later, the client entered the broker's office, accompanied by his wife. Introducing her to the broker, he said to her, "This is the man who gave me such a thrashing about my use of the Lord's name irreverently that last time I was here."

The wife said to the Christian broker, "I am glad you did, because he deserved it. He has been a different man since then."

"Thou shalt not take the name of the LORD thy God in vain: for the LORD will not hold him guiltless that taketh his name in vain" (Exodus 20:7).

* * *

The Family Parrot

So live that you won't be afraid to sell the family parrot to the town gossip.

* * *

Read Like a Book

People may be read like a book, but they can't be shut up as easily: "The tongue can no man tame; it is an unruly evil."

TRUST

The Sure Panacea

From declassified information of the Department of Defense, based on exhaustive study by the U.S. Army to determine what happened to some nine thousand American soldiers in Korean prison camps, it is revealed that these American prisoners suffered the highest death rate of any war in American history, including the Revolutionary War. About 38 percent of the prisoners died, not from starvation or epidemics or mass executions, but from a psychological disease for which the medical corps had no name. The soldiers called it "give-up-itis." When a man became despondent and homesick, he would brood and go into a corner by himself, pull a blanket over his head and turn his face toward the wall. Utterly surrendering to despondency and despair, he often died within forty-eight hours!

It is said that no prior records contain anything like this on such a scale among adult males eighteen to twenty-two years old.

The conclusion of the army's study was that these youths had no inner resources that could give them the courage to rise above their terrible obstacles.

Nothing is so bulwarking and fear-allaying in times of deepest distress as unshakable trust in the provident care and protection of God: "I will trust, and not be afraid" (Isa. 12:2). Lacking this trust, people may go down beneath the bleak waters of defeat and despair.

"The people that do know their God shall be strong, and do exploits" (Dan. 11:32).

* * *

Courage Was Revived

A Canadian pastor was despondent and discouraged. His faith and courage were revived when he read the following true incident.

A parks commission had been ordered to remove the trees from a street which was to be widened. As the workmen began, the foreman observed a robin's nest in one of the trees and a mother robin sitting in the nest. He ordered the men to leave that tree until later.

Later the foreman observed that the nest was occupied by little open-mouthed robins. Again the removal of the tree was delayed.

In time it was observed that the nest was empty. The baby robins had grown and flown away.

When the tree was cut down, a most unusual discovery was made. In the bottom of the nest there was a soiled little white card. When it was separated from the mud and sticks, it was observed that it was a small Sunday school card on which were the words "We trust in the Lord our God!"

Told by C. ERNEST TATHAM

* * *

Just for Today

Lord, for tomorrow and its needs
  I do not pray;
Keep me, my God, from stain of sin
  Just for today.

Now set a seal upon my lips,
  For this I pray;
Keep me from wrong or idle words,
  Just for today.

Let me be slow to do my will,
  Prompt to obey;
And keep me, guide me, use me, Lord,
  Just for today.

* * *

Childlike Trust

He puts his little hand in hers,
  And lifts his trusting eyes;
He walks with her down dangerous paths,
  And on her strength relies.

His heart, rejoicing, hears her voice,
  Which stills his many fears;
He seeks her sympathy and smiles,
  Which chase away his tears.

For he feels safe in Mother's care,
  And trusts her tender love;

Oh, would I had such childlike trust
  In Christ, who dwells above.

OLIVE W. MUMERT

* * *

Canst Thou Not Trust Me?

Canst thou not trust Me, My child,
And to thy cross be reconciled?
I fashioned it thy needs to meet,
Nor were thy discipline complete
Without that very pain and bruise
Which thy weak heart would fain refuse.

* * *

Misplaced Trust

On July 13, 1966, nine student nurses were held captive in their townhouse in Chicago. Eight of them were murdered, one by one. The nine young women had discussed whether they should attack soft-spoken Richard B. Speck or comply with his wishes lest he "do something crazy," according to the only survivor of the massacre, Miss Corazon Amurao. She saved her life by hiding under a bed while the depraved killer methodically murdered her eight fellow student nurses.

In commenting upon the decision of the nurses not to cross their killer, but to remain quiet and calm, Dr. Generoso P. Provido, Philippine Consul General in Chicago, said, "They were too trusting."

The Bible warns us of false trusts: "Confidence in an unfaithful man in time of trouble is like a broken tooth, and a foot out of joint" (Prov. 25:19); "Wilt thou set thine eyes upon that which is not? For riches certainly make themselves wings; they fly away as an eagle toward heaven" (23:5).

* * *

The Outcome Is with God

One night during World War II, General Eisenhower stood with his officers as troop-laden ships sailed out into the mist of the sea while squadrons of planes roared into the sky.

Deeply moved by the sight, the general came to attention and saluted the brave men. Then he bowed his head in silent prayer, his staff joining him in the brief act of devotion.

Turning to his officers, General Eisenhower said, "There comes a time when you've used your brains, your training and your technical skill. The outcome is in the hand of God, and there we must leave it."

The psalmist said, "My times are in thy hand" (Ps. 31:15). Could we be in safer hands?

* * *

The Sure Cure

Dr. S. I. McMillen said in his book *None of These Diseases,* "As many as two-thirds of the patients who go to physicians have symptoms caused by or aggravated by emotional stress."

The sure cure for taut nerves and overwrought minds is quiescent trust in the provident care of God: "I will trust, and not be afraid" (Isa. 12:2); "In returning and rest shall ye be saved; in quietness and in confidence shall be your strength" (30:15).

* * *

A Helping Hand

In his painting *A Helping Hand,* the French artist Emile Ranouf vividly depicts an old fisherman sitting in a boat with a little girl beside him. Both have their hands on a huge oar.

The fisherman is looking encouragingly at the little girl, imparting the thought to her that she is assisting him in the rowing. In reality, his strong hands and muscular arms are mainly moving the boat over the waves.

How helpless we are without God's help: "Without me [Jesus] ye can do nothing" (John 15:5). Let us dependently plead:

Though my faith is feeble,
　Though my strength is small,
I will ever trust Thee
　Who art over all.
I am now persuaded
　Thou wilt keep me true.
Looking unto Jesus
　I can all things do.

J. F. Spink

* * *

If

If we trust, we don't doubt; if we doubt, we don't trust: "I will trust, and not be afraid" (Isa. 12:2).

UNITY

Union Isn't Unity

There is a difference between union and unity. If two cats are tied together by their tails, they have union, but not unity.

Two church bodies with divergent views may join together and have union but not unity. Unity can exist only among born-again believers who know what it is to have a common experience of salvation through faith in Christ's redeeming blood and who believe in and accept the centralities of God's imperishable Word.

Wilber M. Schlichting

* * *

One Only in Christ

Let us liken Christ to the hub of a mammoth wheel, and the children of God to the spokes in the wheel. The closer the spokes get to the hub, Christ, the closer they get to one another.

God's children are one, not in any organization, but one in the Father and the Son: "That they . . . may be one in us" (John 17:21).

* * *

The Unity of Believers

Dr. Vernon Grounds stated, "The ecumenical movement seeks a unity which is visible, external and organizational. The unity of believers in Jesus Christ is a spiritual unity which is personal and voluntary. It is a unity of faith, hope and love."

* * *

Drawing Closer

An ornithologist said, "Swallows leave for the southland on October 23 and return to the northland on March 19. Like true 'birds of a feather,' they gather together beforehand, and fly higher as the time to depart draws nearer. Not one swallow is left behind when they begin their southward flight."

Many of God's children today believe that the Holy Spirit is now gathering the children of God closer together in the bond of love and spiritual fellowship and enabling them to rise above nonessential denominational, divisive and disruptive differences. When Jesus comes to rapture the church, composed of all born-again believers, no saved ones will be left behind.

* * *

The Middle Wall Leveled

On the middle wall, which separated the inner court from the outer court in the temple at Jerusalem, was an inscription which read, "No man of another race is to proceed within the partition and enclosing wall about the sanctuary. Anyone apprehended there will have only himself to blame for the penalty of death which will be imposed as a consequence."

That separating, middle wall disappeared in the rubble when Titus destroyed the temple in A.D. 70.

Long before its destruction, however, Christ broke "down the middle wall of partition" which separated Jew and Gentile. In Him "there is neither Greek nor Jew . . . but Christ is all, and in all" (Col. 3:11).

* * *

Harmony in Variety

John H. Jowett said, "God's glory is expressed through the harmony of variety. We do not need sameness in order to gain union. We have need of one another: 'They helped every one his neighbour; and every one said to his brother, Be of good courage' [Isa. 41:6]. Every note in the organ is needed for the full expression of noble music. God has endowed no two souls alike: 'Having then gifts differing according to the grace that is given to us' [Rom. 12:6]. Every soul is needed to make the music of 'the realm of blest.' "

* * *

Mixed Marriages

Ann Landers stated, "The records show that individuals who share the same religious beliefs have five times as good a

chance of staying married as those who do not. Almost one out of three marriages are flops."

The ancient question is relevant: "Can two walk together, except they be agreed?" (Amos 3:3).

* * *

Our Greatest Need

Billy Graham averred, "Our greatest need is not organizational unity. Our greatest need is for the church to be baptized with the fire of the Holy Spirit and to go out proclaiming the gospel everywhere."

The early Christians were so empowered by the Holy Spirit that wherever they went one of two things occurred—a revival or a revolution: "And many that believed came, and confessed, and shewed their deeds. So mightily grew the word of God and prevailed" (Acts 19:18, 20); "These that have turned the world upside down are come hither also" (17:6).

* * *

United in Unbelief

A survey quoted Lutheran church historian Jaroslav Pelikan of Yale as saying, "It may be that we're developing a kind of ecumenicalism of mutual impoverishment. . . . Maybe we are simply saying that since neither of us believes very much anymore, we might as well unbelieve together."

Prairie Overcomer

* * *

Extravagant Toleration

Bishop J. C. Ryle warned, "One cause of present distress is the extravagant spirit of liberality and toleration which prevails about matters of doctrine. The tendency of the public mind is to ignore all differences and to tolerate anything and everything in religion."

* * *

Cursed Accommodation

Martin Luther stated, "Cursed be that love and unity for whose sake the Word of God must be put to stake."

VICTORY

(*See also* Defeatism)

A Foot and One-Half Too Low!

"Airliner Crash Fatal to 29!" This was the headline of the tragic story about a Bonanza Airlines plane which crashed on a Nevada mountaintop in a blinding snowstorm, killing all aboard.

When the airliner crashed, it was only five minutes from landing at the airport in Las Vegas. A deputy sheriff said at the scene of the wreckage, "If the plane had been a foot and a half higher, it would have cleared the mountaintop."

Let us forsake the miasmic lowlands of defeat and soar triumphantly with Christ on the higher plane of spiritual victory, "more than conquerors through him that loved us" (Rom. 8:37).

* * *

In Nick of Time

Dr. G. Campbell Morgan stated, "The Greek phrase translated 'in time of need' in Hebrews 4:16 is a colloquialism whose exact equivalent is 'in nick of time.' At the moment of assault by the tempter, Satan, you look to Christ and grace is there to help 'in the nick of time.' "

> Just when I need Him,
> Jesus is near;
> Just when I falter,
> Just when I fear.

* * *

How to Live Radiantly

Dr. John H. Jowett said, "I stood one day in a lovely vale in Switzerland in which flowed a gladsome river, full and forceful, and rejoicing in its liberty. I prayed that my life might be as the river —full of power, clearing obstacles by a nimble leap, and hastening on to the great and eternal sea.

"To my voiceless prayer came the reply 'Follow up the stream to its source.' I tracked the buoyant river to the snow line and found in the spreading wastes of virgin snow the river's source. Then I knew that full and forceful Christian lives must have their source in the holiness of God."

To live radiantly and victoriously over sin's defilement we must abide moment by moment in the One who came that God's children "might have life, and that they might have it more abundantly" (John 10:10).

* * *

Which Dog Wins?

In explaining the ceaseless conflict between the Christian's old and new natures, an Indian said, "It seems to me as though two dogs are fighting within me. One is a savage, ferocious dog. The other dog is gentle and good. The bad dog often fights with the good dog."

"And which dog wins?" a friend asked.

Laconically the Indian replied, "Whichever one I say 'sic 'em' to!"

* * *

Hidden Ones

A pastor asked a distraught person who had sought his help, "Would you like to enjoy continuous victory over the trivial things which so often deject and defeat you?"

"I surely would," was the reply.

"Then," said the pastor, "appropriate this sure promise: 'Thou shalt hide them in the secret of thy presence . . .: thou shalt keep them secretly . . . from the strife of tongues' " (Ps. 31:20).

* * *

The Secret

An admiring friend said to an even-tempered woman, "You seem never to become angry and retaliative. Do you feel no injustice or sustain no injuries? You must have a special balm."

"Oh, yes," she replied. "I feel them as much as others do, but they do not hurt me. For hate, I return love. For suffering caused by mistreatment, I have prayer. For every wound, I have Christ's spirit of submission to my heavenly Father's will!"

Rats Live in Lowlands

Hadley Paige landed his plane for re-fueling in Kobar, Arabia. When aloft again, he heard the gnawing of a rat which had gotten into the plane when it was grounded. Paige thought with horror about the damage those cutting teeth could do in the plane. Suddenly he remembered that a rat lives in lowlands and cannot live in the heights. He soared higher and higher, and soon the gnawing ceased. When aground again, he found the rat under his seat—dead.

There is only one way to overcome the surrounding evils which would destroy us: forsake the lowlands of sin and carnality and live on the higher plane of fellowship and communion with God.

VISION

Why Not?

Sen. Robert F. Kennedy, quoting George Bernard Shaw's play *John Bull's Other Island,* said, "Some men see things as they are and say 'Why?' I dream things that never were and say 'Why not?'"

* * *

"I Saw the Lord"

A friend of mine underwent a major operation. She hovered on the borderline between life and death. She said to me, "It was the most terrific time of testing I have ever encountered. I prayed continuously, not for myself only, but for others who shared the hospital ward with me. Then one morning as I prayed, I seemed to see the Saviour in His glory and beauty. I will never forget His angelic, beautiful smile. It will linger with me until I awaken with His likeness in heaven and see Him face to face!"

W. B. K.

* * *

As God Sees Us

A Hebrew scholar said to John Newton, "I am unable to see the doctrine of the atonement in the Hebrew Scriptures."

Newton replied, "I am not surprised. You will not discover it until you see yourself as a sinner in need of the Saviour, although you are a brilliant Hebraist."

When we see ourselves as God sees us, we confess, "Woe is me! For I am undone; because I am a man of unclean lips" (Isa. 6:5).

Both the moral and the immoral man, the religious and the irreligious man, need the Saviour and His forgiveness.

* * *

"I See the Children's Faces!"

Dr. John Sutherland Bonnell said, "Some years before Dwight L. Moody's death two of his grandchildren had died. As the end of his life approached, he looked up and cried in tones of triumph, 'Dwight! Irene! I can see the children's faces!'

"Who is so unbelieving as to say that he didn't?"

* * *

Vision Never Stronger

On his ninety-second birthday, J. C. Penney, the merchant prince, said, "My eyesight is impaired, so I don't travel or accept invitations to speak so much anymore. But my vision is stronger than ever."

In reminiscing on his childhood, he said, "I thought my father was hard on me when he put me on my own, but I thank God every night for his early strict religious training."

* * *

Unseeing Eyes

A lady said to Joseph Mallord Turner, English landscape painter, "I cannot see in nature what you put into your pictures."

The artist replied, "Don't you wish you could, Madam?"

What They Saw

Two men were looking at the sea.
One man saw only quantity;
The other's soul was filled with awe.
The mighty handiwork of God he saw!

* * *

The Dawn

The motto of a group of Protestant monks in France is "Do not be afraid to precede the dawn!"

* * *

A Vision of God

As Isaiah stood in the midst of crumbling thrones and passing kingdoms, God in goodness gave him a vision of Himself "sitting upon a throne, high and lifted up" (Isa. 6:1).

In our day of moral and spiritual confusion, we too need a vision of the changeless God who still rules and overrules and is able to "do exceeding abundantly above all we ask or think" (Eph. 3:20).

As Lord Tennyson neared life's setting sun, someone asked, "Is there anything that you need?"

Tennyson replied, "Yes, a new vision of God."

Handel said after he wrote the *Messiah,* "I did think I did see all heaven before me, and the great God Himself!"

* * *

Seeing God

"I should like to see your God," said Emperor Trajan to a Jewish rabbi.

"No mortal eye can look upon Him," replied the rabbi.

When the emperor insisted, the rabbi said, "Well, suppose we begin by looking on one of His creations." He bade the emperor to gaze at the midday sun in a cloudless sky.

"I cannot," the emperor confessed. "The light dazzles me."

The rabbi said, "If you cannot endure the glory of one of His creations, how can you behold the unclouded glory of the Creator?"

Christian Herald

What Do You See?

William Blake, English artist and poet, stood on the shore watching the sun rise out of the ocean. Sky and sea were brilliant with a million refracted rays. The sun's bright disk was just visible above the water when Blake noticed a man standing beside him. Turning in ecstasy, Blake pointed to the rising sun and exclaimed, "Look! Look! What do you see?"

"I see something that looks like money —gold money. What do you see?" asked the man.

"I see the glory of God," said Blake, "and I hear a multitude of the heavenly host saying, 'Holy, holy, holy is the Lord God Almighty!' "

* * *

A Vision of Lifework

Evangeline Booth said, "What happy visions I had as a little girl of doing something for the poor! When I arranged my dolls' wardrobe or trundled my hoop, I saw myself surrounded by hungry people and feeding them hot soup. I saw myself dressing ragged people with warm jackets and comforting sorrowing people. My mother's training about goodness bringing gladness greatly influenced me at a very early age. I yearned to make very bad people good. These were wonderful daydreams, and the most wonderful feature about them is that they became dearer and more real as the years flew by until they ceased to be daydreams, and I awoke to find they all came true—one by one."

* * *

War's Backwash

Lord Salisbury, British statesman, wrote in 1941: "More than death, wounds and destruction I dread the moral decay that lies ahead. This war is going to destroy the moral sense of nations. Values that it has taken generations to establish will be smashed. I do not mean the political and economic changes that are bound to come. They may be good for us. But the smashing of absolute standards of morality that you and I believe in, the denial of truths of the spirit, the elevation of man's mind and body in place of God—these are the things out

342

of which nothing but darkness and decay can come, and these are the things that I see before us!"

Christianity Today

* * *

Changed by Beholding

Mark Guy Pearse said, "We are changed by beholding. Much depends on the way we look. I walked one May day with a friend in an orchard. How exquisite were the dainty white and pink blossoms! As we returned to the house, I observed a tree without blossoms. Every leaf was blackened and withered. I asked, 'How is this?'

" 'Ah,' said my friend, 'this tree faces east. The others face south. That makes the difference.'

"Some Christians look inward; some look about them. Radiant, triumphant Christians look upward to the Saviour, and are changed 'from glory to glory.' "

* * *

Seeing Eyes That Don't See

Years ago Helen Keller was the special guest of the Society for the Blind, Cleveland, Ohio. Anne Sullivan Macy, her teacher, was with her.

Mrs. Macy demonstrated how Miss Keller had learned to carry on a conversation by touching with her sensitive fingers the lips and throat of another person. She asked Newton D. Baker, chairman of the meeting, to converse with Miss Keller.

When Miss Keller placed her "listening" fingers on his lips and throat, he said, "Blindness is the greatest human handicap, isn't it?"

Quick as a flash, Miss Keller replied, "Oh, no! It is worse to have seeing eyes and not see!"

How great is our need to see ourselves as God sees us—lost sinners—and to see Christ as the only Saviour.

Job said, "I have heard of thee by the hearing of the ear; but now mine eye seeth thee. Wherefore I abhor myself and repent in dust and ashes" (Job 42:5-6).

* * *

God's City

The shining road may seem to lose itself in night;
The valley mist, the winter cloud may hide it from my sight.
I know full well it winds until, or soon or late,
It finds upon the hills of God His shining City gate.

F. GOLDSMITH FRENCH

WAR

"Father, Forgive"

Near Coventry's present stately cathedral in England is the roofless shell of the former cathedral which was bombed and burned during World War II. An altar has been built from rough stones of the ruins. On the altar is a cross made from two pieces of charred wood from the burned cathedral. On the wall behind the altar are these words. "Father, forgive."

How thought-provoking is the omission of the word *them*. The prayer is not exclusively for the enemies who rained destruction from the air upon people and places below. It is also a prayer for God to forgive the wrong madness of all participants in that horrible holocaust.

Before You Press the Button

Young Roger Neal wrote the following letter to the President of the United States:

"Dear Mr. President: I am eleven years old and every night I worry. I worry about what will happen tomorrow, not so much for tomorrow, but for the future. What will be left of this wonderful world in ten years if someone presses the button? What will be left of you and your family? All I am asking for is please think before you press the button, please!"

Myriads of people around the world have the same worries as Roger: "Men's hearts failing them for fear, and for looking after those things which are coming on the earth" (Luke 21:26).

Our National Strength Imperiled

Idealism is praiseworthy, but we imperil our strength and position as a nation if we fail to maintain military security. God gives us no promise of continuing national or international peace until the righteous reign of Jesus, the Prince of peace. Then, the nations "shall beat their swords into plowshares, and their spears into pruninghooks: nation shall not lift up a sword against nation, neither shall they learn war any more" (Micah 4:3); "The whole earth is at rest, and is quiet: they break forth into singing" (Isa. 14:7).

* * *

Will the Sword Devour Forever?

Said Dr. Linus Pauling, who won the Nobel prize for chemistry in 1954 and the Nobel peace prize in 1962, "We have now reached the time in the course of the evolution of civilization when war will be abolished from the world and will be replaced by a system of world law based upon the principles of justice and morality."

This longed-for glorious time will not come in the course of the evolution of civilization. But when Jesus, the Prince of peace, returns as the King of kings and Lord of lords, "nation shall not lift up a sword against nation, neither shall they learn war any more" (Micah 4:3).

* * *

War the Rule, Peace the Exception

A Norwegian statistician computerized the wars of history. His machine quickly indicated that in the 5,560 years of recorded history, there have been 14,531 wars, averaging 2.6135 wars a year. In the recorded history of 185 generations, only 10 generations had unsullied peace.

War has been the rule on earth, and peace the exception.

The Bible asks these pertinent questions: "From whence come wars and fightings among you? Come they not hence, even of your lusts that war in your members?" (James 4:1).

"Father, Forgive Us"

Barrett Wilson said, "During World War II, I was flying as a copilot over the Pacific Ocean. The latest war news crackled over our earphones: 'Fierce fighting on both sides! Casualties high!'

"Suddenly the cockpit seemed to light up! In vision, I saw our world in mortal combat—human beings fighting and behaving like animals in the jungle. I also envisioned the way of Christ in contrast to the way of the world. I silently prayed, 'Father, forgive us; for we know not what we do!'"

* * *

She Shrugged

When a foreigner told Katya, a Russian girl in her early thirties, that Joseph Stalin had killed a million people, she shrugged and said, "A million people? That is only a small part of our two hundred million!"

* * *

So Dangerous It's Safe

Harry S. Truman said, "In Missouri, years ago, there was a particularly dangerous junction of a railroad and a highway. I asked an engineer what should be done about it, and he replied, 'Don't do a thing. It's so dangerous, it's safe!' That's the way I feel about the possibility of a nuclear war."

* * *

Oversupply of People

Said Red Marshal Klementi Voroshilov, proud wearer of a jeweled dagger and a gold revolver, "In Russia we count rifles, planes, missiles and tanks, but never people. Of people we have always had an oversupply!"

* * *

Followers of Cain

Out of the primeval shadows strode the murderer Cain. Behind him have marched the destroying armies of the centuries, in whose wake have lain 15 thousand millions of the slain!

May the righteous reign of Jesus, the Prince of peace, not be distant. His last recorded words are these: "Surely I come quickly" (Rev. 22:20). The responsive plea of myriads of God's children around the world is this: "Even so, come, Lord Jesus."

* * *

Disliked

Pauline Frederick, NBC correspondent at the United Nations, told of a boy who said to his father, "I don't like war because war makes history, and I don't like history."

* * *

Men and Rats

Konrad Lorenz, Austrian-born naturalist, pointed out that men and rats share the dubious distinction of being the only carnivores with no innate inhibitions against attacking members of their own species.

Time, April 19, 1968

Man's Inhumanity

Mussolini's son spoke gleefully and gloatingly of the bombing of Ethiopians. Said he, "I dropped an aerial torpedo right in the center of a cluster of tribesmen, and the group opened up like a flowering rose. It was most entertaining!"

Adapted from *Time,*
April 19, 1968

* * *

Lonely Without War

Sir Winston Churchill said to his physician at the close of World War II, "I feel lonely without war, don't you?"

* * *

Three Armies

A German proverb says "War leaves a country with three armies: an army of cripples, an army of mourners, and an army of thieves."

WILL OF GOD

(*See also* Guidance)

"If the Lord Will"

Henry Martyn prayed, "Lord, let me have no will of my own, or consider my joy as depending, in the smallest degree, on anything that can befall me outwardly, but consisting altogether in conformity to Thy will."

God's children should never say, "I will, or I won't, do this or that." They must say, "If the Lord will, we shall live, and do this, or that" (James 4:15).

Eternity

* * *

Any Wife if It Is Ethel

A young minister attended a summer Bible conference. He prayed out loud when he retired one night. He began quietly and as he prayed he waxed more fervent and louder—so loud indeed that the aged minister in the adjoining room heard his earnest plea: "O Lord, You know how greatly I need a wife in my work. Do give me a wife. Any wife Thou dost give me will be all right, *just so it is Ethel.*"

He knows, He loves, He cares,
  Nothing this truth can dim;
He does the very best for those
  Who leave the choice with Him.

The promise is sure: "The LORD will give grace and glory: no good thing will he withhold from them that walk uprightly" (Ps. 84:11).

* * *

Your Plan for Tomorrow, Lord

Two little sisters, aged three and five, were playing house. After they had pretended to make beds, sweep floors, prepare supper, and wash dishes, the five-year-old girl said to her sister, "Now it is time to go to bed, but first we must say our prayers."

The two knelt beside their beds, folded their hands and bowed their heads. Then the three-year-old sister prayed, "We've had a good day today, Lord. What's Your plan for tomorrow?"

ALICE MARIE KNIGHT

"Make Haste to Help Me, O Lord"

An impatient, energetic Christian man said to his grandmother, "When I pray for something, I want it without delay. I never ask God for anything unless I think it's right. Why should He postpone the answer to my prayer?"

Thoughtfully the grandmother replied, "God sometimes delays the answer to our prayers because we are not ready to receive His answer. Delays are not denials, however. I've known you since you were a small boy and you have always been in too much of a hurry. As a child, you often visited me in early summer before the apples were ripe. I warned you not to eat those hard green apples. Sometimes you disobeyed me, and you got a stomach-ache. You are now a grownup man, but you seem to be the same little boy—you just can't wait for God to mature His plans for you."

God's plans, like lilies, pure and white
    unfold.
We must not tear the close-shut leaves
    apart;
Time will reveal the chalices of gold.

* * *

No Will of My Own

George Müller said, in speaking of God's guidance, "I seek at the beginning to get my heart into such a state that it has no will of its own in regard to a given matter. Nine-tenths of the difficulties are overcome when my heart is ready to do God's will, whatever it be. When I am in this state, it is usually but a little way to the knowledge of what His will is."

* * *

To Do Thy Will

No service in itself is small;
None great, though earth it fill.
But that is small that seeks its own,
And great that seeks God's will.

Then hold my hand, most gracious Lord,
Guide all my goings still;
And let it be my life's one aim
To know and do Thy will.

Rest in the Lord

Dr. F. B. Meyer said, "There is a life in the center of the will of God, so quiet, so at peace with Him, so at rest in His joy, so perfectly content, that the lines in the face are wiped out, the fever gone from the restless eye, and the whole nature still. Rest in the Lord, and wait patiently for Him to use you in helping others from your own experience."

* * *

Only One Mind

Years ago spectators were thrilled as they watched Blondin, the famous tight-rope walker and acrobat, cross over Niagara Falls on a tightrope 1,100 feet long and 160 feet above the water.

Blondin asked a man, "How would you like for me to carry you on my back over the Falls?"

"That would be great!" exclaimed the man.

In giving the man last-minute instructions, Blondin said, "I ask you to remember only one thing: when I take the first step onto the tightrope, there can be only one mind and that is the mind of Blondin. If Blondin leans forward, you must lean forward. If Blondin leans backward, you must lean backward. Remember, there is only one man giving commands—Blondin. Your mind must be utterly one with the mind of Blondin!"

How blessed are God's children when their will is merged utterly with God's will; when they love God with all their heart, soul and mind, and say, "I delight to do thy will, O my God: yea, thy law is within my heart" (Ps. 40:8).

* * *

Not a Tyrant but a Loving Father

"The last thing I want to do is to say to God, 'Thy will be done,' " said a Christian young woman to a minister. Then she added, "If I said this, I am sure I would be compelled to go to Africa as a missionary."

"So that is your idea of God!" exclaimed the minister. "Suppose you told your earthly father, 'Daddy, today I will do those things which bring pleasure to you.' Do you think he would take ad-

346

vantage of your submissive attitude and tell you to do things which make you miserable?"

"Of course not," quickly replied the young woman. "He would tell me to do things which would bring joy to me!"

"Isn't it strange that you have a higher opinion of your earthly father than you have of your heavenly Father?" asked the minister.

"I see it!" joyfully exclaimed the girl. "I now surrender my life to my loving heavenly Father, trusting Him to guide me into paths of His choosing."

Adapted from *Vital Messages in Modern Books*

* * *

Willing to Be Made Willing

Dr. F. B. Meyer testified, "It was a long struggle for me before I submissively prayed, 'Lord, I am willing to be made willing. I give up myself to Thee—body, soul and spirit—to be made willing in sorrow or in joy, in the dark or in the light, in life or in death, to be wholly Thine only forever.'"

When we are totally amenable to the will of God, the divine directive will come speedily: "This is the way, walk ye in it" (Isa. 30:21).

* * *

Has God No Plan for Man?

The architect draws his plans for his stately mansion. The artist sketches the outlines of his masterpiece. The shipbuilder lays down the lines for his ship. Is it conceivable that God has no plan for man, created in His own image, and no eternal destiny for his undying soul?

Baptist Standard

* * *

"None Can Stay His Hand"

An eccentric old man was fond of boasting, "My watch has kept perfect time for forty years. It is never too slow or too fast."

One morning the man was up just before dawn. In glancing at an almanac, he saw the indicated moment when the sun would rise that day. Looking toward the east, he held his watch in his hand and waited for the rising of the sun. He became impatient and exclaimed, "If that sun isn't over the hill in one and a half minutes, it will be too late!"

How vain it is for man to try to regulate God's works. The Bible says, "He doeth according to his will in the army of heaven . . . and none can stay his hand, or say unto him, What doest thou?" (Dan. 4:35).

God's ways and works are perfect. He is never too early or too late: "As for God, his way is perfect" (Ps. 18:30).

* * *

Heart and Head Needed

Sir William Osler, famed physician, speaking to a class of medical students, said, "The practice of medicine is not a trade or an art or a business. It is a divine calling into which you must carry both head and heart."

* * *

Failure—Success

Bernard Edinger stated, "Inside the will of God, there is no failure. Outside the will of God, there is no success."

* * *

Either

If place I choose or place I shun,
My soul is satisfied with none;
But when Thy will directs my way,
'Tis equal joy to go or stay.

* * *

Thine

Thou seemest human and divine,
The highest, holiest manhood, Thou;
Our wills are ours, we know not how,
Our wills are ours, to make them Thine.

ALFRED, LORD TENNYSON

* * *

Conformity to Thy Will

Henry Martyn prayed, "Lord, let me have no will of my own, or consider my true happiness as depending in the smallest degree on anything that can befall me outwardly, but on conformity to Thy will."

Vacant

If you are in the wrong place, the right place is vacant.

* * *

His Blessed Will

All that He blesses is our good,
  An unblessed good is ill;
And all is right that seems most wrong,
  If it be His blessed will.

Would You?

David Livingstone testified, "I had rather be in the heart of Africa in the will of God than on the throne of England out of the will of God."

* * *

Once a Sigh

Frances Ridley Havergal said, in speaking of doing the will of God, "It was once a sigh. Now it is a song."

WORK

Where Edison Went to Relax

One night when Thomas A. Edison came home from work, his wife said, "You've worked too long without a rest. You must take a vacation."

"But where will I go?" he asked.

She replied, "Decide where you would rather be than anywhere else on earth and go there."

"Very well," replied Edison. "I will go there tomorrow." The next morning he went to his laboratory.

* * *

The Best Antidote

Famed cardiologist Dr. Paul Dudley White said, "If we start with a healthy heart, physical labor or exercise helps to keep it healthy. There is no evidence that mental work per se causes heart disease, although in excess it may lead to neglect of proper health habits. The best antidote for the harmful effects of intensive mental work is vigorous physical labor or exercise.

"Physical and mental stresses are needed to live a normal life. A forty-hour workweek is probably too little for healthy humans. We spend so much time trying to entertain ourselves in our leisure time that we are probably less culturally adapted than were our grandparents, who, fortunately for them, did not have automobiles and television—they walked and read. Our important challenge today is to begin with our children and get them to walk to school again, and not get overfed as so many of our teenagers are. If we don't—well, the handwriting is on the wall!"

* * *

The Best Things Are Nearest

Robert Louis Stevenson wrote, "The best things are nearest: breath in your nostrils, light in your eyes, flowers at your feet, duties at your hand, the path of right just before you. Then do not grasp at the stars, but do life's plain, common work as it comes, certain that daily duties and daily bread are the sweetest things of life."

* * *

Mission Accomplished

Dr. Wyn Blair Sutphin, a Presbyterian minister, said, "Some people have too many irons in the fire. They burn up life with small explosions of enthusiasm. They're always cutting ribbon on a new beginning enterprise. They live amid the rubble heap of half-accomplished causes —things half-done, hopes half-built, and dreams half-baked. They spill themselves like shivering quicksilver, and roll off in all directions.

"When the disciples ventured into life, they achieved an impressive record of results. They overturned tradition, upended every obstacle before them, and when they reported to their Lord the mission accomplished, it was with joy!"

Something for Nothing

Commented *Christian Economics,* "In the economic realm you cannot legislate the poor into freedom by legislating the wealthy out of it. You cannot multiply wealth by dividing it. Governments cannot give to the people what they do not first take away from the people. That which one man receives without working for, another man must work for without receiving it.

"Nothing can kill the initiative of a people more quickly than for half of them to get the idea that they need not work because the other half will feed them, and for the other half to get the idea that it does no good to work since someone else receives the rewards of their labors."

* * *

Do and Say

Two brothers once lived down this way,
And one was Do and the other Say;
If streets were dirty, taxes high,
Or schools were crowded, Say would cry:
"My, what a town!" But brother Do
Would set to work and make things new.
And while Do worked, Say still would cry:
"He does it wrong, I know that I
Could do it right." So, all the day,
Was heard the clank of brother Say.
But this one fact from none was hid,
Say always talked, Do always did.

* * *

One Day at a Time

The famed physician William Osler said, "One of my ideals is to do the day's work well and not bother about the next day. I owe whatever success I have had to settling down to the day's work and trying to do the best I can, and letting the future take care of itself."

* * *

You Had Better Slow Down

An elderly lady who had worked hard throughout the years was told by her physician, "You've got to slow down. I am ordering you to lie down each day and take a two-hour rest."

She replied, "All right, doctor, if you say so. But I'll have to get up two hours earlier in the morning."

What! A Missionary?

A Johannesburg businessman, on being informed by Mrs. Agnes Fraser that her husband, Dr. Donald Fraser, was a missionary, said in manifest astonishment, "What! A missionary? Do you mean to tell me that a man of his caliber could not get a better job than that?"

Mrs. Fraser replied, "If he could, you may be sure he would have jumped at it!"

"But, surely," began the businessman. Then he became silent. What she meant slowly began to dawn on him.

* * *

Builders

We are building every day,
In a good, or evil way,
And the structure as it grows,
Will our inmost self disclose.

Build it well, whate'er you do,
Build it straight, and strong and true,
Build it clean, and high and broad,
Build it for the eye of God.

I. E. Dickenza

* * *

What Made the Difference?

A girl in England, who was genuinely converted, worked in a chocolate factory. Sometime after her conversion, a friend said to her, "Tell me the difference your conversion has made in regard to your work."

The girl replied, "Formerly I made chocolates for my employer. Now I make them for God and my employer."

* * *

The Incentive

Three workmen on St. Paul's Cathedral, London, were asked, "What are you doing?"

One replied, "I am making a living for my wife and myself."

The second workman replied, "I am working for Sir Christopher Wren."

The third replied, "I'm building a temple for God!"

Work is glorified when we realize that we are working for God and with Him: "For we are labourers with God" (I Cor. 3:9).

Whom God Uses

God has no place in His service for a lazy, indolent person. When He called Moses to lead His captive people out of Egypt, Moses was occupied, tending sheep in Horeb. When He called Gideon to deliver Israel from the Midianites, Gideon was busy threshing wheat. When He called Elisha, Elisha was busy plowing twelve yoke of oxen. When He called Amos, Amos was busy shepherding his flock. When He called Nehemiah, Nehemiah was busy bearing the king's cup. Peter, Andrew, James, John and Matthew were all occupied when the Saviour called them to follow Him and become His helpers.

One time Moody's students complained, "Nothing turns up." Practical, vigorous Moody flashed, "Go out and turn something up! Keep busy for God!"

* * *

Work Never Begun

Christina Rossetti said, "Can anything be sadder than work left unfinished? Yes. Work never begun."

* * *

How Made

Footprints on the sands of time are never made by sitting down.

* * *

The Unfinished Task

Fred D. Jarvis, a missionary to Japan, stated, "The unfinished task which lies before us is no greater than the unlimited power of God behind us."

* * *

The Danger

Between the great things we cannot do and the little things we will not do, we are in danger of doing nothing.

* * *

That's Success

Before God's footstool to confess,
A poor soul knelt and bowed his head.
"I failed," he cried. The Master said,
"Thou didst thy best! That is success."

Keep Hoeing

Pray for a good harvest, but keep on hoeing.

* * *

No Time to Waste

Agassiz the famed zoologist said, "I have no time to waste in making money. Life is not sufficiently long to enable a man to get rich and do his duty to his fellowman."

* * *

Chisel in Hand

Michelangelo said, "It is only well with me when I have a chisel in my hand."

* * *

A Slave First

A reporter asked Paderewski, "What is the secret of your success?" He replied, "Before I was a master, I was a slave."

* * *

Not What You Have

Said Sir Wilfred Grenfell, "It is not what you have that matters. It is what you do with what you have."

* * *

How Won and Kept

The heights by great men reached and
     kept
Were not attained by sudden flight,
But they, while their companions slept,
     Were toiling upward in the night.

                    LONGFELLOW

* * *

What Genius Is

"You're a wizard," said an admirer to Thomas Edison. Edison quipped, "Pshaw! It's plain hard work that does it. Genius is one percent inspiration and ninety-nine percent perspiration."

* * *

Destroyed

When you destroy man's initiative for work by making it unnecessary for him to work, you have destroyed the man.

Lack of Work

Is it kindness to deprive anyone of all work? Nervous energy should be expended in constructive work. Man was created to work: "And the LORD God took the man and put him into the Garden of Eden to dress it and to keep it" (Gen. 2:15).

Retirement of anyone who is physically and mentally able to work can bring havoc. Dr. Edwin Zabriskie, one of the world's leading neurologists, said, "Retirement can be the severest shock that the human organism can sustain."

WORLDLINESS

Clean Amid Mire and Muck

The lotus flower is one of the loveliest creations in the world of natural beauty. Its delicate hue and spotless texture cause us to gasp in admiration. But look at its setting. Muck, mire and scum surround it. How can it be so immaculately pure and exquisitely beautiful in such an environment? Here's how: the lotus has life within it that enables it to push its stem up through oozy muck and scummy water and blossom with a splendor worthy of onlooking angels. If a lotus could talk to God, it would say, "Dear God, I do not ask that You transplant me where there are no putridity and foul water. I only ask that You keep alive in me that vitality which enables me to bloom in beauty where ugliness and uncleanness hold sway." God does just that!

In a world where sin abounds, God's children can be kept pure in word, thought and deed. In His intercessory prayer, Jesus prayed, "I pray not that thou shouldest take them out of the world, but that thou shouldest keep them from the evil" (John 17:15).

Told by PAUL S. REES

* * *

Separated but Not Insulated

Dr. A. W. Tozer, in *Message of the Open Bible*, wrote, "I believe in separation, not insulation. Evangelicals should not insulate themselves from others. Simon Stylites was a horrible example of those who make an effort to stay good by staying away from people. He ascended a pillar sixty feet high and

perched there for thirty years. He didn't descend for anything, even to take a bath. He was given food on his lofty abode."

Christ was the only sinless One who ever lived. Yet He ate and mingled with publicans and sinners. He moved constantly amid scenes of defilement but maintained His purity.

* * *

A Saved Soul but a Lost Life

Standing at the bedside of a dying woman, a minister simply explained the way of life in Christ. She accepted Christ as her only hope of eternal life. Then a troubled look came upon her face as she lamented, "I do trust Christ to save me and go with me through the valley of the shadow of death. But I am filled with regret because I have lived only for the passing pleasures of the world."

Oh, the tragedy of being a saved soul and having a lost life!

ALAN REDPATH

* * *

Off Course

In 1967 a Boeing 727 airliner collided with an off-course private plane in western North Carolina. Eighty-two perished in the tragedy!

Harold Roberts, chief of the Federal Aviation Administration tower at the Asheville airport, said, "The small plane was about twelve miles south of where it ought to have been."

Aeronautically speaking, twelve miles is a small distance. The private plane was enough off course, however, to cause irreparable loss of lives and plunge scores of loved ones in deep sorrow.

When God's children are off course, where they shouldn't be, they bring sorrow and suffering to themselves and others. When with the enemies of Christ, Peter denied and disowned his Lord.

Not on the Lord's Territory

A Scottish shepherd once slipped into sin. Penitently he confessed the sin to God, then added, "It is but fair, O Lord, to say that when I got into sin, I wasn't on Your territory."

WORRY

Corroding Care

A panel of psychologists declared, as a result of their study, that 40 percent of our worries are over things that will never happen, 30 percent over things in the past, and 22 percent over petty trifles, leaving only 8 percent over things of real consequence—the rightful cares which demand concern.

Worry is putting tomorrow's possible cloud over today's sunshine. It is sinful for God's children to have corroding care or anxious, bothersome thoughts about the unknown tomorrow: "Take . . . no thought for the morrow: for the morrow shall take thought for the things of itself. Sufficient unto the day is the evil thereof" (Matt. 6:34).

* * *

The Worried Cow

The worried cow would have lived till now,
If she had saved her breath;
But she feared her hay wouldn't last all day,
And she mooed herself to death.

* * *

A Built-in Foxhole

During World War II, someone asked President Harry Truman, "How can you bear up so calmly under the strain and stress of the presidency?"

He replied, "I have a foxhole in my mind. Just as a soldier retreats into his foxhole for protection and respite, I periodically retire into my mental foxhole where I allow nothing to bother me."

Strength for Today

W. J. Jeffers said in his book *New Horizons,* "There are two days in the week about which I never worry—yesterday and tomorrow. Yesterday, with its mistakes and blunders, has passed forever beyond recall. I cannot undo any act that I wrought. I cannot unsay a word that I said. All that it holds of my life—of wrongs, regret, and sorrow—is in the hands of God who can bring honey out of the rock, turn weeping into laughter, and give beauty for ashes.

"Tomorrow, with all its possible adversities, burdens, failures and mistakes, is as far beyond my reach as its dead sister —yesterday.

"There is left for me but one day of the week—today. Any man can fight the battles of today. Anyone can resist the temptation of today. It is when we willfully add the burden of yesterday and tomorrow that we break down. Only the mighty God can sustain such burdens. In infinite wisdom, He has carefully measured out to us our day's portion, and He gives the promise 'As thy days, so shall thy strength be' [Deut. 33:25]."

Just for today, Lord,
Tomorrow is not mine;
Just for today I ask Thee
For light and health divine.
Tomorrow's care I must not bear,
The future is all Thine.

Tensions Eased

A burdened mother awoke one morning and sighed as she thought, *Another day's work ahead—meals, children to get ready for school, and many other things to be attended to.*

Observing her stress, her husband said, "Hadn't you better rest? You are worried and feverish."

When alone, she opened her Bible and read Matthew 8:15: "He touched her hand, and the fever left her."

"That's what I need—the Saviour's soothing touch!" Her fears subsided.

"When he giveth quietness, who then can make trouble?" (Job 34:29).

Details

In *Letters to Young Churches,* J. B. Phillips renders Philippians 4:6-7 thus: "Don't worry over anything whatever; tell God every detail of your needs in earnest and thankful prayer, and the peace of God, which transcends human understanding, will keep constant guard over your hearts and minds as they rest in Christ Jesus."

* * *

Shut off the Future

Dr. William Osler said, "The load of tomorrow, added to that of today, makes the strongest falter. Shut off the future as tightly as the past."

WORSHIP

On Tomb of Charles Dickens

Several years ago I visited the Poets' Corner in Westminster Abbey. As I read the epitaphs of England's poets who were interred there, I chanced to look down. I saw that I was standing on the floor-level tomb of Charles Dickens. I felt irreverent and quickly moved elsewhere.

We should ever maintain a reverent attitude for things sacred—the church, God's Word and the name of God.

It would be as easy to grow roses on an iceberg as to create an atmosphere of worship where reverence is lacking.

"The LORD is in his holy temple: let all the earth keep silence before him" (Hab. 2:20).

W. B. K.

* * *

A Particular Time and Place for Worship

Theodore Roosevelt stated, "You may worship God anywhere, at any time, but the chances are that you will not do so unless you have first learned to worship Him in some particular place, at some particular time."

David said, "I was glad when they said unto me, Let us go into the house of the LORD" (Ps. 122:1).

Thomas Carlyle said, "No greater calamity can befall a nation than the loss of worship."

Why Silence Prevailed

A man dreamed that he was escorted into a church by an angel. There was something strange about the service. The organist moved his fingers over the keys, but no music came forth. The choir sang and their lips moved but not a sound was heard. Other phases of the service were routinely carried out, but silence prevailed.

"What does this mean?" asked the dreamer.

The angel replied, "You hear nothing because you see this service just as God sees it. The people are not putting their hearts into the service—only their lips— and God hears nothing."

Jesus said of the empty worship of the scribes and Pharisees, "This people draweth nigh unto me with their mouth, and honoureth me with their lips: but their heart is far from me" (Matt. 15:8).

* * *

The Object of Our Worship

Queen Elizabeth II and Prince Philip went on their honeymoon to Ramsey in Newhampshire. On Sunday morning they worshiped in Ramsey Abbey. Usually the worship services there are sparsely attended. When it was learned that the

353

queen and her husband would attend the service, people filled the church to overflowing. Many stood outside on the tombstones which surrounded the church and peered through the windows. The curious ones who seldom attended church were there, not to worship the King of kings and Lord of lords, but to see the queen and her husband.

Our worship is empty and vain unless the object of our adoration is "the high and lofty One that inhabiteth eternity" (Isa. 57:15).

YOUTH

Sterling Character

A nationwide telecast gave the story of James Kerzman, a nineteen-year-old youth of North Dakota who, upon the tragic automobile deaths of his mother and father, nobly and heroically assumed the responsibility of keeping his fourteen younger brothers and sisters, the youngest one being less than a year old, together as a family in their farm home.

James said that he wouldn't consider his brothers and sisters being placed in an orphanage or in a home with foster parents. He assumed not only their care but also the farming and management of many wheat-producing acres.

When we hear of young people who have cast off restraint and gone into ways of crime, it is inspirational to know that throughout our land there are thousands of respectable, responsibility-assuming youth with sterling character—as fine and upright as the youth of any generation.

* * *

Only Thine

Saviour, while my heart is tender,
　I would yield that heart to Thee;
All my powers to Thee surrender,
　Thine and only Thine to be.

Take me now, Lord Jesus, take me;
　Let my youthful heart be Thine:
Thy devoted servant make me,
　Fill my soul with love divine.

May this solemn consecration
　Never once forgotten be;
Let it know no revocation,
　Accepted, confirmed by Thee.

J. BURTON

"I Must Confess Christ"

Shortly after Frances Havergal entered a girls' school in Dusseldorf, she learned that she was the only Christian among the girls in the school. She was dismayed. Her first thought was *How can I confess Christ among these worldly non-Christians?* Her gentle, sensitive nature shrank from a duty so difficult.

Her second thought was *I cannot refrain from confessing Christ. I am the only one Christ has here, and I must be faithful to Him.* She knew she must walk worthy of her calling for Christ's sake. She must be an exemplary Christian, for any slip in word or in deed would bring discredit to Him. He had placed her there to be a witness for Him, and she must not fail Him.

She didn't fail Him and she had the joy of leading others to Him.

Each Christian is where he is primarily "for the word of God, and for the testimony of Jesus Christ" (Rev. 1:9).

* * *

Are Youth as Bad as They Say?

J. Edgar Hoover said, "I believe that the majority of young Americans are intelligent, stable citizens, ready to accept the responsibilities which this complex world has thrust upon them. I have often decried the stigma which the activities of a few have cast over the entire body of young Americans. I would advise all young people to be idealistic; to know our country's great history and the sterling principles on which it is founded; to be familiar with the Bible; and to work to preserve America's brave pioneer spirit."

354

"They're All Rich Kids"

In Oklahoma City, seven teenage boys abducted a fifteen-year-old girl, horribly mistreated her and forced her to submit to perverted acts.

The boys were apprehended. The arresting police officer, Lt. Jim Reading, said of them, "They're all rich kids—sons of doctors, lawyers, retired colonels and the like."

J. Edgar Hoover was asked, "Why do youths from good homes get into trouble so often?"

Hoover replied, "The so-called 'good home' often is not a good home with respect to the proper training of the children in the home. In most cases of juvenile crime, there is one common factor— *parental neglect*. The parents cringe at even the thought of having to discipline their children."

* * *

Gripped with Despair

A sixteen-year-old boy of Westbrook, Maine, gripped with despair because of crime and evil in our land, took the lives of his sister, mother and father. Then he took his own life!

In speaking of the terrible occurrence, Attorney General Richard S. Cohen said, "Contrary to the rumor, there is no belief that drugs were involved. The boy had no history of misbehavior or of mental or emotional disturbance."

How unbearable are the strain and stress of our distraught world without the sustaining grace and help of God! The crushing cares of this life will cause the strongest to go down beneath the black waters of despair unless they learn to cast every care upon the One who cares for them.

* * *

Rootless

A twenty-six-year-old Navy veteran who was a history major at Johns Hopkins University declared, "We—our generation—are resigned to a position of grayness and indecision. If my generation seems inert, it is not because we do not care. It is because we feel helpless. We are not so much lost as rootless."

"I've Been a Number So Long"

A young man who had all but wrecked his life in crime had completed some years of imprisonment. In prison, he had heard of the mighty power of Christ to change one's life. Now he was seeking help. As he sat in the study of a minister, with tears streaming down his face, he said, "I have been only a *number* so long. Do tell me how I can be somebody. I want to go straight."

How happy the minister was to tell him of the new life Christ gives: "If any man be in Christ, he is a new creature: old things are passed away; behold, all things are become new" (II Cor. 5:17).

* * *

Don't Let Them Down

Your parents have brought you up. Don't let them down!

"Honour thy father and thy mother: that thy days may be long upon the land which the LORD thy God giveth thee" (Exodus 20:12).

* * *

An Irreparable Loss

Gerald Stover, writer and Sunday school specialist, said, "The church and Sunday school lose 70 percent of their teenagers after the junior high age." This figure continues to rise.

What can reverse this tragic situation? Only true sorrow for our sin and for our failure to set the right example before young people plus our sustained effort to enter understandingly into their problems and perplexities.

* * *

Sour Sixteen

A sixteen-year-old girl who signed her name Sour Sixteen expressed her hatred of her father in a letter written to a newspaper columnist. She said, "I hate my father because he is an alcoholic, and he embarrasses me in front of friends."

Another teenager, in commenting upon Sour Sixteen's hatred of her drinking father, wrote, "I am sorry for you, not because your father has caused you embarrassment, but because you are filled with bitterness. This will cause you more harm than anything your father could say or do. I am also sixteen. My father died last year of a liver ailment. He, too, was an alcoholic as far back as I can remember. My father said and did some disgraceful things, too, but he never disgraced me, poor man—only himself. After he sobered up, he was miserable and ashamed.

"Now that my father is gone, I remember the few kind and thoughtful things he did for me. There are so many little things you don't notice, but once they are gone you will miss them. I am sad knowing that when I marry I will not walk down the aisle holding my father's arm. Please give your father a kiss for me because I cherish the memory of the few kisses my own father gave me and I will never know them again!"

* * *

An Ineradicable Scar

Sometime ago throughout the nation a letter from a distraught teenager appeared in newspapers. It said in part:

"I am writing about my parents who fight in front of their children. If they only knew what they drag their kids through, they'd stop. About every three or four weeks, my parents have a terrible argument. Often it lasts for two hours. Right now they are tearing into each other like a couple of jungle animals. After the fight, they don't speak to each other for about a week. The tension in the house during the silent spells is awful, too. We kids feel like we are living in the middle of a battlefield. My sister has headaches and I get bad stomach pains. I can't eat dinner half the time."

It is tragic for parents to thus sin against their children and put an ineradicable scar on their souls. The home is the place where children get their bent for life.

* * *

The Nicest Specimen

A teenager wrote to a newspaper columnist: "I have made up my mind not to drink, but people make it very hard for me to refuse. They keep on insisting and get scornful and angry if I say, 'I'm sorry.

I'd rather have an orangeade.' What's the best way to refuse?"

The columnist replied, "No need to say, 'I'm sorry.' You invite them to persuade you if you sound apologetic. Say only, 'Thank you, but I take only soft drinks.' If you can show that you are proud, glad and grateful for being able to hold onto your standards without being priggish, you are the nicest possible specimen of human beings."

Adapted from *London Daily Mail*

* * *

Apron Strings and Heartstrings

As the teenager matures, apron strings must be severed. Heartstrings must remain intact if stability and understanding are to characterize the relationship between parents and youth.

Weeping, a lovely young lady said to her pastor, "I hate to go home! It's fuss and fight all the time. I didn't notice it so much when I was younger, but now it's just tearing me to pieces. I've stayed with my girl friends and I know what a real home is supposed to be like."

Joyfully a teenager said to his pastor, "I've always loved and respected Mom and Dad because they've treated me like a person. They didn't use me to further their own selfish plans. They made me a part of their plans. We did things together. I know I gave them some sleepless nights, but they always let me know where they stood and how far I could go. I hope I can do half as good a job raising my own kids someday."

* * *

Colors Must Be Mixed in Youth

A teenager was deeply impressed with the graciousness and serenity of an elderly lady. "Mother, I would like to be like her when I become old," she said.

"You may," her mother said, "but you must begin to mix the colors now—love, kindness, patience—if you would portray in old age the one you greatly admire."

356

Everybody's Doing It

Everybody's doing it! So they say,
Everybody's drinking in our day.
Everybody's starting, you'll start, too;
So they say, but it's not true.

Everybody's doing it? No, not yet,
For I'm somebody, don't forget.
Anyone with courage to step aside and
think
Is sure to be somebody—I don't drink!

Many a "somebody" who fell into line
Became a "nobody" in almost no time;
Anyone can follow what the crowds do,
But I'm somebody. How about you?

Everybody's doing it? No, not yet,
For I'm somebody, don't forget.
Anyone with courage to see what's true
Is sure to be somebody. How about you?

Written by a high school student

* * *

Dangers and Glories of Growing Up

As one walked across the old London Bridge to the south end, he saw a lovely gray stone cathedral whose foundations date back to Saxon times. One small side chapel is dedicated to all the young people of the area. In it is the following inscription: "Let us by our prayers and work help to carry the boys and girls safely through the dangers and glories of growing up."

Blessed indeed are those who enter understandingly into the lives of today's youth. They need not so much *advice* but *example*.

Adapted from *National News*,
American Legion Auxiliary

* * *

Understanding Needed

We cannot give young people the reins and say "Drive!" without inviting a smashup. Youth, in their immaturity, lack judgment and experience. Many youth are dominated to a large extent by physical urges. Without a guiding hand they may run amuck. Urgently needed are those who can enter understandingly and helpfully into their problems.

Wanted: Undeserving Boys

Each Christmas the superintendent of a city mission always provided a fine breakfast for poor boys. One year the needed funds were slow in coming in. Going to a Christian businessman, the superintendent said, "I want you to make it possible for me to give the usual Christmas breakfast for a hundred *deserving* boys."

To his surprise and dismay, the businessman flatly refused. The superintendent pleaded, "Why don't you make it possible for me to bring cheer to deserving boys?"

The man flashed, "If you can find one hundred *undeserving* boys, I will be delighted to underwrite the breakfast and bring happiness to them."

God helps us, not because we are worthy or deserving, but because we are needy: "I am poor and needy; yet the LORD thinketh upon me" (Ps. 40:17).

* * *

Confused

The so-called moral revolution is confessedly creating problems which educators are unable to solve or cope with. Promiscuity, dope addiction and alcoholism on the campuses are growing problems, according to college deans and professors who met in a session of the National Conference on Higher Education in Chicago. The conference was reported by Bud Wiedenthal, press staff writer.

"Let's not skirt the issue," said an attractive dean of a college for women. "This thing is tearing us apart. It is pitting faculty against administration and administration against students. What are we supposed to do? What do you do, for instance, when a young girl of eighteen from a fine home and a good finishing school comes to your office and naïvely asks if she should procure a contraceptive. This girl is not promiscuous. She is a good student. But somehow she thinks that this sort of thing is part of going to college."

Another educator said, "Part of the reason we don't come up with answers to these problems is that we just don't know. We are confused."

357

Another educator confessed, "We don't have solutions." Still another said, "We can't take the responsibility of the follies of society. We can only say to the kids, 'You are young adults. You must share the responsibility for your acts.' This is about the best we can do."

The *sure* remedy for the social ills which are so overwhelming and confounding today is so simple that many scorn it: a realistic confrontation with Christ and acceptance of His heart-transforming, restraining gospel.

* * *

A Spunky Teenager

Nina K., a sixteen-year-old Russian girl, fearlessly wrote a letter to the Young Communist League, in which she said, "I am a Young Communist League member. I am a normal girl, but at the same time I am unusual. I'm a Christian. Frankly I do not consider myself a member of the Young Communist League. I have a Komsomal card, but my soul belongs to God. Here at the Baptist church people meet me with warmth and care. Yet Komsomal members pass me without greeting me. My brothers and sisters in God treat me very well. I believe in them and I believe in God."

When Nina's letter was printed, it was captioned "The One Who Has Gone Astray." In reality, she was the one who found the way—Christ.

Told by Tom Olson

* * *

In the Right with Two or Three

They are slaves who fear to speak
For the fallen and the weak;
They are slaves who will not choose
Hatred, scoffing and abuse;
Rather than in silence shrink
From the truth they needs must think;
They are slaves who dare not be
In the right with two or three.

James Russell Lowell

What Waste of Life

At 11:30 P.M. on the night before Eric R. Rosemann was to have departed with other honor students for France, his mother received a phone call and was told that her son was under the weather, or inebriated, at a farewell party in his honor.

When his parents reprimanded him for his immoderate drinking, Eric went to his room and killed himself with a shotgun.

What a waste of life! Rivers of tears flow because of the monstrous evil of alcohol which is increasingly engulfing our youth in a maelstrom of helplessness and hopelessness.

* * *

The Changing Moral Climate

Mrs. Faye Biles, an assistant professor of health and physical education at Kent State University, said, "The moral climate is changing drastically on today's college campuses. For example, homosexuality is more of a problem than it has ever been among American college students. These students know more about contraceptive methods than I do—and I'm a hygiene teacher. I am constantly amazed at the findings of surveys I take in my hygiene classes, and I'm not one who is amazed easily. The most important thing that parents and secondary schools could do for young people is to prepare them to arrive in college with a tremendous sense of maturity and self-discipline."

* * *

"The Fool Hath Said . . ."

In a street meeting in Madison Square, New York City, a blatant atheist shouted, "There is no God. There never was a God. I challenge anyone here to stand on this box and prove that there's a God. God hasn't a friend among you."

A courageous youth came, mounted the box and said, "You are wrong, altogether wrong. I am His friend. I am one of God's children through faith in Jesus Christ the Son of God."

The heroic stand of that youth brought fervid amens from others who had experienced God's saving and keeping power. The atheist was silenced.

Ready

When Lincoln was a boy, a neighbor saw him intently reading a book and asked, "Abe, are you studying law? Do you expect to be President some day?"

Lincoln replied, "I don't know, but I want to be ready for anything God may have for me to do."

* * *

Have Tools Ready

Charles Kingsley said, "Have thy tools ready. God will find thee work."

* * *

The Next Generation

Edmund Burke, English statesman, declared, "Tell me what are the prevailing sentiments that occupy the minds of young men, and I will tell you what is to be the character of your next generation."

Depersonalization

Robert McAfee Brown remarked, "The biggest cause for student rebellion is depersonalization. 'I am a human being. Do not fold, spindle or mutilate' is their cry."

* * *

"Perhaps You May"

Situational ethics assays to change God's changeless "Thou shalt not" to "Perhaps you may." It leaves people in a state of uncertainty, to choose for themselves in any present situation, with no guidance other than the pressure of passion.

* * *

Three Persons in One

You are three persons in one: the person you think you are, the person other people think you are, the person you really are.